2020 Recipe Index

RC = Recipe Card

C

ADDITIONAL COOKBOOKS AVAILABLE FROM THE PUBLISHERS OF COOK'S COUNTRY INCLUDE:

The Complete Plant-Based Cookbook

Meat Illustrated

Foolproof Fish

Cooking for One

The Complete One Pot

How Can It Be Gluten Free Cookbook Collection

The Side Dish Bible

The Complete Summer Cookbook

Bowls

100 Techniques

Easy Everyday Keto

The Perfect Pie

Everything Chocolate

How to Cocktail

Vegetables Illustrated

Spiced

The Ultimate Burger

The New Essentials Cookbook

Dinner Illustrated

The America's Test Kitchen Menu Cookbook

Cook's Illustrated Revolutionary Recipes

Tasting Italy: A Culinary Journey

Cooking at Home with Bridget and Julia

The Complete Diabetes Cookbook

The Complete Slow Cooker

The Complete Make-Ahead Cookbook

The Complete Mediterranean Cookbook

The Complete Vegetarian Cookbook

The Complete Cooking for Two Cookbook

The Complete Cooking for Two Cookbook Gift Edition

Just Add Sauce

How to Braise Everything

How to Roast Everything

Nutritious Delicious

What Good Cooks Know

Cook's Science

The Science of Good Cooking

The Perfect Cake

The Perfect Cookie

Bread Illustrated

Master of the Grill

Kitchen Smarts: Questions and Answers to Boost Your Cooking I.Q.

Kitchen Hacks: How Clever Cooks Get Things Done

100 Recipes: The Absolute Best Way to Make the True Essentials

The New Family Cookbook

The America's Test Kitchen Cooking School Cookbook

The Cook's Illustrated Meat Book

The Cook's Illustrated Baking Book

The Cook's Illustrated Cookbook

The America's Test Kitchen Family Baking Book

The Best of America's Test Kitchen (2007–2021 Editions)

The Complete America's Test Kitchen TV Show Cookbook (2001–2021)

America's Test Kitchen Twentieth Anniversary TV Show Cookbook

Toaster Oven Perfection

Mediterranean Instant Pot

Cook It in Your Dutch Oven

Vegan for Everybody

Sous Vide for Everybody

Air Fryer Perfection

Multicooker Perfection

Food Processor Perfection

Pressure Cooker Perfection

Instant Pot Ace Blender Cookbook

Naturally Sweet

Foolproof Preserving

Paleo Perfected

The Best Mexican Recipes

Slow Cooker Revolution 2: The Easy Prep Edition

Slow Cooker Revolution

The America's Test Kitchen Do-It-Yourself Cookbook

Cook's Illustrated Annual Hardbound Editions
from each year of publication (1993–2020)

THE COOK'S ILLUSTRATED ALL-TIME BEST SERIES

All-Time Best Brunch

All-Time Best Dinners for Two

All-Time Best Sunday Suppers

All-Time Best Holiday Entertaining

All-Time Best Appetizers

All-Time Best Soups

COOK'S COUNTRY TITLES

Big Flavors from Italian America

One-Pan Wonders

Cook It in Cast Iron

Cook's Country Eats Local

The Complete Cook's Country TV Show Cookbook

Visit our online bookstore at www.CooksCountry.com to order any of our cookbooks listed above.
You can also order subscriptions, gift subscriptions, and any of our cookbooks by calling
800-611-0759 inside the U.S., or 515-237-3663 if calling from outside the U.S.

$35.00

Manufactured in the United States of America

ISBN: 978-1-948703-64-2
ISSN: 1552-1990

To get home delivery of Cook's Country magazine, call 800-526-8447 inside the U.S., or 515-237-3663 if
calling from outside the U.S., or subscribe online at www.CooksCountry.com/Subscribe.

Cook's Country

CUBAN SANDWICHES

Our quest for the perfect recipe began in the birthplace of this iconic sandwich: Tampa, Florida.

page 4

ITALIAN MEATLOAF
Red Sauce Supper

CHICKEN PAPRIKASH
Hot from Cleveland

FRENCH ONION SOUP
It's All About the Croutons

SOY SAUCE CHICKEN WINGS
Sticky, Savory, So Good

CHOCOLATE MOUSSE
Deep and Dark but Light as Air

FEBRUARY/MARCH 2020
$6.95 U.S./$7.95 CANADA

03>

0 71486 02742 3

DISPLAY UNTIL MAY 4, 2020

AMERICA'S
TEST KITCHEN

LETTER FROM THE EDITOR

HOW DO YOU make a sandwich? Seems like an easy enough question to answer. You just grab a couple of pieces of bread and put a slice of cheese and some sort of meat or vegetable between 'em. Right?

Well, sure—that would be a sandwich. But a great sandwich can be so much more.

If you want evidence, turn to page 5 to learn about our experience creating a recipe for Cuban sandwiches, that popular Florida-born construction of roast pork, ham, salami, Swiss cheese, and pickles stacked onto sliced bread and lightly toasted. Like other truly remarkable sandwiches, it's really just a pile of ingredients that taste great on their own but, when brought together, create something that's more than the sum of its parts. Something with a story. Something with a soul.

That's what cooking is all about, isn't it? Taking a little of this, a little of that, and putting it together in a careful way to create an experience and tell a story.

TUCKER SHAW

Editor in Chief

P.S. Speaking of a story, visit **CooksCountry.com/thetestcook** to see our behind-the-scenes video series detailing the development of this recipe. You'll see every step of our process in vivid detail. What story will your dinner tell tonight?

Illustration: Hannah Jacobs

BUON APPETITO

Big Flavors from Italian America

This book is an homage to the generous, gutsy, red-sauced family-style cooking born in Italian American kitchens from coast to coast, with 130 tested-and-perfected recipes. This is food we never tire of—simple, hearty weeknight meals; baked pastas and roasts fit for Sunday dinner; and a baker's assortment of rustic breads and sweets. Order your copy at **AmericasTestKitchen.com/bigflavors**.

 Find us on **Facebook**
facebook.com/CooksCountry

 Find us on **Instagram**
instagram.com/CooksCountry

 Follow us on **Pinterest**
pinterest.com/TestKitchen

 Follow us on **Twitter**
twitter.com/TestKitchen

Cook's Country

Chief Executive Officer David Nussbaum
Chief Creative Officer Jack Bishop
Editor in Chief Tucker Shaw
Executive Managing Editor Todd Meier
Executive Food Editor Bryan Roof
Deputy Editor Scott Kathan
Deputy Food Editor Morgan Bolling
Senior Editor Cecelia Jenkins
Associate Editors Alli Berkey, Matthew Fairman
Photo Team/Special Events Manager Tim McQuinn
Test Cooks Mark Huxsoll, Jessica Rudolph
Lead Test Cook, Photo Team Eric Haessler
Assistant Test Cooks, Photo Team Hannah Fenton,
  Jacqueline Gochenouer, Gina McCreadie, Christa West
Copy Editors Christine Campbell, April Poole, Rachel Schow
Contributing Editor Eva Katz
Senior Science Research Editor Paul Adams
Hosts & Executive Editors, Television Bridget Lancaster,
  Julia Collin Davison

Executive Editors, Tastings & Testings Hannah Crowley,
  Lisa McManus
Senior Editors, Tastings & Testings Lauren Savoie, Kate Sh
Associate Editor, Tastings & Testings Miye Bromberg
Assistant Editors, Tastings & Testings
  Riddley Gemperlein-Schirm, Carolyn Grillo, Emily Phares

Creative Director John Torres
Photography Director Julie Cote
Art Director Susan Levin
Associate Art Director Maggie Edgar
Art Director, Tastings & Testings Marissa Angelone
Senior Staff Photographers Steve Klise, Daniel J. van Acke
Staff Photographer Kevin White
Photography Producer Meredith Mulcahy

Senior Director, Creative Operations Alice Carpenter
Senior Editor, Special Projects Christie Morrison
Senior Manager, Publishing Operations Taylor Argenzio
Imaging Manager Lauren Robbins
Production & Imaging Specialists Tricia Neumyer, Dennis N
  Amanda Yong
Deputy Editor, Editorial Operations Megan Ginsberg
Editorial Assistants, Editorial Operations Tess Berger,
  Sara Zatopek
Test Kitchen Director Erin McMurrer
Assistant Test Kitchen Director Alexxa Benson
Test Kitchen Manager Meridith Lippard
Test Kitchen Facilities Manager Kayce Vanpelt
Senior Kitchen Assistant Receiver Heather Tolmie
Senior Kitchen Assistant Shopper Avery Lowe
Kitchen Assistants Gladis Campos, Blanca Castanza,
  Amarilys Merced

Chief Financial Officer Jackie McCauley Ford
Senior Manager, Customer Support Tim Quinn
Customer Support Specialist Mitchell Axelson
Event Coordinator Michaela Hughes

Chief Digital Officer Fran Middleton
VP, Marketing Natalie Vinard
Director, Audience Acquisition & Partnerships Evan Steine
Director, Social Media Marketing Kathryn Przybyla
Social Media Coordinators Charlotte Erritty, Sarah Sandler,
  Norma Tentori

Chief Revenue Officer Sara Domville

Director, Public Relations & Communications Brian Frankl
Public Relations Coordinator Madeleine Cohen

**Senior VP, Human Resources & Organizational
  Development** Colleen Zelina
Human Resources Manager Jason Lynott

Circulation Services PubWorX ProCirc

11

AMERICA'S TEST KITCHEN ®

America's Test Kitchen is a real test kitchen located in Boston. It is the home of more than 60 test cooks, editors, and cookware specialists. Our mission is to test recipes until we understand exactly how and why they work and eventually arrive at the very best version. We also test kitchen equipment and supermarket ingredients in search of products that offer the best value and performance. You can watch us work by tuning in to *America's Test Kitchen* (AmericasTestKitchen.com) and *Cook's Country* (CooksCountry.com) on public television, and you can listen to our weekly segments on *The Splendid Table* on public radio. You can also follow us on Facebook, Twitter, Pinterest, and Instagram.

26

33

Cook's Country magazine (ISSN 1552-1990), number 91, is published bimonthly by America's Test Kitchen Limited Partnership, 21 Drydock Avenue, Suite 210E, Boston, MA 02210. Copyright 2020 America's Test Kitchen Limited Partnership. Periodicals postage paid at Boston, MA, and additional mailing offices, USPS #023453. Publications Mail Agreement No. 40020778. Return undeliverable Canadian addresses to P.O. Box 875, Station A, Windsor, ON N9A 6P2. POSTMASTER: Send address changes to *Cook's Country*, P.O. Box 6018, Harlan, IA 51593-1518. For subscription and gift subscription orders, subscription inquiries, or change of address notices, visit AmericasTestKitchen.com/support, call 800-526-8447 in the U.S. or 515-237-3663 from outside the U.S., or write to us at *Cook's Country*, P.O. Box 6018, Harlan, IA 51593-1518. PRINTED IN THE USA.

by Cecelia Jenkins

Mushroom Cleaning

What's the best way to clean mushrooms? Is it OK to wash them, or will the water make them soggy?
–Emily Scott, Milford, N.H.

Many cooks fear that rinsing mushrooms will cause them to soak up water like a sponge, turn soggy, and steam—rather than brown—in the pan. In the test kitchen, we found that rinsing was actually fine for many mushrooms, as long as we rinsed them whole (before chopping). We proved this by weighing whole mushrooms before and after washing. We found that mushrooms without their gills fully exposed (button, cremini, etc.) did not absorb much water while being rinsed in a colander. Just make sure to dry the mushrooms before prepping and cooking—a quick spin in a salad spinner works well—so they'll be able to brown.

However, varieties with exposed gills, such as portobellos, did absorb a lot of water when rinsed, and that absorption did adversely affect how they cooked, so for these varieties we recommend brushing off the dirt with paper towels or a pastry brush instead.
THE BOTTOM LINE: It's OK to rinse mushrooms such as buttons and cremini; for varieties with their gills exposed, simply brush away the dirt instead.

FEW GILLS EXPOSED
OK to wash with water

GILLS EXPOSED
Brush clean and keep dry

What, Exactly, Is Canadian Bacon?

–Shelly DeSalvo, Boise, Idaho

Canadian bacon, commonly known in Canada as "back bacon" or "peameal bacon" (it is sometimes rolled in ground yellow peas before being sliced), is made from cured and smoked pork loin—which is much leaner than the pork belly used to make American bacon. Canadian bacon is closer to mild ham than it is to assertive American bacon. It is fully cooked and can be eaten directly out of the package—although most cooks like to warm it in a skillet before eating it. It's the traditional choice of meat for eggs Benedict and for a famous American fast-food sandwich.
THE BOTTOM LINE: American bacon comes from fatty pork belly and is assertively seasoned with salt and sugar before being smoked. Canadian bacon is made from lean pork loin and is much milder.

NORTH OF THE BORDER
Canadian bacon is leaner than American bacon.

Searing Scallops

Do you have a preferred method for cooking sea scallops?
–Ronald Thomas, Hamilton, Mont.

Sea scallops are one of our favorite types of seafood to cook (and eat!). But these mollusks are delicate and easily overcooked—and overcooked scallops are rubbery. They are best quickly seared to build a flavorful crust on the outside while the inside remains silky. Cooking scallops successfully starts at the fish counter. Avoid "wet" scallops, which are treated with chemicals to preserve them; they are typically bright white and are often sitting in a pool of cloudy liquid in the case. We much prefer "dry" scallops, which haven't been treated. Dry scallops often have a rosy tint, feel tacky, and taste much better.

Next, make sure to dry the scallops before searing them—the cooking time for searing scallops is so short that extra moisture can throw off the timing. Make sure your skillet (nonstick, traditional, and cast-iron all work well) and oil are thoroughly preheated before adding the scallops. Since salt draws moisture out of foods over time, you don't want to salt scallops too far in advance: Season them just before they go into the hot skillet. And finally, don't overcrowd the skillet; giving each scallop a little room ensures that it will sear, not steam. We like to position the scallops in a ring around the skillet's circumference, starting at the handle so that we can easily remember which of them went into the skillet first.

The cooking goes quickly. You know the scallops are perfectly done when they're translucent in the middle (about 115 degrees) and opaque near the top and bottom, with deep golden crusts. You can baste the cooking scallops with melted butter to add flavor, if you like.

THE BOTTOM LINE: Buy "dry" scallops, and then dry them thoroughly. Preheat a pan to ripping hot, season the scallops at the last minute, don't overcrowd them in the pan, and cook them for just a minute or so per side.

1. Prep Dry the scallops well and season them only when the pan is preheating.

2. Sear Place the scallops in a ring around the circumference of the hot skillet.

3. Finish For even cooking, flip them and pull them out of the pan in the same order.

SIMPLE SEARED SCALLOPS
Serves 4

Be sure to purchase "dry" scallops and remove the tough tendon attached to the side. To ensure that the scallops develop the best crust when cooking on a gas stovetop, place them in a ring around the circumference of the skillet (not directly in the center): Here they sit just above the burner, a spot that will always be hotter than the pan's center. In this orientation, you can use the handle as a marker to help keep track of which scallops went into the skillet first. Start at the handle and add them clockwise so you know the order in which you should flip them (first to last).

1½ pounds large sea scallops, tendons removed
2 tablespoons vegetable oil, divided
¾ teaspoon table salt
¼ teaspoon pepper
Lemon wedges

1. Place scallops on clean dish towel and place second clean dish towel on top. Gently press to blot liquid. Keeping towel on top, let scallops sit at room temperature for 10 minutes while towels absorb moisture.
2. Heat 1 tablespoon oil in 12-inch nonstick skillet over high heat until just smoking, about 2 minutes. Sprinkle scallops on both sides with salt and pepper. Add half of scallops, flat side down, in single layer around circumference of skillet; cook for 3 minutes, flipping halfway through cooking. Transfer scallops to plate and tent with aluminum foil. Repeat with remaining 1 tablespoon oil and remaining scallops. Serve with lemon wedges.

Don't Waste Those Wipes

Anne Hsu Gibson, Boulder, Colo.

I often use cleaning wipes for my kitchen counters, and I've noticed that there's always extra fluid at the bottom of the canister when the wipes run out. Instead of just tossing the whole thing into the recycling bin, I now stick a couple of paper towels into the canister, shake it up, and eke out a few more "cleaning wipes."

Cork It with a Carrot

–Benjamin Musher, Houston, Texas

My wife and I opened a bottle of sparkling wine. We didn't finish the bottle, and we couldn't fit the original cork back into the bottle's mouth. In a pinch, we stuck a peeled carrot into the bottle opening to use as a substitute cork. The tapered shape of the carrot provided a surprisingly tight seal, and the wine was still fizzy the next day.

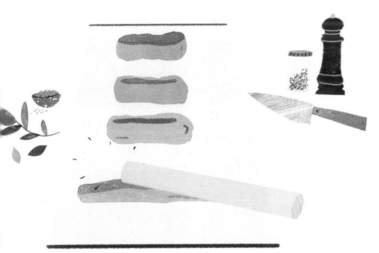

No Meat Pounder, No Problem

–Macon Torterich, Surprise, Ariz.

I don't own a meat pounder, but I've discovered a great substitute that I can use when recipes call for thin cutlets of meat: a dowel-style rolling pin. I hold one end of the pin and gently pound the meat with the other end. The rolling pin is heavy enough to give me good leverage but not so heavy that it tires out my arm or wrist while pounding.

Are All White Chips the Same?

by Carolyn Grillo

PRODUCT
TASTING

IN THE TEST kitchen, we love white chocolate chips in all sorts of sweets. According to the U.S. Food and Drug Administration, white chocolate must contain at least 20 percent cocoa butter. Many products replace some—or all—of that cocoa butter with refined fats; these products can't legally be called white chocolate. Instead, they're labeled white baking chips, morsels, or melting wafers. (For simplicity, we've chosen to refer to these products as "white chips.") We gathered two varieties of white chocolate chips and four varieties of white chips and tasted them plain and in bark; then we pitted the white chocolate chips against our highest-ranking white chips in blondies. Surprisingly, we preferred white chips in both flavor and texture. Some tasters described the white chocolate chips as complex, but others noticed off-putting sour notes. In bark, the white chocolate chips were "too soft," while the white chips were "snappy." Our new favorite chips, Ghirardelli Classic White Baking Chips, are milky, sweet, and smooth. Whether you're adding them to cookies or melting them for bark, they are sure to please.

RECOMMENDED		TASTERS' NOTES
Ghirardelli Classic White Baking Chips **Price:** $4.59 for 11 oz ($0.42 per oz) **Type:** White chips	Our Favorite 	The "mild flavor" was "milky" with hints of "vanilla," "caramel," and "butterscotch." The chips were "creamy" when eaten plain and "smooth" and "dense," with a good "snap and crunch," in bark.
Ghirardelli White Melting Wafers **Price:** $4.99 for 10 oz ($0.50 per oz) **Type:** White chips		The flavor of our runner-up was "subtle" with "caramel notes." It produced a bark with a "firm" consistency and a "nice bite." Tasters really liked its "lovely creamy texture."
Guittard Choc-Au-Lait Baking Chips **Price:** $5.33 for 12 oz ($0.44 per oz) **Type:** White chips		We found these chips, which contain some cocoa butter, "milky," "sweet," and "smooth." One taster described their texture as "firm, which is a good thing for bark," yet "still melts on my tongue."
Nestlé Toll House Premier White Morsels **Price:** $2.99 for 12 oz ($0.25 per oz) **Type:** White chips		The flavor of our lowest-ranking white chips reminded tasters of "marshmallow and coconut." Tasters called this sample "very sweet," with notes of "fake vanilla."
Guittard Collection Etienne Crème Français 31% Cacao White Chocolate Wafers **Price:** $16.98 for 1 lb ($1.06 per oz) **Type:** White chocolate		The bark made with these real chips was "way too soft." However, our tasters liked the chips' "creamy" texture when sampling them plain, describing the flavor as "complex."
Callebaut Recipe No. W2 Finest Belgian White Chocolate Callets **Price:** $30.00 for 2 lb ($0.94 per oz) **Type:** White chocolate		Tasters described these real chips as "nutty" and "sour," with a "rich" texture. The chips didn't perform well in bark because they contain cocoa butter; the bark remained "squishy" and "too soft."

*To learn the secrets to perfecting the iconic **Cuban sandwich**, we went straight to its birthplace: Tampa, Florida.*

The annual Cuban Sandwich Festival, created by Victor Padilla and Jolie Gonzalez-Padilla, has become a massive two-day event that transforms Centennial Park in Tampa's Ybor City neighborhood with music, performances, and, in 2019, a winning attempt at a world record for the longest Cuban sandwich—183 feet.

Ybor City, most historians and other experts agree, is the birthplace of the Cuban sandwich, which reflects the Cuban, Italian, German, and Spanish influences present in Tampa.

The marquee event is a contest to crown the best Cuban sandwich maker in the world. Contestants like Daniel Navarro (top right) and Iliana Cordero (below) often present twists on the theme to a strict panel of judges; for example, cooks from Miami may present sandwiches "Miami-style," in which the salami, essential in Tampa-style versions, is left off.

Made in AMERICA

CUBAN SANDWICH FESTIVAL

Text by Bryan Roof; photos by Steve Klise

I N TAMPA, FLORIDA, the Cuban sandwich is an enduring source of pride, sustenance, and fierce debate. Connoisseurs take strong stands on each element.

Cuban sandwiches are derived from *mixto* sandwiches, which were popular in Cuba more than a century ago. "As the sandwich emigrated from Cuba to Key West and eventually to Tampa, the name evolved from 'mixto' to 'Cubano' and 'Cuban,'" says historian Jeff Houck. They were a common lunch for laborers in the cigar factories, made with a variety of meats that could survive in paper sacks at room temperature. No mayonnaise, tomato, or lettuce.

Illustration: Hannah Jacob

LA SEGUNDA BAKERY

La Segunda Bakery in Ybor City sold its first loaf in 1915. Today, employees including Anthony Sanches (below left) and Bryant Valdez (below right) produce 20,000 loaves of Cuban bread daily. The massive operation lacks climate control, a challenge in Florida. "The bread takes on the personality of the weather—humidity and heat," says co-owner Copeland More. Bakers adjust the process based on the weather that day—the dough might move in and out of the refrigerator or spend extra time in the steam-fed proof box to account for the temperature. Each loaf is baked with a palm frond on top (left) for a signature La Segunda look.

Meanwhile, Back in the Test Kitchen

by Cecelia Jenkins

AFTER EXECUTIVE FOOD Editor Bryan Roof returned from the Cuban Sandwich Festival in Tampa, he set a goal for me: Create a home recipe for Cuban sandwiches that would stand up to the prizewinners he'd tasted.

The sandwich is familiar on a basic level: Roasted spiced pork, ham, Swiss cheese, dill pickles, and yellow mustard on soft bread that's pressed and toasted until golden brown. In Tampa, the sandwich also includes Genoa salami.

That's a fantastic combination any way you look at it, so it's no surprise that there are as many variations of the sandwich as there are fans of it. I wanted to take it back to its Tampa roots: Yes, there'd be salami on it; yes, I'd follow the traditional, particular order of components and amounts of each; yes, I'd even make the bread; yes, all this for a sandwich. And yes (!), it would be worth it.

Let's start with the bread. A Cuban sandwich must be made on golden Cuban bread that's fluffy on the inside and crisp on the outside, which is not easy to find outside Florida. It's traditionally enriched with lard for a savory flavor (not sweet or yeasty like a typical sandwich loaf). When the fully assembled sandwich is toasted on the griddle, the bread is just sturdy enough to hold the many layers together as the flavors fuse.

I found it essential to slice the roast pork very thin. Thick slices interfered with a clean, even press, and shredded pork was harder to distribute evenly on the bread. Cooling the roast so it firmed up a bit before slicing meant that I could achieve the perfect thinness with a good sharp knife.

Taking inspiration from some creative cooks at the Tampa festival, I included a swipe of flavorful *mojo* on each bottom slice of bread for extra complexity and brightness.

After 35 pork butts; 80 loaves of bread; and piles of ham, cheese, pickles, and more, I pressed and toasted my final batch of sandwiches. I cut them into their characteristic triangle shape, and coworkers began to swarm.

The work is worth it. Just make sure you eat it point side up.

COLUMBIA RESTAURANT

Opened in 1905 as Columbia Saloon, Columbia Restaurant in Ybor City originally served as a tasting room for Florida Brewing Company. In addition to beer, they served *café con leche* and *mixto* sandwiches. They've been sourcing bread for their sandwiches, which they consider the definitive Cuban sandwiches, from La Segunda Bakery for nearly 100 years. Andrea Gonzmart-Williams (left) is the fifth-generation owner.

"The architecture of the sandwich is absolutely paramount. It has to be precise to be that original flavor." Even the application of the mustard is given serious consideration, and at Columbia it must go only on the top piece of bread. Historian Jeff Houck tells me, "If [the mustard] goes on the bottom, it coats your tongue. When it's on top, it blossoms on the roof of your mouth and colors the entire experience."

For a link to a video series that details the development of the recipes we used to make our version of a Cuban sandwich, go to **CooksCountry.com/thetestcook.**

OUR RECIPES →

CUBAN SANDWICHES *Serves 4*

We strongly prefer to use our Cuban Bread for this recipe. But if you don't have the time to make it, you can use four 7- to 8-inch soft white Italian-style sub rolls or two 15-inch loaves of soft supermarket Italian or French bread. Do not use a thick-crusted rustic or artisan-style loaf or a baguette. To make slicing the Cuban Roast Pork easier, be sure to chill it thoroughly beforehand. *Mojo* and mayonnaise aren't typical ingredients in Tampa-style Cuban sandwiches, but they make nice additions.

- 1   recipe Cuban Bread (recipe follows)
- ¼   cup mojo from Cuban Roast Pork with Mojo (optional) (recipe follows)
- ¼   cup mayonnaise (optional)
- 12 ounces thinly sliced deli ham
- 10 ounces thinly sliced Cuban roast pork from Cuban Roast Pork with Mojo (2 cups) (recipe follows)
- 3   ounces thinly sliced deli Genoa salami with peppercorns
- 6   ounces thinly sliced deli Swiss cheese
- 16 dill pickle chips
- ¼   cup yellow mustard
- 4   tablespoons unsalted butter, cut into 4 pieces, divided

1. Adjust oven rack to middle position and heat oven to 200 degrees. Set wire rack in rimmed baking sheet. Cut each loaf of bread in half crosswise, then cut each piece in half horizontally.

2. Brush bread bottoms with mojo, if using, and spread with mayonnaise, if using. Layer on ham, followed by pork, salami, Swiss cheese, and pickles, overlapping and/or folding meats as needed to keep them from overhanging sides of bread. Spread mustard on bread tops. Cap sandwiches with bread tops.

3. Melt 1 tablespoon butter in 12-inch nonstick skillet over medium-low heat. Place 2 sandwiches in skillet, right side up, in alternating directions, and spread far apart. Place heavy Dutch oven on top and cook until bottoms of sandwiches are uniformly golden brown and feel firm when tapped, 5 to 7 minutes, rotating sandwiches in skillet as needed. (You will need to flip sandwiches to tap them.)

4. Transfer sandwiches to cutting board. Melt 1 tablespoon butter in now-empty skillet. Return sandwiches to skillet toasted side up. Place Dutch oven on top and continue to cook until second side is uniformly golden brown and feels firm when tapped, 3 to 5 minutes longer.

5. Transfer toasted sandwiches to prepared wire rack and place in oven to keep warm. Wipe skillet clean with paper towels. Repeat with remaining 2 tablespoons butter and remaining 2 sandwiches. Cut sandwiches in half on steep diagonal and serve.

CUBAN SANDWICHES

A great sandwich is built on great parts. This Florida original is no exception.

by Cecelia Jenkins

E Pluribus Sandwich

The traditional ingredients in a Cuban sandwich reflect the unique cultural mix of its birthplace in Ybor City. *Mojo* **roast pork** showcases Cuban and Spanish influences, while **Genoa salami** and **yellow mustard and pickles** have Italian and German roots.

CUBAN ROAST PORK
WITH MOJO *Serves 6 to 8*

Avoid buying a pork butt wrapped in netting; it will contain smaller, separate lobes of meat rather than one whole roast. The pork will take longer to cook in a stainless-steel pot than in an enameled cast-iron Dutch oven, the pot we used while developing the recipe. If using a stainless-steel pot, place a sheet of aluminum foil over the pot before affixing the lid. If you plan to make Cuban sandwiches with the leftovers, it is best to slice only what you want to serve and then slice the chilled leftover pork for the sandwiches. You will need about 10 ounces, or 2 cups, of pork and ¼ cup of *mojo* for the sandwiches. If using table salt, cut the amounts of salt in half.

PORK
- ⅓ cup kosher salt
- ⅓ cup packed light brown sugar
- 1 tablespoon grated lime zest (2 limes)
- 1 tablespoon grated orange zest
- 3 garlic cloves, minced
- 2 teaspoons ground cumin
- 2 teaspoons dried oregano
- ½ teaspoon red pepper flakes
- 1 (5-pound) boneless pork butt roast with fat cap

MOJO
- ⅓ cup extra-virgin olive oil
- 6 garlic cloves, minced
- ⅓ cup pineapple juice
- ⅓ cup orange juice
- ⅓ cup lime juice (3 limes)
- 1 tablespoon yellow mustard
- 1¼ teaspoons ground cumin
- 1 teaspoon kosher salt
- ¾ teaspoon pepper
- ¾ teaspoon dried oregano
- ¼ teaspoon red pepper flakes

  Thinly sliced onion rounds

Cuban roast pork should be tender, juicy, and full of the *mojo* flavors of citrus, garlic, oregano, and cumin. After testing, we nailed down three keys to a flavorful, moist, sliceable roast pork, just right for a sandwich or to serve by itself.

- **For juicier pork** we use an overnight dry rub instead of a wet marinade to season. Don't worry: Our fruity, fresh mojo for serving gives you the citrus punch you expect.
- **For tender meat with a burnished look**, we first braise the pork in water, covered, to break down its tough connective tissue and collagen. We then roast it uncovered to caramelize its exterior.
- **A garnish of crisp raw onion** helps cut through all the porky richness.

1. FOR THE PORK: Combine salt, sugar, lime zest, orange zest, garlic, cumin, oregano, and pepper flakes in bowl. Using sharp knife, trim fat cap on pork to ¼ inch. Cut 1-inch crosshatch pattern in fat cap.
2. Place pork on large double layer of plastic wrap. Sprinkle pork all over with salt mixture. Wrap pork tightly in plastic, place on plate, and refrigerate for at least 12 hours or up to 24 hours.
3. Adjust oven rack to middle position and heat oven to 325 degrees. Unwrap pork; transfer to Dutch oven, fat side up; and pour 2 cups water around pork. Cover, transfer to oven, and cook until meat registers 175 degrees in center, 2½ to 3 hours.
4. Uncover pork and continue to cook until meat registers 195 degrees in center and fork slips easily in and out of meat, 45 minutes to 1¾ hours longer. Transfer pork to carving board, tent with aluminum foil, and let rest for 45 minutes.
5. FOR THE MOJO: While pork rests, heat oil and garlic in small saucepan over low heat, stirring often, until tiny bubbles appear and garlic is fragrant and straw-colored, 3 to 5 minutes. Let cool for at least 5 minutes. Whisk pineapple juice, orange juice, lime juice, mustard, cumin, salt, pepper, oregano, and pepper flakes into cooled garlic oil.
6. Slice pork as thin as possible (some meat may shred; this is OK) and transfer to serving platter. Serve with onion and mojo.

CUBAN BREAD *Makes two 15-inch loaves*

Covering the bread with the disposable pan during baking traps steam to create a crispier crust. You can substitute shortening for the lard, if desired. We prefer the flavor that the overnight fermentation provides, but if you're strapped for time, you can ferment the sponge for at least 1 hour or up to 4 hours at room temperature instead. Be gentle when slashing the shaped loaves or they will bake up wide and squat. As a table bread, these loaves are best eaten warm, but for Cuban sandwiches, we found that two-day-old bread is still acceptable.

SPONGE
- ¼ cup water
- ¼ cup (1¼ ounces) all-purpose flour
- ½ teaspoon instant or rapid-rise yeast

DOUGH
- 3 cups (15 ounces) all-purpose flour
- 2 teaspoons instant or rapid-rise yeast
- 1½ teaspoons table salt
- 1 cup warm water (110 degrees)
- ¼ cup lard

- 1 (16 by 12-inch) rectangular disposable aluminum roasting pan

1. FOR THE SPONGE: Whisk water, flour, and yeast with fork in liquid measuring cup until consistency of thin pancake batter. Cover with plastic wrap and refrigerate overnight (sponge will rise and collapse).
2. FOR THE DOUGH: Whisk flour, yeast, and salt together in bowl of stand mixer. Add warm water, lard, and sponge. Fit mixer with dough hook and mix on low speed until no dry flour remains, about 2 minutes, scraping down bowl as needed. Increase speed to medium and knead for 8 minutes. (Dough will be sticky and clear sides of bowl but still stick to bottom.)
3. Turn out dough onto lightly floured counter, sprinkle top with flour, and knead briefly to form smooth ball, about 30 seconds. Transfer dough to greased large bowl and turn to coat. Cover with plastic and let dough rise at room temperature until doubled in size, about 45 minutes.
4. Line rimless baking sheet with parchment paper. Turn out dough onto floured counter and cut into 2 equal pieces, about 14 ounces each.
5. Working with 1 piece of dough at a time, flatten into 10 by 6-inch rectangle with long side parallel to counter's edge. Fold top edge of rectangle down to midline, pressing to seal. Fold bottom edge of rectangle up to midline, pressing to seal. Fold dough in half so top and bottom edges meet; pinch seam and ends to seal. Flip dough seam side down and gently roll into 15-inch loaf with tapered ends.
6. Transfer loaf, seam side down, to 1 side of prepared sheet. Repeat shaping with second piece of dough and place about 3 inches from first loaf on other side of sheet. Cover loosely with plastic and let rise at room temperature until puffy, about 30 minutes. Adjust oven rack to middle position and heat oven to 450 degrees.

At La Segunda Bakery (see "Made in America" on page 4), the *pan cubano* is airy and light, with a paper-thin crust—just right for sandwiches or for buttering and eating.

- **For a fluffy interior crumb** we make a "sponge" of water, flour, and yeast that we allow to ferment overnight before adding it to the rest of the ingredients. This step helps create the carbon dioxide bubbles that give the finished bread its characteristic airy texture.
- **We cover the loaves** with a rectangular disposable aluminum roasting pan for the first part of baking; the pan traps steam, which then condenses on the bread. This moisture gelatinizes the starches on the outside of the bread, creating the thin, crisp crust we were after.

7. Using sharp paring knife in swift, fluid motion, make ⅛-inch-deep lengthwise slash along top of each loaf, starting and stopping about 1½ inches from ends. Cover loaves with inverted disposable pan. Bake for 20 minutes. Using tongs, remove disposable pan and continue to bake until loaves are light golden brown and centers register 210 degrees, 10 to 12 minutes longer.
8. Transfer loaves to wire rack and let cool for 30 minutes. Serve warm.

TO MAKE AHEAD

Fully cooled loaves can be wrapped in aluminum foil and stored at room temperature for up to 2 days. Cooled bread can also be wrapped in plastic wrap, then in foil, and frozen for up to 1 month. Unwrap and warm before serving.

Garlic Steaks

Garlic goes on the steaks before, during, and after cooking. We're not messing around here. **by Alli Berkey**

WHAT'S THE BEST way to infuse steak with garlic flavor? That was the question I asked myself—and my colleagues—when my editor gave me the assignment to develop a recipe for garlicky strip steaks. (Strip steak is a favorite cut in the test kitchen for its combination of tenderness and big flavor.) Was a garlic rub the best path forward? A garlicky oil marinade? A garlic-laden finishing sauce? I headed into the test kitchen to try them all.

Early tests proved that while steaks rubbed with garlic powder and granulated garlic tasted OK, they lacked the sharp kick of fresh garlic. So next I tested oil-based marinades with fresh garlic prepped in three different ways: minced, sliced, and smashed whole cloves (we know that garlic's flavor compounds are oil-soluble, so the oil helps the garlic express its potential). Minced garlic provided the most garlic flavor by far, which makes sense because the more finely garlic is chopped, the more flavor compounds are exposed. After 4 hours, I rinsed off the marinade (and dried the steaks). Rinsing before cooking prevented the bits of garlic in the marinade from burning in the skillet and turning bitter. I was glad to find that this rinsing didn't diminish the garlic flavor that had penetrated the steaks.

Serving already-garlicky steaks with a potent garlic sauce makes them over-the-top delicious.

The meat tasted great—but, well, I have a thing for garlic and I wanted more. I found that lightly browning whole cloves of garlic in the oil I then used to cook the steaks was a solid move for ramping up the garlic flavor. Serving those mellowed, browned cloves with the steak added yet another layer of garlic flavor. And finally, whisking some of the hot garlic-infused oil into a simple combination of softened butter and minced garlic gave me a potent condiment to serve alongside the steaks.

To minimize smoking and ensure perfectly cooked meat, I started the steaks over medium heat, flipping them every few minutes. Gradually, a dark, savory, seasoned crust developed on each side. The resulting steaks were incredible: deeply browned, perfectly cooked, and smelling and tasting of rich, bright garlic. Fellow garlic lovers, I think we have a new favorite dish.

GARLIC STEAKS *Serves 4*

We developed this recipe using a non-stick skillet, but a cast-iron skillet will also work well. If you're using table salt, use 1½ teaspoons for the steaks and ¼ teaspoon for the garlic sauce and toasted garlic.

STEAKS
- ¼ cup extra-virgin olive oil
- 6 garlic cloves, minced
- 1 tablespoon kosher salt, divided
- 1½ teaspoons pepper, divided
- 2 (1-pound) boneless strip steaks, 1½ inches thick, trimmed

GARLIC SAUCE AND TOASTED GARLIC
- 4 tablespoons unsalted butter, softened
- 1 garlic clove, minced, plus 6 garlic cloves, smashed and peeled
- ½ teaspoon kosher salt
- ¼ teaspoon pepper
- ¼ cup extra-virgin olive oil
- 2 sprigs fresh thyme

1. FOR THE STEAKS: In 1-gallon zipper-lock bag, combine oil, garlic, 2 teaspoons salt, and 1 teaspoon pepper. Place steaks in bag and seal. Turn bag to evenly coat steaks in marinade. Refrigerate for at least 4 hours or up to 24 hours.

2. Remove steaks from marinade and rinse under cold water to remove any pieces of garlic; discard marinade. Pat steaks dry with paper towels. Sprinkle steaks with remaining 1 teaspoon salt and ½ teaspoon pepper; set aside.

3. FOR THE GARLIC SAUCE AND TOASTED GARLIC: Combine butter, minced garlic, salt, and pepper in bowl. Heat oil, thyme sprigs, and smashed garlic in 12-inch nonstick skillet over medium heat until garlic has softened and turned light brown, about 5 minutes, flipping garlic as needed to ensure even browning.

4. Remove smashed garlic from skillet with slotted spoon and set aside; discard thyme sprigs. Add 2 tablespoons hot garlic oil from skillet to butter mixture and whisk to combine (mixture should be emulsified and creamy). Set aside.

5. Heat remaining 2 tablespoons garlic oil in skillet over medium heat until just smoking. Add steaks and cook, flipping every 2 minutes, until well browned and meat registers 115 degrees (for medium-rare), 12 to 16 minutes. Transfer steaks to carving board, tent with aluminum foil, and let rest for 10 minutes. Rewhisk sauce to make fluid again. Slice steaks thin and serve with sauce and reserved smashed garlic.

Using Homemade Garlic Oil to Create Multilayered Garlic Flavor

1. Brown smashed garlic cloves in oil with fresh thyme sprigs.

2. Add some garlic oil to butter and minced garlic to make serving sauce.

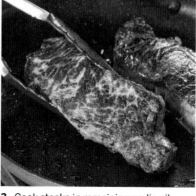

3. Cook steaks in remaining garlic oil; serve with sauce and toasted garlic cloves.

Pork Stroganoff

We love the traditional version of this soothing, creamy dish. But we hate the price tag.

by Natalie Estrada

DURING THE BLEAK winter months here in the Northeast, nothing's quite as comforting as a bowl of warm stroganoff—soft noodles, strips of tender and flavorful meat, and a supercreamy sauce. But instead of using expensive beef tenderloin, the cut most frequently called for in recipes for this dish, I wanted to use pork tenderloin, a favorite in my kitchen for its faintly sweet flavor and relatively low price. Traditional? Nope, and that's OK.

I knew that I had to cook the pork relatively quickly so it wouldn't dry out. I began by cutting the tenderloin in half lengthwise and then sliced each half ¼ inch thick. Next, I dredged the pork in flour to promote browning. I seared the pieces for about 3 minutes and then removed them from the pot with a slotted spoon. The leftover fond served as a base to build a flavorful sauce.

I added mushrooms, onion, sage, garlic, and tomato paste for a savory underpinning. Once these ingredients started to brown, I added chicken broth and wine, scraped up the fond, and continued to cook the sauce until it was silky. I returned the pork to the mix, poured the saucy mixture over cooked egg noodles, and . . . well, let's just say this stroganoff was missing some punch. It was watery and weak without much pork flavor.

My first move was to introduce some pancetta up front. I cut it up and rendered its fat in the pot before cooking the tenderloin. This added deep, meaty, complex notes to enhance the tenderloin's more demure flavors.

Next, I decided to cook the noodles directly in the sauce, allowing them to soak up more flavor while also adding a bit of starchy body to the sauce. A quick 10-minute simmer and the noodles were al dente. Off the heat,

I added tangy sour cream and a bit more sage and sprinkled some chives over the top.

I finally achieved what I'd been searching for: a stroganoff that was satisfying, comforting, and rich—and easy enough (just one pot!) for a weeknight.

PORK STROGANOFF *Serves 4*
Be sure to buy a ¼-inch-thick hunk of pancetta from the deli counter rather than presliced pancetta, as larger chunks are important here.

- 3 ounces pancetta, cut into ¼-inch pieces
- 1 tablespoon extra-virgin olive oil
- 1 (12-ounce) pork tenderloin, trimmed, halved lengthwise, and sliced crosswise ¼ inch thick
- 3 tablespoons all-purpose flour, divided
- 1 teaspoon table salt, divided
- 1 teaspoon pepper, divided
- 3 tablespoons unsalted butter, divided
- 12 ounces cremini mushrooms, trimmed and sliced thin
- 1 large onion, chopped fine
- 4 teaspoons chopped fresh sage, divided
- 3 garlic cloves, minced
- 2 teaspoons tomato paste
- 4 cups chicken broth
- ¼ cup dry white wine
- 8 ounces (4 cups) egg noodles
- ½ cup sour cream
- 2 tablespoons minced fresh chives

1. Cook pancetta and oil in Dutch oven over medium heat until pancetta is lightly browned and crispy, about 10 minutes. Using slotted spoon, transfer pancetta to large plate, leaving fat in pot.
2. Toss pork, 2 tablespoons flour, ½ teaspoon salt, and ½ teaspoon pepper together in bowl. Add 1 tablespoon butter to fat left in pot and melt over high heat. Add pork in single layer, breaking up any clumps, and cook, without stirring, until browned on bottom, about 2 minutes. Stir and continue to cook until pork is no longer pink, about 1 minute longer. Transfer to plate with pancetta.
3. Melt remaining 2 tablespoons butter in now-empty pot over medium heat. Add mushrooms, onion, remaining ½ teaspoon salt, and remaining ½ teaspoon pepper and cook until any liquid has evaporated and vegetables have just begun to brown, 7 to 9 minutes. Add 1 tablespoon sage, garlic, tomato paste, and remaining 1 tablespoon flour and cook until fragrant, about 30 seconds.
4. Stir in broth and wine and bring to simmer, scraping up any browned bits. Stir in noodles and cook, uncovered, stirring occasionally, until noodles are just tender, 9 to 11 minutes.
5. Add pork and pancetta and cook until warmed through, about 1 minute. Off heat, stir in sour cream and remaining 1 teaspoon sage until thoroughly combined. Season with salt and pepper to taste. Sprinkle with chives and serve.

Pork tenderloin cooks in a flash and is supremely tender in this flavorful one-pot dish.

Bovine Inspiration
We used a trick for cooking beef to keep the pork tender and flavor the sauce.

1. Dredge pork in flour, salt, and pepper.

2. Brown in a single layer in butter.

Porky Pancetta
We call for pancetta when we want salty, savory, porky flavor without the overt sweetness or smokiness of bacon. It freezes beautifully, so it's easy to keep at the ready. It's typically sold rolled; to cut even pieces, first unroll the pancetta to flatten it, and then use a sharp knife to cut it into the desired shape.

Italian Meatloaf

*All the soulful flavor
of Sunday supper
with none of the fuss—
meatloaf just got a whole
lot more interesting.*

by Matthew Fairman

THERE ARE A lot of things you can do to jazz up a meatloaf. You can, of course, wrap it in sweet, smoky, salty bacon. You can make a gravy. Glazes—whether ketchup, barbecue, or sweet-and-sour—are always good. The test kitchen even has a recipe for Frosted Meatloaf that calls for covering the loaf in mashed potatoes. But I had another idea, born out of a thought that a meatloaf is really just an oversize, loaf-shaped meatball. I wanted to create a meatloaf with flavors inspired by Italian cuisine. So I topped the whole thing with savory tomato sauce and melted cheese to make meatballs and marinara in meatloaf form.

My recipe starts with an intensely flavorful meat mixture—ground beef, deeply seasoned sweet Italian sausage (you can use hot sausage if you prefer), Parmesan cheese, garlic, and oregano—but instead of rolling dozens of meatballs, you make just one (in a loaf shape, of course). Mixing in a paste of crushed saltines, eggs, and milk ensures that the meatloaf holds its shape and stays perfectly moist.

From there, it's a simple matter of whipping together a bright, garlicky 5-minute tomato sauce; pouring it over the meatloaf in a casserole dish; and baking it all together (covered for the most efficient cooking) for about an hour. During that hour of hands-off cooking, the flavors of the meatloaf and the sauce mingle and meld, elevating and enriching each other in the process.

The bright tomato sauce is mellow, complex, and meaty, and the meatloaf—like the best meatballs—is supersavory and unbelievably tender and juicy. To take this dish to the next level, I topped the meatloaf with creamy, rich fontina (which I melted under the broiler right before serving) and a sprinkling of fresh chopped basil. This combination of meatloaf and sauce is familiar and comforting yet unexpected and exciting—like a surprise visit from an old friend. And if you have leftovers, they make the best meatloaf sandwich ever.

This supersav[...] meatloaf is ma[...] with Italian sausa[...] and seasoned w[...] garlic, herbs, a[...] Parmesan chee[...]

ITALIAN MEATLOAF *Serves 6 to 8*
Grate the Parmesan using a rasp-style grater; shred the fontina on the large holes of a box grater. If making our Italian Meatloaf Sandwich, set aside 1 cup of sauce before slicing the meatloaf.

SAUCE

1 tablespoon extra-virgin olive oil
5 garlic cloves, sliced thin
1 (28-ounce) can crushed tomatoes
1 (15-ounce) can tomato sauce
¼ teaspoon red pepper flakes
¼ teaspoon table salt

MEATLOAF

35 square saltines
¾ cup whole milk
2 large eggs
1 pound 85 percent lean ground beef
1 pound sweet Italian sausage, casings removed
2 ounces Parmesan cheese, grated (1 cup)
1 teaspoon granulated garlic
1 teaspoon dried oregano
½ teaspoon table salt
½ teaspoon pepper
¼ teaspoon red pepper flakes
4 ounces fontina cheese, shredded (1 cup)
3 tablespoons chopped fresh basil

1. FOR THE SAUCE: Adjust oven rack to middle position and heat oven to 400 degrees. Heat oil in large saucepan over medium heat until shimmering. Add garlic and cook until lightly browned, about 1 minute. Stir in tomatoes, tomato sauce, pepper flakes, and salt. Bring to simmer and cook until flavors have melded, about 5 minutes. Remove from heat; cover to keep warm.
2. FOR THE MEATLOAF: Spray broiler-safe 13 by 9-inch baking dish with vegetable oil spray. Place saltines in large zipper-lock bag, seal bag, and crush saltines to fine crumbs with rolling pin. Whisk saltines, milk, and eggs together in large bowl. Let sit until saltines are softened, about 5 minutes.

Whisk saltine mixture until smooth paste forms. Add beef, sausage, Parmesan, granulated garlic, oregano, salt, pepper, and pepper flakes and mix with your hands until thoroughly combined.
3. Transfer beef mixture to prepared dish. Using your wet hands, shape into 9 by 5-inch rectangle; top should be flat and meatloaf should be 1½ inches thick. Pour sauce over meatloaf. Cover dish with aluminum foil and place on rimmed baking sheet. Bake until meatloaf registers 160 degrees, 1 hour 5 minutes to 1¼ hours.
4. Remove sheet from oven, uncover dish, and sprinkle meatloaf evenly with fontina. Heat broiler. Broil meatloaf until cheese is melted, about 2 minutes. Let rest for 15 minutes.
5. Using 2 spatulas, transfer meatloaf to cutting board. Spoon off any excess grease from tomato sauce. Slice meatloaf 1 inch thick. Transfer slices back to sauce in dish, sprinkle with basil, and serve.

35
Saltines? Yes!

This recipe uses a panade (paste) of crushed saltines, milk, and eggs to help keep the meatloaf moist and tender. We found that the meatloaf made with saltines had a better texture than meatloaf made with torn bread.

LEFTOVERS

ITALIAN MEATLOAF SANDWICH
Serves 2
We developed this recipe using Pepperidge Farm Garlic Bread.

1 (12-inch) loaf frozen garlic bread
3 (½-inch-thick) slices Italian Meatloaf
1 cup tomato sauce from Italian Meatloaf
3 ounces mozzarella cheese, shredded (¾ cup)
¼ cup grated Parmesan cheese
½ cup fresh basil leaves, cut into thin strips

1. Cook bread according to package instructions.
2. Adjust oven rack 6 inches from broiler element and heat oven to 400 degrees. Place meatloaf slices in small, ovensafe casserole dish and pour tomato sauce over top. Bake until just heated through, 10 to 15 minutes. Remove dish from oven and heat broiler.
3. Line rimmed baking sheet with aluminum foil. Place bread bottom on prepared sheet. Spread half of tomato sauce on bread bottom, then top with meatloaf, overlapping slices slightly. Spread remaining tomato sauce over meatloaf. Top meatloaf with mozzarella and Parmesan.
4. Broil sandwich bottom until cheese is melted and just beginning to brown, 2 to 4 minutes. Sprinkle with basil. Top with bread top, slice in half, and serve.

Teaching Meatloaf to Speak Italian

1. Make 5-minute tomato sauce.

2. Shape beef mixture into loaf in dish.

3. Pour sauce over beef, cover, and bake.

4. Uncover, top with fontina, and broil.

Parmesan Roasted Cauliflower

Are your roasted vegetables in need of a boost? Parm to the rescue.

by Alli Berkey

PARMESAN CHEESE IS a transformative ingredient. The salty, savory shavings can turn even the blandest bunch of vegetables into something special. I set out to test this idea with roasted cauliflower.

My first stab was to trim a few heads of cauliflower into florets, toss them with a little oil and grated Parmesan, and roast them. But once the cauliflower started giving up its moisture in the hot oven, the cheese steamed right off. Next, I tried roasting the florets for a bit before adding the cheese, but again the cheese slid off the cauliflower and onto the baking sheet. I needed a binder of some sort to act as a glue between the oiled florets and the grated cheese.

Typically, we think of "gluing" agents as wet ingredients such as eggs or milk, but the oily Parmesan needed the opposite. I tried adding a few tablespoons of cornstarch to the cheese, hoping the powdery starch would absorb and trap a bit of the liquid released by the roasting cauliflower and prevent the Parmesan from sliding off. It worked! A flip halfway through roasting ensured even browning and a tasty, crisp Parmesan coating. This one's a keeper.

Parm Appeal

What is it about Parmesan cheese, anyway? The good stuff, real Parmigiano-Reggiano from Italy, is a potent, hard cheese with unrivaled complexity and nuanced flavor. It's sweet, nutty, sharp, fruity, and, most of all, savory. That last quality comes in part from its high levels of naturally occurring glutamates—the chemical compounds that produce umami, or savory, flavor. So Parmesan not only adds cheesy flavor but also brings a background savoriness to dishes. Since a little goes a long way, it is well worth its hefty price tag.

PARMESAN ROASTED CAULIFLOWE

Serves 4

You will need to purchase 3 pounds of whole cauliflower (one to two heads) to yield 2 pounds of florets. You can also use precut cauliflower florets. For the best results, we recommend using freshly grated Parmesan cheese; use a rasp-style grater to grate the Parmesan If using canned Parmesan, omit the sa and season with salt and pepper to tast before serving.

- 3 ounces Parmesan cheese, grated (1½ cups)
- 2 tablespoons cornstarch
- 1 teaspoon minced fresh thyme
- ¾ teaspoon table salt
- ½ teaspoon pepper
- 2 pounds cauliflower florets, cut into 2-inch pieces
- 3 tablespoons extra-virgin olive oil

1. Adjust oven rack to lowest position and heat oven to 450 degrees. Spray rimmed baking sheet with vegetable oil spray. Stir Parmesan, cornstarch, thyme, salt, and pepper in bowl until thoroughly combined; set aside.

2. Toss cauliflower and oil together in large bowl. Add Parmesan mixture to cauliflower mixture and toss until well coated. Pour contents of bowl onto prepared sheet, scraping out any remaining Parmesan from bowl with rubber spatula. Shake sheet to distribute cheese and cauliflower evenly. Where possible, flip florets cut side down.

3. Roast cauliflower until bottom edges of florets begin to brown, about 15 minutes. Remove sheet from oven and flip florets using thin metal spatula. Continue to roast until cauliflower is tender and spotty brown, about 5 minutes longer.

4. Transfer sheet to wire rack and let cool for 5 minutes. Using thin metal spatula, transfer cauliflower and any accompanying cheese to serving platter. Serve.

Step by Step

1. Cut cauliflower florets into 2-inch pieces.

2. Coat florets with Parmesan mixture.

3. Brown 1 side, then flip, taking care not to disturb coating.

Napa Cabbage Salad

Crisp, refreshing napa cabbage is the flavorful salad green you never knew you loved.

By Morgan Bolling

NAPA CABBAGE—THE OBLONG, pale green variety used for kimchi, Asian slaws, and stir-fries—isn't really a salad green. Or is it? A few months back I was intrigued to see a napa cabbage salad on a menu during a trip to, of all places, California's Napa Valley (the vegetable's name has its roots in Japan, not California). The salad featured chopped cabbage scattered with crumbled bacon and topped with blue cheese dressing. The crinkly pieces of cabbage readily clung to lots of dressing (a good thing!) but still maintained a bright flavor and refreshing crunch. It convinced me to bring the idea of a napa cabbage salad into the test kitchen for a closer look.

I started by cutting a small head of napa cabbage into rough pieces and tossing the leaves with a favorite buttermilk–blue cheese dressing. But this dressing was fortified with mayonnaise and felt too heavy and rich here—it overwhelmed the cabbage's fresh flavor. I pivoted to a lemon vinaigrette with blue cheese sprinkled over the salad at the end; this was OK, but not nearly as good as when I whisked the blue cheese right into the lemony dressing. Delicious.

To add substance to the salad, I tossed in some sliced grape tomatoes and cucumber. A bit of red onion, sliced thin, helped balance the richness of the bacon and cheese. Chopped basil added a bright pop of herbal flavor. This refreshing salad casts napa cabbage in a whole new light.

Crispy bacon, pungent red onion, fresh basil, and an easy blue cheese dressing add interest to this refreshing salad.

NAPA CABBAGE SALAD
Serves 4 to 6

For a creamier dressing, buy a wedge of blue cheese (instead of a crumbled product) and crumble it yourself. You can substitute cherry tomatoes for the grape tomatoes, if desired.

- 4 slices bacon, cut into ½-inch-wide strips
- 3 ounces blue cheese, crumbled (¾ cup)
- ¼ cup extra-virgin olive oil
- 2½ tablespoons lemon juice
- 1 teaspoon pepper
- ¾ teaspoon table salt
- 1 small head napa cabbage (1½ pounds), cut into 1½-inch pieces (about 9 cups)
- 8 ounces grape tomatoes, halved
- ½ English cucumber, halved lengthwise and sliced thin crosswise
- ½ cup thinly sliced red onion, rinsed
- ¼ cup chopped fresh basil

1. Cook bacon in 12-inch nonstick skillet over medium heat until crispy, 7 to 9 minutes. Using slotted spoon, transfer bacon to paper towel–lined plate. Let cool for 5 minutes.
2. Whisk blue cheese, oil, lemon juice, pepper, and salt in large bowl until slightly creamy with chunks of blue cheese, about 10 seconds. Add cabbage, tomatoes, cucumber, onion, basil, and bacon; toss to combine. Season with salt and pepper to taste. Serve.

Breaking It Down

1. Halve cabbage lengthwise, then cut each half into 1½-inch strips.

2. Cut crosswise at 1½-inch intervals to make even-size pieces.

A Lighter, Fresher Cabbage
Napa cabbage (sometimes labeled Chinese cabbage) is much more crisp and delicate in texture than the waxy, thick leaves of red or green cabbage. The size of a loaf of sandwich bread, it has a light crunch and refreshingly sweet flavor that is appealing both raw and cooked. In addition to using it in salads, try shredding it for an Asian slaw or adding chopped leaves to stir-fries.

I T'S MIDAFTERNOON AS I make my way through crosstown traffic to Balaton, a strip-mall restaurant in Shaker Square on the outskirts of Cleveland, Ohio. I arrive during quiet time—the period just after lunch but well before dinner. I order chicken paprikash with a side of cucumber salad and *lángos*, a Frisbee-size disk of fried bread that is meant to be torn into pieces and dipped into paprika-dusted sour cream and garlic butter.

Sisters Erika Nagy Johnson and Krisztina Nagy Ponti have worked at Balaton since they immigrated to Cleveland from Budapest in 1989. Erika was 14 and had just finished eighth grade; Krisztina had attended culinary school in Hungary and was just 17.

When they first started working at Balaton, the restaurant was owned by their great aunt, Terezia Nevery. After escaping the violence of the Hungarian Revolution in 1956 and immigrating to the United States, Terezia opened Balaton in 1964; she based the menu on the simple cuisine of her homeland near Lake Balaton in west-central Hungary.

Shortly after relocating the restaurant to its current location in 1998, Terezia passed away and Krisztina took ownership of Balaton with her husband. Erika turns to a picture of Terezia that hangs on the wall near the front of the restaurant and says, "Who knew that one day we were going to continue her legacy?"

Krisztina tells me with passion in her voice, "In order for the recipes to stay the same, to stay in the family, we always have to be here. It's not like you can just show someone what to do. It has to be in your heart, it has to be in your soul, in order to produce the same thing over and over. But you have to do it with love, just like you would do it for your family."

Sister Act

Erika Johnson and Krisztina Ponti carry on their family legacy by serving the foods of their Hungarian homeland.

Text by Bryan Roof; photos by Steve Klise

One of the six iconic Cleveland signs scattered around the city (top); Erika (above) stirs her brick-red paprikash with a wooden paddle stained a deep mahogany after years of use; Krisztina (left, with her sister), does all the baking for the 100-seat restaurant (below).

CHICKEN PAPRIKASH *Serves 4 to 6*
We call for removing the skin from bone-in chicken thighs here. Rather than discarding the skin, try crisping it in a skillet in a little oil set over medium-high heat and setting it aside for a snack. Be sure to use sweet Hungarian paprika here, not hot or smoked, and make sure it's fresh (once opened, paprika loses its flavor quickly). Serve with Buttered Spaetzle (recipe follows) or buttered egg noodles.

- ¼ cup extra-virgin olive oil
- 1 large onion, halved and sliced thin
- 1 red bell pepper, stemmed, seeded, and sliced thin
- 1 (14.5-ounce) can diced tomatoes, drained
- 5 garlic cloves, chopped fine
- 2 teaspoons table salt, divided
- 8 (5- to 7-ounce) bone-in chicken thighs, skin removed, trimmed
- ¾ teaspoon pepper
- 2½ cups chicken broth
- 2 tablespoons paprika, plus extra for serving
- ¼ teaspoon cayenne pepper
- ⅓ cup sour cream, plus extra for serving
- 3 tablespoons all-purpose flour
- 2 tablespoons chopped fresh parsley

1. Heat oil in Dutch oven over medium-high heat until shimmering. Add onion, bell pepper, tomatoes, garlic, and 1 teaspoon salt and cook, stirring often, until vegetables are softened and fond begins to develop on bottom of pot, about 10 minutes. **2.** Sprinkle chicken with pepper and remaining 1 teaspoon salt. Stir broth, paprika, and cayenne into pot, scraping up any browned bits. Submerge chicken in broth mixture and bring to simmer. Reduce heat to medium-low, cover, and simmer until chicken is very tender and registers at least 195 degrees, about 30 minutes, stirring and flipping chicken halfway through simmering. **3.** Whisk sour cream and flour together in bowl. Slowly whisk ½ cup cooking liquid into sour cream mixture. Stir sour cream mixture into pot until fully incorporated. Continue to simmer, uncovered, until thickened, about 5 minutes longer. Off heat, season with salt and pepper to taste. Let stand for 5 minutes. Sprinkle with parsley and serve with extra paprika and extra sour cream.

Paprika is made from dried red peppers that are ground to a powder. There are dozens of varieties. We call for sweet paprika here.

Chicken Paprikash

Paprika gets its time in the spotlight in this rich, comforting dish.

by Jessica Rudolph

A TRADITIONAL HUNGARIAN stew of chicken pieces, onion, peppers, and sour cream, paprikash features the sweet, toasty flavor of paprika as its backbone. But many recipes for this dish seem so loaded with paprika that they end up with a harsh, bitter taste. After visiting Balaton in Cleveland, Ohio (see "Sister Act"), Executive Food Editor Bryan Roof clued me in on why that is: Paprika's delicate flavor is very sensitive to heat, and unlike other ground spices that benefit from blooming in hot oil, paprika becomes acrid almost instantly when cooked over high heat in hot fat. At Balaton, they avoid this by adding paprika to their paprikash and goulash off the heat. This way, the paprika blooms and develops flavor in the braising liquid

rather than in searing-hot oil, avoiding the risk of burning.

Inspired, I hit the test kitchen to develop a recipe for chicken paprikash that I hoped would taste primarily of fruity, earthy paprika. As they do at Balaton, I started by cooking sliced onion, bell pepper, tomatoes, and lots of garlic together until they were softened, sweet, and beginning to brown. I added chicken broth and just 2 tablespoons of paprika (enough to flavor and color the dish without clobbering it) and then nestled chicken pieces into the pot. I chose bone-in thighs, knowing they'd cook up tender and juicy in my braise without any risk of overcooking, and I removed their skin before cooking to avoid a greasy finished dish. I braised the chicken

until it was completely tender and then finished the braise by stirring in a paste of sour cream and flour to thicken and enrich the sauce.

Tasters loved the velvety texture of the sauce and how all the components enhanced—rather than obscured—the natural sweetness of the paprika. For a bit more of a peppery punch, I tried adding just ¼ teaspoon of cayenne. The resulting stew tasted perfectly balanced: The cayenne underlined the subtle warmth of the paprika without adding outright heat. To serve it, I spooned the chicken and ample sauce over homemade spaetzle (though egg noodles were just as good) and topped it all with a dollop of sour cream, a scattering of chopped parsley, and a bit more paprika to highlight the star of the dish.

BUTTERED SPAETZLE *Serves 6 to 8*
The 13 by 9-inch disposable aluminum pan serves as a makeshift sieve for portioning the batter.

  2 **cups all-purpose flour**
  ¾ **teaspoon table salt, plus salt for cooking spaetzle**
  ½ **teaspoon pepper**
  ¼ **teaspoon ground nutmeg**
  ¾ **cup whole milk**
  3 **large eggs**
  1 **(13 by 9-inch) disposable aluminum pan**
  2 **tablespoons unsalted butter, melted**

1. Whisk flour, salt, pepper, and nutmeg together in large bowl. Whisk milk and eggs together in second bowl. Slowly whisk milk mixture into flour mixture until smooth. Cover and let rest for 15 to 30 minutes.
2. While batter rests, use scissors to poke about forty ¼-inch holes in bottom of disposable pan. Bring 4 quarts water to boil in Dutch oven.
3. Add 1 tablespoon salt to boiling water and set prepared disposable pan on top of Dutch oven. Transfer half of batter to disposable pan. Use spatula to scrape batter across holes, letting batter fall into water. Boil until spaetzle float, about 1 minute. Using spider skimmer or slotted spoon, transfer spaetzle to colander set in large bowl to drain. Repeat with remaining batter.
4. Discard any accumulated water in bowl beneath colander. Pour spaetzle into now-empty bowl. Add melted butter and toss to combine. Serve.

Make the batter and let it rest for 15 to 30 minutes.

Create your own noodle maker by using scissors to punch 40 holes in the bottom of a disposable aluminum pan.

Pour half the batter into the pan and use a spatula to press the batter through the holes and into the boiling water.

No-Fail Dark Chocolate Mousse

Fluffy. Rich. And . . . easy?

by Morgan Bolling

You can make this crowd-pleaser up to two days ahead.

CHOCOLATE MOUSSE
Serves 6 to 8

If using pasteurized eggs here, increase the high-speed whipping time to 8 to 10 minutes. To bring the eggs to room temperature quickly, place the whole, uncracked eggs in a bowl of warm water for 15 minutes. We developed this recipe using Ghirardelli 60% Premium Baking Chips. We call for individual serving glasses or ramekins, but this mousse can also be chilled in a large serving dish. Just increase the chilling time to at least 8 hours.

MOUSSE
- 8 large eggs, room temperature
- 2 tablespoons sugar
- 12 ounces bittersweet chocolate chips
- ¼ cup water

WHIPPED CREAM
- 1½ cups heavy cream, chilled
- 4 teaspoons sugar
- 1 teaspoon vanilla extract

1. FOR THE MOUSSE: Using stand mixer fitted with whisk attachment, whip eggs on medium speed until foamy, about 1 minute. Add sugar, increase speed to high, and whip until tripled in volume and ribbons form on top of mixture when dribbled from whisk, 5 to 7 minutes. Set aside.

2. Microwave chocolate chips and water in large bowl at 50 percent power, stirring occasionally with rubber spatula, until chocolate is melted, about 2 minutes.

3. Whisk one-third of egg mixture into chocolate mixture until fully combined. Using clean rubber spatula, gently fold in remaining egg mixture, making sure to scrape up any chocolate from bottom of bowl, until no streaks remain.

4. Portion mousse evenly into 6 to 8 serving glasses or ramekins, cover with plastic wrap, and refrigerate for at least 6 hours or up to 48 hours.

5. FOR THE WHIPPED CREAM: Using stand mixer fitted with whisk attachment, whip cream, sugar, and vanilla on medium-low speed until foamy, about 1 minute. Increase speed to high and whip until stiff peaks form, 1 to 3 minutes.

6. Top mousse with whipped cream before serving.

AIRY, LIGHT, SWEET, and flavorful—what's not to like about chocolate mousse? Unfortunately, the answer is often an overcomplicated recipe. Many versions call for some variation on the following rigmarole: Whipping cream, whipping egg whites, melting chocolate (often with egg yolks and butter), folding in the egg whites, and then adding the whipped cream—all without causing the delicate mixture to deflate. I wanted a foolproof recipe for chocolate mousse that streamlined the process.

To get started, I made half a dozen recipes from well-known dessert cookbooks. The one that best combined simplicity with good flavor called for whisking egg yolks into a mixture of melted chocolate and butter before folding in sweetened whipped egg whites. Without any whipped cream and with minimal sugar, this mousse had an intense dark chocolate flavor. But it also had a marshmallow-like texture that my tasters found unappealing.

When I tried to reduce the number of egg whites, the mousse became too heavy and ganache-like. A coworker suggested whipping whole eggs instead of just whites, a trick she had used to great effect in an olive oil cake. Because whole eggs don't hold as much air as egg whites when whipped, the hope was that my mousse would turn out less poofy. I whipped the whole eggs until they had tripled in volume and reached the ribbon stage, and then I folded them into the melted chocolate. As I'd hoped, this mousse was light and fluffy yet lusciously creamy.

I worked out a few more details through testing. Melting the chocolate with water (instead of butter, which dulled the flavor) resulted in a mousse with an even more pronounced chocolate flavor. Using room-temperature eggs helped prevent lumps in the final mousse—plus, they whipped more efficiently. Deflating the eggs a little while folding was OK, but it was important to use a large bowl and scrape the bottom while folding to incorporate everything thoroughly. Finally, refrigerating the mousse for at least 6 hours gave it just

the right amount of structure: The mousse melts in your mouth, but it can still hold its shape on a spoon.

With just four ingredients and no egg separating, I'd finally found a recipe that was dead easy to make and—better yet—absolutely delicious.

Properly Whipped Eggs

We whip a combination of whole eggs and sugar in a mixer until it's tripled in volume and ribbons form when the mixture is dribbled from the whisk attachment.

Roasted Chicken Breasts with Green Israeli Couscous

30-MINUTE SUPPER

Steak Tips with Sweet Potato Wedges

30-MINUTE SUPPER

Korean-Style Sloppy Joes with Kimchi Slaw

30-MINUTE SUPPER

Greek-Spiced Pork Chops with Warm Zucchini-Feta Salad

30-MINUTE SUPPER

Steak Tips with Sweet Potato Wedges *Serves 4*

Sirloin steak tips are often sold as flap meat. Use small potatoes, about 8 ounces each, because they will fit more uniformly on the baking sheet.

- 2 pounds small sweet potatoes, unpeeled, cut lengthwise into 1½-inch wedges
- ¼ cup vegetable oil, divided
- 1½ teaspoons granulated garlic
- 1½ teaspoons table salt, divided
- ¾ teaspoon pepper, divided
- ¼ cup honey
- 1 tablespoon lime juice
- 1 teaspoon cornstarch
- 2 pounds sirloin steak tips, trimmed and cut into 2-inch chunks
- 1 jalapeño chile, stemmed, halved, seeded, and sliced thin crosswise
- ¼ cup chopped fresh cilantro

1. Adjust oven rack to middle position and heat oven to 450 degrees. Line rimmed baking sheet with parchment paper. Toss sweet potatoes, 2 tablespoons oil, granulated garlic, ½ teaspoon salt, and ¼ teaspoon pepper together in bowl. Arrange potatoes cut side down in single layer on prepared sheet. Roast until tender and bottoms are browned, 25 to 30 minutes.
2. While potatoes roast, whisk honey, lime juice, and cornstarch in second bowl until cornstarch is fully dissolved; set aside. Sprinkle steak tips with remaining 1 teaspoon salt and remaining ½ teaspoon pepper. Heat remaining 2 tablespoons oil in 12-inch nonstick skillet over medium-high heat until just smoking. Add steak tips and cook until browned on all sides and meat registers 120 to 125 degrees (for medium-rare), about 7 minutes. Transfer steak tips to large plate and tent with foil.
3. Pour off fat from skillet. Add honey mixture and jalapeño to now-empty skillet and cook over medium-low heat until mixture is thickened and jalapeño is tender, about 2 minutes. Drizzle steak tips and sweet potatoes with honey mixture and sprinkle with cilantro. Serve.

Greek-Spiced Pork Chops with Warm Zucchini-Feta Salad *Serves 4*

Substitute basil and goat cheese for the oregano and feta for a creamier zucchini salad.

- 4 zucchini (8 ounces each), quartered lengthwise and cut crosswise into 2-inch pieces
- ¼ cup oil-packed sun-dried tomatoes, drained and chopped, plus 3 tablespoons sun-dried tomato oil, divided
- 1 shallot, sliced thin
- 2½ teaspoons kosher salt, divided
- 2 garlic cloves, sliced thin
- 1¼ teaspoons pepper, divided
- 4 (6- to 8-ounce) boneless pork chops, ¾ to 1 inch thick, trimmed
- 2 teaspoons grated lemon zest plus 1 teaspoon juice
- 2 teaspoons dried oregano
- 2 ounces feta cheese, crumbled (½ cup)
- 2 tablespoons fresh oregano leaves

1. Cook zucchini, 2 tablespoons tomato oil, shallot, 1 teaspoon salt, garlic, and ¼ teaspoon pepper in 12-inch nonstick skillet over medium-high heat until zucchini is just tender and lightly browned, 10 to 12 minutes. Transfer to serving bowl. Set aside.
2. Pat pork dry with paper towels and sprinkle with lemon zest, dried oregano, remaining 1½ teaspoons salt, and remaining 1 teaspoon pepper, pressing to adhere. Heat remaining 1 tablespoon tomato oil in now-empty skillet over medium-high heat until just smoking. Add pork and cook, flipping every 2 minutes, until well browned and meat registers 140 degrees, 8 to 10 minutes. Transfer to carving board, tent with foil, and let rest for 5 minutes.
3. Add feta, fresh oregano, sun-dried tomatoes, and lemon juice to zucchini mixture and stir to combine. Slice pork and serve with zucchini.

Roasted Chicken Breasts with Green Israeli Couscous

Serves 4

We recommend using a rasp-style grater to grate the lemon zest.

- 4 cups chicken broth, divided
- 2 cups fresh parsley leaves
- 1 tablespoon grated lemon zest plus 1 tablespoon juice
- 1¼ teaspoons table salt, divided
- ¾ teaspoon pepper, divided
- 4 (10- to 12-ounce) bone-in split chicken breasts, trimmed
- 4 tablespoons unsalted butter, divided
- 1½ cups Israeli couscous
- 1 onion, chopped fine
- 3 garlic cloves, minced
- ¼ cup chopped fresh basil

1. Adjust oven rack to middle position and heat oven to 425 degrees. Process 1 cup broth, parsley, lemon zest, ¾ teaspoon salt, and ½ teaspoon pepper in blender until smooth, about 30 seconds. Set aside.
2. Pat chicken dry with paper towels and sprinkle with remaining ½ teaspoon salt and remaining ¼ teaspoon pepper. Melt 1 tablespoon butter in Dutch oven over medium-high heat. Add chicken and cook until golden brown on both sides, about 6 minutes. Transfer chicken to rimmed baking sheet. Roast until chicken registers 160 degrees, 18 to 20 minutes.
3. While chicken roasts, melt 1 tablespoon butter in now-empty pot over medium heat. Add couscous, onion, and garlic and cook until onion is softened and couscous is lightly toasted, about 4 minutes. Stir in parsley mixture and remaining 3 cups broth and bring to simmer. Cook, uncovered, stirring often, until nearly all liquid has been absorbed, about 14 minutes. Off heat, stir in basil, lemon juice, and remaining 2 tablespoons butter. Serve chicken with couscous.

Korean-Style Sloppy Joes with Kimchi Slaw

Serves 4

One cup of coleslaw mix plus 1 tablespoon of sriracha can be substituted for the kimchi.

- 1 cup kimchi, chopped
- ¼ cup mayonnaise
- ¾ teaspoon pepper, divided
- ½ cup ketchup
- 3 tablespoons soy sauce
- 2 tablespoons toasted sesame oil
- 1 tablespoon packed brown sugar
- 3 garlic cloves, minced
- 1 pound 85 percent lean ground beef
- 4 hamburger buns

1. Combine kimchi, mayonnaise, and ¼ teaspoon pepper in bowl; set aside. In second bowl, whisk ketchup, soy sauce, oil, sugar, and garlic until smooth.
2. Cook beef and remaining ½ teaspoon pepper in 12-inch nonstick skillet over medium heat until beef is no longer pink and begins to brown, 8 to 10 minutes. Stir in ketchup mixture and cook until sauce thickens slightly, about 1 minute.
3. Divide beef mixture and kimchi mixture among bun bottoms. Cover with bun tops and serve.

Spicy Italian Sausage with Cheddar Grits and Cherry Tomatoes

30-MINUTE SUPPER

Seared Scallops with Butternut Squash

30-MINUTE SUPPER

Chickpea Shakshuka

30-MINUTE SUPPER

Curried Chicken Noodle Soup

30-MINUTE SUPPER

Seared Scallops with Butternut Squash

Serves 4

For the best browning, do not move the scallops once you've added them to the skillet, except to flip them.

- 3 **pounds butternut squash, peeled, seeded, and cut into ½-inch pieces (8 cups)**
- ¾ **cup chicken broth**
- 6 **tablespoons unsalted butter, divided**
- 1¾ **teaspoons table salt, divided**
- 1½ **pounds large sea scallops, tendons removed**
- ¾ **teaspoon pepper, divided**
- 2 **tablespoons vegetable oil, divided**
- ½ **cup half-and-half**
- 1 **tablespoon chopped fresh sage**
- ½ **teaspoon grated lemon zest plus 2 teaspoons juice**

1. Combine squash, broth, 4 tablespoons butter, and 1 teaspoon salt in large saucepan. Cover and cook over medium-high heat, stirring occasionally, until squash is tender, about 25 minutes.

2. About 10 minutes before squash is ready, pat scallops dry with paper towels and sprinkle with ¼ teaspoon pepper and remaining ¾ teaspoon salt. Heat 1 tablespoon oil in 12-inch nonstick skillet over high heat until just smoking. Add half of scallops, flat side down, and cook, without moving them, until well browned, about 1½ minutes. Flip and cook until browned on second side, about 1½ minutes. Transfer to plate and tent with foil. Wipe skillet clean with paper towels; repeat with remaining 1 tablespoon oil and remaining scallops.

3. Using potato masher, mash squash until smooth. Stir in half-and-half and remaining ½ teaspoon pepper. Set aside and cover to keep warm. Melt remaining 2 tablespoons butter in now-empty skillet over medium heat. Cook, swirling skillet occasionally, until butter turns dark golden brown and has nutty aroma, 1 to 2 minutes. Off heat, stir in sage and lemon zest and juice. Serve squash topped with scallops and drizzled with sauce.

Spicy Italian Sausage with Cheddar Grits and Cherry Tomatoes

Serves 4

Serve sprinkled with thinly sliced scallions. We developed this recipe using Quaker Quick 5-Minute Grits.

- 3 **cups water**
- 3 **tablespoons unsalted butter**
- 1 **teaspoon table salt, divided**
- ¼ **teaspoon pepper**
- ¾ **cup quick-cooking grits**
- 4 **ounces sharp cheddar cheese, shredded (1 cup)**
- 1 **pound sweet Italian sausage, casings removed**
- 1 **onion, chopped fine**
- 10 **ounces cherry tomatoes, halved**
- 3 **tablespoons chopped jarred hot cherry peppers, plus 1 tablespoon brine**
- ¾ **cup chicken broth**

1. Bring water, butter, ¾ teaspoon salt, and pepper to boil in large saucepan over high heat. Whisk in grits. Cover, reduce heat to low, and cook, whisking occasionally, until grits are cooked through, 5 to 7 minutes. Off heat, stir in cheddar. Set aside and cover to keep warm.

2. Cook sausage and onion in 12-inch nonstick skillet over medium-high heat until sausage is cooked through and onion is lightly browned, 5 to 7 minutes, breaking up sausage with wooden spoon. Off heat, using slotted spoon, transfer sausage and onion to bowl; set aside. Pour off all but 1 tablespoon fat from skillet.

3. Heat fat left in skillet over medium-high heat until just smoking. Add tomatoes and remaining ¼ teaspoon salt and cook, without stirring, until just starting to brown, about 3 minutes. Stir in peppers and cook until tender, about 2 minutes. Add broth, pepper brine, and reserved sausage mixture to skillet and cook until slightly thickened, about 3 minutes. Serve sausage mixture on top of grits.

Curried Chicken Noodle Soup

Serves 4

Serve this soup with lime wedges.

- 2 **tablespoons vegetable oil**
- 1 **onion, halved and sliced thin**
- 3 **carrots, peeled and cut into 2-inch-long matchsticks**
- 1 **teaspoon table salt**
- ½ **teaspoon pepper**
- 6 **cups chicken broth**
- 4 **ounces rice vermicelli**
- ¼ **cup canned coconut milk**
- 2 **tablespoons Asian chili-garlic sauce**
- 1 **(2½-pound) rotisserie chicken, skin and bones discarded, meat shredded into bite-size pieces (3 cups)**
- 1 **cup fresh Thai basil leaves**

1. Heat oil in Dutch oven over medium-high heat until shimmering. Add onion, carrots, salt, and pepper and cook until vegetables are just softened, about 4 minutes.

2. Add broth, noodles, coconut milk, and chili-garlic sauce and bring to boil. Reduce heat to medium-low and simmer until noodles are softened, about 3 minutes.

3. Stir in chicken and cook until chicken is heated through, about 5 minutes. Stir in basil and serve.

Chickpea Shakshuka

Serves 4

We like to sprinkle the *shakshuka* with parsley leaves and serve it with crusty bread.

- 2 **tablespoons extra-virgin olive oil, plus extra for drizzling**
- 1 **onion, chopped fine**
- 1 **cup jarred roasted red peppers, rinsed, patted dry, and chopped coarse**
- 1 **teaspoon table salt**
- ½ **teaspoon pepper**
- 1 **(15-ounce) can chickpeas, rinsed**
- 1½ **teaspoons smoked paprika**
- 1 **teaspoon ground cumin**
- 1 **(28-ounce) can crushed tomatoes**
- 8 **large eggs**
- 2 **ounces goat cheese, crumbled (½ cup)**

1. Heat oil in 12-inch nonstick skillet over medium-high heat until shimmering. Add onion, red peppers, salt, and pepper and cook until onion is softened, about 4 minutes. Add chickpeas, paprika, and cumin and cook until fragrant, about 1 minute. Stir in tomatoes and bring to simmer. Cover, reduce heat to medium-low, and cook until flavors meld, about 5 minutes.

2. Off heat, using back of spoon, make 8 shallow 1½-inch indentations in sauce (seven around perimeter and one in center). Crack 1 egg into each indentation. Spoon sauce over edges of egg whites so that whites are partially covered and yolks are exposed.

3. Return skillet to medium-high heat and bring to simmer. Cover, reduce heat to medium-low, and cook until whites are fully set, about 8 minutes, rotating skillet occasionally for even cooking. Sprinkle shakshuka evenly with goat cheese. Serve, drizzled with extra oil.

Food Processors

One motor, many tasks: A good food processor is incredibly versatile and can save you loads of time and effort in the kitchen—if you know how to get the most out of it. **by Scott Kathan**

Why You Need One

FOR GRINDING MEAT
You can grind different cuts to customize flavor and fat levels. Partially freeze cubed meat to make processing more efficient and overprocessing less likely.

FOR DOUGH
Food processors mix and knead bread dough efficiently, and they're great for making pie and pastry doughs, too.

FOR CHOPPING AND GRINDING VEGETABLES, GRAINS, AND NUTS
Err on the side of underprocessing—there is no going back! We prefer to use the pulse button rather than continuously run the machine.

FOR SLICING AND SHREDDING VEGETABLES AND CHEESE
Slicing: Potatoes for a gratin or homemade chips, cucumbers for salads, cabbage for coleslaw or sauerkraut—the slicing disk makes fast and easy work of prepping them all.
Shredding: A food processor can shred carrots, potatoes, squash, and even cheese. Chilling foods firms them up so they shred cleanly; spraying the feed tube with vegetable oil spray before starting makes cleanup easy and helps prevent the disk from getting gummed up.

Processor Q & A

Can I puree soups and make smoothies in a food processor?
We don't usually recommend it, in part because many food processors leak when filled with liquid (our winner does not). Use a blender—which is designed for use with liquids—for those tasks instead.

When do I pulse rather than let the machine run?
In the test kitchen, we almost always use the pulse button, which gives us greater control and leads to fewer instances of overprocessing.

What's the best way to clean a dirty processor bowl?
Let the machine do the work for you by adding some water and a little dish soap to the bowl and running the machine for a few seconds. Rinse it with hot water, and then let it dry. If you want to soak the bowl (which can help discourage lingering aromas), put a cork in the center hole so you can fill the bowl with soapy water.

What Makes a Good Food Processor?

1 Minimal gap between bottom of feed tube and shredding disk

2 Sharp metal blade

3 Minimal gap between blade and sides and bottom of bowl

4 Heavy base

5 Responsive pulse button

OUR WINNER
Cuisinart Custom 14 Cup Food Processor ($200)

Unexpected Uses

MAKE NUT BUTTERS!
Process 4 cups roasted peanuts or almonds for 5 to 7 minutes, scraping down sides of bowl as needed.

MAKE BREAD CRUMBS!
Tear or cut bread—of any kind—into pieces and pulse.

CRUSH ICE!
Pulse 1 to 2 cups ice cubes until finely ground.

Fully Loaded Twice-Baked Potatoes

The elusive goal: crisp, sturdy skins.

by Natalie Estrada

Twice-baked potatoes, done three ways: with Bacon and Cheddar, Chorizo and Chipotle (below left), and Pancetta and Mozzarella (below right).

THE TWICE-BAKED POTATOES I've eaten in restaurants looked great on the plate, but more often than not, their skin was leathery and bland, and their filling lacked flavor. I wanted to right these wrongs.

The path to better potato skins was blazed by a recent test kitchen recipe for baked potatoes. Instead of brushing the skins with oil, as many recipes instruct but which turns the skins tough, I pricked each spud a few times with a fork and then dunked the potatoes in a saltwater solution before baking. Pricking the potatoes prevents steam from building up inside them, and the salty bath seasons the skins and encourages them to dry and crisp in the oven.

After letting the baked potatoes cool to room temperature and scraping out their insides, I had to figure out the best ingredients for my filling. Cheddar and sour cream packed a ton of flavor, but the half-and-half called for by most versions wasn't doing much. It was better, I found, to replace the half-and-half with butter for a rich (but not too rich) filling. And while some recipes call for sprinkling bacon and scallions over the finished potatoes, we liked them mixed into the filling for maximum impact in every bite.

TWICE-BAKED POTATOES WITH BACON AND CHEDDAR CHEESE
Serves 4
Try to find potatoes of equal size and weight to ensure even cooking. Larger potatoes will work, but the baking time in step 1 will be longer. This recipe can easily be doubled.

- 4 (8- to 10-ounce) russet potatoes, unpeeled
- ¼ teaspoon table salt, plus salt for moistening potatoes
- 4 slices bacon, cut into ½-inch pieces
- 5 tablespoons unsalted butter, melted, divided
- ¼ cup sour cream
- ¼ teaspoon pepper
- 3 ounces sharp cheddar cheese, shredded (¾ cup)
- 4 scallions, sliced thin

1. Adjust oven rack to middle position and heat oven to 450 degrees. Prick each potato lightly with fork in 6 places. Dissolve 1 tablespoon salt in ½ cup water in large bowl. Add potatoes and toss so exteriors are evenly moistened. Place potatoes on wire rack set in rimmed baking sheet. Bake until centers register 205 degrees, 50 minutes to 1 hour. Let potatoes cool for 15 minutes. Reduce oven temperature to 400 degrees.
2. While potatoes bake, cook bacon in 12-inch ovensafe nonstick skillet over medium heat until crispy, 5 to 7 minutes. Using slotted spoon, transfer bacon to paper towel–lined plate; set aside. Discard fat in skillet or reserve for another use. Wipe skillet clean with paper towels.

3. With potatoes sitting on flat sides, cut off top ¼ inch and discard. Using fork, carefully remove potato flesh from remaining portion of potato by poking and twisting at insides to loosen, leaving ¼-inch wall all around inside of potato. Transfer potato flesh to medium bowl. Set aside potato shells.
4. Using potato masher, mash potato flesh until smooth. Stir in 3 tablespoons melted butter, sour cream, pepper, and salt until incorporated. Stir in cheddar, scallions, and reserved bacon until combined. Season with salt and pepper to taste.
5. Divide filling evenly among potato shells (scant ¾ cup each), mounding filling over tops of potatoes. Fluff up top of filling with tines of fork. Brush 1 tablespoon melted butter in now-empty skillet and place potatoes in skillet. Brush remaining 1 tablespoon melted butter over tops of potatoes.
6. Bake until potatoes are warmed through and beginning to brown on top, 20 to 23 minutes. Let cool for 10 minutes before serving.

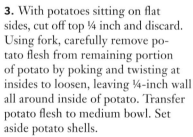

TO MAKE AHEAD
At the end of step 4, let potatoes cool completely. Cover with plastic wrap and refrigerate for up to 24 hours. To serve, continue with step 5, increasing baking time by 10 minutes.

TWICE-BAKED POTATOES WITH CHORIZO AND CHIPOTLE
Substitute 4 ounces Mexican-style chorizo sausage, casings removed, for bacon. Cook chorizo in 12-inch skillet over medium heat, breaking up meat with wooden spoon, until well browned and cooked through, 5 to 7 minutes. Substitute Monterey Jack for cheddar and 1 tablespoon minced canned chipotle chile in adobo sauce for pepper.

TWICE-BAKED POTATOES WITH PANCETTA AND MOZZARELLA
Substitute 4 ounces pancetta, cut into ¼-inch pieces, for bacon; 3 ounces shredded whole-milk mozzarella and ¼ cup grated Parmesan for cheddar; and 1 minced shallot and 1 teaspoon chopped fresh thyme for scallions.

Removing the Potato Flesh
Use a gentle hand.

1. With cooled potatoes arranged so that they are sitting on their most stable sides, cut off top ¼ inch and discard.

2. Use fork to poke, twist, and carefully remove flesh from potatoes.

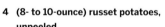

Soy Sauce Chicken Wings

One test cook shares her family's savory, sticky, lightly sweet wings with a wider audience.

by Jessica Rudolph

WHEN I WAS growing up, the best part of family birthday celebrations was my Nana's soy sauce chicken wings. They were so simple—whole wings marinated in soy sauce, vegetable oil, and garlic powder and baked in a dish—but they were intensely seasoned and almost impossibly tender, with a sticky, savory skin that always left us clamoring for more.

More than a decade has passed since we tasted Nana's wings, but after stumbling across an old jotted-down recipe of hers, I have been itching to re-create them. I made a batch for my coworkers, and we agreed that, with just a bit of work, these easy, tasty wings would be a perfect fit for our *Cook's Country* readers. I brought my Nana's recipe into the test kitchen and got to work, hoping to improve it while staying true to its straightforward spirit.

My first tweak was obvious: Nana's whole wings were cumbersome to eat and stayed a bit flabby at the joint. Splitting the wings into flats and drumettes allowed more fat to render out and made them easier to handle.

Next I nixed the garlic powder,

Brown sugar lends a caramelly depth to these garlicky, pleasantly salty wings.

suspecting that I could get better garlic flavor by using fresh garlic in the marinade. Minced garlic stuck to the wings and burned and turned bitter in the oven, but whole smashed garlic cloves imbued the marinade with unmistakable garlic flavor. A pinch of cayenne pepper brought extra verve. The wings were coming together, but my tasters were hoping for a little more depth and a more refined soy flavor. A quarter cup of brown sugar added caramel-like sweetness that brought everything into balance.

With the flavor now spot-on, I just had to nail down the texture. I had been crowding the wings in a baking dish, like Nana had, but when I spread them out on a rimmed baking sheet and gave them room to breathe, the fat in each wing was able to fully render, making the skin sticky-soft all over without any chewy fat pockets. A little more than an hour in a 350-degree oven gave the

fat enough time to render fully while the meat stayed juicy and tender. A final flourish of sliced scallions added a welcome freshness plus visual appeal to boot—I think Nana would approve.

SOY SAUCE CHICKEN WINGS
Serves 4 to 6

We prefer to buy whole chicken wings and butcher them ourselves because they tend to be larger than wings that come presplit. If you can find only presplit wings, opt for larger ones, if possible. Three pounds of chicken wings is about 12 whole chicken wings, which will yield about 24 pieces of chicken (12 drumettes and 12 flats) once broken down.

- ¾ cup soy sauce
- ¼ cup vegetable oil
- ¼ cup packed brown sugar
- 12 garlic cloves, smashed and peeled
- ½ teaspoon cayenne pepper
- 3 pounds chicken wings, cut at joints, wingtips discarded
- 2 scallions, sliced thin on bias

1. Combine soy sauce, oil, sugar, garlic, and cayenne in 1-gallon zipper-lock bag. Add wings to marinade, press out air, seal bag, and turn to distribute marinade. Refrigerate for at least 2 hours or up to 6 hours.

2. Adjust oven rack to middle position and heat oven to 350 degrees. Line rimmed baking sheet with aluminum foil and spray with vegetable oil spray. Remove wings from marinade and arrange in single layer, fatty side up, on prepared sheet; discard marinade. Bake until evenly well browned, about 1 hour 5 minutes. Transfer wings to platter, sprinkle with scallions, and serve.

Breaking Down the Wings

1. To remove wingtips, cut through joints where wingtips meet drumettes.

2. To separate pieces, cut through joints where drumettes meet flats.

French Onion Soup

Crunchy croutons, melty cheese, and savory soup all in one bite. But is there a faster way to French-onion bliss?

by Jessica Rudolph

A CROCK OF savory-sweet French onion soup topped with crunchy croutons and bubbly cheese is as comforting as my favorite slippers. But here in the test kitchen, we're never satisfied with the status quo, so I decided to take another look at this bistro favorite to see if I could create a recipe that cut down on the time needed to caramelize the onions and still produced a great soup.

I tried all manner of "innovative" ingredients to achieve this goal. While most iterations of my soup were fine, I was left facing an unavoidable fact: This classic is a classic for a reason, and there's no beating the understated simplicity of traditional French onion soup. Test after test, tasters preferred slow-cooked onions simmered with just broth, wine, and herbs to any fancy curveball variations I threw at them. I decided to stick with a (mostly) traditional version of this perennial favorite, streamlined as much as possible for the home cook.

Unable to lean on the crutch of distracting additions, I had to nail down perfectly caramelized onions. After dozens of tests, I landed on a method that takes about an hour but requires little more than patience and some stirring. The onions come out meltingly soft, golden brown, and full of flavor.

To pick up all the flavorful bits of fond stuck to the bottom and sides of my pot, I deglazed with a hefty pour of red wine—which had a more richly savory taste than white—before adding beef broth, fresh thyme sprigs, and bay leaves. After a little simmering to meld the flavors, I ladled the soup into crocks, topped it with croutons and cheese, and placed the crocks (on a rimmed baking sheet) in a preheated oven until the cheese was bubbling. The result? A rich, sweet, perfect onion soup topped with soft, melted cheese. *C'est magnifique!*

Large croutons are unwieldy and hard to navigate. Our bite-size croutons are easier to eat.

FRENCH ONION SOUP

Serves 6

Be patient when caramelizing the onions; the entire process takes 55 to 70 minutes. If you don't have oven-safe soup crocks, form six individual piles of croutons on a baking sheet, cover them with the cheese, and broil them on the middle oven rack until the cheese is melted, 1 to 3 minutes. Then use a spatula to transfer the crouton portions to the individual filled soup bowls.

- 4 tablespoons unsalted butter
- 4 pounds onions, halved and sliced thin
- 1¾ teaspoons table salt, divided
- 1 teaspoon sugar
- 1 cup dry red wine
- 8 cups beef broth
- 4 sprigs fresh thyme
- 2 bay leaves
- ¾ teaspoon pepper, divided
- 6 ounces baguette, cut into 1-inch cubes
- 3 tablespoons extra-virgin olive oil
- 8 ounces Gruyère cheese, shredded (2 cups)
- 1½ ounces Parmesan cheese, shredded (½ cup)

1. Melt butter in Dutch oven over medium-high heat. Stir in onions, 1 teaspoon salt, and sugar. Cover and cook, stirring occasionally, until onions release their liquid and are uniformly translucent, about 20 minutes.

2. Uncover and cook until liquid has evaporated and browned bits start to form on bottom of pot, 5 to 10 minutes. Reduce heat to medium and continue to cook, uncovered, until onions are caramel-colored, 30 to 40 minutes longer, stirring and scraping with wooden spoon as browned bits form on bottom of pot and spreading onions into even layer after stirring. (If onions or browned bits begin to scorch, reduce heat to medium-low.)

3. Stir in wine, scraping up any browned bits, and cook until nearly evaporated, about 1 minute. Stir in broth, thyme sprigs, bay leaves, ½ teaspoon pepper, and ½ teaspoon salt. Increase heat to high and bring to boil. Reduce heat to medium-low and simmer, uncovered, for 30 minutes.

4. While onions simmer, adjust oven rack to middle position and heat oven to 350 degrees. Toss baguette, oil, remaining ¼ teaspoon salt, and remaining ¼ teaspoon pepper together in bowl. Transfer to rimmed baking sheet and bake until golden and crisp, 15 to 18 minutes. Remove sheet from oven and set aside. Increase oven temperature to 500 degrees.

5. Set six 12-ounce ovensafe crocks on second rimmed baking sheet. Discard thyme sprigs and bay leaves and season soup with salt and pepper to taste. Divide soup evenly among crocks (about 1½ cups each). Divide 1 cup Gruyère evenly among crocks, top with croutons, and sprinkle with remaining Gruyère, then Parmesan. Bake until cheeses are melted and soup is bubbly around edges, 5 to 7 minutes. Let cool for 5 minutes before serving.

BACKSTORY

It is impossible to know when French-style onion soup was first conceived and cooked; cheap brothy meals were common fare in medieval Europe and likely predate the very concept of France as a political entity.

But in the 18th and 19th centuries, the soup's signature gratiné topping of relatively expensive cheese transformed the humble dish into something that even wealthy eaters rhapsodized over. As kings and emperors rose and fell like so many guillotine blades, the soup remained, achieving renown among the myriad vendors and patrons of the vast Les Halles market in Paris, where it became prized for its restorative (and hangover-soothing) properties.

BROWNING ONIONS

1. GETTING STARTED
Place sliced onions into the pot with butter, salt (which helps them release liquid), and sugar. Cover (to help onions break down) and cook over medium-high heat.

2. AROUND 20 MINUTES
The onions have released most of their liquid. Remove the lid to allow the liquid to evaporate, and then turn down the heat to medium to promote even cooking.

3. AROUND 30 MINUTES
As the liquid continues to cook off, the onions start to brown and flavorful fond continues to form on the bottom of the pot. Scrape up the fond and stir it into the onions.

4. AROUND 60–70 MINUTES
The onions are now fully caramelized: soft, sticky, and deep brown. This is your intensely flavorful base for French onion soup.

Getting the Top Right

1. Toss cubed baguette with olive oil, salt, and pepper in bowl.

2. Toast croutons in 350-degree oven until crisp and golden brown.

3. Top soup with Gruyère, croutons, more Gruyère, and grated Parmesan.

4. Bake in 500-degree oven until cheese is fully melted.

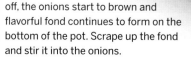

Carrot Snack Cake

With our recipe, carrot cake is easier, faster, and tastier than ever.

by Matthew Fairman

THIS CARROT SNACK cake is an informal, stir-together affair that will make you wonder why you ever spent more time or effort on complicated layer cake versions. There's no stacking of layers, no finicky piping, and no meticulously crafted marzipan carrots here. There's just a simple-to-prepare carrot cake that's moist, sweet, and perfectly spiced. A few uncommon (but easy) techniques helped me ensure consistently delicious results.

Some carrot cakes bake up unpleasantly dry, but my version is perfectly soft and moist. To achieve this, I soaked the still-hot cake in buttermilk syrup. The sweet, mildly tangy buttermilk syrup not only upped the ante texturally but also added a layer of flavor that brightened and balanced the sweetness of the cake while enhancing the tanginess of the cream cheese frosting.

A good carrot cake recipe judiciously employs warm spices and fruit to complement the earthy flavor of the carrots. My recipe calls for just the right amount of convenient pumpkin pie spice—a four-in-one mix of cinnamon, ginger, nutmeg, and allspice—to save time on pulling out and measuring individual spices. I used the time I saved to quickly plump and soften golden raisins in a bit of fragrant orange juice, layering in additional complementary flavors. A generous pinch of salt awakened all these flavors, ensuring that none of them went unnoticed.

And then, of course, there's the one essential component: the cream cheese frosting. I made sure that there was plenty of it and that it wasn't so sugary as to overwhelm the pleasant tang of the cream cheese. I also made it easier by simply processing all the ingredients in a food processor (the same one we used to shred the carrots). Topped with toasted pecans for crunchy contrast and visual appeal, it's a snack cake for any time of day.

> "And then, of course, there's the one essential component: the cream cheese frosting."

CARROT SNACK CAKE *Serves 12 to 16*
Shred the carrots in a food processor fitted with the shredding disk or on the large holes of a box grater. One pound of carrots is about six medium carrots and will yield about 12 ounces of shredded carrots after peeling and trimming.

CAKE
- 1 cup golden raisins
- ¼ cup orange juice
- 2½ cups (12½ ounces) all-purpose flour
- 1 tablespoon pumpkin pie spice
- 2 teaspoons baking powder
- 1 teaspoon baking soda
- ¾ teaspoon table salt
- 1½ cups packed (10½ ounces) light brown sugar
- 1¼ cups vegetable oil
- 4 large eggs
- 1 tablespoon vanilla extract
- 1 pound carrots, peeled and shredded (3 cups)
- 1 cup (4 ounces) confectioners' sugar
- ⅔ cup buttermilk

FROSTING
- 12 ounces cream cheese, softened
- 2 cups (8 ounces) confectioners' sugar
- 8 tablespoons unsalted butter, softened
- 1 teaspoon vanilla extract
- ⅛ teaspoon table salt

- 1 cup pecans, toasted and chopped

1. FOR THE CAKE: Adjust oven rack to middle position and heat oven to 350 degrees. Spray 13 by 9-inch baking pan with vegetable oil spray. Combine raisins and orange juice in small bowl. Microwave, covered, until hot, about 1 minute. Let stand, covered, until raisins are soft, about 5 minutes.

2. Whisk flour, pumpkin pie spice, baking powder, baking soda, and salt together in medium bowl; set aside. Whisk brown sugar, oil, eggs, and vanilla in large bowl until smooth; stir in carrots and raisin mixture. Stir in flour mixture with rubber spatula until just combined.

3. Transfer batter to prepared pan and smooth top with rubber spatula. Bake until toothpick inserted in center of cake comes out clean, 33 to 38 minutes, rotating pan halfway through baking. Transfer pan to wire rack.

4. Immediately whisk confectioners' sugar and buttermilk together until smooth. Brush buttermilk syrup evenly over entire surface of hot cake (use all syrup). Let cake cool completely in pan on wire rack, about 3 hours.

5. FOR THE FROSTING: Process cream cheese, sugar, butter, vanilla, and salt in food processor until smooth, about 30 seconds, scraping down sides of bowl with rubber spatula as needed.

6. Spread frosting evenly over surface of cake, leaving ½-inch border. Sprinkle frosting evenly with pecans. Serve.

TO MAKE AHEAD

Frosted cake can be covered with plastic wrap and refrigerated for up to 2 days.

CARROT-GINGER SNACK CAKE WITH CARDAMOM

Substitute 1 teaspoon ground cinnamon and 1 teaspoon ground cardamom for pumpkin pie spice. Stir in 1½ tablespoons grated fresh ginger with carrots and raisin mixture in step 2. Sprinkle 2 tablespoons finely chopped crystallized ginger over top of frosted cake with pecans in step 6.

asier, Fresher Carrot Cake in Six Simple Steps

Microwave raisins and orange juice (covered) and let stand.

2. Whisk dry ingredients together in bowl.

3. Whisk brown sugar and wet ingredients together in separate bowl.

Stir carrots and raisin mixture into wet ingredients, then stir in dry ingredients.

5. Bake, then brush hot cake with buttermilk syrup.

6. Make cream cheese frosting in food processor, frost cooled cake, and serve.

Searching for the Best Big Spatula *by Miye Bromberg*

NINE TIMES OUT of ten, we grab ish spatula when we want to flip or insfer food. But occasionally we find ourselves wishing we had a tool that was a bit bigger—something that uld help pick up heavier foods, such a roast or a cake, or flip more pieces food, such as roasted vegetables, a time. The solution can be found the short-order line at your local ner. Offset metal turners look like persize offset spatulas: Their heads e broad and long, making them ideal r heavy-duty or high-volume tasks. e wanted to know whether these ols would be worth stocking in home tchens, so we bought eight models, iced from about $6 to about $32, d put them to the test, using them to t tarts and hams; to flip and transfer asted cauliflower and hash browns; d to smash, flip, and transfer burgers. We liked most of the turners, ough some models were better at rtain tasks than others. Testers liked ads with plenty of surface area that uld pick up a significant amount of

food without being unwieldy. They also preferred models with long but relatively narrow heads measuring about 7.5 by 3 inches. These longer heads made it easier for testers to flip and transfer foods and provided more distance between their hands and the hot cooking surfaces.

The thickness of the heads was also important. Our favorite turners were sturdy enough to support a whole tart but flexible enough to wiggle under food easily. Overall, testers preferred unperforated heads with rounded edges that slipped under food more fluidly. Models with a nearly 90-degree

angle between head and handle gave us more leverage and kept our hands higher above the cooking surface than models with shallower angles. Handle design also helped determine our winner. Handles that were about 5 inches long were long enough to accommodate hands of all sizes and allowed for more control when flipping or lifting. We also liked easy-to-grip handles made from soft or textured plastics.

The Dexter Russell Steak Turner (model S286-8PCP) is our winner. Its solid head is long and spacious, so it can scoop up plenty of food at a time. While the back end of the head is thick and sturdy, its front edge is thin, flexible, and rounded, allowing it to slip easily under food. And its textured plastic handle, set at a steep angle, is grippy and allows for good control. For a less expensive option, consider our Best Buy from Mercer Culinary, which performed almost as well.

Go to **CooksCountry.com/mar20** to read the full testing results and see the complete chart.

Our Favorite
HIGHLY RECOMMENDED
Dexter Russell Steak Turner
Comments: With a head that was thin and flexible in the front and thick and sturdy at the back, this long, relatively broad turner scooped up lots of food.
Price: $28.45

RECOMMENDED
Mercer Culinary
M18310 Hell's Handle High Heat 8" x 3" Perforated Rounded Edge Turner
Best Buy
Comments: We liked this model almost as much as we liked our winner, but its perforations caught on food.
Price: $13.99

Winco High Heat Square Edge Turner, Orange Nylon Handle, 7¼" x 3" Blade
Comments: We loved the handle and the broad head. However, the head's squared edges damaged the tart crust.
Price: $5.55

Dexter Russell Rounded 6x3 Turner
Comments: The smaller version of our winner offered more control but couldn't handle as much food.
Price: $19.46

Fresh Hand-Rolled Pasta

Rolling out pasta by hand is fun—and it produces beautifully tender, tasty noodles every time.

by Matthew Fairman

FRESH PASTA

Serves 4 to 6 (Makes 1 pound)

The longer the dough rests in step 2, the easier it will be to roll out. When rolling out the dough in step 4, be sure to avoid dusting the dough with too much flour; that may result in the dough snapping back into shape as you roll. Cook the noodles within 1 hour of cutting them.

- 2 **cups (10 ounces) all-purpose flour**
- 2 **large eggs plus 6 large yolks**
- 2 **tablespoons extra-virgin olive oil**
  Table salt for cooking pasta

1. Process flour, eggs and yolks, and oil in food processor until mixture forms cohesive dough that feels soft and is barely tacky to touch, about 45 seconds. (If dough sticks to your fingers, add up to ¼ cup flour, 1 tablespoon at a time, until barely tacky. If dough doesn't become cohesive, add up to 1 tablespoon water, 1 teaspoon at a time, until it just comes together; process 30 seconds longer.)

2. Turn out dough ball onto clean counter; knead until smooth, about 30 seconds. Shape dough into 6-inch-long cylinder. Wrap in plastic wrap. Let rest at room temperature for at least 1 hour or up to 4 hours.

3. Cut cylinder crosswise into 6 equal pieces. Working with 1 piece of dough (rewrap remaining dough), dust both sides with flour, place cut side down on clean counter, and press into 3-inch square.

4. Using heavy rolling pin, roll into 6-inch square. Dust both sides of dough lightly with flour. Starting at center of square, roll dough away from you in 1 motion. Return rolling pin to center of dough and roll toward you in 1 motion. Repeat rolling steps until dough sticks to counter and measures roughly 12 inches long.

5. Lightly dust both sides of dough with flour. Roll dough until it measures roughly 20 inches long and 6 inches wide, frequently lifting dough to release it from counter. (Outline of your fingers should be easily visible through dough.) If dough firmly sticks to counter and wrinkles when rolled out, dust dough lightly with flour.

6. Transfer pasta sheet to clean dish towel on counter and let stand, uncovered, until firm around edges, about 15 minutes.

Meanwhile, roll out remaining dough. Starting with 1 short end, gently fold first pasta sheet at 2-inch intervals until sheet has been folded into flat, rectangular roll.

7. Using sharp chef's knife, slice crosswise into ⅛-inch-thick noodles for linguine, ¼-inch-thick noodles for tagliatelle, or ½-inch-thick noodles for pappardelle. Use your fingers to unfurl pasta; transfer to rimmed baking sheet. Repeat folding and cutting with remaining pasta sheets.

8. Bring 4 quarts water to boil in large Dutch oven. Add 1 tablespoon salt and pasta and cook until tender but still al dente, about 3 minutes. Reserve 1 cup cooking water. Drain pasta and toss with desired sauce, adjusting consistency with reserved cooking water as needed. Serve immediately.

TO MAKE AHEAD

At end of step 7, place baking sheet in freezer and freeze until pasta is firm. Transfer pasta to zipper-lock bag and freeze for up to 2 weeks. Cook pasta from frozen as directed in step 8.

GARLIC OIL PASTA SAUCE WITH PARSLEY AND PECORINO

Serves 4 to 6
(Makes enough for 1 pound pasta)

For the best results, use a high-quality extra-virgin olive oil.

- ⅓ **cup extra-virgin olive oil**
- 4 **garlic cloves, sliced thin**
- ½ **teaspoon table salt**
- ½ **teaspoon pepper**
- ¼ **teaspoon red pepper flakes**
- 1 **pound cooked pasta, plus ½ cup pasta cooking water**
- ¼ **cup chopped fresh parsley**
- 4 **teaspoons lemon juice**
  Grated Pecorino Romano cheese

1. Combine oil, garlic, salt, pepper, and pepper flakes in 12-inch skillet. Cook over medium heat until garlic is lightly toasted, 2 to 4 minutes.

2. Add pasta and pasta cooking water; toss to combine. Off heat, stir in parsley and lemon juice. Season with salt and pepper to taste. Serve immediately, passing Pecorino separately.

You can custom-cut the dough into different widths (above). We chose to pair ½-inch-wide pappardelle with our Garlic Oil Pasta Sauce with Parsley and Pecorino (below).

...ts of Yolks = Supple Dough

...ugh for pasta that is rolled out with ...asta machine usually calls for two ...gs for 2 cups of flour; our dough, ...ich is rolled much less, ups the ante ...th an additional six egg yolks for ...e same amount of flour. The extra ...t in the yolks makes for a softer ...ugh (and softer noodles) that rolls ...t easily with minimal snapback, in ...rt because the fat interrupts gluten ...ands from forming.

2 WHOLE EGGS

6 EGG YOLKS

Separation Anxiety?

The two best tools for separating egg yolks from whites are your hands and the eggshells themselves.

Hand Method:
Crack egg on flat surface and open shell so yolk and white fall into your cupped hand. Slightly open your fingers so white can slip into bowl below, leaving yolk in your hand.

Shell Method:

Crack egg on flat surface and, working over bowl, tip contents of egg back and forth between pieces of shell, letting white fall into bowl and leaving yolk in 1 half of shell.

Rolling Out Dough: Best Practices

Apply even pressure with your hands throughout rolling motion.	Roll in single, deliberate motions rather than quickly back and forth.	Periodically brush surface of dough with your hands to remove excess flour and monitor thickness.	To prevent pressing and smearing edges too thin, do not roll pin off edges of dough.

 ½ inch   ¼ inch   ⅛ inch

Noodle Guide
1. Pappardelle = ½ inch wide
2. Tagliatelle = ¼ inch wide
3. Linguine = ⅛ inch wide

...en Steps to Fresh Pasta

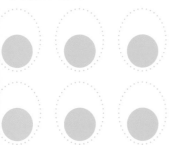

...Weigh flour
...se a digital scale to weigh out ... ounces of all-purpose flour.
...hy? While the recipe will work ...sing the volume equivalent of ...cups, it has less room for error if ...u weigh the flour.

2. Process dough
Process the flour, eggs and yolks, and olive oil in a food processor for 45 seconds.
Why? The efficient mechanical action of the processor brings the dough together quickly.

3. Check and adjust dough
Add either flour or water as needed to create a cohesive dough.
Why? The moisture content of this dough needs to be right in order to produce a workable dough.

4. Knead dough, then let rest
Knead until smooth, shape into a log, wrap, and let rest on the counter.
Why? Resting allows the gluten in the dough to relax, making for a malleable dough that won't spring back excessively when rolled.

5. Divide into 6 pieces
Use a bench scraper or chef's knife to divide the dough into six equal pieces.
Why? Since we roll the dough very thin, each piece has to be fairly small at the start of rolling.

...Prepare to roll
...ust one piece of dough with ...ur, and then pat it into a square.
...hy? Pressing the dough flat ...fore rolling it makes it much ...asier to control the finished ...ape of the pasta sheet.

7. Roll into rectangle
Slowly roll the dough into a thin 20 by 6-inch sheet.
Why? Rolling to these specific dimensions ensures a dough of proper thickness.

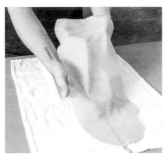

8. Lay sheets out to dry
Transfer the pasta sheet to a dish towel. Let it stand, uncovered, until it's slightly dried and firm. Repeat with the remaining pieces.
Why? Drier dough can be folded up (for cutting) without sticking.

9. Fold and cut
Gently fold one pasta sheet at 2-inch intervals until it's fully rolled up. Then slice it thin.
Why? Slicing the log requires only short, easily controlled knife cuts that help ensure even noodles.

10. Unfurl and cook
Unfurl the noodles and transfer them to a rimmed baking sheet; repeat with the remaining sheets. Boil the noodles for 3 minutes.
Why? Unwinding the noodles before cooking prevents clumping.

Spiced Chicken Kebabs Dinner

We used the oven (and broiler) to make a spiced chicken and vegetable dinner that tastes like it just came off the grill. **by Alli Berkey**

A secret ingredient—red curry paste—adds deep savory flavor to these tasty chicken kebab

WHAT'S NOT TO love about grilled meat on a stick? It's easy to cook (the skewer holds together small pieces that are otherwise hard to manage over the fire), easy to eat (the food is already cut into bite-size pieces), easy to serve (one kebab usually feeds one person), and easy to customize (what you thread onto each skewer is up to you). But do you have to put away the skewers when temperatures are low? I wanted an easy, weeknight-friendly supper of chicken kebabs that tasted of char but could be cooked indoors. And I wanted to cook it all on one pan for easy cleanup.

Step one was choosing between chicken breasts and chicken thighs; I went with the breasts because they require less prep and take less time to cook. I cut four boneless, skinless chicken breasts into 2-inch chunks,

Setup for Success

Timing and positioning on the baking sheet are everything here.

POTATOES Get a head start in the oven

BROCCOLI FLORETS Go in the center of the baking sheet

CHICKEN KEBABS Sit on top of the potatoes, closest to the heat of the broiler element

seasoned the chunks with salt and pepper, threaded them onto skewers, and broiled them for about 15 minutes, flipping them halfway through. Not bad, but the chicken chunks were a tad dry and dull. They needed flavor.

I tried all kinds of marinades, spice rubs, and glazes before landing on a single ingredient that may be unmatched for its combination of potent flavor and ease of use: Thai red curry paste. Marinating the chicken in this aromatic mixture of ginger, chiles, lemongrass, garlic, and spices imbued it with deep flavor; the kebabs tasted superseasoned but didn't necessarily read as Thai. Adding some plain yogurt to the marinade thinned it out so it coated the chicken more evenly and helped the meat brown and char more readily under the broiler's fiery breath.

To round out the meal, I decided on small red potatoes and broccoli, knowing that the potatoes would need more than a quick stint under the broiler to cook through. I experimented with cutting the vegetables into different shapes and broiling and roasting them at different temperatures before landing on a foolproof method. First, I gave halved potatoes a head start in a 475-degree oven until they were browned on their cut side. Then, I removed the baking sheet from the oven, heated the broiler, piled the broccoli florets in the middle of the sheet, placed the kebabs around the perimeter, and broiled the whole lot for about 15 minutes, flipping the kebabs halfway through cooking.

By following this method, I was able to achieve tender and nicely browned potatoes, broccoli florets with a little smoky char, and perfectly charred, deeply seasoned chicken that tasted like it had been cooked on a grill. A quick stir-together yogurt sauce—using more of both the curry paste and the yogurt called for in the marinade, plus lime juice for extra brightness and cilantro for freshness—for serving on the side made all the flavors pop even more. This supper provides a taste of summer all year round—all on one pan.

ONE-PAN CHICKEN KEBABS WITH POTATOES AND BROCCOLI
Serves 4

When shopping, look for small red potatoes measuring 1 to 2 inches in diameter (about the size of a golf ball). We developed this recipe using Thai Kitchen Red Curry Paste; a 4-ounce jar is plenty here. You will need four 12-inch metal skewers for this recipe.

CHICKEN
- ½ cup plain Greek yogurt
- 2 tablespoons red curry paste
- 1 tablespoon vegetable oil
- 1 teaspoon table salt
- ½ teaspoon pepper
- 4 (6- to 8-ounce) boneless, skinless chicken breasts, trimmed and cut into 2-inch chunks

SAUCE
- ½ cup plain Greek yogurt
- ¼ cup chopped fresh cilantro
- 1 tablespoon lime juice
- 1 tablespoon water
- 1 teaspoon red curry paste
- ¼ teaspoon table salt
- ⅛ teaspoon pepper

VEGETABLES
- 1½ pounds small red potatoes, unpeeled, halved
- ¼ cup vegetable oil, divided
- ¾ teaspoon table salt, divided
- ½ teaspoon pepper, divided
- 1 pound broccoli florets, cut into 2-inch pieces

1. FOR THE CHICKEN: Adjust ove rack to middle position and heat oven 475 degrees. Whisk yogurt, curry past oil, salt, and pepper together in mediu bowl. Add chicken and stir to combine Let marinate for at least 30 minutes or up to 1 hour. Thread chicken onto fou 12-inch metal skewers; set aside.

2. FOR THE SAUCE: Whisk all ingredients together in bowl.

3. FOR THE VEGETABLES: Line rimmed baking sheet with aluminum foil. Toss potatoes, 2 tablespoons oil, ½ teaspoon salt, and ¼ teaspoon pepper together on prepared sheet. Arrange potatoes, cut side down, aroun outside of sheet. Bake until bottoms begin to brown, about 15 minutes.

4. Remove sheet from oven and heat broiler. Toss broccoli, remaining 2 tablespoons oil, remaining ¼ teaspoo salt, and remaining ¼ teaspoon pepper together in medium bowl. Place broccoli in center of sheet. Place kebabs around perimeter of sheet on top of potatoes. Return sheet to oven and broil until chicken is lightly charred on top, about 8 minutes. Flip kebabs and continue to broil until lightly charred on second side and chicken registers 160 degrees, 6 to 8 minutes longer. Serve kebabs with vegetables and sauce

Chicken Marbella

he slow cooker can muddy things up. We wanted something brighter.

Natalie Estrada and Morgan Bolling

MONG THE MANY treasured
cipes featured in *The Silver Palate
ookbook*, which was written by Sheila
ukins and Julee Rosso and first pub-
hed in 1982, is Chicken Marbella.
first glance, both then and now, the
mbination of ingredients will surprise
me: Chicken parts stewed with
unes, olives, and wine? But Lukins
d Rosso's bold combination is lovely.
e set out to create an equally lovely
rsion for the slow cooker.

As is common in the test kitchen,
r first move was just to put all the
gredients into the slow cooker, turn
on, and walk away—to see what
uld happen. We chose chicken
ighs because their dark meat is well
ited to the long, gentle cooking of
e slow cooker. After a few hours,
found juicy, tender, beautifully
asoned chicken—swimming in a
uddy, one-note, superfatty sauce.
hile deeply savory, the sauce lacked
e complex sweet, salty, briny, fruity,
eaty profile that made its original
eration so appealing.

Solving the fat issue was easy:
rcooking the chicken thighs for
minutes skin side down in a skillet
fore transferring them to the slow
oker rendered a fair amount of fat in
e skin without sacrificing any mean-
gful flavor. Finishing the parcooked
ighs in the slow cooker was a "set it
d forget it" situation.

Fixing the dull prune-olive sauce
as the tricky part. We tried cook-
g the sauce separately in a saucepan
d introducing it to the slow-cooked
icken only when the dish was ready
serve, but the result felt disjoint-
—the flavors never had a chance to
me together.

Instead, we tried including a portion
the prune-olive mixture (pureed in
food processor for ease of prepara-
n and maximum flavor transfer) in
e slow cooker with chicken broth and
ne to keep the chicken company as it
ewed and then adding the rest of the
uce (boosted with a splash of orange
ice) just before serving. Finally we
ssed in chopped parsley to finish.

There. A complex mix of depth
d brightness, framing juicy chicken
ighs, with inexpensive ingredients and
t a lot of work. With a bit of crusty
ead or couscous on the side, it's just
ght for a rustic supper.

A combination of fruity prunes and briny olives forms the sweet-savory flavor base of this iconic dish.

When *The Silver Palate Cookbook* was published in 1982, it didn't have much competition for its style of cooking—global flavors filtered through an Ameri-

THE AMERICAN TABLE

can lens. But authors Sheila Lukins and Julee Rosso knew American home cooks were ready for cookbooks with a more contemporary vibe. For home cooks whose previous go-tos had included doorstops such as *Joy of Cooking*, *The Silver Palate Cookbook* had a distinct point of view: fresher ingredients (arugula! pesto!); bolder flavors (olives! anchovies!); and a relaxed, friendly, family-style feel. Wear your jeans to dinner, this book said, and don't worry if the silverware doesn't match. Nearly 40 years later, it's still consid-ered an essential cookbook in kitchens across the United States.

SLOW-COOKER CHICKEN MARBELLA
Serves 4 to 6
Serve with crusty bread or couscous.

- 8 (5- to 7-ounce) bone-in chicken thighs, trimmed
- 1½ teaspoons table salt, divided
- 1 teaspoon pepper, divided
- ½ cup pitted green olives
- ½ cup plus ⅓ cup pitted prunes, halved, divided
- 3 tablespoons capers, rinsed, divided
- 1 tablespoon packed brown sugar
- 3 garlic cloves, minced
- 1 teaspoon dried oregano
- ¼ teaspoon red pepper flakes
- 1 cup chicken broth
- ¼ cup dry white wine
- 1 tablespoon orange juice
- 1 tablespoon chopped fresh parsley

1. Pat chicken dry with paper towels and sprinkle with ½ teaspoon salt and ½ teaspoon pepper. Place chicken, skin side down, in cold 12-inch nonstick skil-let. Cook over medium-high heat until fat is rendered and skin is well browned, 8 to 10 minutes. Transfer chicken to slow cooker, skin side up.
2. Pulse olives, ½ cup prunes, 2 table-spoons capers, sugar, garlic, oregano, pepper flakes, remaining 1 teaspoon salt, and remaining ½ teaspoon pepper in food processor until finely chopped, about 10 pulses. Set aside ¼ cup olive mixture.
3. Distribute remaining olive mix-ture over chicken. Add broth, wine, and remaining ⅓ cup prunes. Cover and cook until chicken is tender, 4 to 6 hours on low.
4. Transfer chicken to shallow serving platter. Stir orange juice, reserved olive mixture, and remaining 1 tablespoon capers into sauce in slow cooker. Sea-son with salt and pepper to taste. Pour sauce over chicken and sprinkle with parsley. Serve.

A Cold Start
Starting the chicken thighs skin side down in a cold skillet encourages their fat to render more efficiently.

Sausage Strata for Two

Can't decide between French toast or sausage and eggs? You don't have to! **by Jessica Rudolph**

This savory strata has just a hint of sweetness from a splash of maple syrup.

IT'S A QUESTION as old as brunch itself: Savory or sweet? Eggs and sausage or pancakes and waffles? I'm firmly settled in the "both" camp. That zone on your plate where the syrup has started to seep over and infiltrate the savory side? That's where my favorite bites are, and that's what I wanted my breakfast strata to taste like.

I wanted an easy dish for a lazy day that would serve two people, and I wanted to pack it with all the best parts of breakfast. To start, I browned some bulk breakfast sausage, tossed it with torn sandwich bread and shredded cheddar cheese, poured a simple mixture of milk, eggs, and maple syrup over it, and baked it in a small casserole dish until it was puffy and golden brown.

The strata was beautiful and tasty, but I wanted more complexity. First, I added minced fresh sage to amplify the sausage's flavor. Then I swapped out the white bread for sweet and eggy brioche, which accentuated the maple syrup's sweetness and drove home the strata's French-toast-y flavor. This was a big step in the right direction, but overall the casserole was skewing a little sweet, so I swapped out the regular sausage for hot. The extra heat struck a harmonious balance with the nuttiness of the cheese and the sweetness of the syrup.

Happy with the sweet-savory flavor, I considered my method. I wondered if I could cut down on dishes and bake my strata in the skillet I'd used to brown the sausage. I reached for an 8-inch nonstick ovensafe skillet, the perfect size for a casserole for two, and it worked beautifully: My strata had a custardy-soft inside and a crisp golden crust above and below. Better yet, I found I could refrigerate the fully assembled strata overnight and bake it in the morning for an even more relaxing morning in.

SAUSAGE STRATA FOR TWO

Two small brioche rolls should yield the 4 ounces needed for this recipe. For a less spicy dish, substitute regular pork sausage for the hot. We like the sweetness that maple syrup adds here, but you can omit it for a more savory strata. If you don't have an 8-inch ovensafe nonstick skillet, cook the sausage in a 10-inch skillet and assemble and bake the strata in a greased 9-inch pie plate.

- ¾ cup whole milk
- 3 large eggs
- 1 tablespoon maple syrup
- ¼ teaspoon table salt
- ¼ teaspoon pepper
- 4 ounces brioche, torn into 1-inch pieces (3 cups)
- 4 ounces sharp cheddar cheese, shredded (1 cup)
- 6 ounces hot bulk pork breakfast sausage
- 1 teaspoon minced fresh sage

1. Adjust oven rack to middle position and heat oven to 375 degrees. Whisk milk, eggs, maple syrup, salt, and pepper together in large bowl. Add brioche and cheddar and stir to combine; set aside.
2. Cook sausage in 8-inch ovensafe nonstick skillet over medium heat until browned, about 8 minutes, breaking meat into small pieces with wooden spoon. Add sage and cook until fragrant, about 30 seconds. Transfer to bowl with brioche mixture and stir to combine.
3. Transfer strata mixture to now-empty skillet and smooth into even layer. Bake until puffed and lightly browned, about 30 minutes (strata will puff above rim of skillet). Let rest for 10 minutes. Serve.

TO MAKE AHEAD

At end of step 2, strata mixture can be transferred to greased 9-inch pie plate, covered with plastic wrap, and refrigerated for up to 24 hours. Bake in pie plate.

Cheese Whiz
When we held a taste test of supermarket sharp cheddar cheeses, **Cabot Vermont Sharp Cheddar** came out on top. We were impressed by its "nutty," "almost smoky" flavor and "complex" sharpness.

Top Skillet
An 8-inch nonstick skillet is a useful pan to have when cooking for two. Our favorite is the **OXO Good Grips Hard Anodized Pro Nonstick 8-Inch Fry Pan ($30).**

Buying Maple Syrup
Maple syrup is essential in the test kitchen. A recent taste test surprised us: We didn't find many differences among the products in our lineup. That said, we prefer to use 100% pure maple syrup and like the full flavor of syrups labeled Grade A Dark Amber.

Bacon Jam

Do you like bacon? Then this sweet-savory spread will be your jam. **by Matthew Fairman**

EVERY RECIPE WE publish in *Cook's Country* goes through rigorous testing, not only in our own test kitchens but in dozens of home kitchens across the country. This is, of course, thanks to our dedicated cadre of volunteer home testers (visit the link at the end of the recipe for more information). The feedback we get from our readers—who test our recipes in their home kitchens with their own groceries and pots and pans—is absolutely essential to refining our recipes.

Contributing Editor Eva Katz, an experienced cook and a very tough critic, also runs through and assesses each of our recipes in her home kitchen. If there's a problem with the method or the flavor isn't perfect, she tells us about it. Not every recipe survives her thoughtful, honest, and sometimes heartbreaking review. A thumbs-down from Eva means the test cook has to get back in the kitchen, or possibly even that the recipe has to be scrapped.

Here's what she had to say about this bacon jam: "I ate some of this spread on a slice of toasted whole-grain bread topped with a slice of cheddar cheese. Delicious. It was complex and well balanced. It hits the entire flavor spectrum: smoky, sweet, sour, umami, and salty. It's an easy recipe, and I think anyone who likes bacon would like this jam—9.5 out of 10." When I read her notes, I beamed like a proud parent. I'd tinkered with the recipe for weeks.

I'd tested thick-cut bacon against classic slices and found that the thick-cut bacon remained too chewy in the finished jam. I'd chosen maple syrup over other sweeteners because it perfectly complemented the smoky, salty bacon and yielded a spreadable jam. I'd tested half a dozen cooking methods until I was absolutely sure I had to begin by crisping up the bacon and rendering the fat. Without that step, the jam was greasy and the bacon was flabby.

Once I had the jam where I wanted it—unctuous and spreadable, smoky and salty, with just the right amount of balancing sweetness and acidity—I was unable to stop eating it. I've slathered it on egg sandwiches. I've dipped apple slices into it as an afternoon snack. I've put it out with a fancy cheese plate for my family. I've even whisked it into a vinaigrette.

So here's the recipe. Try it. I can't wait to have your feedback on it, too, and to see what ingenious uses you find for it. As for me, I've got a batch in the fridge and a list of plans. First, burgers with bacon jam. Then I might double down on the bacon in some BLTs. Would it be too much to stir it into some banana pancake batter? We'll see.

BACON JAM

Serves 8 to 10 (Makes about 1¼ cups)
Do not use thick-cut bacon in this recipe. We like cider vinegar here, but you can experiment with other vinegars if you like. You can use more or less cayenne to suit your preferences; the ⅛ teaspoon we call for provides just a hint of heat.

- 1 pound bacon, cut crosswise into ½-inch-wide strips
- 2 cups thinly sliced onion
- 4 sprigs fresh thyme
- 2 garlic cloves, smashed and peeled
- 4 cups water
- ⅓ cup cider vinegar
- ⅓ cup maple syrup
- ⅛ teaspoon cayenne pepper

1. Cook bacon in 12-inch nonstick skillet over medium heat until crispy, 15 to 18 minutes. Using slotted spoon, transfer bacon to paper towel–lined plate; set aside. Pour off all but 2 tablespoons fat from skillet.
2. Heat fat left in skillet over medium heat until shimmering. Add onion, thyme sprigs, and garlic and cook until onion is softened and browned, 5 to 7 minutes. Stir in water, vinegar, maple syrup, cayenne, and reserved bacon. Increase heat to medium-high and bring to boil. Cook, stirring occasionally, until nearly all liquid has evaporated and mixture begins to sizzle loudly, 22 to 28 minutes.
3. Remove from heat and let cool for 15 minutes. Discard thyme sprigs. Transfer bacon mixture to food processor and pulse until minced, 15 to 20 pulses. Serve warm. (Jam can be refrigerated for up to 4 days. To serve, cover and microwave for 1 minute, stirring halfway through microwaving.)

Cook bacon in skillet and transfer to
per towel–lined plate.

2. Sauté aromatics in bacon fat until onion is softened and browned.

Add liquids, cayenne, and bacon to pan.
il and cook until liquid evaporates.

4. Discard thyme sprigs and pulse bacon mixture in food processor until minced.

Join our thousands of home recipe testers! Visit **CooksCountry.com/recipetesting** to sign up.

Tasting Cornmeal

Our favorite product produced a tender cornbread with a pleasant flavor. **by Emily Phares**

Our Favorite

WE RECOMMEND EVERY CORNMEAL WE TASTED.

① ② ③ ④ ⑤

CORNMEAL IS A pantry essential, whether we're making cornbread or corn pancakes. When our former favorite was discontinued, we chose five nationally available products to test. We made Southern-Style Skillet Cornbread and (to see how the products performed when combined with flour) Cornmeal Buttermilk Pancakes.

Every cornmeal produced satisfactory pancakes. The cornbreads were much more revealing—their textures ranged from smooth, moist, and tender to grainy and crumbly.

To assess the grind sizes of the cornmeals, we sifted them. Despite being labeled as "fine," one product was much finer than the rest, while another was much coarser. The grind sizes of the other three products fell somewhere in between. Tasters found cornbread made with the very coarse cornmeal to be "grainy" and "gritty." But overall, tasters cared more about how moist the cornbreads were than how rough or fine they were in texture; tasters strongly preferred the two "moist" cornbreads to the three that were perceived as drier.

To learn why only some of the cornmeals produced moist cornbreads, we talked to Dr. Charles Hurburgh, professor of agricultural and biosystems engineering at Iowa State University. He explained that the moistness of a cornbread probably has more to do with whether or not the corn kernels were degerminated prior to grinding than how finely or coarsely they were ground.

Dr. Hurburgh said it's standard practice for high-capacity mills to remove the germ—the part of the corn kernel

that contains vitamins, enzymes, and corn oil—prior to grinding the corn. There are two reasons for this. First, manufacturers can sell the corn oil they harvest from the germ. Second, the oil in the germ will turn rancid over time, so removing the germ prior to grinding helps prolong a cornmeal's shelf life.

According to our science research editor, a cornmeal's label may report that it contains 0 grams of fat, but that doesn't mean it contains no fat at all. The amounts are just too small to register when calculating the nutritional information. He also noted that, on average, the fat content of degerminated cornmeal is 1.75 percent, whereas the fat content of germ-in cornmeal is almost 4 percent. Though this difference may be small, it can have a big impact: Cornmeals made from kernels with their fatty germs intact would be more likely to produce a moist cornbread. Sure enough, our two favorite products—the ones that produced particularly moist cornbreads—were made from corn that was not degerminated.

As for flavor, tasters noted that some of the cornbreads were more "subdued" in flavor, while others had a "prominent" corn taste. We preferred the more neutral, "buttery" flavor of our favorite cornmeal to the "very strong" corn flavor of our lowest-ranked product.

Ultimately, we can recommend every cornmeal we tasted. Our favorite, Anson Mills Antebellum Fine Yellow Cornmeal, made tender, cakey cornbread. Since we had to order this cornmeal online, we also chose a winning supermarket brand: Goya Fine Yellow Corn Meal.

RECOMMENDED

① Anson Mills Antebellum Fine Yellow Cornmeal
Price: $5.95 for 12 oz ($0.50 per oz), plus shipping ($9.44 for four 12-oz bags)
Ingredients: Organic John Haulk corn
Degerminated: No **Fat:** Not listed

② Goya Fine Yellow Corn Meal
Price: $1.99 for 24 oz ($0.08 per oz)
Ingredients: Yellow corn meal enriched with iron, niacin, thiamin, riboflavin, folic acid
Degerminated: No **Fat:** 0 g per serving

③ Aunt Jemima Yellow Corn Meal
Price: $11.00 for 80 oz ($0.14 per oz)
Ingredients: Degerminated yellow corn meal, niacin, reduced iron, thiamin mononitrate, riboflavin, folic acid
Degerminated: Yes **Fat:** 0 g per serving

④ Bob's Red Mill Fine Grind Cornmeal
Price: $2.59 for 24 oz ($0.11 per oz), plus shipping ($13.34 for two 24-oz bags)
Ingredients: Whole grain corn
Degerminated: No **Fat:** 1.12 g per serving

⑤ Quaker Yellow Corn Meal
Price: $2.69 for 24 oz ($0.11 per oz)
Ingredients: Degerminated yellow corn meal, niacin, reduced iron, thiamin mononitrate, riboflavin, folic acid
Degerminated: Yes **Fat:** 0.5 g per serving

TASTERS' NOTES

This germ-in cornmeal produced a cornbread that was "moist," soft, and tender, with a smooth, cakey texture that was "not too crumbly." Instead of being corn-forward its flavor was more muted, with some tasters noting a "nice butter flavor."

Another germ-in product, our runner-up produced a really moist cornbread. Its smooth texture "holds together well" without crumbling. It had an understated yet "pleasant" and "savory" flavor that we liked

This cornmeal was degerminated, which likely contributed to the relatively dry (but not too dry) crumb in the cornbread made from it. We liked the "nice medium texture" and "buttery" flavor.

Labeled "fine grind," this cornmeal looked a lot coarser than the rest. In cornbread, it was "earthy" in flavor and "grainy" in texture. One taster lamented that the "flavor is pleasant, but it feels like I'm eating couscous."

Our lowest-ranked cornmeal was "dry," with a "crumbly" texture that one taster said "falls apart very easily." Some liked the "nice, gritty texture." This cornmeal also ha a "prominent" corn flavor that, as one taste put it, "reminded me of a tortilla chip."

Germ = Fat = Moist Cornbread

Sometimes a corn kernel's germ—which contains vitamins, enzymes, and corn oil—is removed before the corn is ground, which can lead to drier baked goods. Cornmeals made from kernels with their germ intact are more likely to produce moist cornbread.

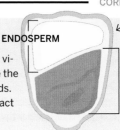

CORN KERN

ENDOSPERM

EMBRY (GERM

Countertop Vacuum Sealers

f you regularly buy or prepare food in bulk, this appliance can save you time and money—
ut only if it's easy to use. **by Kate Shannon**

YOU REGULARLY buy or
epare food in bulk, a vacuum sealer
n save you time and money. These
achines remove air from storage
gs before sealing them tightly,
ich protects the foods inside from
oisture loss or gain and helps them
y fresher longer. To find the best
oduct, we purchased seven models
iced from about $49 to about $385
d used them to vacuum-seal various
ods, from berries to blade steaks.
e then stashed the sealed bags in our
eezer or pantry and checked them
gularly over a period of months for
ose seals or signs of food degrada-
on. We also rated each machine on
e user-friendliness of its design.

Based on performance alone, we
uld recommend every machine we
ted. Each machine removed air,
lling the bags tight around every
e of food, and then melted a sturdy
al into the plastic. We measured each
achine's vacuum power on a scale
om 0 percent (normal atmosphere) to
0 percent (every single molecule of
removed from bags). The machines
performed respectably, with scores
nging from about 68 percent to about
percent. The vacuum-sealed foods
o held up well over time: After six
onths, all the pantry bags were still
htly sealed, and, with the exception
the steaks, most of the frozen food
mples showed no signs of ice. (The
aks developed small patches of ice
ystals after about six weeks.)

Next we evaluated ease of use. We
ed clearly labeled control panels that
ade it easy to select a setting. Every

Vacuum sealing removes most of the air around foods (such as the strawberries above), so they last longer and freeze better.

machine had an automatic and a manual
setting, both of which we found essential; additional controls such as a pulse
button or a gentle setting were nice but
not critical. Before any of the machines
could pull air from bags, their lids had
to be firmly locked. On some machines
this was surprisingly difficult, thanks
to lids that were awkwardly positioned
or that required a good deal of force to
close; this made us worry that we would
break them. The size of the machines
also mattered: Some were sturdy but
too heavy to easily move and store,
while some lighter models felt flimsy.

In the end, our favorite was the
Nesco Deluxe Vacuum Sealer, a
sturdy yet relatively light and compact
machine with an easy-to-read display
screen and a lid that we could easily
lock firmly into place. Less expensive
than some of the other models tested,
it's a great choice for home cooks who
vacuum-seal regularly.

 Go to **CooksCountry.com/mar20** to read the full testing results and see the complete chart.

KEY Good ★★★ Fair ★★ Poor ★

HIGHLY RECOMMENDED

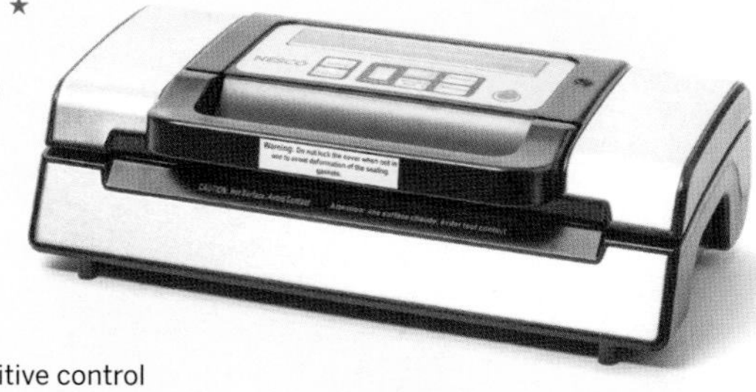

Nesco Deluxe Vacuum Sealer
Model: VS-12 **Price:** $90.02
Vacuum Strength: 75.20%
Compatible with Generic Bags: Yes
Weight: 6 lb, 1 oz
Dimensions: 15¾ x 7¾ x 4¾ in

Comments: We liked this model's intuitive control panel and stellar performance. The handle locked the lid into place with a reassuring click, and the "gentle" setting and pulse modes both worked well when vacuum-sealing fragile foods such as strawberries.

Performance ★★★
Ease of Use ★★★
Handling ★★★

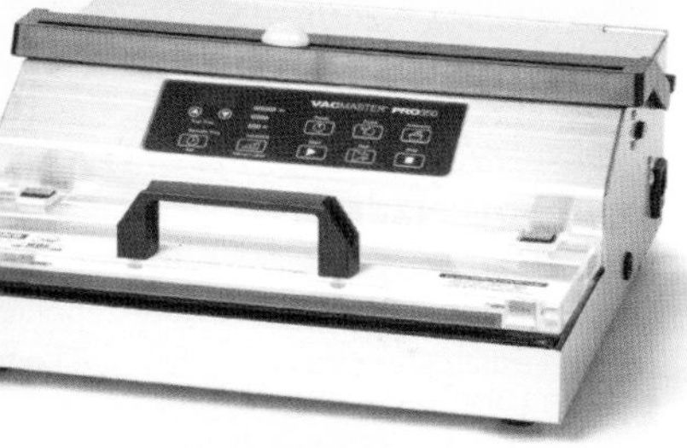

VacMaster PRO350
Professional Vacuum
Sealer - 12" Seal Bar
Model: PRO350 **Price:** $298.19
Vacuum Strength: 77.99%
Compatible with Generic Bags:
Yes, but company rep discouraged use
Weight: 19 lb, 8 oz
Dimensions: 15 x 13¾ x 6¼ in

Comments: If you like tinkering with vacuum strength and seal times to find the optimal set-tings for your favorite foods, this heavy-duty and highly customizable machine might be for you.

Performance ★★★
Ease of Use ★★★
Handling ★★½

The FoodSaver FM2000
Vacuum Sealing System
Model: FM2000
Price: $71.03
Vacuum Strength: 70.19%
Compatible with Generic Bags: Yes, but company rep discouraged use
Weight: 3 lb, 14¼ oz
Dimensions: 16 x 5¾ x 4 in

Comments: We loved this sealer's slim, compact design; sleek user interface; and manual control setting (which came in handy when sealing delicate foods). It didn't have a countdown screen but was otherwise very easy to use.

Performance ★★★
Ease of Use ★★½
Handling ★★★

RECOMMENDED

Gourmia Vacuum Sealer
Model: GVS455 **Price:** $49.99
Vacuum Strength: 76.87%
Compatible with Generic Bags: Yes
Weight: 5 lb, 4½ oz
Dimensions: 15¾ x 8 x 3½ in
Comments: First-time users had a hard time figuring out this machine. It sealed foods well, but closing the lid required a lot of force.

Crenova VS100S Food Vacuum Sealer
Model: VS100S **Price:** $59.99
Vacuum Strength: 76.87%
Compatible with Generic Bags: Yes
Weight: 2 lb, 10⅜ oz
Dimensions: 13½ x 5¾ x 2¾ in
Comments: This model kept pace with others, but we had to press hard on the lid to close it.

RECOMMENDED WITH RESERVATIONS

Weston Pro-2300 Vacuum Sealer
Model: 65-0201 **Price:** $382.00
Vacuum Strength: 67.96%
Compatible with Generic Bags: Yes, but company rep discouraged use **Weight:** 21 lb, 15 oz
Dimensions: 19 x 13½ x 5¾ in
Comments: This machine was the heaviest, bulkiest, and priciest model we tested, but it performed well.

NOT RECOMMENDED

NutriChef Vacuum Sealer
Model: PKVS35STS **Price:** $74.71
Vacuum Strength: 73.53%
Compatible with Generic Bags: Yes
Weight: 3 lb, 5 oz
Dimensions: 16 x 5¼ x 2¾ in
Comments: It took a lot of trial and error to use this machine successfully.

Pizza Dip

This dip is creamy, savory, and hot—just perfect for a movie night or game day. It smells too good to resist, but don't skip the cooling time. Right out of the oven, the dip is hot enough to burn your tongue.

HEIRLOOM PIZZA DIP
Serves 6
For the best results, buy a stick of pepperoni, not packaged presliced pepperoni. Serve with breadsticks, crackers, or toasted baguette slices.

8	**ounces cream cheese, cut into 8 pieces**
¾	**cup jarred pizza sauce**
1	**garlic clove, minced**
½	**teaspoon dried oregano**
¼	**teaspoon red pepper flakes**
4	**ounces whole-milk mozzarella cheese, shredded (1 cup)**
3	**ounces pepperoni, cut into ¼-inch pieces**
1	**ounce Parmesan cheese, grated (½ cup)**
6	**tablespoons thinly sliced scallions, divided**

1 Adjust oven rack to middle position and heat oven to 425 degrees.

2. Microwave cream cheese in large bowl until soft, 20 to 30 seconds. Stir in pizza sauce, garlic, oregano, and pepper flakes until thoroughly combined. Stir in mozzarella, pepperoni, Parmesan, and ¼ cup scallions.

3. Transfer cream cheese mixture to 1-quart casserole dish and smooth top with rubber spatula. Bake until spotty brown and bubbling at edges, 17 to 20 minutes. Let cool for 10 minutes. Sprinkle with remaining 2 tablespoons scallions. Serve.

We're looking for recipes that you treasure—the ones that have been handed down in your family for a generation or more, that always come out for the holidays, and that have earned a place at your table and in your heart through many years of meals. Send us the recipes that spell home to you. Visit CooksCountry.com/recipe_submission (or write to Heirloom Recipes, Cook's Country, 21 Drydock Avenue, Suite 210E, Boston, MA 02210) and tell us a little about the recipe. Include your name and address. If we print your recipe, you'll receive a free one-year subscription to Cook's Country.

COMING NEXT ISSUE

*Last year in Asheville, North Carolina, Executive Food Editor Bryan Roof came face-to-face with an extraordinary **Banana Pudding Pie** with a beautiful toasted meringue top, and he knew it was something we had to share with the world. We'll publish our recipe next issue, along with recipes for **Green Chicken Enchiladas**, **Pork with 40 Cloves of Garlic**, **Slow-Cooker Pork Ramen**, **Strawberry-Rhubarb Crisp**, and more.*

FIND THE ROOSTER!

A tiny version of this rooster has been hidden in a photo in the pages of this issue. Write to us with its location, and we'll enter you in a random drawing. The first correct entry drawn will win ou[r] favorite inexpensive blender, and each o[f] the next five will receive a free one-year subscription to Cook's Country. To ente[r] visit CooksCountry.com/rooster by Feb[ru]ary 29, 2020, or write to Rooster FM20, Cook's Country, 21 Drydock Avenue, Suite 210E, Boston, MA 02210. Include your name and address. Pat Vignocchi of Northbrook, Illinois, found the rooste[r] in the October/November 2019 issue o[n] page 9 and won our favorite broiler-safe baking dish.

WEB EXTRAS

Free for four months online at
CooksCountry.com/mar20

Chocolate Layer Cake Rounds
Food-Processor Vanilla Frosting

READ US ON IPAD

*Download the **Cook's Country** app for iPad and start a free trial subscription o[r] purchase a single issue of the magazin[e;] issues are enhanced with Cooking Mod[e] slide shows that provide step-by-step instructions for completing recipes, plu[s] expanded reviews and ratings. Go to CooksCountry.com/iPad to download app through iTunes.*

Kahlúa Cheesecake

Coffee, cheesecake, and chocolate cake come together in a dessert that's sure to hit the bull's-eye. **by Sarah Ewald**

TO MAKE THIS CAKE, YOU WILL NEED:

- 1½ teaspoons unflavored gelatin
- ½ cup Kahlúa
- 6 ounces white chocolate, chopped
- 1 cup heavy cream
- 1 pound cream cheese, softened
- ½ cup (3½ ounces) sugar
- 2 (9-inch) Chocolate Layer Cake Rounds*
- 1 recipe Food-Processor Vanilla Frosting*
- 6 ounces bittersweet chocolate, melted and cooled slightly
- 2½ tablespoons (½ ounce) Dutch-processed cocoa powder

FOR THE CHEESECAKE:

Sprinkle gelatin over Kahlúa in small saucepan and let sit until gelatin softens, about 5 minutes. Cook gelatin mixture over low heat until edges are just bubbling. Add white chocolate and continue to cook, stirring constantly, until just melted and smooth, about 2 minutes longer. Set aside and let cool for 15 minutes.

Using stand mixer fitted with whisk attachment, whip cream on medium-high speed until soft peaks form, 1 to 2 minutes; transfer to medium bowl and set aside. Fit now-empty mixer with paddle and beat cream cheese and sugar on medium-high speed until light and fluffy, 2 to 3 minutes. Reduce speed to medium-low, add cooled white chocolate mixture, and beat until just combined, about 30 seconds, scraping down bowl as needed. Using rubber spatula, gently fold in whipped cream until combined.

TO ASSEMBLE:

Set 1 cake round in 9-inch springform pan. Spread cheesecake mixture over cake round in pan in even layer. Place remaining cake round on top of cheesecake mixture. Cover with plastic wrap and refrigerate until set, about 6 hours. Run thin knife between cake and side of pan; remove side of pan. Transfer cake to cake stand or plate. Run offset spatula around cake sides to smooth cheesecake flush with cake.

TO DECORATE:

Fit 3 pastry bags with small star tips. Transfer ½ cup vanilla frosting to 1 pastry bag. Whisk bittersweet chocolate into remaining frosting in bowl until fully combined. Transfer 2½ cups chocolate frosting to second pastry bag. Whisk cocoa into remaining chocolate frosting in bowl until fully combined, then transfer to third pastry bag. (You will have 2 shades of chocolate frosting: light and dark.) Cover sides of cake with stars of light chocolate frosting. Pipe bull's-eye pattern of stars over top of cake, starting with dark chocolate frosting at edge and alternating colors with each row. Refrigerate until frosting is firm, about 45 minutes. Serve.

*Our recipes for Chocolate Layer Cake Rounds and Food-Processor Vanilla Frosting are available for free for four months at **CooksCountry.com/ kahluacake**.

INSIDE THIS ISSUE

Cook's Country

This Pie Is Bananas

Banana Pudding Pie
PAGE 21

APRIL/MAY 2020
6.95 U.S./$7.95 CANADA

05>

71486 02742 3

ISPLAY UNTIL MAY 7, 2020

AMERICA'S
TEST KITCHEN

* PLUS

Savory Bronx-Style **Jamaican Beef Patties**
Spicy Weeknight **Chicken Arrabbiata**
Fresh Springtime **Strawberry-Rhubarb Crisp**
Green Chile Chicken Enchiladas in a Flash
Tasting Supermarket **Corn Tortillas**

LETTER FROM THE EDITOR

Illustration: Hannah Jacobs

MOST OF THE banana pudding pies I've encountered in my life have let me down. Sure, they've made my sweet tooth happy, but for the effort involved, they've always seemed dull. Lacking in pizzazz.

Our new recipe for Banana Pudding Pie (pictured on the cover) delivers that pizzazz and then some. Our Executive Food Editor, Bryan Roof, was inspired by a version at Buxton Hall Barbecue in Asheville, North Carolina. Test Cook Jessica Rudolph took his notes into the kitchen, where she spent weeks developing a recipe that any home cook can tackle with confidence. Make it (see page 22) and you will have achieved something remarkable—and earned major bragging rights.

While on the subject of bragging rights: If you turn to page 24, you'll see our recipe for American Sandwich Bread. This one is particularly special to me; as someone who in the past only briefly dipped his toes into bread making, I now make this loaf every week. It takes very little effort and makes the house smell fantastic. It's perfect for beginning bread bakers but won't disappoint old pros.

TUCKER SHAW

Editor in Chief

P.S. Did you know that our recipes are tested in home kitchens around the country? Thousands of cooks like you put our recipes to the test at home well before we publish them, giving us their honest feedback. We'd love to have your voice in the mix. Find out more at **AmericasTestKitchen.com/recipe_testing**.

FOOLPROOF FISH

Modern Recipes for Everyone, Everywhere

The typical supermarket seafood counter reveals a wide variety of fish, from mild and flaky to rich and meaty. In Foolproof Fish, we offer 219 approachable recipes, most of which can be made with more than one kind of fish. You're guaranteed a flavorful meal no matter what you bring home from the market or fishmonger. Order your copy today at AmericasTestKitchen.com/foolproof-fish.

 Find us on **Facebook**
facebook.com/CooksCountry

 Find us on **Instagram**
instagram.com/CooksCountry

 Follow us on **Pinterest**
pinterest.com/TestKitchen

 Follow us on **Twitter**
twitter.com/TestKitchen

Cook's Country

Chief Executive Officer David Nussbaum
Chief Creative Officer Jack Bishop
Editor in Chief Tucker Shaw
Executive Managing Editor Todd Meier
Executive Food Editor Bryan Roof
Deputy Editor Scott Kathan
Deputy Food Editor Morgan Bolling
Senior Editor Cecelia Jenkins
Associate Editors Alli Berkey, Matthew Fairman
Test Cooks Mark Huxsoll, Jessica Rudolph
Lead Test Cook, Photo Team Eric Haessler
Assistant Test Cooks, Photo Team Hannah Fenton, Jacqueline Gochenouer, Gina McCreadie, Christa West
Copy Editors Christine Campbell, April Poole, Rachel Scho[...]
Contributing Editor Eva Katz
Senior Science Research Editor Paul Adams
Hosts & Executive Editors, Television Bridget Lancaster, Julia Collin Davison

Executive Editors, Tastings & Testings Hannah Crowley, Lisa McManus
Senior Editors, Tastings & Testings Lauren Savoie, Kate S[...]
Associate Editor, Tastings & Testings Miye Bromberg
Assistant Editors, Tastings & Testings Chase Brightwell, Riddley Gemperlein-Schirm, Carolyn Grillo, Emily Phares

Creative Director John Torres
Photography Director Julie Cote
Art Director Susan Levin
Associate Art Director Maggie Edgar
Art Director, Tastings & Testings Marissa Angelone
Senior Staff Photographers Steve Klise, Daniel J. van Acke[...]
Staff Photographer Kevin White
Photography Producer Meredith Mulcahy

Senior Director, Creative Operations Alice Carpenter
Senior Editor, Special Projects Christie Morrison
Senior Manager, Publishing Operations Taylor Argenzio
Imaging Manager Lauren Robbins
Production & Imaging Specialists Tricia Neumyer, Dennis [...], Amanda Yong
Deputy Editor, Editorial Operations Megan Ginsberg
Editorial Assistants, Editorial Operations Tess Berger, Sara Zatopek
Test Kitchen Director Erin McMurrer
Assistant Test Kitchen Director Alexxa Benson
Test Kitchen Manager Meridith Lippard
Test Kitchen Facilities Manager Kayce Vanpelt
Senior Kitchen Assistant Receiver Heather Tolmie
Senior Kitchen Assistant Shopper Avery Lowe
Kitchen Assistants Gladis Campos, Blanca Castanza, Amarilys Merced

Chief Financial Officer Jackie McCauley Ford
Senior Manager, Customer Support Tim Quinn
Customer Support Specialist Mitchell Axelson

Chief Digital Officer Fran Middleton
VP, Marketing Natalie Vinard
Director, Audience Acquisition & Partnerships Evan Steine[...]
Director, Social Media Marketing & Emerging Platforms Kathryn Przybyla
Social Media Manager Charlotte Errity
Social Media Coordinators Sarah Sandler, Norma Tentori

Chief Revenue Officer Sara Domville

Director, Public Relations & Communications Brian Frankl[...]

Senior VP, Human Resources & Organizational Development Colleen Zelina
Human Resources Manager Jason Lynott

Circulation Services PubWorX ProCirc

® AMERICA'S TEST KITCHEN

erica's Test Kitchen is a real test kitchen located
Boston. It is the home of more than 60 test cooks,
tors, and cookware specialists. Our mission is to
t recipes until we understand exactly how and
y they work and eventually arrive at the very
st version. We also test kitchen equipment and
permarket ingredients in search of products that
er the best value and performance. You can watch
work by tuning in to **America's Test Kitchen**
mericasTestKitchen.com) and **Cook's Country**
poksCountry.com) on public television, and you
n listen to our weekly segments on *The Splendid*
ple on public radio. You can also follow us on
ebook, Twitter, Pinterest, and Instagram.

28

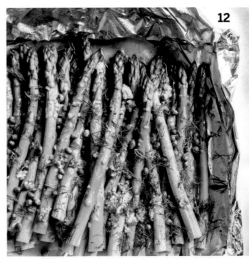

12

23

Cook's Country magazine (ISSN 1552-1990), number 92, is published bimonthly by America's Test Kitchen Limited Partnership, 21 Drydock Avenue, Suite 210E, Boston, MA 02210. Copyright 2020
America's Test Kitchen Limited Partnership. Periodicals postage paid at Boston, MA, and additional mailing offices, USPS #023453. Publications Mail Agreement No. 40020778. Return undeliverable Canadian addresses to P.O. Box 875, Station A, Windsor, ON N9A 6P2. POSTMASTER: Send address changes to *Cook's Country*, P.O. Box 6018, Harlan, IA 51593-1518. For subscription and gift
subscription orders, subscription inquiries, or change of address notices, visit AmericasTestKitchen.com/support, call 800-526-8447 in the U.S. or 515-237-3663 from outside the U.S., or write to
us at *Cook's Country*, P.O. Box 6018, Harlan, IA 51593-1518. PRINTED IN THE USA.

*Compiled by Cecelia Jenkins
and Morgan Bolling*

Encourage-mint

I want to grow mint in my garden this year, but I don't know which kind to plant. What is the difference between spearmint and peppermint?
–Emily Wells, Saratoga, N.Y.

There are more than 30 species of mint, but peppermint and spearmint are the most common. Peppermint has smooth green leaves and stems with a purple tinge, while spearmint (the type of mint most grocery stores carry) has bright green or gray-green leaves with a more crinkly texture.

To compare their flavors, we had tasters sample raw peppermint and spearmint leaves side by side and then had them try our recipes for Fresh Mint Sauce (an accompaniment for our Crumb-Crusted Rack of Lamb) and Cucumber-Mint Lemonade prepared with each type of mint. Since peppermint contains more menthol, it makes sense that our tasters found it spicier and much sharper than spearmint, commenting that it was "supercooling," "prickly," and "tingly," while spearmint had a "sweeter," "milder" minty flavor with a bitter finish.

Tasters had only a slight preference for the spearmint in the mint sauce since the olive oil masked some of the peppermint's sharpness. But they had a stronger preference for spearmint in the lemonade, finding it "vibrant," "herbaceous," and "rounded." The peppermint sample had a more distinct "herbal tea" flavor and astringency that several tasters described as "toothpaste-y."

THE BOTTOM LINE: Peppermint is more pungent than spearmint. We found the two kinds interchangeable in recipes with fat and other strong flavors, but we preferred spearmint overall for delivering refreshing mint flavor.

PEPPERMINT
Spicy and "supercooling"

SPEARMINT
Sweet, refreshing mint flavor

Roots in Coffee

A neighbor just served me chicory coffee. What is it?
–Samantha Edgar, Billerica, Mass.

Chicory is a plant in the endive family. Its curly, bitter leaves can be cooked or, when young and tender, enjoyed raw in salads. Your neighbor may have spent some time in New Orleans, where many people enjoy coffee bolstered with the dried and ground roots of the chicory plant. The story goes that chicory root was first added to coffee as an extender during the Union Army blockade of New Orleans during the Civil War (although there is some evidence of chicory coffee being an older French tradition). Chicory root adds a mild, earthy bitterness to the brew.

THE BOTTOM LINE: Coffee made with ground chicory root is a New Orleans tradition.

The Dark Side

I recently purchased "dark" Chinese soy sauce. How should I use it?
–Paul Graham, Burlington, Vt.

Most soy sauces can be classified as either "light" or "dark." Chinese light soy sauces (sometimes labeled "thin," "pure bean," or "fresh") are assertively salty and have a watery texture; our tasters described their flavor as "earthy," "intensely meaty," "bright," and "almost boozy." Chinese dark soy sauces are fermented longer and are therefore much thicker, deeper in color, sweeter, and significantly less salty than light soy sauces; dark soy sauces also often contain molasses. Tasters described the flavor of the dark soy sauces as milder and more balanced, not as one-note salty, and almost nutty with plum/bitter notes and found it much more syrupy and viscous in texture. Dark soy sauce is not commonly found in American supermarkets.

By comparison, Japanese soy sauce is generally sweeter, thinner, and less opaque than Chinese soy sauce, but both Japanese and Chinese light soy sauces are saltier than their darker counterparts and are used for seasoning. Chinese and Japanese dark soy sauces are richer in color and flavor, heavier in texture, and less salty than light versions.

THE BOTTOM LINE: Generally, light soy sauces (not always labeled as such) from both China and Japan can be considered all-purpose sauces and are the standard. Dark soy sauces are sweeter and more syrupy. They are most often used to color marinades and for basting.

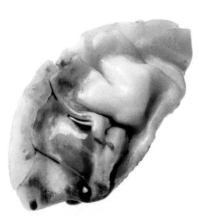
REGULAR (LIGHT) SOY SAUCE
Thinner and saltier

DARK SOY SAUCE
Thicker and sweeter

Hidden Morsel

I've heard the tastiest bits of meat on a roast chicken are the oysters and that most of us usually throw them away. What and where are they?
–Frederic Allen, Bellingham, Wash.

Every chicken has two "oysters," little oyster-size bits of tender, flavorful dark meat tucked along the backbone on the underside of a breast-side-up roast chicken. Many cooks consider it a well-deserved treat to eat these morsels in the kitchen.

Why are these bits of meat so great? As a chicken roasts breast side up in the oven, the oysters underneath the bird are protected from the direct heat of the oven and are constantly basted in the rendering chicken fat; this helps them stay ultrasilky, tender, and flavorful. They are easily carved out—you could even push them out of their cavities with your thumb—and since there are only two of these juicy gems, they're highly coveted. When breaking a whole raw chicken into parts, a good butchering job will leave the oyster attached to the thigh so that you get as much meat off the bird as possible.

THE BOTTOM LINE: When you roast and carve a chicken, don't forget about the oysters on the back of the bird (for a cook's treat!).

Chicken "oysters": Some say they're the tastiest bites on the bird.

These two pieces of meat sit on either side of the middle of the backbone on a roast chicken.

Compiled by Matthew Fairman

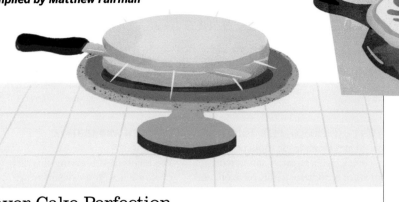

Makeshift Pizza Stone
–Terry Shearer, New Haven, Conn.

I just started baking my own pizzas, but I don't own a baking stone. Thankfully, I found another way to cook my pizza on a superhot surface. I place an overturned large cast-iron skillet on a baking sheet (for easy handling) and preheat it like a pizza stone. I have to bake slightly smaller pizzas, but since I'm baking for only two anyway, the size is perfect. My crusts turn out crisp every time, so I don't think I'll be buying a baking stone anytime soon.

Layer Cake Perfection
–Stephanie Roberts, Broken Arrow, Okla.

I'm an avid baker, and I love making tall, showstopping layer cakes for special occasions (and sometimes just because it's Thursday). But I've never been any good at cutting a single cake round into two even layers. After botching another one, I finally got fed up and figured out a way to cut the cake without having to eyeball it. I set the round on my rotating cake stand and placed eight toothpicks halfway up the side of the cake around the perimeter (using a ruler to make sure that they're even) to act as a guide for my knife. I then worked my way around the outside of the cake, cutting right above the toothpicks. Now it's easy to get even layers every time!

Faster Slow Cooking
–Jerry Lawson, Charleston, W. Va.

I love my slow cooker, but sometimes I just want to speed it up! I often make slow-cooker soups and stews using chicken stock that I've also made in the slow cooker and stored in the fridge. It takes forever for a couple of quarts of cold chicken stock to get hot in the slow cooker, so I simply microwave the stock for 5 to 10 minutes first to warm it up. I've found that this can shave up to an hour off the cooking time.

Deep-Fryers: Sizzle or Substance?
by Miye Bromberg

ELECTRIC DEEP-FRYERS promise to make frying easier, safer, and less messy than frying in a Dutch oven with a probe thermometer attached, which is how we typically deep-fry foods in the test kitchen. The machines are essentially metal bins with an electrical heating element suspended inside: To use them, you pour oil up to a maximum fill line, turn the machine on, and, in most cases, set the desired temperature for the oil. Once the oil is ready, you lower the food into the oil (usually via a basket) and often stick on a lid, which helps reduce any mess and supposedly contains unwanted odors.

To find out if any of these machines had advantages over a Dutch oven, we bought six deep-fryers and used them to cook frozen mozzarella sticks, french fries, fried chicken, vegetable tempura, and cider doughnuts. In almost every test, every model performed well, heating to within 5 degrees of the temperature we selected and making crispy, well-browned, evenly cooked food. And most models did a good job of letting us know when the temperature had been reached, either with a beep or by turning an indicator light on or off. They faltered only when making tempura, as they couldn't heat to the correct frying temperature of 400 degrees. We preferred deep-fryers that came with large fry baskets, which made it safer to add and remove food and allowed us to cook more food in a single batch. And while almost all the models kept our counter neat, there were many parts to wash: To get them completely clean, we had to wipe down each component and scrub them before placing the dishwasher-safe parts in the dishwasher.

Our favorite, the T-Fal Ultimate EZ-Clean Fryer, is easy to use, offers effortless temperature control, and can cook just as much food in one batch as a Dutch oven can—and just as well, as long as you're not frying at temperatures above 375 degrees. A built-in filter cleans the oil, which is stored in a handy container in its base.

Our Favorite

Web subscribers can read the entire testing and complete chart at CooksCountry.com/may20.

RECOMMENDED					RECOMMENDED WITH RESERVATIONS
1 T-Fal Ultimate EZ-Clean Fryer **Model:** FR7008002 **Price:** $94.68 **Comments:** Its basket held lots of food, and its high walls were good at containing messes. We liked its built-in oil filter and oil storage container.	**2 DeLonghi** Livenza Deep Fryer **Model:** D44528DZ **Price:** $129.99 **Comments:** It made excellent food, but its small fry basket required us to make extra batches. Its high walls and lid kept things tidy.	**3 Hamilton Beach** 12-Cup Oil Capacity Deep Fryer **Model:** 35033 **Price:** $44.99 **Comments:** Food was OK. A small basket meant many batches. Its high walls and lid reduced mess. It had many parts to clean.	**4 Breville** Smart Fryer **Model:** BDF500XL **Price:** $129.95 **Comments:** It gave us good cooking results, but its basket was the smallest of the lot, so it took more batches and time to cook all the recipes.	**5 Cuisinart** Digital Deep Fryer **Model:** CDF-170 **Price:** $49.99 **Comments:** It cooked most foods well, but its basket was too small, requiring us to use more batches to cook a recipe. It kept our counter neat.	**6 Presto** GranPappy Electric Deep Fryer **Model:** 05411 **Price:** $36.92 **Comments:** This small fryer had no basket, heated only to one temperature, and was messy (but easy to clean).

Dark-meat chicken leg quarters stay moist in the fiery sauce.

Chicken Arrabbiata

We wanted a spicy sauce that would assert itself but not take over.

by Alli Berkey

JUST HEARING THE Italian word *arrabbiata* leads some people to break into a sweat. A simmered mixture of tomato, garlic, olive oil, and a heavy-handed dose of crushed red pepper flakes helps this classic Italian sauce live up to its name: "Arrabbiata" translates as "angry."

Me, I love arrabbiata sauce. It's full of personality and surprise, its beautiful red hue just hinting at the heat within. This sauce is usually used to coat pasta or is paired with various types of seafood, but I wanted to tap into its spicy kick to ramp up my weeknight chicken routine.

With such a short list of ingredients, there was nothing to hide behind, so I knew that each item would have to be perfect. A quick comparison of tomato products was a good place to start. Fresh tomatoes, canned diced tomatoes, and canned crushed tomatoes were all decent options, but the crushed delivered the most concentrated tomato flavor with minimal cooking.

Next, I needed to add punch and complexity. I turned to chopped onion, salty anchovies (just a couple of fillets added savory notes without tasting fishy) and sharp, briny pickled pepperoncini. A couple of tablespoons of tomato paste added sweetness and enhanced the tomato flavor. Plenty of minced garlic and 1½ teaspoons of red pepper flakes sealed in the heat while also adding complexity.

My lively sauce was ready to meet the chicken. I used bone-in, skin-on leg quarters here for their tender, juicy meat and deep chicken flavor. I tried browning the pieces first in olive oil before draining off the fat and finishing the sauce in the skillet, but I couldn't help thinking that all that rendered fat was going to waste. For my next round, I browned the chicken, removed it from the skillet, and used the rendered fat to cook the sauce. This added depth and body, and after I nestled the browned chicken pieces back into the sauce and slipped the skillet into the oven to finish, I found that the sauce was complex, cohesive, spicy, and satisfying. And angry—but not too angry.

CHICKEN ARRABBIATA
Serves 4

We recommend serving this dish over polenta. You can substitute eight 5- to 7-ounce bone-in chicken thighs for the leg quarters, if desired. Good-quality olive oil makes a difference here. The anchovies add a background savory richness without tasting like fish; we encourage even nonfans to give them a try here. Be sure to remove the stems from the pepperoncini before mincing them. You can substitute Parmesan for the Pecorino Romano, if desired.

- 4 (10- to 12-ounce) chicken leg quarters, trimmed
- 1 teaspoon table salt, divided
- ½ teaspoon pepper
- ¼ cup extra-virgin olive oil
- 1 small onion, chopped fine
- 2 tablespoons minced pepperoncini
- 2 anchovy fillets, rinsed and minced
- 2 tablespoons tomato paste
- 4 garlic cloves, minced
- 1½ teaspoons red pepper flakes
- 1 (28-ounce) can crushed tomatoes
- ¼ cup grated Pecorino Romano cheese plus extra for serving

1. Adjust oven rack to middle position and heat oven to 350 degrees. Pat chicken dry with paper towels and sprinkle with ½ teaspoon salt and pepper.

2. Heat oil in Dutch oven over medium heat until just smoking. Add chicken, skin side down, and cook until skin is browned, about 9 minutes. Transfer chicken to large plate; set aside.

3. Add onion, pepperoncini, and anchovies to now-empty pot. Cook until onion is just softened, about 3 minutes. Add tomato paste, garlic, and pepper flakes and cook until fragrant, about 1 minute. Stir in tomatoes, Pecorino, and remaining ½ teaspoon salt, scraping up any browned bits.

4. Nestle chicken into sauce, skin side up, and bring to boil. Transfer pot to oven and cook, uncovered, until chicken registers 200 degrees, 35 to 40 minutes. Transfer chicken to serving platter. Stir sauce to recombine and spoon over chicken. Serve.

What's in a Name?

Reading the names of Italian dishes, whether in cookbooks or on menus, can be confusing if you're not familiar with the language. While knowing that *ragù* is a meat sauce and *melanzane* is eggplant, for instance, can help with decoding, some dishes have less literal names. ***Arrabbiata*** means "angry" and refers to this dish's fiery bite from the garlic and pepper flakes; our version also includes pepperoncini.

Some other Italian sauces to know: ***Amatriciana*** (from the Roman town of Amatrice) sauce is made from tomato, pancetta, and chile. **Carbonara** sauce contains egg, pancetta or *guanciale*, and lots of black pepper. Sauce ***alla norma*** is made from eggplant and tomatoes. **Puttanesca** sauce is a bold mix of tomatoes, anchovies, olives, capers, and garlic. Sauce ***alla vesuviana*** is made by bolstering tomatoes with olives, oregano, and capers. **Genovese** sauce is a rich ragu of meat and slow-cooked onions.

THREE "ANGRY" INGREDIENTS
Pepperoncini, garlic, and red pepper flakes

Pork Roast with 40 Cloves of Garlic

[W]on't add a little garlic to your next pork roast— [a]dd a lot. **by Cecelia Jenkins**

[I] LOVE TO EAT the traditional [di]sh of chicken with 40 cloves of gar[lic], but, to the uninitiated, the name of [th]is recipe can be a bit shocking. Forty [cl]oves of garlic sounds like enough to [m]ake your breath peel paint, but in [bo]th the garlic in the dish is slowly [co]oked and becomes sweet, nutty, [an]d mild. There is plenty of garlic [fla]vor, sure, but it isn't harsh or fiery. [I t]hought that sweet, mellow garlic [fla]vor would be a perfect match for the [su]btle natural sweetness of pork loin.

For my first few attempts, I seasoned [th]e pork with salt and pepper, put it in [a b]aking dish, scattered peeled garlic [cl]oves around it, and roasted it, testing [ov]en temperatures ranging from 300 to [40]0 degrees. The pork fared best—stay[in]g juicy and tender—when cooked at [a l]ower temperature; the garlic fared [be]st—caramelized and sweet—at a [hi]gher temperature. I wanted to cook [th]e two elements together for ease and [so] that their flavors could commingle.

After a bit of trial and error, I found [a] solution: I seared the pork roast in a [sk]illet on the stovetop to develop flavor[fu]l browning, added the peeled garlic [cl]oves, and then roasted them together [in] a 300-degree oven until the pork was [pe]rfectly done. Then I removed the [po]rk from the skillet and put the skillet

on the stovetop to finish browning the garlic in the flavorful juices.

A creamy sauce full of mellow garlic flavor is the standard for this dish, so after the cloves had browned, I added chicken broth, white wine, thyme, and a bit of cream to the skillet on the stovetop. I watched it bubble away and, when it had reduced to a thick, glossy sauce, I sliced the pork thin and poured the sauce over it.

It was really, really good . . . but not quite great. The dish needed a bolder hit of seasoning to take it over the top. The answer, I found, was to rub the raw pork with a potent mix of herbs and seasonings before searing at the start. Rosemary and pork go great together, so I'd use that. I already had thyme in the sauce, so it made sense to double down by using it on the pork, too. Ground fennel added its signature licorice flavor, and red pepper flakes provided just a hint of heat. This mix brought a balanced and complex depth to the entire dish.

Don't let the name—or the amount of garlic—scare you. Roast Pork Loin with 40 Cloves of Garlic is a savory, lightly sweet dish with a foundation of flavor built on the back of mellow, nutty roasted garlic. It's the perfect weeknight meal.

Sweet garlic is the star here; thyme, rosemary, and fennel are the supporting players.

ROAST PORK LOIN WITH 40 CLOVES OF GARLIC
Serves 4 to 6

You can use a blade-end or center-cut pork loin here. Three to four heads of garlic will yield 40 cloves. Note that the pork needs to be salted and refrigerated for at least an hour before cooking.

- 4 teaspoons minced fresh thyme, divided
- 1 tablespoon minced fresh rosemary
- 1 tablespoon kosher salt
- 2 teaspoons ground fennel
- 1 teaspoon pepper
- ¼ teaspoon red pepper flakes
- 1 (3-pound) boneless pork loin roast, trimmed
- 2 tablespoons vegetable oil
- 40 garlic cloves, peeled
- 1¼ cups chicken broth
- ⅓ cup dry white wine
- ⅓ cup heavy cream

1. Combine 2 teaspoons thyme, rosemary, salt, fennel, pepper, and pepper flakes in bowl. Sprinkle pork with thyme mixture. Wrap pork in plastic wrap and refrigerate for at least 1 hour or up to 24 hours.

2. Adjust oven rack to middle position and heat oven to 300 degrees. Heat oil in 12-inch ovensafe nonstick skillet over medium-high heat until

1 Head = About 12 Cloves
We don't mind peeling garlic cloves the old-fashioned way: Slice off the hard nub, lightly crush with the broad side of a knife, and peel. But we're also fans of tubular rubber peelers; our favorite is the **Zak! Designs E-Z Rol Garlic Peeler ($8.79)**.

just smoking. Unwrap pork and place in skillet. Cook until browned on all sides, about 7 minutes.

3. Scatter garlic around pork and transfer skillet to oven. Roast until pork registers 130 degrees, 40 to 50 minutes. Transfer pork to carving board, tent with aluminum foil, and let rest for 20 minutes.

4. While pork rests, place skillet with garlic over medium-high heat (skillet handle will be hot) and cook, stirring occasionally, until garlic is sizzling and light golden brown all over, about 3 minutes. Add broth, wine, cream, and remaining 2 teaspoons thyme and bring to boil. Cook until sauce has reduced to slightly more than 1 cup and is thick enough to coat back of spoon, about 10 minutes. Remove from heat and cover to keep warm.

5. Slice pork thin. Serve with sauce.

[M]aximizing Garlic's Sweetness

[W]e wanted sweet, deep, and mellow garlic flavor from all 40 cloves—and achieved just [th]at through our hybrid roasting-sautéing method.

[1.] Roast We roast the garlic cloves along [wi]th the pork to soften them.

2. Brown We then brown them on the stovetop for extra depth and sweetness.

Chicken Croquettes

A high crunch factor was our number one goal.

by Morgan Bolling

Use a knife and fork if you must, but our crunchy, creamy croquettes make fantastic finger food

CHICKEN CROQUETTES WITH LEMON-SCALLION SAUCE

Serves 4 to 6

An average-size rotisserie chicken should yield between 3 and 4 cups of shredded meat, which is more than enough for this recipe.

LEMON-SCALLION SAUCE

- ½ cup mayonnaise
- 1 scallion, minced
- 1 teaspoon grated lemon zest plus 1 tablespoon juice
- 1 tablespoon water

CROQUETTES

- 3 slices hearty white sandwich bread, torn into 1-inch pieces
- 1 tablespoon all-purpose flour
- 2 large eggs
- 1½ cups finely shredded rotisserie chicken
- 1¼ cups plain instant mashed potato flakes
- 4 scallions, sliced thin
- 2 garlic cloves, minced
- 1¼ teaspoons table salt
- 1 teaspoon pepper
- ⅛ teaspoon cayenne pepper
- 1½ cups half-and-half
- 2 tablespoons unsalted butter
- 2 cups vegetable oil for frying

1. FOR THE LEMON-SCALLION SAUCE: Combine all ingredients in bowl. Cover with plastic wrap and refrigerate until ready to serve.

2. FOR THE CROQUETTES: Process bread and flour in food processor until finely ground, about 30 seconds; transfer to shallow dish. Beat eggs together in second shallow dish. Set aside bread-crumb mixture and eggs.

3. Combine chicken, potato flakes, scallions, garlic, salt, pepper, and cayenne in large bowl. Combine half-and-half and butter in 2-cup liquid measuring cup and microwave, covered, until butter is melted and mixture is hot, about 3 minutes. Add to chicken mixture and stir to combine (mixture will thicken as it sits).

4. Divide chicken mixture into 20 equal portions (about 2 tablespoons each). Using your moistened hands, shape each portion into 3-inch log with pointed ends. Working with 3 to 4 croquettes at a time, dip in eggs, turning to coat and allowing excess to drip off; then coat with bread-crumb mixture. Transfer to rimmed baking sheet. (Breaded croquettes can be covered with plastic wrap and refrigerated for up to 24 hours.)

5. Line second rimmed baking sheet with triple layer of paper towels. Heat oil in 12-inch nonstick skillet over medium heat to 350 degrees. Add 10 croquettes and cook until deep golden brown on first side, about 2 minutes. Using tongs, carefully flip croquettes and continue to cook until deep golden brown on second side, about 3 minutes longer. Adjust burner, if necessary, to maintain oil temperature between 300 and 350 degrees.

6. Transfer croquettes to paper towel–lined sheet. Return oil to 350 degrees and repeat with remaining croquettes. Serve with lemon-scallion sauce.

It's Time for Croquettes

No mallet or wickets required.

1. Divide into 20 equal portions.

2. Shape into 3-inch logs with pointed ends.

3. Dip in egg mixture, turning to coat all over.

4. Dip in bread-crumb mixture.

THE WORD "CROQUETTE" comes from the French word *croquer*, meaning "to crunch." When biting into a good chicken croquette, you should not just feel the crunch but hear it, too, as you crack through the exterior into the soft, rich chicken filling. A hundred years ago they were a popular lunch, but they've fallen out of vogue. It's time to bring them back.

To get started with my recipe development, I made a few different styles of croquettes using existing recipes. Two promising lessons made my path forward clear: Shallow frying worked just as well as deep frying (and saved a ton of oil), and shredded rotisserie chicken was a perfectly acceptable shortcut.

Most of these croquette recipes called for making an extra-thick white sauce of flour and dairy, stirring in shredded chicken before chilling the mixture (to help it set), and then scooping, shaping, breading, and frying the mixture in nugget-size portions. This yielded croquettes with nice creamy centers, but the time and mess it required did not feel worth it. An easier set of recipes instructed to bind the chicken with cubed bread (like stuffing), but the resulting croquettes were dense.

While it was less common, we loved a light, fluffy version of croquettes that combined shredded chicken with leftover mashed potatoes for a binder. However, calling for leftover mashed potatoes was a nonstarter. Cooks add different amounts of butter and cream to their spuds, so no two people would have the same mashed potatoes in their refrigerators. I tried making mashed potatoes from scratch, but this took nearly as long as preparing and chilling a cream sauce.

In a moment of inspiration, I made a batch of chicken croquettes using instant potato flakes and kept the box hidden from coworkers as they sampled them. The flakes were a breeze to use, and my coworkers devoured the croquettes without ever knowing. Perfect.

I tested coating the croquettes with panko and dried bread crumbs, but we preferred fresh bread crumbs—which are as easy to make as dropping bread (and a little flour) in the food processor—for the best crunch. Dipping the shaped chicken mixture into beaten egg helped the bread crumbs adhere to the croquettes before frying. Not as quick as prefab crumbs, but worth it.

For maximum flavor, I added fresh scallions, garlic, and spicy cayenne pepper into the chicken-potato mixture. And to make them even better, I stirred together a quick lemon-scallion sauce for dipping.

Stifado: Simple Greek Beef Stew

This Mediterranean rendition will rekindle your love for beef stew.

Matthew Fairman

WITH ULTRATENDER BEEF, wine-and-spice-infused tomato sauce, and a sweet underpinning of braised pearl onions, this *stifado* (which basically means "stew" in Greek) offers an easy, intriguing take on beef stew. Though there are countless variations (with rabbit or seafood, with or without tomatoes, etc.), the stew always features loads of baby onions and varying amounts of warm spices such as cinnamon, cumin, allspice, and cloves. It's typically served over buttery pasta (orzo is a traditional choice), and it's often topped with salty feta cheese.

The version I offer here applies a few easy, effective techniques gleaned from test kitchen experience. First, since stifado always includes generous amounts of onion, recipes for this stew sometimes turn out sour. That wouldn't do. I wanted sweet, creamy onions with complex caramelized flavor. I began by sautéing pearl onions with just a pinch of sugar to jump-start the development of flavorful browning. Using pearl onions straight from the freezer—no thawing—makes this step a snap.

Unfortunately, some of the existing stifado recipes I made during my research phase were overwhelmed by an intense potpourri of warm spices. For a balanced stew in which each ingredient exists in subtle harmony with the others, I included a cinnamon stick (rather than easy-to-overdo ground cinnamon), a generous amount of earthy cumin, and only ⅛ teaspoon of floral allspice—just enough to be noticed and appreciated.

As for the beef, I tested chuck versus boneless short ribs, and we liked them equally; since the chuck is cheaper and easier to find, I went with it. I found it better to buy a whole roast—a well-marbled roast is ideal—and cut it up myself for the best-quality meat. Then, to limit hands-on cooking and intensify the flavor of the stifado, I skipped the tedious step of browning the beef in batches. Instead, I seasoned the cubed beef, stirred it into the stew, and placed the pot in a 300-degree oven without a lid. When exposed to the hot oven, the broth-wine mixture reduces, intensifies, and thickens into a full-bodied sauce, and the beef develops deep, delectable browning.

Frozen pearl onions, which are already peeled and thus require zero work to prep, provide this stew with sweet pops of flavor.

GREEK BEEF STEW (STIFADO)
Serves 4 to 6

Be sure to buy a chuck-eye roast and cube it yourself. Do not use precubed stew meat. One 14.4-ounce bag of frozen pearl onion contains about 3½ cups. Do not thaw the onions before cooking. Serve over orzo or with pita bread.

2½	pounds boneless beef chuck-eye roast, trimmed and cut into 1-inch pieces
2	teaspoons kosher salt, divided
½	teaspoon pepper
3½	cups frozen pearl onions
2	tablespoons extra-virgin olive oil
½	teaspoon sugar
2	tablespoons tomato paste
3	garlic cloves, minced
1	teaspoon ground cumin
⅛	teaspoon ground allspice
2	tomatoes, cored and chopped
2¼	cups chicken broth
¾	cup dry white wine
1	cinnamon stick
2	bay leaves
¼	cup chopped fresh parsley
	Crumbled feta cheese

1. Adjust oven rack to middle position and heat oven to 300 degrees. Sprinkle beef with 1½ teaspoons salt and pepper; set aside.

2. Cook onions, oil, sugar, and remaining ½ teaspoon salt in large Dutch oven over medium-high heat until onions are softened and deeply browned, 10 to 12 minutes. Add tomato paste, garlic, cumin, and allspice and cook until fragrant, about 1 minute. Add tomatoes and cook until tomatoes break down and mixture is darkened and thick, about 5 minutes.

3. Add broth, wine, cinnamon stick, bay leaves, and beef to pot, scraping up any browned bits. Increase heat to high and bring to simmer. Transfer to oven and cook, uncovered, for 1 hour.

4. Remove pot from oven and stir to redistribute beef. Return pot to oven and continue to cook, uncovered, until meat is tender, 1½ to 2 hours longer.

5. Discard cinnamon stick and bay leaves. Skim excess fat from surface of stew. Stir in parsley. Serve, sprinkled with feta cheese.

Breaking Down the Roast

The origins of precubed stew meat at the supermarket can be mysterious. For the best results, we prefer to buy a chuck-eye roast and cube it ourselves. Here's what that process looks like.

WHOLE BONELESS 2½-POUND CHUCK-EYE ROAST

SEPARATED AT NATURAL SEAM

TRIMMED AND CUT INTO 1-INCH PIECES

FLAKY GOLDEN PASTRY folded around deeply seasoned ground meat, beef patties are a street food staple in Jamaica and other islands in the West Indies. These handheld meat pies are an evolution of the Cornish pasties brought by British colonizers, and they started appearing in Jamaican communities in New York in the 1960s. These days, mass-produced frozen patties are sold in supermarkets, though you can find many bakeries in the United States turning out scratch-made patties, too (see "50 Years of Flavor").

To get my bearings before crafting my own version, I prepared a handful of beef patty recipes from Caribbean cookbooks. Most of the crusts turned out short and crumbly, not flaky. The fillings were savory and spicy—fragrant with curry powder, scallions, and fiery Scotch bonnet chiles—but most were pebbly and dry and messily fell out of the crusts while my tasters and I snacked. I had my work cut out for me.

I used a basic pie dough as a starting point for my crust. In the food processor I blitzed together flour, salt, a little sugar, and some turmeric for color and a hint of gingery flavor. I pulsed in cold butter and then just enough ice water to bring the dough together. The resulting crust had picturesque layers but was a little tough and brittle. I introduced some sour cream for tenderness (ditching the water), plus an egg for added structure and richness. Perfect.

I still had two problems to solve with the filling: dry, pebbly meat and a lack of cohesion. For the first issue, I tossed the ground beef with baking soda before cooking it, a test kitchen trick that tenderizes meat and keeps it juicy. After browning the meat and adding traditional aromatics (scallions; garlic; curry powder; thyme; allspice; and minced habanero chile, which is more widely available than Scotch bonnet), I simmered the lot with a little water and a torn-up slice of bread to help it bind together, solving the second problem.

Once it was cooked, I took a potato masher to the mixture until the texture was uniform and the bread had broken down and thickened the sauce. This filling was rich, deeply spiced, and just sticky enough to stay together.

To shape the patties, I encased scoops of filling in rectangles of dough and sealed them shut with the tines of a fork. The patties baked up beautifully golden with brown-tinged edges.

Here's my favorite part: After some tests, I found that you can stash a batch of fully assembled patties in your freezer and bake them up whenever a craving strikes. Like store-bought—but better.

Spicy beef encased in tender crust, these hand pies are your new favorite snack. And lunch. And breakfast.
by Jessica Rudolph

Jamaican Beef Patties

JAMAICAN BEEF PATTIES
Serves 8

For a spicier filling, include the seeds and ribs of the habanero chile. If you're able to find Scotch bonnet chiles, you can substitute one for the habanero. We recommend wearing rubber gloves to protect your hands while prepping the chile. We prefer sweet (not hot) curry powder here.

CRUST

- ⅔ cup sour cream, chilled
- 1 large egg, lightly beaten
- 3 cups (15 ounces) all-purpose flour
- 1 tablespoon sugar
- 1¼ teaspoons table salt
- 1 teaspoon ground turmeric
- 16 tablespoons unsalted butter, cut into ½-inch pieces and chilled

FILLING

- 1 tablespoon plus 1 cup water, divided, plus extra for brushing
- ¾ teaspoon table salt
- ¼ teaspoon baking soda
- 1 pound 85 percent lean ground beef
- 1 tablespoon vegetable oil
- 12 scallions, chopped fine
- 4 garlic cloves, minced
- 1 habanero chile, stemmed, seeded, and minced
- 1 teaspoon dried thyme
- ¾ teaspoon curry powder
- ¾ teaspoon ground allspice
- ½ teaspoon pepper
- 1 slice hearty white sandwich bread, torn into 1-inch pieces

1. FOR THE CRUST: Whisk sour cream and egg together in small bowl.

Process flour, sugar, salt, and turmeric in food processor until combined, about 3 seconds. Scatter butter over top and pulse until butter is no larger than size of peas, about 10 pulses. Add half of sour cream mixture and pulse until combined, about 5 pulses. Add remaining sour cream mixture and pulse until dough begins to form, about 15 pulses.

2. Turn out dough onto sheet of plastic wrap and shape into 6-inch square, smoothing any cracks. Wrap tightly in plastic and refrigerate for 1 hour. (Dough can be refrigerated for up to 2 days.)

3. FOR THE FILLING: Combine 1 tablespoon water, salt, and baking soda in large bowl. Add beef and mix until thoroughly combined. Let sit at room temperature for 10 minutes.

Patty Construction

1. Pulse crust ingredients in food processor until dough begins to form.

2. Shape dough into 6-inch square, wrap in plastic wrap, and refrigerate for 1 hour.

3. Roll one-quarter of dough into rectangle and place 2 mounds of filling on top.

4. Fold dough over filling, press to adhere, and cut between mounds to make 2 patties.

4. Heat oil in 12-inch nonstick skillet over medium-high heat until just smoking. Add beef mixture and cook, breaking up meat with wooden spoon, until beginning to brown, 5 to 7 minutes. Add scallions, garlic, habanero, thyme, curry powder, allspice, and pepper and cook, stirring frequently, until scallions are softened, about 3 minutes.

5. Add bread and remaining 1 cup water and stir to incorporate. Bring to boil, then reduce heat to low and simmer, stirring occasionally, until sauce thickens and coats beef, 8 to 10 minutes. Off heat, mash beef mixture with potato masher until fine-textured and bread is fully incorporated, about 2 minutes. Transfer to clean bowl and let cool completely. (Filling can be covered with plastic and refrigerated for up to 24 hours.)

6. Adjust oven rack to upper-middle position and heat oven to 375 degrees. Line rimmed baking sheet with parchment paper. Remove dough from refrigerator and cut into 4 equal pieces (about 7½ ounces each); cover with plastic. Working with 1 piece at a time, sprinkle dough with flour and roll into rough 11 by 9-inch rectangle (about ⅛ inch thick) on lightly floured counter, with long side parallel to counter edge, reflouring counter and dough as needed.

7. Place 2 scant ⅓-cup mounds of filling on bottom half of dough, about 4 inches apart and about 2 inches from bottom edge of dough. Flatten mounds to roughly 3-inch rounds. Lightly brush bottom half of dough with water. Fold top half of dough over filling, pressing along sides, bottom edge, and between filling to adhere.

8. Cut between mounds and trim edges to form two 5 by 4-inch rectangles. Crimp edges with floured tines of fork to seal, then transfer patties to prepared sheet.

9. Bake until patties have puffed and exteriors have lightly browned, about 30 minutes. Transfer patties to wire rack and let cool for 10 minutes before serving.

TO MAKE AHEAD

At end of step 8, transfer patties on baking sheet to freezer. Once frozen solid, patties can be transferred to zipper-lock bag and frozen for up to 1 month. To cook from frozen, extend baking time to 40 to 45 minutes, until bottoms are crisp.

50 Years of Flavor

ON THE ROAD
Text by Bryan Roof; photos by Steve Klise

KINGSTON TROPICAL BAKERY sits under the train tracks at the corner of White Plains Road and East 226th Street in the Bronx. A sidewalk-facing case filled with golden Jamaican-style beef patties lures customers inside, where shelves are loaded with fresh breads, buns, and other Caribbean treats.

But this is more than a bakery. After fifty years in business, Kingston is a neighborhood institution and gathering place for the local Jamaican community. Manager Caroline Sinclair grew up in Jamaica and worked in banking before a career change brought her to the Bronx thirty years ago; today she oversees operations with a sharp eye on quality.

Kingston isn't the only bakery selling patties in town, but it's one of the few that makes them from scratch. Others have switched to industrialized methods for efficiency—by Sinclair's account, at the expense of flavor.

"We're very old-fashioned," she says, her arms filled with fresh Scotch bonnet chiles and thyme. As she eyes retirement, Sinclair is concerned about Kingston's future. "When you get to my age, you have to think about what you're going to do after," she says with a pensive gaze. "But for now, I love what I'm doing and that makes a difference."

Kingston Tropical Bakery, managed by Caroline Sinclair (above), sells beef patties that taste notably of green bell peppers and fresh thyme, with a touch of warm spice and plenty of heat from Scotch bonnet chiles. In the kitchen, baker Lorraine Benjamin (top) prepares massive blankets of dough for the patties. The crust is slightly sweet to help temper the heat of the chiles, and just sturdy enough to contain the substantial filling.

Adding panko bread crumbs to the seasoned flour coating gives these fried tomatoes extra crunch.

Fried Green Tomato BLTs

What if the T in your BLT was a fried green tomato?

by Matthew Fairman

I'M A FOOD-LOVING Southerner from one of America's great eating cities: Charleston, South Carolina. As such, there are dishes I'm expected to know and love, most of them rightly so. For instance, shrimp and grits—delicious!

Fried green tomatoes are on that list, too (see "The American Table"). And until a couple of months ago, I'd have been on board with the most avid fan of those tart, cornmeal-crusted tomatoes. But when I began my assignment for fried green tomato BLTs, I uncovered something downright dishonorable: My professed love for this Southern favorite was a lie.

Let me explain. I researched dozens of recipes, picking the most delicious-sounding ones to fry up in the test kitchen. I took pains to keep the fried tomatoes hot and crispy for each tasting. My colleagues and I dug in, and as it turned out, the only thing I like about (most) fried green tomatoes is the creamy, tangy dipping sauce, which can cover up a multitude of sins. I'm talking culinary transgressions: soggy, grainy, chewy breading and bland, steamy tomatoes. These attempts were not fried green tomatoes at their best. They ought to have been crunchy, crispy, sweet-tart little jewels, well seasoned with a kick of spice.

I let my disappointment motivate me to make fried green tomatoes so good that they could stand alone—only then would I put them on a BLT. The recipe here is what emerged from that sad, soggy valley, and it's one I'm proud of. To eradicate sogginess and erase the memory of those steamy, bland tomatoes, I sprinkled healthy amounts of salt and sugar on the sliced tomatoes, drawing out their moisture and intensifying their flavor before breading them. I ditched the all-too-often chewy, gritty cornmeal in favor of panko bread crumbs, which are unfailingly crunchy. And I doubled down on crunch by dredging twice in a boldly seasoned breading enhanced by Old Bay seasoning.

After an easy shallow fry, the slices came out golden and crispy. A quick bite confirmed they were ready for the BLT treatment. I mixed together a quick and tangy spicy mayo; slathered it on a big, soft brioche roll; and then piled on the bacon, shredded lettuce, and crispy fried tomatoes. I hope you'll do the same, but do treat yourself to a bite of one of the fried tomatoes by itself; it's worth it.

BACON, LETTUCE, AND FRIED GREEN TOMATO SANDWICHES Serves 4

Look for green tomatoes that are about 3 inches in diameter. It's best to slice the tomatoes closer to ⅛ inch thick if possible, but as long as they're less than ¼ inch thick they will work well in this sandwich.

- 3 green tomatoes
- 1 tablespoon sugar
- 1½ teaspoons table salt, divided
- ½ cup mayonnaise
- 2 teaspoons Tabasco sauce
- 1½ cups all-purpose flour
- 1½ cups panko bread crumbs
- 1 tablespoon Old Bay seasoning
- 4 large eggs
- 1½ cups vegetable oil for frying
- 4 large brioche sandwich rolls, split and toasted
- 12 slices cooked bacon, halved
- 2 cups shredded iceberg lettuce

1. Core tomatoes and cut off rounded top and bottom. Slice tomatoes into twelve ⅛- to ¼-inch-thick slices (you may have some left over). Line rimmed baking sheet with triple layer of paper towels. Place tomatoes on prepared sheet and sprinkle both sides with sugar and 1 teaspoon salt. Cover tomatoes with triple layer of paper towels and let sit for 1 hour.

2. Meanwhile, whisk mayonnaise and Tabasco together in bowl; set aside.

3. Whisk flour, panko, Old Bay, and remaining ½ teaspoon salt together in large bowl. Beat eggs together in shallow dish. Remove top layer of paper towels from tomatoes. Transfer tomatoes to flour mixture and toss to coat.

4. Remove remaining paper towels from sheet and wipe sheet dry. Return tomatoes to now-empty sheet. Working with 1 slice at a time, dip tomatoes in egg, allowing excess to drip off, and return to flour mixture, pressing firmly so coating adheres. Return tomatoes to sheet.

5. Line large plate with triple layer of paper towels. Add oil to 12-inch nonstick skillet and heat over medium-high heat to 350 degrees. Fry half of tomatoes until golden and crispy, about 2 minutes per side, reducing heat as needed if oil gets too hot. Using tongs, transfer fried tomatoes to prepared plate. Return oil to 350 degrees and repeat with remaining tomatoes.

6. Spread 1 tablespoon mayonnaise mixture on each roll bottom, then follow with 6 half-slices bacon and 3 fried tomatoes, overlapping slightly in center. Toss lettuce with remaining ¼ cup mayonnaise mixture in bowl and divide evenly among sandwiches. Cover with roll tops and serve.

THE AMERICAN TABLE

Fried green tomatoes are an iconic Southern food. Right?

Not so fast.

In 2011, food historian Robert F. Moss published *The Fried Green Tomato Swindle and Other Southern Culinary Adventures*, a book in which he debunked the idea that fried green tomatoes have deep roots in the South. In fact, the earliest references he could find to the dish were from turn-of-the-century cookbooks published in New York, Pennsylvania, and Ohio. This makes sense if you think about it; there are a lot more green tomatoes up North, where the summer growing season is shorter and not every tomato gets a chance to ripen on the vine.

We can blame Fannie Flagg's best-selling 1987 novel, *Fried Green Tomatoes at the Whistle Stop Cafe*, and the 1991 movie adaptation *Fried Green Tomatoes* starring Kathy Bates and Jessica Tandy (above) for introducing the idea that these are a treasured Southern tradition.

The Whistle Stop Cafe is based on a real restaurant, the Irondale Cafe in Irondale, Alabama, which is still open today.

Singular Seasonings

This recipe relies on two of our—and America's—favorite seasonings. First up is Old Bay seasoning, a celery salt– and paprika-heavy mix that is a staple of seafood boils (and particularly crab boils in and around Maryland). We use it to give our coating a deep, complex seasoning.

Tabasco sauce needs no introduction, but it's worth noting that it's not the test kitchen's taste test winner for an all-around hot sauce. However, we found its sharp, vinegary, peppery bite to be perfect for putting a little kick in the mayonnaise that dresses the buns of these sandwiches.

Keys to the Crunchiest Fried Green Tomatoes

1. Slice the green tomatoes ⅛ to ¼ inch thick. Even slices mean even cooking.

2. Sprinkle with sugar and salt and drain on paper towels to remove moisture.

3. Dip in a mixture of flour, panko bread crumbs, Old Bay seasoning, and salt.

4. Place the floured tomatoes on a rimmed baking sheet.

5. Dip the floured tomatoes in beaten egg and then in the flour mixture a second time.

6. Shallow-fry the slices in hot oil for about 2 minutes per side.

Asparagus Baked in Foil

To coax the most flavor out of mild asparagus, we kept it contained.

by Morgan Bolling

AT MY FRENCH technique–based culinary school, we learned the benefits of cooking delicate foods such as vegetables, fish fillets, and chicken breasts *en papillote*, which means enclosed in parchment-paper packets. The food cooks in steam created by its own juices and emerges from the packets tasting clean and deeply of itself—this is a good thing.

An even better thing—an intensely flavored sauce—is made by adding butter and aromatics to the packets. There's some theater at the table, too, as the bundles release a fragrant plume of steam when you cut into them. As an overworked, overtired culinary student, I fondly remember that the cleanup for these dishes was as simple as throwing away the remnants of the packets.

With the abundance of asparagus this time of year, I wanted to develop a recipe to cook it using this tried-and-true technique. To start, I washed and trimmed 2 pounds of medium-width asparagus. I started to assemble a packet made with parchment, but folding the paper's edges to hold a crimp was finicky. So I switched to easy-to-fold, readily available aluminum foil.

After a few rounds of asparagus that was either too crunchy or too mushy, I landed on baking the packet in a 400-degree oven for 18 minutes. While the timing seemed a little too precise, it was ideal for getting snappy yet tender, bright green stalks. Letting the packet rest undisturbed for 5 minutes out of the oven provided a gentle finish that ensured all the spears were cooked through. To make this spring side extra-vibrant, I tossed the asparagus with some briny capers, dill, and lemon juice right before serving it. Perfect.

Trimming Tip

To trim the ends from the spears, bend one spear near its base until it breaks—this is the point where the base will be naturally woody. Then use that spear's trimming point as a guide to trim the rest of the bunch with your knife.

ASPARAGUS BAKED IN FOIL WITH CAPERS AND DILL
Serves 4 to 6

Look for asparagus spears that are about ½ inch thick at the base.

- 2 **pounds (½-inch-thick) asparagus, trimmed**
- 4 **tablespoons unsalted butter, cut into ½-inch pieces**
- 1 **shallot, minced**
- 2 **garlic cloves, minced**
- 1½ **teaspoons table salt**
- ½ **teaspoon pepper**
- 1 **tablespoon capers, rinsed**
- 1 **tablespoon chopped fresh dill**
- 1 **teaspoon lemon juice**

1. Adjust oven rack to middle position and heat oven to 400 degrees. Line rimmed baking sheet with 16 by 12-inch sheet of aluminum foil.
2. Arrange asparagus in center of foil with spears running parallel to short side of sheet, leaving 1½-inch border between bottom of spears and edge of foil. Sprinkle butter, shallot, garlic, salt, and pepper evenly over asparagus.
3. Place second 16 by 12-inch sheet of foil over asparagus. Starting with 1 edge, pinch sheets together and fold foil in toward center by ½ inch. Repeat folding 1 or 2 times to create tight seal. Continue folding remaining 3 edges of foil to create tightly sealed packet.
4. Transfer sheet to oven and cook for 18 minutes. Remove sheet from oven and let asparagus continue to steam in unopened packet 5 minutes longer (if using slightly thicker or thinner asparagus, increase or decrease this resting time by 2 minutes).
5. Using scissors or paring knife, carefully cut open top of packet, allowing steam to escape away from you. Sprinkle asparagus with capers, dill, and lemon juice. Toss gently with tongs to combine. Using tongs, transfer asparagus to serving platter, then pour sauce from packet over top and serve. (Alternatively, serve directly from packet.)

 A bonus recipe for Asparagus Baked in Foil with Parmesan and Thyme is available for free for four months at **CooksCountry.com/may20.**

Potent capers and garlic, shallot, butter, and dill combine to create a tasty sauce.

Hot Rice

This Ohio favorite belongs on tables everywhere.

by Alli Berkey

WHEN I WAS growing up in north-eastern Ohio, my grandmother Mary Lou used to serve a memorable dish called "hot rice." The buttery rice was cooked in a tomato-rich sauce spiked with hot red peppers that provided the dish's signature bite. (The famous fried chicken from nearby Barberton is often served with a similar rice, but they call it "hot sauce.") Sadly, Mary Lou's recipe has been lost.

Longing for her version, I started sampling some recipes from Ohio cookbooks. The recipes typically call for canned tomatoes, jalapeño chiles or red pepper flakes for heat, bell pepper for sweetness, and white rice. Most call for everything to be cooked together until the tomatoey liquid is absorbed. Common issues: clumpy rice and a searing, unbalanced heat.

My goal was to combine strong tomato flavor with perfectly tender rice and controlled heat and spice. I started by using canned crushed tomatoes (diced tomatoes were too watery). But an entire can of crushed tomatoes contributed too much "canned" flavor, so I cut back to half a can supplemented by some chicken broth for savoriness. Rinsing the raw rice before cooking it got rid of excess starch and prevented it from clumping.

For a well-rounded flavor that actually tasted of peppers (and not just heat), I used paprika (made from dried peppers) for color and punch, red pepper flakes for spark, and sautéed red bell peppers for sweetness. And for a twist of acidity and even more pepper flavor and heat, I added pickled cherry peppers. A bit more butter (as a nod to Mary Lou's rich version) and this one was ready for the table.

HOT RICE Serves 6

One 28-ounce can of crushed tomatoes will contain more than enough for this recipe. Rinse the rice in a fine-mesh strainer under cold running water until the water runs almost clear, about 1½ minutes, stirring the rice with your hand every so often. You can substitute brown sugar for the granulated sugar, if desired. For a spicier dish, add extra chopped cherry peppers.

6 tablespoons unsalted butter, divided
2 red bell peppers, stemmed, seeded, and chopped fine
1 onion, chopped fine
1¼ teaspoons table salt, divided
1 tablespoon sugar
1 tablespoon paprika
1½ teaspoons red pepper flakes
4 cups chicken broth
1½ cups canned crushed tomatoes
1½ cups long-grain white rice, rinsed
2 tablespoons jarred hot cherry peppers, stemmed, seeded, and chopped fine

1. Melt 3 tablespoons butter in large saucepan over medium heat. Add bell peppers, onion, and ½ teaspoon salt and cook until softened, 6 to 8 minutes.
2. Stir in sugar, paprika, and pepper flakes and cook until fragrant, about 30 seconds. Add broth, tomatoes, rice, and remaining ¾ teaspoon salt and bring to boil. Cover, reduce heat to low, and simmer, stirring occasionally, until rice is tender and liquid is mostly absorbed, 13 to 15 minutes.
3. Remove from heat and let sit, covered, for 10 minutes. Stir in cherry peppers and remaining 3 tablespoons butter until combined. Serve.

Skillet-Braised Fennel

What's the best way to draw out maximum flavor from this gentle-tasting vegetable?

by Alli Berkey

WHEN FENNEL BULBS are roasted in a hot oven, they develop a sweet, almost nutty flavor, with an enchanting licorice undertone. But roasting them in the oven can take upwards of an hour. I wanted a speedy way to make deliciously sweet, tender, nicely browned fennel on the stovetop.

I started by chopping fennel bulbs into different-size wedges and sautéing them in olive oil. Small wedges fell apart, and those that were too big were a challenge to cook through evenly. One-inch wedges were just right for serving, and I found that they cooked most evenly when I added some water to help them steam through.

Through testing, I landed on placing the wedges in a skillet; adding a cup of water, a few tablespoons of oil, and some fresh thyme; and bringing the mixture to a boil. Then I reduced the heat, covered the skillet, and let the fennel steam until it was tender, about 8 minutes. I uncovered the pan to let the water evaporate so that the wedges could pick up flavorful browning. Finally, I stirred together a simple dressing of lemon juice, honey, and more oil and thyme to drizzle over the fennel.

SKILLET-BRAISED FENNEL
Serves 4

Be sure to buy fennel with the stalks still attached. If you can find only stalkless bulbs, then look for those that weigh from 10 to 12 ounces each; they will weigh between 6 and 8 ounces when fully trimmed.

4 (1-pound) fennel bulbs, stalks discarded
1 cup water
¼ cup extra-virgin olive oil, divided
2 sprigs fresh thyme, plus ½ teaspoon minced
¾ teaspoon plus ⅛ teaspoon table salt, divided
¼ teaspoon pepper
2 teaspoons lemon juice
1 teaspoon honey

1. Halve fennel bulbs through core. Trim away and discard tough outer leaves. Cut halves into 1-inch-thick wedges through core, leaving core intact.
2. Arrange fennel, cut side down when possible, in 12-inch nonstick skillet. Add water, 2 tablespoons oil, thyme sprigs, ¾ teaspoon salt, and pepper to skillet and bring to boil over medium-high heat. Reduce heat to medium, cover, and cook until fennel is just tender and can be easily pierced with tip of paring knife, about 8 minutes.
3. Uncover and continue to cook until water has evaporated, 6 to 10 minutes longer. Increase heat to medium-high and cook, turning fennel as needed, until browned on cut sides, about 6 minutes. Transfer fennel to serving platter.
4. Whisk lemon juice, honey, minced thyme, remaining 2 tablespoons oil, and remaining ⅛ teaspoon salt together in bowl. Pour vinaigrette over hot fennel. Serve.

White Beans

How to cook them and how to use them.

by Bryan Roof and Morgan Bolling

CANNED WHITE BEANS are impossible to beat for convenience. But for those recipes where beans take center stage, starting with dried beans is well worth the extra time and effort. The creamy texture and earthy flavor of homemade cooked-from-dried beans are more satisfying than anything you get from a can. Plus, there's just something comforting and wholesome about making a big pot of beans to eat throughout the week.

Such flavorful beans are great eaten with a drizzle of oil and some salt and pepper but also lend themselves well to other applications. So we developed four quick recipes featuring these beans: stirred into a salad with tuna, simmered with tomatoes and capers, sautéed with garlic and sage, and pureed into a dip.

NEVER TRIED COOKING DRIED BEANS? HERE'S OUR FOOLPROOF METHOD.

1 Brine the Beans
Brining the beans for 8 to 24 hours takes forethought. But this step seasons them thoroughly and helps them maintain their shape throughout cooking. (Be sure to pick through them to discard any funky-looking beans or pebbles before brining.)

2 Cook Uncovered
The cooking time for dried beans can vary a lot based on bean type, brand, and age; cooking them uncovered on the stovetop gives you the ability to watch and taste them as they cook.

3 Slowly Simmer
Maintaining a gentle simmer prevents the beans from rupturing. (Boiling water causes the beans to knock into each other and break.)

4 Taste for Texture
After 40 to 50 minutes of simmering, the beans should be just barely al dente; to check, simply bite into a few to see. Note that the doneness levels of the beans in the pot may vary, so be sure to sample more than one.

5 Finish Off Heat
Turning off the heat, covering the pot, and letting the beans steep allows them to gently finish cooking through without any skins rupturing.

WHITE BEAN AND TUNA SALAD *Serves 4 to 6*

We prefer the flavor and texture of cooked-from-dried beans here, but you can substitute two 15-ounce cans of cannellini beans, if desired.

1	(6-ounce) container olive oil–packed tuna
3½	cups cooked cannellini beans
¼	cup extra-virgin olive oil
¼	cup very coarsely chopped fresh parsley
1	shallot, sliced into thin rings
4	teaspoons sherry vinegar
¼	teaspoon table salt
¼	teaspoon red pepper flakes

Remove tuna from container and discard packing oil. Coarsely flake tuna into medium bowl. Add beans, oil, parsley, shallot, vinegar, salt, and pepper flakes and stir to combine. Serve.

WHITE BEANS WITH TOMATOES AND CAPERS *Serves 4 to 6*

We prefer the flavor and texture of cooked-from-dried beans here, but you can substitute two 15-ounce cans of cannellini beans, if desired.

6	tablespoons extra-virgin olive oil, divided
3	garlic cloves, sliced thin
3½	cups cooked cannellini beans
5	ounces grape tomatoes, halved
1	tablespoon capers, rinsed
½	teaspoon dried oregano
½	teaspoon red pepper flakes
¼	teaspoon table salt

1. Combine ¼ cup oil and garlic in 12-inch nonstick skillet and cook over medium heat until garlic begins to brown lightly at edges, about 3 minutes. Add beans, tomatoes, capers, oregano, pepper flakes, and salt and cook until tomatoes just begin to soften, about 5 minutes, stirring occasionally.
2. Transfer bean mixture to shallow dish and drizzle with remaining 2 tablespoons oil. Serve.

WHITE BEANS
Serves 8 (Makes 7 cups)
Soaking the beans in a saltwater solution for at least 8 hours results in creamier beans that cook more evenly than if just soaked in water.

1½ **tablespoons table salt for brining**
  1 **pound dried cannellini beans, picked over and rinsed**
  1 **tablespoon table salt**

1. Dissolve 1½ tablespoons salt in 2 quarts cold water in large container. Add beans and soak at room temperature for at least 8 hours or up to 24 hours.
2. Drain beans in colander and rinse well. Combine beans, 10 cups fresh water, and salt in Dutch oven and bring to boil over high heat. Reduce heat to medium and cook at gentle simmer until beans are barely al dente, 40 to 50 minutes. (During simmer, bubbles should just break surface of water.)
3. Turn off heat, cover pot, and let beans steep until tender, 20 to 30 minutes. Serve beans from pot using slotted spoon or drain in colander for later use. (Beans can be refrigerated in airtight container for up to 3 days. Alternatively, beans can be cooled, transferred to zipper-lock bags, and frozen for up to 1 month.)

Storing Beans
Dried beans degrade over time, so we recommend using them within six months of purchase. Cooked dried beans can be refrigerated for up to three days before use or frozen for up to one month. To freeze cooked beans, lay them flat on a plate or baking sheet and pop them in the freezer; once frozen, transfer the beans to a zipper-lock bag or other airtight container. Save frozen beans for applications where they will be pureed, such as in our recipe for White Bean Dip (below).

Choosing Dried Beans
Dried white beans look similar but cook differently. Use only cannellini here. (Beans shown here are to scale.)

CANNELLINI   **GREAT NORTHERN**   **NAVY**

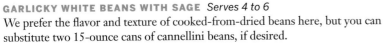

GARLICKY WHITE BEANS WITH SAGE *Serves 4 to 6*
We prefer the flavor and texture of cooked-from-dried beans here, but you can substitute two 15-ounce cans of cannellini beans, if desired.

  6 **tablespoons extra-virgin olive oil, divided**
  3 **garlic cloves, sliced thin**
  6 **fresh sage leaves**
  ¼ **teaspoon red pepper flakes**
3½ **cups cooked cannellini beans**
  ¼ **teaspoon table salt**

Combine ¼ cup oil and garlic in 12-inch nonstick skillet and cook over medium heat until garlic begins to brown lightly at edges, about 3 minutes. Add sage and pepper flakes and cook until fragrant, about 30 seconds. Add beans and salt and cook, stirring and tossing often, until just heated through, about 2 minutes. Transfer to shallow serving dish and drizzle with remaining 2 tablespoons oil. Serve.

WHITE BEAN DIP *Serves 4 to 6*
The texture of this dip can vary depending on the beans. If it seems too thick in the food processor, add extra water 1 tablespoon at a time, and adjust the seasoning at the end if necessary. Serve with crudités, crackers, or bread.

  1 **recipe Garlicky White Beans with Sage (left)**
  5 **tablespoons water**
  1 **tablespoon lemon juice**
    Extra-virgin olive oil
  1 **tablespoon chopped fresh parsley**

Combine beans, water, and lemon juice in food processor and process until smooth, about 2 minutes, scraping down sides of bowl as needed. Transfer bean dip to shallow serving dish and spread into even layer. Drizzle liberally with oil and sprinkle with parsley. Serve.

Cast Iron Potato Kugel

This simple, flavorful potato side is perfect for Passover.

by Jessica Rudolph

A cast-iron skillet allows us to start the kugel on the stove and finish it in the oven.

POTATO KUGEL, SAVORY cousin to the Jewish home-style favorite noodle kugel, sounds so promising: shredded potatoes mixed with onion, eggs, and fat (often schmaltz, rendered chicken fat) and baked until crisp on the outside and fluffy on the inside. It's like one giant, sliceable latke.

But the recipes I tried were disappointing. Some kugels were eggy and rubbery, some were slimy, and all were overpowered by the sour tang of raw onion. I learned some things right off the bat: We preferred cooked onion to raw, savory schmaltz was our fat of choice, and squeezing the shredded potatoes dry reduced slipperiness.

Armed with this knowledge, I took a stab at an improved kugel. I softened 2 cups of finely chopped onions with a sizable dollop of schmaltz and used the food processor to quickly shred 3 pounds of peeled potatoes (starchy russets since a fluffy interior was the goal). I wrung the potatoes dry with a clean dish towel and mixed them together with the onions, beaten eggs, and generous amounts of salt and pepper. I spread this mixture in a casserole dish I had brushed with additional schmaltz and baked it until tender.

The resulting kugel had great flavor, and the interior texture was improved as well: fluffy yet still creamy. But the exterior was a tad too soft, and the potatoes had an unattractive gray cast.

To encourage more flavorful crusty browning at the edges, I made the next batch in a preheated cast-iron skillet. This worked beautifully. As for potato oxidation, I tried a technique we've used before in the test kitchen and tossed the shreds in a saltwater solution (since salt inhibits the enzyme responsible for discoloration). This made a marked difference, giving my next kugel a creamy white hue throughout.

Topped with a shower of minced chives, this kugel is as welcome on your springtime holiday table as it is next to your weeknight roast chicken.

Color Saver

Shredding potatoes releases an enzyme that can cause them to turn a blue-gray color. A simple toss with salted water neutralizes this reaction and keeps the spuds white.

LIGHT AND LOVELY
The salt water preserves the spuds' color.

GRAY AND GHOULISH
The shreds turn gray without the salt water.

CAST IRON POTATO KUGEL
Serves 8

You can find rendered chicken fat (schmaltz) in the frozen foods section of larger supermarkets. If you can't find it, you can substitute extra-virgin olive oil. We prefer using the shredding disk of a food processor to shred the potatoes, but you can also use the large holes of a box grater. Making this kugel in a well-seasoned cast-iron skillet ensures that it will have a crisp crust, but if you don't have one, you can use a 10-inch oven-safe nonstick skillet. Serve with sour cream, if desired.

- 6 tablespoons rendered chicken fat (schmaltz), divided
- 2 cups finely chopped onions
- ¾ teaspoon table salt, plus salt for tossing potatoes
- 3 pounds russet potatoes, unpeeled
- 4 large eggs
- 1¼ teaspoons pepper
- 1 tablespoon minced fresh chives

1. Adjust oven rack to upper-middle position and heat oven to 425 degrees. Heat 2 tablespoons chicken fat in 10-inch cast-iron skillet over medium-high heat until shimmering. Add onions and cook, stirring occasionally, until softened, about 3 minutes. Transfer to bowl and set aside.

2. Whisk 2 cups water and 2 tablespoons salt in large bowl until salt is dissolved. Fit food processor with shredding disk. Peel potatoes and halve or quarter lengthwise as needed to fit through processor feed tube. Shred potatoes. Transfer potatoes to salt water and toss briefly to coat.

3. Drain potatoes in colander. Place one-quarter of shredded potatoes in center of clean dish towel. Gather ends of towel and twist tightly to wring out excess moisture from potatoes. Transfer dried potatoes to now-empty bowl. Repeat 3 more times with remaining potatoes. Stir eggs, pepper, onions, and remaining ¾ teaspoon salt into potatoes until thoroughly combined.

4. Heat remaining ¼ cup chicken fat in now-empty skillet over medium-high heat until just smoking. Add potato mixture to skillet and distribute into even layer but do not press down or smooth top. Cook for 1 minute to set bottom.

5. Transfer to oven and bake until kugel is lightly browned on top, about 45 minutes. Let cool for 5 minutes. Cut into wedges in skillet. Sprinkle with chives and serve.

Flank Steak with Farro and Mango Salsa

30-MINUTE SUPPER

Italian Chicken Sausage Pizzas

30-MINUTE SUPPER

Spicy Soy-Bourbon Shrimp

30-MINUTE SUPPER

Grilled and Glazed Pork Chops with Radicchio Salad

30-MINUTE SUPPER

Italian Chicken Sausage Pizzas *Serves 4*

We developed this recipe using Rao's Homemade Marinara Sauce.

- ¼ cup extra-virgin olive oil
- 1 pound pizza dough
- ½ cup jarred marinara sauce
- 8 ounces hot or sweet Italian chicken sausage, casings removed
- 8 ounces mozzarella cheese, shredded (2 cups)
- 1 ounce Pecorino Romano cheese, grated (½ cup)
- 2 jarred hot cherry peppers, halved, seeded, and sliced thin
- ¼ cup chopped fresh basil

1. Adjust oven rack to middle position and heat oven to 500 degrees. Brush rimmed baking sheet with oil (use all of it).

2. Divide dough into 4 equal pieces. Roll each piece of dough into 5 by 7-inch rectangle and transfer to prepared sheet. Spread 2 tablespoons marinara on each rectangle, leaving ½-inch border. Break sausage into ½-inch chunks and divide evenly among rectangles. Sprinkle evenly with mozzarella and Pecorino.

3. Bake until cheese is spotty brown and crust is golden, 12 to 14 minutes. Let pizzas cool on sheet for 5 minutes. Sprinkle with cherry peppers and basil. Serve.

Flank Steak with Farro and Mango Salsa
Serves 4

To make four equal-size steaks, cut the steak in half lengthwise with the grain, and then cut each piece in half crosswise against the grain.

- 2 cups whole farro
- 1½ teaspoons table salt, divided, plus salt for cooking farro
- 1 (2-pound) flank steak, trimmed and cut into 4 equal steaks
- 1 tablespoon ground cumin
- 1 teaspoon pepper, divided
- 3 tablespoons extra-virgin olive oil, divided, plus extra for drizzling
- 1 mango, peeled, pitted, and cut into ¼-inch pieces
- 1 red bell pepper, stemmed, seeded, and cut into ¼-inch pieces
- ½ cup finely chopped red onion
- ½ cup chopped fresh cilantro
- 2 tablespoons lime juice

1. Bring 2 quarts water to boil in large saucepan. Add farro and 1 tablespoon salt. Return to boil, reduce heat to medium-low, and simmer until farro is tender with slight chew, about 20 minutes. Drain farro well.

2. Meanwhile, pat steaks dry with paper towels and sprinkle with cumin, ½ teaspoon pepper, and ¾ teaspoon salt. Heat 2 tablespoons oil in 12-inch nonstick skillet over medium-high heat until just smoking. Cook steaks until well browned and meat registers 125 degrees (for medium-rare), 5 to 7 minutes per side. Transfer to carving board, tent with aluminum foil, and let rest for 5 minutes.

3. Combine mango, bell pepper, onion, cilantro, lime juice, remaining ¾ teaspoon salt, remaining ½ teaspoon pepper, and remaining 1 tablespoon oil in bowl. Measure out and reserve ½ cup salsa. Toss remaining salsa with farro in bowl. Slice steaks against grain on bias. Serve steaks with farro and reserved salsa, drizzled with extra oil.

Grilled and Glazed Pork Chops with Radicchio Salad *Serves 4*

If you can't find a Gala apple, you can substitute a Honeycrisp, Braeburn, or Fuji apple.

- 6 tablespoons apple jelly
- 6 tablespoons extra-virgin olive oil
- 1 head radicchio (10 ounces), halved, cored, and torn into bite-size pieces
- 1 Gala apple, cored and cut into 2-inch-long matchsticks
- 2 ounces blue cheese, crumbled (½ cup)
- ½ cup pecans, toasted and chopped coarse
- ¼ cup sour cream
- 2 tablespoons sherry vinegar
- 1½ teaspoons table salt, divided
- 1 teaspoon pepper, divided
- 4 (6- to 8-ounce) bone-in pork rib chops, ¾ to 1 inch thick, trimmed

1. Whisk jelly and oil in large bowl until combined; measure out and reserve ½ cup jelly mixture. Add radicchio, apple, blue cheese, pecans, sour cream, vinegar, ½ teaspoon salt, and ½ teaspoon pepper to remaining jelly mixture and toss to combine. Cover and refrigerate until ready to serve.

2. Pat chops dry with paper towels and sprinkle with remaining 1 teaspoon salt and remaining ½ teaspoon pepper. Measure out ¼ cup reserved jelly mixture and set aside. Brush each chop all over with 1 tablespoon remaining jelly mixture. Grill chops, covered, over hot fire until browned and meat registers 140 degrees, about 3 minutes per side.

3. Transfer chops to large plate and, using clean brush, brush with reserved ¼ cup jelly mixture. Tent with foil and let rest for 5 minutes. Serve chops with radicchio salad.

Spicy Soy-Bourbon Shrimp *Serves 4*

Serve with white rice.

- 2 pounds extra-large shrimp (21 to 25 per pound), peeled and deveined, shells reserved
- ½ cup water
- ¼ cup soy sauce
- ¼ cup bourbon
- 2 tablespoons packed brown sugar
- 1 tablespoon cornstarch
- 1 teaspoon red pepper flakes
- 2 tablespoons toasted sesame oil
- 4 scallions, white parts minced, green parts sliced thin on bias
- 4 garlic cloves, minced

1. Combine shrimp shells, water, soy sauce, and bourbon in bowl. Microwave until fragrant and shells are pink, about 2 minutes. Strain liquid through fine-mesh strainer set over bowl; reserve soy sauce mixture and discard solids. Whisk sugar, cornstarch, and pepper flakes into soy sauce mixture until cornstarch is dissolved.

2. Heat oil in 12-inch nonstick skillet over high heat until just smoking. Stir in shrimp, scallion whites, and garlic and cook until shrimp are just pink, about 3 minutes.

3. Add soy sauce mixture and continue to cook until sauce has thickened slightly and shrimp are cooked through, about 3 minutes longer. Off heat, stir in scallion greens. Serve.

Pan-Seared Salmon with Curried Couscous

30-MINUTE SUPPER

Rigatoni with Quick Mushroom Bolognese

30-MINUTE SUPPER

Picadillo-Style Beef Chili

30-MINUTE SUPPER

Coriander Chicken Thighs with Cauliflower and Herbed Yogurt

30-MINUTE SUPPER

Rigatoni with Quick Mushroom Bolognese

Serves 4

We like to sprinkle the pasta with sliced chives and red pepper flakes before serving.

- 1 pound rigatoni
- ¾ teaspoon table salt, plus salt for cooking pasta
- 1 pound cremini mushrooms, trimmed and quartered
- 3 tablespoons extra-virgin olive oil
- 1 small onion, chopped fine
- 1 carrot, peeled and chopped fine
- ¼ cup tomato paste
- 3 garlic cloves, minced
- ¼ cup dry white wine
- ¼ cup grated Pecorino Romano cheese, plus extra for serving

1. Bring 4 quarts water to boil in Dutch oven. Add pasta and 1 table-spoon salt and cook, stirring occasionally, until al dente. Reserve 1 cup cooking water, then drain pasta and return it to pot.

2. Meanwhile, pulse mushrooms in food processor until finely chopped, about 10 pulses. Heat oil in 12-inch skillet over medium-high heat until just smoking. Add mushrooms, onion, carrot, and salt and cook until mushrooms appear dry and begin to stick to bottom of skillet, about 14 minutes.

3. Stir in tomato paste and garlic and cook until fond forms on bottom of skillet, about 1 minute. Stir in wine, scraping up any browned bits, and cook until evaporated, about 2 minutes. Stir in reserved cooking water and bring to boil. Add sauce and Pecorino to pasta in pot and stir to combine. Serve with extra Pecorino.

Pan-Seared Salmon with Curried Couscous *Serves 4*

Serve with lemon wedges.

- 1½ cups chicken broth
- 2 tablespoons extra-virgin olive oil
- 1 tablespoon curry powder
- 1 teaspoon table salt, divided
- 1 cup couscous
- 1 (15-ounce) can chickpeas, rinsed
- 1 cup baby spinach, chopped coarse
- 4 (6- to 8-ounce) skin-on salmon fillets, 1 to 1½ inches thick
- 1 teaspoon cayenne pepper
- 2 ounces feta cheese, crumbled (½ cup)

1. Bring broth, oil, curry powder, and ½ teaspoon salt to boil in medium saucepan over medium-high heat. Stir in couscous, cover, and let sit off heat for 5 minutes. Stir chickpeas and spinach into couscous. Cover and set aside.

2. Sprinkle salmon flesh with cayenne and remaining ½ teaspoon salt. Arrange salmon skin side down in 12-inch nonstick skillet. Place skillet over medium-high heat and cook until fat is rendered and skin becomes crispy, about 7 minutes.

3. Flip salmon and continue to cook until center is still translucent when checked with tip of paring knife and registers 125 degrees (for medium-rare), about 7 minutes longer. Stir feta into couscous and serve with salmon.

Coriander Chicken Thighs with Cauliflower and Herbed Yogurt *Serves 4*

Fresh basil can be substituted for the mint, if desired.

- 8 (5- to 7-ounce) bone-in chicken thighs, trimmed
- 1¾ teaspoons table salt, divided
- 1½ teaspoons ground coriander
- 1 teaspoon pepper, divided
- 2 tablespoons extra-virgin olive oil
- 1 head cauliflower (2 pounds), cored and cut into 1-inch florets
- 10 ounces cherry tomatoes, quartered
- 1 garlic clove, minced
- ½ cup plain whole-milk yogurt
- 3 tablespoons chopped fresh mint, plus ½ cup torn leaves
- 1 tablespoon lemon juice

1. Adjust oven rack to middle position and heat oven to 450 degrees. Sprinkle chicken with ¾ teaspoon salt, coriander, and ½ teaspoon pepper. Heat oil in 12-inch nonstick skillet over medium-high heat until just smoking. Cook chicken, skin side down, until skin is browned and crispy, about 7 minutes. Flip chicken and continue to cook 3 minutes longer. Transfer chicken, skin side up, to rimmed baking sheet and roast until chicken registers 175 degrees, about 17 minutes.

2. Meanwhile, heat fat left in skillet over medium-high heat until shimmering. Add cauliflower, ¾ teaspoon salt, and ¼ teaspoon pepper and cook until tender and browned, stirring occasionally, 12 to 14 minutes. Off heat, stir in tomatoes and garlic.

3. Combine yogurt, chopped mint, lemon juice, remaining ¼ teaspoon salt, and remaining ¼ teaspoon pepper in bowl. Transfer cauliflower to platter and sprinkle with mint leaves. Serve chicken with cauliflower and yogurt sauce.

Picadillo-Style Beef Chili *Serves 4*

Serve this chili with warm flour tortillas, sour cream, and hot sauce.

- 1 pound 85 percent lean ground beef
- 1¾ teaspoons table salt, divided
- 1 teaspoon pepper
- 1 onion, chopped fine
- 1 jalapeño chile, stemmed, halved, seeded, and sliced thin
- 1½ tablespoons chili powder
- 3 garlic cloves, minced
- 2 (14.5-ounce) cans fire-roasted diced tomatoes, drained
- 2 cups chicken broth
- 1 pound Yukon Gold potatoes, peeled and cut into ½-inch pieces
- ½ cup pimento-stuffed green olives, sliced thin

1. Combine beef, 1 teaspoon salt, and pepper in Dutch oven and cook over medium-high heat, breaking up meat with wooden spoon, until beginning to brown, about 10 minutes.

2. Stir in onion, jalapeño, chili powder, and garlic and cook until vegetables are softened, about 2 minutes. Stir in tomatoes, broth, potatoes, and remaining ¾ teaspoon salt and bring to boil, scraping up any browned bits.

3. Reduce heat to medium, cover, and simmer until potatoes are tender, 15 to 17 minutes. Stir in olives and serve.

Fresh Herbs

GETTING TO KNOW

Using fragrant, flavorful fresh herbs—whether delicate or hardy—can elevate your cooking. Here's what you need to know. *by Scott Kathan*

xpand Your orizons

markets now carry interesting
ties of common herbs. Look for Thai
which has a deeper, more peppery
a than Italian basil; substitute lemon
e for regular thyme in almost any
and experiment with purple sage
ad of green. There are countless
ties of herbs to try.

expected Uses

EN GRILLING OVER RCOAL

stripped stems of hardy
s such as thyme and
mary can be tossed onto
lit charcoal while you're grilling;
erfumed smoke will add an extra
nsion of flavor to your food.

KING FLAVORED VINEGAR

can make flavorful herbed vinegars—
thus incredible vinaigrettes—by
ng fresh herbs to distilled white
gar, letting the mixture steep for two
ks, and then straining it.

CHIVES
This tender herb is oniony and grassy.

TEST KITCHEN TIP
Don't chop chives with a knife—snip them with kitchen shears.

CILANTRO
It's aromatic and refreshing, with a peppery finish.

TEST KITCHEN TIP
Use the stems, too! They're tender and packed with flavor.

DILL
These feathery fronds have a bright, lemony flavor.

BASIL
Genovese (or Italian) basil has a licorice flavor.

TARRAGON
Easy to overdo, it tastes of citrus and anise.

MINT
Both spearmint (shown here) and peppermint, the two most common types of mint, feature a cooling, bright bite.

DELICATE
Delicate herbs are most potent and fragrant with little to no cooking. Use them raw as a garnish or add them to dishes in the last moments on the heat.

PARSLEY
These leaves are mildly astringent and pleasantly grassy-tasting.

MARJORAM
This potent, lightly picy herb tastes like mix of oregano (for hich it is often mis- taken) and juniper.

HARDY
Hardy herbs can be added to long-cooked foods at the beginning of cooking. We often add sprigs of rosemary or thyme to soups, stews, or braises and then remove them before serving.

OREGANO
Mediterranean oregano has a pleasantly perfume-y, musty, slightly spicy bite.

THYME
Its distinct menthol flavor is slightly grassy.

ROSEMARY
Piney and floral, a little goes a long way.

SAGE
These fuzzy leaves taste minty and musky.

Storing Herbs

SHORT-TERM

If you are lucky enough to obtain delicate herbs with the roots still attached, you can store them at room temperature in a glass with about an inch of water; change the water every day, and make sure the leaves are never submerged. Store all other herbs, both delicate and hardy, wrapped in damp paper towels in a plastic bag in the crisper drawer of the refrigerator. Using either method, the herbs should stay fresh for about a week (herbs with roots attached typically last a little longer).

LONGER STORAGE

Freezing is an option, but delicate herbs will lose their bright color. That's why it's best to mix chopped delicate herbs with oil, which helps preserve their color, before freezing them. Pesto lovers, for instance, can puree fresh basil with oil and freeze the paste (portioning it in ice cube trays for freezing is a neat trick) for up to three months.

Easy Green Chile Chicken Enchiladas

Our mission: maximum satisfaction, minimum stress. **by Cecelia Jenkins**

I LOVE SAVORY, spicy, satisfying enchiladas—especially when someone else makes them. They're just too much work for me on a weeknight.

But do they need to be? I challenged myself to create a streamlined recipe for fresh, tangy baked green chile enchiladas with melty cheese, one that I could pull off even after a long and taxing day at work.

Cooking through a handful of existing recipes revealed a range of supposed shortcuts; some were acceptable, and some were definitely not. In a side-by-side tasting of enchiladas made with shredded rotisserie chicken and chicken that I'd poached or roasted, my tasters barely detected a difference in flavor—there was my first acceptable shortcut.

The sauce proved to be a trickier challenge. Store-bought green enchilada sauce (*salsa verde* made with tomatillos, green chiles, onions, and cilantro) was out, as tasters found that it was too acidic for the more balanced flavors I was after. Homemade enchilada sauces had more subtlety, but many of these recipes called for fresh tomatillos, which I had a hard time finding out of season. Other recipes yielded tight, dried-up sauces or out-of-balance flavors.

I turned to canned tomatillos (which are always available) and bolstered them with fresh poblano and jalapeño chiles. To add an extra layer of complexity to the mix, I broiled the chiles and tomatillos with an onion and some whole garlic cloves to enhance the tomatillos' pleasant bitterness and concentrate the flavors of the chiles. This hands-off process gave me time to shred the chicken.

While many recipes called for painstakingly scraping off the dried, blackened skins of the chiles and tomatillos, I skipped this step and simply dumped the broiled vegetables into the blender. In a smooth puree, the skins weren't bothersome; in fact, they added lovely charred notes. I threw in a bunch of cilantro—stems and leaves—for a punch of fresh flavor.

A bit of water helped the sauce stay fluid throughout cooking, and a teaspoon of sugar kept sourness in check. I rolled right into enchilada assembly. In a surprise twist, tasters preferred sharp cheddar cheese to milder Monterey Jack for the final essential ingredient.

Bright, flavorful, totally satisfying enchiladas after a long day at work? Challenge accepted, success achieved.

GREEN CHILE CHICKEN ENCHILADAS *Serves 4 to 6*

For more heat, reserve the jalapeño seeds and add them to the blender in step 3. Don't spend a lot of time chopping the cilantro stems and leaves for the sauce; chop them just enough to measure them, and then let the blender do the bulk of the work. Serve with hot sauce, if desired.

SAUCE

- 1 **(28-ounce) can whole tomatillos, drained**
- 3 **poblano chiles, stemmed, halved, and seeded**
- 1 **onion, cut into 8 wedges through root end**
- 1 **jalapeño chile, stemmed, halved, and seeded**
- 5 **garlic cloves, peeled**
- 1 **tablespoon vegetable oil**
- ¼ **cup water**
- ¼ **cup coarsely chopped fresh cilantro leaves and stems**
- 1 **teaspoon ground cumin**
- 1 **teaspoon dried oregano**
- 1 **teaspoon sugar**
- 1 **teaspoon table salt**
- 1 **teaspoon pepper**

ENCHILADAS

- 1 **(2½-pound) rotisserie chicken, skin and bones discarded, meat shredded into bite-size pieces (3 cups)**
- 12 **ounces sharp cheddar cheese, shredded (3 cups), divided**
- 12 **(6-inch) corn tortillas**
- 1 **tablespoon chopped fresh cilantro**
  Sour cream
  Lime wedges
  Avocado
  Finely chopped onion

1. FOR THE SAUCE: Adjust oven rack 6 inches from broiler element and heat broiler. Line rimmed baking sheet with aluminum foil.

2. Place tomatillos, poblanos, onion, jalapeño, and garlic on prepared sheet. Drizzle with oil and toss gently to coat. Arrange poblanos and jalapeño skin side up. Broil until poblanos, jalapeño, and tomatillos are blistered and blackened and onion wedges are dark at edges, about 15 minutes, rotating sheet halfway through broiling. (Vegetables may appear to be burning, but they are not.) Let vegetables cool on sheet for 15 minutes.

3. Turn off broiler and heat oven to 400 degrees. Transfer broiled vegetables and any accumulated juices to blender. Add water, cilantro, cumin, oregano, sugar, salt, and pepper and process until smooth, about 30 seconds, scraping down sides of blender jar as needed (you should have about 3½ cups sauce).

4. FOR THE ENCHILADAS: Spread ½ cup sauce in bottom of 13 by 9-inch baking dish. Combine chicken, 1½ cups cheddar, and 1 cup sauce in bowl. Stack tortillas and wrap in damp dish towel. Microwave until hot and pliable, about 1½ minutes.

5. Arrange tortillas on counter and place ¼ cup filling in center of each. Distribute any remaining filling evenly among tortillas. Roll tortillas tightly around filling and place seam side down in prepared dish.

6. Pour remaining 2 cups sauce over enchiladas and spread evenly with back of spoon. Sprinkle with remaining 1½ cups cheddar and cover dish with foil. Bake until enchiladas are heated through and cheese is melted, about 30 minutes.

7. Uncover and let cool for 15 minutes. Sprinkle with cilantro and serve with sour cream, lime wedges, avocado, and onion.

For this quicker weeknight version, we cut down on the preparation, not the flavor.

TO MAKE AHEAD

After dish is covered with aluminum foil in step 6, unbaked enchiladas can be refrigerated for up to 24 hours. When ready to serve, bake enchiladas as directed, extending baking time by 15 minutes.

Building Flavor

reat enchiladas require great sauce.

Broil tomatillos, chiles, onion, and arlic until blackened.

Blend broiled vegetables with water, ilantro, and spices.

Are All Store-Bought Corn Tortillas Equal? No, They Are Not. *by Carolyn Grillo*

PRODUCT TASTING

CORN TORTILLAS HAVE been a dietary staple in Mexico and other Latin American countries for centuries. While we enjoy making corn tortillas at home, it's more convenient to use supermarket products. To find our favorite, we gathered seven nationally available 6-inch corn tortillas, the size we call for most frequently in our recipes. Five of the products were made from corn, and two were made from blends of corn, wheat gluten, and/or wheat flour. We gently warmed the tortillas and sampled them plain and in pork tacos.

Our ideal corn tortilla has corn-forward flavor, mild sweetness, and a slight nuttiness developed from nixtamalization, the chemical process that prepares corn for use in tortillas (and other applications). A few of the tortillas we tasted hit all those notes, exhibiting "slightly sweet," "pleasant corn flavor." In comparison, other samples tasted "bland" and had "very little corn flavor." One tortilla tasted slightly "musty." Since most commercial corn tortillas are produced from the same high-yield commodity corn, we wondered why some of the tortillas had more corn flavor than others.

During our research, we learned that several factors influence flavor: the length of the nixtamalization

time, how the masa (dough traditionally made by grinding nixtamalized corn kernels) is processed, and how the tortillas are cooked. Another factor is the amount of sugar and sodium in each tortilla. Higher-rated tortillas contained sugar (which occurs naturally in corn) and/or sodium. The lowest-ranked, "musty" tortilla was the only product in our lineup that didn't contain either.

Many factors related to manufacturing processes also influence a tortilla's texture. Companies were reluctant to share details about their processes, so we examined the ingredient lists on the labels and measured the tortillas. The ingredient lists revealed that all but one tortilla contained preservatives. Those that did were pliable and tender; the one that didn't was "dry" and "stale."

We also noticed that the two tortillas that contained wheat products were sturdy yet flexible and tender. When we measured the thickness of all the tortillas, we discovered two things: Most of the all-corn tortillas were thinner than those that contained wheat, and our favorite all-corn tortilla was the thinnest in the lineup.

Two of the tortillas stood out in our tastings. We loved the all-corn Guerrero White Corn Tortillas for their "sweet corn flavor" and their "delicate but not dry" texture that made them easy to fold. We also loved Maria and

The best corn tortillas will bend but not break when loaded with taco fixings.

Ricardo's Soft Yellow Corn Tortillas. Made from a corn/wheat blend, they had a "subtle corn flavor" and were "sturdy but not too doughy."

Since one of our top two tortillas contains wheat gluten and one doesn't, we compared them in enchiladas and tostadas. Both made great enchiladas, but the corn/wheat blend tortillas never fully crisped up for tostadas. For this reason, we recommend using Guerrero White Corn Tortillas when frying. In every other application, either winner will serve you well.

	Best All-Corn	Best Corn/Wheat Blend			
RECOMMENDED	**Guerrero** White Corn Tortillas **Price:** $1.75 for 18 tortillas ($0.10 per tortilla) **Thickness:** 2.08 mm **Sodium:** 23.5 mg **Sugar:** 2 g	**Maria and Ricardo's** Soft Yellow Corn Tortillas **Price:** $3.49 for 8 tortillas ($0.44 per tortilla) **Thickness:** 3.05 mm **Sodium:** 108.9 mg **Sugar:** 0 g	**La Tortilla Factory** Handmade Style Yellow Corn & Wheat Tortillas **Price:** $3.19 for 8 tortillas ($0.40 per tortilla) **Thickness:** 2.78 mm **Sodium:** 217.8 mg **Sugar:** 0 g	**La Banderita** Yellow Corn Tortillas **Price:** $2.49 for 30 tortillas ($0.08 per tortilla) **Thickness:** 2.27 mm **Sodium:** 15 mg **Sugar:** 1 g	**Mission** Yellow Corn Tortillas **Price:** $4.88 for 30 tortillas ($0.16 per tortilla) **Thickness:** 2.43 mm **Sodium:** 10 mg **Sugar:** 2 g
TASTERS' NOTES	Our favorite all-corn tortillas were "thin but not frail." Tasters liked their "sweet corn flavor" that "didn't overpower the pork" in tacos. They were "delicate" in enchiladas and became light, airy, and crisp when fried for tostadas.	The addition of wheat gluten makes these thicker tortillas pleasantly "chewy." Tasters liked their "subtle corn flavor" in enchiladas. One small drawback: This product didn't become fully crisp when fried for tostadas.	The third-thickest tortillas in our lineup contain gluten, and tasters described them as "thick and hearty," with "great chew." A few thought they were "a little too bulky." They had mild corn flavor.	These tortillas had "a neutral corn flavor" with "a little sweetness." Most on our panel agreed that they were "soft and pliable yet sturdy enough to hold the meat" for tacos. A few tasters found them "slightly dry."	Some tasters found these tortillas to be "soft but sturdy," noting that they "held together and didn't sog out or tear." Other tasters griped that they were "tough" and that "not much corn" came through in their flavor.

Sodium and sugar amounts are based on serving sizes of 47 grams.

Web subscribers can see the complete results chart at CooksCountry.com/may20.

In Asheville, N.C., pastry chef Ashley Capps aims to surprise. "When I have an idea, it's not gonna leave me until I try it."

Text by Bryan Roof; photos by Steve Klise

Buxton Hall sits in a 1930s building that used to hold a roller-skating rink. Two barbecue pits loaded with pork and chicken (below right) provide a prelude to pie.

I T'S EARLY MORNING at Buxton Hall Barbecue in Asheville, North Carolina. Sunlight creeps through skylights to illuminate battered wood floors and mingle with smoke from a wood fire burning down to coals for two adjacent barbecue pits. I'm not here for barbecue; I'm here for banana pudding pie, a Buxton specialty that pastry chef Ashley Capps has agreed to make for me. This is no small favor; the pie is a complex, multilayered beast. "You know the term 'easy as pie'? It's so false. It's just easy to eat," she says with a laugh.

As a child, Capps was fond of her mother's meringue-topped banana pudding. Transforming the childhood dessert into a pie fit for a restaurant was "a combination of technique and nostalgia," a blending of her "inner child and Southern roots."

She builds the pie with a mesmerizing confidence, carefully forming the crumb crust into the corner of the pie plate, the "neck" of the pie, so the slices stay sturdy. She stirs the pudding with a spatula, not a whisk, so the custard won't curdle in the corners of the pot. She insists that cooking the egg whites to 168 degrees is the key to a stable meringue, "although the textbooks disagree."

While she works, she talks about the arc of a culinary career: the struggle of learning the process and techniques; the discipline of repetition; and after sufficient growth and self-awareness, the feeling of fulfillment from making the same thing as close to perfect every time. Her passion for the process is evident.

The banana pudding pie was a hit on the Buxton Hall menu from day one. And even though Ashley left the restaurant on good terms last year to pursue other opportunities, the pie remains. Call it a little slice of nostalgia.

This Pie Is Bananas

by Jessica Rudolph

WHEN EXECUTIVE FOOD Editor Bryan Roof returned to Boston after visiting Buxton Hall Barbecue in Asheville, North Carolina (see "On the Road"), I wanted to hop on a plane and go sample all the tasty, smoky, porky morsels he described.

But of all the dishes he told us about, it was the banana pudding pie, a reimagining of the classic layered dessert, that I couldn't get out of my head. Bryan described a toasty, buttery crust of homemade vanilla wafers; a lusciously creamy yet sliceable vanilla pudding studded with a tumble of banana slices; and airy swoops of a brown sugar meringue kissed with torch until lightly charred. I was anxious to get in the kitchen and make this treat for myself.

For my version, I started with the crust. I pulsed Nilla Wafers (some recipes call for making your own wafers, but Nilla's familiar vanilla flavor worked well here) in a food processor, moistened the crumbs with melted butter, and added a touch of flour for structure and a bit of brown sugar for extra depth of flavor. I transferred the crumb mixture to a pie plate, and, like pastry chef Ashley Capps did at Buxton Hall, I formed the walls of my crust before the bottom to ensure that I'd have enough crumbs for a strong, supportive outer edge.

For the pudding base, I turned to a pastry cream from our recipe archives. I started with a base mixture of half-and-half, egg yolks, sugar, and flour cooked together on the stovetop until the mixture was bubbling and thickened. Following Capps' guidance again, I added a pinch each of ground cinnamon and ground allspice to round out the sweet, creamy flavor. Into the still-warm custard I stirred butter, vanilla, and softened gelatin (to help

the pie hold its shape when sliced). I folded two sliced ripe bananas into the pudding, poured it all into my par-baked pie shell, and let it firm up in the refrigerator for a couple of hours.

All that remained was the meringue top. I wanted a cooked meringue, since those made with just raw egg whites whipped with sugar are less stable and therefore prone to weeping. I combined egg whites with granulated and brown sugars (to get the right balance of caramel notes without an overpowering molasses flavor) and

a pinch of cream of tartar and cooked the mixture gently over simmering water until it registered around 165 degrees. I used a stand mixer to whip the meringue until it formed pearly stiff peaks and spread it over the surface of my chilled pie, making decorative swoops and dips with my spatula.

Placing the pie for a minute or two under the oven's broiler (or passing a torch, if you have one, over the pie's

surface) created a beautifully browned exterior that tasted like a campfire marshmallow, the slight toasty bitterness nicely offsetting the pie's sweetness.

As my tasters and I gobbled down the pie, savoring the perfect balance of sweet and salty, buttery and fruity, and creamy and crunchy, I breathed easy; though I still look forward to one day sampling Buxton Hall's delicacies myself, I have this darn good pie to tide me over until then.

Turn the page for *step-by-step* instructions on how to make this *bananas* pie!

8 Steps to Delicious, Showstopping Banana Pudding Pie

1. Pulse cookies, brown sugar, flour, and salt in food processor until finely ground. Add butter and pulse until combined.

2. Transfer crumbs to pie plate. Use your hands to press crumbs firmly up sides of plate to ¼-inch thickness.

3. Press remaining crumbs firmly into bottom and corners of plate to ¼-inch thickness.

4. Make stovetop pudding, then stir in sliced bananas.

5. Cook meringue in bowl over simmering water until it registers 160 to 165 degrees.

6. Whip meringue to stiff peaks in mixer.

7. Spread meringue evenly over filling, using spatula or spoon to create swirls.

8. Broil briefly or use torch to brown meringue.

BANANA PUDDING PIE *Serves 8*
For the best results, use either fully yellow or lightly spotted bananas here (avoid bananas that are green on top or all brown). Peel and slice the bananas just before using to help prevent browning. Plan ahead: The pie needs to be refrigerated for at least 4 hours or up to 24 hours before it's topped. Chilling the topped pie for longer than 4 hours may cause the top to deflate. Don't worry; it will still be delicious.

CRUST
4   cups (8⅓ ounces) Nilla Wafer cookies
3   tablespoons packed light brown sugar
1   tablespoon all-purpose flour
¼   teaspoon table salt
6   tablespoons unsalted butter, melted

FILLING
2   teaspoons unflavored gelatin
1¾   cups half-and-half, divided
¾   cup (5¼ ounces) granulated sugar
5   large egg yolks
2   tablespoons all-purpose flour
¼   teaspoon table salt
     Pinch ground cinnamon
     Pinch ground allspice
2   tablespoons unsalted butter, cut into 2 pieces and chilled
1   tablespoon vanilla extract
2   ripe bananas, peeled and sliced ¼ inch thick (1½ cups)

MERINGUE
⅓   cup (2⅓ ounces) granulated sugar
⅓   cup packed (2⅓ ounces) light brown sugar
4   large egg whites
¼   teaspoon cream of tartar
⅛   teaspoon table salt

1. FOR THE CRUST: Adjust oven rack 8 inches from broiler element and heat oven to 325 degrees. Pulse cookies, sugar, flour, and salt in food processor until finely ground, about 10 pulses. Add melted butter and pulse until combined, about 8 pulses, scraping down sides of bowl as needed. Transfer mixture to 9-inch pie plate (it will seem like a lot of crumbs).
2. Using your hands, press crumbs firmly up sides of plate, building walls about ¼ inch thick and leveling top edge. Press remaining crumbs into even layer on bottom of plate, firmly pressing crumbs into corners of plate. Bake until fragrant and beginning to darken at edges, 18 to 20 minutes. Transfer plate to wire rack.
3. FOR THE FILLING: Meanwhile, sprinkle gelatin over ½ cup half-and-half in small bowl and let mixture sit until gelatin softens, about 5 minutes. Whisk sugar, egg yolks, flour, salt, cinnamon, allspice, and remaining 1¼ cups half-and-half in large saucepan until fully combined. Cook over medium heat, whisking constantly and scraping corners of saucepan, until mixture thickens, bubbles burst across entire surface, and mixture registers 180 degrees in several places, 5 to 7 minutes. Off heat, whisk in butter, vanilla, and gelatin mixture until combined.
4. Stir bananas into hot filling. Pour filling into crust (crust needn't be completely cooled). Press parchment paper directly onto surface of filling and refrigerate until set, at least 4 hours or up to 24 hours.
5. FOR THE MERINGUE: Whisk all ingredients together in bowl of stand mixer. Place bowl over saucepan filled with 1 inch of barely simmering water, making sure water does not touch bottom of bowl. Whisking gently but constantly, cook until mixture registers 160 to 165 degrees, 5 to 8 minutes.
6. Fit mixer with whisk attachment and whip on high speed until meringue forms stiff peaks and is smooth and creamy, 2 to 3 minutes.
7. Gently peel off parchment from filling (if any filling sticks to parchment, scrape off and smooth back over surface of pie). Spread meringue over filling, making sure meringue touches edges of crust. Working gently, use spatula or spoon to create swirls over surface.
8A. FOR A BROILER: Heat broiler. Broil until meringue is well browned, 1 to 2 minutes, rotating plate as needed for even browning.
8B. FOR A TORCH: Ignite torch; continuously sweep flame about 2 inches above meringue until well browned.
9. Slice pie into wedges with wet knife, wiping knife clean between slices. Serve immediately. (Topped pie can be refrigerated for up to 4 hours.)

Strawberry-Rhubarb Crisp

Don't let spring pass by without making this easy, foolproof seasonal dessert.

by Matthew Fairman

STRAWBERRIES THAT RIPEN in late spring have an unmistakable sweet, floral perfume that seems to lead us by the nose toward summer. When combined with bright, tart, pleasantly tannic rhubarb, they make for a beautiful dessert with compelling contrast and complexity.

And is there an easier, more satisfying way to enjoy this combination than baked into a crisp? Making a crisp is much easier than making a pie, as the dessert takes little more than stirring together a topping in a bowl, tossing cut-up fruit with some sugar, and throwing it all in the oven. But baker beware! Follow the wrong recipe (or worse, no recipe at all) and you might end up with a strawberry-rhubarb soup and a soggy topping—decidedly not crisp.

That's the real lesson of this carefully tested recipe: Different batches of strawberries and rhubarb will exude varying amounts of moisture when combined with sugar and baked. So how do you create a recipe that will result in the perfect (slightly jammy but never stodgy) texture every time?

The simplest answer is to cook the filling briefly on the stovetop, over moderately high heat, to coax out the excess liquid, reduce it, and thicken it to the consistency you're after. Then you can top the fruit and quickly brown the crisp in the oven. Applying this simple technique also ensures that your topping remains crisp.

An unusual ingredient in our topping—panko bread crumbs—bears mentioning. There was a fair amount of debate on whether we were developing a recipe for a crisp or a crumble (and debate on the difference between the two). Suffice it to say that I wanted a crisp, and I wanted to end all confusion on the matter. A crisp topping should be crispy, and panko is an excellent way to give the topping a lasting, light, airy crispness. Try it and see.

STRAWBERRY-RHUBARB CRISP
Serves 6

If using frozen strawberries, there's no need to thaw them completely; you can chop them as soon as they're soft enough. If using frozen strawberries and frozen rhubarb, you may need to increase the stovetop cooking time by up to 4 minutes. Depending on the amount of trimming required, you may need to buy more than 1 pound of rhubarb to ensure that you end up with 3½ cups. Serve with vanilla ice cream.

TOPPING
- ¾ cup (3¾ ounces) all-purpose flour
- ½ cup panko bread crumbs
- ¼ cup packed (1¾ ounces) light brown sugar
- ½ teaspoon table salt
- ¼ teaspoon ground cinnamon
- 6 tablespoons unsalted butter, melted

FILLING
- 1 pound fresh rhubarb, trimmed and cut into ½-inch pieces, or frozen rhubarb, thawed and cut into ½-inch pieces (3½ cups)
- 12 ounces fresh strawberries, hulled and chopped coarse, or frozen strawberries, thawed and chopped coarse (2 cups)
- 1¼ cups packed (8¾ ounces) light brown sugar
- 2 tablespoons cornstarch
- ⅛ teaspoon table salt

1. FOR THE TOPPING: Whisk flour, panko, sugar, salt, and cinnamon together in bowl. Add melted butter and stir until no dry spots of flour remain and mixture forms clumps. Refrigerate until ready to use.

2. FOR THE FILLING: Adjust oven rack to middle position and heat oven to 375 degrees. Toss all ingredients in large bowl until thoroughly combined. Transfer to 10-inch ovensafe skillet. Cook over medium-high heat, stirring frequently, until fruit has released enough liquid to be mostly submerged, rhubarb is just beginning to break down, and juices have thickened, about 8 minutes. Remove skillet from heat.

3. Squeeze topping into large clumps with your hands. Crumble topping into pea-size pieces and sprinkle evenly over filling. Bake until topping is browned and filling is bubbling around sides of skillet, about 20 minutes. Let cool for 15 minutes. Serve.

A surprise ingredient—panko bread crumbs—creates a crispy top.

Rhubarb Primer

Well over 1,000 years ago, a brave human first ate rhubarb stems; they had probably watched a friend get horribly sick (or worse!) from eating the leaves, which contain toxic levels of oxalic acid. But the supertart stems are perfectly safe to eat, and they pair incredibly well with sweet fruits and berries.

Rhubarb doesn't need to be peeled, but it's a good idea to trim the stems of any small bits of leaves and to rinse the stems before chopping. Some supermarkets sell frozen sliced rhubarb stems, which work fine in many recipes (including this one). Keep in mind that rhubarb stems come in varying thicknesses (oftentimes even within the same bunch), so make sure that you're cutting them down to the same size to ensure even cooking. If you have extra stems, chop them and freeze the uncooked pieces for up to three months.

White Sandwich Bread

Light, tender, sliceable: This is the perfect bread for BLTs, PB&Js, or morning toast.

AMERICAN SANDWICH BREAD
Makes 1 loaf

- 2½ **cups (13¾ ounces) bread flour**
- 2 **teaspoons instant or rapid-rise yeast**
- 1½ **teaspoons table salt**
- ¾ **cup (6 ounces) whole milk, room temperature**
- ⅓ **cup (2⅔ ounces) water, room temperature, plus extra for misting**
- 2 **tablespoons unsalted butter, melted**
- 2 **tablespoons honey**

1. Whisk flour, yeast, and salt together in bowl of stand mixer. Whisk milk, room-temperature water, melted butter, and honey in 4-cup liquid measuring cup until honey is dissolved.
2. Fit mixer with dough hook. Slowly add milk mixture to flour mixture on low speed until cohesive dough starts to form and no dry flour remains, about 2 minutes, scraping down bowl as needed. Increase speed to medium-low and knead until dough is smooth and elastic and clears sides of bowl, about 8 minutes.
3. Transfer dough to lightly floured counter and knead to form smooth, round ball, about 30 seconds. Place dough seam side down in lightly greased large bowl, cover tightly with plastic wrap, and let rise until doubled in size, 1½ to 2 hours.
4. Grease 8½ by 4½-inch loaf pan. Press down on dough to deflate. Turn out dough onto lightly floured counter (side of dough that was against bowl should now be facing up). Press and stretch dough into 8 by 6-inch rectangle, with long side parallel to counter edge.

Our bread has a light, tender crumb and a subtle sweetness.

5. Roll dough away from you into firm cylinder, keeping roll taut by tucking it under itself as you go. Pinch seam closed and place loaf seam side down in prepared pan, pressing dough gently into corners.
6. Cover loosely with greased plastic and let rise until loaf reaches 1 inch above lip of pan and dough springs back minimally when poked gently with your knuckle, 1 to 1½ hours.

7. Adjust oven rack to lower-middle position and heat oven to 350 degrees. Mist loaf with water and bake until loaf is deep golden brown and registers 205 to 210 degrees, 35 to 40 minutes, rotating pan halfway through baking.
8. Let loaf cool in pan for 15 minutes. Remove loaf from pan and let cool completely on wire rack, about 3 hours, before slicing and serving.

WHOLE-WHEAT AMERICAN SANDWICH BREAD
Reduce bread flour to 1½ cups (8¼ ounces) and add 1 cup (5½ ounces) whole-wheat flour and 3 tablespoons wheat germ to yeast and salt in step 1. Increase honey to 3 tablespoons.

Step by Step

1. Combine dry ingredients
Whisk together flour, yeast, and salt in the bowl of a stand mixer.
Why? Whisking ensures even distribution of the yeast and salt.

2. Combine wet ingredients
Whisk together room-temperature milk, water, melted butter, and honey in a liquid measuring cup.
Why? Yeast works best at room temperature. If it's mixed with ingredients that are too hot or too cold, it can lose its effectiveness.

3. Make dough in mixer
Slowly add the wet ingredients to the dry and knead for 8 minutes.
Why? Eight minutes of kneading helps develop the gluten for a soft, stretchy texture.

4. Let dough rise
Form the dough into a smooth, round ball. Place the dough in a greased bowl, cover it tightly, and let it rise for 1½ to 2 hours.
Why? Covering the bowl tightly helps keep it from drying out during this initial rise.

5. Deflate and stretch
Press down on the dough to deflate it, and then stretch it into a rectangle.
Why? Deflating the dough before the second rise pops any large air bubbles and makes it easier to shape.

Equipment

...ke a Stand (Mixer)
...knead dough well, a stand mixer should be ...avy enough to keep it from shimmying off ... counter and have a motor that's sturdy ...ough to manhandle the dough. We love the ...chenAid KSM75WH Classic Plus Series ...-Quart Tilt-Head Stand Mixer ($207.99). ...knead your bread like a champ.

...ck the Right Pan
...r favorite loaf pans (our winner, pictured ...the steps below, is the USA Pan Loaf Pan, ...Volume [$14.95]) measure approxi-...tely 8½ inches by 4½ inches (lip to lip). If ...ur loaf pan measures 9 inches by 5 inches, ...crease the second rise by about 20 to ...minutes (your visual cue of 1 inch above ...lip still holds true—it'll just take longer) ...d start checking for doneness about ...minutes earlier.

...ke the Temperature
...e best way to know when your bread is ...ne is to insert an instant-read thermometer ...to the middle of the loaf. When it hits 205 to ...0 degrees, its protein structures have fully ...t, but the interior crumb is still tender ...d soft. Our favorite thermometer is the ...ermoWorks Thermapen Mk4 ($99.00).

...read Knife
...cing bread with a nonserrated knife is an ...ercise in disappointment. Instead, use a ...arp serrated knife with a blade long enough ...allow you to do long back-and-forth sweeps ...thout squishing the loaf. Another key to even ...ces? Letting the loaf cool completely. It's ...t easy when the kitchen smells so good, but ...s essential for sandwich-ready slices. Our ...vorite serrated knife is the Mercer Culinary ...illennia 10" Wide Bread Knife ($22.10).

Dough Rising 101

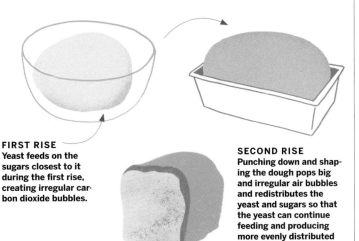

FIRST RISE
Yeast feeds on the sugars closest to it during the first rise, creating irregular carbon dioxide bubbles.

SECOND RISE
Punching down and shaping the dough pops big and irregular air bubbles and redistributes the yeast and sugars so that the yeast can continue feeding and producing more evenly distributed carbon dioxide during the second rise.

Why Two Rises?

Most bread recipes call for letting the dough rise and then punching it down before shaping. To understand why you punch down a risen dough, you need to know how yeast works. Yeast is composed of fungi that, when hydrated, convert starches in the flour into sugars; the fungi then consume the sugars and produce many flavorful compounds in addition to carbon dioxide gas. The gas is what physically causes the dough to rise—it's like slowly blowing air into a balloon. The carbon dioxide bubbles created through this process are held in place by the bread's gluten network, which relaxes during rising to be flexible enough to stretch (instead of ripping or breaking, which would cause the gas to escape) as the dough grows.

During the first rise, the yeast fungi consume most of the available natural sugars around them in the dough; punching the dough down and shaping it into a loaf redistributes the yeast particles so that they come in contact with more natural sugars to feed on, creating more carbon dioxide and more flavor compounds in turn. Thus the second rise contributes to better flavor. It also helps produce a more even texture by deflating any large pockets of carbon dioxide that would create large holes in the bread and also by acting as additional kneading to strengthen the gluten network and therefore improve the texture of the bread.

If you baked the bread after only one rise, it would have an uneven shape, big pockets of air, and underdeveloped flavor.

Why Bread Flour?
Bread flour has the highest protein percentage of any supermarket flour—usually between 12 and 14 percent. This makes it particularly good at forming gluten, which gives bread structure and chew. Compare a great piece of sliceable, toastable, sandwich-ready bread made with bread flour with a great slice of tender, fluffy, airy cake made with cake flour, which contains about 6 to 8 percent protein. That's the difference. All-purpose flour is in the middle of the pack with about 10 percent protein.

THE AMERICAN TABLE

Fun fact: The first presliced loaves of bread available for sale came on the market in 1928, when Otto Rohwedder fired up his slicing machine in Chillicothe, Missouri. Rohwedder calibrated his contraption to create ½-inch slices, which he deemed just right for everyday sandwiches. The local newspaper gushed that customers would experience "a thrill of pleasure" when they first encountered a loaf of slices, with "each slice the exact counterpart of its fellows."

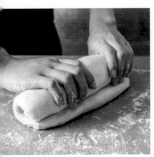

...Shape and place in pan
...oll the dough tightly and place it ...a greased pan for a second rise. ...hy? A tight log ensures that the ...af rises properly to create the ...erfect crumb.

7. Let dough rise again
Allow the shaped loaf to rise until it reaches 1 inch above the lip of the pan.
Why? This second rise creates more air pockets and a beautiful, smooth dome.

8. Spray loaf with water
Uncover the loaf and mist it with water before baking.
Why? A quick spritz helps the loaf achieve a slightly firm crust.

9. Bake
Bake until the loaf is deep golden brown and registers 205 to 210 degrees.
Why? At this target temperature, the bread is baked through but not dried out.

10. Cool
Remove the loaf from the pan and let it cool completely on a wire rack before slicing.
Why? Slicing into a hot loaf will lead to tearing. Let it cool for perfect, even slices.

Steak Dinner

We wanted our meat, potatoes, and vegetables, all in a single pan.

by Alli Berkey

1. Sear steaks on stovetop until browned, then remove them from pan.

2. Add potatoes and mushrooms and cook until lightly browned.

3. Add asparagus and seared steaks, then roast to doneness in oven.

A simple, bright horseradish sauce is the perfect complement to the savory steak and vegetables.

PERFECTLY ROASTED POTATOES, buttery mushrooms, a savory strip steak, and maybe something green to lighten things up. I mentioned my dinner desires to my wife one Sunday evening, and she laughed. "I bet you can't do it in one pan!" On Sundays, our deal is that I cook and she's in charge of doing dishes, so she clearly had an ulterior motive in issuing this challenge. Well, challenge accepted.

I started with a cast-iron skillet to cook my steaks, knowing that—because cast iron gets ripping hot and retains heat really well—I'd get a beautiful brown crust. I seared the steaks in a bit of butter because, well, butter and steak

are best friends. Just a few minutes in the hot skillet on each side produced a perfect crust and a lovely fond in the pan that would add flavor to my vegetables. I removed the steaks (they were not fully cooked yet—I'd finish them in a moment) and set them aside while I got on with the rest.

Next came the potatoes and the mushrooms. After experiments with staggering their introduction to the pan, I found that I could add the potatoes and mushrooms all at once, with a bit more butter to brown them. After about 10 minutes, I added sliced garlic and shallot for their savory-sweet flavors (a perfect match for the steak),

plus a good handful of potent fresh thyme—shy flavors are not my style.

After a couple of minutes, I topped the potato mixture with a layer of seasoned asparagus spears followed by the already browned (but not fully cooked) steaks and sent everything into the oven to finish cooking, hopefully in unison.

Fifteen minutes later my multicomponent, rustic bistro dinner was ready for guests (this recipe serves four)—and yes, sweetheart, I'd done it all in just one pan. All that was left to do was to set out a stir-together horseradish sauce (just horseradish, sour cream, salt, pepper, and a little water to thin it) and open the wine.

IE-PAN STEAK WITH POTATOES, SHROOMS, AND ASPARAGUS
rves 4
u can use a 12-inch nonstick skillet tead of a cast-iron pan, but make e it's ovensafe to 400 degrees. Buy rigerated prepared horseradish, not shelf-stable kind, which contains servatives and additives.

- ½ cup sour cream
- 2 tablespoons prepared horseradish
- 2 tablespoons water
- ¼ teaspoons kosher salt, divided
- ¼ teaspoons pepper, divided
- 2 (1-pound) strip steaks, about 1½ inches thick, trimmed and cut in half crosswise
- 3 tablespoons unsalted butter, divided, plus 1 tablespoon melted
- 1 pound Yukon Gold potatoes, unpeeled, cut into ¾-inch pieces
- 2 ounces cremini mushrooms, trimmed and quartered
- 1 shallot, halved and sliced thin
- 3 garlic cloves, sliced thin
- 1 tablespoon chopped fresh thyme
- 1 pound asparagus, trimmed

Adjust oven rack to middle position d heat oven to 400 degrees. Come sour cream, horseradish, water, teaspoon salt, and ¼ teaspoon pepr in bowl; set aside.
Heat 12-inch cast-iron skillet over dium-high heat for 5 minutes. t steaks dry with paper towels and inkle with 1½ teaspoons salt and teaspoon pepper. Melt 1 tablespoon tter in preheated skillet. Add steaks d cook until well browned on both les, about 3 minutes per side. Transsteaks to plate; set aside.
Add 2 tablespoons butter to w-empty skillet over medium-high at. Stir in potatoes, mushrooms, easpoon salt, and remaining teaspoon pepper. Cook, stirring casionally, until vegetables are htly browned, about 10 minutes. d shallot, garlic, and thyme and ok until shallot is just softened, out 2 minutes.
Off heat, place asparagus in gle layer on top of vegetables skillet. Drizzle asparagus with elted butter and sprinkle with maining ¼ teaspoon salt. Place aks on top of asparagus.
Transfer skillet to oven and roast til steaks register 125 degrees (for edium-rare), 10 to 15 minutes. Tent illet with aluminum foil and let aks rest for 10 minutes. Serve with rseradish sauce.

Pasta Primavera

How does this sound? An elegant plate of fresh comfort food that's perfect for spring and won't take forever. **by Matthew Fairman**

YOU WANT AN elegant dinner that's light yet satisfying, but you don't want to spend all afternoon making it. Pasta primavera is the solution. The joy of this dish is that it's simultaneously healthy and incredibly flavorful all at once. There are heaps of vibrantly colored, lightly cooked vegetables, but they're rooted firmly in a foundation of pasta, olive oil, and Parmesan cheese. It's a sophisticated meal, but it comes together in minutes.

It's as easy as can be. Start by cutting up a big handful of bright-red cherry tomatoes, some marinated artichoke hearts, and a stack of sweet, emerald asparagus. Then toss them with some garlic, salt, lemon, and Parmesan and let them get acquainted with each other in a bowl while your pasta cooks. Boil your pasta water, and you're nearly there already.

All that's left is to slice your shallot and soften it, with a pinch of red pepper flakes, in a generous glug of olive oil and put everything you've prepped into the pan. Add frozen peas and a little bit of the starchy pasta water to make it creamy and cohesive, and then sprinkle on a bit of fresh mint and more shredded cheese to finish it off. You'll find that it tastes as irresistible as it looks.

Jarred marinated artichoke hearts contribute lots of flavor with minimal work.

PASTA PRIMAVERA FOR TWO

Look for asparagus spears that are roughly ¼ inch thick. We recommended using a rasp-style grater to zest the lemon; you can also use it to mince the garlic. You can substitute 6 ounces (2½ cups) of farfalle for the orecchiette. There's no need to thaw the peas.

- 4 ounces cherry tomatoes, halved
- 4 ounces thin asparagus, trimmed and sliced on bias ½ inch thick
- ¾ cup marinated artichoke hearts, patted dry and chopped coarse
- ¼ cup shredded Parmesan cheese, plus extra for serving
- 1 teaspoon grated lemon zest plus 1 tablespoon juice
- 1 garlic clove, minced
- ½ teaspoon table salt, divided, plus salt for cooking pasta
- 6 ounces (1¾ cups) orecchiette
- ¼ cup extra-virgin olive oil
- 1 shallot, sliced thin
- ¼ teaspoon pepper
- ⅛ teaspoon red pepper flakes
- ⅓ cup frozen peas
- 1 tablespoon chopped fresh mint

1. Combine tomatoes, asparagus, artichokes, Parmesan, lemon zest and juice, garlic, and ¼ teaspoon salt in bowl; set aside.

2. Bring 2 quarts water to boil in large saucepan over high heat. Add pasta and 1 tablespoon salt and cook, stirring often, until al dente. Reserve ¼ cup cooking water, then drain pasta and return it to saucepan.

3. Heat oil in 12-inch nonstick skillet over medium heat until shimmering. Add shallot, pepper, pepper flakes, and remaining ¼ teaspoon salt and cook until shallot is just softened, about 2 minutes. Stir in peas, tomato mixture, pasta, and reserved cooking water and cook, stirring constantly, until hot throughout and sauce is thickened, about 2 minutes. Sprinkle with mint and serve, passing extra Parmesan separately.

Gravlax

The hardest part of making cured salmon at home is the waiting.

by Morgan Bolling

THE ONLY THING better than gravlax layered on a bagel with a smear of cream cheese at your favorite deli is having homemade gravlax at your fingertips—no need to swap your pj's for real clothes to visit that deli on a Sunday morning.

Gravlax is an ancient salmon preparation. Fishing communities in northern Europe and Russia, surrounded by an abundance of salmon, acquired most of their catch during the time of year when the fish swim upstream to spawn. To preserve the fish for the rest of the year, they'd salt and bury it—this curing process gave them easy access to protein during the lean winter months.

Today the process relies on refrigeration rather than shovels. Instead of being buried in the earth, modern gravlax is made by "burying" salmon in a mixture of sugar and salt to extract liquid and cure the flesh. Depending on the cook, herbs, spices, or even booze are added to enhance flavor and preservation.

For our recipe, you simply coat a large piece of salmon evenly with a mixture of salt, brown sugar (we liked the deep flavor it gave the fish), and dill in a zipper-lock bag. Dill is our flavoring of choice here, but you could experiment with other flavors such as coriander or juniper.

The bag contains the mess and is easy to flip, a step that helps the salmon cure more evenly. To give the fish a firmer texture and infuse it with flavor more quickly, you weight the bag while curing.

After the three-day cure, you remove the fish from the salt mixture and rinse off the excess salt. All that's left to do is slice it thin on the bias, a step that is easier if you halve the fish lengthwise first.

GRAVLAX

Serves 8 to 10 (Makes about 1½ pounds)
We prefer using farmed salmon here; if you choose to use wild salmon, reduce the curing time in step 2 to 36 hours, flipping the bag halfway through the curing period.

- ½ cup kosher salt
- ½ cup chopped fresh dill
- ⅓ cup packed light brown sugar
- 1 (1½-pound) center-cut skinless salmon fillet, about 1½ inches thick

1. Combine salt, dill, and sugar in bowl. Place salmon in 1-gallon zipper-lock bag. Spread half of salt mixture evenly over top of salmon. Flip bag and spread remaining half of salt mixture over bottom of salmon (salmon should be well coated all over). Press out air and seal bag.
2. Place bag on large plate or rimmed baking sheet, making sure salmon sits flat. Place square baking dish filled with 2 large, heavy cans on top of bag. Refrigerate for 3 days, flipping bag once each day.
3. Remove gravlax from salt mixture; discard salt mixture. Rinse gravlax well with cold water and pat dry with paper towels. To serve, slice gravlax in half lengthwise, then slice crosswise on bias as thin as possible with sharp knife. (Gravlax can be wrapped tightly in plastic wrap and refrigerated for up to 3 days.)

Bring on the accoutrements: bagels, sliced cucumber and red onion, lemon wedges, capers, chives, and cream cheese.

1. Coat Cover the salmon in the salt mixture in a 1-gallon zipper-lock bag. The bag contains the mess and is easy to flip—an essential step for even curing.

2. Press Place the bag on a large plate or rimmed baking sheet; top it with a square baking dish; and weight with two large, heavy cans.

3. Rinse After 3 days, take the gravlax out of the salt mixture and rinse it off so that it is not too salty to eat. Pat it dry with paper towels before slicing.

4. Slice Slice the fillet in half lengthwise before slicing crosswise—against the grain—to make it easier to create paper-thin slices.

Pork Ramen

Truly great ramen isn't built on a powdered soup mix—it's built on a deeply flavorful homemade broth. Enter the slow cooker. **by Matthew Fairman**

MY FIRST FORAYS into making ramen involved a microwave, a squiggly brick of dried noodles, and a little pouch of powdered chicken flavoring. And while I'll still slurp down the instant stuff, I've gotten a little more ambitious about making my own ramen. These days, I'll trek all over town to eat in the best ramen shops and then spend the better part of a three-day weekend taking pains to re-create the "perfect bowl" by simmering stock overnight, doting on slow-roasted pork belly, and marinating soft-cooked eggs.

But I've also learned that you don't need to put in that much work to make truly incredible homemade ramen. The one shortcut I employ is using the noodles (but not the seasoning packets) from packages of instant ramen (you could use fresh noodles, too, if you prefer). But the bedrock of all great ramen is the broth, and here I used the slow cooker to make easy work of it. The broth in a good bowl of ramen should be rich, salty, supersavory, and so complex that it leaves you in disbelief, wondering how on earth a liquid could be filled with so much flavor.

The key to achieving that kind of irresistible soup broth in this slow-cooker version is slowly simmering a pork butt. The pork butt—a fatty cut from the shoulder of the hog—produces an intensely porky broth and loads of silky, savory meat to add back to the soup before serving.

Two powerhouse ingredients, miso and kombu, further bolster the broth's flavor. Miso—a paste made from fermented soybeans—adds an irreplaceable salty-sweet, savory depth to the broth and also gives it body, making it seem almost creamy. Good news: Miso has become more familiar to American home cooks and is usually available in well-stocked supermarkets.

Kombu, a type of dried kelp, may be harder to find, but it is a staple of Japanese soup making that's worth seeking out for this recipe. When steeped in a hot liquid for a short amount of time, it provides an instant boost of savory flavor (or umami). In this ramen, adding kombu turns an already great soup into something otherworldly. I hope you'll seek it out and try it in this recipe—and maybe even see what it can do to your other favorite soups, too.

Rich, tender pork is the crowning jewel of this savory noodle soup.

At the Fish Counter
Look for a center-cut, 1½-inch-thick, skinless salmon fillet. Without the skin, the fish cures faster and more evenly. Using center-cut salmon means that you don't have a tapered tail end that would cure unevenly; however, if your salmon fillet has the thin belly portion on the side attached, you can leave that on.

SLOW-COOKER MISO-PORK RAMEN
Serves 4 to 6
You can substitute 1¾ pounds of fresh ramen noodles for the dried. This recipe makes more pork than needed, but cooking the full amount is essential to the broth's flavor. Kombu can be found in well-stocked grocery stores, Asian markets, or online. We like to serve this soup with Soy-Marinated Eggs (page 32) and Sichuan Chili Oil, but plain soft-cooked eggs and toasted sesame oil are great, too. Our recipe for Sichuan Chili Oil is available for free for four months at CooksCountry.com/may20.

- 8 cups chicken broth
- ½ cup white miso
- 4 ounces shiitake mushrooms, stemmed and sliced thin
- 4 scallions, white and green parts separated, green parts sliced thin on bias
- 6 garlic cloves, smashed and peeled
- 1 (1½-inch) piece ginger, peeled and sliced into ½-inch-thick rounds
- 1 (2½-pound) boneless pork butt roast, trimmed
- ½ teaspoon pepper
- 1 (4-inch) square piece kombu (optional)
- 6 (3-ounce) packages ramen noodles, seasoning packets reserved for another use

1. Whisk broth and miso together in slow cooker. Add mushrooms, scallion whites, garlic, and ginger. Sprinkle pork with pepper and transfer to slow cooker. Cover and cook until pork is tender and registers 195 degrees, 4 to 6 hours on high or 8 to 10 hours on low. Transfer pork to cutting board and let rest for 20 minutes.

2. Meanwhile, add kombu, if using, to broth mixture in slow cooker and cook, covered, on high for 10 minutes. Using slotted spoon, remove and discard scallion whites, garlic, ginger, and kombu, leaving mushrooms in slow cooker.

3. Bring 4 quarts water to boil in large Dutch oven. Add noodles and cook until tender but still chewy. Drain noodles and divide evenly among serving bowls. Slice pork in half lengthwise, then slice crosswise ¼ inch thick. Ladle broth into bowls. Serve ramen topped with 3 or 4 slices of pork and scallion greens.

12-Inch Nonstick Skillets

Step 1: Buy the best skillet. Step 2: Treat it right. **by Kate Shannon**

KEY **Good** ★★★ **Fair** ★★ **Poor** ★

THERE'S NOTHING LIKE a good nonstick skillet. You can crack an egg into it and count on a perfect fried egg sliding out a few minutes later, even if you get distracted for a bit or are a little clumsy with your spatula. It's our go-to pan for all sorts of delicate and fast-cooking foods. We know which nonstick skillets we like: those with a slick and durable coating, a wide cooking surface, and a comfortable handle. Finding that several intriguing new models have hit the market recently, we gathered nine nonstick skillets and used them to make stir-fry, frittata, and pan-fried sole—recipes selected to test the pans' capacity, browning ability, and maneuverability. We also cooked eggs in the dry skillets back-to-back, stopping either when they began to stick or when we had made 50 consecutive eggs, both at the beginning and end of testing, to see if the nonstick coatings deteriorated with use.

All the pans' nonstick coatings were made with polytetrafluoroethylene (PTFE), a compound best known by the brand name Teflon. The exact names and formulations of the coatings varied, and manufacturers told us that they applied between two and five layers of these coatings to their skillets. Despite these differences, most skillets performed similarly. Every skillet was ovensafe to at least 400 degrees, and none of the coatings flaked or wore off. All the skillets aced our egg tests, both when the pans were brand-new and at the end of user testing. We also used a paring knife to see if making cuts in the skillets' cooking surfaces would result in scratching. All the pans were marred by scratches, proving that you should follow manufacturers' instructions and not use knives in nonstick cookware. We also recommend avoiding metal utensils.

Next we considered ease of use. When we cook in a nonstick skillet, we often move food around quickly—sliding it around the pan with a spatula or tossing it up in the air in a rolling motion. One skillet's walls were too short, and food went overboard. Another model featured tall, straight sides that were set at almost a 90-degree angle to the cooking surface. When we joggled the frittata over the walls and out of this pan, it wobbled and nearly belly flopped onto the plate. Frittatas slid easily out of every other skillet. The weight of each skillet was another major factor in our considerations. In general, lighter was better; our favorites weighed less than 3 pounds and were easy to lift and maneuver.

Two pans surpassed the rest, with broad, impressively nonstick surfaces; light and maneuverable designs; and walls just high enough to prevent spilling. Our overall favorite was the affordable OXO Good Grips Non-Stick Pro 12" Open Frypan. If you require an induction-compatible model, the All-Clad Stainless 12" Nonstick Fry Pan is an excellent, though more expensive, choice.

How to Take Care of Your Nonstick Cookware

If you don't properly care for these skillets, their coatings won't last long with regular use. For some tips on extending the life of your nonstick cookware, see "The Dos and Don'ts of Nonstick Cookware" at **CooksCountry.com/nonstick**.

Web subscribers can read the entire testing and complete chart at **CooksCountry.com/may20**.

HIGHLY RECOMMENDED

OXO Good Grips Non-Stick Pro 12" Open Frypan
Model: CW000960-003 **Price:** $42.49
Weight: 2.40 lb **Cooking Surface:** 9¾ in
Ovensafe to: 430°F **Induction Compatible:** No
Pros: Slick cooking surface, food never stuck, lightweight, easy to lift and maneuver, resisted denting, comfortable handle
Cons: Surface scratched when cuts were made in pan, not induction compatible

Nonstick Ability ★★★   **Capacity** ★★★   **Ease of Use** ★★★   **Durability** ★★½

All-Clad Stainless 12" Nonstick Fry Pan
Model: 4112 NS R2 **Price:** $181.49
Weight: 2.75 lb **Cooking Surface:** 9¼ in
Ovensafe to: 500°F **Induction Compatible:** Yes
Pros: Induction compatible, slick, durable, generous cooking surface, gently sloped walls, lightweight, sturdy, feels balanced
Cons: Uncomfortable handle, surface scratched when cuts were made in pan

Nonstick Ability ★★★   **Capacity** ★★★   **Ease of Use** ★★½   **Durability** ★★½

RECOMMENDED

T-Fal Professional Non-Stick Fry Pan
Model: H9090564 **Price:** $33.48
Weight: 2.50 lb **Cooking Surface:** 9¾ in
Pros: Spacious and slippery surface, lightweight, comfortable handle
Cons: Cooking surface is domed, so food slides to edges of pan; too wide to fit a 12-inch lid

Nonstick Ability ★★★
Capacity ★★★
Ease of Use ★★
Durability ★★½

Made In Stainless Steel Non Stick Frying Pan
Model: n/a **Price:** $95.00
Weight: 3.30 lb **Cooking Surface:** 9 in
Pros: Superslick surface that kept food from sticking, walls were perfect height
Cons: Felt unbalanced and heavy when we lifted pan full of food

Nonstick Ability ★★★
Capacity ★★★
Ease of Use ★★
Durability ★★½

Misen 12" Nonstick Skillet
Model: n/a **Price:** $65.00
Weight: 3.19 lb **Cooking Surface:** 9 in
Pros: Slick surface, spacious, good wall height
Cons: Silicone handle sleeve was shorter than the handle; pan felt heavy, unbalanced

Nonstick Ability ★★★
Capacity ★★★
Ease of Use ★★
Durability ★★½

RECOMMENDED WITH RESERVATIONS

Tramontina
PRO3004 12 In. Restaurant Fry Pan
Nonstick Ability ★★★ **Capacity** ★★★
Ease of Use ★½ **Durability** ★★

Le Creuset
Toughened Nonstick 12" Fry Pan
Nonstick Ability ★★★ **Capacity** ★★
Ease of Use ★★ **Durability** ★★½

NOT RECOMMENDED

Cuisinart Multiclad Pro Triple Ply
Stainless Cookware 12" Nonstick Skillet
Nonstick Ability ★★★ **Capacity** ★★★
Ease of Use ½ **Durability** ★★

Calphalon
Classic Nonstick 12-in. Fry Pan
Nonstick Ability ★★★ **Capacity** ★★
Ease of Use ★★ **Durability** ★½

Very) Dark
Chocolate Bars

e found a 90-percent-cacao bar that's more "beautiful" than bitter.

Emily Phares

RKER CHOCOLATE BARS—
se with 70- to 80-plus cacao per-
tages—are more popular than ever.
d very dark chocolate bars—those
h cacao percentages in the 90-plus
ge—not only contain less sugar
bar than lower-cacao chocolates
also offer a more nuanced and
netimes more complex chocolate
or, making them an ideal choice
chocolate connoisseurs and health
husiasts alike.

To experience these very dark
ocolates for ourselves, we selected
nationally available bars ranging
m 90 to 95 percent cacao and ate
m plain. While some tasters weren't
ially thrilled about eating very dark
ocolate (completely unsweetened
ocolate can be hard to stomach),
ny were delighted to discover that
ne of these bars, which contained
y small amounts of sugar, were
ually delicious.

Most of the bars we tasted had pleas-
, smooth textures, except for one
t was gritty and grainy. The gritty
was divisive; a few tasters loved the
ture, but others said it was "almost
eating sand." Our science research
tor said many factors contribute
a chocolate bar's texture. One is
ching, one of the last steps in the

manufacturing process, during which
the chocolate is heated and constantly
stirred. The result is a chocolate with
a very smooth texture. The company
that manufactures the gritty chocolate
we tasted does not conche. Most of the
other companies confirmed that their
chocolate had been conched, and we
found their bars to be much smoother.
Another factor: cocoa butter, the fat in
the cacao bean. Bars made with added
cocoa butter—more than the amount
existing naturally in the bean—are typically smoother than ones without added
cocoa butter. Indeed, we found that
bars with higher fat levels were much
smoother.

Although the bars had similar sugar
contents—roughly 2 to 3 grams per
40-gram serving—we saw a range of
bitterness. The experience of eating our
least favorite bar was "like biting into
a lemon," while our favorite chocolate
bar had a faint bitterness that was nicely
balanced with sweet, fruity notes. Our
science research editor said that apart
from its sugar content, a bar's bitterness
also corresponds to its ratio of cocoa
solids to cocoa butter (the two elements
that determine a chocolate bar's cacao
percentage). Fewer cocoa solids means
more cocoa butter—or fat—which
produces a less bitter chocolate.

Tasters also noted a range of flavors,
from stone fruit and berries to coffee
and espresso. Fermentation, drying,
and storing procedures can all influence
a chocolate's flavor, as can roasting.
Lightly roasted beans will often have
more acidity, which can impart fruitiness, and strongly roasted beans convey
toasty or fudgy flavors. Bean origin
matters, too. According to Megan
Giller, food writer and the author of
*Bean-to-Bar Chocolate: America's Craft
Chocolate Revolution* (2017), "Cocoa
beans have terroir, just like wine grapes
and coffee beans." Some chocolate is
single origin, meaning the cacao beans
used to make it come from only one location and may have flavors distinct to

Nutrition information
is based on a 40-gram
serving size.

Our Favorite

HIGHLY RECOMMENDED

Alter Eco 90% Deepest Dark
Super Blackout Organic
Chocolate Bar
Price: $2.99 for 2.65 oz ($1.13 per
oz), plus shipping
Fat: 24.2 g **Sugar:** 3.2 g **Cocoa Solids:** 11.8 g

Comments: Our winning bar had a "good balance
of bitter and sweet," with a "really nice, creamy
texture" that was impressively "smooth." We also
enjoyed the fruity undertones, with some tasters
noting hints of berries, cherries, and peaches. As
one taster put it, "What a beautiful chocolate!"

**AN IDEAL CHOICE
FOR CHOCOLATE
LOVERS AND HEALTH
ENTHUSIASTS ALIKE**

that region. Other products are made
from blends of beans sourced from
multiple places.

Our clear winner was Alter Eco
90% Deepest Dark Super Blackout
Organic Chocolate Bar. We loved this
bar's supersmooth texture and optimal
balance of bitter and sweet notes, with
fruity undertones. One taster summed
it up nicely: "I could eat a lot of this."

Web subscribers can read the entire
testing and see the complete chart
at **CooksCountry.com/may20**.

RECOMMENDED

Lindt EXCELLENCE 90% Cocoa
Price: $3.29 for 3.5 oz ($0.94 per oz)
Fat: 22 g **Sugar:** 3 g **Cocoa Solids:** 14 g
Comments: This chocolate was "surprisingly
nice to eat" despite its mild sweetness, and
we liked its "well-rounded chocolate flavor." It
tasted "balanced" and had a smooth texture.

Ghirardelli Moonlight Mystique 92%
Intense Dark Bar
Price: $2.50 for 3.5 oz ($0.71 per oz)
Fat: 23.5 g **Sugar:** 2.4 g **Cocoa Solids:** 13.3 g
Comments: Another "smooth" bar, this one
offered "rich cocoa" and "fruity" notes; some
tasters even detected a hint of coffee.

RECOMMENDED WITH RESERVATIONS

Madecasse 92% Pure Dark
Chocolate Bar
Price: $3.99 for 2.64 oz ($1.51 per oz)
Fat: 21.3 g **Sugar:** 3.2 g **Cocoa Solids:** 15.5 g
Comments: Tasters noted that this "extremely
dark" bar tasted "pleasantly bitter," and they
liked its "silky" texture.

Taza 95% Wicked Dark Bar
Price: $5.00 for 2.5 oz ($2.00 per oz)
Fat: 16 g **Sugar:** 2.3 g **Cocoa Solids:** 22 g
Comments: This bar's "gritty" texture set it
apart from the rest. Tasters liked its "very
interesting, fruity flavor" and the "balance of
sweet and bitter."

Soy-Marinated Eggs

SOY-MARINATED EGGS
Makes 8 eggs

Mirin can be found in your super-market's Asian foods section. The soy marinade can be reused to marinate up to three batches of soft-cooked eggs; it can be refrigerated for up to one week and frozen for up to one month.

- 1 cup soy sauce
- ¼ cup mirin
- 2 scallions, sliced thin
- 2 tablespoons grated fresh ginger
- 2 tablespoons sugar
- 2 garlic cloves, minced
- 8 large eggs

1. Combine soy sauce, mirin, scallions, ginger, sugar, and garlic in small saucepan and bring to simmer over medium-high heat. Remove from heat and stir in 1 cup cold water; set aside.
2. Bring 3 quarts water to boil in large saucepan over high heat. Fill large bowl halfway with ice and water.
3. Using spider skimmer or slotted spoon, gently lower eggs into boiling water and cook for 7 minutes. Transfer eggs to ice bath and let cool for 5 minutes.
4. Gently tap eggs on counter to crack shells. Begin peeling off shell at wider end of egg, making sure to break membrane between shell and egg white. Working under gently running water, carefully peel membranes and shells off eggs.
5. Combine soy sauce mixture and eggs in large zipper-lock bag and place bag in medium bowl. Press out as much air as possible from bag so eggs are fully submerged in liquid, then seal bag. Refrigerate for at least 3 hours or up to 4 hours (any longer and eggs may become too salty). Remove eggs from marinade using slotted spoon. Serve.

We're looking for recipes that you treasure—the ones that have been handed down in your family for a generation or more, that always come out for the holidays, and that have earned a place at your table and in your heart through many years of meals. Send us the recipes that spell home to you. Visit CooksCountry.com/recipe_submission (or write to Heirloom Recipes, Cook's Country, 21 Drydock Avenue, Suite 210E, Boston, MA 02210) and tell us a little about the recipe. Include your name and address. If we print your recipe, you'll receive a free one-year subscription to Cook's Country.

COMING NEXT ISSUE

*Summer is coming, and we'll help you throw the perfect backyard barbecue with recipes such as **Grilled Chicken Teriyaki** (a Seattle favorite), **North Carolina Barbecue Pork**, homemade **Sweet Pickle Relish**, and beautiful **Mixed Berry Buckle**. In the mood for some big, bold flavors? Try **Slow-Cooker Adobo-Braised Beef**, **S'mores Bars**, **Cashew Chicken**, **Couscous Tabbouleh**, or **French Bread Pizza**. Yum!*

FIND THE ROOSTER!

A tiny version of this rooster has been hidden in a photo in the pages of this issue. Write to us with its location, and we'll enter you in a random drawing. T first correct entry drawn will win a cop The Complete Cook's Country TV Sho Cookbook, and each of the next five w receive a free one-year subscription to our website. To enter, visit CooksCoun com/rooster by April 30, 2020, or writ to Rooster AM20, Cook's Country, 21 Drydock Avenue, Suite 210E, Boston, 02210. Include your name and address Lynda Reaves of Inola, Oklahoma, four the rooster in the December/January 2 issue on page 10.

WEB EXTRAS

Free for four months online at
CooksCountry.com/may20

Asparagus Baked in Foil with Parmes and Thyme
Browned Butter Frosting
Pretzel Cake Layers
Sichuan Chili Oil

READ US ON IPAD

Download the Cook's Country app for iPad and start a free trial subscription purchase a single issue of the magazir issues are enhanced with Cooking Moo slide shows that provide step-by-step instructions for completing recipes, plu expanded reviews and ratings. Go to CooksCountry.com/iPad to download app through iTunes.

RC=Recipe Card

TO MAKE THIS CAKE, YOU WILL NEED:

- 1 (13.4-ounce) can dulce de leche
- 1¼ cups heavy cream, chilled
- 1 recipe Pretzel Cake Layers*
- 1 recipe Browned Butter Frosting*
- 1½ ounces thin pretzel sticks, broken roughly in half (1 cup)
- 8 small pretzel twists

FOR THE FILLING:

Measure out ¼ cup dulce de leche and set aside. Using stand mixer fitted with whisk attachment, whip cream and remaining dulce de leche on low speed until combined, about 1 minute. Increase speed to medium-high and whip until stiff peaks form, 2½ to 3 minutes (do not overwhip).

TO ASSEMBLE:

Using long serrated knife, cut 1 horizontal line around sides of each cake layer; following scored line, cut each layer into 2 even layers. Place 1 cake layer on platter. Spread 1 cup filling evenly over top, right to edge of cake. Repeat with 2 more cake layers, pressing lightly to adhere and spreading 1 cup filling evenly over each layer. Top with remaining cake layer. Refrigerate for 45 minutes.

Measure out 1¼ cups frosting and set aside. Spread thin layer of remaining frosting over top and sides of cake. Refrigerate until frosting is firm, 30 to 45 minutes. Spread remaining frosting evenly over top and sides of cake. Arrange pretzel sticks upright along bottom of cake.

Fill pastry bag fitted with large closed star tip with reserved 1¼ cups frosting. Pipe 8 rosettes around top edge of cake. Place pretzel twists between rosettes. Microwave reserved ¼ cup dulce de leche in small bowl at 50 percent power for 30 seconds, then transfer to clean pastry bag fitted with ⅛-inch round tip. Pipe dulce de leche in circles in center of cake. Serve.

*Our recipes for Pretzel Cake Layers and Browned Butter Frosting are available for free for four months at CooksCountry.com/pretzelcake.

Salted Caramel Pretzel Cake

Pretzels and caramel are a perfect pair for a cake that's both salty and sweet.

by Sarah Ewald

INSIDE THIS ISSUE

Cook's Country

PICK YOUR PORK

Lexington style:
*coarse chop,
tangy-sweet sauce*

**North
Carolina
BBQ Pork**

Eastern style:
*fine chop,
spicy-vinegary
sauce*

NE/JULY 2020
95 U.S. / $7.95 CANADA

71486 02742 3

SPLAY UNTIL JULY 7, 2020

**AMERICA'S
TEST KITCHEN**

07>

LETTER FROM THE EDITOR

Illustration: Hannah Jacobs

WHEN I WAS growing up, I often spent a couple of weeks during the summer with my grandparents, who lived in a small New England town with white clapboard houses and old brick civic buildings and a beautiful little Carnegie library, where my grandmother was head librarian. They both grew up in remote rural areas, farm kids, so they ate seasonally and locally as a matter of habit and necessity, not as a matter of choice. Berries came around in the summer, and if you didn't have the foresight to put them in jars or freeze them, those were the only berries you'd see all year. Gram would sometimes take us into the woods to pick raspberries, blackberries, and blueberries.

She'd tell us it was for fun, which it was, but it was also for practicality: More pickers meant more berries, and my speedy hands could fill a bucket fast. I'd sometimes get scraped up by the bushes, but the plump, sweet berries, still warm from the sunshine, helped salve the discomfort.

We never put them in jars though. We'd eat most of them out in the field. Then Gram would assemble and freeze a few blueberry pies to bake over the course of the year, often for breakfast. She'd make muffins and quick breads, too, and sometimes a crumble or a crisp or a grunt or a slump or a buckle.

If you've never had a buckle, which is a lot like a coffee cake only less fussy and more friendly, now is your chance. Turn to page 23 to see our new recipe by Mark Huxsoll.

TUCKER SHAW

Editor in Chief

P.S. JOIN OUR TEAM

Did you know that our recipes aren't just tested in our kitchens here but in home kitchens across the country? More than 20,000 home cooks help us work out the final kinks in our recipes by volunteering to cook up to three recipes a month and giving us unvarnished feedback. Did it work? Did it turn out well? Did you like it? Unless 80 percent of people say they'd make the recipe again, we won't publish it. We'd love for you to join in! Visit **CooksCountry.com/recipetesting**.

READY TO TAKE IT OUTSIDE?

The Complete Summer Cookbook

In this book, you'll find all you need for casual patio meals prepared entirely on the grill (from meat to vegetables to pizza). Visited the farmers' market? Find ideas for main dishes as well as sides inspired by the seasonal bounty, plus the best fruit desserts worth turning on the oven for. To end your meal on a cooler note, turn to a chapter on icebox desserts and no-bake sweets. Order your copy at **AmericasTestKitchen.com/summer**.

 Find us on **Facebook**
facebook.com/CooksCountry

 Find us on **Instagram**
instagram.com/CooksCountry

 Follow us on **Pinterest**
pinterest.com/TestKitchen

 Follow us on **Twitter**
twitter.com/TestKitchen

Cook's Country

Chief Executive Officer David Nussbaum
Chief Creative Officer Jack Bishop
Editor in Chief Tucker Shaw
Executive Managing Editor Todd Meier
Executive Food Editor Bryan Roof
Deputy Editor Scott Kathan
Deputy Food Editor Morgan Bolling
Senior Editor Cecelia Jenkins
Associate Editor Matthew Fairman
Test Cooks Mark Huxsoll, Amanda Luchtel, Jessica Rudolph
Photo Team Manager Alli Berkey
Lead Test Cook, Photo Team Eric Haessler
Assistant Test Cooks, Photo Team Hannah Fenton, Jacqueline Gochenouer, Gina McCreadie, Christa West
Copy Editors Christine Campbell, April Poole, Rachel Schow
Managing Editor, Web Mari Levine
Digital Content Producer Danielle Lapierre
Contributing Editor Eva Katz
Senior Science Research Editor Paul Adams
Hosts & Executive Editors, Television Bridget Lancaster, Julia Collin Davison

Executive Editors, Tastings & Testings Hannah Crowley, Lisa McManus
Senior Editors, Tastings & Testings Lauren Savoie, Kate Shannon
Associate Editor, Tastings & Testings Miye Bromberg
Assistant Editors, Tastings & Testings Chase Brightwell, Riddley Gemperlein-Schirm, Carolyn Grillo

Creative Director John Torres
Photography Director Julie Cote
Art Director Maggie Edgar
Associate Art Director Kristen Jones
Art Director, Tastings & Testings Marissa Angelone
Senior Staff Photographers Steve Klise, Daniel J. van Acker
Staff Photographer Kevin White
Photography Producer Meredith Mulcahy

Senior Director, Creative Operations Alice Carpenter
Senior Editor, Special Projects Christie Morrison
Senior Manager, Publishing Operations Taylor Argenzio
Imaging Manager Lauren Robbins
Production & Imaging Specialists Tricia Neumyer, Dennis Amanda Yong
Deputy Editor, Editorial Operations Megan Ginsberg
Assistant Editors, Editorial Operations Tess Berger, Sara Zatopek
Test Kitchen Director Erin McMurrer
Assistant Test Kitchen Director Alexxa Benson
Test Kitchen Manager Meridith Lippard
Test Kitchen Facilities Manager Kayce Vanpelt
Senior Kitchen Assistant Receiver Heather Tolmie
Senior Kitchen Assistant Shopper Avery Lowe

Chief Financial Officer Jackie McCauley Ford
Senior Manager, Customer Support Tim Quinn
Customer Support Specialist Mitchell Axelson

Chief Digital Officer Fran Middleton
VP, Marketing Natalie Vinard
Director, Audience Acquisition & Partnerships Evan Stein
Director, Social Media Marketing & Emerging Platforms Kathryn Przybyla
Social Media Manager Charlotte Errity
Social Media Coordinators Sarah Sandler, Norma Tentori

Chief Revenue Officer Sara Domville

Director, Public Relations & Communications Brian Frank

Senior VP, Human Resources & Organizational Development Colleen Zelina
Human Resources Manager Jason Lynott

Food Stylist Elle Simone

Circulation Services PubWorX ProCirc

...rica's Test Kitchen has been teaching home
...ks how to be successful in the kitchen since 1993.
...mission is to empower and inspire confidence,
...munity, and creativity in the kitchen. Millions
...ch our two shows on public television; read
...two flagship magazines (*Cook's Country* and
...*'s Illustrated*); and rely on our books, websites,
...os, podcasts, and educational products for
...lren. America's Test Kitchen is located in a
...e-of-the-art Boston facility with 15,000 square
... of test kitchen and studio space. Learn more at
...ericasTestKitchen.com.

9   12

7

Cook's Country magazine (ISSN 1552-1990), number 93, is published bimonthly by America's Test Kitchen Limited Partnership, 21 Drydock Avenue, Suite 210E, Boston, MA 02210. Copyright 2020
America's Test Kitchen Limited Partnership. Periodicals postage paid at Boston, MA, and additional mailing offices, USPS #023453. Publications Mail Agreement No. 40020778. Return undeliverable Canadian addresses to P.O. Box 875, Station A, Windsor, ON N9A 6P2. POSTMASTER: Send address changes to *Cook's Country*, PO Box 6018, Harlan, IA 51593-1518. For subscription and gift
subscription orders, subscription inquiries, or change of address notices, visit AmericasTestKitchen.com/support, call 800-526-8447 in the U.S. or 515-237-3663 from outside the U.S., or write to
us at *Cook's Country*, P.O. Box 6018, Harlan, IA 51593-1518. PRINTED IN THE USA.

22

by Cecelia Jenkins

Twice the Tomato?

My tube of tomato paste says that it is "double concentrated." Should I use only half the amount called for in recipes?
–*Norma Dudley, Lynnwood, Wash.*

Of the tomato pastes sold in American supermarkets, most tubed pastes are made in Italy and most canned pastes are made in the United States. The term "double concentrated" refers to an Italian manufacturing method that differs from the method used to make canned pastes but yields essentially the same product (and concentration). In Italy, manufacturers heat ground tomatoes to a lower temperature, and the resulting tomato paste undergoes a longer evaporation period (hence "double concentrated"). In the United States, manufacturers heat the tomatoes to a higher temperature and evaporate them for a shorter time—two different ways to arrive at the same place. In recipes, double-concentrated tomato paste is interchangeable with single-concentrated paste. In a recent tasting, we ultimately recommended all the tomato pastes we tried, both from tubes and from cans. We do, however, prefer tubed tomato paste for its ease of use and storage.

THE BOTTOM LINE: The term "double concentrated," which appears on the packaging of some tomato pastes, refers to the manufacturing method, not the concentration of the tomato paste. You can use double-concentrated and regular tomato pastes interchangeably.

"DOUBLE" IN NAME ONLY
Same concentration as regular paste

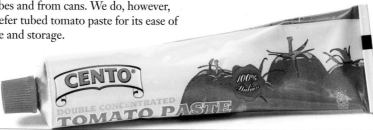

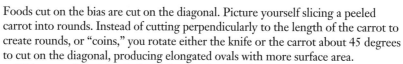

Biased Thinking

Some of your recipes call for slicing foods such as carrots and scallions on the bias. What does that mean?
–*Ted Bachmann, St. Augustine, Fla.*

Foods cut on the bias are cut on the diagonal. Picture yourself slicing a peeled carrot into rounds. Instead of cutting perpendicularly to the length of the carrot to create rounds, or "coins," you rotate either the knife or the carrot about 45 degrees to cut on the diagonal, producing elongated ovals with more surface area.

This type of cut is typical with longer foods such as carrots, baguettes, scallions, cucumbers, asparagus, zucchini, and summer squash. You can take this concept even further by angling the plane of your knife so that your cutting strokes hit the cutting board on the diagonal.

THE BOTTOM LINE: Slicing foods on the bias involves rotating and/or angling your knife to produce slices with more surface area.

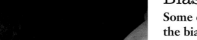

Dish Dilemma

What's the difference between a baking pan and a baking dish?
–*Emily Muldoon, Andover, Mass.*

When we call for a baking pan in our recipes, we're referring to a metal pan, ideally one with straight sides and crisp corners that will give well-defined, professional-looking edges to baked goods. Our favorite 13 by 9-inch metal baking pan, from Williams Sonoma, is nonstick and has a gold color that produces perfectly browned baked goods (an 8-inch square version is also available). The only downside to this pan is that the nonstick coating can scratch and that it's ovensafe only up to 450 degrees (it's not broiler-safe).

Baking dishes, on the other hand, are those made of either tempered glass or ceramic, with rounded corners to make it easy to scoop out soupy desserts and casseroles. Neither glass nor ceramic reacts with acidic foods like some uncoated metals, and both are scratchproof and safe to use with metal utensils. Glass is transparent, so you can easily track browning. The downside for glass dishes is that they are ovensafe only up to around 425 degrees, can't go under the broiler, and shouldn't be exposed to sudden temperature changes. Our favorite glass dish is the Pyrex Easy Grab 3-Quart Oblong Baking Dish.

Some ceramic baking dishes can withstand direct-heat cooking such as broiling (up to 550 degrees) because the material is hardened by being fired in a kiln at temperatures well over 1,000 degrees. Our favorite ceramic baking dish is Mrs. Anderson's Baking Lasagna Pan with Handle (Rose), which measures about 13 inches by 9 inches.

Season It

Can I use unseasoned rice vinegar in a recipe that calls for seasoned rice vinegar?
–*Morgan Affleck, Arvada, Colo.*

Rice vinegar is made from steamed rice. Also called rice wine vinegar (not to be confused with rice wine), it has a mild acidity and gentle sweetness. It is available both seasoned and unseasoned. Because the seasoned version contains added salt and sugar, we usually call for the unseasoned kind so that we can control the seasoning in a dish.

That said, through testing we came up with a way to add "seasoning" to convert plain rice vinegar into a facsimile of the seasoned version.

HOMEMADE SEASONED RICE VINEGAR
Makes ½ cup
Table salt dissolves most readily here, but if all you have is kosher salt, increase the amount to 2 tablespoons.

- ½ cup unseasoned rice vinegar
- ¼ cup sugar
- 1 tablespoon table salt

1. Combine all ingredients in bowl and let sit for 5 minutes.
2. Whisk constantly until sugar and salt dissolve, about 3 minutes. (Seasoned vinegar can be stored in airtight container at room temperature for up to 1 week.)

THE BOTTOM LINE: Baking pans are made of metal, and baking dishes are made of glass or ceramic.

OUR FAVORITE BAKING PAN AND BAKING DISHES

BAKING PAN	GLASS BAKING DISH	CERAMIC BAKING DISH
Williams Sonoma Goldtouch Nonstick Rectangular Cake Pan, 9" x 13", $33	**Pyrex** Easy Grab 3-Quart Oblong Baking Dish, $7	**Mrs. Anderson's Baking** Lasagna Pan with Handle (Rose), $50
Use for: • Cakes • Brownies • Sticky buns	**Use for:** • Stuffings • Cobblers	**Use for:** • Lasagna • Gratins • Broiling
Don't use for: • Anything that needs to be cut in the pan with a sharp knife	**Don't use for:** • Dishes that require high heat or the broiler	**Don't use for:** • Foods where you need to track the bottom browning

Infuse It and Reuse It

—Leslie Goodman, Saratoga, N.Y.

I don't keep cheesecloth on hand, so when a soup recipe calls for making a spice bundle (bouquet garni), I put my tea infuser to work instead. It's a cinch compared to tying up the spices and herbs myself, and it's reusable, so there's no waste. Plus, it comes with a little tether that I can just wrap around the pot handle for easy removal later.

More Appealing Garlic Peeling

—John Dutton, Dover, N.H.

I recently saw an ad for a silicone garlic peeler and realized I might already own something that could do the job just as well: my silicone baking mat. I grabbed a handful of unpeeled garlic cloves; rolled them up inside the mat; and then, using both of my hands, pressed and rolled them back and forth. To my delight, the silicone baking mat peeled the garlic just like the garlic peeler had in the commercial. Maybe now I'll get some more use out of the baking mat.

Bring Home the Bacon (and Freeze It)

—Devon Starhill, Plano, Texas

Around my house, bacon is a pantry staple, and I like to have it at the ready at all times. So when I get it from the store, I'll buy two pounds—1 pound to cook into strips for BLTs or breakfast and 1 pound to cut up into roughly ½-inch pieces and freeze (I freeze it on a plate first so that it doesn't stick together, and then I transfer it to a zipper-lock bag). Then I have cut-up bacon ready to cook straight from the freezer for salads, pastas, baked potatoes, etc. It's easier than trying to peel off a couple of strips from the frozen mass and cutting them up every time I need just a little bit.

Finding a Good Pasta Substitute

by Carolyn Grillo

DUE TO THE demand driven by diverse culinary restrictions, chickpeas, lentils, and dried beans have been popping up in everything from chips and burgers to bread crumbs. Another food category they've entered? Pasta.

To find out if gluten-free legume pasta was worth the hype, we tasted eight nationally available products, including two chickpea pastas, four lentil pastas, one mung bean pasta, and one pasta made with both chickpeas and lentils. The pastas were available in an assortment of shapes, but for the sake of consistency, we settled on widely available rotini or spiral shapes. We tasted the pastas plain; with our Quick Tomato Sauce; and in our recipe for Pasta with Pesto, Potatoes, and Green Beans.

PRODUCT TASTING

We can fully recommend three of the products in our lineup, but Modern Table Rotini, made from lentils, was the best. This pasta had a "great chewy, real-pasta texture and a nicely seasoned, buttery flavor." It was the only sample in our lineup that contained rice flour, which gave it a more neutral flavor, and pea protein, which enhanced its cohesiveness and chew. One taster remarked, "I would have no idea this wasn't regular pasta."

RECOMMENDED		TASTERS' NOTES
Modern Table Rotini **Price:** $3.67 for 8-oz box ($0.46 per oz) **Ingredients:** Red lentil flour, white rice, pea protein **Protein:** 11 g **Fiber:** 3 g		Tasters loved that this pasta "held its shape but had some chew." It's the only product in our lineup that contained rice flour, which gave it a neutral flavor.
Banza Chickpea Rotini **Price:** $2.86 for 8-oz box ($0.36 per oz) **Ingredients:** Chickpeas, tapioca, pea protein, xanthan gum **Protein:** 13 g **Fiber:** 5 g		The flavor of this pasta was "neutral" and "buttery." Our tasters liked it better when served with pesto than when served with tomato sauce.
Chickapea Spirals **Price:** $3.88 for 8-oz box ($0.49 per oz) **Ingredients:** Organic chickpea flour, organic lentil flour **Protein:** 15 g **Fiber:** 8 g		Tasters enjoyed this pasta with both tomato sauce and pesto. One noted that its flavor was "not too strong." However, its texture "becomes a bit mushy when chewed."

RECOMMENDED WITH RESERVATIONS		
Barilla Chickpea Rotini **Price:** $3.25 for 8.8-oz box ($0.37 per oz) **Ingredients:** Chickpea flour **Protein:** 11 g **Fiber:** 8 g		This pasta clashed with the acidic tomato sauce but fared better with pesto. Many tasters noted a "crumbly" texture that "fell apart."
Tolerant Foods Green Lentil Rotini **Price:** $3.99 for 8-oz box ($0.50 per oz) **Ingredients:** Organic green lentil flour **Protein:** 14 g **Fiber:** 6 g		This sample's flavor was "neutral in a good way" when tried with each sauce. But tasters still found the texture "too firm."
Barilla Red Lentil Rotini **Price:** $6.20 for 8.8-oz box ($0.70 per oz) **Ingredients:** Red lentil flour **Protein:** 13 g **Fiber:** 6 g		Tasters liked this pasta's "pleasant lentil flavor," but it had textural issues. It was "grainy," "dry," and "mealy."
Explore Cuisine Mung Bean Rotini **Price:** $4.50 for 8-oz box ($0.56 per oz) **Ingredients:** Organic mung bean flour **Protein:** 13 g **Fiber:** 6 g		This pasta had "a pretty strong flavor compared with the others." When eaten plain, it was "grassy-tasting with a bitter edge."
Ancient Harvest POW! Pasta Red Lentil Rotini **Price:** $2.99 for 8-oz box ($0.37 per oz) **Ingredients:** Red lentil flour, organic quinoa flour **Protein:** 14 g **Fiber:** 7 g		This sample's flavor was "very neutral" with a "mild buttery flavor." It contained quinoa flour, which helped retain moisture, but it was still "gritty" and "grainy."

Nutrition information based on 2-ounce serving

Web subscribers can see the complete results chart at **CooksCountry.com/jul20.**

Charcoal Snake
This simple arrangement of carefully counted charcoal briquettes provides a long-burning, low, smoky fire that you need to reload only once for this recipe.

TWO LAYERS OF 60 BRIQUETTES WITH 6-INCH GAP

EASTERN N.C. STYLE
+ Finer chop, thinner sauce
+ Best served with collard greens, coleslaw, and cornbread

North Carolina Barbecue Pork

Eastern style or Lexington style? Plate or sandwich? Use our recipes to choose your own N.C. BBQ adventure.

by Morgan Bolling

WHEN YOU'RE TALKING barbecue in North Carolina, you're talking pork. But that's just the beginning: Different parts of the state treat the pork differently. I reached out to food historian and barbecue expert Robert Moss for context.

Moss explained that pitmasters in the eastern part of the state traditionally cook whole hogs on open pits. But in the area in and around Lexington, closer to the middle of the state, they usually cook hulking bone-in pork shoulders—often several at a time—in closed brick pits.

Both styles use low, direct heat and plenty of smoke, ideally from smoldering hickory logs. There are distinctions in how the pork is served and sauced, too, but I'll get to those in a moment.

I set out with an audacious goal: to emulate each of these two styles using a single method, with a recipe engineered for a backyard grill.

After some initial tests, I opted for a smoking technique we've used before at *Cook's Country*: a charcoal snake (see "Charcoal Snake"). With a water-filled pan directly below the pork to moderate the grill's temperature, I was able to get the pork cooked through with only one charcoal reload. The

> **Got buns? See the sandwiches on the cover!**

meat was mostly tender, but its exterior char was too dark and bitter-tasting.

The fix was pulling the pork off the grill and wrapping it in aluminum foil when it reached 170 degrees. This gave the meat 4 to 5 hours to absorb smoke and get nice and crusty on the outside before it was wrapped; the foil prevented further browning while allowing the pork to finish cooking to doneness (200 degrees). Pausing to wrap the pork also provided the perfect opportunity to refuel the snake. Once the pork registered 200 degrees, I pulled it off the grill, still wrapped, to rest for 1½ hours to let the juices inside redistribute.

The pork was cooked perfectly, but I still had work to do. Moss explained that in eastern North Carolina you're more likely to get finely chopped whole hog 'cue, while in Lexington people can choose "chopped, sliced, or chopped coarse with the option to request outside brown" (aka extra smoky bark). And while the sauces in both parts of the state are tangy, eastern North Carolina sauce should be simply "salty, fiery, and vinegary." Lexington-style sauce contains a little ketchup, which makes it redder, sweeter, and a touch thicker.

On a sandwich or on a plate? The choice is yours

NORTH CAROLINA BARBECUE PORK

Serves 8 to 10

We developed this recipe using a 22-inch Weber kettle grill. Pork butt roast is often labeled Boston butt in the supermarket. Plan ahead: The pork butt must be seasoned at least 18 hours before it is cooked.

- 3 **tablespoons kosher salt**
- 1½ **tablespoons pepper**
- 1 **(6-pound) bone-in pork butt roast, with ¼-inch fat cap**
- 1 **(13 by 9-inch) disposable aluminum pan**
- 4 **(3-inch) wood chunks**
- 1 **recipe Lexington-Style Barbecue Sauce or Eastern North Carolina–Style Barbecue Sauce**

1. Combine salt and pepper in bowl. Place pork on large sheet of plastic wrap and sprinkle all over with salt mixture. Wrap tightly with plastic and refrigerate for 18 to 24 hours.
2. Open bottom grill vent completely.

Set up charcoal snake: Arrange 60 briquettes, 2 briquettes wide, around perimeter of grill, overlapping slightly so briquettes are touching, leaving 6-inch gap between ends of snake. Place second layer of 60 briquettes, also 2 briquettes wide, on top of first. (Completed snake should be 2 briquettes wide by 2 briquettes high.)
3. Starting 4 inches from 1 end of snake, evenly space wood chunks on top of snake. Place disposable pan in center of grill so short end of pan runs parallel to gap in snake. Fill pan with 4 cups water.
4. Light chimney starter filled with 15 briquettes. When coals are partially covered with ash, pour over 1 end of snake. Make sure lit coals touch only 1 end of snake. Use tongs if necessary to move any coals that touch other end of snake.
5. Set cooking grate in place. Clean and oil cooking grate. Unwrap pork and position fat side down over water pan. Insert temperature probe into

thickest part of pork. Cover grill, positioning lid vent over gap in snake, and open lid vent completely. Cook, without opening grill, until pork registers 170 degrees, 4 to 5 hours.
6. Place 2 large sheets of aluminum foil on rimmed baking sheet. Remove probe from pork. Using oven mitts, lift pork and transfer to center of 1 sheet of foil, fat side down. Wrap tightly with first sheet of foil, minimizing air pockets between foil and pork. Wrap with second sheet of foil. (Use additional foil, if necessary, to completely wrap pork.) Foil wrap should be airtight. Make small mark on foil with marker to keep track of fat side.
7. Remove cooking grate. Starting at still-unlit end of snake, pour 2 quarts unlit briquettes about one-third of way around perimeter of grill over gap in snake and spent coals. Replace cooking grate. Return wrapped pork

to grill over water pan, fat side down. Reinsert probe into thickest part of pork. Cover grill and continue to cook until pork registers 200 degrees, 1 to 1½ hours longer.
8. Remove probe. Transfer pork to carving board, fat side up, and let rest in foil for 1½ hours. Remove bone from pork. For Lexington style, chop pork with cleaver into 1-inch pieces. For eastern North Carolina style, chop pork into ¼-inch pieces. Toss with ⅔ cup sauce. Serve, passing remaining sauce separately.

Our recipes for the coleslaws shown on the plates here—Creamy Buttermilk Coleslaw and Carolina Red Slaw—are available for free for four months at **CooksCountry.com/jul20**.

EASTERN NORTH CAROLINA–STYLE BARBECUE SAUCE

Makes about 2½ cups

This sauce is meant to be tangy and spicy to balance the rich smoked pork. One 12-ounce bottle of Texas Pete Original Hot Sauce will yield more than enough for this recipe.

- 1½ **cups cider vinegar**
- 1 **cup Texas Pete Original Hot Sauce**
- ¼ **cup packed light brown sugar**
- 2 **teaspoons kosher salt**
- 1 **teaspoon pepper**
- 1 **teaspoon red pepper flakes**

Whisk all ingredients together in bowl.

LEXINGTON-STYLE BARBECUE SAUCE

Makes about 2½ cups

This sauce is meant to be tangy and salty to balance the rich smoked pork.

- 2 **cups cider vinegar**
- 1 **cup ketchup**
- 2 **teaspoons granulated garlic**
- 2 **teaspoons pepper**
- 1½ **teaspoons kosher salt**
- 1 **teaspoon red pepper flakes**

Combine all ingredients in small saucepan and bring to boil over medium-high heat. Reduce heat to medium-low and simmer for 5 minutes. Transfer sauce to bowl and let cool completely.

LEXINGTON STYLE

+ Coarser chop, thicker sauce
+ Best served with hush puppies, french fries, and red slaw

Brighter, Fresher Succotash

Let's let summertime shine. **by Morgan Bolling**

SUCCOTASH, A SAVORY medley of sweet corn, beans, and zucchini or summer squash, should taste clean and fresh. But all too often it is under-seasoned, overloaded with dairy, or muddy—not good. When seasonal produce is at its best, it should shine.

To begin my testing, I made five recipes for succotash that either omitted or restrained the cream and butter. Most tasted like lackluster sautéed mixed vegetables. Our favorite tasted the freshest and featured raw corn, butter beans, zucchini, and tomatoes tossed in a vinegar-based dressing.

Inspired by this, I auditioned a variety of dressings and landed on an ultrasimple, refreshing white wine vinaigrette. I found that if I let the zucchini and tomatoes soak in this dressing for a few minutes before I added the rest of the ingredients, the vegetables softened a bit and tasted more deeply seasoned.

Testing revealed that the flavor of fresh corn was far superior to that of canned or frozen—no surprise there. But rather than leave the kernels raw, I browned them in a skillet to bring out more of their sweetness. Fresh basil added its licorice-like flavor, and scallions contributed a light savoriness and a pop of green.

I knew that I wanted either lima or butter beans here, so I developed versions using both (the butter beans were canned, the lima beans frozen). And I made a third iteration with chickpeas and dill to give you three variations on this simple and fresh summer staple.

Bean Primer

Our succotash recipes here use the following three varieties of beans.

BUTTER BEAN
Creamy and mild

CHICKPEA (GARBANZO BEAN)
Nutty and firm

LIMA BEAN
Soft and earthy

SUCCOTASH SALAD WITH BUTTER BEANS AND BASIL
Serves 4 to 6
Do not use frozen or canned corn for this recipe. Fresh basil is a must.

- ⅓ cup extra-virgin olive oil, divided
- ¼ cup white wine vinegar
- 2 teaspoons table salt, divided
- 1 teaspoon pepper
- 1 (15-ounce) can butter beans, rinsed
- 8 ounces cherry tomatoes, halved
- 1 zucchini, cut into ½-inch chunks
- 4 scallions, sliced thin
- 4 ears corn, kernels cut from cobs (3 cups)
- 1 garlic clove, minced
- 2 tablespoons chopped fresh basil

1. Whisk ¼ cup oil, vinegar, 1½ teaspoons salt, and pepper together in large bowl. Add butter beans, tomatoes, zucchini, and scallions and toss to combine.
2. Heat remaining oil in 12-inch nonstick skillet over medium-high heat until shimmering. Add corn and remaining ½ teaspoon salt and cook, stirring occasionally, until softened and just beginning to brown, 5 to 7 minutes. Add garlic and cook until fragrant, about 30 seconds.
3. Transfer corn mixture to bowl with butter bean mixture and toss to combine. Let sit for at least 30 minutes to allow flavors to meld. (Salad can be covered with plastic wrap and refrigerated for up to 2 days.)
4. Stir in basil and season with salt and pepper to taste. Serve.

SUCCOTASH SALAD WITH CHICKPEAS AND DILL
Substitute 1 (15-ounce) can rinsed chickpeas for butter beans, lemon juice for vinegar (2 lemons), and fresh dill for basil.

SUCCOTASH SALAD WITH LIMA BEANS AND CILANTRO
Add 1 tablespoon honey to oil mixture in step 1. Substitute 1½ cups thawed frozen lima beans for butter beans, ¼ teaspoon red pepper flakes for pepper, and fresh cilantro for basil.

Lightly browning the freshly stripped corn kernels amplifies their sweetness.

Grow Together, Go Together

You'd have a hard time coming up with a list of three vegetables that go together better than corn, beans, and squash—and that affinity doesn't exist only on the plate. It exists in the garden, too.

This textbook example of "companion gardening" is perfectly balanced. As stalks of corn grow tall, they offer beans a trellis-like structure to climb without compromising their own productivity. The beans also help stabilize the stalks in windy conditions. Squat squash plants grow around the base of the two, deterring pests with their fuzzy, prickly leaves and blocking sunlight from the soil to inhibit pesky weeds. What's more, the three vegetables produced by these plants provide excellent nutrition, including all nine essential amino acids.

Native Americans have taken advantage of this relationship for millennia; the three crops have been called the "Three Sisters" for their unique bond.

Couscous Tabbouleh

For a faster take on the classic, we chose couscous as our canvas.

by Mark Huxsoll

COME SUMMER, I crave lighter, fresher, grain-and-vegetable-based dishes such as tabbouleh, a salad from the eastern Mediterranean that's become a refrigerated supermarket staple in the United States.

Tabbouleh is usually made from lightly steamed (or soaked) bulgur (though other grains are often substituted), lots of parsley, and a mix of aromatics including onion and garlic. A simple dressing of extra-virgin olive oil and fresh lemon juice keeps it light, flavorful, and uncomplicated. The dish is bright and refreshing but substantial enough to satisfy.

When researching and testing existing tabbouleh recipes, I found wide variance in ingredients, seasonings, and proportions. Through experimentation and some thoughtful debate and discussion among my colleagues, I decided to follow the couscous trail. The tiny balls of pasta cook quickly, which fits my weeknight schedule.

To maximize the herbal appeal, I used nearly twice as much fresh chopped parsley as most other recipes call for. This gave the tabbouleh serious punch and a beautiful green color. I added mint for a cool hit and even more herbal complexity.

Now to create a balanced dressing. Too much lemon juice made the tabbouleh sour and harsh, while too little left it lackluster. A quarter cup (squeezed fresh from two lemons) was the right amount to bring the dressing into balance.

I chose minced shallot over onion for its milder flavor, and where other recipes included lots of garlic, I stuck with a single clove for a tame but present pungency. To keep these alliums under control, I found that soaking them in the lemon juice and olive oil while the couscous cooled took the edge off and resulted in a more rounded flavor.

COUSCOUS TABBOULEH
Serves 4 to 6

For the best results, be sure to use a high-quality olive oil. Freshly squeezed lemon juice and a ripe, seasonal tomato are also essential here. Make sure to truly mince the shallot and garlic, since big pieces of either will be too pungent. Look for bright green herbs with firm, healthy leaves. It's OK to use the tender, thin stems at the base of the parsley leaves.

- ¾ cup water
- 1 tablespoon plus ½ cup extra-virgin olive oil, divided
- 1 teaspoon table salt, divided
- ¾ cup couscous
- ¼ cup lemon juice (2 lemons)
- ¼ cup minced shallot
- 1 garlic clove, minced
- 2 cups finely chopped fresh parsley
- 1 cup finely chopped fresh mint
- 1 vine-ripened tomato, cored and cut into ¼-inch pieces

1. Bring water, 1 tablespoon oil, and ½ teaspoon salt to boil in small saucepan over high heat. Stir in couscous, cover, and remove from heat. Let sit for 5 minutes. Fluff with fork and let cool completely, uncovered, about 30 minutes.

2. Meanwhile, combine lemon juice, shallot, garlic, remaining ½ cup oil, and remaining ½ teaspoon salt in large bowl.

3. Add parsley, mint, tomato, and cooled couscous to lemon juice mixture and toss to combine. Serve.

TO MAKE AHEAD

Tabbouleh can be refrigerated in airtight container for up to 2 days.

Tabbouleh is powered by lots of lemon juice and plenty of chopped herbs.

Parsley Stems

You can chop the thin, tender stems along with the parsley leaves—but don't use the thicker, woodier stalks, which will be tough and chewy even when finely chopped.

CHOP ALL OF THIS

BUT NOT THIS

WASTE NOT
Chop the tender parsley stems, too.

Grain versus Pasta

Tabbouleh is typically made with bulgur, a grain that can be hard to find in supermarkets. Our version calls for couscous instead—it's easier to find and cooks more quickly than bulgur; plus, it has a nutty, mild, light flavor that allows the lemon and parsley to shine.

BULGUR
Whole grain, earthy flavor

COUSCOUS
Lighter flavor—and easier to cook

ON THE ROAD

The Titan of Teriyaki

A stalwart of the Seattle restaurant scene invites us into his kitchen. **Text by Bryan Roof; photos by Steve Klise**

WHEN SEATTLE COOKING legend Toshi Kasahara invited me for a teriyaki lunch at his restaurant in Mill Creek, Washington, about 30 minutes outside of the city, I hadn't pictured a strip-mall storefront with just three tables and a view of Staples and Rite Aid out front. But that's where I find him, tucked away in the tiny kitchen of Toshi's Teriyaki Grill, a space filled with the iconic aromas of ginger, garlic, and grilled meats.

Toshi smiles as he cooks, sharing his story in a soft voice that is nearly drowned out by the dull hum of the range hood. He arrived in Seattle in 1976 with a business degree and a plan: to change the city's understanding of what teriyaki should be. Toshi's teriyaki sauce is simple, tasting only of soy sauce, sugar, and a mildly boozy splash of mirin. The sauce doubles as a marinade when he adds ginger and garlic. It's a balanced combination that resembles nothing of the cloying, overly sweet versions of teriyaki that pass at many restaurants.

Customers responded favorably, and Toshi's business grew. He franchised the concept, and at one time, more than 30 restaurants bore his name. Many still do, but Toshi is no longer involved with them. His focus is here at his shop in Mill Creek, where his attention is on the food. Its pristine execution is what fulfills him.

Today, regulars line up for Styrofoam containers of chicken and beef teriyaki served with rice and slaw. Toshi moves with focus and intensity to fill the orders. He knows what he's doing.

Susie Seo (top) greets a customer at Toshi's Teriyaki Grill in Mill Creek, Washington. The dining room is small, so most customers come for takeout; at just over $8, a chicken teriyaki lunch with rice and slaw is a good deal. Toshi Kasahara (above) poses in front of a 1976 photograph of a previous location of the restaurant.

Grilled Chicken Teriyaki

imple, shiny, and acked with flavor.

Jessica Rudolph

JAPANESE, TERIYAKI ughly translates as "shiny grilled" d describes a cooking style in which eats are marinated in a thin but potent ixture of soy sauce, sugar, and mirin (a eet Japanese wine) or sometimes sake d then quickly grilled or broiled. The gar and sweet wine reduce and cara- elize to produce the dish's signature ster and complex flavor.

Chef Toshi Kasahara employs this aditional method for his chicken riyaki at his restaurant outside of eattle, Washington (see "The Titan Teriyaki"). It's a simple but sophis- cated dish, with its success lying in e quality of a few ingredients and the uanced balance between them.

When developing my own take, knew I'd use the hot fire of a grill d choose boneless, skinless chicken ighs so that they'd stay juicy and cook rough quickly. I started building my uce, tweaking the proportions of soy uce, sugar, and mirin and cooking the ixture briefly to achieve the ideal bal- ce of sweet, salty, and savory.

Taking another page from Toshi's ook, I decided to marinate the chick- n before grilling it to deeply imbue it ith teriyaki flavor. I pureed a portion f the sauce with fresh ginger and gar- c to add some pungent warmth and oured it over the chicken. I'd serve e rest of the smooth sauce (with no verly pungent garlic or ginger bits) ith the finished chicken.

After marinating the chicken for a ouple of hours (longer is better—it can narinate up to 24 hours), I threw it on hot grill. The thighs took on a gor- eous mahogany color as they cooked, icking up flavorful char around the dges where the marinade caramelized. sliced the cooked chicken and plated up with steamed white rice and the emainder of my teriyaki sauce.

As my tasters gathered, they seemed keptical: This dish looked almost aus- ere compared to what they expected. No pineapple rings?" one colleague ked. But they were instant converts fter one bite of this robust, juicy, and erfectly balanced chicken teriyaki. ometimes simple is best.

The sugar in the marinade caramelizes on the grill to create a flavorful mahogany crust.

CHICKEN TERIYAKI
Serves 6 to 8

Mirin is a sweet rice wine that is a common ingredient in Japanese cook- ing. It can be found in the international section of most supermarkets. Serve with white rice.

- 1 **cup soy sauce**
- ½ **cup sugar**
- 2 **tablespoons mirin**
- 1 **(2-inch) piece ginger, peeled and sliced thin**
- 5 **garlic cloves, peeled**
- 3 **pounds boneless, skinless chicken thighs, trimmed**

1. Bring soy sauce, sugar, and mirin to boil in small saucepan over medium-high heat, stirring to dis- solve sugar. Remove from heat and let teriyaki sauce cool completely.
2. Combine ¾ cup teriyaki sauce, ginger, and garlic in blender and process until smooth, about 20 seconds. Set aside remaining teriyaki sauce for serv- ing (you should have about ½ cup).
3. Place chicken in 1-gallon zipper-lock bag and add teriyaki sauce–ginger mixture. Press out air, seal bag, and turn to coat chicken with marinade. Refrigerate for at least 1 hour or up to 24 hours.
4A. FOR A CHARCOAL GRILL: Open bottom vent completely. Light large chimney starter filled with charcoal briquettes (6 quarts). When top coals are partially covered with ash, pour evenly over grill. Set cooking grate in place, cover, and open lid vent completely. Heat grill until hot, about 5 minutes.
4B. FOR A GAS GRILL: Turn all burners to high, cover, and heat grill until hot, about 15 minutes. Turn all burners to medium-high.
5. Clean and oil cooking grate. Place chicken on grill and cook (covered if using gas) until chicken is lightly charred and registers at least 175 degrees, 6 to 8 minutes per side, rearranging as needed to ensure even browning. Transfer to cutting board, tent with aluminum foil, and let rest for 5 minutes. Slice crosswise ½ inch thick and serve with reserved teriyaki sauce.

Building Teriyaki Flavor

1. Cook teriyaki sauce.

2. Puree ¾ cup teriyaki sauce with ginger and garlic in blender.

3. Marinate chicken in teriyaki sauce– ginger mixture for 1 to 24 hours.

4. Grill chicken, slice, and serve with reserved teriyaki sauce.

Sausage-Stuffed Peppers

Can stuffed peppers really be exciting?
Yes, they can! **by Matthew Fairman**

Leaving the stems on the peppers adds visual flair and makes a handy handle.

STUFFED PEPPERS HAVE a retro charm I've always found appealing. But exemplary versions are rare; when I made a selection of promising-looking recipes for my colleagues, we were all disappointed. Most of the fillings were tasty enough, but the peppers in each version seemed like an afterthought. They were bland and either mushy or squeaky, and they toppled over on the plate, slumped over sideways, or split open and spilled their stuffing. Why couldn't the pepper be just as enticing as the filling—and not just a vessel?

From my initial tests, red bell peppers emerged as the definitive favorite for their mild sweetness. And my tasters were especially taken with one stuffing made from richly spiced Italian sausage, rice, and plenty of cheese, so including those was an easy decision.

But how could I elevate the pepper? While other recipes call for blanching the peppers to soften them before they're stuffed, I wanted to add flavor in the softening step—so I decided to char them. I halved four peppers through the stems (for stability and ease of stuffing); tossed them with olive oil, salt, and pepper; and then broiled them until they were lightly browned, which enhanced their sweetness and added caramelized complexity.

While the peppers cooled, I steamed rice in a flavorful base of browned sausage and onion and stirred in a handful of shredded Monterey Jack cheese for cohesiveness. After stuffing the pepper halves and topping them with a shower of crunchy panko bread crumbs and grated Parmesan, I popped them back into the oven to brown the topping and further cook the peppers until they were tender and almost creamy.

My tasters approved, but they wanted an additional element for enhanced complexity. So to make a sauce, I added an extra bell pepper and some garlic cloves to the broiling step. When they were softened and charred, I tossed them in the blender with some jarred cherry peppers (including a splash of the brine) and a little bit of the panko mixture to bind it. Delicious.

Seeds Begone

Use a paring knife to trim out the seed pod and any large white ribs.

SAUSAGE-STUFFED PEPPERS WITH SPICY RED PEPPER SAUCE
Serves 4 to 6
Look for large bell peppers that weigh at least 8 ounces each.

- 5 large red bell peppers
- 2 garlic cloves, lightly crushed and peeled
- 5 tablespoons extra-virgin olive oil, divided
- 1 teaspoon plus ⅛ teaspoon table salt, divided
- ½ teaspoon pepper
- 1 pound sweet Italian sausage, casings removed
- 1 onion, chopped
- 1 cup long-grain white rice
- 2 teaspoons Tony Chachere's Original Creole Seasoning
- 2 cups chicken broth
- 4 ounces Monterey Jack cheese, shredded (1 cup)
- ½ cup panko bread crumbs
- ¼ cup grated Parmesan cheese
- 2 teaspoons finely chopped jarred hot cherry peppers, plus 2 tablespoons brine

1. Adjust oven rack 6 inches from broiler element and heat broiler. Line rimmed baking sheet with aluminum foil. Using paring knife or scissors, halve bell peppers lengthwise through stem. Using paring knife, remove seed pod at base of stem, leaving stem intact.
2. Toss bell peppers and garlic with 2 tablespoons oil on prepared sheet, then sprinkle with 1 teaspoon salt and pepper. Arrange bell peppers cut side down. Broil until bell peppers and garlic are spotty brown, 4 to 7 minutes. Set aside and let cool.
3. Meanwhile, heat oven to 400 degrees. Cook sausage and onion in 12-inch nonstick skillet over medium-high heat, breaking up meat with wooden spoon, until sausage is cooked through and onion is softened and beginning to brown, 8 to 10 minutes.
4. Add rice and Creole seasoning and cook until fragrant, about 1 minute. Stir in broth and bring to boil. Cover, reduce heat to low, and cook for 20 minutes. Off heat, stir in Monterey Jack until melted and combined. Set aside and let cool for 10 minutes.
5. Meanwhile, combine panko, Parmesan, and 1 tablespoon oil in bowl. Discard stems from 2 bell pepper halves; chop stemmed halves coarse (you should have 1 cup chopped bell pepper; reserve excess for another use). Process chopped bell pepper, 2 tablespoons panko mixture, cherry peppers and brine, garlic, remaining 2 tablespoons oil, and remaining ⅛ teaspoon salt in blender until smooth, about 1 minute. Set aside sauce.
6. Arrange remaining bell pepper halves cut side up on baking sheet and divide sausage and rice mixture evenly among halves, packing in mixture and mounding it slightly. Sprinkle remaining panko mixture over top, pressing lightly to adhere. Bake until bell peppers are heated through and panko mixture is well browned, about 25 minutes. Let cool for 15 minutes. Serve with sauce.

TO MAKE AHEAD
After filling bell peppers in step 6, do not sprinkle panko mixture on top. Let bell peppers cool, transfer them to large plate, and wrap them in plastic wrap. Transfer sauce and panko mixture to separate airtight containers. Refrigerate all ingredients for up to 24 hours. To serve, extend baking time by about 10 minutes and cover with foil for final 10 minutes of baking if tops begin to get too dark.

Cashew Chicken

This skillet supper comes together in a matter of minutes.

By Matthew Fairman

CRUNCHY, GOLDEN-BROWN, BUTTERY cashews and tender morsels of juicy stir-fried chicken all awash in a salty-sweet, glossy brown sauce—what more could you ask from a recipe you can pull together in less time than it takes to steam some rice? Our version hits all the right notes, and once it's made at home, it's hotter and fresher than takeout.

To ensure that the chunks of chicken are flavorful and remain tender and juicy, we briefly marinate them in a mixture of soy sauce, dry sherry, toasted sesame oil, and cornstarch. The cornstarch not only coats the lean chicken and protects its exterior from becoming dry and tough but also thickens the stir-fry sauce, giving it an attractive glossy sheen.

We prepare the other ingredients while the chicken marinates. For an easy, intensely flavored sauce, we start with a base of sweet-savory hoisin (a multilayered ingredient that includes soybeans, vinegar, and chiles), stir in a bit more soy sauce for balance, and thin it with some water. A tablespoon of balsamic vinegar brightens the sauce and stands in for the more traditional (but less readily available) Chinese black vinegar, and a mix of scallions, garlic, ginger, and red pepper flakes adds fresh, pungent bite. Sliced celery is a common addition, and we liked it for its crisp texture and mild vegetal flavor.

As for those cashews, most recipes call for quickly toasting cashew pieces and dropping them in at the end. And while the results of that method are OK, we wanted our recipe to treat the cashews as more than just a garnish. To that end, we add more cashews than most recipes call for, and we use whole nuts rather than pieces to make certain that they don't get lost in the finished dish. More important, we deeply toast the cashews in the same oil we later use for the stir-fry, so their flavor permeates the whole dish. Using moderate heat and stirring frequently turns them a beautiful golden brown, gets them thoroughly crisp, and deepens and concentrates their nutty flavor.

Our version packs potent flavor without being too saucy or sweet.

BACKSTORY

Cashews extend from an "apple" that grows on the cashew tree (below). Native to Brazil, the cashew tree was brought to India in the 16th century by Portuguese colonists; from there, the trees spread throughout Southeast Asia and Africa. Today, Vietnam and India are the largest exporters of shelled cashews; there is no significant commercial cashew production in the United States.

CASHEW CHICKEN
Serves 4

Be sure to have all the ingredients prepared and close by so that you're equipped for fast cooking. Serve with white rice.

- 1½ pounds boneless, skinless chicken breasts, trimmed and cut into ¾-inch pieces
- 5 tablespoons soy sauce, divided
- 2 tablespoons cornstarch
- 1 tablespoon dry sherry
- 1 teaspoon toasted sesame oil
- ⅓ cup hoisin sauce
- ⅓ cup water
- 1 tablespoon balsamic vinegar
- 3 tablespoons vegetable oil
- 1 cup raw cashews
- 2 celery ribs, sliced on bias ¼ inch thick
- 6 scallions, white parts sliced thin, green parts cut into 1-inch pieces
- 2 garlic cloves, minced
- 1 teaspoon grated fresh ginger
- ½ teaspoon red pepper flakes

1. Combine chicken, 2 tablespoons soy sauce, cornstarch, sherry, and sesame oil in bowl. Combine hoisin, water, vinegar, and remaining 3 tablespoons soy sauce in separate bowl.

2. Heat vegetable oil in 12-inch nonstick skillet over medium heat until shimmering. Add cashews and cook, stirring constantly, until golden brown, 4 to 6 minutes, reducing heat if cashews begin to darken too quickly. Using slotted spoon, transfer cashews to small bowl.

3. Heat oil left in skillet over medium-high heat until just smoking. Add chicken and cook, stirring frequently, until beginning to brown and no longer translucent, about 3 minutes. Add celery, scallion whites, garlic, ginger, and pepper flakes and cook until celery is just beginning to soften, about 2 minutes.

4. Add hoisin mixture, bring to boil, and cook until chicken is cooked through and sauce is thickened, 1 to 3 minutes. Off heat, stir in scallion greens and cashews. Serve.

Toasting Deeply

Toasting nuts brings out and intensifies their flavor and makes them crunchier. Properly toasted nuts are golden brown not just on the outside but also all the way through their interior. Be sure to stir constantly when toasting nuts to prevent them from scorching.

GOLDEN BROWN THROUGHOUT

Hot-Honey Chicken

Hidden among my grandmother's stack of recipes was a sweet, sneaky-hot surprise.

by Morgan Bolling

Hot honey is trendy these days, sure, but it's an idea that has been around for a long time.

MY GRANDMOTHER, "MOOMOO" as I called her, knew her way around the kitchen. My mother tells tales of her carrying a rolling pin in one hand, not only for rolling out doughs but also for protection against a pet rooster that terrorized the house.

I keep her recipe binder in my kitchen, both for inspiration and nostalgia. I recently noticed a page titled "Hot Honey Butter Chicken." Sweet honey, a prick of heat, and lots of butter sounded like a delicious combination. But this was more like scribbled notes than an actual recipe. In her recognizable hand it said, "Cut up a chicken. Bake one hour in equal parts honey, hot sauce, butter, and flavorings to taste. Start the pieces skin-side down but flip halfway."

I channeled my grandmother and took a stab at the "recipe." I combined ¼ cup each of honey, hot sauce (I started with a test kitchen favorite, Frank's RedHot), and butter in a skillet. I added cut-up chicken pieces and roasted them in a low 300-degree oven for a full hour, flipping the pieces halfway through roasting. The butter, honey, and Frank's, mixed with the chicken juices, made a lively concoction that tasted like a sweet take on buffalo sauce. But the chicken was pale, the sauce was greasy, and I had no idea what "flavorings" to add. MooMoo taught me that a little improvisation in the kitchen goes a long way, so I figured she wouldn't mind my taking some liberties.

For my next test, I seared the chicken parts before roasting them, which eliminated the need to flip them halfway through cooking. And searing gave me a chance to pour off the chicken fat to get rid of the greasiness before I added the honey and hot sauce. Withholding the butter until right before serving (I stirred it into the reduced pan juices and spooned the resulting sauce over the chicken) preserved its clean flavor. To speed up the cooking time, I cranked the oven temperature to 425 degrees. Finally, I found that drizzling the honey mixture on top of the browned chicken before baking it gave the pieces an appealing gloss.

For the flavorings my grandmother alluded to, I tried a few different spices before sprinkling earthy, complex cumin on the chicken before searing it. Just right. A final splash of lime juice and a handful of sliced scallions added brightness. Is this my grandmother's exact recipe? No, but I know it would have made MooMoo proud.

Building the Perfect Sweet Heat

1. Season chicken and sear on stovetop.

2. Pour hot-honey sauce over chicken and roast chicken to doneness in oven.

3. Remove chicken and reduce sauce and skillet juices back on stovetop.

4. Stir butter and lime juice into reduced sauce and pour over chicken.

A Tempered Heat

Frank's RedHot is our favorite
all-around hot sauce; we
love its tang and mild heat.
Hotter sauces are often too
spicy for some palates and
don't taste balanced in the
dishes you make with them.
Frank's is just right here,
producing a punchy, but
not overpowering, flavor.

Greek Potatoes

Just like the rest of us, potato salad sometimes needs a change of scenery. How about the Mediterranean?

by Morgan Bolling

Pickled hot peppers
add kick and acidity
to this lively side.

MY CURRENT FAVORITE side
dish is the roasted Greek potatoes
served at a restaurant near my apartment. The spuds arrive at the table
doused in enough olive oil and lemon
juice to give them a balanced mix of
brightness and richness.

I wanted to create my own recipe so
that I could make this spunky dish at
home. So I read up on Greek potatoes
and made half a dozen existing recipes.
The two basic camps were those that
called for boiling the potatoes and
those that went the roasting route.

My tasters had a strong preference
for the roasted version; they loved
the contrasting textures of the creamy
insides and the crisp, roasted edges.
So I halved 2 pounds of small Yukon
Gold potatoes (a favorite variety for
their creamy interiors), tossed them in
lemon juice and olive oil, and roasted
them cut side down on a rimmed baking sheet in a 400-degree oven until
the cut sides were well browned.

The flavor of lemon changes when
you cook it. While that's sometimes a
good thing, in this case the potatoes
emerged from the oven unpleasantly
sour. So instead of seasoning the potatoes with lemon before cooking them,
I roasted them first and only then
tossed them with a lemony vinaigrette
made from extra-virgin olive oil,
lemon juice, and lemon zest. With this
technique, the warm potatoes soaked
up the vibrant dressing without
becoming soggy. These potatoes were
good, but they got even better when
I bumped up the flavor of the vinaigrette with the mild sting of briny
pepperoncini and some potent garlic,
dried oregano, and fresh parsley.

THE AMERICAN TABLE

Potato salad is a truly transatlantic
dish. Potatoes, which are native to the
Americas, were first brought to Europe
in the 16th century by Spanish explor-
ers. There, cooks made potato salad by
boiling potatoes in wine or vinegar and
dressing them up with various additions.

Eventually potatoes made their way to
Germany, where a more sour/sweet style
of potato salad developed, with onions,
mustard, and sometimes sugar or bacon.

This German style, in turn, crossed
the Atlantic in the 19th century, quickly
spreading throughout the United States.
Today, we have innumerable variations
on potato salad, but that's no surprise:
Inexpensive potatoes are a beautiful
canvas to paint on.

GREEK ROASTED POTATOES

Serves 4 to 6
For the best results, look for small
Yukon Gold potatoes measuring 1½ to
2 inches in diameter (about the size of
a golf ball).

2	pounds small Yukon Gold potatoes, unpeeled, halved
5	tablespoons extra-virgin olive oil, divided
1¼	teaspoons table salt, divided
3	tablespoons finely chopped pepperoncini
1	teaspoon grated lemon zest plus 4 teaspoons juice
2	garlic cloves, minced
1½	teaspoons dried oregano
⅓	cup chopped fresh parsley, divided

1. Adjust oven rack to middle position
and heat oven to 400 degrees. Spray
rimmed baking sheet with vegetable
oil spray.
2. Toss potatoes, 2 tablespoons oil,
and 1 teaspoon salt in bowl until potatoes are well coated. Arrange potatoes
in single layer on prepared sheet,
cut side down. Roast until bottoms
of potatoes are golden brown, 35 to
40 minutes.
3. Meanwhile, combine pepperoncini,
lemon zest and juice, garlic, oregano,
remaining 3 tablespoons oil, and
remaining ¼ teaspoon salt in large bowl.
4. Transfer potatoes to pepperoncini
mixture in bowl. Add half of parsley and toss to combine. Transfer
potatoes to serving dish. Sprinkle with
remaining parsley. Serve warm.

Country-Fried Steak

This classic chuck wagon recipe needed to be lassoed in.

by Cecelia Jenkins

The thick, creamy gravy and the crunch of the steak's fried coating make a great textural contrast.

COUNTRY-FRIED STEAK IS a thin cut of beef dredged in seasoned flour, fried, and smothered in a peppery gravy made with the steak drippings. This classic cowboy dish is usually made with cube steak, a tough cut from the round that is mechanically tenderized. I wanted to stick to the spirit of this dish's frugal roots but give it a refresh.

I started by making several recipes that called for cube steak. When my tasters and I sampled them, we were surprised to find that the mechanically tenderized steaks were still chewy. To add insult to injury, most of the fried coatings lacked crunch or—worse—peeled off in the frying oil. I set out to find a way to make the cube steak work.

Since cube steaks can be inconsistent, I gently pounded them to an even ¼-inch thickness so that they'd fry quickly and evenly. While a simple flour coating is traditional, it didn't provide enough crunch. A few recipes called for adding crushed saltines to make the coating more substantial. I did this and also added some cornstarch for lightness, a few seasonings (cayenne, granulated garlic, and oregano), and baking powder (to aerate the coating and keep it from becoming dense and tough). Next, I shifted my focus to making sure the coating would stick.

Soaking the steaks in buttermilk is a common first step because the acidic buttermilk adds tangy flavor, helps tenderize the meat, and helps the flour coating adhere. This method gave me mixed results: The meat was more flavorful and slightly more tender, but the coating didn't adhere, making a mess of the skillet and leaving bald spots on the fried steaks. Adding an egg to the buttermilk thickened it, but the coating still sloughed off. The solution was to dry the meat with paper towels and then dip it first in flour before subsequent dips in the buttermilk-egg mixture and seasoned saltine crumb mixtures. Now the coating was adhering, and it was frying up crisp and flavorful. I was almost home.

But without the buttermilk soak, the cube steaks were still a little too tough to declare victory. A colleague suggested a test kitchen trick for tenderizing meat: tossing it with a little baking soda mixed with water and salt. This worked great and took just 15 minutes. Once the steaks were breaded, I let them sit in the refrigerator to give the coating time to adhere to the meat. I wound up "medium-frying" two steaks at a time in 1½ cups of oil in a 12-inch skillet.

Now it was time for the gravy. I found that using a few tablespoons of the frying oil—flavored from the steaks and seasoned breading—as the base of

 Go to **CooksCountry.com/taters** for our Crushed Red Potatoes with Garlic and Herbs recipe (above).

How to Make a Cheap Cut Eat Like a Million Bucks

1. Pound the steaks to an even thickness to tenderize them and for even cooking.

2. Treat the steaks in a baking soda brine; the baking soda helps tenderize the beef.

3. Dip the steaks in flour and then in a mixture of buttermilk and beaten egg.

4. Finally, coat the steaks with a seasoned saltine crumb mixture before frying.

y gravy, per tradition, added savory
∎vor. I stirred a little flour into the
∎l, let it brown, and whisked in milk
∎d plenty of salt and pepper. Simple
∎d delicious. Come and get it!

∎OUNTRY-FRIED STEAK
∎erves 4

∎here are about 35 crackers in one
∎eeve of saltines. Use more or less
∎ayenne to suit your taste.

∎TEAK
- 4 (4- to 6-ounce) cube steaks,
  trimmed
- ¼ cup water
- ∎½ teaspoons table salt, divided
- ¼ teaspoon baking soda
- 1 cup all-purpose flour, divided
- ¾ cup buttermilk
- 1 large egg
- 35 square saltines
- ½ cup cornstarch
- 2 teaspoons pepper
- 1 teaspoon baking powder
- 1 teaspoon dried oregano
- 1 teaspoon granulated garlic
- ¼ teaspoon cayenne pepper
- ∎½ cups peanut or vegetable oil
  for frying

∎RAVY
- 2 tablespoons all-purpose flour
- ∎½ cups whole milk
- ¼ teaspoon table salt
- ¼ teaspoon pepper

∎. FOR THE STEAK: Using meat
∎ounder, pound each steak to even
∎4-inch thickness between 2 sheets of
∎lastic wrap. Whisk water, 1 teaspoon
∎alt, and baking soda in medium
∎owl until baking soda and salt are
∎issolved. Add steaks and toss until
∎oated and no liquid pools at bottom
∎f bowl. Let sit for 15 minutes.
∎. Meanwhile, place ½ cup flour in
∎hallow dish. Whisk buttermilk and
∎gg together in second shallow dish.
∎lace saltines in large zipper-lock bag,
∎eal bag, and crush to fine crumbs

with rolling pin. Whisk saltine
crumbs, cornstarch, pepper, baking
powder, oregano, granulated garlic,
cayenne, remaining ½ teaspoon salt,
and remaining ½ cup flour together in
third shallow dish.
3. Pat steaks dry with paper towels.
Working with 1 steak at a time, dredge
steaks in flour, shaking off excess; dip
in buttermilk mixture, allowing excess
to drip off; then coat with saltine
mixture, pressing firmly to adhere.
Transfer steaks to parchment paper–
lined rimmed baking sheet; refrigerate
for at least 1 hour or up to 2 hours.
4. Adjust oven rack to middle position and heat oven to 200 degrees.
Set wire rack in second rimmed baking sheet and line half of rack with
triple layer of paper towels. Heat
oil in 12-inch nonstick skillet over
medium-high heat to 375 degrees
(to take temperature, tilt skillet so
oil pools to 1 side). Carefully place
2 steaks side by side in skillet (they
may overlap slightly; this is OK).
5. Cook until evenly well browned on
bottom, 3 to 5 minutes. Using 2 spatulas, carefully flip steaks and continue
to cook until evenly well browned on
second side, 3 to 5 minutes longer,
gently pressing on steaks with spatula
as needed for even browning.
6. Transfer steaks to paper towel–lined
side of prepared rack to drain for about
15 seconds per side, then move to
unlined side of rack and transfer sheet
to oven. Return oil to 375 degrees and
repeat with remaining steaks.
7. FOR THE GRAVY: Carefully
pour hot oil from skillet into heatproof container. Add 2 tablespoons
hot oil back to skillet and place skillet
over medium heat (discard remaining
oil). Whisk in flour and cook until
mixture is peanut butter–colored,
about 3 minutes, whisking often.
Gradually whisk in milk, salt, and
pepper. Bring to boil and cook until
thickened, about 2 minutes.
8. Serve with steaks with gravy.

Come and Git It!
In the early days of the film industry, "westerns"
were reliable moneymakers for the big studios,
partly because of geography. In the 1910s, '20s,
and '30s, when Los Angeles was still in its early
stages of growth, Hollywood was surrounded by
rural areas; the hills were still undeveloped, so
it was easy to find locations that looked "wild."
The chuck wagon cook was a stock character in
dozens of Westerns, right up there with saloon
keepers and rough-riding sheriffs.

Bird's Beak Paring Knives
by Miye Bromberg

A BIRD'S BEAK paring knife features a curved blade shaped like a bird's beak.
Fans of these knives use them for precise detail work. To see if any deserve a place
in our kitchens, we bought eight and pitted them against our favorite paring knife,
the Victorinox Swiss Army Fibrox Pro 3¼" Spear Point Par-
ing Knife, as we hulled and quartered strawberries, cored and
peeled tomatoes, peeled and segmented lemons, removed the
eyes from whole peeled pineapples, and peeled ginger.
We were impressed. In fact, we preferred using most of the bird's beak paring knives to using the standard paring knife. Why? The blades of the bird's beak
paring knives were, on average, about an inch shorter than the blade of the paring
knife, so they were easier to maneuver around irregularly shaped foods.

Still, features including sharpness, narrowness, blade length, handle length
and thickness, weight, and handle material separated the good models from the
bad. By the end of testing, most of us were completely
smitten with these unusual knives. If you do a lot of
detail work with your paring knife, the MAC Paring
Knife, Bird's Beak, 2½" would be an excellent addition to your collection. Featuring a relatively long,
very narrow, razor-sharp blade, it effortlessly peeled,
hulled, cored, and sliced all the produce we put in front
of it. And because it was lightweight and had a grippy
handle, it nearly disappeared into our hands, making it
especially easy to use.

Ways to Use
- Remove eyes from potatoes
- Trim brussels sprouts
- Peel fruits and vegetables

KEY **Good** ★★★ **Fair** ★★ **Poor** ★

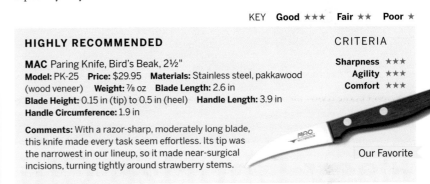

HIGHLY RECOMMENDED

MAC Paring Knife, Bird's Beak, 2½"
Model: PK-25 **Price:** $29.95 **Materials:** Stainless steel, pakkawood
(wood veneer) **Weight:** ⅞ oz **Blade Length:** 2.6 in
Blade Height: 0.15 in (tip) to 0.5 in (heel) **Handle Length:** 3.9 in
Handle Circumference: 1.9 in

CRITERIA
Sharpness ★★★
Agility ★★★
Comfort ★★★

Comments: With a razor-sharp, moderately long blade,
this knife made every task seem effortless. Its tip was
the narrowest in our lineup, so it made near-surgical
incisions, turning tightly around strawberry stems.

Our Favorite

RECOMMENDED

Misono Molybdenum Peeling Knife
Model: HMI-MOPL-050 **Price:** $29.00
Weight: ⅞ oz **Blade Length:** 2.0 in

Sharpness ★★★
Agility ★★½
Comfort ★★½

Mercer Culinary Renaissance Forged Peeling Knife
Model: M23640 **Price:** $22.52
Weight: 1⅞ oz **Blade Length:** 2.6 in

Sharpness ★★★
Agility ★★½
Comfort ★★

Shun Classic Bird's Beak Knife
Model: DM0715 **Price:** $84.95
Weight: 2 oz **Blade Length:** 2.5 in

Sharpness ★★★
Agility ★★½
Comfort ★★

RECOMMENDED WITH RESERVATIONS

Victorinox Swiss Army Bird's Beak Paring Knife
Model: 6.7503 **Price:** $14.92
Weight: ⅝ oz **Blade Length:** 2.2 in

Sharpness ★½
Agility ★★
Comfort ★★★

Zwilling Pro 2.75-inch Bird's Beak Peeling Knife
Model: 38400-053 **Price:** $59.95
Weight: 2⅛ oz **Blade Length:** 2.5 in

Sharpness ★★½
Agility ★★
Comfort ★★

Wüsthof Classic 2¾-inch Peeling Knife
Model: 4062-7 **Price:** $64.95
Weight: 2 oz **Blade Length:** 2.4 in

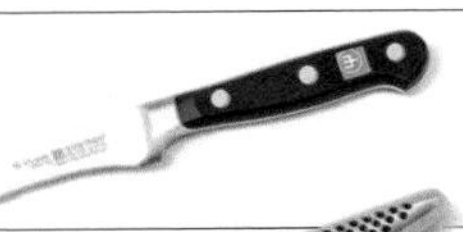

Sharpness ★★
Agility ★★
Comfort ★★

Global Classic 2.75" Peeler
Model: GS-8 **Price:** $49.95
Weight: 2⅞ oz **Blade Length:** 2.5 in

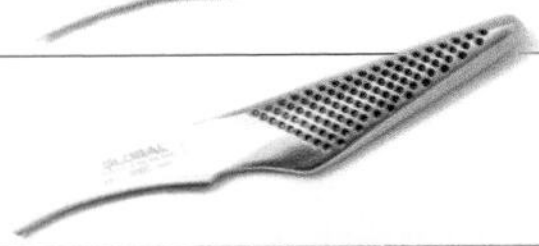

Sharpness ★★★
Agility ★★
Comfort ★

Web subscribers can read the complete results at **CooksCountry.com/jul20**.

Chilaquiles make for
a lively breakfast,
lunch, or dinner.

Easy Chorizo Chilaquiles

Our goals: incredibly easy and incredibly good. **by Morgan Bolling and Bryan Roof**

CHILAQUILES ARE A classic thrifty dish: You take stale corn tortillas, crisp them up, and then soften them in a pan of red sauce. They're typically draped in shredded cheese and bulked up with eggs, vegetables, or whatever leftover meat the cook has on hand, making the dish rich and ultracomforting for breakfast, lunch, or dinner.

We were after an easy version loaded with flavorful chorizo sausage (the fresh Mexican kind, not the cured, salami-like Spanish variety). Many recipes we found took the simplified approach of tossing store-bought chips—straight from the bag—with jarred salsa, cooked meat, and shredded cheese and then baking or broiling the mixture. It sounded too good to be true.

In a first test, we browned chorizo and tossed it with tortilla chips and store-bought salsa in a skillet. The resulting chilaquiles were good, but we lost too many chips over the edge of the skillet when mixing everything together.

For the next round of tests, we moved the operation to a Dutch oven to make stirring easier. These chilaquiles were fast and easy and were tasting really good. To cover our bases, we went back and made batches with homemade salsa and home-fried tortilla strips. Both were great, but so was the version we were making with the convenience products. We'd stick with this easier, faster method.

We knew that the right toppings were the key to making the dish truly exceptional. After a lot of delicious testing, we landed on an attractive, flavorful mix of melty Monterey Jack cheese, sliced red onion, chopped cilantro, sliced avocado, and a drizzle of tangy Mexican crema (a mixture of sour cream, lime juice, and a little salt works, too). These chilaquiles were fast, easy, and incredibly flavorful. Mission accomplished.

Chips Ahoy!

Traditionally, chilaquiles were made with stiff, dry, day-old tortillas. But nowadays, many recipes rely on the convenience of store-bought tortilla chips. Their texture is key—you want them softened yet not mushy, so the trick is to add chips at just the right time to ensure that they'll yield to the other ingredients, but not too much. Our suggestion: Call people to the table before you add the chips to the other ingredients, and serve promptly—chilaquiles don't hold well.

A trickier issue, with commercial chips especially, is salt. We tried using unsalted chips, but our recipe testers told us they had a hard time finding them, so we proceeded with regular salted chips. Our winning (salted) chips, from On the Border, worked fine, but we don't recommend Tostitos (second place in our taste test) here, as they add too much salt. Use your bag of Tostitos for dipping in salsa instead.

EASY CHORIZO CHILAQUILES
Serves 4

We developed this recipe with Fronte medium-hot red salsa. Our favorite tortilla chips are On the Border Café Style Tortilla Chips; we don't recommend using our second-place chips, Tostitos, because they can make the dish too salty. Mexican crema can be found near the sour cream in many supermarkets. If you can't find it, you can substitute a mixture of ⅓ cup of sour cream, 1 tablespoon of lime juice and ¼ teaspoon of table salt.

- 1 pound Mexican-style chorizo sausag casings removed
- 1 (16-ounce) jar medium-hot red salsa
- 1 cup water
- 8 ounces tortilla chips
- 4 ounces Monterey Jack cheese, shredded (1 cup)
- ¼ cup thinly sliced red onion
- ¼ cup very coarsely chopped fresh cilantro leaves and stems
- 1 avocado, sliced thin
- ⅓ cup Mexican crema, plus extra for serving

1. Cook chorizo in Dutch oven over medium-high heat, breaking up meat with wooden spoon, until cooked through and starting to brown, about 7 minutes.

2. Add salsa and water to chorizo. Add tortilla chips and bring to a boil. Reduc heat to medium-low. Using large spoo gently fold chips into sauce to coat, tak ing care to minimize breakage. Transfe mixture to shallow platter.

3. Sprinkle with Monterey Jack, onion, and cilantro; top with avocado and drizzle with crema. Serve with extra crema.

Can't Find Chorizo?
If you can't locate chorizo, you can use this pork filling instead. Substitute it for the chorizo, proceeding with step 2 above.

PORK FILLING FOR CHILAQUILES

- 1 tablespoon vegetable oil
- 1 pound ground pork
- 1 tablespoon chili powder
- ¾ teaspoon table salt

Heat oil in Dutch oven over medium-high heat until shimmering. Add pork, chili powder, and salt and cook, breaking up meat with wooden spoon, until no longer pink, about 7 minutes.

Zucchini and Goat Cheese Frittata with Cherry Tomato Sauce

30-MINUTE SUPPER

Steak Fried Rice

30-MINUTE SUPPER

Roasted Pork Tenderloin with Romaine and Cremini Salad

30-MINUTE SUPPER

Chicken Curry with Green Beans

30-MINUTE SUPPER

Steak Fried Rice

Serves 4

We developed this recipe with Kikkoman Soy Sauce.

- 3 quarts water
- 1½ cups long-grain white rice
- 5 tablespoons soy sauce
- 2 tablespoons hoisin sauce
- 1 tablespoon sriracha, plus extra for serving
- 1 (12-ounce) skirt steak, trimmed
- 2 tablespoons toasted sesame oil, divided
- 4 scallions, white parts minced, green parts sliced thin on bias
- 4 garlic cloves, minced
- 4 large eggs, lightly beaten
- 1 cup frozen peas and carrots, thawed

1. Bring water to boil in large saucepan over high heat. Add rice and cook, stirring occasionally, until just cooked through, about 12 minutes. Drain rice in fine-mesh strainer; set aside. Combine soy sauce, hoisin, and sriracha in bowl; set aside.

2. Cut steak with grain into 2-inch-wide pieces, then slice pieces thin against grain. Heat 1 tablespoon oil in 12-inch nonstick skillet over high heat until just smoking. Add steak and 2 tablespoons soy sauce mixture to skillet and cook until steak is well browned, about 4 minutes. Transfer steak to bowl; set aside.

3. Add remaining 1 tablespoon oil, scallion whites, and garlic to now-empty skillet and cook until fragrant, about 15 seconds. Stir in rice and remaining soy sauce mixture. Cook, stirring often, until rice is sizzling and popping loudly, about 4 minutes. Push rice to 1 side of skillet. Pour eggs into empty side of skillet and cook until just set, about 1 minute. Stir eggs, steak, scallion greens, and peas and carrots into rice. Serve with extra sriracha.

Zucchini and Goat Cheese Frittata with Cherry Tomato Sauce *Serves 4*

Shred the zucchini on the large holes of a box grater.

- 10 large eggs
- ½ cup half-and-half
- 1¼ teaspoons table salt, divided
- ¼ teaspoon pepper
- 4 tablespoons unsalted butter, divided
- 1 pound cherry tomatoes, halved
- 3 tablespoons thinly sliced shallot, divided
- 2 tablespoons chopped fresh basil, divided
- 1 teaspoon seasoned rice vinegar
- 2 zucchini, shredded
- 3 ounces goat cheese, crumbled (¾ cup)

1. Adjust oven rack to upper-middle position and heat oven to 375 degrees. Whisk eggs, half-and-half, 1 teaspoon salt, and pepper together in bowl; set aside.

2. Melt 1 tablespoon butter in 12-inch ovensafe nonstick skillet over medium-high heat. Add tomatoes, 1 tablespoon shallot, and remaining ¼ teaspoon salt. Cook until tomatoes release their juice and just begin to break down, about 5 minutes. Transfer tomatoes to bowl and stir in 1 tablespoon basil and vinegar; set aside.

3. Add zucchini, remaining 3 tablespoons butter, and remaining 2 tablespoons shallot to now-empty skillet. Cook over medium heat until zucchini has softened, about 7 minutes. Stir in egg mixture and sprinkle evenly with goat cheese and remaining 1 tablespoon basil. Transfer skillet to oven and bake until frittata is just set in center, about 12 minutes. Let rest for 5 minutes. Slide frittata onto platter, cut into wedges, and serve with tomato sauce.

Chicken Curry with Green Beans

Serves 4

Serve with chopped fresh cilantro and naan.

- 8 (3- to 5-ounce) boneless, skinless chicken thighs, trimmed and cut into 1-inch chunks
- ½ teaspoon table salt
- ½ teaspoon pepper
- 1 tablespoon vegetable oil
- 8 ounces green beans, trimmed and cut on bias into 1-inch lengths
- 1 red bell pepper, stemmed, seeded, and sliced thin
- 1 small onion, minced
- 3 tablespoons curry powder
- 2 garlic cloves, minced
- 1 (15-ounce) can tomato sauce
- 1 cup chicken broth

1. Pat chicken dry with paper towels and sprinkle with salt and pepper. Heat oil in 12-inch nonstick skillet over medium-high heat until just smoking. Add chicken and cook until lightly browned, 6 to 8 minutes. Using slotted spoon, transfer chicken to large plate; set aside.

2. Add green beans, bell pepper, and onion to fat left in skillet and cook over medium-high heat until onion is softened and beginning to brown, about 4 minutes. Add curry powder and garlic and cook until fragrant, about 30 seconds. Stir in tomato sauce, broth, and chicken and bring to boil. Reduce heat to medium and simmer, covered, until chicken is cooked through, about 10 minutes. Serve.

Roasted Pork Tenderloin with Romaine and Cremini Salad *Serves 4*

Top the salad with lots of shaved Parmesan cheese.

- 2 (1-pound) pork tenderloins, trimmed
- 1¾ teaspoons table salt, divided
- ¾ teaspoon pepper, divided
- 6 tablespoons extra-virgin olive oil, divided
- 4 teaspoons Dijon mustard, divided
- 10 ounces cremini mushrooms, trimmed and quartered
- 3 tablespoons cider vinegar
- 1 teaspoon honey
- ¼ teaspoon red pepper flakes
- 2 romaine lettuce hearts (12 ounces), torn into bite-size pieces
- ¼ cup pine nuts, toasted

1. Adjust oven rack to upper-middle position and heat oven to 425 degrees. Pat pork dry with paper towels and sprinkle with 1 teaspoon salt and ½ teaspoon pepper. Heat 1 tablespoon oil in 12-inch nonstick skillet over medium-high heat until just smoking. Cook pork until well browned on all sides, about 7 minutes. Transfer pork to rimmed baking sheet and brush with 1 tablespoon mustard. Transfer sheet to oven and roast until pork registers 140 degrees, 12 to 15 minutes.

2. Meanwhile, heat 1 tablespoon oil in now-empty skillet over medium-high heat until shimmering. Add mushrooms and ¼ teaspoon salt and cook until golden brown, about 6 minutes. Transfer to large bowl. Add vinegar, honey, pepper flakes, remaining ½ teaspoon salt, remaining ¼ teaspoon pepper, remaining ¼ cup oil, and remaining 1 teaspoon mustard to mushrooms and stir to combine.

3. Let pork rest for 5 minutes. Add romaine and pine nuts to mushroom mixture and toss to combine. Slice pork and serve with salad.

Prosciutto-Wrapped Chicken Breasts with Cantaloupe-Cucumber Salad

30-MINUTE SUPPER

Grilled Green Chile Chorizo Burgers

30-MINUTE SUPPER

Spicy Shrimp Soup

30-MINUTE SUPPER

Grilled Rib-Eye Steaks with Summer Squash and Smoky Paprika Lemon Butter

30-MINUTE SUPPER

Grilled Green Chile Chorizo Burgers

Serves 4

We developed this recipe using Frontera Tomatillo Salsa. For more heat, serve with jarred sliced jalapeños.

- 1 (4-ounce) can chopped green chiles, drained
- 3 tablespoons jarred salsa verde
- 2 tablespoons finely chopped onion
- 1 pound ground pork
- 1 pound Mexican-style chorizo sausage, casings removed
- 1 teaspoon table salt
- 1 teaspoon pepper
- 4 ounces Monterey Jack cheese, shredded (1 cup)
- 4 hamburger buns, toasted
- ¼ cup mayonnaise
- 1 cup shredded iceberg lettuce

1. Combine chiles, salsa verde, and onion in small bowl; set aside. Combine pork and chorizo in separate bowl. Form pork mixture into 8 equal balls, then press into 5-inch patties. Sprinkle patties with salt and pepper.

2. Grill patties, covered, over hot fire until well browned on first side, about 5 minutes. Flip patties and top each with 1 tablespoon chile mixture and 2 tablespoons Monterey Jack. Continue to grill, covered, until cheese is melted and burgers are cooked through, about 5 minutes longer. Transfer to platter, arranging burgers in stacks of two. Let rest for 5 minutes.

3. Spread 1 tablespoon mayonnaise on each bun top. Place 1 burger stack on each bun bottom, followed by ¼ cup lettuce and bun top. Serve.

Prosciutto-Wrapped Chicken Breasts with Cantaloupe-Cucumber Salad *Serves 4*

Packaged, presliced prosciutto tends to yield more consistent slices than prosciutto from the deli counter.

- 4 (6- to 8-ounce) boneless, skinless chicken breasts, trimmed and pounded ½ inch thick
- 1 teaspoon table salt, divided
- ½ teaspoon pepper, divided
- 4 ounces thinly sliced prosciutto
- 5 tablespoons extra-virgin olive oil, divided
- 1½ tablespoons lemon juice
- 5 ounces (5 cups) baby arugula
- 2 cups ½-inch cantaloupe pieces
- ½ English cucumber, halved lengthwise and sliced thin crosswise
- 4 ounces feta cheese, crumbled (1 cup)
- ¼ cup chopped fresh mint

1. Pat chicken dry with paper towels and sprinkle with ½ teaspoon salt and ¼ teaspoon pepper. Wrap each breast with 2 slices prosciutto.

2. Heat 1 tablespoon oil in 12-inch nonstick skillet over medium heat until shimmering. Add chicken and cook, covered, until well browned on first side, about 6 minutes. Gently flip and continue to cook, uncovered, until chicken registers 160 degrees, about 6 minutes longer. Transfer chicken to platter and let rest while preparing salad.

3. Whisk lemon juice, remaining ½ teaspoon salt, remaining ¼ teaspoon pepper, and remaining ¼ cup oil together in large bowl. Add arugula, cantaloupe, cucumber, feta, and mint to dressing and toss to combine. Slice chicken and serve with salad.

Grilled Rib-Eye Steaks with Summer Squash and Smoky Paprika Lemon Butter *Serves 4*

Strip steaks can be substituted for the rib eyes, if desired.

- 8 tablespoons unsalted butter, softened
- 2 tablespoons minced fresh chives, divided
- 2 teaspoons smoked paprika
- 1 teaspoon grated lemon zest, plus 1 tablespoon juice, divided
- 1¾ teaspoons table salt, divided
- 1⅛ teaspoons pepper, divided
- 4 yellow summer squashes, sliced on bias ½ inch thick
- 2 tablespoons extra-virgin olive oil
- 2 (1-pound) boneless rib-eye steaks, 1½ to 1¾ inches thick, trimmed

1. Combine butter, 1 tablespoon chives, paprika, lemon zest and 2 teaspoons juice, ¼ teaspoon salt, and ⅛ teaspoon pepper in bowl; set aside. Toss squash with oil, ½ teaspoon salt, and ½ teaspoon pepper in large bowl.

2. Pat steaks dry with paper towels and sprinkle with remaining 1 teaspoon salt and remaining ½ teaspoon pepper. Grill steaks over hot fire, flipping every 2 minutes, until well browned and meat registers 125 degrees (for medium-rare), 10 to 12 minutes. Transfer to carving board. Top each steak with 1 tablespoon butter mixture and tent with foil. Let rest for 10 minutes.

3. Grill squash until lightly charred and tender, about 3 minutes per side. Return squash to bowl. Add 1 tablespoon butter mixture and remaining 1 teaspoon lemon juice and toss to combine. Slice steaks and serve with squash, sprinkling squash with remaining 1 tablespoon chives and passing remaining butter mixture separately.

Spicy Shrimp Soup

Serves 4

You can use kielbasa sausage in place of the linguica.

- 2 tablespoons vegetable oil
- 4 carrots, peeled and sliced ½ inch thick
- 1 onion, halved and sliced thin
- 2 celery ribs, sliced ½ inch thick
- 1½ tablespoons Old Bay seasoning
- 5 cups water
- 8 ounces red potatoes, unpeeled, cut into ¾-inch pieces
- 6 ounces mild linguica sausage, sliced on bias ½ inch thick
- ½ teaspoon pepper
- ¼ teaspoon table salt
- 1 pound extra-large shrimp (21 to 25 per pound), peeled, deveined, and tails removed
- ¾ cup fresh or thawed frozen corn

1. Heat oil in Dutch oven over medium-high heat until shimmering. Add carrots, onion, and celery and cook until onion is softened, 5 to 7 minutes.

2. Stir in Old Bay and cook until fragrant, about 15 seconds. Stir in water, potatoes, sausage, pepper, and salt and bring to boil. Reduce heat to medium, cover, and simmer until potatoes are tender, about 10 minutes.

3. Stir in shrimp and corn. Cover and continue to cook until shrimp is cooked through, about 4 minutes longer. Serve.

BACON

Food trends come and go, but bacon never goes out of style. That's because it strikes the perfect balance between sweet, salty, smoky, and meaty.

by Scott Kathan

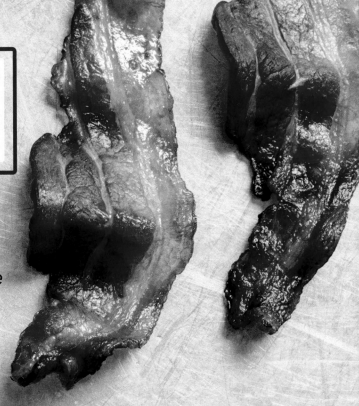

Grease Is the Word

you're not saving your bacon fat, it's not oo late to start. Simply strain the cooled ut still liquid) fat through a fine-mesh trainer into a glass jar or bowl, cover it, nd refrigerate it until you're ready to use . It will make anything you cook with —soups and stews, fried eggs, German otato salad, cornbread, biscuits, mashed otatoes, and beans—taste better.

Bacon's Best Friends

PERFECT PARTNERS
Bacon pairs well with eggs, potatoes, pears, corn, apples, shrimp, cabbage, cheese, and cream.

Unexpected Uses

- Add some crispy bacon bits to sweets—crispy rice cereal treats, chocolate chip cookies, caramel ice cream, and even apple pie take well to this sweet-savory treatment.
- Use bacon fat to supplement the oil in salad dressings and homemade mayonnaise.
- Weave slices of bacon around your favorite roast or meatloaf.
- Make bacon jam. Find our recipe at **CooksCountry.com/baconjam**.

Best Cooking Methods

A general rule of thumb is to never cook bacon too quickly or aggressively—the fat needs time to be rendered. For evenly cooked bacon with minimal mess, turn to the oven. Arrange slices on a rimmed baking sheet and place the sheet in a 400-degree oven. Cook for 6 minutes, rotate the sheet, and continue to cook until the bacon is crispy, 6 minutes longer for thin-cut bacon or 9 minutes longer for thick-cut. No flipping required.

To cook only a few slices, place the bacon in a skillet and add just enough water to barely cover it. Bring the water to a boil over high heat, and then lower the heat to medium and cook until the water has evaporated and the bacon is crispy. The water helps the bacon retain its moisture and stay tender—it also helps prevent burning and uneven cooking.

BIG BATCH

SMALL BATCH

 Feel like taking your bacon fixation to the next level? Make your own bacon! Our sister publication has a recipe at **CooksIllustrated.com/DIYbacon**.

Test Kitchen Taste Test Winners

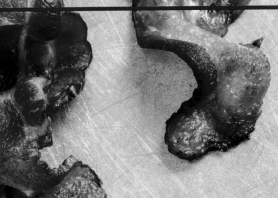

SUPERMARKET
Oscar Mayer Naturally Hardwood Smoked Bacon
This "classic" bacon (about $7 per pound) hit all the right notes."

ARTISANAL
Vande Rose Applewood Smoked Artisan Dry Cured Bacon
With a "thick and chewy" texture and a "savory," flavor, this fantastic yet expensive bacon (about $29 per pound) had "balanced" salt, sugar, and smoke levels.

THICK-CUT
Sugardale Thick Sliced Bacon
This "very meaty" bacon (about $4 per pound) stood out for its sweet, "distinctly maple taste."

TURKEY
Wellshire All Natural Uncured Turkey Bacon
This product (about $9 per pound) is closer to Canadian bacon than it is to American-style bacon. Still, we liked its balance of smoky, salty, and sweet flavors.

FRENCH BREAD PIZZA

What do you get when you combine garlic bread and pizza? Layers of flavor.

by Jessica Rudolph

BEFORE DEVELOPING MY own recipe for French bread pizza, I first had to gauge my competition. So I picked up some boxed versions from the frozen foods aisle of the supermarket and brought them back to the test kitchen. Judging by the responses from my coworkers, you'd have thought I'd spent all day building artisan pizzas from scratch. Many a wide-eyed test cook paused as they wandered past, longingly ogling the picture-perfect pizzas or excitedly recounting adolescent afternoons spent in front of their TVs with a plate of French bread pizza in their laps.

I set out to make a hearty, delicious French bread pizza that was easy to prepare and that was ready in less time than it takes to bake the frozen kind. I began by testing different types of bread. After auditioning what felt like the entire supermarket bakery, I settled on a soft French loaf for its thin crust and tender interior (baguettes had great flavor but were a bit too chewy for this application). Toasting the bread before adding toppings proved necessary to crisp the cut surface and discourage its porous insides from absorbing too much sauce. Since I was doing an initial

bake, why not gild the lily and give the bread a garlic-bread treatment? I brushed the cut side with melted butter, granulated garlic, and a pinch of pepper flakes before toasting it in the oven. To produce the crisp exterior I sought during this initial baking step, I brushed the outside crust with olive oil.

With my crispy crust settled, I turned to the sauce. A simple stir-together mix of canned crushed tomatoes, olive oil, Italian seasoning, and sugar made a bold and bright sauce that couldn't have been easier.

I saved the fun part for last. My coworkers and I had different ideas for how to top the pizzas, but we all agreed to start with a classic base of shredded low-moisture mozzarella (the fresh kind was too rubbery once it was melted) plus a sprinkling of grated Parmesan for nutty depth. Some purists wanted to leave it at that, while others were happy only once pepperoni joined the party. But there's no reason to stop there; unlike flimsy pizza dough, the hearty French bread base can withstand a mountain of toppings. As a nod to my favorite pizzas as a child, I made both pineapple-bacon and supreme variations as well. Pizza party, anyone?

BEYOND BAGUETTE
Soft supermarket French bread is best for these pizzas; traditional baguettes are a tad too chewy.

PEPPERONI FRENCH BREAD PIZZA

Serves 4

A 24 by 4-inch loaf of supermarket French bread, which has a soft, thin crust and fine crumb, works best here. If you can't find soft French bread, you can substitute one and a half 18-inch baguettes, though the crust will be slightly tougher. Cut the baguettes into six equal pieces, and distribute the toppings evenly.

PIZZA
- 1 (24 by 4-inch) loaf soft French bread
- 1 tablespoon extra-virgin olive oil
- 8 tablespoons unsalted butter, melted
- 2 teaspoons granulated garlic
- ½ teaspoon table salt
- ¼ teaspoon red pepper flakes
- 12 ounces mozzarella cheese, shredded (3 cups)
- 1 ounce Parmesan cheese, grated (½ cup)
- 2 ounces thinly sliced pepperoni

SAUCE
- 1½ cups canned crushed tomatoes
- 1 tablespoon extra-virgin olive oil
- 1½ teaspoons Italian seasoning
- ½ teaspoon sugar
- ½ teaspoon table salt
- ½ teaspoon pepper

1. FOR THE PIZZA: Adjust oven rack to upper-middle position and heat oven to 450 degrees. Line rimmed baking sheet with aluminum foil. Cut bread in half crosswise, then halve each piece horizontally to create 4 equal pieces. Arrange pieces cut side down on prepared sheet. Brush crust with oil.

2. Combine melted butter, granulated garlic, salt, and pepper flakes in bowl. Flip bread cut side up and brush cut side evenly with melted butter mixture. Bake, cut side up, until browned around edges, about 5 minutes.

3. FOR THE SAUCE: Meanwhile, combine all ingredients in bowl. (Sauce can be refrigerated for up to 24 hours.)

4. Spread sauce evenly over toasted bread, then top with mozzarella, followed by Parmesan and pepperoni (in that order). Bake until cheese is melted and spotty brown, about 15 minutes. Let pizza cool for 5 minutes. Serve.

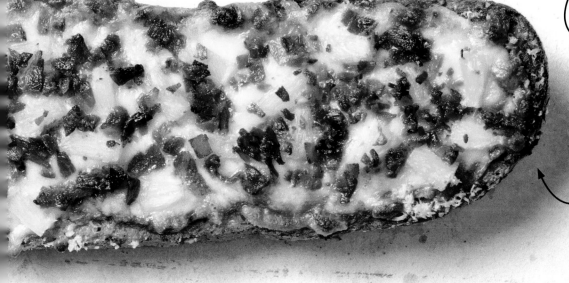

SUPREME FRENCH BREAD PIZZA
Decrease pepperoni to 1½ ounces. Add 2½ ounces sweet Italian sausage, casings removed, meat pinched into ½-inch pieces; ½ cup thinly sliced red onion; ½ cup thinly sliced green bell pepper, cut into 2-inch lengths; and ½ cup sliced black olives with pepperoni.

PINEAPPLE AND BACON FRENCH BREAD PIZZA
Substitute ¾ cup crumbled cooked bacon and ¾ cup canned pineapple tidbits, drained and patted dry, for pepperoni.

Building a Better French Bread Pizza

1. Cut bread, place on rimmed baking sheet, and brush crust with olive oil.

2. Flip bread and brush cut side with garlic-butter mixture.

3. Bake until nicely browned around edges.

4. Top with sauce, cheese, and toppings and bake.

Stroud's Cinnamon Rolls

In Kansas City, these fluffy, sweet rolls are served at dinner. We like them anytime. **by Jessica Rudolph**

THEY MAY NOT be the image you conjure when you think of cinnamon rolls, but the rolls served at Stroud's Oak Ridge Manor (see "Kansas City's Sweet Surprise") use a similar buttery cinnamon sugar mixture as well as just enough salt to be noticeable. Instead of being swirled up inside, however, the mixture coats the outside of the rolls. And unlike traditional cinnamon rolls, these are not covered in frosting— they're served with lunch or dinner alongside fried chicken.

In the test kitchen, I started with a yeasted dough from our archives. It produces a pillowy and lightly sweet roll that's enriched with butter, milk, and eggs—perfect for this application. I mixed the dough in a stand mixer and let it rise for an hour before portioning and rolling it into smaller dough balls.

For the good stuff, I stirred together melted butter, sugar, cinnamon, and salt. I poured some of this goo into the bottom of a baking dish, like they do at Stroud's, and then tucked my dough balls into the dish to let them rise again. Topped with more goo and baked, the golden rolls smelled heavenly, but they were stickier than I wanted.

Rethinking the goo, I tried rolling individual dough balls in melted butter and cinnamon sugar to avoid the sugar collecting in empty spaces between the rolls. This batch was more promising, cleanly releasing from the dish with an even sugary coating, but it was missing butteriness. The solution was easy: I brushed a second, smaller batch of the sugar-butter mixture onto the baked rolls while they were still hot from the oven. As they rested, the rolls absorbed buttery richness, and the extra sugar made the coating even more crunchy.

I wanted to have cinnamon rolls any time of day, so I made a batch through the sugar-rolling step and refrigerated it overnight. I baked the rolls the next morning, and they were indistinguishable from a same-day batch. So go ahead and make these for breakfast, too.

Keys to Sturdy, Salty-Sweet Dinner Rolls

1. Roll raw dough balls in butter, then in cinnamon sugar.

2. Transfer dough balls to baking dish and let rise until doubled in size.

3. Bake until rolls are golden brown and register 200 degrees.

4. Brush baked rolls with sugar-butter mixture and let cool for 10 minutes.

These sticky rolls are a little sweet, a little savory, and fully delicious.

STROUD'S CINNAMON ROLLS
Makes 15 rolls

We developed this recipe using a 4½-quart stand mixer. If using a larger mixer, you may need to increase the mixing time after adding the butter in step 2 to about 10 minutes. If the dough doesn't come together in the mixer, switch to a paddle attachment and mix just until the dough comes together. Then switch back to the dough hook and keep kneading. Use an instant-read thermometer to make sure that the milk is the correct temperature. We developed this recipe using a ceramic baking dish. If you choose to use a metal baking pan, reduce the baking time to 20 minutes. The slight tackiness of the dough aids in rolling it into smooth balls in step 4, so do not dust your counter with flour.

DOUGH

- ½ cup plus 2 tablespoons warm milk (110 degrees)
- 1 large egg
- 2 cups plus 2 tablespoons (10⅝ ounces) all-purpose flour
- 1½ teaspoons instant or rapid-rise yeast
- 2 tablespoons sugar
- 1 teaspoon table salt
- 4 tablespoons unsalted butter, softened

COATING

- 1¼ cups (8¾ ounces) sugar
- 4 teaspoons ground cinnamon
- ½ teaspoon table salt
- 12 tablespoons unsalted butter, melted, divided

1. FOR THE DOUGH: Whisk milk and egg together in bowl of stand mixer. Add flour and yeast. Fit mixer with dough hook and mix on low speed until all flour is moistened, about 2 minutes, scraping down dough hook and bowl as

THE ENTRANCE TO STROUD'S TAKES
YOU THROUGH A NEARLY 200-YEAR-OLD CABIN.

ON THE ROAD

eded. Let stand for 15 minutes.
Add sugar and salt and mix on
edium-low speed for 5 minutes.
ith mixer running, add butter,
tablespoon at a time. Continue to
ix on medium-low speed 5 min-
es longer, scraping down dough
ok and bowl occasionally (dough
ill stick to bottom of bowl). Trans-
r dough to greased large bowl.
over tightly with plastic wrap and
t rise at room temperature until
ubled in size, about 1 hour.

FOR THE COATING: Com-
ne sugar, cinnamon, and salt in
wl. Reserve ¾ cup cinnamon sug-
. Place remaining cinnamon sugar
shallow dish. Place 6 tablespoons
elted butter in second shallow dish.
. Grease 13 by 9-inch baking dish.
urn out dough onto counter and
vide into fifteen 1⅓-ounce por-
ons; divide any remaining dough
enly among portions. Working
ith 1 portion at a time, cup dough
ith your palm and roll against
unter into smooth, tight ball.
. Working with 3 or 4 dough balls
a time, roll dough balls in melted
tter in shallow dish, then roll in
nnamon sugar in shallow dish.
ace dough balls in prepared dish
3 rows of five. Cover loosely with
astic and let rise at room tempera-
re until doubled in size, about
hour (cinnamon sugar coating
ay crack during rising; this is OK).
djust oven rack to middle position
d heat oven to 350 degrees.
. Bake until rolls are puffed and
lden brown and register at least
00 degrees in center, about 25 min-
tes. Whisk reserved cinnamon
gar and remaining 6 tablespoons
elted butter in bowl until com-
ined (mixture may look separated).
rush tops and sides of hot rolls
ith cinnamon sugar–butter mixture
se all of it) and let cool in dish for
0 minutes. Remove rolls from dish
nd serve warm.

TO MAKE AHEAD

efore letting dough balls rise for
econd time in step 5, cover baking
ish with plastic wrap and refriger-
te for up to 24 hours. Let dough
alls sit at room temperature for
hour before baking.

Kansas City's Sweet Surprise

Sweet rolls for supper? You better believe it.

Text by Bryan Roof; photos by Steve Klise

AT STROUD'S OAK Ridge Manor in Kansas City, Missouri, customers line up for the famous pan-fried chicken. But it's what's served on the side of your lunch or dinner plate that intrigued us most: cinnamon rolls.

Far from the overly sweet, frosted monsters you'd find at the mall or at a breakfast café, these fluffy, buttery little rolls rolled in cinnamon sugar offer a surprising complement to the savory main course.

After 40 years as a barbecue restaurant, Stroud's refreshed their menu in the 1970s and introduced their cinnamon rolls. They've been a customer favorite ever since.

In the kitchen at Stroud's, a cook tends 16 skillets full of oil for frying chicken (below). Stroud's serves hundreds of orders of pan-fried chicken daily. Cinnamon rolls, which are proofed in a syrup of cinnamon, sugar, and butter, are served as a side.

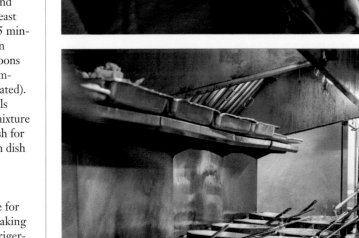

MAPLE PARK

KANSAS CITY

S'mores Bars

Summer's sweetest taste. **by Jessica Rudolph**

THERE IS NO more iconic summertime treat than a s'more—toasty marshmallow and snappy-soft milk chocolate sandwiched between graham cracker squares—enjoyed around a campfire. I wanted to translate the best parts of a s'more into a portable bar cookie that could be made anytime.

I knew I'd need a crunchy graham cracker base that was thick enough to support a heavy filling. I started with a recipe for a shortbread-like cookie, swapping out two-thirds of the flour for graham cracker crumbs (made in the food processor). I added sugar and salt and cut in cold butter to ensure a tender yet sturdy cookie. I pressed the dough into an 8-inch square baking pan and baked it until it was browned. The cookie texture was just right, but the flavor was a bit delicate; swapping in brown sugar for white added a caramelly depth.

As for chocolate, Hershey's is the classic choice for good reason: Other chocolates were too bitter and not soft enough. I topped my cooled crust with an even layer of chocolate bars and moved on to the marshmallows.

Marshmallows scattered on top of the chocolate and baked until toasty turned chewy and tough. Marshmallow crème baked into a sliceable yet gooey layer, but it also toasted unevenly, leaving leopard spots of char.

Using both products worked the best: A thin layer of marshmallow crème covered with mini marshmallows produced a gooey marshmallow layer with a toasty top. A sprinkling of chopped chocolate was the perfect finishing touch. S'mores just became a year-round treat.

Scout's Honor

In 1927, the book *Tramping and Trailing with the Girl Scouts* included a recipe for "some mores," but it wasn't the first published recipe for the graham cracker, chocolate, and marshmallow stack. That distinction belongs to Gladys Williams, who developed a recipe for campfire graham cracker sandwiches in the early 1920s for the Campfire Marshmallow Company. By the late 1930s, the treat took the name "s'mores."

S'MORES BARS
Makes 16 bars

We developed this recipe using Fluff brand marshmallow crème. Hershey's Milk Chocolate bars are best here; if you're using our favorite milk chocolate from Endangered Species, use four 3-ounce bars. Note that the baked s'mores bars need to cool for about 4 hours to set the chocolate; if you're in a hurry, you can put the bars in the refrigerator for 1 hour, but don't refrigerate them for much longer because the crust will become too hard.

7	whole graham crackers, broken into rough pieces
½	cup (2½ ounces) all-purpose flour
¼	cup packed (1¾ ounces) brown sugar
½	teaspoon table salt
8	tablespoons unsalted butter, cut into ½-inch pieces and chilled
6	(1.55-ounce) Hershey's Milk Chocolate bars, divided
1	cup marshmallow crème
1½	cups mini marshmallows

Browned marshmallows add to the "right from the campfire" appeal.

1. Adjust oven rack to middle position and heat oven to 425 degrees. Make foil sling for 8-inch square baking pan by folding 2 long sheets of aluminum foil so each is 8 inches wide. Lay sheets of foil in pan perpendicular to each other, with extra foil hanging over edges of pan. Push foil into corners and up sides of pan, smoothing foil flush to pan. Generously spray foil with vegetable oil spray.
2. Process cracker pieces in food processor until finely ground, about 30 seconds. Add flour, sugar, and salt and pulse to combine, about 5 pulses.

Add butter and pulse until mixture is uniform and resembles wet sand, about 20 pulses. Press dough into even layer in bottom of prepared pan. Bake until crust is set and well browned around edges, about 13 minutes. Let cool completely. (Cooled crust can be wrapped in plastic wrap and stored at room temperature for up to 2 days.)
3. Cover crust with 5 chocolate bars, breaking bars as necessary to create even layer (you will have some chocolate left over). Chop remaining chocolate fine and set aside. Spray offset spatula with oil spray. Using prepared spatula, spread marshmallow crème over chocolate. Sprinkle marshmallows evenly over marshmallow crème.
4. Bake bars until edges are set and marshmallows are puffed and dark brown, about 15 minutes. Transfer pan to wire rack and sprinkle with chopped chocolate. Let bars cool until chocolate is set, at least 4 hours.
5. Lightly spray chef's knife with oil spray. Using foil overhang, lift bars out of pan. (Marshmallows may stick to foil. Use knife to separate, if necessary.) Cut bars into 16 squares. Serve. (Do not cut bars until ready to serve. Bars can be stored in airtight container at room temperature for up to 2 days.)

Building Better Bars
Construction is the key to keeping these bars tender but also portable and sturdy enough to eat out of hand.

1. Make crust in food processor, press into pan, and bake.

2. Lay chocolate over baked crust.

3. Top with marshmallow crème and marshmallows and bake.

Mixed Berry Buckle

A sweet proposition from the past for peak-season berries.

by Mark Huxsoll

THE BUCKLE—COUSIN to crumble, crisp, and coffee cake—consists of a thick cake batter mixed with chopped fruit or berries and baked under a crunchy streusel topping. Friendly and rustic, it's been a favorite of New England home cooks for hundreds of years.

But when I tested five existing recipes for buckles, the results were all over the place. Some versions were on the dry side and too cake-like, while others called for more liquid and had fruit that sank to the bottom, reminding me of cobblers. I wanted to find that sweet spot with the perfect amount of fruit suspended in a buttery, supermoist (almost creamy) cake.

The berries were a vexing variable. I tested several different methods of pretreating the fresh berries so that, when baked, they were luscious and summery. I found that halving the raspberries and blackberries and tossing them with the blueberries and sugar brought out their natural sweetness and evened out the variance between sweet and sour. A bit of lemon zest added punch.

As is often the case, the best batter was a dead-simple one: milk, eggs, melted butter, and vanilla whisked together and then flour, sugar, baking powder, lemon zest, and salt stirred in. I found that folding half the fruit into the batter and then sprinkling the rest of the berries on top evenly distributed the berries and looked good, too.

Finally, I added a crumbly streusel topping for texture and sweetness. This buckle was the perfect way to celebrate summer's bounty.

MIXED BERRY BUCKLE *Serves 8*

We prefer the flavor of fresh mixed berries here, but you can also use a single variety of berries as long as the total amount still equals 15 ounces (3 cups). If using all fresh blueberries, omit the ¼ cup sugar for tossing the berries in step 4; blueberries are sweet enough on their own. You can also use 15 ounces (3 cups) of frozen mixed berries that have been thawed, drained for 30 minutes in a colander, and then patted dry with paper towels.

STREUSEL
- 1 cup (5 ounces) all-purpose flour
- ½ cup packed (3½ ounces) light brown sugar
- 6 tablespoons unsalted butter, melted
- ½ teaspoon table salt

CAKE
- ½ cup whole milk
- 2 large eggs
- 4 tablespoons unsalted butter, melted
- 1 teaspoon vanilla extract
- 1 cup (5 ounces) all-purpose flour
- ½ cup (3½ ounces) granulated sugar, divided
- 1½ teaspoons baking powder
- 1 teaspoon grated lemon zest
- ½ teaspoon table salt
- 5 ounces (1 cup) blackberries, cut in half crosswise
- 5 ounces (1 cup) blueberries
- 5 ounces (1 cup) raspberries, cut in half crosswise

1. FOR THE STREUSEL: Stir all ingredients in bowl until no dry spots remain and mixture forms clumps. Refrigerate until streusel is firm, at least 10 minutes. Keep refrigerated until ready to use.

2. FOR THE CAKE: Adjust oven rack to middle position and heat oven to 350 degrees. Grease light-colored 9-inch round cake pan, line with parchment paper, grease parchment, and flour pan.

3. Whisk milk, eggs, melted butter, and vanilla in bowl until well combined. Whisk flour, ¼ cup sugar, baking powder, lemon zest, and salt together in large bowl. Stir milk mixture into flour mixture until just combined.

4. Toss blackberries, blueberries, and raspberries with remaining ¼ cup sugar in separate bowl until coated. Using rubber spatula, gently fold half of berry mixture into batter until evenly distributed. Transfer batter to prepared pan and spread to edges of pan with spatula. Sprinkle remaining half of berry mixture evenly over top.

5. Break streusel into pea-size crumbs and distribute evenly over berries. Bake until top of buckle is golden brown and toothpick inserted in center comes out clean, about 50 minutes, rotating pan halfway through baking. Let buckle cool in pan on wire rack for 2 hours.

6. Run paring knife around edges of pan to release buckle from pan. Place inverted plate on top of pan (do not use plate or platter on which you intend to serve buckle). Invert buckle, remove pan, and discard parchment. Reinvert buckle onto serving platter. Cut into wedges and serve.

Summer berries are more than an afterthought in this easy dessert.

Berry Important Stuff
How you treat the berries can make or break your buckle.

1. Cut blackberries and raspberries in half crosswise. Toss with blueberries and sugar.

2. Fold half of sugared berries into batter.

3. Sprinkle remaining berries on top of batter before baking.

Basil Pesto

An extra step pays outsize dividends in this recipe for a classic summertime sauce. **by Cecelia Jenkins**

BASIL PESTO

Serves 4 to 6 (Makes 1¾ cups)

This recipe yields enough to sauce 1 pound of pasta. We prefer the flavor of Italian pine nuts here; the container should indicate where they're grown. Use a good-quality, relatively mild extra-virgin olive oil for the best results. When shopping for basil, look for a 4-ounce plastic container of leaves with stems; after stemming, you should have 4 cups of leaves (3 ounces by weight). If you don't have a scale to measure the Parmesan, the amount of processed Parmesan should be about ½ cup plus 2 tablespoons. This pesto is also good on crostini, in sandwiches, on fish, or stirred into soup.

½	cup pine nuts
¾	cup extra-virgin olive oil, divided
4	ounces fresh basil leaves and stems
¾	teaspoon table salt, plus salt for blanching basil
1¼	ounces Parmesan cheese
2	garlic cloves, peeled

1. Combine pine nuts and 1 tablespoon oil in 8-inch skillet. Cook over medium heat, stirring often, until pine nuts are light golden, 3 to 6 minutes. Spread pine nuts out on plate and let cool for 15 minutes.
2. Meanwhile, bring 2 quarts water to boil in medium saucepan. Remove and discard basil stems from leaves (you should have 4 cups leaves [3 ounces by weight]). Add basil leaves and 1½ teaspoons salt to boiling water and cook until basil is wilted and bright green, 5 to 10 seconds. Using spider skimmer or slotted spoon, transfer basil directly to salad spinner and spin to remove excess water. Spread basil on clean dish towel to dry. (If you don't have a salad spinner, drain basil on clean dish towel and thoroughly pat dry with paper towels.)
3. Process Parmesan in food processor until finely ground, about 30 seconds; transfer to medium bowl. Process garlic, pine nuts, basil, salt, and remaining oil in now-empty processor until smooth, about 1 minute, scraping down sides of bowl as needed. Transfer pesto to bowl with Parmesan and stir to combine. Serve.

TO MAKE AHEAD

Place pesto in sealable 1-pint container and cover with additional 1 tablespoon extra-virgin olive oil. Refrigerate for up to 2 days or freeze for up to 1 month.

SPAGHETTI WITH PESTO

Serves 4 to 6

If you're planning on making the pesto specifically for coating pasta, you can blanch the basil in the salted pasta cooking water before cooking your pasta.

1	pound spaghetti
	Salt for cooking pasta
1	recipe Basil Pesto
	Parmesan cheese

Bring 4 quarts water to boil in large pot. Add pasta and 1 tablespoon salt and cook, stirring often, until al dente. Reserve ½ cup cooking water, then drain pasta and transfer to large bowl. Add pesto and reserved cooking water to pasta and toss to combine. Season with salt to taste. Serve immediately, passing Parmesan separately.

Step by Step

1. Measure basil
Measure out 4 lightly packed cups (3 ounces) of stemmed leaves.
Why? This method provides consistency in measuring.

2. Toast pine nuts
Combine the pine nuts and 1 tablespoon of oil in an 8-inch skillet. Cook over medium heat, stirring often.
Why? We toast the pine nuts in oil to bring out their flavor and to ensure that they brown more thoroughly and evenly.

3. Let pine nuts cool
Transfer the pine nuts to a plate, spread them into an even layer, and let them cool.
Why? Hot pine nuts will turn the pesto dark green or brown. Spreading them out disperses the heat, so they cool in 15 minutes.

4. Blanch basil
Add the basil and 1½ teaspoons of salt to boiling water and cook until the basil is bright green, 5 to 10 seconds.
Why? Blanching denatures the browning enzymes in the basil and helps it hold on to its bright green color.

5. Spin dry
Transfer the basil to a salad spinner and spin to remove the excess water.
Why? After blanching, the basil leaves become limp, clump together, and retain water. The salad spinner is the most effective way to dry them.

Ingredients

Extra-Virgin Olive Oil

Basil pesto is a prime example of how a recipe can be only as good as its ingredients. The test kitchen has two favorite supermarket olive oils, **Bertolli Extra-Virgin Olive Oil, Original, Rich Taste** and **California Olive Ranch Destination Series Everyday Extra Virgin Olive Oil**. Our tasters found these oils to have a light, medium-fruity flavor and lightly peppery aftertaste. Freshness is key with olive oils, and both of these products list a harvest date on the label so that you know when the olives were picked.

Parmesan

While both Parmesan and Pecorino Romano are traditional in pesto, we prefer the milder, nutty flavor of Parmesan. For pesto with a stronger profile, use Pecorino. Our taste test–winning supermarket Parmesan is **Boar's Head Parmigiano-Reggiano**, which costs about $20 per pound.

Not All Pine Nuts Are Created Equal

Did you know that there are two varieties of pine nuts commonly sold in the United States? We prefer Italian pine nuts, which are easily identifiable by their thin, oblong shape; they taste creamier and nuttier. Chinese and Russian pine nuts, on the other hand, are shorter and rounder and, in our experience, taste oily and are more prone to rancidity. This recipe will work with Chinese or Russian pine nuts as long as they haven't gone rancid. But as far as pine nuts go, we say, *viva L'Italia*!

ITALIAN PINE NUTS

½ inch

CHINESE AND RUSSIAN PINE NUTS

¼ inch

Adding pasta cooking water helps the pesto cling to the pasta.

Setting the Color

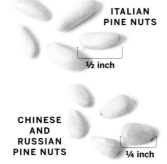

Blanching the basil before making pesto may sound fussy, but we found it essential to pesto that held its bright green color (see bowl on left). How does this work? Chlorophyll gives basil its green color. When cells containing chlorophyll are damaged—by being chopped in a food processor or by being bruised—the basil can turn an olive green (see bowl on right). A quick dip in boiling water activates an enzyme that inhibits this discoloration. Pesto made with blanched basil stays bright green for several days.

The Importance of Pasta Water

Our recipe for Spaghetti with Pesto calls for reserving ½ cup of the pasta cooking water to stir into the pasta with the pesto; the water turns the chunky pesto into a silky sauce that evenly clings to each noodle. We tested using plain hot water instead, but without the starch from the pasta, the dish was watery and thin. Without any added water, we found that the pesto slipped off the noodles and didn't cling, resulting in bland noodles and a pile of pesto at the bottom of the bowl.

Lay on clean dish towel
Arrange the leaves on a clean dish towel so that they're lying flat.
Why? It's important to remove any residual moisture from the leaves so that it doesn't water down the pesto.

7. Process Parmesan
Process the chunk of Parmesan in a food processor until it's finely ground, about 30 seconds. Transfer to a medium bowl.
Why? Since we were using the food processor already, we save ourselves some work and use it to grate the cheese, too.

8. Process pesto base
Add garlic, pine nuts, basil, salt, and the remaining oil to the processor and process until the mixture is smooth.
Why? Processing the remaining ingredients with the oil engages the blade to make an ultra-smooth pesto.

9. Combine with Parmesan
Transfer the pesto to the bowl with the grated cheese and stir to combine.
Why? The ground Parmesan provides concentrated pops of flavor in the pesto, which we preferred to thin shavings of cheese that disappear into the pesto.

10. Use or store
If not eating right away, transfer the pesto to a pint container, cover it with 1 tablespoon of oil, and refrigerate it for up to two days or freeze it for up to one month.
Why? The oil on top seals the pesto from contact with the air so that it doesn't discolor over time.

Turkey Meatballs with Coconut Rice

Turkey meatballs make a great canvas for flavor.

by Jessica Rudolph

Adding bold seasonings to turkey meatballs is a recipe for success.

Four Steps to a Tasty Dinner

1. Brown meatballs and remove from skillet.

2. Sauté peppers, then add raw rice and toast in flavorful fat for a nutty flavor.

3. Add liquid and return meatballs to skillet; cover and cook.

4. Add peas, peanuts, scallions, and cilantro off heat before serving.

FOR ME, THE most comforting weeknight meals start with a bowl of perfectly cooked rice. Add coconut milk and vegetables to the rice and top it with savory meatballs packed with deep, rich flavors, and that comforting meal gets a lot more enticing. But do you know what's not very enticing? A sinkful of dirty dishes on a weeknight. I'd aim to cook everything together using a single skillet.

I tackled the meatballs first, adding cilantro, scallions, ginger, fish sauce, and chili-garlic sauce to a mixture of ground beef and pork for a fresh, savory, and spicy flavor profile. But both the beef and pork tasted a little heavy here, so I switched to ground turkey: Its mild taste was the perfect backdrop for the aromatic mix-ins. Some panko bread crumbs and an egg bound everything together and helped the turkey stay moist. The mixture was quite soft at first, but a brief stint in the refrigerator firmed up the balls so that they stayed round as I browned them in the skillet.

After searing and setting aside the meatballs, I sautéed sliced red bell peppers. I then added rice and lightly toasted it, both to bring out its nuttiness and to combat future clumping. I knew from previous test kitchen recipes how much water to use for perfectly cooked rice, but I swapped out one-third of the water for canned coconut milk (just enough for subtle coconut flavor and creaminess without the rice turning stodgy). A tablespoon of fish sauce provided a savory backbone and kept the coconut flavor from veering too sweet. Once everything was boiling, I added the meatballs back in to finish cooking and simmered everything together, covered, for 20 minutes.

After I let the rice rest for 10 minutes off the heat to ensure that it absorbed all the flavorful liquid, I stirred in some peas for a burst of color. More scallions and cilantro on top amped up the fresh flavor, and a sprinkling of chopped peanuts added welcome crunch. A squeeze of lime juice was the only thing missing from this comforting, flavor-packed dish, made all the more satisfying without dish duty looming overhead.

ONE-PAN TURKEY MEATBALLS WITH COCONUT RICE *Serves 4*

Do not use 99 percent lean ground turkey; it will make dry meatballs. We like the flavor of jasmine rice here, though any long-grain white rice will work. Rinse the rice in a fine-mesh strainer under running water until the water runs almost clear, about 1½ minutes, agitating the rice a few times with your hand. We developed this recipe with Aroy-D Coconut Milk. A 12-inch nonstick skillet with a tight-fitting lid is essential. Turn the meatballs gently in step 2 so that they won't break.

- 1 **pound ground turkey**
- ½ **cup panko bread crumbs**
- 6 **scallions, sliced thin, divided**
- ½ **cup chopped fresh cilantro, divided**
- 1 **large egg, lightly beaten**
- 2 **tablespoons Asian chili-garlic sauce, plus extra for serving**
- 2 **tablespoons fish sauce, divided**
- 1 **tablespoon grated fresh ginger**
- 1 **teaspoon table salt, divided**
- 2 **tablespoons vegetable oil**
- 2 **red bell peppers, stemmed, seeded, and sliced into ¼-inch-thick strips (2 cups)**
- 1 **cup long-grain white rice, rinsed**
- 1½ **cups water**
- ⅔ **cup canned coconut milk**
- ½ **cup frozen peas, thawed**
- ¼ **cup dry-roasted peanuts, chopped coarse**
  Lime wedges

1. Combine turkey, panko, two-thirds of scallions, ¼ cup cilantro, egg, chili-garlic sauce, 1 tablespoon fish sauce, ginger, and ½ teaspoon salt in bowl and mix with your hands until thoroughly combined. Divide mixture into 20 portions, about 2 tablespoons each. Roll portions between your wet hands to form meatballs. Transfer meatballs to plate and refrigerate for 15 minutes.

2. Heat oil in 12-inch nonstick skillet over medium-high heat until shimmering. Add meatballs and cook until well browned all over, 5 to 7 minutes. Return meatballs to plate, leaving fat in skillet.

3. Add bell peppers to now-empty skillet; cook until beginning to brown, about 2 minutes. Add rice and cook, stirring frequently, until edges of grains begin to turn translucent, about 1 minute. Stir in water, coconut milk, remaining 1 tablespoon fish sauce, and remaining ½ teaspoon salt and bring to boil.

4. Return meatballs to skillet. Cover, reduce heat to low, and cook for 20 minutes.

5. Without removing lid, remove skillet from heat and let sit, covered, for 10 minutes. Gently stir peas into rice. Sprinkle with peanuts, remaining one-third of scallions, and remaining ¼ cup cilantro. Serve with lime wedges and extra chili-garlic sauce.

Sweet Pickle Relish

Do you really know what's on your hot dog? With our easy recipe, you will. **by Matthew Fairman**

SWEET PICKLE RELISH, my favorite style of relish, is a must-have topping for hot dogs. It's also irreplaceable in every mayo-based salad from potato to egg to tuna, and if it's not in my tartar sauce or rémoulade when I'm eating fried seafood, then I'm in shambles. Simply put, I need a jar of it in my fridge door at all times. But why make my own sweet pickle relish when there's a dozen perfectly good products in the store?

It's a cliché to criticize store-bought condiments for their mysterious ingredients, but the sentiment has merit. Take a look at the ingredient list on one of the top-selling relishes and you'll see that high-fructose corn syrup is high up on the list, followed by a litany of preservatives, "natural flavors," and food dyes. To be fair, I am not above eating squeeze packets of the stuff at the ballpark. But the recipe I developed is miles better—more balanced, a little savory, and more wholesome. You can actually identify all the ingredients without a degree in chemistry!

My recipe starts with a pound of cucumbers, ½ cup each of chopped red bell pepper and onion, and a clove of garlic. The onion and garlic add a savory bite, and the bell pepper adds color and a pleasant sweetness. I use a food processor to streamline the chopping, and then I salt the vegetables for an hour, drain them, and squeeze them

dry in a dish towel to remove excess liquid. (Skipping this step means that you have to simmer and reduce the relish for longer, which muddies the flavor and turns the relish mushy.)

From there, I simply combine the chopped, salted, and drained vegetables with 1 cup of distilled white vinegar and ½ cup of sugar in a large saucepan and simmer them for about 15 minutes until the vegetables are translucent, the flavors have melded, and the liquid is reduced until slightly syrupy. Brilliant.

SWEET PICKLE RELISH

Makes about 1¾ cups
You can substitute pickling cucumbers (sometimes called Kirby cucumbers) for the English cucumbers, if you like.

- 1 **pound English cucumbers, cut into 1-inch pieces**
- ½ **cup coarsely chopped red bell pepper**
- ½ **cup coarsely chopped onion**
- 1 **tablespoon kosher salt**
- 1 **garlic clove, minced**
- 1 **cup distilled white vinegar**
- ½ **cup sugar**
- ½ **teaspoon ground turmeric (optional)**

1. Pulse cucumbers in food processor until pieces measure roughly ¼ inch, 8 to 10 pulses, scraping down sides of bowl as needed. Transfer to large bowl. Pulse bell pepper and onion until pieces measure roughly ¼ inch, about 10 pulses, scraping down sides of bowl as needed. Transfer to bowl with cucumbers. Stir in salt and garlic. Cover and refrigerate for 1 hour.
2. Drain vegetables in colander, transfer to clean dish towel, and squeeze to remove excess liquid. Combine vegetables; vinegar; sugar; and turmeric, if using, in large saucepan and bring to boil over medium-high heat. Reduce heat to medium and simmer until vegetables are translucent and mixture has thickened slightly, 10 to 15 minutes.
3. Let relish cool completely, about 2 hours. Transfer relish to airtight container and refrigerate until ready to serve.

TO MAKE AHEAD

Relish can be refrigerated in airtight container for up to 4 months.

SWEET AND TANGY TARTAR SAUCE

Makes about 1 cup

- ¾ **cup mayonnaise**
- 2 **tablespoons capers, rinsed and minced**
- 2 **tablespoons Sweet Pickle Relish**
- 1 **tablespoon minced shallot**
- 1½ **teaspoons distilled white vinegar**
- ½ **teaspoon Worcestershire sauce**
- ½ **teaspoon pepper**

Mix all ingredients together in bowl. Cover with plastic wrap and let sit for 15 minutes to allow flavors to blend. Serve.

This relish is far brighter, fresher, and tastier than the store-bought stuff.

1. Pulse cucumbers, then pepper and onion.

2. Stir salt and garlic into vegetables.

3. Drain vegetables in colander, then squeeze dry in clean dish towel.

4. Combine vegetables, vinegar, sugar, and turmeric and simmer until thickened.

Chicken Noodle Casserole

We wanted all the homey comfort of this retro dish without the leftovers. **by Cecelia Jenkins**

IN THE 1940s, the Campbell Soup Company introduced Americans to chicken noodle casserole. The recipe, printed on the back of cream of mushroom soup cans, called for the condensed soup plus milk, precooked chicken and egg noodles, and some canned or frozen vegetables to be stirred together and baked, maybe with some crackers crushed over the top. I wanted a homemade version totally from scratch that was still easy and that was scaled down to make a cozy dinner for two.

To emulate the base flavors of mushroom soup, I began by cooking sliced mushrooms and chopped shallots. Once they started to brown, I turned to the chicken. Rotisserie chicken worked fine, but it tends to be overcooked and dry; in a side-by-side test, my tasters preferred the juicier chicken that was cooked in the casserole. I decided on boneless, skinless chicken thighs (more flavorful and less prone to drying out than breast meat) and cut them into chunks so that they'd cook faster and be easier to eat.

For a homemade white sauce, I sprinkled a little flour over the vegetables and chicken in the pan and then tested whisking in both milk and half-and-half; my tasters preferred the richness of the latter. A big handful of shredded cheddar added body and flavor.

Next up were the egg noodles. Instead of boiling them in water in a separate pot, I wanted to simply cook the noodles directly in the sauce (before adding the cheese). After a bit of testing, I got it to work by adding an equal amount of chicken broth with the half-and-half; though some noodles poked out of the shallow liquid in the skillet, frequent stirring ensured even cooking, and in just 8 minutes the noodles were done and infused with the flavors of the sauce. Some bright green peas—added straight from the freezer—completed the picture.

I tried sprinkling on a crunchy, flavorful topping of panko bread crumbs and Parmesan and running the pan under the broiler, but I found it easier to toast the topping in the pan before starting with the rest of the dish. I then reserved it to sprinkle over the casserole before serving.

CHICKEN NOODLE CASSEROLE FOR TWO

You can substitute cremini mushrooms for the white mushrooms, if desired. There is no need to thaw the frozen peas before adding them in step 4.

- 3 tablespoons extra-virgin olive oil, divided
- ½ cup panko bread crumbs
- ½ teaspoon table salt, divided
- ½ teaspoon pepper, divided
- 3 tablespoons grated Parmesan cheese
- 4 ounces white mushrooms, trimmed and sliced thin
- 2 shallots, chopped
- 8 ounces boneless, skinless chicken thighs, trimmed and cut into 1-inch pieces
- 4 teaspoons all-purpose flour
- 1 cup half-and-half
- 1 cup chicken broth
- 3 ounces (1½ cups) wide egg noodles
- 2 ounces sharp cheddar cheese, shredded (½ cup)
- ½ cup frozen peas

1. Combine 1 tablespoon oil, panko, ⅛ teaspoon salt, and ⅛ teaspoon pepper in 10-inch nonstick skillet. Cook over medium heat, stirring frequently, until evenly browned, 3 to 5 minutes. Off heat, sprinkle Parmesan evenly over panko mixture and stir to combine, breaking up any clumps. Transfer panko mixture to bowl; set aside.
2. Heat remaining 2 tablespoons oil in now-empty skillet over medium heat until shimmering. Add mushrooms, shallots, ¼ teaspoon salt, and ¼ teaspoon pepper and cook until moisture has evaporated and mushrooms are golden brown, about 8 minutes.
3. Add chicken and flour and stir until no dry flour remains. Cook for 1 minute. Stir in half-and-half and broth and bring to simmer. Stir in noodles, submerging them as much as possible, and cook, uncovered, stirring often, until noodles are tender and sauce is thickened (rubber spatula will leave trail that takes about 3 seconds to fill in), about 8 minutes.
4. Stir in cheddar, peas, remaining ⅛ teaspoon salt, and remaining ⅛ teaspoon pepper until cheese is completely melted and peas are warmed through, about 2 minutes. Off heat, sprinkle evenly with reserved panko mixture. Serve.

Chunks of flavorful boneless, skinless chicken thighs stay tender and juicy.

THE AMERICAN TABLE

"Casserole" is a flexible word. It can be used to mean the cooking vessel you use or the dish you cook in it. In other words, you can make a casserole in a casserole.

It's also a flexible concept, one that exploded in popularity in mid-century America. Use of the term started to spike in the 1950s, a time when American shoppers started to find a wider range of ingredients in the supermarket, including convenience products such as canned soups. Creative cooks saw opportunities to imprint their tastes and ideas on the simple concept, and soon variations on the theme were showing up on dinner tables and in potluck spreads everywhere. Today, the idea of a casserole has burst the bonds of its namesake vessel, as it does in this recipe.

The Comfort of Egg Noodles

What makes dried egg noodles different from other dried pastas at the supermarket? Eggs, naturally. Eggs give egg noodles added richness and their signature light yellow hue. In a recent taste test of egg noodles, we found that we preferred products that used egg yolks, not just egg whites as some do, and that were made with semolina flour. Our favorite product was from Pennsylvania Dutch.

PENNSYLVANIA DUTCH WIDE EGG NOODLES
The best of the bunch

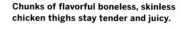

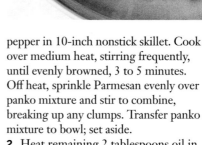

Adobo-Braised Beef

Once you've got the recipe for this remarkable adobo sauce, your slow cooker can take it from there.

Matthew Fairman

ADOBO-BRAISED BEEF—WITH
intensely flavored, glossy, mahogany
sauce and its hunks of tender, juicy
meat—may stand at the pinnacle of
Tex-Mex cooking. When I first tried a
version of this a few years ago (*Cook's
Country* readers and TV viewers
might recall our popular recipe for
Flank Steak in Adobo), I was stunned
at how good it was. Spicy, garlicky,
sweet, sour, meaty, fruity, rich—the
complex sauce, at once comforting
and invigorating, had me want-
ing more. I set out to make a great
slow-cooker version that was almost as
easy as it was flavorful.

The secret to adobo's otherworldly
appeal (or at least a big part of it) is
in dried chiles. Even if you haven't
cooked much with dried chiles, don't
let their presence here dissuade you
from making this recipe; they're easy
to use and can transform your cooking.
Once toasted to coax out their complex
flavors, rehydrated and softened in
warm water, and blitzed in a blender,
they form the backbone of a braising
sauce that is thick and glossy and has
an irreplaceable array of flavors. Prefab
chili powders don't compare.

Adobo sauces vary greatly but always
contain dried chiles, onion and garlic,
spices, and an acidic element. Through
research and testing I found that the
best mixes include orange and lime
juice for a bright citrus spark, sweet-tart
tomatillos, dried cumin and oregano,
and a combination of two dried chiles:
fruity anchos and earthy, pleasantly bitter pasillas. To save work in the kitchen,
I used jarred salsa verde to cover the
tomatillo and onion components.
Instead of browning the beef (boneless chuck worked best) on the stovetop
and sautéing the aromatics in the rendered fat before transferring everything
to the slow cooker, I took a big chance
and simply tossed the seasoned beef and
adobo sauce together in the slow cooker
before hitting the "start" button.

To my delight, this simplified version was excellent, with deep, rich
flavor and tender, silky chunks of beef.
What's more, you can make the adobo
sauce a day in advance and then just
throw everything in the slow cooker
on the day you plan to eat it. As one
tester commented, "This is not just a
good slow-cooker recipe, it's a good
recipe—full stop."

Flour tortillas are the perfect vehicle for mopping up the complex, glossy sauce.

Two Dried Chiles for Complex Flavor

You can make adobo sauce with chili powder, but using dried chiles provides deeper,
more potent flavor. Here we use raisiny ancho chiles (dried poblanos) and slightly bitter
pasillas, both of which can be found in many supermarkets (or can be ordered online).
The combination brings incredible depth and complexity to the sauce.

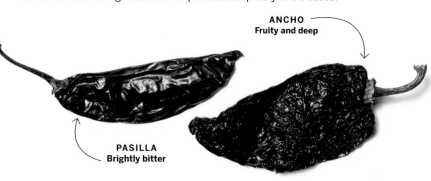

ANCHO
Fruity and deep

PASILLA
Brightly bitter

SLOW-COOKER ADOBO-BRAISED BEEF
Serves 4 to 6

Salsa verde is a green salsa made
from tomatillos and green chiles. We
developed this recipe using Frontera
Tomatillo Salsa. When buying the dried
chiles, 1½ ounces of ancho chiles will
be two to three chiles, and 1 ounce of
pasilla chiles will be about four chiles.
Both light and dark brown sugars work
for this recipe. We like flour tortillas
here, but corn tortillas work well, too.
If queso fresco is unavailable, you can
substitute farmer's cheese or a mild feta.
This dish is also great served over rice.

- 1½ ounces dried ancho chiles, stemmed
- 1 ounce dried pasilla chiles, stemmed
- ¾ cup salsa verde
- ½ cup orange juice
- ¼ cup lime juice (2 limes)
- 3 tablespoons packed brown sugar
- 2 teaspoons ground cumin
- 2 garlic cloves
- 2 teaspoons table salt, divided
- 1½ teaspoons dried oregano
- 1 teaspoon pepper, divided
- 2½ pounds boneless beef chuck-eye roast, trimmed and cut into 1-inch pieces
- 12 (8-inch) flour tortillas, warmed
- 4 ounces queso fresco, crumbled (1 cup)
- ½ cup coarsely chopped fresh cilantro

1. Using kitchen shears, cut anchos and
pasillas in half lengthwise and discard
seeds, then cut into 1-inch pieces. Place
anchos and pasillas in 12-inch skillet
and cook over medium heat, stirring
often, until fragrant, about 5 minutes.
Immediately transfer anchos and pasillas to bowl and cover with hot water.
Let stand until soft and pliable, about
5 minutes. Drain.

2. Process salsa verde, orange juice,
lime juice, sugar, cumin, garlic, 1 teaspoon salt, oregano, ½ teaspoon pepper,
and anchos and pasillas in blender until
smooth, 1 to 2 minutes. Pour adobo
sauce into slow cooker. Sprinkle beef
with remaining 1 teaspoon salt and
remaining ½ teaspoon pepper, transfer
to slow cooker, and stir to combine
with sauce.

3. Cover slow cooker and cook until
beef is tender, 4 to 5 hours on high or
6 to 8 hours on low. Serve with tortillas,
sprinkled with queso fresco and cilantro.

The Best Graters

Want the best grater? Look for the stamp of approval.

by Miye Bromberg

① ② ③ ④ ⑤ ⑥ ⑦ ⑧

IT HAD BEEN a while since we last tested graters, and we wanted to know if our favorite, the Rösle Coarse Grater, still held up to the competition. We bought eight models and used them to shred cheese, potatoes, and carrots. Two of the graters (including the Rösle model) were paddle-style, one was two-sided, and the other five were box graters. For testing, we focused on the graters' large-hole side, which is best for shredding.

All the graters worked, but a few factors made some perform better than others. One factor was the type of teeth. Teeth that are chemically etched on the grating surface lie flatter, creating narrower openings in which soft foods such as mozzarella can get stuck. We much preferred teeth that are mechanically stamped out of the grater's surface because they rise higher, providing more clearance for foods of all textures to pass through the grater's holes.

Right from the start, the teeth on some of the graters were dull, which meant that it took more time and effort to shred food on those graters. Dull teeth also tended to chew through produce, rupturing cell walls and splattering juice all over.

Another factor affecting performance was the area and length of the grating surface. The larger and longer the grating surface, the more ground we could cover before starting a new stroke and the less time it took to get through a batch of food.

Some testers liked paddle graters

TYPES OF TEETH
The teeth on stamped graters (top) rise higher above the grating surface than the teeth on etched graters (bottom).

because they could be hooked over a bowl or positioned at different angles on a cutting board. They were also easy to store and clean. Others preferred box graters because they sat securely on the cutting board, and their shape contained the shreds.

Regardless of the style, we liked graters with plastic bumpers or feet tipped with rubber, which prevented slipping and skidding. We also preferred graters with big, thick handles made from rubbery materials, which were more comfortable to hold—especially when wet—and accommodated a variety of grips.

We have two winning graters: one paddle and one box. We again liked the Rösle Coarse Grater for its flexible positioning, easier cleanup, and smaller footprint. We also liked the Cuisinart Box Grater for its greater security and shred containment. Both models feature large grating surfaces full of sharp, stamped teeth, so they're able to shred hard vegetables and soft cheeses alike. With big handles and rubber-tipped feet or bases, they are easy to hold and sit stably on a cutting board. We don't recommend either tool for slicing foods or grating them more finely (we tried with the winning box grater and the results were not good), but we're happy to reach for our favorite mandoline or rasp-style grater when we need to perform those tasks.

 Web subscribers can see the full testing results and complete chart at CooksCountry.com/jul20.

Web subscribers can see the full testing results and complete chart at CooksCountry.com/jul20.

KEY **Good** ★★★ **Fair** ★★ **Poor**

HIGHLY RECOMMENDED

Best Paddle-Style Grater
❶ Rösle Coarse Grater
Model: 95022 **Price:** $35.93
Performance: ★★★ **Ease of Use:** ★★½
Style: Paddle **Hole Type:** Stamped

COMMENTS: With one of the largest, longest grating surfaces and ultrasharp teeth, our previous favorite effortlessly shredded foods of all sizes and textures.

Best Box-Style Grater
❷ Cuisinart Box Grater
Model: CTG-00-BG **Price:** $11.95
Performance: ★★½ **Ease of Use:** ★★★
Style: Box **Hole Type:** Stamped

This box grater had a large, long grating surface studded with stamped teeth that were just a hair less keen than those of our favorite paddle grater.

RECOMMENDED

❸ Microplane Specialty Series 4-Sided Box Grater
Model: 34006 **Price:** $34.47
Performance: ★★½ **Ease of Use:** ★★
Style: Box **Hole Type:** Etched

With fairly sharp etched teeth, this box grater did a good job of shredding most foods. Cheese was a little difficult to shred.

RECOMMENDED WITH RESERVATIONS

❹ OXO Good Grips Etched Box Grater with Removable Zester
Model: 11231700 **Price:** $29.95
Performance: ★★ **Ease of Use:** ★★

We loved this model's large, rubbery handle and stable, grippy base, but it struggled to grate soft cheese.

❺ Cuisipro 4-Sided Box Grater
Model: 746850 **Price:** $31.00
Performance: ★★ **Ease of Use:** ★★

The handle of this etched grater was comfy, but the narrow holes clogged easily.

NOT RECOMMENDED

❻ KitchenAid Gourmet Stainless Steel Box Grater with Detachable Storage Container
Model: KN300OSOBA **Price:** $18.41
Performance: ★★ **Ease of Use:** ★½

With the dullest teeth in the lineup, this stamped grater made shredding difficult, requiring a ton of effort.

❼ Norpro Stainless Steel Coarse Grater
Model: 354 **Price:** $15.83
Performance: ★★½ **Ease of Use:** ★

This model was a pain: Its wire handle was uncomfortable, and it slid around during grating.

❽ Progressive Prep Solutions 2-Way Grate & Measure
Model: PS-9024 **Price:** $9.95
Performance: ★½ **Ease of Use:** ★

This two-way grater didn't deliver on its promise to allow us to grate both up and down.

Whole Dill Pickles

Whether you're enjoying a pickle as a satisfying side or as a quick snack, it should be three things: crunchy, tangy, and garlicky. **by Kate Shannon**

AMERICANS SPENT MORE than 2 billion on pickles last year, according to data from IRI, a Chicago-based market research firm. We set out to find the best whole dill pickles to enjoy alongside a meal or as a snack. We rounded up eight top-selling, nationally available products and sampled them plain—served chilled at a blind tasting—judging their flavor and texture.

Our lineup included a mix of styles. Seven products were vinegar pickles. Of those, four were shelf-stable and three were refrigerated. We also included one lacto-fermented pickle (cucumber immersed in a salt brine and allowed to ferment for days or weeks).

When we reviewed dill pickle spears, the shelf-stable products were soft and soggy, while the refrigerated pickles were crisp and crunchy. That's because the heat applied to shelf-stable spears during pasteurization essentially cooks them, softening their texture. But with whole dill pickles, the differences between the refrigerated and shelf-stable products were more subtle. The refrigerated whole pickles were crunchy, but the shelf-stable options were only "a little less crisp." We quickly came to understand why what was true for spears wasn't true for whole pickles. First, the skin surrounding a whole pickle holds it together and keeps it crisp. Second, whole pickles tend to have more mass than spears and thus are less affected by the heat of pasteurization, so they are more likely to retain their crunch and snap. We slightly preferred the texture of the refrigerated whole pickles, but all the pickles in our lineup were crunchy.

Flavor was a different story. Although all the products contained garlic and dill in some form, those flavors didn't always

come through. Some contained visible pieces of garlic and/or dill, while others used highly concentrated flavorings similar to those used in beef broth or other packaged foods. To our surprise, we didn't have a preference for a particular source of the garlic or dill—but we did want to taste those key ingredients. Some products were described by tasters as "garlicky," with "big emphasis on the dill," while others were milder and mainly just tangy. One was very heavily seasoned with warm spices that reminded tasters of "nutmeg," "five-spice powder," "cinnamon," and "anise." Another tasted like "licorice." These flavors felt out of place and overshadowed the garlic and dill.

Another thing that mattered? Tanginess. The concentration of the vinegars that manufacturers use for pickling can differ, and it can impact a pickle's flavor. Two of the vinegar pickles in our lineup tasted too sharp and too sour, so they were most likely made with a highly acidic vinegar. The other products, including the lacto-fermented pickle, were pleasantly tangy and vibrant.

After crunching our way through dozens of whole dill pickles, Boar's Head Kosher Dill Pickles—the sibling of our favorite dill pickle spears—emerged as the favorite. These refrigerated pickles were "firm" and had "great crunch." We also loved that they tasted almost like a "homemade" pickle, with lots of garlic and dill, balanced tanginess, and no bold competing spices. For a refreshingly tangy, garlicky whole dill pickle, Boar's Head is our top pick.

 Web subscribers can see the full tasting results and complete chart at **CooksCountry.com/jul20**.

RECOMMENDED

Our Favorite

Boar's Head Kosher Dill Pickles
Price: $4.79 for 26 oz ($0.18 per oz)
Style: Vinegar **Refrigerated:** Yes
Ingredients: Cucumbers, water, vinegar, carrots, salt, fresh dill, garlic, spices, $\frac{1}{10}$ of one percent sodium benzoate (as a preservative), calcium chloride, natural flavors, EDTA (to preserve freshness), turmeric (for color)

Comments: These refrigerated pickles were perfectly crisp and "extra-crunchy." They also earned top marks for flavor: Due to the strong presence of garlic and dill, tasters said these pickles "tasted almost homemade." A few slices of carrot, which do not affect flavor, are added to each jar.

Mt. Olive Kosher Dills
Price: $5.19 for 46 oz ($0.11 per oz)
Style: Vinegar **Refrigerated:** No
Ingredients: Cucumbers, water, vinegar, salt, calcium chloride, 0.1% sodium benzoate (preservative), natural flavors, polysorbate 80, and yellow 5

Comments: These shelf-stable pickles were crisp and crunchy. They had "the right amount of tang" and tasted "very familiar," with a hint of garlic and dill and no strong spices.

Dietz & Watson Kosher Pickles
Price: $4.99 for 32 oz ($0.16 per oz)
Style: Vinegar **Refrigerated:** Yes
Ingredients: Cucumbers, water, salt, vinegar, spices, garlic, dill, $\frac{1}{10}$ of 1% sodium benzoate (preservative), turmeric, natural spices, flavorings

Comments: Tasters liked the texture of these "very firm and crunchy" refrigerated pickles. They also liked that they were "heavy on the garlic flavor" and "actually tasted of dill."

Woodstock Organic Whole Kosher Dill Pickles
Price: $5.84 for 24 oz ($0.24 per oz)
Style: Vinegar **Refrigerated:** No
Ingredients: Organic cucumbers, water, organic vinegar, salt, contains less than 2% of dehydrated organic garlic, calcium chloride, natural flavors (contains mustard), organic gum arabic, organic turmeric extract (color)

Comments: These shelf-stable pickles stayed crisp through the pasteurization process. The vinegar flavor was a little too strong. We preferred pickles that weren't quite so bracingly sour.

RECOMMENDED WITH RESERVATIONS

Claussen Kosher Dill Wholes
Price: $4.49 for 32 oz ($0.14 per oz) **Style:** Vinegar
Refrigerated: Yes
Ingredients: Fresh cucumbers, water, distilled vinegar, salt, contains less than 2% of high fructose corn syrup, dried garlic, calcium chloride, sodium benzoate (to preserve flavor), spice, mustard seed, natural flavor, dried red peppers, polysorbate 80

Comments: We liked the "substantial crunch" of these pickles. They were heavily spiced, which was a turnoff for some.

Vlasic Kosher Dill Wholes
Price: $4.59 for 46 oz ($0.10 per oz) **Style:** Vinegar
Refrigerated: No
Ingredients: Cucumbers, water, distilled vinegar, salt, calcium chloride, polysorbate 80, natural flavors, yellow 5

Comments: These shelf-stable pickles were "slightly less crisp" than our favorites but weren't too soft or soggy. Tasters liked their mild, briny flavor; there were "no surprises."

Bubbie's Kosher Dill Pickles
Price: $8.39 for 33 oz ($0.25 per oz)
Style: Lacto-fermented
Refrigerated: Yes
Ingredients: Cucumbers, water, salt, garlic, dill, spices, mustard seed, calcium chloride

Comments: The one naturally fermented pickle in our lineup was crunchy, snappy, and satisfying. Most tasters thought the pickles were "too heavy on the seasonings," but some did say that they reminded them of good deli pickles.

NOT RECOMMENDED

McClure's Pickles Whole Garlic & Dill
Price: $10.00 for 32 oz ($0.31 per oz) **Style:** Vinegar
Refrigerated: No
Ingredients: Cucumbers, distilled vinegar, salt, garlic, dill

Comments: The smallest pickles in our lineup drew comparisons to gherkins and cornichons, and they stayed crunchy enough after pasteurization. Although their texture was crisp, their flavor was described as "way too sharp" and "overly vinegary." Tasters found this mouth-puckering tartness to be overwhelming.

Malted Milk Whipped Cream

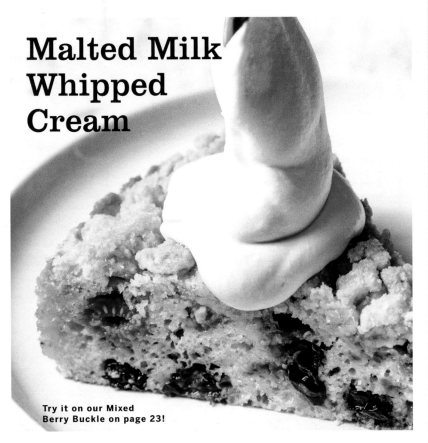

Try it on our Mixed Berry Buckle on page 23!

This sweet and savory whipped cream pairs well with all kinds of desserts, including pies, cakes, puddings, and more.

MALTED MILK WHIPPED CREAM

Serves 8 (Makes 2 cups)

We found that chilled heavy cream can be whipped to peaks more quickly and easily than room-temperature heavy cream.

- 2 **cups heavy cream, chilled**
- ½ **cup malted milk powder**
- 3 **tablespoons sugar**

Using stand mixer fitted with whisk attachment, whip cream, malted milk powder, and sugar on medium-low speed until foamy, about 1 minute. Increase speed to medium-high and whip until stiff peaks form, 1 to 3 minutes. Serve.

We're looking for recipes that you treasure—the ones that have been handed down in your family for a generation or more, that always come out for the holidays, and that have earned a place at your table and in your heart through many years of meals. Send us the recipes that spell home to you. Visit CooksCountry.com/recipe_submission (or write to Heirloom Recipes, Cook's Country, 21 Drydock Avenue, Suite 210E, Boston, MA 02210) and tell us a little about the recipe. Include your name and address. If we print your recipe, you'll receive a free one-year subscription to Cook's Country.

COMING NEXT ISSUE

*Celebrate summer outside with our recipes for **Grilled Tuna Steaks** and **Tacos al Pastor**. Keep things light with **One-Pan Salmon with White Beans, Fennel, and Tomatoes** or **Mexican Chile-Garlic Shrimp**. Or feed your sweet tooth with **Pecan Pralines**, summery **Peach Pie**, or **German Apple Pancake**. This is just a taste of the great recipes coming in our August/September 2020 issue!*

RECIPE INDEX

FIND THE ROOSTER!

A tiny version of this rooster has been hidden in a photo in the pages of this issue. Write to us with its location, and we'll enter you in a random drawing. The first correct entry drawn will win a copy The Complete Cook's Country TV Show Cookbook, and each of the next five will receive a free one-year subscription to website. To enter, visit CooksCountry.co rooster by June 30, 2020, or write to Ro JJ20, Cook's Country, 21 Drydock Aven Suite 210E, Boston, MA 02210. Include y name and address. Dorothy Girardi of S City Center, Florida, found the rooster in February/March 2020 issue on page 12.

WEB EXTRAS

Free for four months online at
CooksCountry.com/jul20

Carolina Red Slaw
Creamy Buttermilk Coleslaw

READ US ON IPAD

Download the Cook's Country app for iPad and start a free trial subscription or purchase a single issue of the magazine All issues are enhanced with Cooking Mode slideshows that provide step-by-s instructions for completing recipes, plus expanded reviews and ratings. Go to CooksCountry.com/iPad to download o app through iTunes.

Cornmeal Cake with Cream Cheese Frosting and Strawberries

Crunchy cornmeal and sweet strawberries combine for a cake that sings of summer.

by Rebeccah Marsters and Morgan Bolling

CORNMEAL CAKE WITH CREAM CHEESE FROSTING AND STRAWBERRIES

Serves 8 to 10

We developed this recipe using Quaker Yellow Corn Meal. Our favorite cream cheese is Philadelphia Cream Cheese Brick Original, and our favorite honey is Nature Nate's 100% Pure Raw and Unfiltered Honey.

CAKE
- ¾   cup (3¾ ounces) cornmeal, plus extra for pan
- 1½ cups (7½ ounces) all-purpose flour
- 2   teaspoons baking powder
- ½   teaspoon table salt
- 1½ cups (10½ ounces) plus 2 tablespoons granulated sugar, divided
- 1   cup buttermilk, room temperature
- 14 tablespoons unsalted butter, melted
- 3   large eggs, room temperature
- ½   teaspoon vanilla extract
- ¼   teaspoon almond extract

FROSTING
- 6   ounces cream cheese, softened
- 4   tablespoons unsalted butter, softened
- 1   cup (4 ounces) confectioners' sugar
- ½   teaspoon vanilla extract
- Pinch table salt

TOPPING
- 12 ounces strawberries, hulled and halved or quartered if large
- 2   tablespoons honey
- 2   tablespoons chopped toasted pistachios

FOR THE CAKE:
Adjust oven rack to lower-middle position and heat oven to 350 degrees. Grease bottom, sides, and center of 10-cup tube pan, then dust pan with cornmeal, tapping out excess.

Whisk flour, baking powder, salt, and cornmeal together in bowl. Whisk 1½ cups sugar, buttermilk, melted butter, eggs, vanilla, and almond extract in separate bowl until fully combined. Whisk flour mixture into sugar mixture until just combined. Transfer batter to prepared pan, smoothing into even layer with rubber spatula, and sprinkle with remaining 2 tablespoons sugar.

Bake until top is browned and paring knife inserted in center comes out clean, about 50 minutes. Let cake cool in pan on wire rack for 30 minutes. Run paring knife around edges and center of pan. Invert cake onto parchment paper–lined baking sheet (cake will be sugared side down). Remove pan, place wire rack on top of cake, and reinvert cake sugared side up. Let cake cool completely, about 2 hours.

FOR THE FROSTING:
Using stand mixer fitted with whisk attachment, whip cream cheese and butter on medium-high speed until fluffy, about 1 minute. Add sugar, vanilla, and salt and mix on low speed until sugar is moistened, about 30 seconds. Increase speed to medium-high and beat until light and smooth, about 3 minutes. Cover and refrigerate until slightly firm, at least 30 minutes or up to 2 hours.

FOR THE TOPPING:
Spread frosting evenly over top of cake. Pile strawberries evenly over top of frosting. Drizzle with honey and sprinkle with pistachios. Serve.

INSIDE THIS ISSUE

STEP-BY-STEP FOCACCIA / TASTE TEST: SHREDDED CHEDDAR / HOMEMADE PRALINES

Cook's Country

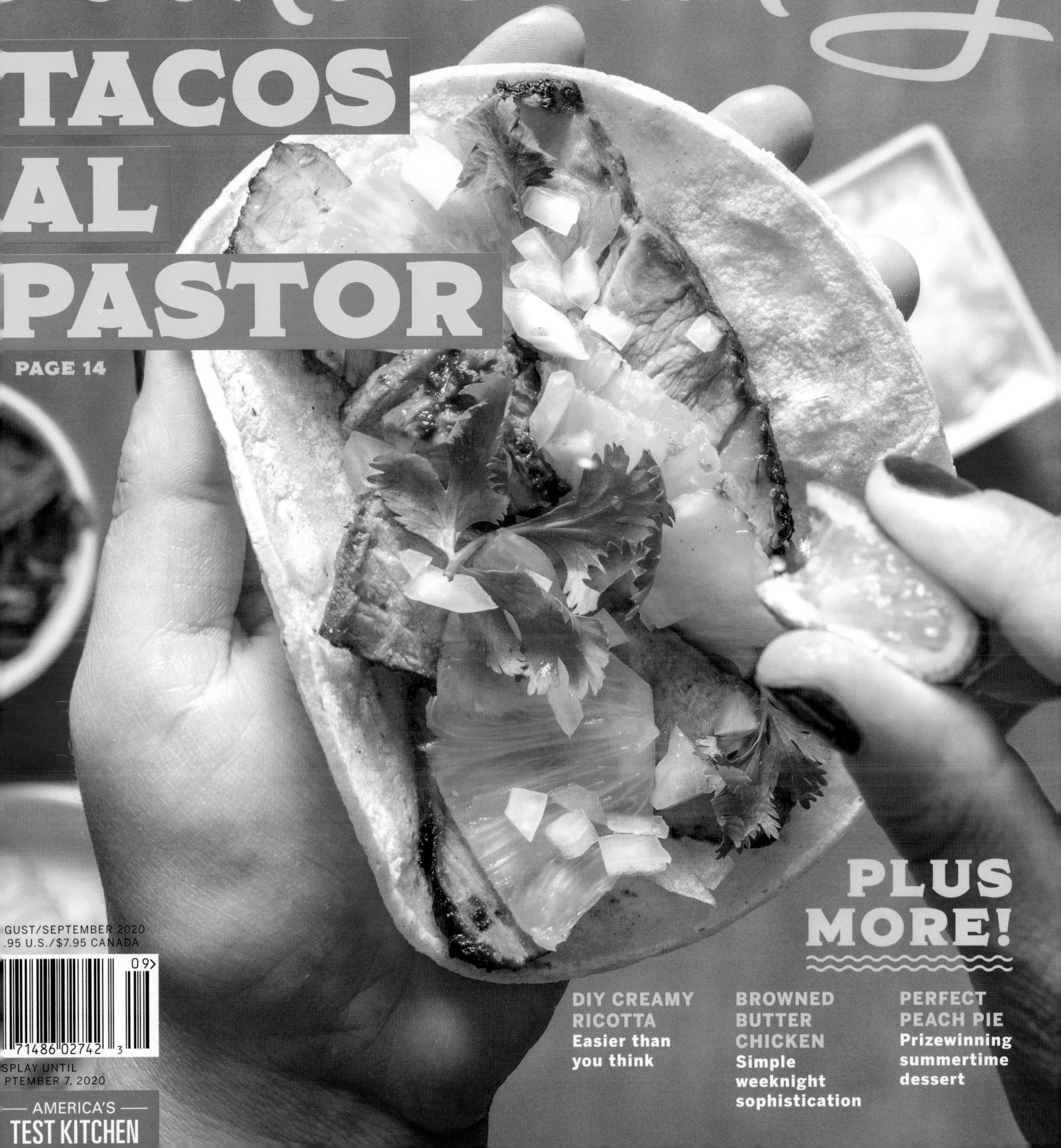

TACOS AL PASTOR

PAGE 14

PLUS MORE!

DIY CREAMY RICOTTA
Easier than you think

BROWNED BUTTER CHICKEN
Simple weeknight sophistication

PERFECT PEACH PIE
Prizewinning summertime dessert

GUST/SEPTEMBER 2020
.95 U.S./$7.95 CANADA
09>
71486 02742 3
SPLAY UNTIL
PTEMBER 7, 2020

— AMERICA'S —
TEST KITCHEN

LETTER FROM THE EDITOR

Cook's Country

Chief Executive Officer David Nussbaum
Chief Creative Officer Jack Bishop
Editor in Chief Tucker Shaw
Executive Managing Editor Todd Meier
Executive Food Editor Bryan Roof
Deputy Editor Scott Kathan
Deputy Food Editor Morgan Bolling
Senior Editor Cecelia Jenkins
Associate Editors Matthew Fairman, Jessica Rudolph
Test Cooks Mark Huxsoll, Amanda Luchtel
Photo Team Manager Alli Berkey
Lead Test Cook, Photo Team Eric Haessler
Test Cooks, Photo Team Hannah Fenton, Jacqueline Goche
Assistant Test Cooks, Photo Team Gina McCreadie, Chris
Copy Editors Christine Campbell, April Poole, Rachel Scho
Managing Editor, Web Mari Levine
Digital Content Producer Danielle Lapierre
Contributing Editor Eva Katz
Senior Science Research Editor Paul Adams
Hosts & Executive Editors, Television Bridget Lancaster,
    Julia Collin Davison

Executive Editors, Tastings & Testings Hannah Crowley,
    Lisa McManus
Senior Editors, Tastings & Testings Lauren Savoie, Kate S
Associate Editors, Tastings & Testings Miye Bromberg,
    Riddley Gemperlein-Schirm, Carolyn Grillo
Assistant Editor, Tastings & Testings Chase Brightwell

Creative Director John Torres
Photography Director Julie Cote
Art Director Maggie Edgar
Associate Art Director Kristen Jones
Art Director, Tastings & Testings Marissa Angelone
Senior Staff Photographers Steve Klise, Daniel J. van Acke
Photographer Kevin White
Photography Producer Meredith Mulcahy

Senior Director, Creative Operations Alice Carpenter
Deputy Editor, Culinary Content and Curriculum
    Christie Morrison
Senior Manager, Publishing Operations Taylor Argenzio
Imaging Manager Lauren Robbins
Production & Imaging Specialists Tricia Neumyer, Dennis
    Amanda Yong
Deputy Editor, Editorial Operations Megan Ginsberg
Assistant Editors, Editorial Operations Tess Berger,
    Sara Zatopek
Test Kitchen Director Erin McMurrer
Assistant Test Kitchen Director Alexxa Benson
Test Kitchen Manager Meridith Lippard
Test Kitchen Facilities Manager Kayce Vanpelt
Test Kitchen Shopping & Receiving Lead Heather Tolmie
Senior Kitchen Assistant Shopper Avery Lowe

Chief Financial Officer Jackie McCauley Ford
Senior Manager, Customer Support Tim Quinn
Customer Support Specialist Mitchell Axelson

Chief Digital Officer Fran Middleton
VP, Marketing Natalie Vinard
Director, Audience Acquisition & Partnerships Evan Stein
Director, Social Media Marketing & Emerging Platforms
    Kathryn Przybyla
Social Media Manager Charlotte Errity
Social Media Coordinators Sarah Sandler, Norma Tentori

Chief Revenue Officer Sara Domville

Director, Public Relations & Communications Brian Frank

Senior VP, Human Resources & Organizational
    Development Colleen Zelina
Human Resources Manager Jason Lynott

Food Stylists Ashley Moore, Elle Simone Scott

Circulation Services PubWorX ProCirc

I AM A LUCKY man. Every day at *Cook's Country* I get to learn from talented test cooks, thoughtful writers, skilled designers, sharp-eyed photographers, smart copy editors . . . and, also, many of you.

I'm talking, of course, about the tens of thousands of volunteer home cooks across the country who help test our recipes. You've heard about them. Maybe you are one—I hope so!

If you're not, here's how it works. You sign up online, and then every few weeks you receive an email with a recipe or two to test. If a recipe appeals to you, and you have the time and inclination (there is literally zero obligation), you cook through it, and then you fill out a short survey to let us know what you think. Were the instructions clear? Did the dish meet your expectations? Did you have any difficulty finding any of the ingredients?

And the most important question: Would you make it again?

Nearly every one of our recipes goes through this gauntlet. If a theme comes up in the feedback (too salty! too spicy! too boring!), or if it doesn't achieve an 80 percent score on that "Would you make it again?" question, we take it back into the test kitchen to tinker with things. Then we send it back around. If, after a few swings, it doesn't hit that 80 percent score, we set it aside. And we do this all the time: The list of recipes that never found the spotlight is long.

But even if a recipe fails to make it to publication, I don't call it a failure. We've still learned something, and the next recipe will be better for it. Kind of like in life. Lemons, lemonade—you know how it works.

> **P.S.**
> Sign up to be a recipe tester at **AmericasTestKitchen.com/recipe_testing**

TUCKER SHAW
Editor in Chief

Illustration: Hannah Jacobs

 Find us on **Facebook**
facebook.com/CooksCountry

 Find us on **Instagram**
instagram.com/CooksCountry

 Follow us on **Pinterest**
pinterest.com/TestKitchen

 Follow us on **Twitter**
twitter.com/TestKitchen

AMERICA'S TEST KITCHEN ®

America's Test Kitchen has been teaching home cooks how to be successful in the kitchen since 1993. Our mission is to empower and inspire confidence, community, and creativity in the kitchen. Millions watch our two shows on public television; read our two flagship magazines (*Cook's Country* and *Cook's Illustrated*); and rely on our books, websites, videos, podcasts, and educational products for children. America's Test Kitchen is located in a state-of-the-art Boston facility with 15,000 square feet of test kitchen and studio space. Learn more at AmericasTestKitchen.com.

18

Recipe Card

Cook's Country magazine (ISSN 1552-1990), number 94, is published bimonthly by America's Test Kitchen Limited Partnership, 21 Drydock Avenue, Suite 210E, Boston, MA 02210. Copyright 2020 America's Test Kitchen Limited Partnership. Periodicals postage paid at Boston, MA, and additional mailing offices, USPS #023453. Publications Mail Agreement No. 40020778. Return undeliverable Canadian addresses to P.O. Box 875, Station A, Windsor, ON N9A 6P2. POSTMASTER: Send address changes to *Cook's Country*, P.O. Box 6018, Harlan, IA 51593-1518. For subscription and gift subscription orders, subscription inquiries, or change of address notices, visit AmericasTestKitchen.com/support, call 800-526-8447 in the U.S. or 515-237-3663 from outside the U.S., or write to us at *Cook's Country*, P.O. Box 6018, Harlan, IA 51593-1518. PRINTED IN THE USA.

22

Compiled by Cecelia Jenkins

READY TO GO

Start Me Up

I just bought a charcoal chimney starter to light briquettes for the grill. Any tips for how to use it?

–Luke Norman, Berwick, Maine

Chimney starters safely ignite charcoal without the need for lighter fluid. These simple gadgets consist of a cylindrical body with a handle, plus two stacked chambers inside. The large top chamber is for charcoal, and the smaller bottom chamber is for newspaper. You fill the bottom chamber with newspaper (two gently crumpled sheets should do the trick), load the top chamber with the desired amount of charcoal, and then light the newspaper. Depending on the amount and type of charcoal (and the weather conditions), it can take 20 to 40 minutes for the top layer of charcoal to become covered in a fine layer of white ash—the visual cue that it's ready to use.

Once the charcoal is fully lit, it is ready to be poured out onto the bottom grate inside the grill in the desired configuration for whatever you're cooking. Place the cooking grate over the coals, let the grill preheat, and you are ready to grill.

THE BOTTOM LINE: Charcoal chimney starters light charcoal in a controlled manner and are our top choice for charcoal grillers. Our testing winner, the Weber Rapidfire Chimney Starter (about $15), features a roomy charcoal chamber, an insulated handle, and a helper handle to make it easier to precisely distribute the lit coals.

CHARCOAL

NEWSPAPER

A FEW TIPS

- Light the starter on the lower grate in your grill; it's a firesafe location with plenty of airflow (with the bottom vent open).
- When pouring out hot coals, wear grill gloves to shield your hands and arms from heat and sparks.
- To dispose of spent coals after grilling, first suffocate the flow of oxygen: Cover the grill with the lid and close both the bottom grill vent and top lid vent and then let the coals and ash cool for at least 48 hours. Finally, we suggest dumping the coals and ash into a metal bin and pouring water over them to keep any dormant embers from reigniting. The completely cooled charcoal and ash mixture can then be disposed of in a noncombustible outdoor trash receptacle.

Edgy Veggies

Are habanero and Scotch bonnet chiles the same?

–April Niles, St. Paul, Minn.

While both habanero and Scotch bonnet chiles are among the spiciest chiles sold at grocery stores, and they come from the same genus and species of pepper (*Capsicum chinense*), there are significant distinctions between the two, particularly regarding their heat levels. (We've commonly seen them mislabeled at the grocery store, so it's important to know the difference.)

Chiles get their fire from a class of spicy compounds called capsaicinoids, the most prominent of which is capsaicin. The Scoville scale measures chile spiciness in Scoville Heat Units (SHU); the larger the number, the spicier the chile. Scoville scores are often presented as ranges because even within the same type of chile, some specimens will be hotter than others. Habaneros and Scotch bonnets share the same range—from 150,000 to 350,000 SHU—but Scotch bonnets are typically hotter (for reference, a jalapeño is about 1,000 to 4,000 SHU).

As for other differences, the habanero ("from Havana" in Spanish) was named for the pepper trade that once flourished in Havana, Cuba. Habanero are bulbous, with wavy indentations a waxy, firm skin, and they average about 2 inches in length. They are usually orange, orange red, or red in color and are grown around the world and used salsas, marinades, and hot sauces.

The Scotch bonnet is named for its resemblance to the traditional Scottish Tam o' Shanter cap. These peppers are squatter and have more prominent gnarled ridges than habaneros. Simila to habaneros in size, they also have waxy, firm skin. As they mature they turn from green to yellow, orange, an then red. Scotch bonnets are popular throughout the Caribbean but are esp cially prominent in Jamaican cuisine.

THE BOTTOM LINE: Scotch bonnet chiles have a squatter shape—and a hotter bite—than habaneros. Both are significantly hotter than jalapeños.

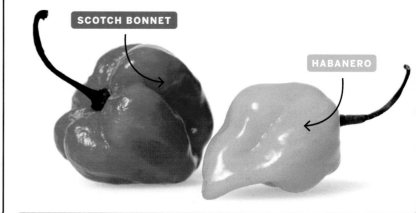

SCOTCH BONNET

HABANERO

Smoked Salmon

Cured and hot- or cold-smoked; salty, smoky flavor

Gravlax *(pictured)*

Cured in salt (and usually sugar) and flavored with dill, juniper, and often liquor; weighted during curing for a more compact texture; mild, salty flavor

Lox

Salt-cured salmon belly

Nova Lox

Traditionally from Nova Scotia–fished salmon; cured and cold-smoked

FINISH LINE

All four methods result in beautiful, sliceable cured salmon. Whichever style you choose, it'll be great on a bagel piled high with fixings.

Salmon: Salt, Sugar, and Smoke

How do smoked salmon, lox, nova lox, and gravlax differ?

–Evan Records, Sacramento, Calif.

Fans of cured and smoked salmon have a lot of options for topping their bagels. Here's a quick breakdown: Smoked salmon can be either hot- or cold-smoked; the words pretty much say it all. Cold-smoked salmon is technically not cooked, as the fish usually never gets hotter than 85 degrees, but the combination of the smoke and a presmoke cure (in salt and sugar) make it safe to eat.

Lox comes from the belly of the salmon and is salt-cured but not smoked. Nova lox is traditionally made from Nova Scotia–fished salmon and is cold-smoked after curing (although you can now buy "nova lox" fished and smoked in other parts of the world).

Similar to lox, gravlax is salt-cured and not smoked, but it is traditionally seasoned with dill and often includes sugar and other seasonings (such as juniper, horseradish, pepper, and/or liquor) in the cure. Gravlax is weighted during curing; this speeds up the curing process and gives it a more compact texture. Traditional Scandinavian methods call for burying the salmon in the ground; in Swedish, "grav" means "grave" and "lax" means "salmon."

THE BOTTOM LINE: Although differences are hard to see with the naked eye, each style of cured salmon has a unique character and flavor.

mpiled by *Matthew Fairman*

etter Peanut utter Beater

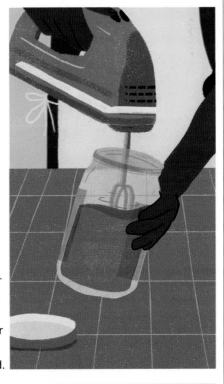

hat do you do with a just-opened of natural peanut butter (or nini)? The separated oil on top eds to be stirred back in, but the is full. We've tried methods such simply stirring it with a fork (very essy and ineffective) and dumping all into a bowl and whisking it until s smooth (too much work). But e've recently found a better way. ab your handheld electric mixer d attach just one of the beaters. rmly grasp the jar with one hand, ess the beater into the peanut butr until it touches the bottom of the , and mix on **low speed** for about minute. The oil stays in the jar, your m isn't tired from stirring, and the anut butter gets thoroughly mixed.

Clumps Begone

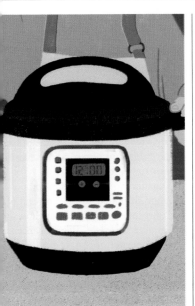

Joan Lennon of Grand Rapids, Mich., knows just what to do when the humidity gets to her onion powder or garlic powder and it begins to clump. She doesn't throw out the bottle; rather, she processes the clumps in her spice grinder (she uses a coffee grinder dedicated solely to spices). Voilà. Perfect powder again.

Multipurpose Multicooker

atty Riek of Sussex, Wis., has a new vorite method for transporting the bups and stews she makes in her ulticooker. It may seem obvious, but stead of letting the food cool and en transferring it to a storage coniner for transport, she simply fully leases the pressure and puts the lid ack on. With a lid that stays locked in ace, there's no need to worry about bills in the car.

*OUR FAVORITE

PRODUCT TASTING

Tasting Bottled Teriyaki Sauce

by Riddley Gemperlein-Schirm

IN JAPAN, TERIYAKI sauce is a simple combination of soy sauce, sake, mirin, and sugar; it has a thin consistency and a glossy appearance. It is typically used as finishing sauce, brushed on grilled meat toward the end of cooking to give it a shiny glaze and a sweet, salty flavor. In the United States, most of the bottled teriyaki sauces sold in supermarkets are thicker than typical Japanese sauces and have more flavoring ingredients. To find the best product, we rounded up six supermarket offerings and tasted them plain and in our recipe for Teriyaki Stir-Fried Beef with Green Beans and Shiitakes.

We were after a sauce that was thin enough to pour but not runny, with a flavor that balanced teriyaki sauce's characteristic sweet and salty notes. Some of the sauces contained starchy thickening agents, which made them goopy. Our favorite sauce, Soy Vay Veri Veri Teriyaki Marinade & Sauce, struck the perfect balance of sweet and salty, and most tasters thought that the inclusion of sesame seeds, dried ginger, and dried garlic made the sauce more "complex" and rich. Tasters also liked the consistency, which glazed the meat and vegetables well in the stir-fry.

Sodium and sugar levels are based on a 1-tablespoon serving.

RECOMMENDED	TASTERS' NOTES
Soy Vay Veri Veri Teriyaki Marinade & Sauce **Price:** $4.99 for 21 oz ($0.24 per oz) **Added Thickeners:** No **Sodium:** 580 mg **Sugar:** 7 g	This sauce struck the perfect balance of sweet and salty, and the inclusion of sesame seeds, dried ginger, and dried garlic made the sauce more "complex." Tasters also liked the consistency.
La Choy Teriyaki Marinade & Sauce **Price:** $2.39 for 10 oz ($0.24 per oz) **Added Thickeners:** Yes **Sodium:** 620 mg **Sugar:** 8 g	Tasters compared this thick, viscous sauce to "molasses" when sampled plain. But its "rich," "smoky" flavor paired well with the stir-fried beef.
Annie Chun's Japanese-Style Gluten-Free Teriyaki Sauce **Price:** $4.99 for 9.9 oz ($0.50 per oz) **Added Thickeners:** Yes **Sodium:** 370 mg **Sugar:** 5 g	Tasters liked the texture of this sauce, which was neither too thick nor too thin, and thought that it tasted "homemade" and "complex" when they sampled it plain.
P.F. Chang's Teriyaki Sauce **Price:** $9.98 for 14 oz ($0.71 per oz) **Added Thickeners:** Yes **Sodium:** 380 mg **Sugar:** 5 g	In the stir-fry, this "citrusy" sauce was "rich and thick" and "clung to the meat well," but it was very thick and tasted a bit "harsh" when sampled plain.

RECOMMENDED WITH RESERVATIONS	
San-J Gluten-Free Teriyaki Stir-Fry & Marinade **Price:** $4.69 for 10 oz ($0.47 per oz) **Added Thickeners:** Yes **Sodium:** 410 mg **Sugar:** 3 g	Tasters liked the "smooth" texture of this sauce when sampled plain, but they described the flavor as "boozy" and "sour." Its texture was a bit "runny."
Kikkoman Teriyaki Marinade & Sauce **Price:** $2.99 for 10 oz ($0.30 per oz) **Added Thickeners:** No **Sodium:** 610 mg **Sugar:** 2 g	This sauce's consistency, which was reminiscent of a traditional Japanese teriyaki sauce, was "thin," and its flavor was "more salty than sweet."

Web subscribers can see the complete results chart at CooksCountry.com/sept20.

Khao Man Gai
(Thai-Style Chicken and Rice)

This simple cooking method gets a boost from a remarkable sauce. **by Matthew Fairman**

A FTER FEASTING ON the deservedly famous chicken and rice at Nong's Khao Man Gai in Portland, Oregon (see "Old-School Flavors with a Smile"), we came back to the test kitchen to create a recipe for home cooks. Following the lead of the cooks at Nong's, we began by poaching the chicken whole with garlic and ginger, simultaneously creating perfectly juicy meat and flavorful chicken broth. Then, while the bird rested, we cooked fragrant jasmine rice in the poaching liquid to make a rich, poultry-infused rice to serve alongside the sliced and shredded chicken.

The ultracomforting, subtly flavored chicken and rice could stand on their own, but at Nong's it's the bright, savory, spicy sauce that wakes it all up and keeps customers coming back for more. The sauce is a combo of soy sauce, vinegar, ginger, fresh Thai chiles, Thai pickled garlic, and fermented soybeans.

With some testing, we were able to work out some substitutions for ingredients that may be hard to find in your area (see "Ingredient Notes").

A couple of things to keep in mind: When grating ginger on a rasp-style grater, be sure to scrape up the flavorful juice that is exuded onto your work surface after grating and include it in your measurement. And don't forget to wash your hands after mincing the Thai chiles. They are hot!

Ingredient Notes

We call for fresh Thai chiles to give the sauce an unapologetic kick of heat. If you can't find them, Asian chili-garlic sauce makes a good substitute. Also note that while we call for Thai soybean paste (sometimes labeled as yellow bean sauce or soybean sauce) for a deeply savory flavor, you can substitute Japanese red miso for similar results.

SPICE SUBSTITUTE
There's more than one way to bring the heat.

▉ THAI-STYLE CHICKEN AND RICE (KHAO MAN GAI)
Serves 4 to 6

One tablespoon of Asian chili-garlic sauce can be substituted for the Thai chiles, if desired. Use a Dutch oven with at least a 7-quart capacity to comfortably fit the chicken. Thai soybean paste is sometimes labeled as yellow bean sauce or soybean sauce. If this ingredient is unavailable, you can substitute Japanese red miso.

CHICKEN AND BROTH
- 12 cups water
- 1 (2-inch) piece ginger, peeled and sliced into ¼-inch-thick rounds
- 2 tablespoons table salt
- 6 garlic cloves, smashed and peeled
- 1 (3½- to 4-pound) whole chicken, giblets discarded

RICE
- 1 tablespoon vegetable oil
- 1 shallot, chopped fine
- 1 (2-inch) piece ginger, peeled and cut in half lengthwise
- 2 garlic cloves, minced
- ¼ teaspoon table salt
- 2 cups jasmine rice, rinsed
- 1 cup fresh cilantro leaves and stems
- ½ English cucumber, sliced into thin rounds

SAUCE
- ¼ cup Thai soybean paste
- ¼ cup soy sauce
- ¼ cup distilled white vinegar
- 2 tablespoons sugar
- 3 garlic cloves, minced
- 2 Thai chiles, stemmed and minced
- 1 teaspoon grated fresh ginger

- 2 scallions, sliced thin

1. FOR THE CHICKEN AND BROTH: Combine water, ginger, salt, and garlic in large Dutch oven. Add chicken to pot, breast side up, and bring to simmer over high heat. Place large sheet of aluminum foil over pot, then cover with lid. Reduce heat to low and simmer until breast registers 160 degrees and thighs register at least 175 degrees, 25 to 35 minutes.
2. Transfer chicken to bowl, tent with foil, and let rest while making

rice. Using slotted spoon, skim foamy residue from surface of chicken broth. Set aside 3 cups broth for cooking rice. Cover remaining broth.
3. FOR THE RICE: Heat oil in large saucepan over medium heat until shimmering. Add shallot, ginger, garlic, and salt and cook until shallot is softened, about 2 minutes. Add rice and cook, stirring frequently, until edges begin to turn translucent, about 2 minutes.
4. Stir in reserved 3 cups broth and bring to boil over medium-high heat. Stir once more, then cover and reduce heat to low. Cook for 20 minutes. Without removing lid, remove saucepan from heat and let sit, covered, for 10 minutes.
5. FOR THE SAUCE: Whisk all ingredients in bowl until sugar is dissolved, about 1 minute. (Sauce can be refrigerated for up to 2 days.)
6. Rewarm remaining broth over medium heat. Using boning knife, remove breast meat from chicken carcass; discard skin. Remove chicken leg quarters by dislocating thigh joint from carcass. Using 2 forks, shred

leg quarter meat into bite-size pieces discard skin and bones. Slice breasts crosswise ½ inch thick.
7. Transfer rice to large serving platt Arrange shredded chicken on top of rice. Arrange sliced breast meat on to of shredded chicken. Place cilantro ir pile in 1 corner of platter and shingle cucumber along side of platter.
8. Portion four to six 1-cup servings of remaining hot broth into individua soup bowls and sprinkle with scallion (you will have more than 6 cups broth reserve extra broth for another use). Serve chicken and rice with sauce and portions of broth.

TO MAKE AHEAD
Follow recipe through step 2 and let chicken and broth cool completely. Remove breasts and leg quarters from chicken carcass (as in step 6), but do not slice breasts or shred meat from leg quarters. Refrigerate broth and chicken for up to 24 hours. To serve, proceed with step 3. Reheat chicken in brot before shredding and slicing.

Once the chicken is poached, we us the resulting broth for cooking th rice and save some to sip on the side

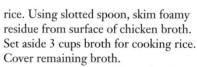

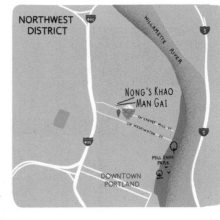

NORTHWEST DISTRICT

WILLAMETTE RIVER

NONG'S KHAO MAN GAI

MILL ENDS PARK

DOWNTOWN PORTLAND

Old-School Flavors with a Smile

Text by Bryan Roof; photos by Steve Klise

JUST BEFORE THE lunch rush, Nong Poonsukwattana greets me with an easy smile at her namesake Nong's Khao Man Gai in downtown Portland, Oregon. Giant pots of whole chickens bubble in the open kitchen, and the aromas of ginger, garlic, and floral pandan leaves fill the air in the tiny restaurant. The focus here is khao man gai, a classic, comforting chicken and rice dish that's filled with flavor; Nong has been making and selling her version since 2009, when she opened her first food cart in town.

Nong comes from a family of cooks in Bangkok, Thailand. She grew up watching her mother work 16-hour days in restaurant kitchens, her arms scarred and blistered from hot cooking grease. "To be honest, I never thought of opening a restaurant," Nong tells me. "I always imagined a different life. Like working in an office." As a child, Nong applied herself in school, where she was often at the top of her class. Looking back, she acknowledges that her academic success was a "cover-up" for a difficult home life.

But Nong learned to cook from her mother, who taught her the foundational techniques. "My mom grew up with her grandma, so her side is old-school; everything we cooked was from scratch. Even coconut milk would come from whole, green coconuts," she says. As the youngest in the family, Nong was often delegated the laborious tasks of extracting the coconut milk and pounding the curry paste with a mortar and pestle. "My mom was the chef, my sister was like the sous chef, and I was always the one who had to do the prep." By 13, Nong was working alongside her mother in restaurants.

Nong moved to Portland in 2003 and began working front-of-the-house restaurant jobs to support her family. Eventually, she turned her focus back to the kitchen, and in 2008, she landed a job at Pok Pok, the award-winning Thai restaurant run by American chef Andy Ricker.

"[The experience] resonated with me. It taught me to trust my gut." It also taught her how to run a restaurant kitchen. Nine months later she decided to branch out on her own.

Searching for a concept, Nong thought back to the food stalls of Bangkok, where khao man gai vendors were usually one-person operations. The dish held a certain nostalgia and, most important, it was something she could pull off on her own in the confined space of a food cart. A few months later, Nong's Khao Man Gai was up and running. "I was happy there. I came from nothing. For me to have that, I was happy. That was a dream." But the dream got even bigger, and in 2011, the operation moved to a brick-and-mortar location. In 2018, she opened her second location.

There's very little difference between preparing khao man gai in restaurant kitchens and preparing it in home kitchens. You begin by gently simmering a whole chicken in salted water along with garlic and ginger. While the chicken rests, you cook the rice in the chicken broth you've just created. As it steams, you stir together the sauce. Finally, you shred the dark meat and slice the breasts and serve it all with a small bowl of broth for sipping and cilantro and cucumber for a fresh, simple, beautiful finish.

Exposed wood beams and colorful decorations accent the industrial space (top). Nong Poonsukwattana (middle) and her team focused on delivery service during the height of the COVID-19 crisis in 2020 and donated many meals to frontline workers. Some of the restaurant's accolades adorn the walls at Nong's (bottom).

Browning the capers makes them less briny and more savory.

Browned Butter Chicken

This easy weeknight supper rests on a foundation of a delicious tongue twister: Browning makes butter better. **by Cecelia Jenkins**

ARE YOU IN a midweek dinner rut? We're here to help with this easy recipe for an intensely flavorful dish: sautéed chicken breasts coated in a lemony browned butter sauce that's studded with capers. It's like chicken piccata's more refined cousin.

The heart of the dish is the browned butter. To brown butter, you melt it and keep it on the heat until the water in the butter evaporates and the milk solids take on a caramelized, golden (or darker) hue. This browning (see the progression from melted to browned in "Butter-Browning Tips") creates new flavor compounds that give the butter a deep, rich, toasty, nutty flavor. It's irresistible.

But first, the chicken. I pounded out four breasts so that they'd cook quickly and evenly. Then I dipped them in flour, which kept the exterior tender and added eventual thickening power to the sauce. Covering the chicken for part of the time helped it cook through in a traditional skillet (which gave me a better view of the browning butter). I then removed the chicken from the pan and tented it with foil to keep it warm while I got on with the sauce.

After testing nearly every shade of browned butter, I found that I liked

butter the color of milk chocolate best in this recipe. I cooked the capers in the butter the entire time to take off some of their briny edge and transform the buds into crisp, savory nubs. And finally, I added lemon juice just as the butter reached the perfect color. This halted the browning so that it didn't veer into burnt territory and provided enough liquid to loosen all the concentrated fond on the pan floor.

Butter-Browning Tips

- Use a light-colored pan so that you can monitor the change in color.
- Don't walk away, especially when the butter has melted and started foaming; things will move quickly.
- Stop the cooking when you reach the desired color; remove the pan from the heat and either add a cold ingredient (such as lemon juice) or transfer to another container.

1 MELTED
Little depth

2 BEGINNING TO BROWN
Flavor deepening

4 TOO DARK
Tastes bitter and acrid

3 NICELY BROWNED
Rich, nutty flavor

◼ PAN-SEARED CHICKEN BREAST WITH BROWNED BUTTER SAUCE
Serves 4

This recipe calls for a stainless-steel skillet, which makes it easier to see the butter browning. If you can't tell the color of the butter through the foam in step 4, quickly spoon some onto a white plate. Once the lemon juice is added, much of the fond on the bottom of the skillet will incorporate into the butter and color it further.

- **4** (6- to 8-ounce) boneless, skinless chicken breasts, trimmed
- **1¼** teaspoons table salt, divided
- **½** teaspoon pepper
- **¼** cup all-purpose flour
- **2** tablespoons extra-virgin olive oil
- **6** tablespoons unsalted butter, cut into 6 pieces
- **2** tablespoons capers, rinsed
- **2** tablespoons lemon juice
- **3** tablespoons minced fresh chives, divided

1. Sandwich chicken between 2 sheets of plastic wrap on cutting board. Using meat pounder, gently pound thickest part of each breast to ¾-inch thickness to match thin part of breast. Pat chicken dry with paper towels and sprinkle with 1 teaspoon salt and pepper.
2. Place flour in shallow dish. Dredge chicken in flour to coat both sides, shake off excess, and transfer to plate. Heat oil in 12-inch skillet over medium heat until just smoking. Add chicken, smooth side down. Cover and cook until light golden brown on first side, about 8 minutes.
3. Flip chicken and continue to cook, uncovered, until registering 160 degrees, about 4 minutes longer. Using metal spatula, loosen chicken stuck to skillet and transfer to cutting board. Tent with aluminum foil and let rest for 10 minutes.
4. Meanwhile, melt butter in now-empty skillet over medium heat. Add capers and cook, swirling skillet and scraping skillet bottom occasionally with wooden spoon, until milk solids in butter are color of milk chocolate and have toasty aroma, 3 to 5 minutes (it's OK if skillet bottom is very browned and bits don't release when scraped).
5. Immediately remove skillet from heat and stir in lemon juice, scraping up browned bits. Stir in 2 tablespoons chives and remaining ¼ teaspoon salt.
6. Slice chicken and transfer to serving platter. Spoon sauce over chicken and sprinkle with remaining 1 tablespoon chives. Serve.

Chile and Garlic Shrimp

*uick-cooking shrimp and ultraflavorful dried
*hiles team up to kick the midweek dinner blues
* the curb.* **by Morgan Bolling**

Glossy, saucy, and packed with flavor.

T'S WEDNESDAY NIGHT, but
that doesn't mean I'm willing to
ke compromises when planning
nner. Enter this bold, exciting,
exican-inspired meal of plump, juicy
rimp simmered in a deeply flavorful,
rlicky, chile-infused sauce.

The first building block of this dish
dried guajillo chiles. These long,
ky chiles are fruity and lightly spicy.
a big fan of dried chiles, I knew to
ed them, cut them into pieces, and
ast the pieces in a skillet to bring out

eir flavor and add a subtle smokiness.
ext, I tossed the toasted chiles into
y blender, which I used as a makeshift
ice grinder. It turned the guajillos
to a vibrant, complex homemade chile
wder that packed way more depth
an a supermarket version would.
olended in water, Worcestershire
uce, and fresh garlic to make a thick,
imson-colored sauce.

To tackle the shrimp, I first tossed
em with cumin, salt, and cayenne
pper. I tried searing 2 pounds of
rimp (to feed four people) in one
tch, but the shrimp overcrowded the
n and steamed rather than seared. For
e next round, I sautéed the shrimp
two batches, just browning one side
d then getting them out of the pan
fore they finished cooking (they'd fin-
h cooking in the sauce momentarily).
his method gave the shrimp a lightly
ramelized exterior without overcook-
g them and turning them rubbery.

Now it was time to unite the shrimp
d the sauce. To add another layer of
vor, I doubled down on the garlic
hich I'd already added to the sauce)
sautéing sliced garlic in a little oil.
then added my chile sauce and the
rimp and let the shrimp finish cook-
g through. Off the heat, I stirred in a
uirt of lime juice, a couple pats of but-
r, and some fresh cilantro. Perfection.

▢ CHILE-GARLIC SHRIMP
Serves 4

One ounce of guajillo chiles is about
four chiles. New Mexican chiles can be
substituted for the guajillos. We prefer
untreated shrimp—those not treated
with sodium or additives such as sodium
tripolyphosphate. Most frozen E-Z peel
shrimp have been treated (check the
ingredient list). If you're using treated
shrimp, omit the ½ teaspoon of salt for
seasoning the shrimp in step 3. Serve
with warm tortillas or rice.

- 1 **ounce dried guajillo chiles**
- ½ **cup water**
- 1 **tablespoon Worcestershire sauce**
- 6 **garlic cloves (2 chopped,
  4 sliced thin)**
- 1 **teaspoon table salt, divided**
- 2 **pounds extra-large shrimp
  (21 to 25 per pound), peeled,
  deveined, and tails removed**
- ½ **teaspoon ground cumin**
- ¼ **teaspoon cayenne pepper**
- 3 **tablespoons extra-virgin olive oil,
  divided**
- 2 **tablespoons lime juice**
- 2 **tablespoons unsalted butter,
  cut into 2 pieces**
- 2 **tablespoons chopped fresh cilantro**

1. Using kitchen shears, stem guajillos, cut in half lengthwise, and discard
seeds. Cut guajillos into 1-inch pieces.
Place guajillos in 12-inch nonstick skillet and cook over medium heat, stirring
often, until fragrant, 3 to 5 minutes.
2. Transfer guajillos to blender jar
and process until finely ground, about
2 minutes. Add water, Worcestershire,
chopped garlic, and ½ teaspoon salt
and blend until smooth, about 2 minutes; set aside.
3. Pat shrimp dry with paper towels
and sprinkle with cumin, cayenne,
and remaining ½ teaspoon salt. Heat
1 tablespoon oil in now-empty skillet
over high heat until just smoking.
Add half of shrimp in even layer and
cook, without stirring, until beginning to brown on underside but still
raw on top, about 2 minutes. Transfer
to bowl. Repeat with 1 tablespoon oil
and remaining shrimp, then transfer
to bowl with first batch.
4. Reduce heat to low and add remaining 1 tablespoon oil and sliced garlic
to now-empty skillet. Cook until garlic
is fragrant and golden brown, about
2 minutes. Stir in reserved chile sauce
and shrimp and cook until shrimp is
just cooked through, about 1 minute.
Off heat, stir in lime juice and butter
until butter is melted, about 1 minute.
Transfer to serving dish. Sprinkle with
cilantro and serve.

Getting the Most out of Dried Chiles

1. Using scissors, stem and halve chiles.
Seed chiles and then cut into pieces.

2. Toast chile pieces in nonstick skillet
until fragrant.

3. Add toasted chile pieces to blender,
grind, then add sauce ingredients.

Cajun Meatball Fricassee

To power up your stew, start with a chocolate roux.

by Matthew Fairman

The roux gives the gravy a complex, toasted flavor.

The stew is best served over steamed white rice with sliced scallions on top.

CAJUN-SPICED MEATBALLS IN a roux-based gravy are a real thing and a popular weeknight supper in Louisiana. This deeply seasoned dish has everything I love about good Cajun cooking: bold flavors, rich meatiness, plenty of spice, a balanced kick of heat, and the savory toastiness that comes from a dark-cooked roux. And the white rice and hot sauce are important parts of the mix, so don't serve this dish without them.

■ CAJUN MEATBALL FRICASSEE
Serves 4 to 6

We recommend using a #16 portion scoop to divvy up the meatball mixture. To make shaping easier, wet your hands slightly. Serve with a dash of Louisiana-style hot sauce.

MEATBALLS
- 22 square saltines
- 1 cup milk
- 2 tablespoons Worcestershire sauce
- 2 pounds 85 percent lean ground beef
- 2 ounces Parmesan cheese, grated (1 cup)
- 1 tablespoon Tony Chachere's Original Creole Seasoning
- 1½ teaspoons dried thyme
- 1 teaspoon pepper

STEW
- ⅓ cup vegetable oil
- ⅓ cup all-purpose flour
- 1 onion, chopped
- 1 green bell pepper, stemmed, seeded, and chopped
- 1 celery rib, chopped
- 2 slices bacon, cut into ½-inch pieces
- 6 scallions, white and green parts separated and sliced thin
- 3 garlic cloves, minced
- ½ teaspoon Tony Chachere's Original Creole Seasoning
- 4 cups chicken broth
- 1 tablespoon Worcestershire sauce
  Cooked white rice

1. FOR THE MEATBALLS: Adjust oven rack to upper-middle position and heat oven to 425 degrees. Set wire rack in aluminum foil–lined rimmed baking sheet and spray rack evenly with vegetable oil spray.
2. Place saltines in large zipper-lock bag, seal bag, and crush saltines fine with rolling pin. Whisk saltines, milk, and Worcestershire together in large bowl. Let sit for 5 minutes to soften saltines. Whisk saltine mixture until smooth paste forms. Add beef,

Parmesan, Creole seasoning, thyme, and pepper and mix with your hands until thoroughly combined.
3. Divide mixture into about 24 scant ¼-cup portions. Roll portions between your slightly wet hands to form meatballs and evenly space on prepared wire rack. Roast meatballs until lightly browned on top, about 25 minutes.
4. FOR THE STEW: Meanwhile, heat oil in large Dutch oven over medium-high heat until just smoking. Using rubber spatula, stir in flour and cook, stirring constantly, until mixture is color of peanut butter, 2 to 5 minutes. Reduce heat to medium and continue to cook, stirring constantly, until roux has darkened to color of milk chocolate, 5 to 10 minutes longer.
5. Stir in onion, bell pepper, celery, and bacon and cook until vegetables are softened, 7 to 10 minutes. Stir in scallion whites, garlic, and Creole seasoning and cook until fragrant, about 1 minute. Whisk in broth and Worcestershire until thoroughly combined. Bring to boil over medium-high heat.
6. Add meatballs to stew; reduce heat to low; and cook, covered, until flavors have melded, about 20 minutes. Uncover; increase heat to medium-high; and cook until thickened to texture of heavy cream, 8 to 12 minutes. Serve over rice, sprinkled with scallion greens.

> **66** Louisiana food is two things to me: It's Cajun and Creole. Two completely distinctive things that developed side by side over the years. Cajun food is country food, and Creole food is city food. Creole food is a food of the city of New Orleans. [. . .] Cajun food is different. Cajun food was evolved by the people coming from Nova Scotia into Louisiana and isolating themselves in the swamps and the bayous and living off the land and making do with what they had. **99**
>
> **The late chef Paul Prudhomme on Cajun and Creole cooking**

Shades of Roux

A roux is simply a mixture of flour and fat (butter or oil) cooked together. In Louisiana-style cooking, a roux is almost always made with oil; Cajun cooks often cook the roux for an hour or more to get the nutty, complex flavors a dark roux provides. Our technique takes only 15 minutes. The three important steps are preheating the oil until it's just smoking, stirring the roux constantly, and adding the vegetables to the pot right when you've reached the desired milk-chocolate color; the vegetables stop the roux from darkening further.

PEANUT-BUTTER COLOR　　**MILK-CHOCOLA COLOR**

Palomilla Steak

This Cuban American favorite delivers outsize flavor. **by Mark Huxsoll**

THE PROMISE OF bistec de palomilla (which translates as "butterfly steak," indicating the way in which the steaks are sliced and/or pounded to resemble a butterfly) is meat deeply flavored with vibrant garlic and citrus flavors and smothered in gently sweet, golden-brown onions. It's a celebrated Cuban tradition in thousands of American and Caribbean homes.

Many of the recipes I found in my initial research called for marinating less expensive steaks such as round or cube steak with garlic and lime juice to help tenderize the meat and introduce flavor. But my experiments consistently yielded steaks with muted flavor and uneven texture—a result of the meat sitting in the acidic lime juice. Did I need to marinate the steaks at all, or could I introduce these flavors in a different way to keep them vibrant and fresh?

After trying various cuts of steak, from flank to top round to cube, I settled on skirt steak for its wonderfully intense beef flavor. Plus, with this cut there was no need to marinate or pound the meat to improve its texture, since skirt steak, when sliced thin against the grain, has just a slight pleasant chew.

To streamline the process and dirty just one pan, I tried searing the steaks and then cooking the onions in the pan while the steaks rested, but onions don't cook in a flash, and by the time they were just the right texture, the steaks weren't just rested—they were cold. I found that cooking the onions first, setting them aside while I cooked the meat, and then reheating the onions while the meat rested was the easiest approach. I added the garlic to the pan 2 minutes before the onions were done to release its flavor just enough without burning.

By using a nonstick skillet I could simply (but carefully) wipe the pan clean after the onions finished and cook the steaks. Then, as the meat rested, I quickly reheated the onions in the warm pan off of the heat. It took a little back and forth, but the process wasn't complicated and it was all done in one pan for easy cleanup.

A squeeze of lime juice and some chopped cilantro added freshness and acidity, producing a dish with deep savory-sweet flavor and a vibrant punch. My palomilla steak was flavorful, satisfying, and simple.

▇ PALOMILLA STEAK
Serves 4

You'll need about three medium onions for this recipe. Try to find skirt steaks with an even thickness throughout to allow for more even cooking. It is difficult to take an accurate temperature on skirt steaks because they are so thin; if you have trouble getting a reading, rely on the times in the recipe. Depending on the length of your whole skirt steaks, you will get anywhere from five to eight portions once the steaks are cut into 3-inch sections. Fresh lime juice is essential here. You'll need a 12-inch nonstick skillet with a lid for this recipe.

- 2 tablespoons unsalted butter
- 3 cups (¼-inch-thick) sliced onions
- 1¼ teaspoons table salt, divided
- 3 garlic cloves, minced
- 1½ pounds skirt steak, trimmed and cut with grain into 3-inch portions
- 1 teaspoon pepper
- 2 tablespoons vegetable oil
- 2 tablespoons chopped fresh cilantro
- 1 tablespoon lime juice

1. Melt butter in 12-inch nonstick skillet over medium heat. Add onions and ½ teaspoon salt. Cover and cook, stirring occasionally, until onions have softened, about 10 minutes. Uncover and continue to cook until onions begin to brown, about 2 minutes longer. Add garlic and cook until fragrant, about 2 minutes. Transfer to bowl and tent with aluminum foil. Wipe skillet clean with paper towels.

2. Pat steaks dry with paper towels and sprinkle with pepper and remaining ¾ teaspoon salt. Heat oil in now-empty skillet over high heat until just smoking. Add steaks and cook, without moving them, until well browned on first side, about 3 minutes.

3. Flip steaks and cook, without moving them, until browned on second side and registering 130 to 135 degrees, about 2 minutes. Transfer steaks to carving board, tent with foil, and let rest for 10 minutes. Pour off fat from skillet. Add onion mixture to now-empty skillet, cover, and let sit off heat to rewarm while steaks rest.

4. Stir cilantro and lime juice into onion mixture. Slice steaks thin against grain and transfer to platter. Spoon onion mixture over top. Serve.

Buttery onions make a perfect foil for the simply seasoned steak.

Mind the Grain

Skirt steaks have a distinct grain of muscle fibers running parallel to their short sides. To make skirt steak less chewy, it's important that the slices you eat are cut against this grain. Here's how to get there.

1. Lay the steak lengthwise on the counter. You'll see the grain running up and down.

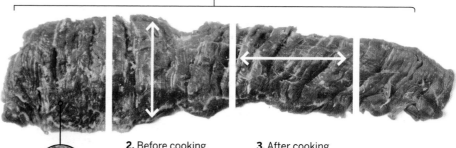

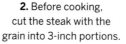

2. Before cooking, cut the steak with the grain into 3-inch portions.

3. After cooking, slice the steak thin against the grain.

Kansas City
BBQ-Style Cheesy Corn

Think of it as mac and cheese, only with corn standing in for pasta. **by Cecelia Jenkins**

TO BE FAIR, the barbecue-style cheesy corn in Kansas City is more cheese than corn. As Executive Food Editor Bryan Roof discovered on a recent visit to Missouri, it is so cheesy that you eat it with a spoon. In addition, its pleasant pops of bright, sweet corn and savory nubs of meat provide a creamy, stick-to-your-ribs counterpoint to a barbecue lunch tray of smoked meat.

To mimic the meaty spread it goes with (and since barbecue joints often stir barky bits of leftover smoked meats into it), I started re-creating this cheese-packed side by rendering two strips' worth of cut-up bacon in a saucepan, a shortcut substitute for those chewy, smoky, meaty morsels of leftover barbecue scraps.

Once the bacon was crisp and its fat had rendered, I dumped in 3 cups of corn kernels (kernels freshly cut from the cob are best, but frozen corn works well here, too), cream cheese for a rich and tangy base, and milk to thin it out (we found that this added just enough richness; cream was a little too much),

plus granulated garlic and cayenne pepper for a kick.

By the time the cream cheese was melted and smooth, the fresh corn kernels had softened to give the dish a pleasant, tender, sweet pop. Shredded yellow cheddar cheese (which we preferred to less flavorful varieties such as American and mozzarella) stirred in gave it the right look and topped off the cheesy flavor. As I ladled out rich, molten pools of cheese dotted with corn and bacon, the approving nods from my teammates told me I was nearly there.

The question arose: Were two strips of bacon enough meat? When I swapped in cubed ham steak for the bacon, my tasters were excited to sink their teeth into the plump, juicy squares of ham poking through the veil of cheese on their spoons . . . but they missed the smoky flavor and chewy texture the bacon provided. Did we have to choose? Using both meats gave us the perfect varied combination of meaty flavors and textures. This is a corn dish that will stick to your ribs.

Our version of this cheesy corn side dish is studded with bits of bacon and ham.

Sitting Pretty in Kansas City

Text by Bryan Roof; photos by Steve Klise

ON *the* ROAD

UNLIKE SOME OTHER barbecue meccas, Kansas City, Missouri, is a melting pot of barbecue ingenuity. It's a city where beef and pork are represented in equal measure and the uniqueness and bold character of a well-made barbecue sauce is valued above all else.

Kansas City also takes great pride in its barbecue side dishes, of which cheesy corn is a predominant standout. The best versions, like the one at Slap's BBQ (right, shown with brisket burnt ends and a half rack of pork ribs), are slightly soupy, rich, and intensely flavorful, with the sharp tang of cheddar cheese. It's a special side dish fit for any meal, not just barbecue.

KANSAS CITY–STYLE CHEESY CORN *Serves 6 to 8*

Frozen corn can be substituted for the fresh corn, if desired. A 14-ounce bag of frozen kernels will yield 3 cups. You will need a broiler-safe 1½-quart baking dish for this recipe. Do not use a Pyrex dish; it is not broiler-safe.

- 2 slices bacon, cut into ½-inch pieces
- 4 ears corn, kernels cut from cobs (3 cups)
- 4 ounces ham steak, cut into ½-inch pieces
- 1 cup whole milk
- 8 ounces cream cheese
- 1 teaspoon granulated garlic
- ½ teaspoon table salt
- ½ teaspoon pepper
- ¼ teaspoon cayenne pepper
- 6 ounces yellow cheddar cheese, shredded (1½ cups), divided

Adjust oven rack 6 inches from broiler element and heat broiler. Cook bacon in large saucepan over medium heat until crispy, 5 to 7 minutes. Add corn, ham, milk, cream cheese, granulated garlic, salt, pepper, and cayenne to saucepan, breaking up cream cheese with rubber spatula. Cook, stirring occasionally, until cream cheese is melted and mixture just begins to bubble at edges of saucepan, 8 to 10 minutes (mixture will be liquid-y). Off heat, stir in 1 cup cheddar until melted, about 30 seconds. Transfer corn mixture to 1½-quart broiler-safe baking dish and top with remaining ½ cup cheddar. Broil until cheese is spotty brown, about 3 minutes. Serve immediately.

Kentucky has its red slaw, the Carolinas have their hush puppies, and Texas has its beans. In Kansas City, it's all about the rich, satisfying cheesy corn. We found this savory side at many restaurants across the city, including Fiorella's Jack Stack Barbecue, and fell in love.

Cider vinegar helps bring out the tomatoes' fruitiness.

Tomato and Onion Salad

With good tomatoes, simpler is better. **by Alli Berkey**

RIPE SUMMER TOMATOES need nothing more than a little olive oil, vinegar, salt, and pepper to help them taste their best. Many cooks, myself included, like to add a little sliced onion to the mix; the onion's pungency accents the sweetness and tartness of the tomatoes.

A few tips on making the best version: Use a sweet onion, such as a Vidalia, to balance the vinegar, and slice it thin. Fruity cider vinegar calls out the tomatoes' sweetness. And letting the dressed salad sit for an hour allows the flavors to meld and draws liquid out of the tomatoes that mixes with the dressing to become an elixir so tasty that, when the tomatoes themselves are gone, you'll want to pick up the bowl and drink the dregs.

TOMATO AND VIDALIA ONION SALAD
Serves 4 to 6

If you cannot find Vidalia or other sweet onions, you can substitute a regular white or yellow onion. If substituting, place the sliced onion in a colander and rinse under cold running water for about 20 seconds before patting the slices dry with paper towels and combining them with the tomatoes. For the best results, we recommend using seasonal heirloom tomatoes here.

- ¼ cup extra-virgin olive oil
- 3 tablespoons cider vinegar
- 1 teaspoon table salt
- 1 garlic clove, minced
- ¼ teaspoon pepper
- 2 pounds ripe heirloom or vine-ripened tomatoes, cored
- 1 small Vidalia onion, quartered through root end and sliced thin crosswise

1. Whisk oil, vinegar, salt, garlic, and pepper together in large bowl. Halve tomatoes through core, cut into 1-inch wedges, then cut wedges in half crosswise.

2. Add tomatoes and onion to vinaigrette and fold gently with rubber spatula to combine. Let salad sit for 1 hour at room temperature, stirring once after 30 minutes. Serve. (Salad can be refrigerated for up to 2 days.)

Here's How to Prep the Vegetables for This Bright, Fresh Salad

1. Garlic: Use knife or rasp-style grater to mince

2. Tomatoes: Core, halve, cut into wedges, and halve wedges crosswise

3. Onion: Quarter through root end, then slice thin crosswise

Cotija cheese adds a salty pop of flavor.

■ POTATOES WITH CHORIZO AND TOMATO
Serves 4 to 6

Use a dry-cured, Spanish-style chorizo in this recipe.

- 3 tablespoons extra-virgin olive oil
- 1½ pounds Yukon Gold potatoes, unpeeled, cut into ½- to ¾-inch dice
- ¾ teaspoon table salt
- 5 ounces Spanish-style chorizo sausage, sliced ¼ inch thick (1 cup)
- 1 onion, cut into ½-inch dice
- 3 garlic cloves, minced
- 1 teaspoon chipotle chile powder
- 1 (8-ounce) can tomato sauce
- ½ cup coarsely chopped fresh cilantro leaves and stems
- 4 ounces cotija cheese, crumbled (1 cup)

1. Heat oil in 12-inch nonstick skillet over medium heat until shimmering. Add potatoes and salt. Cover and cook until fork inserted into potatoes meets little resistance, 10 to 12 minutes, shaking skillet periodically to redistribute potatoes.

2. Uncover; add chorizo and onion; and cook until onion is softened, about 8 minutes, stirring occasionally. Add garlic and chile powder and cook until fragrant, about 1 minute. Stir in tomato sauce; reduce heat to low; and cook until sauce has thickened slightly, about 2 minutes.

3. Stir in cilantro and transfer to serving platter. Sprinkle with cotija. Serve.

Potatoes with Chorizo and Tomato

We were after saucy, meaty spuds. **by Morgan Bolling**

WHEN POTATOES, SMOKY chorizo sausage, and tangy tomato sauce come together—as they sometimes do in Spanish cuisine—it's a beautiful thing. The potatoes soak up the flavors of everything else in the skillet to make for a hearty, mildly spicy dish that is equally good as a side for chicken or steak; as a meal with an egg on top; or simply on a plate with some cheese, served next to a tall glass of sangria.

To get there, I started with creamy Yukon Gold potatoes, knowing that their medium-starchy texture and lightly buttery flavor would be perfect in this dish. I tried dicing the spuds (I found no need to peel them) and simmering them right in canned tomato sauce, but the potatoes took too long to soften in the acidic liquid. Instead, I steamed the potatoes, alone, in a

covered nonstick skillet. This process took a little care: shaking the pan regularly, listening to the sizzle, and lifting the lid every so often to poke a potato piece with a fork to check it for doneness. But this method ensured that the potatoes were fully tender every time. It also gave them some light browning, which added a roasty flavor.

Once the potatoes were fully cooked, I tossed in slices of highly spiced Spanish-style chorizo. To amplify the chorizo's flavor, I sautéed an onion with some smoky, spicy chipotle chile powder and garlic before finally stirring in an 8-ounce can of tomato sauce. After the sauce thickened just enough to cling to the potatoes, I showered the pan with some chopped fresh cilantro. A sprinkle of cotija cheese made this rich yet bright dish something worth writing home about. Now, where's that sangria?

SPANISH-STYLE CHORIZO
Hard like pepperoni

MEXICAN-STYLE CHORIZO
Soft like Italian sausage

A Tale of Two Chorizos

This recipe calls for Spanish-style chorizo (left), which is a hard, dry-cured salami that is intensely flavored with paprika. Mexican-style chorizo (right) is also flavored with paprika, along with garlic, cumin, chile powder, and oregano, but it is softer in texture. We prefer the texture and flavor of the Spanish variety here.

Marinated Zucchini

Time to squash the haters. **by Morgan Bolling**

Fresh thyme, lemon, Parmesan, and flavorful browning add interest to mild zucchini.

THE ONLY WAY I would eat zucchini growing up was doused in bottled Italian dressing. I loved how the mild, porous zucchini soaked up that tangy, salty, herbed vinaigrette.

My tastes have (thankfully) evolved, but I wanted to see if I could create something similar—just a little more grown-up. This wasn't a unique idea, as I found tons of recipes that called for marinating either raw or cooked zucchini in an Italian-inspired dressing. I made a handful of those recipes and dug in.

A few of the recipes called for tossing raw, bite-size pieces of zucchini in the dressing and letting the acid and salt in the dressing do the work of softening it. But the squash released a lot of water, and these samples became too diluted. And bite-size pieces of zucchini that were cooked before or after marinating ended up mushy. I knew I needed to precook the zucchini to drive off some of its water, but I needed to cook it gently enough that it didn't turn to mush when dressed.

To strike the right balance, I cut three medium zucchini in half lengthwise, patted them dry (to minimize splatter), and seared the halves in a hot skillet. Cooking the zucchini this way drove off some of the squash's water and built flavor by lightly caramelizing the outside without cooking it through.

Once seared, I cut the zucchini into bite-size pieces; tossed it with a dressing of olive oil, lemon juice, thyme, garlic, and red pepper flakes; and let it sit for an hour. The zucchini soaked up the flavorful marinade without releasing too much water. Stirring in some shaved Parmesan cheese added richness and nutty savoriness.

MARINATED ZUCCHINI
Serves 4 to 6

You will need one medium shallot to yield the 3 tablespoons called for here. Buy medium zucchini that weigh about 8 ounces each.

- 5 tablespoons extra-virgin olive oil, divided
- 3 tablespoons minced shallot
- 1½ tablespoons lemon juice
- 1½ teaspoons table salt
- 1 teaspoon chopped fresh thyme
- 1 garlic clove, minced
- ⅛ teaspoon red pepper flakes
- 1½ pounds zucchini, trimmed and halved lengthwise
- 1½ ounces Parmesan cheese, shaved with vegetable peeler (about ⅔ cup)

1. Combine ¼ cup oil, shallot, lemon juice, salt, thyme, garlic, and pepper flakes in medium bowl.

2. Pat zucchini dry with paper towels. Heat remaining 1 tablespoon oil in 12-inch nonstick skillet over medium heat until shimmering. Add half of zucchini to skillet cut side down and cook until browned, about 3 minutes. Flip and cook until skin side is spotty brown, about 3 minutes. Transfer to large plate. Repeat with remaining zucchini. Let cool for 5 minutes.

3. Slice zucchini crosswise ¼ inch thick. Transfer zucchini to bowl with oil mixture and toss to evenly coat. Marinate for at least 1 hour or up to 24 hours. (If marinating longer than 1 hour, cover with plastic wrap and refrigerate. Let sit at room temperature for 1 hour before serving.)

4. Season zucchini with salt to taste. Transfer zucchini to shallow platter and sprinkle with Parmesan. Serve.

THE AMERICAN TABLE

Hold on to your hat: Botanically, zucchini are berries. Berries!

Today, we consider zucchini a vegetable because, with a few exceptions, it's usually served in savory dishes. But it's really a fruit.

The current form of zucchini that we find most frequently in grocery stores in the United States is a variety developed in Italy in the 19th century. But its native roots, like all squashes, are in the Americas.

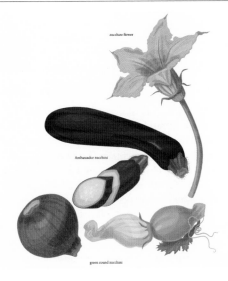

Zucchini is easy to cultivate, as anyone with a vegetable garden knows. So it's no surprise that it has become a culinary staple around the world, from Egypt to Britain to Singapore. Depending on where in the world you are (and the age of the fruit), you may find it called zucchini, courgette, or marrow.

Tacos
al Pastor

Savory and sweet come together in this, the world's favorite taco.

by Alli Berkey

TACOS AL PASTOR contain an irresistible combination of flavorful components: deeply seasoned pork, charred fresh pineapple, warm corn tortillas, and a bounty of lively toppings.

Traditional versions are made by slicing fatty pork (usually shoulder) thin and then marinating it in what is essentially an adobo sauce of dried chiles, spices, and often citrus or vinegar. The marinated slices are then stacked high on a vertical spit and cooked slowly—as they spin around and around—until they're tender. When it's time to make the tacos, the heat is cranked up so that the outer layer of meat on the spit gets lightly charred; the cook slices the charred pork off the rotating spit right onto warm tortillas and then adds toppings before handing the tacos over to waiting taco fiends. So . . . how could I make this process work at home on a simple backyard grill?

After researching and reading through dozens of recipes, I started my testing with the marinade, eventually landing on a combination of (toasted and rehydrated) guajillo and ancho chiles, garlic, dried oregano, cider vinegar, and some pineapple juice, all liquefied together in a blender.

I tested several cuts of meat but ended up back at the beginning, with a boneless pork butt roast. Since the meat wouldn't be stacked on a spit, there was no need to slice it thin; instead, I cut the roast into steaks that had enough surface area to drink up lots of marinade and would cook through relatively quickly.

I found that grilling the marinated pork steaks over indirect heat for about an hour was the best route to tender meat. Then, for the pork's signature char, I brushed the steaks with some of the reserved marinade and moved them over the direct heat to crackle and brown. Since the pineapple just needed to soften a bit and warm through, this was the time to toss it on the grill.

All that was left to do was to let the meat rest, slice it thin, warm the tortillas, and set out the toppings. And to my delight, my leftover pork was just as good the next day.

CHILES, SPICES, AND CHAR FLAVOR THE MEAT

PINEAPPLE ADDS A BURST OF SWEETNESS AND ACIDITY

The cooked pork makes great leftovers for sandwiches, stir-fries, or more tacos.

Now, About Those Tortillas . . .

In a recent taste test of supermarket corn tortillas, Guerrero White Corn Tortillas came out as the top-rated all-corn brand; we also liked Maria and Ricardo's Soft Yellow Corn Tortillas, which are made with a mixture of corn and wheat. The pro move here is to make your own corn tortillas from scratch; you can find our recipe at **CooksCountry.com/corntortillas**. And to keep them warm, we're big fans of the Imusa 12" Cloth Tortilla Warmer, which costs about $10.

CORN TORTILLAS
Taste test winner

TORTILLA WARMER
Best way to keep them warm

Piece of Piña

This recipe uses one-quarter of a fresh pineapple; having extra pineapple around is never a bad thing, right?

TACOS AL PASTOR
Serves 8 to 10

Note that 1½ ounces of guajillos is about six chiles, and 1 ounce of anchos is about two chiles. The pineapple doesn't need to be charred in step 8. Any leftover pork can be used to make sandwiches, stir-fries, or more tacos.

- 1½ ounces dried guajillo chiles, stemmed
- 1 ounce dried ancho chiles, stemmed
- ½ cup cider vinegar
- ½ cup pineapple juice
- 1 tablespoon table salt
- 4 garlic cloves, peeled
- 1 tablespoon dried oregano
- 2 teaspoons ground cumin
- 1½ teaspoons pepper
- ½ teaspoon ground cinnamon
- 1 (2½-pound) boneless pork butt roast, trimmed
- 1 pineapple
- 24 (6-inch) corn tortillas, warmed
  Finely chopped onion
  Fresh cilantro leaves
  Lime wedges

1. Using kitchen shears, cut guajillos and anchos in half lengthwise and discard seeds and stems. Cut guajillos and anchos into 1-inch pieces. Place guajillos and anchos in 12-inch skillet and cook over medium heat, stirring often, until fragrant and darkened slightly, about 6 minutes. Immediately transfer guajillos and anchos to bowl and cover with hot water. Let sit until soft, about 5 minutes.

2. Using slotted spoon, lift guajillos and anchos from water and transfer to blender; discard soaking water. Add vinegar, pineapple juice, salt, garlic, oregano, cumin, pepper, and cinnamon and process until smooth, about 1 minute, scraping down sides of blender jar as needed. Set aside ¼ cup marinade.

3. Cut pork crosswise into approximate 1½-inch-thick steaks. Transfer pork to 1-gallon zipper-lock bag. Add remaining marinade to bag with pork. Seal bag and turn to distribute marinade evenly. Refrigerate for at least 1 hour or up to 24 hours.

4. Using sharp chef's knife, cut top and bottom from pineapple, then peel. Quarter pineapple lengthwise through core. Reserve 3 quarters for another use. Remove and discard core from remaining pineapple quarter; set aside.

5A. FOR A CHARCOAL GRILL: Open bottom vent completely. Light large chimney starter filled with charcoal briquettes (6 quarts). When top coals are partially covered with ash, pour evenly over half of grill. Set cooking grate in place, cover, and open lid vent completely. Heat grill until hot, about 5 minutes.

5B. FOR A GAS GRILL: Turn all burners to high; cover; and heat grill until hot, about 15 minutes. Adjust primary burner to medium-high and turn off other burners. (Adjust burner as needed to maintain grill temperature of 350 degrees.)

6. Clean and oil cooking grate. Remove pork from marinade and place on cooler side of grill. Cover and cook until pork registers 150 degrees, about 50 minutes for charcoal or 1 hour 5 minutes to 1 hour 10 minutes for gas.

7. Brush tops of steaks with 2 tablespoons reserved marinade. Flip steaks marinade side down onto hotter side of grill. Brush second side of steaks with remaining 2 tablespoons reserved marinade. Place reserved pineapple on hotter side of grill next to steaks.

8. Cook, uncovered for charcoal and covered for gas, until pork is well charred and registers 175 degrees, 6 to 8 minutes per side for charcoal or 12 to 15 minutes per side for gas. Cook pineapple until warmed through, about 10 minutes. Transfer pork and pineapple to wire rack set in rimmed baking sheet, tent with aluminum foil, and let rest for 15 minutes.

9. Transfer pork and pineapple to carving board and slice thin. Season with salt to taste. Fill tortillas with few slices of pork and pineapple. Top tacos with onion and cilantro. Serve with lime wedges.

A Many-Layered History

What do shepherds, spinning tops, and pineapple have in common? They're all part of the history of tacos al pastor. This dish was first created by Lebanese immigrants in Mexico who replicated the shawarma of their homeland by cooking meat (pork and lamb) on vertical spits called trompos. "Trompo" is the Spanish word for "spinning top," the shape the spitted meat resembles. "Pastor" means "shepherd," a nod to the lamb. And the pineapple? While some sources suggest it may help tenderize the meat, its real role is to introduce sweet, bright flavor.

Let's Get Cooking!
Here's how to make our version of tacos al pastor.

1. Dry-toast dried chile pieces in skillet.

2. Transfer chiles to bowl and rehydrate with hot water.

3. Transfer chiles to blender jar and blend with other marinade ingredients.

4. Reserve ¼ cup marinade for grilling.

5. Marinate pork steaks for at least 1 hour or up to 24 hours in refrigerator.

6. Grill steaks to internal temperature of 150 degrees.

7. Brush both sides of steaks with reserved marinade and grill over coals.

8. Lightly grill pineapple quarter, then slice thin.

A simple sauce of sour cream enhanced with brown sugar provides the perfect sweet-tart punch to this pancake.

This custardy, apple-filled, crisp-edged pancake is perfect for a showstopping breakfast.

by Jessica Rudolph

German Apple Pancake

GERMAN APPLE PANCAKE WITH BROWN SUGAR SOUR CREAM
Serves 4 to 6

You can substitute low-fat or skim milk for the whole milk, if desired, but the pancake will taste slightly eggier. You will need a 12-inch ovensafe skillet for this recipe. We do not recommend using a nonstick or cast-iron skillet here, as the bottom of the pancake will get too dark. The pancake will puff up during baking and deflate shortly after it comes out of the oven—that's supposed to happen. The interior will be no less delicious.

- ½ cup sour cream
- ½ cup packed (3½ ounces) brown sugar, divided
- ¾ cup (3¾ ounces) all-purpose flour
- 1 teaspoon table salt, divided
- 5 large eggs
- 1 cup whole milk
- 1 teaspoon vanilla extract
- 4 tablespoons unsalted butter
- 1¼ pounds Granny Smith apples, peeled, halved, cored, and sliced ¼ inch thick
- ¼ teaspoon ground cinnamon
  Confectioners' sugar

1. Adjust oven rack to lowest position and heat oven to 425 degrees. Combine sour cream and 2 tablespoons brown sugar in small bowl; set aside.
2. Whisk flour, ¾ teaspoon salt, and 2 tablespoons brown sugar together in large bowl. Whisk eggs, milk, and vanilla together in separate bowl. Whisk half of egg mixture into flour mixture until no lumps remain. Slowly whisk in remaining egg mixture until smooth; set aside batter.
3. Melt butter in 12-inch ovensafe skillet over medium-high heat. Add apples, cinnamon, remaining ¼ cup brown sugar, and remaining ¼ teaspoon salt. Cook, stirring frequently, until apples are softened, browned, and glazy, 8 to 10 minutes.
4. Scrape any apples off sides of skillet and distribute evenly over bottom of skillet. Working quickly, pour batter around and over apples. Immediately transfer skillet to oven and bake until edges of pancake are browned and have risen above skillet, about 18 minutes.
5. Transfer skillet to wire rack. Cut pancake into wedges in skillet and dust with confectioners' sugar. Serve hot from skillet with reserved sour cream mixture.

Glossary of Puffy Things
These three items, all made from a similar batter, rely on the leavening power of steam for their signature puff.

Supercustardy flat portion, crispy edges

Dutch baby/German pancake: The term "Dutch baby" once described a pancake designed to serve just one, but now it's used interchangeably with "German pancake" to refer to a large pancake, made in a 12-inch skillet, that can serve four to six

Peaks and valleys with contrasting textures

Yorkshire pudding: Yorkshire pudding batter is flavored with beef drippings rather than sugar, so it has a savory taste. It is traditionally served with roast beef.

More crackly crust a handheld packag

Popovers: Baked in much smaller vessels (muffin tins or popover pans, which are deeper and more narrow) than German pancakes, popovers grow tall as the air inside them expands, resulting in a much higher ratio of crispy, airy exterior to custardy interior.

ALSO KNOWN AS a Dutch baby, a German pancake features a giant puffed rim that makes for a festive presentation—and it comes together in a flash. It's traditionally made by pouring a thin, eggy batter into a hot skillet and baking it; the heat from the skillet and oven convert moisture in the batter to steam, which causes the pancake to balloon dramatically (and then fall). The end result, like Yorkshire pudding or popovers, features a creamy, custardy center surrounded by a crispy browned lip. Classic versions include apples baked right in.

I started with a batter of flour, milk, eggs, brown sugar, salt, and vanilla, which I stirred together by hand. Pancakes from early tests with raw or only lightly cooked apples baked up too wet, and bites of crunchy apples were jarring against the soft-textured pancake, so I began by cooking down apples until they had softened and some of their

moisture had evaporated. My tasters liked tart Granny Smith apples, which provided an excellent foil for the rich pancake. To coax out extra complexity, I added butter, brown sugar, and cinnamon to the skillet and cooked the apples until they began to brown and their juices reduced to a caramel-like glaze.

I poured the batter around the apples, put the skillet in a 425-degree oven, and held my breath. Every single time I make this pancake, the doubt starts to creep in, and I fear that the steam science will somehow fail me. But it never does! I watched the pancake puff before my eyes and pulled out a gorgeously rumpled, golden-brown pancake with a towering rim about 20 minutes later.

The finishing touch was a tasty, if unconventional, accompaniment: a dollop of sour cream sweetened with a bit of brown sugar. It was creamy, tangy, and just right.

Chicken Parmesan Pasta Bake

30-MINUTE SUPPER

Blackened Salmon Tacos with Slaw, Avocado, and Grapefruit

30-MINUTE SUPPER

Spiced Chickpea Gyros with Tahini Yogurt

30-MINUTE SUPPER

Lemony Steak Tips with Zucchini and Sun-Dried Tomato Couscous

30-MINUTE SUPPER

Blackened Salmon Tacos with Slaw, Avocado, and Grapefruit

Serves 4

We like to serve these tacos with an assertive hot sauce such as Tabasco.

- 2 cups thinly sliced red cabbage
- ¼ cup Mexican crema, plus extra for serving
- ¼ cup chopped fresh cilantro
- 1 tablespoon lime juice
- ½ teaspoon table salt
- ¼ teaspoon pepper
- 4 (6-ounce) skin-on center-cut salmon fillets, 1½ inches thick
- 1½ tablespoons blackening seasoning
- 12 (6-inch) flour tortillas, warmed
- 1 avocado, halved, pitted, and sliced thin
- 1 grapefruit, segmented

1. Combine cabbage, crema, cilantro, lime juice, salt, and pepper in bowl; set aside.

2. Adjust oven racks to upper-middle and lower-middle positions and heat broiler. Line rimmed baking sheet with foil. Sprinkle salmon all over with blackening seasoning, then place skin side down on prepared sheet. Broil salmon on upper rack until well browned, about 6 minutes.

3. Transfer sheet to lower rack and continue to cook until salmon registers 135 degrees, about 8 minutes longer. Using fork, gently flake salmon apart on sheet; discard skin. Divide salmon evenly among tortillas. Top with reserved slaw, avocado, and grapefruit segments. Serve with extra crema.

Chicken Parmesan Pasta Bake

Serves 4

Sprinkle with chopped fresh basil before serving.

- 3 tablespoons extra-virgin olive oil, divided
- 1 small onion, chopped fine
- 4 garlic cloves, minced, divided
- 12 ounces (3¾ cups) penne
- 1 (28-ounce) can crushed tomatoes
- 3 cups water
- 2 teaspoons table salt, divided
- ½ teaspoon red pepper flakes
- ½ cup panko bread crumbs
- 1 (2½-pound) rotisserie chicken, skin and bones discarded, meat shredded into bite-size pieces (3 cups)
- 8 ounces whole-milk mozzarella cheese, shredded (2 cups)

1. Heat 2 tablespoons oil in Dutch oven over medium heat until shimmering. Add onion and three-quarters of garlic and cook until softened, about 4 minutes. Add pasta, tomatoes, water, 1¾ teaspoons salt, and pepper flakes and bring to boil. Reduce heat to medium; cover; and simmer until pasta is tender, about 10 minutes, stirring occasionally.

2. Meanwhile, combine panko, remaining 1 tablespoon oil, remaining garlic, and remaining ¼ teaspoon salt in bowl. Microwave until golden brown, 2 to 3 minutes, stirring occasionally; set aside.

3. Adjust oven rack to middle position and heat broiler. Stir chicken into pasta and sprinkle mozzarella over top. Broil until mozzarella is melted and spotty brown, about 5 minutes. Sprinkle with reserved panko mixture. Serve.

Lemony Steak Tips with Zucchini and Sun-Dried Tomato Couscous

Serves 4

Use a medium-size zucchini here, or swap in yellow summer squash if desired. Sirloin steak tips are often sold as flap meat.

- 1½ cups Israeli couscous
- 1½ teaspoons table salt, divided, plus salt for cooking couscous
- 1 zucchini, quartered lengthwise and sliced thin
- ½ cup frozen peas, thawed
- 1 ounce Parmesan cheese, grated (½ cup)
- ⅓ cup chopped fresh basil
- ¼ cup oil-packed sun-dried tomatoes, drained and chopped fine, plus 2 tablespoons sun-dried tomato oil
- 3 tablespoons extra-virgin olive oil, divided
- 1 tablespoon grated lemon zest plus 2 tablespoons juice
- 2 pounds sirloin steak tips, trimmed and cut into 2-inch chunks
- ½ teaspoon pepper

1. Bring 2 quarts water to boil in large saucepan over medium-high heat. Add couscous and 1½ teaspoons salt and cook until tender, about 12 minutes. Drain couscous and rinse with cold water until cool, about 1 minute; drain thoroughly.

2. Combine couscous, zucchini, peas, Parmesan, basil, tomatoes and tomato oil, 2 tablespoons olive oil, lemon juice, and ½ teaspoon salt in large bowl; set aside.

3. Sprinkle steak tips with lemon zest, pepper, and remaining 1 teaspoon salt. Heat remaining 1 tablespoon oil in 12-inch nonstick skillet over medium-high heat until just smoking. Add steak tips and cook until well browned all over and registering 120 to 125 degrees (for medium-rare), about 7 minutes. Transfer steak tips to large plate, tent with foil, and let rest for 5 minutes. Serve steak tips with reserved couscous.

Spiced Chickpea Gyros with Tahini Yogurt

Serves 4

For more heat, serve with extra Asian chili-garlic sauce.

- 1 cup plain Greek yogurt
- ¼ cup tahini
- 1 teaspoon table salt, divided
- 2 (15-ounce) cans chickpeas, rinsed
- 2 tablespoons Asian chili-garlic sauce
- 2 teaspoons ground cumin
- 4 (8-inch) pita breads, lightly toasted
- ½ English cucumber, halved lengthwise and sliced thin on 3-inch bias
- ½ cup pepperoncini, stemmed and sliced into thin rings
- ¼ cup thinly sliced red onion

1. Combine yogurt, tahini, and ½ teaspoon salt in small bowl; set aside.

2. Using potato masher, very coarsely mash chickpeas in medium bowl. Stir chili-garlic sauce, cumin, and remaining ½ teaspoon salt into chickpeas; set aside.

3. Spread reserved yogurt sauce evenly over 1 side of each pita (use all of it). Divide reserved chickpea mixture, cucumber, pepperoncini, and onion evenly among pitas. Fold pitas in half, wrap tightly in parchment paper, and serve.

Grilled Chicken with Charred Scallions and Peanut Sauce

30-MINUTE SUPPER

Tuna and Heirloom Tomato Salad with Olives and Parsley

30-MINUTE SUPPER

Chipotle Chopped Steak Salad

30-MINUTE SUPPER

Pork Chops with Sweet Potatoes and Rosemary-Maple Sauce

30-MINUTE SUPPER

Tuna and Heirloom Tomato Salad with Olives and Parsley

Serves 4

We like to serve this salad with grilled bread. You can substitute vine-ripened tomatoes for the heirlooms.

- 4   heirloom tomatoes, cored and sliced ½ inch thick
- 1¼ teaspoons table salt, divided
- ⅓   cup extra-virgin olive oil
- 1½ tablespoons lemon juice
- 1   tablespoon Dijon mustard
- 1   garlic clove, minced
- ¼   teaspoon pepper
- 3   (6-ounce) jars oil-packed tuna, drained (1½ cups)
- 1   cup fresh parsley leaves
- ½   cup pitted kalamata olives, halved
- 1   shallot, sliced thin

1. Shingle tomatoes on 4 dinner plates and sprinkle with ½ teaspoon salt.
2. Whisk oil, lemon juice, mustard, garlic, pepper, and remaining ¾ teaspoon salt together in large bowl. Reserve 2 tablespoons vinaigrette.
3. Add tuna, parsley, olives, and shallot to remaining vinaigrette in bowl and toss gently to combine. Divide salad evenly among plates on top of tomatoes. Drizzle reserved vinaigrette over salads. Serve.

Grilled Chicken with Charred Scallions and Peanut Sauce

Serves 4

Serve with rice or Chinese egg noodles.

- ¼   cup creamy peanut butter
- 3   tablespoons warm water
- 2   tablespoons soy sauce
- 2   tablespoons toasted sesame oil, divided
- 1   tablespoon sriracha
- ¾   teaspoon table salt, divided
- ½   teaspoon pepper, divided
- 4   (6- to 8-ounce) boneless, skinless chicken breasts, trimmed and pounded ½ inch thick
- 16 scallions, trimmed
- ¼   cup salted dry-roasted peanuts, chopped

1. Whisk peanut butter, warm water, soy sauce, 1 tablespoon oil, and sriracha together in bowl. Transfer 3 tablespoons peanut sauce to small bowl and stir in ½ teaspoon salt and ¼ teaspoon pepper. Set aside.
2. Pat chicken dry with paper towels. Brush both sides of chicken with reserved 3 tablespoons peanut sauce. Brush scallions with remaining 1 tablespoon oil and sprinkle with remaining ¼ teaspoon salt and remaining ¼ teaspoon pepper.
3. Grill chicken and scallions over hot fire until chicken registers 160 degrees, about 5 minutes per side, and scallions are lightly charred, about 3 minutes per side. Transfer chicken and scallions to platter, tent with foil, and let rest for 5 minutes. Slice chicken on bias ½ inch thick and cut scallions into 2-inch pieces. Sprinkle with peanuts. Serve with remaining peanut sauce.

Pork Chops with Sweet Potatoes and Rosemary-Maple Sauce   *Serves 4*

Fresh thyme can be substituted for the rosemary, if desired.

- 2   pounds sweet potatoes, unpeeled, cut into ¾-inch-thick rounds
- 2   red onions, cut through root end into 1½-inch-thick wedges
- 2   tablespoons unsalted butter, melted, plus 4 tablespoons unsalted butter, divided
- 2   teaspoons table salt, divided
- 1½ teaspoons pepper, divided
- 4   (10- to 12-ounce) bone-in pork rib chops, 1 inch thick, trimmed
- ½   teaspoon cayenne pepper
- 1   cup chicken broth
- 1   tablespoon minced fresh rosemary
- 1   tablespoon maple syrup

1. Adjust oven rack to lower-middle position and heat oven to 450 degrees. Toss potatoes, onions, melted butter, 1 teaspoon salt, and ½ teaspoon pepper together on rimmed baking sheet. Bake until vegetables are browned and tender, about 30 minutes.
2. Meanwhile, pat pork dry with paper towels and sprinkle with cayenne, remaining 1 teaspoon salt, and remaining 1 teaspoon pepper. Melt 1 tablespoon butter in 12-inch nonstick skillet over medium-high heat. Add pork and cook until well browned, about 6 minutes per side. Transfer pork to platter, tent with foil, and let rest while vegetables finish cooking.
3. Add broth, rosemary, and maple syrup to now-empty skillet and bring to boil over medium-high heat, scraping up any browned bits. Cook until reduced by half, about 4 minutes. Off heat, whisk in remaining 3 tablespoons butter until incorporated. Serve pork and vegetables with sauce.

Chipotle Chopped Steak Salad

Serves 4

We like to serve this salad with crumbled cotija cheese and cilantro leaves.

- 1   pound flank steak, halved lengthwise with grain, trimmed
- 1¾   teaspoons table salt, divided
- ¾   teaspoon pepper, divided
- 2   tablespoons vegetable oil
- ½   cup sour cream
- 2   tablespoons water
- 1   tablespoon lime juice, plus lime wedges for serving
- 1   tablespoon minced canned chipotle chile in adobo sauce
- 1   large head romaine lettuce (14 ounces), halved lengthwise and sliced thin crosswise
- 1   (15-ounce) can black beans, rinsed
- 1   avocado, halved, pitted, and cut into ½-inch pieces
- 2   ounces tortilla chips, crushed coarse (1 cup)

1. Pat steak dry with paper towels and sprinkle with 1 teaspoon salt and ½ teaspoon pepper. Heat oil in 12-inch nonstick skillet over medium-high heat until just smoking. Add steak and cook until well browned and registering 125 degrees (for medium-rare), 5 to 7 minutes per side. Transfer steak to carving board, tent with foil, and let rest for 5 minutes.
2. Meanwhile, whisk sour cream, water, lime juice, chipotle, remaining ¾ teaspoon salt, and remaining ¼ teaspoon pepper together in large bowl.
3. Add lettuce, beans, avocado, and chips to dressing in bowl and toss to coat. Divide salad evenly among 4 plates. Slice steaks thin against grain on bias and divide among salads. Serve with lime wedges.

Pickling

Pickling foods in vinegar or brine is an ancient method of food preservation—properly pickled foods can last for months without refrigeration. The pickling process also creates textures and flavors we love. *by Scott Kathan*

Classic Cucumber Pickles

The soft, porous texture of cucumbers—and their naturally short shelf life—makes them a historically popular choice for pickling. Here's a breakdown of some of the most common pickled cukes.

1 SWEET PICKLES: Bread-and-butter pickles are typically made with waffle-cut cucumber rounds that are seasoned with sugar; mustard; celery seed; and turmeric, which adds color. Crunchy gherkins and cornichons—made with pinkie-size cucumbers that are seasoned with clove and garlic—are classic accompaniments to cheese and charcuterie boards.

2 LACTO-FERMENTED PICKLES: These are the big sour and half-sour kosher dill pickles traditionally made in (and sold from) barrels. "Full-sour" pickles are fermented longer than half-sours, so they have a stronger flavor and less crunch. There's no vinegar added; the acid you taste is from the lactic acid created in the fermentation process.

3 DILL PICKLES: Vinegar, salt, and the namesake herb play a starring role in standard dill pickles—as does garlic in kosher dill pickles. Our favorite supermarket whole dill pickles are **Boar's Head Kosher Dill Pickles**, which our tasters praised for their strong dill and garlic flavors and "extra-crunchy" texture.

Vinegar Pickles versus Lacto-Fermented Pickles

VINEGAR PICKLES
Pour (usually hot) seasoned vinegar over food and let cool

↓

Hot-water canned for long storage (acid in vinegar prevents/slows bacterial growth)

LACTO-FERMENTED PICKLES	
METHOD 1 Chop food, add salt, press (draws out liquid, creates brine)	**METHOD 2** Mix brine of salt and water, pour over food to cover

↓

Anaerobic environment produces new, flavorful compounds (e.g., lactic acid and flavorful esters)

To make vinegar pickles, simply pour (usually hot) seasoned vinegar over the food and let it cool. Many vinegar pickles are subsequently hot-water canned for long storage. The acid in the vinegar prevents/slows the bacterial growth that leads to spoilage; it also adds flavor and changes the texture of the food.

There are two methods for making lacto-fermented pickles, neither of which requires vinegar. For the first method, chop or grate the food into pieces, toss them with salt, and press; the salt draws liquid out of the chopped food, and this liquid mixes with the salt to create a brine that covers the food. The second method calls for mixing a brine of salt and water and pouring it over the food to cover it. At this point, the two methods converge; in this anaerobic (oxygen-free) environment, friendly bacteria consume sugars in the food and, in turn, produce new, flavorful compounds, among them lactic acid.

And More . . .

Canning Pickles

Quick vinegar pickles (such as our Quick Pickled Onions, right) are designed to last for about a week in the refrigerator. For longer storage (up to a year in a cool place), pickles have to be hot-water canned. The process may seem daunting, but each step is straightforward. Here are the basics.

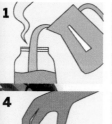

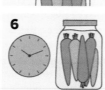

1. Heat jars (you do not need to sterilize them as long as you process the food for at least 10 minutes).
2. Using tongs or your clean hands, fill jars with food to be pickled.
3. Heat vinegar mixture and pour over food (taking care not to overfill jars).
4. Stir and press food to release air bubbles, then wipe jar rims clean and add lids and rings. Seal.
5. Submerge filled, sealed jars in boiling water for at least 10 minutes (recipes vary). Turn off heat and let jars sit in hot water to begin sealing.
6. Use jar lifter to remove jars from liquid and let sit at room temperature for 24 hours to cool and fully seal. Store in cool place out of sunlight for up to 1 year.

QUICK PICKLED ONIONS
Makes about 1 cup

- 1 red onion, halved and sliced thin
- 1 cup distilled white vinegar
- ⅓ cup sugar
- ¼ teaspoon table salt

Place onion in medium heatproof bowl. Bring vinegar, sugar, and salt to boil in small saucepan over medium-high heat, stirring occasionally until sugar dissolves. Pour vinegar mixture over onion and cover loosely. Let onion cool completely, about 30 minutes. (Pickled onions can be refrigerated for up to 1 week.)

Pickled Proteins

While we primarily think of pickles as being made from vegetables, meats, eggs, and seafood are commonly preserved via pickling, too. Think pickled pigs' feet, a jar of pickled eggs (sometimes stained red with beet juice), anchovies packed in salt or vinegar, or pickled herring or whitefish.

Other Pickled Products

Capers
Cocktail onions
Dilly beans
Giardiniera
Kimchi
Olives
Pepperoncini
Pickled ginger
Sauerkraut

This crispy fried chicken tastes extra-savory.

Indiana-Style
Lard-Fried
Chicken

Chicken fried in oil is already one of our favorite foods. Swap in lard and it gets even better.

by Morgan Bolling

FRYING CHICKEN PIECES in lard, aka rendered pork fat, is hardly a newfangled idea. Back in 1836, Mary Rudolph's cookbook, *The Virginia Housewife*, included a recipe for "Fried Chickens" that starts: "Cut [the chickens] up as for the fricassee, dredge them well with flour, sprinkle them with salt, put them into a good quantity of boiling lard, and fry them a light brown . . . "

Rudolph wasn't the only one calling for frying chicken in lard. At the time, lard was more readily available to cooks in many regions of the country than other fats. And even with the advent of more commonly available frying mediums, cooks across the United States—including a personal hero of mine, chef and cookbook author Edna Lewis—stuck to lard for the rich flavor and consistent results it produced.

But you don't see lard called for as a frying medium much in contemporary cookbooks. Over the course of the 20th century, the fat fell out of fashion. This happened in large part as a result of health reports—many of which have since been discredited—that denounced animal fats.

But in many kitchens, in the South and Midwest especially, this old-school method has survived. Our inspiration here comes from Indiana.

In this recipe, chicken pieces are seasoned with salt and plenty of freshly ground black pepper before being dunked in a very light coating of flour—unlike what's called for in typical batter-fried chicken recipes, this coating is a bit more delicate and restrained.

After the pieces are cooked in a pot full of bubbling lard, they emerge supremely flavorful, with tender, juicy interiors and crispy, supersavory exteriors. While the lard doesn't make it taste like pork, it adds a big, bold savory flavor that makes this one of our favorite fried chicken recipes ever.

Even better: It all cooks in a single batch, which means supper is on the table even faster. Just give it a few minutes to cool down, so you don't burn your tongue.

At the Grocery Store
We noticed significant flavor differences among chicken fried in various lard products. John Morrell Snow Cap Lard (pictured above) gave the chicken a savory and rich yet not overpowering flavor. Both Goya Lard and Armour Premium All Natural Lard imparted more distinctly porky flavor (good for those who want to lean into it). U.S. Dreams Lard was the most neutral product we tested. If desired, you can swap in 1 quart of peanut or vegetable oil for the lard and still get equally crisp chicken, but it will be missing the unique savory quality we love about this recipe.

LARD-FRIED CHICKEN *Serves 4*

Use a Dutch oven that holds 6 quarts or more for this recipe. We developed this recipe using John Morrell Snow Cap Lard, but you can substitute 1 quart of peanut or vegetable oil, if desired, although the taste will be different. If you're breaking down a whole chicken for this dish, a 4½-pound chicken would yield the necessary pieces. If you're using table salt, reduce the amount by half. To take the temperature of the chicken pieces, take them out of the oil and place them on a plate; this is the safest way and provides the most accurate reading.

- 3 pounds bone-in chicken pieces (2 split breasts cut in half crosswise, 2 drumsticks, and 2 thighs), trimmed
- 5 teaspoons kosher salt, divided
- 1 tablespoon pepper
- 1½ cups all-purpose flour
- 1½ teaspoons baking powder
- 4 cups water
- 2 pounds lard

1. Sprinkle chicken all over with 2 teaspoons salt and pepper. Whisk flour, baking powder, and remaining 1 tablespoon salt in large bowl until combined. Place water in medium bowl.
2. Working with 1 piece of chicken at a time, dredge chicken in flour mixture, shaking off excess; dunk in water, letting excess drip off; then dredge again in flour mixture, pressing to adhere. Transfer to large plate and refrigerate for at least 30 minutes or up to 2 hours.
3. Set wire rack in rimmed baking sheet and line half of rack with triple layer of paper towels. Melt lard in large Dutch oven and heat over medium-high heat to 350 degrees.
4. Add all chicken to lard, skin side down, in single layer (some slight overlap is OK) so pieces are mostly submerged. Fry for 10 minutes, rotating pot 180 degrees after 5 minutes. Adjust burner, if necessary, to maintain oil temperature between 300 and 325 degrees.
5. Carefully flip chicken and continue to fry until golden brown and breasts register 160 degrees and drumsticks/thighs register 175 degrees, 5 to 9 minutes longer. Transfer chicken to paper towel–lined side of prepared rack and drain for about 10 seconds per side, then move to unlined side of rack. Let cool for 10 minutes. Serve.

Breaking Down a Chicken in Six Simple Steps

1. Orient bird on board breast side up with wings away from you. Gather chef's knife, boning knife, and shears.

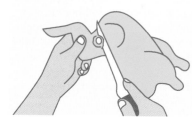

2. Use boning knife to slice between wing joint and breast to free wing. Repeat on other side. Reserve wings for another use.

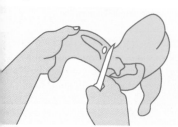

3. Bend leg quarters down to "pop" and expose joint. Maneuver tip of boning knife around base of joint and cut leg free. Repeat on other side.

4. Flip chicken breast side down with cavity facing you. Using shears, cut on both sides of backbone to remove it. Reserve backbone for stock.

5. Flip chicken breast side up. With both your hands on chef's knife, cut through breastbone to split breasts in two.

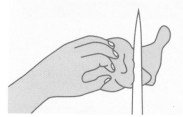

6. Use chef's knife to cut at seam that naturally separates drumstick from thigh. Repeat with other leg.

Testing Serrated Utility Knives
by Miye Bromberg

A UTILITY KNIFE is a handy, multi-purpose kitchen knife. It falls somewhere between a paring knife and a chef's knife in size, with a blade that's usually between 5 and 6 inches long; it can come in both serrated and straight-bladed styles. We bought eight, focusing on serrated-style knives, and used them to slice tomatoes, baguettes, kaiser rolls, and salami and to quarter avocados and loaded BLT sandwiches.

Our favorite is the Zwilling Pro 5.5" Serrated Prep Knife. Its blade features 5 inches of scalloped and pointed serrations, providing the perfect amount of power and grip when we cut food. A narrow tip let us core tomatoes easily, and a relatively tall heel gave our hands plenty of clearance as we cut. Best of all, it's razor-sharp. A few testers thought the handle could have been a touch longer and thicker, but most found it comfortable to use. At about $100, it's not cheap, but it made quick work of all the smaller tasks for which we wouldn't want to pull out a large serrated knife.

Winning Traits
- Sharp, stiff blade with serrated length of about 5 inches
- Wedge-shaped blade: tall at heel, narrow at tip
- Razor-sharp, with scalloped and pointed serrations interspersed
- Handle of moderate length and circumference

KEY **Good** ★★★ **Fair** ★★ **Poor** ★

HIGHLY RECOMMENDED   CRITERIA

Zwilling Pro 5.5" Serrated Prep Knife
Model: 38425-143 **Price:** $99.95
Serrated Blade Length: 5 in
Serration Types: Pointed and scalloped
Handle Length: 4.25 in
Our Favorite
Sharpness ★★★
Blade Design ★★★
Handle Design ★★½

Shun Classic 6-in. Serrated Utility Knife
Model: DM0722 **Price:** $109.95
Serrated Blade Length: 5.1 in
Serration Type: Scalloped
Handle Length: 4.5 in
Sharpness ★★★
Blade Design ★★½
Handle Design ★★★

RECOMMENDED

Cangshan TS Series 5-Inch Serrated Utility Knife and Wood Sheath Set
Model: 1020588 **Price:** $55.97
Serrated Blade Length: 4.25 in
Serration Type: Pointed **Handle Length:** 4.5 in
Best Buy
Sharpness ★★★
Blade Design ★★
Handle Design ★★★

RECOMMENDED WITH RESERVATIONS

Wüsthof Classic 5" Serrated Utility Knife
Model: 4110-7 **Price:** $84.95
Serrated Blade Length: 4.5 in
Serration Type: Pointed
Sharpness ★★★
Blade Design ★½
Handle Design ★★

Global Classic 6" Serrated Utility Knife
Model: GS-14 **Price:** $67.95
Serrated Blade Length: 5.25 in
Serration Type: Pointed
Sharpness ★★½
Blade Design ★★½
Handle Design ★

Mercer Millennia 6-Inch Utility Knife-Wavy Edge
Model: M23406 **Price:** $10.49
Serrated Blade Length: 5.25 in
Serration Type: Pointed
Sharpness ★★½
Blade Design ★★
Handle Design ★½

NOT RECOMMENDED

Victorinox Serrated Utility Knife
Model: 6.7833 **Price:** $7.85
Sharpness ★½
Blade Design ★
Handle Design ★★★

OXO Good Grips Pro 5-in Serrated Utility Knife
Model: 11191200 **Price:** $14.99
Sharpness ★
Blade Design ★½
Handle Design ★★★

Web subscribers can see the complete results chart at CooksCountry.com/sept20.

After baking the pizza, brush it with garlic butter and sprinkle it with oregano.

Alternating layers of meat and cheese help the slices stay intact.

Stuffed Pizza

The key to creating this remarkable centerpiece: patience. **by Mark Huxsoll**

THE STUFFED PIZZA at Michelangelo's in Sarasota, Florida (see "A Life of [Pizza] Pie"), a behemoth packed with meat and cheese, is truly special. But is it a reasonable dish to make at home? I was determined to find out.

The concept is simple enough: two layers of pizza dough with "toppings" in between. But I suspected that the pizza's tricky architecture could lead to spillage. I wondered if baking the pizza in a cake pan would help, so I tested a basic recipe once on a rimmed baking sheet and once in a 9-inch cake pan. The pan helped with structure, but the pie didn't develop the deep golden color I wanted.

When I tried building the pizza directly on the baking sheet, however, the rim impeded my ability to seal it tightly. I built the next pie on a lightly floured piece of parchment paper, and then, once it was sealed, I used the parchment to transfer it to the sheet. After some experimenting, I found that baking the pizza on the lowest rack of the oven produced perfectly even browning on both sides.

Stuffing the pizza generously but carefully (not overstuffing) and sealing it tightly (take your time) are the keys to a sliceable pie that won't explode. Also essential: letting the pizza cool for at least 45 minutes to allow the cheese to set up so that the slices stay intact. A short stint in a hot oven rewarms the pie for serving.

In a series of tests, I found that store-bought pizza dough worked just as well as homemade; once you brush the hot pizza with melted garlic butter and dried oregano, either type of dough is transformed into something utterly irresistible.

STUFFED PIZZA *Serves 8*

Plan ahead: Once baked, this pizza needs to rest for at least 45 minutes so that it can be sliced cleanly without the filling oozing out. Do not use canned pizza dough such as Pillsbury Pizza Crust here. When using store-bought pizza dough, it is helpful to let it come to room temperature to make it easier to roll out and shape. Buy a 4-ounce chunk of salami rather than sliced salami from the deli.

PIZZA

- 4 ounces hot Italian sausage, casings removed
- 4 ounces thinly sliced pepperoni, quartered
- 4 ounces thinly sliced Black Forest deli ham, cut into ½-inch pieces
- 4 ounces salami, cut into ¼-inch cubes
- ¾ teaspoon dried oregano, divided
- 2 (1-pound) balls pizza dough, room temperature
- 1 pound whole-milk mozzarella cheese, shredded (4 cups)
- 2 tablespoons unsalted butter, cut into 2 pieces
- 1 garlic clove, minced

SAUCE

- 1 (14.5-ounce) can whole peeled tomatoes, drained
- 1½ teaspoons extra-virgin olive oil
- 1 small garlic clove, minced
- ½ teaspoon red wine vinegar
- ½ teaspoon table salt
- ½ teaspoon dried oregano

1. FOR THE PIZZA: Adjust oven rack to lowest position and heat oven to 425 degrees. Cook sausage in 8-inch nonstick skillet over medium heat,

Putting It All Together

1. Layer meats and cheese over rolled-out bottom dough.

2. Brush edges of bottom dough with water to help seal.

3. Using rolling pin, cover filled bottom dough with rolled-out top dough.

4. Press dough edges together to seal, then trim excess dough from perimeter.

breaking up meat with wooden spoon, until no longer pink, 5 to 7 minutes. Transfer to medium bowl and let cool completely, about 20 minutes. Add pepperoni, ham, salami, and ½ teaspoon oregano to bowl with sausage and toss to combine.

2. Turn out 1 dough ball onto lightly floured 16 by 12-inch sheet parchment paper. Using your hands, flatten into 8-inch disk. Using rolling pin, roll dough into 12-inch circle, dusting lightly with flour as needed.

3. Sprinkle 1 cup mozzarella evenly over dough, leaving ½-inch border. Sprinkle one-third of sausage mixture (about 1 heaping cup) over cheese. Repeat layering until cheese and meat mixture are used up (top layer should be cheese).

4. Roll remaining dough ball into 12-inch circle on lightly floured counter, dusting lightly with flour as needed. Brush edges of dough on parchment with water. Loosely roll dough on counter around rolling pin and gently unroll it directly over dough on parchment and filling. Press dough edges together firmly to seal. Using pizza cutter, trim and discard dough just beyond sealed edge of pizza, about ¼ inch from filling.

5. Using paring knife, cut 1-inch hole in top center of pizza. Lifting parchment, transfer pizza to rimmed baking sheet. Using your hands, press down on top of pizza to compress filling into even layer. Bake until deep golden brown, 20 to 25 minutes.

6. Slide pizza from sheet onto wire rack. Microwave butter and garlic in small bowl until butter is melted and mixture is fragrant, about 1 minute. Brush top of hot pizza with garlic butter, then sprinkle with remaining ¼ teaspoon oregano. Let pizza cool on rack for at least 45 minutes. (Cooled pizza can be covered loosely with aluminum foil and refrigerated for up to 2 days.)

7. FOR THE SAUCE: Meanwhile, process all ingredients in food processor until smooth, about 30 seconds. Transfer to serving dish. (Sauce can be refrigerated for up to 3 days or frozen for up to 1 month.)

8. To serve, adjust oven rack to lowest position and heat oven to 425 degrees. Slice pizza into 8 wedges and place on parchment paper–lined rimmed baking sheet. Bake pizza slices until hot throughout, about 10 minutes. Microwave sauce until hot, about 2 minutes, stirring occasionally. Serve pizza with sauce.

A Life of (Pizza) Pie

Text by Bryan Roof; photos by Steve Klise

THE RAIN IS heavy when I pull up to Michelangelo's Pizzeria and Italian Restaurant in Sarasota, Florida. The dining room is empty at 11:09 a.m., but the glass display case is full. A pizzaiolo wearing a white T-shirt, white apron, and motivated white socks takes my order for stuffed pizza. After putting my slice into the oven to warm, he introduces himself with a heavy New York accent.

Mike Iannucci started working at his cousin's pizzeria in Long Island, New York, when he was 15 and has been in the pizza business in some capacity ever since, bringing his expertise with him when he moved to Florida 30 years ago. He doesn't own Michelangelo's and says he's content with that. He tells me that, from experience, "When you own a restaurant, it's like a baby. You worry about it constantly. I'm much happier this way."

While he works, the radio in the open kitchen pumps out classic rock and Mike sings along: "We gotta get out of dis place, if it's the last thing we ever do." His accent is even thicker when he sings.

Mike presses the dough against the marble counter, spinning it into a large circle before sliding it onto a well-floured pizza peel. He alternates layers of meat—pepperoni, meatballs, sausage, ham, salami—with fistfuls of mozzarella cheese. He makes small talk with a regular who's just stepped through the door. "How's it going, Sherry? Did you make it in here dry?" "Not really," she responds.

ON *the* **ROAD**

Mike chuckles and spins a second dough ball into a circle, which he delicately drapes over the mountain of meat and cheese. He presses it around the edges to seal and, with a dramatic flourish, pinches the center to create a steam vent. After a brush with garlicky oil, he slides the weighty pie into the oven.

When it's done, Mike will let the pie set up overnight before slicing it so that the filling doesn't run out. He steps back and admires his work. "It's like making pottery. When it comes out of the kiln, it's like 'WOW!' Of course, it also doesn't hurt that I'd like to eat it."

Mike Iannucci (right) puts the final touches on a stuffed pizza. During the COVID-19 crisis in 2020, Michelangelo's continued making pies for curbside takeout and home delivery.

TURN TO PAGE 32
FOR THE SALTED
BUTTERSCOTCH
SAUCE RECIPE

"Endless Summer"
Peach Pie

There's a problem with fresh peaches, and it's high time we talked about it.

by Jessica Rudolph

IS THERE A more highly anticipated time of year than peach season? I don't think so. And once it's here, the best way to celebrate is to capture the essence of a perfectly ripe peach in a freshly baked pie . . . right?

The sad truth is that all of a fresh peach's best qualities can become roadblocks to a great pie. The juices you love when they're running down to your elbows can make a pie a soupy mess. Those subtle floral and creamy flavors you crave in the fresh fruit tend to flatten out when baked. And not every peach is sweet and juicy, even in peak season. How can you best account for the variability in sweetness, tartness, and juiciness in less-than-perfect peaches?

Good news! We have the ideal fix at our disposal: frozen peaches. While they're not as lively or rewarding as fresh peaches when eaten straight, frozen peaches are a far more consistent product and are available anytime, anywhere. And with a little care, they make a dynamite pie.

To bolster the muted flavor of the frozen peaches, I had to first drive off excess moisture to concentrate their fruity taste. I did this by cooking down frozen peaches in a Dutch oven with some sugar and a pinch of salt. As the peaches cooked, they thawed and released liquid, which then reduced with the sugar and turned syrupy and glazy, lightly candying the peaches. Unlike fresh peaches, frozen peach slices start out quite firm and will hold their shape without breaking down while simmering.

Once cooked and cooled, the peaches needed little more than a squeeze of lemon to perk them up, plus some cornstarch to thicken the remaining liquid and contribute sliceable structure to the finished pie.

Tucked into a simple, buttery pie crust and topped with a decorative lattice and a sprinkle of satisfyingly crunchy turbinado sugar, the peaches baked into a beautiful, fragrant pie that could sway even the most die-hard of fresh seasonal peach fans. Endless summer, indeed.

Let It Go: Frozen Is Better

Eaten plain, ripe fresh peaches taste so much better than thawed frozen peaches. But we found that frozen peaches are much better (and more consistent) in a pie, since fresh peaches weep too much liquid and make for soggy slices.

ENDLESS SUMMER PEACH PIE

Serves 8 to 10

When purchasing frozen peaches, look for a no-sugar-added product; we like Earthbound Farm, Cascadian Farm, and Welch's frozen peaches. There is no need to thaw the frozen peaches. If you can't find turbinado sugar, simply omit the sugar topping (do not substitute granulated sugar). Plan ahead: The pie filling needs to cool for at least 2 hours and the dough needs to chill for at least 1 hour before rolling. This pie is best when baked a day ahead of time and allowed to rest overnight. Serve with Salted Butterscotch Sauce (page 32) and whipped cream.

FILLING

- 3 pounds frozen sliced peaches
- 1 cup (7 ounces) granulated sugar
- ¾ teaspoon table salt
- 1½ tablespoons lemon juice
- 2 tablespoons cornstarch
- 2 tablespoons unsalted butter, cut into ½-inch pieces

PIE DOUGH

- 7 tablespoons ice water
- ¾ cup sour cream
- 2½ cups (12½ ounces) all-purpose flour
- 1 tablespoon granulated sugar
- 1 teaspoon table salt
- 16 tablespoons unsalted butter, cut into ½-inch pieces and chilled
- 1 large egg, lightly beaten
- 2 tablespoons turbinado sugar

FOR THE FILLING: Combine peaches, sugar, and salt in Dutch oven. Cook peach mixture over medium-high heat, stirring occasionally, until juice is reduced to thick syrup and spatula dragged through mixture leaves trail that doesn't fill in immediately, 25 to 30 minutes. Transfer to large bowl and refrigerate until completely cooled, at least 2 hours. (Filling can be refrigerated for up to 3 days.)

FOR THE PIE DOUGH: Meanwhile, mix ice water and sour cream in bowl. Process flour, granulated sugar, and salt in food processor until combined, about 5 seconds. Scatter butter over top and pulse until butter pieces are no larger than peas, about 10 pulses. Add half of sour cream mixture to flour mixture and pulse until incorporated, about 4 pulses. Scrape down sides of bowl; add remaining sour cream mixture; and pulse until dough forms large clumps and no dry flour remains, about 6 pulses.

Transfer dough to counter and knead briefly until it comes together. Divide dough in half. Form 1 half into 5-inch disk and second half into 5-inch square, pressing any cracked edges back together. Wrap separately in plastic wrap and refrigerate for 1 hour. (Wrapped dough can be refrigerated for up to 2 days or frozen for up to 1 month. If frozen, let dough thaw completely on counter before rolling.)

5. Adjust oven rack to lowest position and heat oven to 375 degrees. Let chilled dough sit on counter to soften slightly before rolling, about 10 minutes. Roll dough disk into 13-inch circle on lightly floured counter. Loosely roll dough around rolling pin and gently unroll it onto 9-inch pie plate, letting excess dough hang over edge. Ease dough into plate by gently lifting edge of dough with your hand while pressing into plate bottom with your other hand.

6. Wrap dough-lined plate loosely in plastic and refrigerate until dough is firm, about 30 minutes. Roll dough square into 13 by 11-inch rectangle on lightly floured counter, with long side parallel to counter's edge. Using pizza cutter or chef's knife, trim ½ inch of dough from short sides of rectangle (sides perpendicular to counter's edge) to create clean edges. Cut six 2-inch-wide strips of dough perpendicular to counter's edge. Transfer strips to parchment paper–lined baking sheet, cover with plastic, and refrigerate for 30 minutes.

7. Stir lemon juice and cornstarch together in small bowl, add to cooled peach mixture, and stir to combine. Transfer peach mixture to dough-lined pie plate, spread into even layer, and dot with butter.

8. To make lattice, lay 1 dough strip across center of pie, parallel to counter's edge. Lay second strip across center of pie to form cross. Lay 2 strips across pie, parallel to counter's edge, on either side of middle parallel strip, about ¾ inch away from middle strip.

9. Fold back left side of middle parallel strip. Lay 1 strip across left side of pie, perpendicular to counter's edge, about ¾ inch away from middle perpendicular strip. Unfold middle parallel strip to cover. Repeat with right side of middle parallel strip and remaining dough strip.

10. Shift strips as needed so they are evenly spaced over top of pie. Pinch edges of lattice strips and bottom crust together firmly. Trim overhang to ½ inch beyond lip of plate. Tuck overhang under itself; folded edge should be flush with edge of plate. Crimp dough evenly around edge of plate using your fingers.

11. Brush lattice top and crimped edge with egg and sprinkle with turbinado sugar. Set pie on parchment-lined baking sheet. Bake until well browned and juices bubble around outer edge between lattice strips, about 1 hour, rotating sheet halfway through baking. Let cool on wire rack for at least 6 hours. Slice and serve.

Go Big or Go Home

You don't need a degree in physics or an origami manual to get this simple lattice right.

1. Cut six 2-inch-wide strips of dough, chill, then lay first strip across pie.

2. Make cross with second strip.

3. Lay third strip parallel to first.

4. Lay fourth strip below first.

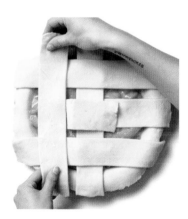
5. Fold back left side of first strip and lay fifth strip in place.

6. Unfold first strip to cover.

7. Fold back right side of first strip and lay final strip in place.

8. Unfold and seal lattice pieces to bottom dough.

Rosemary Focaccia

We simplify this chewy, rosemary-scented bread by baking it in two cake pans. **by Andrew Janjigian**

ROSEMARY FOCACCIA
Makes two 9-inch round loaves
The bread can be kept for up to two days well wrapped at room temperature or frozen for up to two months wrapped in aluminum foil and placed in a zipper-lock bag.

SPONGE
- ½ cup (2½ ounces) all-purpose flour
- ⅓ cup (2⅔ ounces) water, room temperature
- ¼ teaspoon instant or rapid-rise yeast

DOUGH
- 2½ cups (12½ ounces) all-purpose flour
- 1¼ cups (10 ounces) water, room temperature
- 1 teaspoon instant or rapid-rise yeast
- 1 tablespoon kosher salt, divided
- ¼ cup (1¾ ounces) extra-virgin olive oil
- 2 tablespoons chopped fresh rosemary

1. FOR THE SPONGE: Stir flour, water, and yeast in large bowl with wooden spoon until well combined. Cover tightly with plastic wrap and let sit at room temperature until sponge has risen and begins to collapse, about 6 hours (sponge can sit at room temperature for up to 24 hours).
2. FOR THE DOUGH: Stir flour, water, and yeast into sponge with wooden spoon until well combined. Cover bowl tightly with plastic; let dough rest for 15 minutes.
3. Stir 2 teaspoons salt into dough with wooden spoon until thoroughly incorporated, about 1 minute. Cover bowl tightly with plastic and let dough rest for 30 minutes.
4. Using greased bowl scraper or rubber spatula, fold dough over itself by gently lifting and folding edge of dough toward middle. Turn bowl 45 degrees and fold dough again; repeat turning bowl and folding dough 6 more times (total of 8 folds). Cover tightly with plastic and let rise for 30 minutes. Repeat folding and let dough rise for 30 minutes longer. Fold dough one final time, then cover bowl tightly with plastic and let dough rise until nearly doubled in size, 30 minutes to 1 hour.
5. One hour before baking, adjust oven rack to upper-middle position, place baking stone on rack, and heat oven to 500 degrees. Coat two 9-inch round cake pans with 2 tablespoons oil each. Sprinkle each pan with ½ teaspoon salt. Transfer dough to lightly floured counter and dust

top with flour. Divide dough in half and cover loosely with greased plastic. Working with 1 piece of dough at a time (keep remaining piece covered), shape into 5-inch round by gently tucking under edges.
6. Place dough rounds seam side up in prepared pans. Coat tops and sides with oil, then flip rounds so seam side is down. Cover loosely with greased plastic and let dough rest for 5 minutes.
7. Using your fingertips, gently press each dough round into corners of pan, taking care not to tear dough. (If dough resists stretching, let it relax for 5 to 10 minutes before trying to stretch it again.) Using fork, poke surface of dough 25 to 30 times, popping any large bubbles. Sprinkle 1 tablespoon rosemary evenly over top of each loaf; cover loosely with greased plastic; and let dough rest until slightly bubbly, about 10 minutes.
8. Place pans on baking stone and reduce oven temperature to 450 degrees. Bake until tops are golden brown, 25 to 30 minutes, rotating pans halfway through baking. Let loaves cool in pans for 5 minutes. Remove loaves from pans and transfer to wire rack. Brush tops with any oil remaining in pans and let cool for 30 minutes. Serve warm or at room temperature.

FOCACCIA WITH CARAMELIZED RED ONION, PANCETTA, AND OREGANO
Cook 4 ounces finely chopped pancetta in 12-inch skillet over medium heat, stirring occasionally, until well rendered, about 10 minutes. Using slotted spoon, transfer pancetta to medium bowl. Add 1 chopped red onion and 2 tablespoons water to fat left in skillet and cook over medium heat until onion is softened and lightly browned, about 12 minutes. Transfer onion to bowl with pancetta and stir in 2 teaspoons minced fresh oregano; let mixture cool completely before using. Substitute pancetta mixture for rosemary.

What's in a Word?
Focaccia is a descendent of an everyday ancient Roman flatbread called "panis focacius." The term derives from the Latin word "focus," which translates as "hearth"—in other words, the center of the home. The modern English word "focus" comes from the same root.

CHOPPED ROSEMARY ADDS A PINEY PUNGENCY

CHEWY TEXTURE, WITH LOTS OF HOLES

NEED TO KNEAD

[Ge]ntly turning the dough over itself at regular [int]ervals takes the place of kneading in our focaccia [rec]ipe. This technique aerates the dough to replen-[ish] the oxygen that yeast needs to work; elongates [an]d redistributes the bubbles; and ensures a chewy, [bu]t not tough, interior.

[SA]LTING THE PAN?

[A li]ttle coarse salt sprinkled into the pan means [cru]nchy salty bits on the outsides of the finished [br]eads for some textural contrast.

[RO]SEMARY

[Ro]semary is a traditional herb in focaccia. Its piney, [su]mmery flavor and beautiful flecks amplify this [br]ead's rustic nature.

[Y]EAST

[Th]is recipe calls for instant or rapid-rise yeast. Both [th]ese yeasts are gently dehydrated so that every [dri]ed particle is living, or active. Unlike active-dry [ye]ast, instant and rapid-rise yeast do not need to be [bl]oomed or activated in water before using.

ABOUT THAT OIL

Many focaccia recipes call for adding olive oil directly to the dough, but after experimenting, we found that adding olive oil to only the exterior of the dough yielded more consistent results. This keeps the insides of our breads light while adding rich olive-oil flavor to the outsides, where it has the most impact.

TASTE TEST CO-WINNER Bertolli Extra Virgin Olive Oil, Original, Rich Taste

BAKING STONE

Focaccia requires a hot, evenly heated oven to create its signature crisp crust. A baking stone is just the thing, absorbing heat during the warm-up period and maintaining that heat at an even level throughout cooking. Our favorite is the **Pizzacraft All-Purpose Baking Stone** ($29).

CAKE PAN

Some focaccia is made in a rimmed baking sheet or rectangular pan, but we chose to bake ours in round cake pans to maximize the mix of tender, stretchy interior and crisp, crunchy exterior; every wedge gets a bit of both. We developed this recipe using the **Chicago Metallic Non-Stick 9" Round Cake Pan** ($11), which gave us the best browning.

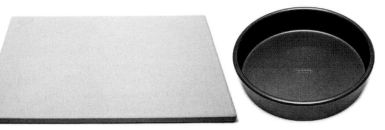

TOP-RATED PIZZA STONE
It has a large surface, and it's ovensafe to 800 degrees.

BEST CAKE PAN FOR BREADS
The dark finish promotes deep browning.

[1.] Make sponge
[Sti]r together sponge ingredients, cover, [an]d set aside for 6 hours.
[W]hy? This "pre-fermentation" step leads [to] more complex flavor and better chew.

2. Add flour, water, and yeast
Stir flour, water, and yeast into sponge and let rest for 15 minutes.
Why? Adding these ingredients after the sponge has rested helps achieve balanced structure.

3. Add salt
Stir salt into dough until incorporated.
Why? Salt slows down yeast activity, so waiting a few minutes to add it gives the yeast a head start.

4. Fold dough over itself
Use spatula to fold dough over itself 8 times, then let rest and repeat.
Why? Gently folding the dough as it rises takes the place of kneading.

[5.] Divide dough
[Pr]eheat oven, split dough in half, and [sh]ape each half into 5-inch rounds.
[W]hy? This recipe makes two smaller [lo]aves, ensuring textural contrast in [ev]ery wedge.

6. Prepare pans and add dough
Add oil and salt to cake pans and add 1 dough round to each pan. Coat tops and sides of dough with oil in pan, then flip dough so seam side is down.
Why? Plenty of olive oil adds flavor and sheen and keeps the bread from sticking.

7. Press dough into pans
Gently press each dough round into corners of pan and pierce bubbles with fork. Sprinkle rosemary on top.
Why? Pressing and piercing helps release excess gas so that the bread maintains its shape in the oven.

8. Bake, remove from pan, and brush tops with oil
Place pans on baking stone and bake. Remove bread and brush tops with oil remaining in pan.
Why? There's flavor in that oil! And it will give your loaves a lovely sheen.

Roasted Salmon with White Beans, Fennel, and Tomatoes

The key to the tastiest salmon and roasted vegetables: a flavor-packed compound butter.

by Jessica Rudolph

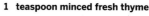

SALMON IS A perennial favorite in the test kitchen for quick and versatile weeknight dinners. For this easy one-pan supper, I wanted to highlight fresh summer flavors by roasting fennel and tomatoes alongside my salmon and then tie it all together with a garlic-lemon-herb compound butter.

To ensure that the licorice-y fennel became caramelized and sweet, I gave it a head start by spreading it out on a baking sheet and letting it get some color in the oven before adding my other ingredients. I stirred in halved cherry tomatoes and sliced garlic before adding the salmon fillets and let it all roast together while I stirred lemon zest, minced garlic, and minced thyme into softened butter. By the time the salmon was cooked, the tomatoes had slumped and released some juices that, when stirred together with the butter mixture, became a luscious sauce just thick enough to coat all the vegetables. It was delicious, but the meal was in need of some bulking up.

In looking for a starch to add, I bypassed the typical options such as pasta or potatoes and settled on cannellini beans instead; their nutty, earthy flavor complemented the bright, buttery tomatoes, and their creamy texture made the whole dish even more cohesive.

Now to fine-tune the flavor. To add pizzazz to the salmon itself, I coated the raw fillets with some of the compound butter I was stirring in at the end. I also added a splash of white wine with the beans and tomatoes and a squeeze of lemon juice at the very end—the extra acid helped all the flavors pop. Lastly, a shower of chopped parsley added a fresh note to brighten up the entire meal.

ONE-PAN ROASTED SALMON WITH WHITE BEANS, FENNEL, AND TOMATOES *Serves 4*

We purchased fennel with the stalks still attached. If you can find only stalkless bulbs, then look for those that weigh around 10 to 12 ounces each. To ensure uniform pieces of salmon that cook at the same rate, buy a whole 2-pound center-cut fillet and cut it into four equal pieces. For a nonalcoholic version of this recipe, omit the wine.

- 2 (1-pound) fennel bulbs, stalks discarded
- 2 tablespoons extra-virgin olive oil, divided
- 1¼ teaspoons table salt, divided
- ¾ teaspoon pepper, divided
- 2 (15-ounce) cans cannellini beans, rinsed
- 10 ounces cherry tomatoes, halved (2 cups)
- ¼ cup dry white wine
- 3 garlic cloves (2 sliced thin, 1 minced)
- 6 tablespoons unsalted butter, softened

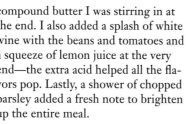

- 1 teaspoon minced fresh thyme
- 1 teaspoon grated lemon zest plus 1 tablespoon juice
- 4 (6- to 8-ounce) skinless center-cut salmon fillets, 1 to 1½ inches thick
- 2 tablespoons chopped fresh parsley

1. Adjust oven rack to middle position and heat oven to 450 degrees. Halve fennel bulbs through core, then trim away and discard tough outer leaves. Cut away core and slice fennel ¼ inch thick. Toss fennel, 1 tablespoon oil, ¼ teaspoon salt, and ¼ teaspoon pepper together on rimmed baking sheet. Spread fennel into even layer and roast until beginning to brown around edges, about 15 minutes.

2. Meanwhile, toss beans, tomatoes, wine, sliced garlic, ½ teaspoon salt, ¼ teaspoon pepper, and remaining 1 tablespoon oil together in bowl. Combine butter, thyme, lemon zest, and minced garlic in small bowl. Pat salmon dry with paper towels and sprinkle with remaining ½ teaspoon salt and remaining ¼ teaspoon pepper. Spread 1 tablespoon butter mixture on top of each fillet.

3. Remove sheet from oven. Add bean mixture to sheet with fennel, stir to combine, and spread into even layer. Arrange salmon on top of bean mixture, butter side up. Roast until center of fillets register 125 degrees (for medium-rare), 17 to 20 minutes.

4. Transfer salmon to serving platter. Stir lemon juice and remaining 2 tablespoons butter mixture into bean mixture, transfer to serving platter with salmon, and sprinkle with parsley. Serve.

What you can't see: a flavorful seasoned butter melted into the mix.

1. Brown sliced fennel.

2. Stir in beans, tomatoes, and garlic.

3. Add seasoned butter–topped salmon.

4. Stir vegetables with butter and lemon

THE CUT: Cost-effective chicken leg quarters provide a generous portion per person. Plus, their silky, rich dark meat is less prone to drying out and more forgiving to cook than white meat.

THE SAUCE: A bit of flour cooked with the vegetables gives the finished sauce enough body to make a cohesive dish. Garlic and dried oregano add complexity.

CHAR FOR FLAVOR: We brown red bell pepper and onion so that they pick up flavorful char and serve as the savory-sweet backbone for the bold sauce.

MOP IT: Don't toss that sauce! Mop it all up with crusty bread.

MEATY ACCENT: Juicy crumbles of meaty browned sausage amplify the heartiness of this weeknight supper.

CHERRY ON TOP: Just 1 tablespoon of chopped hot pickled cherry peppers, plus a splash of their spicy brine, delivers the dish's signature shot of bright heat.

Chicken Scarpariello

Want an easy chicken dinner with big, bold flavors? We've got you covered.

By Cecelia Jenkins

OUR VERSION OF this Italian American dish of browned chicken, sausage, and tender strips of sautéed onion and bell pepper gets a bold boost of flavor from hot pickled cherry peppers.

Though its exact origins are murky, Italian immigrants—particularly from in and around Naples—popularized the dish in New York City in the early 1900s. "Scarpariello" loosely translates "shoemaker-style," a description earned perhaps because it features ingredients inexpensive enough for a poor cobbler to afford or maybe because, much like a shoe, the dish was originally "cobbled" together with whatever ingredients were on hand.

More Uses for Hot Pickled Cherry Peppers

Here are some other handy uses for the peppers and brine.

- In sandwiches
- Minced and added to meatballs or meatloaf
- In salads
- In scrambled eggs
- As a taco topping
- As a burger topping
- Minced and stirred into mayo
- In a vinaigrette (brine)

CHICKEN SCARPARIELLO FOR TWO

We call for sweet Italian sausage here to balance the spiciness of the cherry peppers. Feel free to substitute hot Italian sausage if you prefer a spicier dish. Serve with crusty bread.

    2   (10-ounce) chicken leg quarters, trimmed
    ¼   teaspoon table salt
    ¼   teaspoon pepper
    2   teaspoons extra-virgin olive oil
    6   ounces sweet Italian sausage, casings removed
    1   cup thinly sliced red bell pepper
    1   cup thinly sliced onion
    1   tablespoon chopped hot pickled cherry peppers, plus 1 tablespoon brine
    2   garlic cloves, minced
    1   teaspoon all-purpose flour
    ½   teaspoon dried oregano
    ¾   cup chicken broth
    1   tablespoon chopped fresh parsley

1. Pat chicken dry with paper towels and sprinkle with salt and pepper. Heat oil in 10-inch nonstick skillet over medium-high heat until just smoking. Add chicken skin side down and cook, without moving it, until well browned, about 5 minutes. Flip chicken and continue to cook until browned on second side, about 4 minutes longer. Transfer chicken to plate.

2. Add sausage to fat left in skillet and cook until browned, breaking up meat with wooden spoon, about 2 minutes. Using slotted spoon, transfer sausage to paper towel–lined plate.

3. Heat leftover fat in skillet over medium-high heat until shimmering. Add bell pepper and onion and cook until vegetables are softened and charred in spots, stirring occasionally, about 7 minutes. Add cherry peppers, garlic, flour, and oregano and cook until fragrant, about 1 minute. Stir in broth, sausage, and cherry pepper brine and bring to simmer, scraping up any browned bits.

4. Nestle chicken, skin side up, into sauce and pour in any accumulated juices. Reduce heat to medium-low; cover; and simmer until chicken registers 200 degrees, about 20 minutes.

5. Off heat, let chicken rest in skillet, uncovered, for 10 minutes. Sprinkle with parsley and serve.

We like this sauce with short pasta shapes, but feel free to mix it up.

Sausage Ragu

A supersavory, slow-cooked red sauce supper, plus plenty more for leftovers. **by Matthew Fairman**

IT'S THURSDAY AT 7:45 p.m., and I'm just wrapping up a long day. I remember that Lauren (my wife) is working late and this is my day to take care of dinner. There's nothing in the cupboards or the refrigerator, and I've got no clue what I'm going to pull together for food. Searching the kitchen, hoping I can avoid resorting to takeout, I swing open the freezer. Relief. There in the back corner sits more than a quart of Slow-Cooker Sausage Ragu, a half batch from my final go-around with the recipe in the test kitchen.

Twenty-five minutes later, my wife comes home to the aromas of slow-simmered tomatoes, garlic, fennel, and Italian sausage—as I'm just showering our portions with grated Pecorino Romano cheese. With a stroke of luck, I've timed it perfectly. We dig in, and it's even more delicious than I remembered. The best part? It hardly took any work to prepare the first time around.

If you haven't yet used your slow cooker to do the hard part of making your pasta sauce, let me tell you: It's a game changer. With hardly any hands-on cooking (5 minutes on the stove to soften and sweeten some chopped onion and fennel), you're practically done with all the work for tonight's supper, and you've set yourself up for one or two more future suppers. Walk away from the kitchen and let the Italian sausage work its magic on the canned tomatoes, glug of red wine, and aromatic vegetables. Come back with a potato masher to break up the cooked sausage once you've boiled your pasta. It's that simple. Do your future self a favor and try it out.

◼ SLOW-COOKER SAUSAGE RAGU
Serves 8 to 10

This recipe yields about 10 cups of sauce (enough to coat 2 pounds of pasta). Serve the ragu with grated Pecorino Romano cheese and chopped fresh basil.

- 2 tablespoons extra-virgin olive oil
- 1 fennel bulb, stalks discarded, bulb halved, cored, and chopped fine
- 1 onion, chopped fine
- 4 garlic cloves, minced
- 3 tablespoons tomato paste
- 2 pounds hot Italian sausage, casings removed
- 1 (28-ounce) can crushed tomatoes
- 1 (15-ounce) can tomato sauce
- ½ cup red wine
- 1 teaspoon pepper
- ½ teaspoon table salt

1. Heat oil in 12-inch nonstick skillet over medium-high heat until shimmering. Add fennel, onion, and garlic and cook until softened, about 5 minutes. Add tomato paste and cook, stirring constantly, until mixture is uniformly colored, about 1 minute. Transfer vegetable mixture to slow cooker.
2. Add sausage, crushed tomatoes, tomato sauce, wine, pepper, and salt to slow cooker and stir to combine. Cover and cook until sausage is cooked through and tender, 6 to 7 hours on high or 8 to 10 hours on low.
3. Skim excess fat from surface of sauce with spoon. Using potato masher, mash sausage in slow cooker until uniformly broken into small pieces. Season with salt and pepper to taste. Serve. (Cooled sauce can be refrigerated for up to 3 days.)

◼ FREEZE IT
This sauce freezes beautifully for up to two months. To freeze it, let the sauce cool completely and then spoon it into a zipper-lock bag or an airtight storage container. You can reheat the sauce right from frozen in a saucepan or Dutch oven over medium-low heat (stirring frequently and taking care to not let it scorch) with a little extra water added.

Powerhouse Ingredients

Italian Sausage
Several ingredients in one: savory pork, fennel seeds, garlic, and red pepper flakes.

Red Wine With long, low cooking, the wine's flavor mellows, leaving a mild, complex acidity.

Tomato Paste
Concentrated tomatoes bring umami and body to the sauce.

Mash-Up
Your potato masher isn't just for spuds. Use it to shred slow-cooked meats, such as those in our recipes for Slow-Cooker Mexican Shredded Pork Tostadas and Slow-Cooker Pork Ragu. Our favorite is the **Zyliss Stainless Steel Potato Masher** ($13).

Try this creamy ricotta smeared on toast and drizzled with olive oil.

HOMEMADE CREAMY RICOTTA CHEESE

Makes about 2 cups

Do not use ultra-pasteurized (UHT) milk or cream in this recipe. Use a large fine-mesh strainer to drain the ricotta. If you don't have one, you can also use a colander lined with a single layer of cheesecloth, but you may need to stir longer in step 4 to drain off 5½ cups of whey. This recipe yields a creamy ricotta cheese with much smaller curds than many other homemade versions.

- 8 cups whole milk
- ¾ teaspoon table salt
- ¼ cup distilled white vinegar
- ¼–½ cup heavy cream

1. Set large fine-mesh strainer over large bowl. Heat milk and salt in large saucepan over medium-high heat, stirring frequently with rubber spatula to prevent scorching, until milk registers 185 degrees.

2. Remove saucepan from heat. Add vinegar and stir until mixture curdles, about 10 seconds. Let sit, undisturbed, until mixture fully separates into curds and cloudy whey, about 5 minutes.

3. Using ladle, transfer curds and whey to prepared strainer. Let sit until most of whey has drained from ricotta but center is still moist, about 10 minutes.

4. Using rubber spatula, stir ricotta in strainer, gently scraping sides and bottom of strainer, until any excess whey has drained from ricotta, about 90 seconds (you should have at least 4½ cups whey; if not, continue stirring until you have 5½ cups whey). Discard whey. Transfer ricotta to airtight container and refrigerate until cold, about 2 hours.

5. Process ricotta and ¼ cup cream in food processor until ricotta is uniformly smooth and spreadable, about 1 minute, scraping down sides of bowl as needed. (Finished ricotta should have texture of buttercream frosting.) If ricotta is too stiff, add remaining cream, 1 tablespoon at a time, and pulse until desired consistency is achieved. Serve.

TO MAKE AHEAD

Ricotta can be refrigerated for up to 5 days; stir to recombine before using.

Creamy Ricotta

Miles better than grainy supermarket versions and delightfully easy to make. **by Matthew Fairman**

FOR MOST OF my life, I knew ricotta cheese only as a bland, sometimes stale-tasting, always grainy cheese available in a plastic tub at the supermarket. But then I had it at a restaurant where they made their own. Served simply—spread on toasted sourdough with a sprinkle of sea salt and a drizzle of olive oil—it was a rich, thick, mildly sweet, ultracreamy, and even buttery revelation.

A bit of research uncovered the secrets to that creamy homemade ricotta, and to my delight the actual process of making it turned out to be a breeze. To make ricotta yourself, you typically just heat milk with some salt, add a bit of lemon juice or vinegar to separate the dairy into curds (solids) and whey (liquid), and then drain off the whey. The same simple process is used for

my version here but with some simple, crucial refinements. (Many commercial producers shortcut the draining process by adding stabilizers, which hold the bland excess liquid in suspension, creating a gummy and inferior ricotta.)

For extra-tender curds, I found that I needed to make sure that I didn't overheat the milk (185 degrees was the target temperature; any hotter and the curds could overcook and toughen). And for that over-the-top, velvety, luscious texture, the key turned out to be pureeing the chilled curds in a food processor with a little heavy cream. The processor blades broke down the large curds and smoothed the texture of the cheese while the cream added lightness and richness, ensuring that it was perfectly spreadable. It was everything ricotta should be.

HAVE EXTRA RICOTTA? MAKE THIS!

RICOTTA BRUSCHETTA WITH CARROT AND OLIVE SALAD *Serves 4*

Any type of pitted olives will work here. Shred the carrot on the large holes of a box grater. One large carrot should yield about ¾ cup shredded.

- ¾ cup shredded carrot
- ½ cup pitted green olives, chopped coarse
- ½ cup very coarsely chopped fresh parsley
- ¼ cup extra-virgin olive oil
- 2 teaspoons lemon juice
- 1 small garlic clove, minced
- ½ teaspoon table salt
- ¼ teaspoon red pepper flakes
- 4 ounces (½ cup) Homemade Creamy Ricotta Cheese
- 4 slices rustic bread, toasted

1. Combine carrot, olives, parsley, oil, lemon juice, garlic, salt, and pepper flakes in bowl. Let sit for 10 minutes to allow flavors to meld.

2. Divide ricotta evenly among bread slices. Divide carrot salad evenly over ricotta. Serve.

Outdoor Flat-Top Grills

With large, smooth cooking surfaces, these aren't your typical grills: They're good for searing smashed burgers, cooking pancakes, and even frying bacon.

by Riddley Gemperlein-Schirm

We liked cooktops that were big enough to accommodate enough food for four people.

A FLAT-TOP GRILL is similar to a traditional grill (it's propane powered and meant for outdoor use), but it features a carbon-steel sheet instead of cooking grates. In recent years, the popularity of flat-top grills has surged. A 2018 article by *Popular Science* reports that manufacturers have seen a 150 to 600 percent increase in sales.

To find out which model was best, we selected four grills, priced from about $170 to around $350. Three models had four burners under their rectangular cooktops, and one model had just two burners and a round cooktop. On each grill, we made pancakes, bacon, and eggs over easy; seared smashed burgers and toasted burger buns; and made chopped cheese sandwiches. We also used an infrared thermometer to measure the temperature of each grill's cooktop.

Before we could start grilling, we had to unpack and assemble all the grills and season their carbon-steel cooktops to prevent rusting and keep food from sticking. It took us from 20 to 65 minutes to assemble each grill and from 10 minutes to about an hour to season each grill's cooking surface.

Most of the grills produced well-seared, crispy-edged smashed burgers and toasted buns; crispy bacon and evenly cooked pancakes and eggs; and chopped cheese sandwiches with uniformly browned meat and onions. We preferred the models with cooking surfaces that measured at least 35 inches long by 20 inches wide, since they could easily accommodate enough food for four people. Larger cooking surfaces also gave us ample room for flipping and maneuvering food on the cooktop.

To measure the heat levels of the grills' cooking surfaces, we set half of each grill's burners to high heat and half to low heat and took the temperatures of the cooktops at the 30-minute mark. Our favorite grill had distinct hotter and cooler zones, with temperatures that varied by almost 100 degrees. This allowed us to sear burgers on the hotter side and toast burger buns on the cooler side.

A few design features made some of the grills easier to use than others: We liked the models with four wheels for easy transport and high back and side walls that helped contain food and grease. Our favorite grill had two well-positioned side tables that made transferring food easy.

When it came to cleaning, our two highest-rated grills had large openings at the rear of their cooktops, with drip cups positioned directly under the openings. We simply scraped any bits of residual gunk through the openings and into the grease cups before wiping down and cleaning the cooktops.

Our favorite, the Nexgrill 4-Burner Propane Gas Grill in Black with Griddle Top, produced well-cooked and evenly browned food. A heads-up: The cooktop arrives covered with a sticky coating to protect the surface, but it is easy to remove during the seasoning process. The grill is smartly designed, with four wheels for easy moving, walls that helped contain food, and two well-positioned side tables for keeping food organized. Two of the wheels could be locked, so it stayed put during use, and it had distinct hotter and cooler zones. Another plus: Its well-positioned drip cup made it easy to clean.

A Fervid Fan of Flat-Top Grills

Cook's Country television host Julia Collin Davison loves her flat-top grill for two reasons: "First, it's seriously fun to cook on. Second, I can cook a ton of food at once, which minimizes kitchen mess. It's also great for crowded weekends and parties. Rarely do I fire it up just to cook a single thing."

SOME THINGS JULIA LIKES TO COOK ON HER GRILL

• Smashed burgers

• Breakfast, including pancakes, bacon, eggs, and homemade breakfast sausage

• Seared steaks and chops

• Crispy-skinned fish and seared scallops

• Charred vegetables

KEY **Good** ★★★ **Fair** ★★ **Poor** ★

HIGHLY RECOMMENDED

Nexgrill 4-Burner Propane Gas Grill in Black with Griddle Top
Model: 720-0786 **Price:** $299.00 **Number of Burners:** 4
Dimensions of Cooktop: 35.75 x 20.50 in (732.88 sq in)
Temperature Difference Between Hotter and Cooler Zones: 90°
Number of Wheels: 4 **Drip Cup Location:** Rear
Side Tables: 2 **Assembly Time:** 20 min
Assembly: ★★½ **Cooking:** ★★★ **Capacity:** ★★★
Ease of Use: ★★★ **Cleanup:** ★★★

Comments: Our favorite model made evenly cooked and well-browned food, and its large cooktop easily accommodated enough food to feed a crowd. The cooktop also had distinct hotter and cooler zones, so we could successfully sear burgers and toast burger buns at the same time. The grill is equipped with two well-positioned side tables, a large opening and drip cup at the back that make for easy cleanup, and four wheels for easy transport. Two of the wheels can be locked to keep the grill stationary while in use. While the cooktop emerged from its packaging covered in a sticky factory coating, it came off easily as we seasoned it.

RECOMMENDED   COMMENTS

Blackstone 36" Griddle Cooking Station in Classic Black
Model: 1554 **Price:** $279.99
Number of Burners: 4
Dimensions of Cooktop: 35.75 x 21.50 in (768.63 sq in)
Temperature Difference Between Hotter and Cooler Zones: 88°
Drip Cup Location: Rear
Side Tables: 2 **Assembly Time:** 65 min
Assembly: ★★ **Cooking:** ★★ **Capacity:** ★★★
Ease of Use: ★★★ **Cleanup:** ★★★

This grill had a large cooktop that produced well-cooked food. It was easy to use and clean, but a large hot spot ran through the middle of the grill, so we had to be attentive while cooking to avoid burning delicate items such as burger bun. It also took more than an hour to assemble. We liked that it ha four wheels for easy transport and two side tables.

RECOMMENDED WITH RESERVATIONS

Camp Chef Flat Top Grill
Model: FTG600 **Price:** $349.00
Number of Burners: 4
Dimensions of Cooktop: 31.00 x 18.75 in (581.25 sq in)
Temperature Difference Between Hotter and Cooler Zones: 95°
Drip Cup Location: Front left
Side Tables: 2 **Assembly Time:** 45 min
Assembly: ★★★ **Cooking:** ★★ **Capacity:** ★★
Ease of Use: ★ **Cleanup:** ★½

While this grill was easy to assemble and produced well-cooked food, it was hard to tell if the burners were lit. Plus, its regulator needed to be securely tightened and opened slowly so as not to trigger the safety mechanism. (Once triggered, the burners will shut off.) The cooktop's drip cup often clogged and made cleanup difficult.

NOT RECOMMENDED

Cuisinart 360° Griddle Cooking Center
Model: CGWM-041 **Price:** $174.00
Number of Burners: 2 **Diameter of Cooktop:** 22.00 in (380.13 sq in)
Temperature Difference Between Hotter and Cooler Zones: 56°
Drip Cup Location: Rear
Side Tables: 1 **Assembly Time:** 65 min
Assembly: ★★ **Cooking:** ★½ **Capacity:** ★
Ease of Use: ½ **Cleanup:** ★½

While this grill's round cooktop seared burgers well, it was frustrating to cook on, use, and clean. The small cooktop lacke sides, so it was hard to flip and contain food. The cooktop offered no clearly defined heat zones and ran hot, which resulted in burnt burger buns. Its drip cup was wobbly.

Web subscribers can see the complete results chart at CooksCountry.com/sept20

Shredded **Sharp Cheddar Cheese**

reshredded cheddar is a timesaver, but how does it compare to block cheddar you shred yourself?

Lauren Savoie

ERICANS SPEND MORE money shredded cheese than cheese in any er form. Last year, shredded cheese t out block cheese by more than billion in sales, according to IRI, a icago-based market research firm. Could we find a good shredded ched-? We chose six, focusing on sharp ddar. Three of the products were nge and three were white; all were aditional," "thick," or "farmstyle" . We sampled the six products plain melted atop nachos.

When sampled plain, the strands med dry, with a slightly duller flavor n we're used to in sharp cheddar. l, tasters found all the cheeses to "savory" and "sharp." When we npled the cheeses melted on nachos, ters zeroed in on differences in melt-lity. Some cheeses were "smoother"

and "more stretchy," while others were a bit "greasy" and "slightly separated." To understand why, we compared ingredient labels, but there were no glaring differences. It's likely that lower-ranked cheeses were more dried out, reducing their ability to melt smoothly.

Flavor differences were harder to discern. Some cheeses were "sharp" and "punchy" when tasted plain, but most were "mellow" and "mild" when melted for the nachos. Experts told us that some of the compounds responsible for sharpness can dissipate during cooking, which is likely why the flavors of the melted cheeses were rated more evenly.

We liked all the cheeses we tried, but Kraft Sharp Cheddar Shredded Natural Cheese came out on top for its "subtly sharp," "buttery" flavor and its "softer," "smoother" texture when melted.

But how did our favorite shredded cheddar compare to block cheddar we shredded ourselves? To find out, we pitted it against shreds of our favorite block cheddar, Cabot Vermont Sharp Cheddar, in three more blind tastings: plain, on nachos, and in Simple Stovetop Macaroni and Cheese.

In the plain tasting, the Cabot block cheese had a sharper flavor. Tasters also preferred the silky texture of the melted Cabot cheese in the nachos. It was hard to discern the differences between the two in the macaroni and cheese. So when should you opt for shredded cheese? If you have the time, we recommend shredding block cheese by hand. However, for dishes where the cheese will be melted or combined with other ingredients, we think the shredded stuff is a perfectly acceptable shortcut.

Pros and Cons

BLOCK CHEDDAR

+ Often higher quality
+ Can shred into whatever size you want
+ Doesn't have cellulose or starch, which can have a drying effect
+ Lack of starch makes for better melting
- Takes time and tools to shred

SHREDDED CHEDDAR

+ Easy to use
+ Saves prep time
+ Often less expensive than block cheese
- No control over shred size
- A dry, chalky texture that is noticeable when eaten plain; not as smooth when melted

OUR FAVORITE

We tested six shredded cheddar cheeses ranging in color and shape!

RECOMMENDED

Kraft Sharp Cheddar Shredded Natural Cheese
Price: $3.29 for 8 oz ($0.41 per oz)
Comments: Our favorite cheese was "bright" and "sweet," with a subtle sharp-ness and a hint of "tang." The cheese melted easily and was "mellow" and "mild" atop nachos. When tasted plain, the strands had a slightly dry texture.

Crystal Farms Shredded Wisconsin Sharp Cheddar Cheese
Price: $3.49 for 8 oz ($0.44 per oz)
Comments: These long, thin white shreds were subtly sharp and slightly sweet. The cheese was a little "sticky" and clumped a bit in the bag. When melted, it was "mellow" and "sweet," with a hint of sharpness.

Kraft Sharp White Cheddar Shredded Natural Cheese
Price: $3.29 for 8 oz ($0.41 per oz)
Comments: The white version of our favorite product, this cheese was similar in flavor, with the same "long, thin" strands. This product uses cornstarch to prevent caking. As a result, it was a bit dry when tasted plain.

Sargento Shredded Sharp Cheddar Cheese Traditional Cut
Price: $3.29 for 8 oz ($0.41 per oz)
Comments: These "thick" orange shreds resembled "hand-shredded" cheese. Though the "chunky" shreds were a bit harder to sprinkle on nachos, they tasted pleasantly "milky" and melted easily.

Tillamook Farmstyle Cut Sharp Cheddar Shredded Cheese
Price: $3.19 for 8 oz ($0.40 per oz)
Comments: These "chunky" strips were "mellow" and a bit "tangy" both when eaten plain and when melted. While they were a tad "dry" when tasted plain, they were perfectly "melty" atop nachos.

Cabot Vermont Sharp Shredded Cheddar Cheese
Price: $3.69 for 8 oz ($0.46 per oz)
Comments: This product had the "tang" and "sharp-ness" we like in cheddar but was unfortunately a bit "too chalky" when eaten plain. Starches gave the shreds a "drier" mouthfeel and a "dulled" flavor.

Web subscribers can see the complete results chart at CooksCountry.com/sept20.

Salted Butterscotch Sauce

SALTED BUTTERSCOTCH SAUCE
Serves 8 to 10 (Makes 1½ cups)
We like to serve this sauce warm with our Endless Summer Peach Pie (page 23), but it can also be drizzled over ice cream, bread pudding, or cake.

- 1   cup packed (7 ounces) light brown sugar
- ½   cup heavy cream
- 8   tablespoons unsalted butter, cut into 8 pieces and chilled, divided
- ½   teaspoon table salt
- ½   teaspoon vanilla extract

1. Combine sugar, cream, 4 tablespoons butter, and salt in medium saucepan. Cook over medium-high heat, stirring often with rubber spatula, until large bubbles burst on surface of sauce, about 4 minutes. Remove from heat.

2. Carefully stir in vanilla and remaining 4 tablespoons butter until fully combined, about 1 minute. Carefully transfer sauce to bowl and let cool for 30 minutes (sauce will thicken as it cools). Serve. (Sauce can be refrigerated for up to 1 week. Reheat in microwave before serving.)

We're looking for recipes that you treasure—the ones that have been handed down in your family for a generation or more, that always come out for the holidays, and that have earned a place at your table and in your heart through many years of meals. Send us the recipes that spell home to you. Visit CooksCountry.com/recipe_submission (or write to Heirloom Recipes, Cook's Country, 21 Drydock Avenue, Suite 210E, Boston, MA 02210) and tell us a little about the recipe, and be sure to include your name and address.

COMING NEXT ISSUE
*This year, Thanksgiving will take on an extra-special meaning, and we've got some extra-special ideas for you to consider for your table. We're really excited about our **Maple Cheesecake**, which we plan on making an annual tradition. We're also working on a new **Roast Turkey Breast with Stuffing**; a crowd-pleasing **Cheesy Mashed Potato Casserole**; and for the morning after, our most banana-filled **Banana Bread** ever.*

RECIPE INDEX

FIND THE ROOSTER!

A tiny version of this rooster has been hidden in a photo in the pages of this issue. Write to us with its location, and we'll enter you in a random drawing. The first correct entry drawn will win a copy The Complete Cook's Country TV Show Cookbook, and each of the next five will receive a free one-year subscription to website. To enter, visit CooksCountry.co rooster by August 31, 2020, or write to Rooster AS20, Cook's Country, 21 Drydock Avenue, Suite 210E, Boston, MA 02210. Include your name and address. Jesse Hamilton of Houston, Texas, foun the rooster in the April/May 2020 issue page 23.

WEB EXTRAS

Free for four months online at
CooksCountry.com

Corn Tortillas

READ US ON IPAD

Download the Cook's Country app for i and start a free trial subscription or pur chase a single issue of the magazine. G CooksCountry.com/iPad to download app through iTunes.

RC=Recipe Card

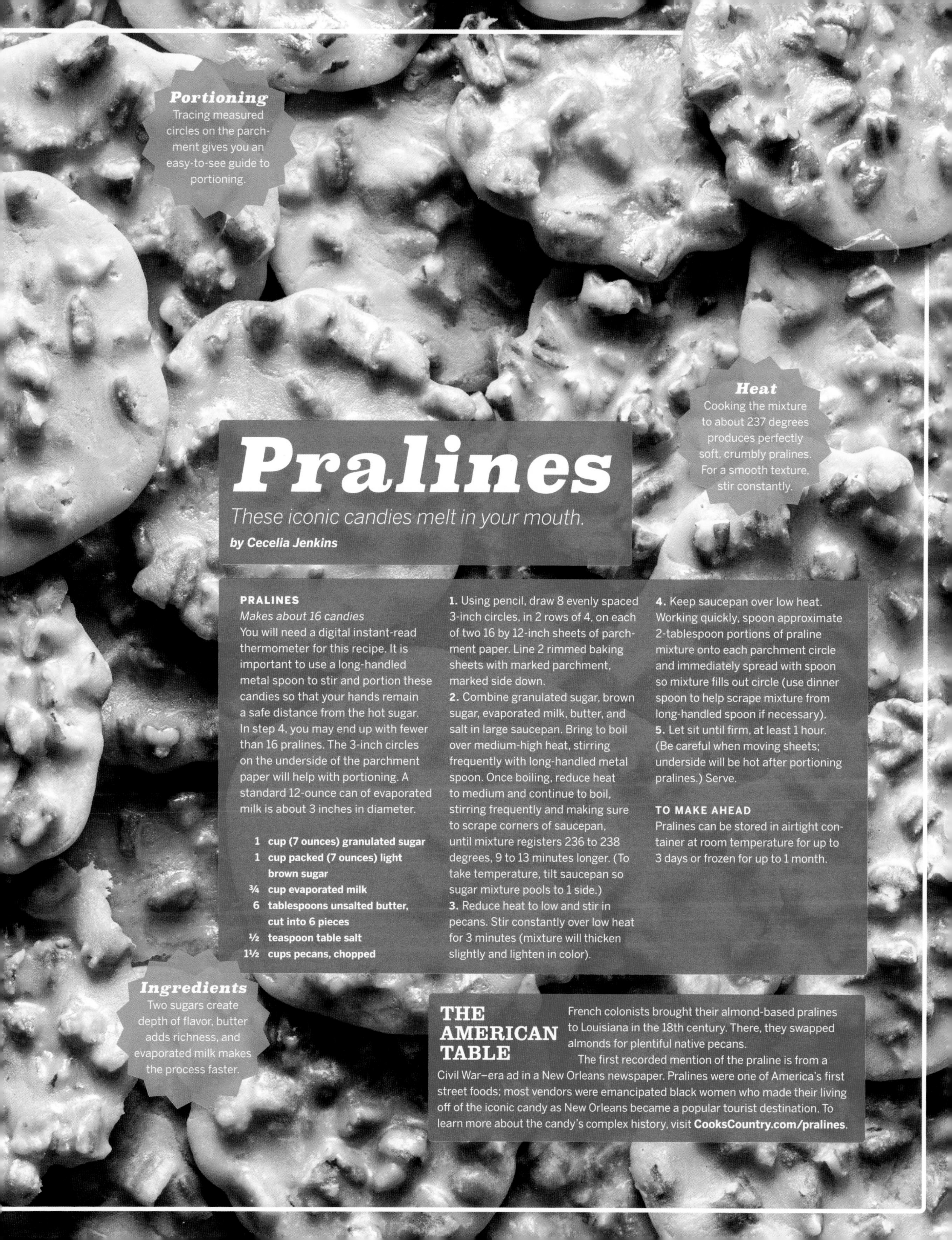

Pralines

These iconic candies melt in your mouth.

by Cecelia Jenkins

Portioning
Tracing measured circles on the parchment gives you an easy-to-see guide to portioning.

Heat
Cooking the mixture to about 237 degrees produces perfectly soft, crumbly pralines. For a smooth texture, stir constantly.

Ingredients
Two sugars create depth of flavor, butter adds richness, and evaporated milk makes the process faster.

PRALINES

Makes about 16 candies

You will need a digital instant-read thermometer for this recipe. It is important to use a long-handled metal spoon to stir and portion these candies so that your hands remain a safe distance from the hot sugar. In step 4, you may end up with fewer than 16 pralines. The 3-inch circles on the underside of the parchment paper will help with portioning. A standard 12-ounce can of evaporated milk is about 3 inches in diameter.

- 1 **cup (7 ounces) granulated sugar**
- 1 **cup packed (7 ounces) light brown sugar**
- ¾ **cup evaporated milk**
- 6 **tablespoons unsalted butter, cut into 6 pieces**
- ½ **teaspoon table salt**
- 1½ **cups pecans, chopped**

1. Using pencil, draw 8 evenly spaced 3-inch circles, in 2 rows of 4, on each of two 16 by 12-inch sheets of parchment paper. Line 2 rimmed baking sheets with marked parchment, marked side down.

2. Combine granulated sugar, brown sugar, evaporated milk, butter, and salt in large saucepan. Bring to boil over medium-high heat, stirring frequently with long-handled metal spoon. Once boiling, reduce heat to medium and continue to boil, stirring frequently and making sure to scrape corners of saucepan, until mixture registers 236 to 238 degrees, 9 to 13 minutes longer. (To take temperature, tilt saucepan so sugar mixture pools to 1 side.)

3. Reduce heat to low and stir in pecans. Stir constantly over low heat for 3 minutes (mixture will thicken slightly and lighten in color).

4. Keep saucepan over low heat. Working quickly, spoon approximate 2-tablespoon portions of praline mixture onto each parchment circle and immediately spread with spoon so mixture fills out circle (use dinner spoon to help scrape mixture from long-handled spoon if necessary).

5. Let sit until firm, at least 1 hour. (Be careful when moving sheets; underside will be hot after portioning pralines.) Serve.

TO MAKE AHEAD

Pralines can be stored in airtight container at room temperature for up to 3 days or frozen for up to 1 month.

THE AMERICAN TABLE

French colonists brought their almond-based pralines to Louisiana in the 18th century. There, they swapped almonds for plentiful native pecans.

The first recorded mention of the praline is from a Civil War–era ad in a New Orleans newspaper. Pralines were one of America's first street foods; most vendors were emancipated black women who made their living off of the iconic candy as New Orleans became a popular tourist destination. To learn more about the candy's complex history, visit **CooksCountry.com/pralines**.

INSIDE THIS ISSUE

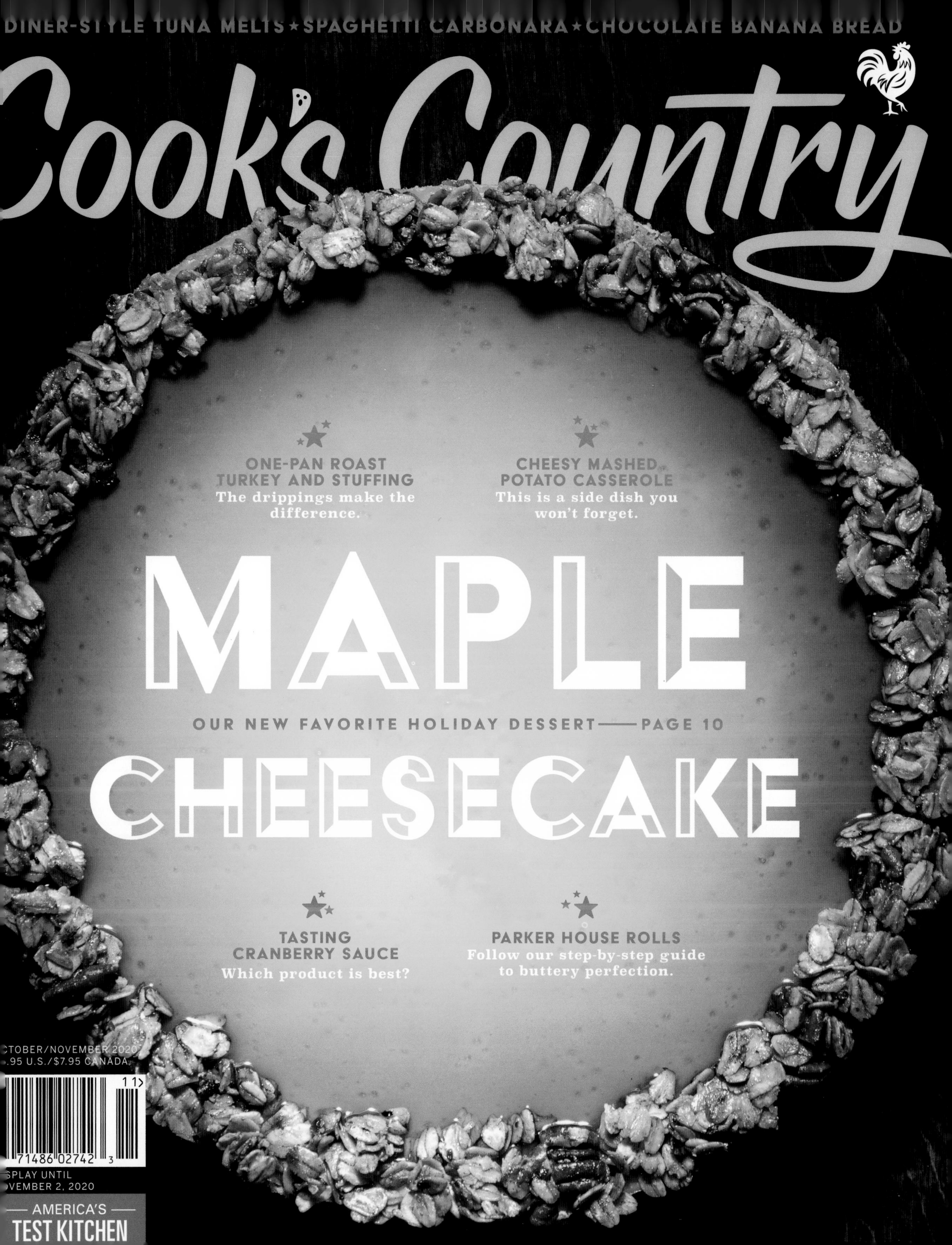

DINER-STYLE TUNA MELTS ★ SPAGHETTI CARBONARA ★ CHOCOLATE BANANA BREAD

Cook's Country

ONE-PAN ROAST
TURKEY AND STUFFING
The drippings make the
difference.

CHEESY MASHED
POTATO CASSEROLE
This is a side dish you
won't forget.

MAPLE

OUR NEW FAVORITE HOLIDAY DESSERT —— PAGE 10

CHEESECAKE

TASTING
CRANBERRY SAUCE
Which product is best?

PARKER HOUSE ROLLS
Follow our step-by-step guide
to buttery perfection.

OCTOBER/NOVEMBER 2020
$5.95 U.S./$7.95 CANADA

DISPLAY UNTIL
NOVEMBER 2, 2020

AMERICA'S
TEST KITCHEN

0 71486 02742 3

11>

Letter from the EDITOR

L IKE MANY OF us, I have been spending more time at home over the past few months. It hasn't been easy to have my old wings clipped (figuratively and temporarily), but I have enjoyed the chance to dig deeper into the stacks of old cookbooks I've collected over the years.

As I've run through some of the oldest books, the 19th-century titles in particular, I'm struck by how sound the advice is. Take, for example, this snippet from the introduction to one of my all-time favorite cookbooks, *Common Sense in the Household* (1871) by Marion Harland: "We may as well start from the right point, if we hope to continue friends. You must learn the rudiments of the art [of cooking] for yourself. Practice, and practice alone, will teach you certain essentials. The management of the ovens, the requisite thickness of boiling custards, the right shade of brown upon bread and roasted meats—these and dozens of other details are hints which cannot be imparted by written or oral instructions. But, once learned, they are never forgotten, and henceforward your fate is in your own hands."

This is perfect cooking advice, I think, because it is true. Reading and learning instructions is very important, and at *Cook's Country* we do our best to make sure that our recipes are easy to follow and produce good results. But ultimately, there is no replacement for hands-on experience in the kitchen. The more you cook, the more confident you become and the more success you have.

I think this is what I love most about cooking. There is always something new (or old) to learn. You can live an entire life in the kitchen and just scratch the surface. That's what makes it interesting.

TUCKER SHAW
Editor in Chief

P.S. The COVID-19 crisis interrupted our production schedule for this issue of *Cook's Country*. To make sure that you have a full package of excellent recipes, we've curated a few of our favorites from our coworkers on the ATK books team. You'll see them in the Recipe Cards and in a handful of other features in this issue.

Illustration: Hannah Jacobs

 Find us on **Facebook**
facebook.com/CooksCountry

 Find us on **Instagram**
instagram.com/CooksCountry

 Follow us on **Pinterest**
pinterest.com/TestKitchen

 Follow us on **Twitter**
twitter.com/TestKitchen

Cook's Country

Chief Executive Officer David Nussbaum
Chief Creative Officer Jack Bishop
Editor in Chief Tucker Shaw
Executive Managing Editor Todd Meier
Executive Food Editor Bryan Roof
Deputy Editor Scott Kathan
Deputy Food Editor Morgan Bolling
Senior Editor Cecelia Jenkins
Associate Editors Matthew Fairman, Jessica Rudolph
Test Cooks Mark Huxsoll, Amanda Luchtel
Photo Team Manager Alli Berkey
Lead Test Cook, Photo Team Eric Haessler
Test Cooks, Photo Team Hannah Fenton, Jacqueline Gochenour
Assistant Test Cooks, Photo Team Gina McCreadie, Christa
Copy Editors Christine Campbell, April Poole, Rachel Schow
Managing Editor, Web Mari Levine
Digital Content Producer Danielle Lapierre
Contributing Editor Eva Katz
Senior Science Research Editor Paul Adams
Hosts & Executive Editors, Television Bridget Lancaster,
   Julia Collin Davison

Executive Editors, ATK Reviews Hannah Crowley, Lisa McM
Senior Editors, ATK Reviews Lauren Savoie, Kate Shannon
Associate Editors, ATK Reviews Miye Bromberg,
   Riddley Gemperlein-Schirm, Carolyn Grillo
Assistant Editor, ATK Reviews Chase Brightwell

Creative Director John Torres
Photography Director Julie Cote
Art Director Maggie Edgar
Associate Art Director Kristen Jones
Art Director, ATK Reviews Marissa Angelone
Senior Staff Photographers Steve Klise, Daniel J. van Acker
Photographer Kevin White
Photography Producer Meredith Mulcahy

Senior Director, Creative Operations Alice Carpenter
Deputy Editor, Culinary Content and Curriculum
   Christie Morrison
Senior Manager, Publishing Operations Taylor Argenzio
Imaging Manager Lauren Robbins
Production & Imaging Specialists Tricia Neumyer, Dennis N
   Amanda Yong
Deputy Editor, Editorial Operations Megan Ginsberg
Assistant Editors, Editorial Operations Tess Berger, Sara Za
Test Kitchen Director Erin McMurrer
Assistant Test Kitchen Director Alexxa Benson
Test Kitchen Manager Meridith Lippard
Test Kitchen Facilities Manager Kayce Vanpelt
Test Kitchen Shopping & Receiving Lead Heather Tolmie
Senior Kitchen Assistant Shopper Avery Lowe

Chief Financial Officer Jackie McCauley Ford
Senior Manager, Customer Support Tim Quinn
Customer Support Specialist Mitchell Axelson

Chief Digital Officer Fran Middleton
VP, Marketing Natalie Vinard
Director, Audience Acquisition & Partnerships Evan Steine
Director, Social Media Marketing & Emerging Platforms
   Kathryn Przybyla
Social Media Manager Charlotte Errity
Social Media Coordinators Sarah Sandler, Norma Tentori

Chief Revenue Officer Sara Domville

Director, Public Relations & Communications Brian Frankl

Senior VP, Human Resources & Organizational
   Development Colleen Zelina
Human Resources Manager Jason Lynott

Food Stylists Ashley Moore, Elle Simone Scott

Circulation Services PubWorX ProCirc

AMERICA'S ® TEST KITCHEN

America's Test Kitchen has been teaching home cooks how to be successful in the kitchen since 1993. Our mission is to empower and inspire confidence, community, and creativity in the kitchen. Millions watch our two shows on public television; read our two flagship magazines (*Cook's Country* and *Cook's Illustrated*); and rely on our books, websites, videos, podcasts, and educational products for children. America's Test Kitchen is located in a state-of-the-art Boston facility with 15,000 square feet of test kitchen and studio space. Learn more at americasTestKitchen.com.

6

16

15

Cook's Country magazine (ISSN 1552-1990), number 95, is published bimonthly by America's Test Kitchen Limited Partnership, 21 Drydock Avenue, Suite 210E, Boston, MA 02210. Copyright 2020 America's Test Kitchen Limited Partnership. Periodicals postage paid at Boston, MA, and additional mailing offices, USPS #023453. Publications Mail Agreement No. 40020778. Return undeliverable Canadian addresses to P.O. Box 875, Station A, Windsor, ON N9A 6P2. POSTMASTER: Send address changes to *Cook's Country*, P.O. Box 6018, Harlan, IA 51593-1518. For subscription and gift subscription orders, subscription inquiries, or change of address notices, visit AmericasTestKitchen.com/support, call 800-526-8447 in the U.S. or 515-237-3663 from outside the U.S., or write to us at *Cook's Country*, P.O. Box 6018, Harlan, IA 51593-1518. PRINTED IN THE USA.

Compiled by Cecelia Jenkins

Bird Buying

Do you recommend buying a fresh turkey or buying a frozen one?

–Terry Lennox, Bloomington, Ind.

Well, it's complicated. If you have access to a truly fresh, recently butchered turkey (usually from a farm or high-end butcher), by all means buy it. But at the supermarket, most turkeys sold as "fresh" are actually kept right around the freezing point, which is a bad thing because they run the risk of repeatedly thawing and refreezing; this can damage the cell walls in the meat, causing the turkeys to cook up mushy and/or dry.

We prefer to buy frozen turkeys at the supermarket and thaw them ourselves; this way we can control the thawing and make sure that it happens only once. To keep it food-safe, always thaw your turkey in the refrigerator. Plan on a defrosting time of at least one day for every 5 pounds of turkey (round up if needed); this gives you some leeway as well as time to brine or salt the turkey, if desired. So if you have a 12-pound turkey, you'll need three full days to thaw it completely.

DAY 1 **Sunday morning to Monday morning:** *The turkey is rock-hard in the refrigerator.*

DAY 2 **Monday morning to Tuesday morning:** *The turkey is thawing.*

DAY 3 **Tuesday morning to Wednesday morning:** *The turkey is fully thawed; you can now salt or brine the turkey (or have peace of mind knowing that it's thawed and ready to cook).*

Emergency Quick Thaw

If you absolutely must rush the thawing, submerge the turkey (in its wrapper) in a bucket filled with cold water and thaw for 30 minutes per pound. Change the water every 30 minutes to prevent bacterial growth. (For a 12-pound bird, this will take 6 to 8 hours, switching the water 12 or more times.)

When Is It Done?

Turkey (and chicken) is done when the breasts register 160 degrees and the drumsticks/thighs register 175 degrees; an instant-read **digital thermometer** (see our winners below) is the best tool for taking the bird's temperature. The cooking time depends on many factors, such as the size of the turkey and the temperature of the oven. We recommend checking for doneness 30 minutes earlier than advised in the recipe.

To take the temperature of the breast, insert the thermometer at the neck end, holding it parallel to the bird. To take the temperature of the thigh, insert the thermometer between the breast and drumstick and into the thickest part of the thigh, staying away from the bone. Check the temperatures of the breast and thigh on both sides of the bird.

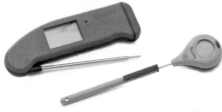

THERMOWORKS THERMAPEN MK4 ($99) AND THERMOWORKS THERMOPOP ($29)
The best digital thermometers

What Size Turkey Should You Buy?

WHOLE TURKEY
WEIGHT/SERVINGS
12–15 pounds = 10–12 servings
15–18 pounds = 14–16 servings
18–22 pounds = 20–22 servings

BONE-IN BREAST
WEIGHT/SERVINGS
6–7 pounds = 8–10 servings
A regular or "true" cut turkey breast includes the whole front of the bird: two breast halves separated by the breastbone, the ribs, a portion of the wing meat, and a portion of the back and neck skin.

BONELESS BREAST
WEIGHT/SERVINGS
3–4 pounds = 6–8 servings
A boneless turkey breast can be perfect for a smaller gathering.

Resting: The Pause Between Cooking and Carving

Once the turkey has finished roasting and you've taken it out of the oven, you need to wait at least 30 minutes before carving it. This resting time allows the turkey's juices to redistribute throughout the meat so that it will be more moist when it's served. There is no need to tent a resting turkey with aluminum foil, as the turkey will stay warm uncovered. Plus, covering the crisped skin can make it soggy.

Thanksgiving Tips from the Test Kitchen

▷ Once it's hot, you can hold gravy in a slow cooker or insulated carafe to keep it warm and out of the way.

▷ Keep a small saucepan of hot chicken broth on the stove to help rewarm/adjust the consistency of dishes when it's go time.

▷ You can reheat fully baked pies in a low, 200-degree oven until they're warm in the middle (you might sacrifice the crispness of the bottom crust a little).

▷ Reheat mashed potatoes in the microwave (you may need to add butter or hot broth or milk to loosen them before serving).

▷ You can warm your plates and platters in a low oven (or you can pour hot water into serving dishes) to help keep food hot once it reaches the table.

Turkey Carving 101

Carving is a messy job. We prefer to do it in the kitchen, where you can break down the turkey and carve neat, picture-perfect slices without worrying as much about mess or the pressure of an audience.

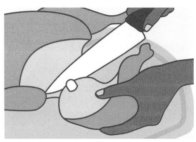

1. Slice through skin between breast and leg and pull leg quarter down until joint is exposed. Remove leg by cutting between hip joint and any attached skin. Repeat on opposite side.

2. Remove wings by bending wing out to expose joint and then cutting down through joint.

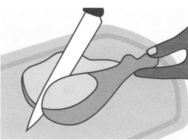

3. Separate thighs from drumsticks by cutting between joint connecting them. Leave drumsticks whole. Cut thigh meat from both sides of bone and then slice. Repeat with second thigh.

4. To remove breast meat from carcass, gently start cutting across top of breast half, right up against bone.

5. Use your free hand to hold and pull meat from bone as you cut down along breastbone, following its contours so entire breast half comes off in 1 piece.

6. Once both breast halves are fully removed, use slicing knife to slice meat crosswise roughly ¼ inch thick.

Make-Ahead Gravy Tip

Marie Westblanc of Rapid City, S.D., has a secret for make-ahead gravy: rotisserie chicken. In the weeks leading up to Turkey Day, she freezes the wings and carcasses from rotisserie birds that she uses for weeknight dinners in order to make one "superstrong" batch of stock for gravy, adding plenty of carrots, onions, and celery to the pot. Then she uses the measurements from our recipe for Turkey and Gravy for a Crowd (October/November 2017)—6 cups of broth or stock, ⅔ cup of flour, and ½ cup of reserved chicken fat (or oil)—to make gravy in the days before the holiday. Finally, when reheating the gravy the day of, she adds turkey drippings to fortify it with the flavors of roasted turkey.

No Cake Stand, No Problem

Marcia Entzel of Moses Lake, Wash., doesn't own a rotating cake stand. So when she decorates a cake, she uses her Rubbermaid lazy Susan—which usually sits in the middle of the dinner table with condiments on it—instead. She simply sets her crystal cake platter on the turntable and places strips of waxed paper under the cake to keep frosting from getting on the edges of the platter. That way, she never needs to move the decorated cake.

Caramelized Onions at the Ready

Renie Wilson of West Des Moines, Iowa, loves caramelized onions, but she doesn't always have time to make them. When she does, she makes a big batch and freezes them in a silicone ice cube tray. Once they're solid, she pops them out and throws them in a freezer bag. When she needs caramelized onions—say, to top a burger or slather on a grilled cheese—she simply grabs a cube from the freezer and quickly thaws it for 45 seconds in the microwave.

What's the Best All-Purpose Wooden Spoon? *by Lisa McManus*

WOODEN SPOONS ARE one of the oldest cooking tools—and home cooks still love them. They're useful for many tasks, such as mixing cookie dough, browning roux, scraping up fond for stews and sauces, sautéing onions, and breaking up ground beef as it cooks.

ATK REVIEWS

We bought 13 spoons in innovative and classic styles and prepared vegetable curry, Bolognese sauce, and oatmeal cookies, rating their performance, comfort, and durability and how easy they were to clean.

Our top two models were light and easy to maneuver, with scooped heads and thin front edges that helped us scoop and scrape. Their rounded, longer handles felt comfortable and kept our hands far from the heat. Both were easy to keep clean and didn't break or crack. Our co-winners were the Spootle from Jonathan's Spoons, an innovative spatula-like model with a scooped bowl and thin leading edge, and the classic FAAY 13.5" Teak Cooking Spoon (also our Best Buy). We'd be happy to reach for either one in the kitchen.

Can They Go in the Dishwasher?

Spoons stay closer to their original condition when washed by hand. After 10 trips through the dishwasher, most spoons look bleached and feel as dry as driftwood. Any spoons with a shellac-like finish lose most of it after about five dishwasher cycles. To prolong a spoon's life span, hand-wash it.

KEY **Good** ★★★ **Fair** ★★ **Poor** ★

HIGHLY RECOMMENDED

Jonathan's Spoons Spootle
Model: UH **Price:** $28.00
Material: Wild cherry
Weight: 1.6 oz **Length:** 12.25 in

Performance ★★★
Ease of Use ★★★
Cleanup/Durability ★★★

Comments: This "spootle" (combination spoon and spatula) won fans for its light, maneuverable weight; slim, long scraping edge and rounded bowl for scooping food; and comfortable handle. It didn't overly dry out, even after 10 dishwasher cycles.

FAAY 13.5" Teak Cooking Spoon
Model: 8541966738 **Price:** $10.99
Material: Teak
Weight: 1.8 oz **Length:** 13.5 in

Performance ★★★
Ease of Use ★★★
Cleanup/Durability ★★★

Comments: Light, long, and maneuverable, this classic spoon kept our hands far from the heat, and its rounded, tapered handle was comfortable and easy to grip. Made of teak, the wood resisted staining or drying out, even after 10 dishwasher cycles.

Best Buy

RECOMMENDED

Jonathan's Spoons Lazy Spoon Original
Model: TNO **Price:** $36.00 **Material:** Wild cherry **Weight:** 1.8 oz **Length:** 12 in

Performance ★★★
Ease of Use ★★½
Cleanup/Durability ★★½

Lancaster Cast Iron Handmade Wooden Lazy Spoon
Model: n/a **Price:** $24.99 **Material:** Black cherry **Weight:** 2.6 oz **Length:** 12 in

Performance ★★½
Ease of Use ★★½
Cleanup/Durability ★★½

Le Creuset VW302 Revolution Wood Scraping Spoon, 12.5 x 2.5-Inch
Model: VW302 **Price:** $25.04
Material: Beech **Weight:** 2.5 oz **Length:** 12.5 in

Performance ★★½
Ease of Use ★★½
Cleanup/Durability ★★

OXO Good Grips Large Wooden Spoon
Model: 1058024 **Price:** $5.78
Material: Beech **Weight:** 2.5 oz **Length:** 12 in

Performance ★★★
Ease of Use ★★
Cleanup/Durability ★★

OXO Good Grips Corner Wooden Spoon
Model: 1130880 **Price:** $12.31
Material: Beech **Weight:** 3.5 oz **Length:** 12.5 in

Performance ★★½
Ease of Use ★★
Cleanup/Durability ★★

Web subscribers can see the complete results chart at **CooksCountry.com/nov20.**

RUSTIC BREAD CUBES
Soak up flavor and have nice chew

ITALIAN SAUSAGE
Adds deep seasoning and meaty complexity

HEAVY-DUTY ROASTING PAN
Starts on the stovetop, finishes in the oven

POP OF POMEGRANATE
Balances richness with bright flavor

One-Pan Turkey Breast and **Stuffing**

Turkey and stuffing are already a perfect pair on the plate. With a little know-how, they can be in the oven, too. **by Morgan Bolling**

THANKSGIVING IS MY favorite holiday. But even as a professional chef, I've had my fair share of near meltdowns trying to juggle the cooking, hosting, and—let's face it—guests who don't always get along. So I'm all for any recipe that streamlines my efforts. This led me to my goal this year: a holiday-worthy turkey and stuffing cooked together in one pan. Not only would this save me from cleaning extra dishes, but the turkey would slowly render its fat into the stuffing below and infuse it with savory poultry flavor.

I opted to use a bone-in turkey breast rather than a whole turkey. A 6-pound breast is easier to carve than a whole bird and is plenty to feed about eight to 10 diners—or just four with lots of leftovers for sandwiches.

Plus, by using a breast, I didn't have to deal with one of the hardest parts of cooking turkey: trying to sync the cooking times for white and dark meat. And opting for a bone-in breast, as opposed to boneless, made for more-flavorful drippings for the stuffing below.

Given my already nontraditional approach, I wanted to tweak the stuffing by making it both more rustic and more flavorful. The combination of sage, thyme, onion, wine, and chicken broth was an homage to classic Thanksgiving flavors and a perfect jumping-off point. Hot Italian sausage added deep meaty savoriness and a bit of heat (which I augmented with red pepper flakes). And instead of small cubes of sandwich bread, I opted for large chunks of ciabatta; the bigger pieces retained some chew even as they soaked up the flavors from the turkey and sausage.

I roasted the turkey breast on top of the stuffing, and, when the breast was done, I removed it and returned just the stuffing to the oven to create a crisp top that nicely contrasted with the chewy chunks of bread below.

For a final holiday flourish, I stirred together a vibrant, bright, and gorgeous sauce with pomegranate seeds and parsley. (Don't worry, I'll still serve gravy on the side.)

Visit CooksCountry.com/GravyMA for our recipe for Make-Ahead Turkey Gravy.

◻ ONE-PAN TURKEY BREAST AND STUFFING WITH POMEGRANATE-PARSLEY SAUCE
Serves 8 to 10
Estimated Time: 3½ to 4 hours, plus 2 hours salting

The salted turkey needs to be refrigerated for at least 2 hours before cooking. If you can't find a loaf of ciabatta, you can substitute 2 pounds of another rustic, mild-tasting white bread. Do not use sourdough here; its flavor is too assertive.

TURKEY
- 1½ tablespoons kosher salt
- 1 tablespoon pepper
- 1 tablespoon minced fresh thyme
- 1 (5- to 7-pound) bone-in turkey breast, trimmed

STUFFING
- ½ cup extra-virgin olive oil
- 3 cups chopped onion
- 1¾ teaspoons kosher salt, divided
- 6 garlic cloves, minced
- 3 cups chicken broth
- ⅓ cup dry white wine
- 2 tablespoons minced fresh sage
- 1 tablespoon minced fresh thyme
- ¼ teaspoon red pepper flakes
- 2 pounds ciabatta, cut into 1-inch cubes (about 20 cups)
- 1 pound hot Italian sausage, casings removed
- 1½ cups coarsely chopped fresh parsley

SAUCE
- ¾ cup chopped fresh parsley
- ¾ cup pomegranate seeds
- ½ cup extra-virgin olive oil
- 1 shallot, minced
- 2 tablespoons lemon juice
- 2 garlic cloves, minced
- ¾ teaspoon kosher salt

1. FOR THE TURKEY: Combine salt, pepper, and thyme in bowl. Place turkey on large plate and pat dry with paper towels. Sprinkle all over with salt mixture. Refrigerate, uncovered, for at least 2 hours or up to 24 hours.

2. FOR THE STUFFING: Adjust oven rack to lower-middle position and heat oven to 325 degrees. Spray large heavy-duty roasting pan with vegetable oil spray, then add oil to pan. Heat oil in roasting pan over medium heat until shimmering. Add onion and ¼ teaspoon salt and cook until onion is golden brown, about 10 minutes. Add garlic and cook until fragrant, about 30 seconds.

3. Off heat, stir in broth, wine, sage, thyme, pepper flakes, and remaining 1½ teaspoons salt, scraping up any browned bits. Add bread and, using tongs or your hands, toss until bread is evenly coated. Break sausage into ¾-inch chunks and toss with bread mixture to combine.

4. Nestle turkey, skin side up, into stuffing in center of roasting pan. Roast until thickest part of turkey registers 160 degrees, 2¼ to 2¾ hours.

5. FOR THE SAUCE: Meanwhile, combine all ingredients in bowl; set aside.

6. Transfer turkey to carving board, skin side up, and let rest, uncovered, for at least 30 minutes or up to 1 hour.

7. Meanwhile, stir stuffing in roasting pan. Return pan to oven and cook until top of bread looks golden brown and is evenly dry, 10 to 15 minutes.

8. Remove breast meat from bone and slice thin crosswise. Toss parsley with stuffing in roasting pan. Arrange turkey over stuffing in pan. Drizzle with sauce. Serve, passing remaining sauce separately.

TO USE A DISPOSABLE ROASTING PAN
Heat oil in 12-inch skillet over medium heat until shimmering. Add onion and ¼ teaspoon salt and cook until onion is golden brown, about 10 minutes. Add garlic and cook until fragrant, about 30 seconds. Off heat, stir in broth, wine, sage, thyme, pepper flakes, and remaining 1½ teaspoons salt, scraping up any browned bits. Transfer mixture to 16 by 12-inch disposable aluminum roasting pan. Add bread and sausage as described in step 3. Place disposable pan on rimmed baking sheet before roasting for added stability. Increase roasting time for turkey in step 4 to 2½ to 3 hours. Increase cooking time for stuffing in step 7 to 30 to 35 minutes.

To perk up this substantial salad, we add lots of chopped fresh cilantro.

Sweet Potato Salad

A fresh new take on a Thanksgiving favorite. **by Mark Huxsoll**

WE LOVE SWEET potatoes for their deep earthy flavor, but this year I wanted to take them in a fresh new direction inspired by simple, vinaigrette-based potato salads. My goal was a mix of bright, fresh, lively flavors anchored by the trusty sweet potato that we all love.

I started by cutting up a few sweet potatoes into ¾-inch pieces. It doesn't matter if the pieces are all exactly the same shape as long as they're about the same size; this is necessary for them to cook at the same rate. I gave the potatoes a quick toss in extra-virgin olive oil and a sprinkle of salt, spread them into a single layer on a baking sheet, and slid them into a 450-degree oven to roast and cook through. Thirty minutes later (with a quick stir halfway through), the sweet potatoes were perfectly tender.

I set them aside to cool completely and scanned the pantry for inspiration.

I like strong flavors, so I assembled a rogues' gallery of my favorites: sharp scallions, punchy lime juice, spicy minced jalapeño (I chose to remove the seeds to keep the heat in check, but if you love heat, you can include them, too), ground cumin to amplify the earthiness, smoked paprika, black pepper, pungent minced garlic, and ground allspice for its unbeatable complexity. I combined these with a bit more extra-virgin olive oil in a large bowl to make my flavorful dressing.

Once the potatoes had cooled, I tossed them with the dressing and added chopped fresh cilantro. But the dish was missing some texture. I wanted a little something to offset the soft sweet potatoes.

The answer? Some toasted almonds. I had some almonds in the pantry already, so after I quickly toasted them (3 to 5 minutes in a dry skillet over medium heat was all they needed), I chopped them up and added them into the mix.

After a few more run-throughs, I got the ratio of nuts to sweet potatoes right. And I also learned that I could roast the sweet potatoes and stir together the dressing ahead of time and keep them in the refrigerator until I needed them. (The potatoes need about an hour out of the refrigerator to take the chill off before serving; don't dress them until you're ready to serve them.)

I'll always have room in my heart for a marshmallow-topped sweet potato casserole, but this year, I'm making room for this fresh take.

■ SWEET POTATO SALAD WITH CUMIN, SMOKED PAPRIKA, AND ALMONDS
Serves 6 to 8
Estimated Time: 1½ hours
A high-quality extra-virgin olive oil will add depth and complexity here.

- 3 pounds sweet potatoes, peeled and cut into ¾-inch pieces
- 3 tablespoons plus ¼ cup extra-virgin olive oil, divided
- 2 teaspoons table salt
- 3 scallions, sliced thin
- 3 tablespoons lime juice (2 limes)
- 1 jalapeño chile, stemmed, seeded, and minced
- 1 teaspoon ground cumin
- 1 teaspoon smoked paprika
- 1 teaspoon pepper
- 1 garlic clove, minced
- ½ teaspoon ground allspice
- ½ cup fresh cilantro leaves and stems, chopped coarse
- ½ cup whole almonds, toasted and chopped

1. Adjust oven rack to middle position and heat oven to 450 degrees. Toss potatoes with 3 tablespoons oil and salt in bowl. Transfer to rimmed baking sheet and spread into even layer. Roast until potatoes are tender and just beginning to brown, 30 to 40 minutes, stirring halfway through roasting. Let potatoes cool for 30 minutes.
2. Meanwhile, combine scallions, lime juice, jalapeño, cumin, paprika, pepper, garlic, allspice, and remaining ¼ cup oil in large bowl. (Cooled sweet potatoes and scallion mixture can be refrigerated, separately, for up to 24 hours; let both come to room temperature before proceeding with recipe.)
3. Add cilantro, almonds, and potatoes to bowl with scallion mixture and toss to combine. Serve.

SWEET POTATO SALAD WITH SOY SAUCE, SRIRACHA, AND PEANUTS
Substitute 1 tablespoon soy sauce, 1 tablespoon sriracha, 1 teaspoon sugar, and 1 teaspoon grated fresh ginger for cumin, smoked paprika, pepper, and allspice. Substitute salted dry-roasted peanuts for almonds.

Skillet Squash Casserole

Plenty of melted cheese and a crunchy cracker top transform simple summer squash into a spectacular holiday side. **by Morgan Bolling**

HER SQUASH CASSEROLE almost made us break up.

You see, a man I was dating knew about my disapproval of this side dish and brought me home to try his mother's rendition. She was a great cook, and when he described her squash casserole—mild summer squash, melted cheese, sour cream, and a crunchy Ritz Cracker topping—it sounded great. But it was not. It was watery and sad.

I was young and hadn't yet learned that there are times when you can be too honest. And one of those times is a face-to-face assessment of a Southern mom's cooking.

I apologized and we got past it. He and I didn't last in the long run (maybe the squash scars were too deep), but his mom was fighting an uphill battle. Yellow squash is, by nature, a watery vegetable. Throw it in a casserole dish with salt, which pulls out moisture, and it's no wonder things turn out bland and wet. I wanted to give this dish another shot to live up to its full potential by making something deliciously rich and cheesy, pleasantly moist but not wet, and finished with buttery crackers on top.

After researching and making half a dozen existing recipes from Southern sources, I cobbled together my own. I started by cooking sliced onions and squash in a skillet with plenty of salt to drive off moisture and soften the squash. Rather than switching to a separate baking dish (why dirty another dish?), I stirred cheese, sour cream, and scallions directly into the skillet with the softened squash. I scattered crushed Ritz Crackers over top and moved the skillet to the oven to melt the cheese and brown the topping.

The texture was good, but the flavor was bland. I swapped in mayonnaise for the sour cream (both are common here) because mayonnaise has a more savory flavor. I increased the amount of cheese (a mix of intense sharp cheddar and creamy, silky American cheese) to create a rich, smooth sauce. Two peppers, black and cayenne, added just enough heat to contrast the sweet squash.

This was a squash casserole that was excited to eat. If you read this, Mrs. Chapman, I hope all is forgiven.

SKILLET SQUASH CASSEROLE
Serves 6 to 8
Estimated Time: 1¼ hours

The skillet will be full when you add the squash in step 2. This is OK; the squash will shrink as it cooks.

- 2 tablespoons extra-virgin olive oil
- 3 cups thinly sliced onion (3 onions)
- 1 teaspoon table salt, divided
- 2 pounds yellow summer squash, halved lengthwise and sliced ¼ inch thick
- 2 garlic cloves, minced
- 6 ounces sharp cheddar cheese, shredded (1½ cups)
- 2 ounces American cheese, chopped (½ cup)
- ½ cup mayonnaise
- 4 scallions, sliced thin
- ½ teaspoon pepper
- Pinch cayenne pepper
- 30 Ritz Crackers, crushed coarse

1. Adjust oven rack to middle position and heat oven to 375 degrees. Heat oil in 12-inch ovensafe skillet over medium-high heat until shimmering. Add onion and ¼ teaspoon salt and cook until onion is lightly browned, about 6 minutes.
2. Add squash, garlic, and remaining ¾ teaspoon salt and cook until any liquid exuded by squash has evaporated and squash is tender, about 10 minutes. Reduce heat to low and stir in cheddar cheese, American cheese, mayonnaise, scallions, pepper, and cayenne until fully combined, about 2 minutes.
3. Off heat, use rubber spatula to scrape down sides of skillet. Scatter crackers over top. Transfer skillet to oven and bake until bubbling around edges and hot throughout, about 18 minutes. Let cool for 10 minutes. Serve.

TO MAKE AHEAD
At end of step 2, transfer mixture to 8-inch square baking pan and let cool completely. Cover with aluminum foil and refrigerate for up to 24 hours. To serve, keep covered and bake until casserole is heated through, about 20 minutes. Uncover, top with crackers, and continue to bake 15 minutes longer.

The secret to a supercreamy sauce that never breaks? American cheese mixed in with the cheddar.

Ritz Crackers
In 1934, the Nabisco Biscuit Company needed a name and a marketing hook for its newest snack, a crisp round cracker with ridged edges, so they turned to employee Sydney Stern. His pitch: Ritz.

THE AMERICAN TABLE Executives were concerned that the snazzy (even ritzy) name was out of touch with Depression-era America, but customers loved it. The name stuck. Since then, it's remained one of the best-selling crackers in the country.

Cheesy Mashed Potato Casserole

Irresistibly cheesy potatoes that can be made ahead? Your Thanksgiving just got a whole lot easier (and tastier). **by Jessica Rudolph**

SOME THANKSGIVING classics are untouchable, right? I wouldn't dare suggest you upend tradition by replacing the trusty turkey or stuffing, and I'm not about to propose you go without creamy, comforting mashed potatoes either. But maybe there's room for improvement, especially if it means crossing an item off your to-do list on the big day.

Typically, mashed potatoes are made and served right away, which can take up precious time on a high-pressure holiday. But you can assemble a creamy, buttery mashed potato casserole ahead of time, getting most of the work out of the way the day before. While you're at it, why not up the flavor ante with almost too much cheese and a crispy, buttery topping to boot? Here's how.

To start, slice 4 pounds of Yukon Gold potatoes (enough for a full casserole dish; you'll want leftovers) and boil them in well-seasoned water. Once they are completely tender, drain and mash them with butter until they're smooth and lump-free. Adding two full sticks of butter in this step prevents the potatoes from becoming gluey as you work them; plus, the residual heat from the potatoes melts the butter. Then stir in a hefty pour of half-and-half (heavy cream is just a tad too rich here, and milk is not quite rich enough)—the mixture should be loose enough to slump when scooped but not so loose that it pools.

Now the cheese. My tasters loved Gruyère's nutty depth but also wanted something that melted more readily.

Mozzarella fit the bill: Its mild flavor allowed the Gruyère to sing, and it gave the potatoes a supple, stretchy texture that screamed "cheesy." Stir in a generous 1½ cups of each, plus ½ cup of minced chives.

At this point, you can go ahead and bake the casserole—the potatoes will be looser than they would be if they were made ahead, but they will still be delicious. Alternatively, you can refrigerate the casserole for up to three days, during which time the potatoes will firm up a tiny bit but will still be sumptuously creamy when baked. Either way, before baking top the potatoes with cheesy, buttery panko bread crumbs, which will crisp up into the perfect crunchy foil for the luscious potatoes underneath.

CHEESY MASHED POTATO CASSEROLE

Serves 10 to 12
Estimated Time: 1½ hours,
plus 30 minutes cooling

This recipe can easily be halved: Boil the potatoes in a large saucepan and bake them in an 8-inch square baking dish. If made ahead, the casserole will be slightly more firm and set than a freshly made one; we liked both versions.

POTATOES

- **4 pounds Yukon Gold potatoes, peeled and sliced ½ inch thick**
- **1 teaspoon table salt, plus salt for cooking potatoes**
- **16 tablespoons unsalted butter, cut into 16 pieces**
- **1½ cups half-and-half**
- **1 teaspoon pepper**
- **6 ounces Gruyère cheese, shredded (1½ cups)**
- **6 ounces whole-milk mozzarella cheese, shredded (1½ cups)**
- **½ cup minced fresh chives**

TOPPING

- **¾ cup panko bread crumbs**
- **2 ounces Gruyère cheese, shredded (½ cup)**
- **2 tablespoons unsalted butter, melted**

1. FOR THE POTATOES: Adjust oven rack to upper-middle position and heat oven to 400 degrees. Place potatoes and 2 tablespoons salt in Dutch oven, add water to cover by 1 inch, and bring to boil over high heat. Reduce heat to medium and simmer until potatoes are tender and can be easily pierced with paring knife, 18 to 20 minutes.

2. Drain potatoes and return them to pot. Add butter and mash with potato masher until smooth and no lumps remain. Stir in half-and-half, pepper, and salt until fully combined. Stir in Gruyère, mozzarella, and chives until incorporated. Transfer potato mixture to 13 by 9-inch baking dish and smooth top with spatula.

3. FOR THE TOPPING: Combine bread crumbs, Gruyère, and melted butter in bowl. Sprinkle topping evenly over potato mixture.

4. Bake until casserole is heated through and topping is crisp and golden brown, about 30 minutes. Let cool for 30 minutes. Serve.

Why Yukon Golds?

We love all potatoes, but Yukon Golds are perfect here for their lovely flavor and supercreamy texture once cooked.

Mashed potatoes reach their full potential when you add cheese and a crunchy topping.

TO MAKE AHEAD

At end of step 2, let potato mixture cool completely in dish, cover tightly with plastic wrap, and refrigerate for up to 3 days. When ready to bake, remove plastic, cover dish tightly with aluminum foil, and bake for 25 minutes. Remove foil and proceed with step 3.

Half Size!

As good as these potatoes are, sometimes a full batch is too much. To serve six, halve the measurements of all the ingredients, cook the potatoes in a large saucepan, and bake them in an 8-inch square baking dish. Leftovers can be gently warmed in a low oven or on the stovetop; they're excellent the next morning with a poached egg on top.

Tasting Cranberry Sauce *by Chase Brightwell*

PREPARING AND EXECUTING a memorable Thanksgiving meal is hard work, and buying a canned or jarred cranberry sauce is an easy way to streamline things. Prepared cranberry sauces are either "jellied" (smooth and gelatinous) or "whole berry" (with cranberry pieces or whole cranberries mixed in). For this tasting, we purchased 10 sauces (three jellied, seven whole berry) and sampled them plain and with roast turkey breast to evaluate their flavors, textures, and levels of sweetness.

The textures of the sauces varied widely within each category. We expected jellied sauces to be firm and jiggly, but some didn't hold their shape. We were also surprised that one whole-berry sauce was thin and had hardly any berries. Tasters were drawn to jellied sauces with "smooth," "melt-in-your-mouth" textures. They also liked "jammy" whole-berry sauces that had the "pop of whole berries."

Flavor preferences among our tasters were clear and consistent across both styles: the less

sweet and the fewer added ingredients, the better. Our top three finishers contained only cranberries, sugar or corn syrup, and water, and they were among the tartest in our lineup. Tasters praised their "classic" and "straightforward" flavors. In contrast, sauces with added fruit juices, warm spices, and nuts generally performed poorly. Tasters "lost the cranberry" flavor in those "aggressively spiced" mixtures. We also didn't like sauces that were too sweet; instead of tasting like cranberry, they reminded us of "cough syrup" or "liquid candy."

In the end, we picked a favorite in each style. Ocean Spray Jellied Cranberry Sauce earned our top spot among the jellied sauces. Tasters loved its "classic," "smooth" texture and "fresh" flavor. New England Cranberry Colonial Cranberry Sauce was our winning whole-berry sauce. It had a "good mixture of sweet and sour," and tasters noted that the whole berries and jammy sauce "don't compete with each other; they blend together nicely."

TEXTURE MATTERS
The textures of the sauces we tasted varied widely, from smooth (top) to studded with chewy skins (middle) to weepy and watery (bottom).

Sugar amounts are based on a ¾-cup serving size.

RECOMMENDED | | TASTERS' NOTES

Best Jellied Sauce

Ocean Spray Jellied Cranberry Sauce
Price: $2.29 for 14-oz can ($0.16 per oz)
Style: Jellied **Sugar:** 25 g **Ingredients:** Cranberries, high fructose corn syrup, corn syrup, water

Our winning jellied sauce had a "tangy," "tart" flavor that tasted "so classic." Tasters noted that it was "smooth" and "melt-in-your-mouth." It was "a great foil for salty, savory, fatty holiday foods."

Best Whole-Berry Sauce

New England Cranberry Colonial Cranberry Sauce
Price: $7.99 for 12-oz jar ($0.67 per oz)
Style: Whole berry **Sugar:** 51 g
Ingredients: Cranberries, sugar, water

Our favorite whole-berry sauce offered a jammy texture and large berries interspersed throughout. It contained the most sugar per serving in our lineup, but its whole berries added "complex," "balanced," slightly "bitter" flavors.

Ocean Spray Whole Berry Cranberry Sauce
Price: $2.29 for 14-oz can ($0.16 per oz)
Style: Whole berry **Sugar:** 22 g
Ingredients: Cranberries, high fructose corn syrup, corn syrup, water

This sauce finished only slightly behind our whole-berry winner, and tasters praised the "pop of whole berries" and the "variation in texture" between the berries and the smooth sauce. One taster wrote that it tasted "like my childhood, just elevated."

RECOMMENDED WITH RESERVATIONS

Gefen Whole Berry Cranberry Sauce
Price: $2.99 for 16-oz can ($0.19 per oz)
Style: Whole berry **Sugar:** 24 g
Ingredients: Cranberry, cane sugar, water

Some tasters found this sauce's flavor "nice and tangy," and others found it "passable but forgettable." Texture-wise, some tasters were put off by the sheer number of furled, "spiky"-looking cranberry skins, which made the sauce "stringy" and "tough."

Woodstock Organic Jellied Cranberry Sauce
Price: $2.29 for 14-oz can ($0.16 per oz)
Style: Jellied **Sugar:** 24 g
Ingredients: Organic cranberries, organic sugar, filtered water, organic lemon juice concentrate

While some tasters praised this sauce, noting that it tasted "like home" and that they "could eat it plain," in general it failed to stand out. Most thought it was "bland and lacked depth" and that the flavor was "too one-note."

Stonewall Kitchen New England Cranberry Relish
Price: $6.49 for 12-oz jar ($0.54 per oz)
Style: Whole berry **Sugar:** 14 g
Ingredients: Cranberries, pure cane sugar, water, orange juice, orange peel, tapioca starch, spices, citric acid

Many tasters found this sauce "aggressively spiced but also bright-tasting." However, most found this sauce's citrus and spice notes "overpowering." "I've lost all the cranberry and all I can taste is warm spice and orange," wrote one taster.

Web subscribers can see the complete results chart at CooksCountry.com/nov20.

HEESY MASHED POTATO ASSEROLE WITH BLUE CHEESE, ACON, AND ROSEMARY
ubstitute 1 cup crumbled blue cheese for ruyère and 2 teaspoons minced fresh roseary for chives in potatoes. Add 12 ounces rumbled cooked bacon with cheeses in ep 2. Omit Gruyère from topping.

HEESY MASHED POTATO ASSEROLE WITH PARMESAN, ROWNED BUTTER, AND SAGE
ubstitute 2 cups shredded Parmesan for ruyère in potatoes. Omit Gruyère from topping. While potatoes boil, melt butter for otatoes in 10-inch skillet over medium-high eat. Cook, swirling skillet constantly, ntil milk solids in butter are color of milk hocolate and have toasted aroma, 3 to minutes. Off heat, stir in 2 tablespoons inced fresh sage and 4 minced garlic loves. Transfer to heatproof bowl. Add rowned butter mixture to drained potatoes n pot before mashing. Omit chives.

For the cleanest slices, warm the blade of your knife under hot water and wipe it dry before cutting.

Our easy homemade granola (page 32) adds a welcome crunch to this creamy cheesecake.

A little extra syrup on top? Yes, absolutely.

Maple Cheesecake

Dense and creamy and full of pure maple flavor, this cheesecake is just right for Thanksgiving. **by Jessica Rudolph**

A SIMPLE CHEESECAKE IS, in my mind, the ultimate dessert: velvety and smooth, with a crisp, buttery crust and a richness that's restrained by an underlying tang. But for Thanksgiving this year, I wanted to give the classic an autumnal twist, and sweetening the cheesecake with maple syrup instead of sugar was just the way to get there.

But first, the crust. I tried a basic graham cracker crust as well as a few unorthodox variations; we loved the way a handful of pecans added to our tried-and-true graham cracker crust provided a nutty accent to the maple-y filling. To make it, grind up graham crackers and pecans in a food processor until they're fine crumbs. To this, add sugar, salt, and flour (the flour is the key to the crisp texture of this crust, as it combines with the butter to waterproof the cracker crumbs and prevent the crust from sogging out). After moistening this mixture with melted butter, tumble it into a greased 9-inch springform pan (the pop-off collar will make unmolding a breeze when it's time to serve) and press it into an even, compact layer on the bottom of the pan—the flat bottom of a dry measuring cup is a great tool for this, but a

Maple Syrup

It takes about 40 gallons of maple sap to make 1 gallon of syrup—that's a lot of boiling down! In a recent taste test, we found that all the syrups in our lineup tasted very similar. That's because most commercial syrups are blends of lighter syrup (from earlier in the sugaring season) and darker syrup (from later in the season); this blending produces a consistent product. There is no universal grading standard in the industry. Our advice? Buy the cheapest 100 percent pure syrup you can find.

40:1
GALLONS OF SAP TO GALLONS OF SYRUP

straight-edged drinking glass works, too. Bake it until it's toasty and crisp, let it cool while making the filling, and drop the oven temperature down to ensure a gentle bake on the cheesecake.

For maximum maple impact, you need to use a lot of maple syrup (not pancake syrup, which is corn syrup–based and cloying). Through several rounds of testing, I landed on 1¼ cups of syrup for 2 pounds (that's four bricks) of cream cheese.

The cheesecake batter couldn't be easier to make. Start by blitzing the syrup and cream cheese together in the food processor. Once the mixture is totally smooth, add four eggs, one at a time, until they're incorporated (adding them individually helps ensure even blending), and then pour this batter into your cooled crust. Rap the pan on the counter a couple times, let the mixture settle for 10 minutes to release air bubbles, and then drag a fork around the surface to pop them (it's not essential to eliminate every single bubble; the cheesecake will still be delicious with a less-than-smooth top!).

Once your oven has cooled down to 225 degrees (use an oven thermometer to be sure), pop the cheesecake in and bake it for a full 3 hours. The low oven temperature cooks the cheesecake superslowly, setting the filling to a just barely firm, custardy texture that's completely free of cracks, without the need for a sloshy water bath.

After chilling completely, this beauty is ready to wow at your next dinner party as is. But to make it extra-spectacular, a border of crunchy granola (after all, we already borrowed the syrup from the breakfast table) plus an extra drizzle of maple syrup will make the cheesecake look as stunning as it tastes.

Springform Pans

Springform pans consist of two pieces: a round, flat base and a circular collar with a latch that opens and closes it, allowing delicate cakes to be unmolded upright. They are great for cheesecakes and other fragile cakes that could break or tear when being tipped out of the pan.

Our testing winner, the **Nordic Ware 9" Leakproof Springform Pan**, almost lives up to the "leakproof" in its name (every springform pan we've tested occasionally leaks a little). This pan produced beautiful, evenly browned cheesecakes that were easy to release from the pan. At about $17, it's a great value.

■ MAPLE CHEESECAKE
Serves 12 to 16
Estimated Time: 3½ hours, plus 8 hours cooling

Do not substitute pancake syrup for the maple syrup. Reduce the oven temperature as soon as the crust is finished baking, and use an oven thermometer to check that it has dropped to 225 degrees before you bake the cheesecake. Thoroughly scrape the processor bowl as you make the filling to eliminate lumps. For the topping, try our Maple-Pecan Skillet Granola on page 32.

CRUST
- 4 whole graham crackers, broken into pieces
- ¼ cup pecans
- ½ cup (2½ ounces) all-purpose flour
- ⅓ cup (2⅓ ounces) sugar
- ¼ teaspoon table salt
- 4 tablespoons unsalted butter, melted

CHEESECAKE
- 2 pounds cream cheese, softened
- 1¼ cups maple syrup
- 4 large eggs

TOPPING
- ⅓ cup granola
- ½ cup maple syrup

1. FOR THE CRUST: Adjust oven rack to middle position and heat oven to 325 degrees. Grease bottom and side of 9-inch springform pan. Process cracker pieces and pecans in food processor until finely ground, about 30 seconds. Add flour, sugar, and salt and pulse to combine, about 2 pulses. Add melted butter and pulse until crumbs are evenly moistened, about 5 pulses.

2. Using your hands, press crumbs into even layer on prepared pan bottom. Using bottom of dry measuring cup, firmly pack crumbs into pan. Bake until crust smells toasty and is browned around edges, about 18 minutes. Reduce oven temperature to 225 degrees. Let crust cool completely.

3. FOR THE CHEESECAKE: In clean, dry processor bowl, process cream cheese and maple syrup until smooth, about 2 minutes, scraping down sides of bowl as needed. With processor running, add eggs, one at a time, until just incorporated, about 30 seconds total. Pour batter onto cooled crust.

4. Firmly tap pan on counter and set aside for 10 minutes to allow air bubbles to rise to top. Gently draw tines of fork across surface of batter to pop air bubbles that have risen to surface.

5. Once oven has reached 225 degrees, bake cheesecake on aluminum foil–lined rimmed baking sheet until edges are set and center jiggles slightly when shaken and registers 165 degrees ½ inch below surface, about 3 hours.

6. Transfer pan to wire rack and let cool completely, about 2 hours. Refrigerate cheesecake, uncovered, until cold, about 6 hours. (Once fully chilled, cheesecake can be covered with plastic wrap and refrigerated for up to 4 days.)

7. To unmold cheesecake, run tip of paring knife between cake and side of pan; remove side of pan. Slide thin metal spatula between crust and pan bottom to loosen, then slide cheesecake onto serving platter. Let cheesecake stand at room temperature for 30 minutes.

8. FOR THE TOPPING: Sprinkle granola around top edge of cheesecake. Drizzle maple syrup inside ring of granola. Spread with back of spoon, as needed, to fill area inside granola ring.

9. Warm knife under hot water, then wipe dry. Cut cheesecake into wedges and serve.

We toss the cauliflower in sauce to add sweetness, heat, and depth.

Gobi
Manchurian

This satisfying, multitextured dish is perfect for sharing—or eating all by yourself. **by Mark Huxsoll**

G OBI MANCHURIAN IS a beautiful, complex dish with roots in the Chinese community of Kolkata, India. It's a popular dish in cities across the United States, too, including Asheville, North Carolina, where chef Meherwan Irani serves a version at his restaurant Chai Pani (see "An Asheville Staple"). Gobi Manchurian features cauliflower florets that are battered, fried, and then served with a spicy-sweet sauce. Its powerful mix of textures and flavors makes it a popular vegetarian dish that's served as a meal or a snack.

Gobi Manchurian comes in at least two styles. The "dry" style features fried cauliflower florets with a vibrant dipping sauce on the side, while the "wet" style marries the florets and the sauce in the same dish. The recipe here, inspired by the version served at Chai Pani, is the "wet" style.

The first order of business is to fry the cauliflower. Ideally, the fried pieces will have crisp exteriors and creamy centers. To achieve this, you create a thick, sticky batter of cornstarch, flour, and water, plus a bit of baking powder to create a lighter, crispier texture.

After dunking the florets in the batter and ensuring that they are completely coated, you fry them for about 5 minutes in oil heated to 375 degrees; the florets emerge perfectly crisp. Keep an eye on the oil temperature after you add the florets to make sure that it doesn't dip too low. (Peanut or vegetable oil works best here.) Once the coating is golden and firm, use a spider skimmer or slotted spoon to carefully transfer the florets to a paper towel–lined baking sheet to drain.

Next up, the sauce. While sauces vary from kitchen to kitchen, most include a mixture of alliums, spices, citrus, and tomato sauce or ketchup for a balanced mix of heat, sweetness, and depth. The first step is to gently cook aromatic scallions, garlic, and ginger in a saucepan until they are soft and fragrant; then you stir in a mixture of ingredients including chili-garlic sauce, lime juice, soy sauce, and cumin. After a short time on the stove, the flavors come together and the mixture thickens into a sauce that clings perfectly to the fried florets. Once you toss the fried cauliflower and sauce together, be ready to eat! While the crisp exterior will keep its crunch for a little while, it won't last forever.

Simple to make, packed with flavor, and featuring a beautiful range of textures, Gobi Manchurian is best enjoyed with good friends and cold drinks.

■ GOBI MANCHURIAN
Serves 4
Estimated Time: 1 hour

A whole 2½-pound head of cauliflower should yield 1 pound of florets. You can also buy precut florets if available. Use a Dutch oven that holds 6 quarts or more.

CAULIFLOWER
- 1 **cup water**
- ⅔ **cup cornstarch**
- ⅔ **cup all-purpose flour**
- 1 **teaspoon table salt**
- 1 **teaspoon baking powder**
- 1 **pound (1½-inch) cauliflower florets (4 cups)**
- 2 **quarts peanut or vegetable oil for frying**

SAUCE
- ¼ **cup ketchup**
- 3 **tablespoons water**
- 2 **tablespoons soy sauce**
- 1 **tablespoon Asian chili-garlic sauce**
- 2 **teaspoons lime juice, plus lime wedges for serving**
- ¾ **teaspoon pepper**
- ½ **teaspoon ground cumin**
- 2 **tablespoons vegetable oil**
- 3 **scallions, white and green parts separated and sliced thin**
- 1 **tablespoon grated fresh ginger**
- 3 **garlic cloves, minced**

1. FOR THE CAULIFLOWER: Whisk water, cornstarch, flour, salt, and baking powder in large bowl until smooth. Add cauliflower florets to batter and toss with rubber spatula to evenly coat; set aside.

2. Line baking sheet with triple layer of paper towels. Add oil to large Dutch oven until it measures about 1½ inches deep and heat over medium-high heat to 375 degrees.

3. Using tongs, add florets to hot oil 1 piece at a time. Cook, stirring occasionally to prevent florets from sticking, until coating is firm and very lightly golden, about 5 minutes. (Adjust burner, if necessary, to maintain oil temperature between 300 and 325 degrees.) Using spider skimmer, transfer florets to prepared sheet.

4. FOR THE SAUCE: Combine ketchup, water, soy sauce, chili-garlic sauce, lime juice, pepper, and cumin in bowl. Heat oil in small saucepan over medium-high heat until shimmering. Add scallion whites, ginger, and garlic and cook, stirring frequently, until fragrant, about 1½ minutes. Stir in ketchup mixture and bring to simmer, scraping up any bits of ginger mixture from bottom of saucepan. Transfer sauce to clean large bowl.

5. Add cauliflower and scallion greens to bowl with sauce and toss to combine. Transfer to platter and serve with lime wedges.

From Head to Floret
Here's how to prep the cauliflower.

1. Cut the stem flush with the base of the head, then snap off the leaves.

2. Place the head on the cutting board, rounded side down. Using a paring knife, cut down through the floret stems, rotating the head after each cut.

3. Pull off the loose florets, then continue cutting until all the florets are removed. Cut the florets into 1½-inch pieces.

An Asheville Staple

Text by Bryan Roof; photos by Steve Klise

MEHERWAN IRANI, the owner of popular restaurant Chai Pani in Asheville, North Carolina, entered the restaurant business in 2009. At the time, he felt that the Indian food he grew up eating—his mother's cooking specifically—was underrepresented in the South. It deserved more fans. The best way to spread the word? Open a restaurant.

"I wasn't trying to be groundbreaking. I was just trying to do what I knew people would love. I was thinking, 'Wait till they try Indian street food. They'll lose their minds.'"

Owning and operating an Indian street-food restaurant in the South required Meherwan to think deeply about his product and goals as well as his own identity as a Southerner.

A turning point came a few years ago when a fellow Indian chef

working in the southern United States encouraged Meherwan to attend a conference of food professionals in Oxford, Mississippi.

The conference was about the Latinx experience in the South and how Latinx immigrants have influenced the ever-changing food culture of the region. The experience inspired Meherwan to consider and tell his own story. "The South isn't only Latino, it's Korean and Vietnamese and Indian."

Meherwan began asking himself, "At what point do I stop saying that I'm an Indian living in the South and start saying that I'm a Southerner that happens to be Indian?"

"The South today is changing," Meherwan tells me. "It looks completely different than what someone from Boston or Philly or New York thinks it is. That's because people like me are standing up and saying, 'I'm a Southerner.'"

Chai Pani suspended operations during the early months of the COVID-19 pandemic, but it reopened for evening take-out service in June 2020.

Tuna Melts

Crunchy, creamy, gooey tuna melts at home? We show you the way.

by Cecelia Jenkins

Put your skillet away. We cook these tuna melts four at a time in the oven.

■ **TUNA MELTS**

Serves 4
Estimated Time: 45 minutes

For the best results, do not use chunk light tuna here. You can substitute two 6.7-ounce jars of our winning oil-packed tuna, Tonnino Tuna Fillets in Olive Oil, if desired. The sandwiches will just be a little bigger. Serve with potato chips, if desired.

TUNA SALAD

- 2 (5-ounce) cans solid white tuna in water, drained and flaked
- ¼ cup mayonnaise
- ¼ cup finely chopped onion
- ¼ cup chopped bread-and-butter pickles
- ¼ cup minced celery
- 1 tablespoon Dijon mustard
- 2 teaspoons lemon juice
- ½ teaspoon pepper
- ⅛ teaspoon table salt

SANDWICHES

- 8 slices hearty white sandwich bread
- 6 tablespoons unsalted butter, melted
- 4 slices deli sharp cheddar cheese (4 ounces)
- 4 slices deli American cheese (4 ounces)

1. FOR THE TUNA SALAD: Adjust oven rack to middle position and heat oven to 425 degrees. Combine all ingredients in bowl. (Tuna salad can be refrigerated for up to 3 days.)

2. FOR THE SANDWICHES: Line rimmed baking sheet with aluminum foil. Brush 1 side of each slice of bread with melted butter. Place 4 slices of bread, buttered side down, on prepared sheet. Top each slice of bread with 1 slice of cheddar, one-quarter of tuna salad, 1 slice of American cheese, and 1 remaining slice of bread, buttered side up.

3. Bake sandwiches until golden brown on top, about 8 minutes. Flip sandwiches and continue to bake until golden brown on second side and cheese is melted, 5 to 8 minutes longer. Let cool for 5 minutes. Cut in half and serve.

WHEN I THINK of classic diner sandwiches, tuna melts are right up there with BLTs, meatloaf sandwiches, and patty melts. But creamy, crispy tuna melts don't have to be relegated to diners—you can make them at home! The one obstacle is that, without the big flat-top griddle found in diners, it's difficult to make more than one sandwich at a time. I set out to clear that hurdle and develop a recipe for bright, tasty tuna melts that were easy to make anytime, four at a time.

Tuna melts start with tuna salad. I decided right away to work with the most basic canned tuna, the kind that's packed in water. That way I knew my recipe would work with any tuna; if you have fancier stuff, the sandwiches will be all the better for it.

It is an undeniable truth that a tuna melt needs pickles. I found that slices layered on top of the tuna salad were too assertive; it was better to chop up sweet bread-and-butter pickles (which my tasters preferred to dill pickles) and mix them right in with the tuna.

Mayo was a must, and we liked it best spiked with a little Dijon mustard and lemon juice for brightness. Chopped onion and minced celery added freshness and crunch. Salt and plenty of pepper rounded out this supercharged tuna salad. Now, on to the logistics of making the sandwiches.

Since I wanted to make four at a time, I knew the skillet was not an option. So I turned to the oven. At first I tried oven-toasting all the bread on a rimmed baking sheet, assembling the sandwiches on the toast, and quickly baking them to melt the cheese. But this didn't warm the tuna salad enough, and the bread was a little dry. It was better, I found, to fully assemble four sandwiches on untoasted bread (which I generously buttered), lay them on a rimmed baking sheet, and slide the sheet into a hot oven so that the bread could toast while the salad warmed and the cheese melted. Aside from flipping them halfway through (it's easiest to remove the sheet from the oven and do this on the empty stovetop) to toast the bottom, these sandwiches were hands-off, and they were ready all at once.

Oh, and about that cheese: I tried all the usual suspects and, in the end, landed on a combination of American (which melts beautifully and is a nod to the diner version) and sharp cheddar cheese for its flavorful kick.

CANNED TUNA PRIMER

ALBACORE ("WHITE" TUNA)
This species of tuna has the lightest-colored flesh and mildest flavor. It's also known as bonito del norte or "white" tuna (although the actual color of albacore tuna can range from cream to pink to tan).

YELLOWFIN OR SKIPJACK ("LIGHT" TUNA)
These are different species of tuna with richer flavor and darker, tan to brownish flesh. When the label doesn't specify the species of "light" tuna, it's likely a mix.

SOLID VERSUS CHUNK
Tuna labeled "solid" is packed in one layer, generally as a single fillet cut from the tuna loin. Alternatively, "chunk" refers to tuna packed in flakes of varying sizes.

OIL VERSUS WATER
Oil-packed tuna is generally of a higher quality than water-packed. At its best, this fish has a moist, silky texture and rich, clean, meaty taste that is enhanced by being preserved with oil.

Water-packed tuna is often cooked twice, which can result in a drier texture. It needs plenty of fat (such as mayo or olive oil) to be enjoyable.

Halibut **Puttanesca**

Our motto for mild fish fillets: Go big (on flavor) or go home. **by Morgan Bolling and Bryan Roof**

Fish spatulas aren't just good for fish—they are our all-around favorite metal spatulas.

■ **HALIBUT PUTTANESCA**
Serves 4
Estimated Time: 40 minutes
This may seem like a lot of anchovies, and it is, but their flavor mellows as they cook. Note that we do not drain the canned tomatoes before adding them to the sauce. One 2-ounce can of anchovies equals roughly 1½ tablespoons once chopped. You can substitute other types of white fish, such as cod, haddock, and hake, for the halibut, if desired. Serve with crusty bread.

   4 (6- to 8-ounce) skinless center-cut
      halibut fillets, 1 inch thick
 ½ teaspoon table salt
 ½ teaspoon pepper
 ¼ cup extra-virgin olive oil,
      plus extra for drizzling
   1 shallot, minced
   5 garlic cloves, sliced thin
   1 (2-ounce) can anchovies, drained
      and chopped
   2 teaspoons dried oregano
 ½ teaspoon red pepper flakes
   1 (14.5-ounce) can diced tomatoes
 ½ cup pitted kalamata olives
 ¼ cup capers, rinsed
 ¼ cup fresh parsley leaves

1. Adjust oven rack to middle position and heat oven to 375 degrees. Sprinkle halibut with salt and pepper; set aside. Add oil, shallot, garlic, anchovies, oregano, and pepper flakes to 12-inch ovensafe nonstick skillet and cook over medium-low heat until fragrant and shallot softens, about 4 minutes.
2. Stir in tomatoes and their juice, olives, and capers. Nestle halibut into sauce and bring to simmer over medium-high heat. Transfer skillet to oven and bake until fish registers 135 degrees, 13 to 16 minutes.
3. Using spatula, transfer halibut to platter. Stir sauce to recombine, then spoon over halibut. Sprinkle with parsley and drizzle with extra oil. Serve.

> **Tiny Fish, Big Flavor**
> Anchovies are a "secret ingredient" that can boost the savoriness of many dishes without tasting like fish. We call for a whole tin in this recipe, but they don't overwhelm the dish. If you prefer a stronger anchovy flavor here, reserve and add some of the oil they are packed in. To make their flavor less assertive, rinse them under running water and pat them dry.

WE'RE ALWAYS ON the lookout for ways to bring bold, exciting flavors to our weeknight dinners. Enter halibut puttanesca, a dish of mild fish simmered in a tomato sauce that's punched up with spicy pepper flakes, garlic, briny olives and capers, and plenty of savory anchovies.

To begin our testing for this saucy supper, we started by searing four halibut fillets in extra-virgin olive oil; the plan was to build a tomato sauce around the browned fish. But even with a preheated nonstick skillet, some halibut stuck to the pan, and it took a delicate hand to flip the fish without it flaking apart.

We scrapped that approach and instead made the sauce first, sautéing shallot, garlic, a few anchovies, oregano, and red pepper flakes before adding canned tomatoes. Only then did we nestle the halibut fillets into the pan of sauce. Cooking on the stovetop worked, but we found it easier to maintain an even, gentle heat (so as not to overcook the fish) by moving the skillet to the oven. The tomato sauce slowly reduced as it cooked, concentrating its flavor. And this gentle approach made for halibut that not only held its shape but also stayed moist.

We love halibut here, but testing showed that other white fish varieties such as cod and haddock worked just as well with this forgiving method—as long as the fillets were similarly sized and 1 inch thick.

For the canned tomatoes, we tried crushed (too thick and jammy) and whole tomatoes (didn't break down enough). Diced tomatoes proved perfect. A standard 14.5-ounce can made enough sauce to coat the four fillets. Rather than throwing away the canning juice, we chose to add it to the skillet to give the sauce more body and flavor.

A mixture of kalamata olives and capers added pops of savory salinity to the sauce. As for the anchovies, our tasters clamored for more, so we slowly added them, test by test, until we'd used the whole 2-ounce can. It sounds like a lot—and it is—but the anchovies mellow in the sauce and give it an incredible depth of flavor. A shower of whole parsley leaves before serving added freshness and color to this bold, simple supper.

Spaghetti Carbonara

This "bacon and eggs" pasta is a restaurant staple. We show you how to make it at home. **by Mark Huxsoll**

WHEN PASTA CARBONARA—a Roman dish of pasta, cured pork, and sharp cheese—is done well, its bold flavors and creamy texture are a revelation. But it's also one of those seemingly simple dishes that can go wrong at several turns. The two most common failures are unbalanced flavor caused by the wrong ratios of ingredients and a gummy or runny texture from an improperly emulsified sauce.

As for the ingredients, sharp, bold Pecorino Romano is the traditional cheese. This cheese's pleasantly funky flavor is the key to a potent but well-rounded carbonara. You can make this dish with Parmesan and it will be great, but it won't be quite as assertive. With Pecorino, you generally get what you pay for, and this is the time to splurge on the good stuff if it's available to you (see "Parmesan's Funky Cousin").

The cured pork product we use is salty, meaty guanciale (see "The Cheekiest of Cured Meats"). We cut it into chunks and render some of the fat; this fat, in turn, serves as the backbone of

the sauce. With ingredients this potent, balance proved to be key; through weeks of testing, we landed on just the right proportions of cheese and meat.

One last note on flavor: Use freshly ground black pepper if possible, as the dusty preground stuff is too mild to hold its own here. Freshly ground pepper makes a big difference.

The keys to ensuring that your carbonara has great texture are threefold: the eggs, the pasta water, and the tossing. We call for three whole eggs plus two yolks for added richness and creaminess; the raw eggs are tossed into the hot pasta and (just barely) cook from the heat of the noodles. Reserved pasta cooking water is integral here, as its starches help bind the sauce so that it coats and clings to every strand of spaghetti. And in order for that to happen, you have to vigorously toss the sauced pasta for a few minutes (it's tiring!) right before serving.

We also recommend heating your serving bowls or plates right before you eat; this will help the carbonara stay warm and fluid.

The Cheekiest of Cured Meats

Guanciale is an Italian spiced, cured meat product made from pork jowls or cheeks. "Guancia" is the Italian word for cheek. It has a richer pork flavor than pancetta does (but you can use pancetta in this recipe if you can't find guanciale). For this recipe, buy a 4-ounce chunk and cut it into planks, then into strips, and then crosswise into chunks. Any extra guanciale can be tightly wrapped in plastic wrap and refrigerated for a few weeks; it also freezes well. Try it in bean soups, with sautéed greens, or tossed in with browning onions to start stews and braises. And remember: A little goes a long way.

Parmesan's Funky Cousin

Since we were trying to create a spaghetti alla carbonara that was as true to its Roman origin as possible, using a cheese produced in the area surrounding Rome (though now produced elsewhere, too) made sense. Pecorino Romano is a traditional Roman cheese made from 100 percent sheep's milk, the source of its signature tang. Its flavor is stronger than Parmesan's.

■ **SPAGHETTI CARBONARA**
Serves 4
Estimated Time: 45 minutes

It is important to immediately add the egg mixture to the hot pasta in step 5. The hot pasta cooks the eggs, which thickens them and creates a luscious, creamy sauce that coats the pasta. We call for Pecorino Romano here, but Parmesan can be used, if preferred. If guanciale is difficult to find, you can substitute pancetta; just be sure to buy a 4-ounce chunk and not presliced pancetta. It's best to use freshly ground black pepper here.

- 3 large eggs plus 2 large yolks
- 2½ ounces Pecorino Romano cheese, grated (1¼ cups), plus extra for serving
- 1 teaspoon pepper, plus extra for serving
- ¼ teaspoon table salt, plus salt for cooking pasta
- 4 ounces guanciale, cut into ½-inch chunks
- 2 tablespoons extra-virgin olive oil
- 1 pound spaghetti

1. Bring 4 quarts water to boil in large Dutch oven.

2. Meanwhile, beat eggs and yolks, Pecorino, pepper, and salt together in bowl; set aside. Combine guanciale and oil in 12-inch nonstick skillet and cook over medium heat, stirring frequently, until guanciale begins to brown and is just shy of crisp, about 6 minutes. Remove skillet from heat.

3. Add pasta and 1 tablespoon salt to boiling water and cook, stirring often, until al dente.

4. Reserve ½ cup cooking water, then drain pasta and immediately return it to pot. Add guanciale and rendered fat from skillet and toss with tongs to coat pasta.

5. Working quickly, whisk ¼ cup reserved cooking water into egg mixture, then add egg mixture to pasta in pot. Toss pasta until sauce begins to thicken and looks creamy, 1 to 2 minutes. Adjust consistency with remaining reserved cooking water as needed. Serve immediately, passing extra Pecorino and pepper separately.

Panko-Crusted Chicken with Cabbage Salad

QUICK SUPPER

Roasted Chicken with Harissa and Bulgur

QUICK SUPPER

Spicy Lamb with Lentils and Yogurt

QUICK SUPPER

Chopped Winter Salad with Butternut Squash

QUICK SUPPER

Roasted Chicken with Harissa and Bulgur

Serves 4

For a simple sauce to accompany the chicken, season Greek yogurt with salt and pepper.

- 3 **pounds bone-in chicken pieces (split breasts cut in half, drumsticks, and/or thighs), trimmed**
- 1½ **teaspoons table salt, divided**
- ¾ **teaspoon pepper, divided**
- 1 **teaspoon plus 2 tablespoons extra-virgin olive oil, divided**
- 3 **cups cooked bulgur**
- 1 **English cucumber, chopped**
- 1 **cup jarred roasted red peppers, rinsed, patted dry, and chopped**
- 2 **tablespoons chopped fresh dill**
- 1 **teaspoon grated lemon zest plus 3 tablespoons juice**
- 1 **small garlic clove, minced**
- 3 **tablespoons harissa**

1. Adjust oven rack to middle position and heat oven to 450 degrees. Pat chicken dry with paper towels and sprinkle with 1 teaspoon salt and ½ teaspoon pepper. Heat 1 teaspoon oil in 12-inch ovensafe skillet over medium-high heat until just smoking. Cook chicken, skin side down, until well browned on skin side, 6 to 8 minutes. Flip chicken; transfer skillet to oven; and roast until breasts register 160 degrees and drumsticks/thighs register 175 degrees, 15 to 20 minutes.

2. Meanwhile, toss bulgur, cucumber, red peppers, dill, lemon zest and juice, garlic, remaining ½ teaspoon salt, remaining ¼ teaspoon pepper, and remaining 2 tablespoons oil together in large bowl. Season with salt and pepper to taste; set aside.

3. Transfer chicken to platter, reserving juices in skillet. Whisk harissa with 3 tablespoons reserved juices in bowl. Brush harissa mixture onto chicken, tent with foil, and let rest for 5 minutes. Serve chicken with bulgur salad.

Panko-Crusted Chicken with Cabbage Salad

Serves 4

Sliced scallions are a great addition to the cabbage salad. Serve with rice.

- 4 **cups thinly sliced green cabbage**
- 1 **tablespoon soy sauce, divided**
- 2 **teaspoons lemon juice**
- 1 **teaspoon toasted sesame oil**
- ¾ **teaspoon table salt, divided**
- ¼ **cup ketchup**
- 2 **tablespoons Worcestershire sauce**
- 1 **teaspoon Dijon mustard**
- 2 **cups panko bread crumbs**
- 2 **large eggs**
- 8 **(3- to 4-ounce) chicken cutlets, ½ inch thick, trimmed**
- ½ **cup vegetable oil for frying, divided**

1. Toss cabbage, 1 teaspoon soy sauce, lemon juice, sesame oil, and ¼ teaspoon salt together in bowl; set aside. Whisk ketchup, Worcestershire, mustard, and remaining 2 teaspoons soy sauce together in small bowl; set aside.

2. Place panko in large zipper-lock bag and lightly crush with rolling pin. Transfer panko to shallow dish. Beat eggs with remaining ½ teaspoon salt in second shallow dish. Working with 1 cutlet at a time, dip cutlets in egg, then coat all sides with panko, pressing gently to adhere.

3. Line large plate with triple layer of paper towels. Heat ¼ cup vegetable oil in 12-inch nonstick skillet over medium-high heat until shimmering. Add 4 cutlets and cook until deep golden brown, 2 to 3 minutes per side. Transfer cutlets to prepared plate. Wipe out skillet with additional paper towels and repeat with remaining ¼ cup oil and remaining 4 cutlets. Slice cutlets ½ inch thick, then drizzle with sauce. Serve cutlets with cabbage salad.

Chopped Winter Salad with Butternut Squash

Serves 4

We prefer Fuji, but any sweet apple will work here.

- 1 **(1½- to 2-pound) butternut squash, peeled, seeded, and cut into ½-inch pieces (4½ cups)**
- ¼ **cup extra-virgin olive oil, divided**
- 3 **tablespoons balsamic vinegar, divided**
- ⅜ **teaspoon table salt, divided**
- ⅜ **teaspoon pepper, divided**
- 1 **tablespoon Dijon mustard**
- 1 **small head radicchio (6 ounces), halved, cored, and cut into ½-inch pieces**
- 1 **romaine lettuce heart (6 ounces), cut into 1-inch pieces**
- 1 **Fuji apple, cored and cut into ½-inch cubes**
- ½ **cup hazelnuts, toasted, skinned, and chopped**
- 2 **ounces feta cheese, crumbled (½ cup)**

1. Adjust oven rack to lowest position and heat oven to 450 degrees. Toss squash, 1 tablespoon oil, 1½ teaspoons vinegar, ¼ teaspoon salt, and ¼ teaspoon pepper together on rimmed baking sheet. Roast until well browned and tender, 20 to 25 minutes, stirring halfway through roasting. Remove sheet from oven and let squash cool for 5 minutes.

2. Meanwhile, whisk mustard, remaining 3 tablespoons oil, remaining 2½ tablespoons vinegar, remaining ⅛ teaspoon salt, and remaining ⅛ teaspoon pepper together in large bowl.

3. Add radicchio, lettuce, and apple to bowl with dressing and toss to combine. Season with salt and pepper to taste. Divide salad among 4 plates. Top with squash, then sprinkle with hazelnuts and feta. Serve.

Spicy Lamb with Lentils and Yogurt

Serves 4

Serve with chopped fresh cilantro and naan.

- ¼ **teaspoon baking soda**
- 2 **tablespoons plus 1 cup water, divided**
- 1 **pound ground lamb**
- ¾ **teaspoon table salt, divided**
- 2 **tablespoons extra-virgin olive oil**
- 1 **onion, chopped**
- 1 **tablespoon tomato paste**
- 3 **garlic cloves, minced**
- 2 **teaspoons garam masala**
- 1 **teaspoon grated fresh ginger**
- ½ **teaspoon red pepper flakes**
- 2½ **cups cooked lentilles du Puy**
- 2 **tomatoes, cored and chopped**
- ¾ **cup plain Greek yogurt, divided**

1. Dissolve baking soda in 2 tablespoons water in medium bowl. Add lamb and ½ teaspoon salt and mix until thoroughly combined; let sit for 10 minutes.

2. Heat oil in 12-inch skillet over medium heat until shimmering. Add onion and remaining ¼ teaspoon salt and cook until softened, about 5 minutes. Stir in tomato paste, garlic, garam masala, ginger, and pepper flakes and cook until fragrant, about 1 minute. Stir in 1 cup water and bring to boil. Add lamb to skillet; cover; and cook until lamb is cooked through, about 10 minutes, stirring and breaking up lamb with wooden spoon halfway through cooking.

3. Stir in lentils and cook, uncovered, until liquid has mostly evaporated, 3 to 5 minutes. Off heat, stir in tomatoes and 2 tablespoons yogurt. Serve, passing remaining yogurt separately.

Skillet Steak Tips with Cheesy Roasted Potatoes and Mesclun Salad

QUICK SUPPER

Glazed Salmon with Black-Eyed Peas, Walnuts, and Pomegranate

QUICK SUPPER

Pan-Seared Thick-Cut Boneless Pork Chops with Apples and Spinach

QUICK SUPPER

Rioja-Style Potatoes with Chorizo and Peas

QUICK SUPPER

Glazed Salmon with Black-Eyed Peas, Walnuts, and Pomegranate

Serves 4

One bunch of parsley should yield the ½ cup minced parsley needed for this recipe.

2	(15-ounce) cans black-eyed peas, rinsed
½	cup pomegranate seeds
½	cup walnuts, toasted and chopped
½	cup minced fresh parsley
4	scallions, sliced thin
¼	cup pomegranate molasses, divided
3	tablespoons plus 1 teaspoon extra-virgin olive oil, divided
2	tablespoons lemon juice
¾	teaspoon table salt, divided
½	teaspoon pepper, divided
4	(6- to 8-ounce) skin-on salmon fillets, 1 to 1½ inches thick

1. Combine black-eyed peas, pomegranate seeds, walnuts, parsley, scallions, 2 tablespoons pomegranate molasses, 3 tablespoons oil, lemon juice, ¼ teaspoon salt, and ¼ teaspoon pepper in large bowl. Season with salt and pepper to taste; set aside.

2. Adjust oven rack to upper-middle position and heat oven to 450 degrees. Line rimmed baking sheet with foil. Place salmon skin side down on sheet and brush tops of fillets with remaining 1 teaspoon oil and 1 tablespoon pomegranate molasses. Sprinkle fillets with remaining ½ teaspoon salt and remaining ¼ teaspoon pepper. Roast until center is still translucent when checked with tip of paring knife and registers 125 degrees (for medium-rare), about 12 minutes.

3. Remove sheet from oven and brush fillets with remaining 1 tablespoon pomegranate molasses. Serve salmon with black-eyed pea salad.

Skillet Steak Tips with Cheesy Roasted Potatoes and Mesclun Salad

Serves 4

Sirloin steak tips are often sold as flap meat.

1½	pounds Yukon Gold potatoes, unpeeled, sliced ¼ inch thick
6	tablespoons extra-virgin olive oil, divided
2½	teaspoons kosher salt, divided
1¼	teaspoons pepper, divided
2	ounces feta cheese, crumbled (½ cup)
4	scallions, white parts minced, green parts sliced thin
1½	pounds sirloin steak tips, trimmed and cut into 2-inch chunks
1	tablespoon balsamic vinegar
1	teaspoon Dijon mustard
5	ounces (5 cups) mesclun
3	radishes, trimmed and sliced thin

1. Adjust oven rack to middle position and heat oven to 475 degrees. Toss potatoes, 2 tablespoons oil, ½ teaspoon salt, and ¼ teaspoon pepper together on parchment paper–lined rimmed baking sheet and arrange in single layer. Roast until spotty brown and tender, 15 to 20 minutes. Sprinkle potatoes with feta and bake until feta is melted, about 5 minutes. Sprinkle with scallion greens.

2. Meanwhile, pat steak dry with paper towels and sprinkle with remaining 2 teaspoons salt and remaining 1 teaspoon pepper. Heat 1 tablespoon oil in 12-inch nonstick skillet over medium-high heat until just smoking. Add steak and cook until well browned all over and meat registers 125 degrees (for medium-rare), 7 to 10 minutes. Transfer to plate and tent with foil.

3. Whisk vinegar, mustard, remaining 3 tablespoons oil, and scallion whites together in large bowl. Toss mesclun and radishes with dressing and season with salt and pepper to taste. Serve steak with potatoes and salad.

Rioja-Style Potatoes with Chorizo and Peas

Serves 4

We like to stir in chopped fresh parsley at the end for a hit of freshness. Serve with crusty bread.

2	tablespoons extra-virgin olive oil, plus extra for drizzling
1	leek, white and light green parts only, halved lengthwise, sliced thin, and washed thoroughly
1	red bell pepper, stemmed, seeded, and cut into ½-inch pieces
¼	teaspoon table salt
8	ounces Spanish-style chorizo sausage, halved lengthwise and sliced ½ inch thick
4	garlic cloves, minced
1	teaspoon smoked paprika
¼	teaspoon red pepper flakes, plus extra for seasoning
1½	pounds Yukon Gold potatoes, peeled and cut into ¾-inch pieces
1	cup dry white wine
2	cups chicken broth
1¼	cups frozen peas, thawed

1. Heat oil in Dutch oven over medium heat until shimmering. Add leek, bell pepper, and salt. Cover; reduce heat to medium-low; and cook, stirring occasionally, until vegetables are softened, 5 to 7 minutes.

2. Stir in chorizo, garlic, paprika, and pepper flakes and cook, uncovered and stirring frequently, until chorizo is softened, about 2 minutes. Stir in potatoes and cook over medium heat until edges are translucent, 2 to 4 minutes.

3. Stir in wine and cook until reduced by half, about 2 minutes. Stir in broth and bring to simmer over high heat. Reduce heat to medium-low; cover; and simmer vigorously until potatoes are tender, about 20 minutes, stirring occasionally. Stir in peas. Season with salt and extra pepper flakes to taste. Serve, drizzling individual portions with extra oil.

Pan-Seared Thick-Cut Boneless Pork Chops with Apples and Spinach

Serves 4

Look for a pork loin roast that is 7 to 8 inches long and 3 to 3½ inches in diameter.

1	(2½-pound) boneless pork loin roast, trimmed
2	teaspoons ground coriander
1	teaspoon table salt, divided
½	teaspoon pepper
3	tablespoons vegetable oil, divided
2	apples, cored and cut into 1-inch wedges
1	red onion, chopped
12	ounces (12 cups) baby spinach
1	tablespoon minced fresh tarragon

1. Cut pork loin crosswise into 4 chops of equal thickness. Pat chops dry with paper towels, then sprinkle with coriander, ¾ teaspoon salt, and pepper. Heat 12-inch cast-iron skillet over medium heat for 5 minutes. Add 1 tablespoon oil and heat until just smoking. Add chops and cook, flipping every 2 minutes, until well browned and registering 135 degrees, 14 to 18 minutes. Transfer chops to cutting board, tent with foil, and let rest while preparing apples.

2. While chops rest, heat 1 tablespoon oil in now-empty skillet over medium-low heat until shimmering. Add apples, cut side down, and cook until caramelized and tender, about 2 minutes per side. Transfer to serving platter.

3. Heat remaining 1 tablespoon oil in now-empty skillet over medium heat until shimmering. Add onion and remaining ¼ teaspoon salt and cook until softened, about 3 minutes. Add spinach and cook until wilted, about 2 minutes. Season with salt and pepper to taste. Sprinkle apples with tarragon. Serve pork with apples and spinach.

GETTING TO KNOW Stock

At its most basic level, stock (or broth) is water infused with the flavors of the meat, bones, vegetables, and seasonings simmered in it. This simple liquid is a transformative ingredient—good stock can truly elevate your cooking. **by Scott Kathan**

SIMMER

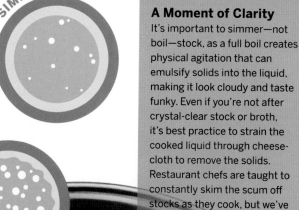

BOIL

A Moment of Clarity

It's important to simmer—not boil—stock, as a full boil creates physical agitation that can emulsify solids into the liquid, making it look cloudy and taste funky. Even if you're not after crystal-clear stock or broth, it's best practice to strain the cooked liquid through cheese-cloth to remove the solids. Restaurant chefs are taught to constantly skim the scum off stocks as they cook, but we've found straining at the end to be easier and plenty effective for most recipes.

Stock versus Broth

Technically, stock is made primarily with bones (plus vegetables and seasonings) and is cooked until concentrated, while broth is made primarily with meat (often on the bone) and is lighter-tasting and more diluted. The bones provide stock with gelatin, which gives it a fuller body; it takes on a jellied consistency when chilled. Broth has a thinner consistency. But most commercial producers (and recipe writers) don't distinguish between the two, so if you're going the store-bought route, either broth or stock will work in most recipes.

Stock
Made with bones; rich and full-bodied

Broth
Made with meat; light and versatile

Keeping Stock at the Ready

Stock freezes beautifully, so many cooks like to make a big batch to stash in the freezer. We recommend letting stock cool completely before portioning and freezing it. While most any airtight container will make a suitable storage vessel, we like to use reusable containers when possible and to err on the side of smaller portions, which have a wider range of uses. In fact, freezing some stock in ice cube trays and then transferring the frozen cubes to another container for airtight freezer storage is a great move for cooks who sometimes need small amounts of stock for recipes such as pan sauces. Stock keeps well for up to three months in the freezer.

Defatting Stock

Depending on the cuts of meat you use, homemade stock can contain a significant amount of fat. While fat adds flavor, too much fat can make a stock greasy and unappealing, so most cooks like to defat stock. Here are the three most common methods.

SPOON SKIMMING
Pros: Fast, easy
Con: Slightly less effective

OVERNIGHT CHILL AND REMOVE
Pros: Easy, very effective
Cons: Takes time, requires fridge space

FAT SEPARATOR
Pros: Tidy, does a thorough job if you wait 5 to 10 minutes for the liquid to settle and the fat to rise
Con: Limited capacity means you have to defat larger volumes in batches

Stock Ingredients

You can make stock with virtually any meat or vegetable, but here are some of the more common base ingredients. What they all share is affordability and deep flavor. For darker, richer stocks, you can roast the bones and vegetables before adding them to the water. Note that vegetable and especially seafood stocks require less cooking than meat-and-bone stocks.

Alliums
Onions, shallots, garlic, leeks

Vegetables
Carrots, celery, mushrooms, tomatoes, fennel (especially for seafood stocks)

Seasonings
Peppercorns, bay leaves

Pork
Boston butt, neck bones, ribs

Poultry
Backs, carcasses, and wingtips

Beef
Shanks, oxtails, meaty bones

Seafood
Fish heads and tails; fish bones; shells from shrimp, crab, and lobster

Add salt to stock judiciously while it cooks, as the relative saltiness will increase as you reduce and concentrate the stock. **BE CAREFUL!**

Pho toppings: lime, cilantro, bean sprouts, basil, scallions, and onion

Thin slices of raw eye-round roast are gently cooked in the hot broth.

Beef Pho

The aromas and flavors in this deeply delicious meal are nothing short of transcendent.

by Matthew Fairman

■ BEEF PHO

Serves 6
Estimated Time: 4 hours

This version of pho is slightly sweeter and heavier on warm spices than other versions. If you prefer a broth that is less sweet, feel free to halve the amount of sugar, although the amount called for in the recipe helps provide balance. The broth should taste overseasoned before it's poured over the noodles. We developed this recipe using Red Boat 40°N Fish Sauce. If you can't find Thai basil, you can substitute any other type of sweet basil.

BEEF BROTH

- 4½ pounds bone-in, cross-cut beef shanks, trimmed
- 2 onions, halved
- 1 (3-inch) piece ginger, halved lengthwise
- 5 garlic cloves, smashed and peeled
- 10 star anise pods
- 1 tablespoon black peppercorns
- 1 tablespoon coriander seeds
- ½ cinnamon stick
- 5 whole cloves
- ½ cup fish sauce
- ½ cup sugar
- 2 tablespoons table salt

NOODLES AND GARNISHES

- 10 ounces boneless eye-round roast, trimmed and sliced in half with grain
- 21 ounces rice vermicelli
- 1 cup fresh cilantro leaves and stems
- 6 scallions, sliced thin
- ½ cup very thinly sliced onion, rinsed
  Mung bean sprouts
  Fresh Thai basil leaves
  Lime wedges
  Sriracha

1. FOR THE BEEF BROTH: Combine 6 quarts water, beef shanks, onions, ginger, garlic, star anise, peppercorns, coriander seeds, cinnamon stick, and cloves in large stockpot. Bring to boil over high heat. Reduce heat to medium-low and simmer gently for 3 hours.

2. FOR THE NOODLES AND GARNISHES: Meanwhile, place eye round on plate and freeze until very firm, 35 to 45 minutes. Once firm, slice against grain ⅛ inch thick. Return eye round to plate, cover with plastic wrap, and refrigerate until needed.

3. Bring 4 quarts water to boil in large pot. Add noodles and cook until tender. Drain noodles and divide among 6 individual bowls.

4. Using spider skimmer or tongs, remove large solids from broth. Shred beef shanks and either reserve for another use or use to garnish soup in step 6. Let broth settle for 5 minutes and then skim any fat that rises to surface with ladle.

5. Line colander with triple layer of cheesecloth, then set prepared colander over large Dutch oven. Pour broth through colander into Dutch oven; discard any remaining solids. Whisk fish sauce, sugar, and salt into broth (broth should taste overseasoned).

6. When ready to serve, bring broth to rolling boil over high heat. Divide eye round among individual bowls, about 3 slices per bowl, shingling slices on top of noodles. Divide cilantro; scallions; onion; and shredded beef, if using, among bowls. Ladle broth into each bowl to cover noodles. Serve immediately, passing bean sprouts, basil, lime wedges, and sriracha separately.

TO MAKE AHEAD

Prepare broth through step 5 and let cool completely. Refrigerate broth and beef shanks separately for up to 3 days or freeze for up to 1 month. To serve, prepare eye round and noodles and continue with step 6.

Fragrant and Flavorful

Two heavy hitters that contribute to the knockout flavor of our pho broth are star anise pods and fish sauce. Beautiful star anise pods have a warm, licorice-y flavor and an intense, sweet aroma. Fish sauce brings an incredible depth of savory flavor while enhancing—but not overwhelming—the beef flavor.

PHO, AN EXTRAORDINARY Vietnamese soup consisting of broth, rice noodles, meat, and herbs, is a favorite around the world. The soup has countless variations; one incredible example is the version served by Hà VL in Portland, Oregon (see "Soup's on in Portland").

At Hà VL, the pho is built on a deeply spiced, aromatic, savory-sweet broth and boasts slightly chewy noodles and a crown of thinly sliced beef. At the table, an array of vibrant garnishes—Thai basil, scallions, cilantro, and lime—can be mixed and matched to add a range of fresh and bright flavors. It is a wonderfully complex dish.

For our version, we found that beef shanks, simmered slowly, added extra richness and body to the broth and that generous measurements of spices were essential. For the beef served with the soup, eye round proved perfect for its ease of slicing and beefy flavor.

It's essential to slice the eye round as thinly as you can because it must cook through in the residual heat from the broth. (Don't worry, it will cook through.) The best way to get those superthin slices is to freeze the meat before slicing it.

One big benefit of homemade pho: Your kitchen will smell fantastic as you work.

Soup's on in Portland

Text by Bryan Roof; photos by Steve Klise

R EGULARS LINE UP outside Hà VL on SE 82nd Avenue in Portland, Oregon, a good half-hour before the 8:00 a.m. opening. The menu offers two Vietnamese noodle soups each day on a rotating six-day menu; on Sunday, the options are northern beef pho and turmeric yellow noodles, a sun-colored, wide-noodle soup with pork and shrimp.

Owner Peter Vuong (pictured above) offers me my choice of hot or cold Vietnamese coffee in strong or medium when we meet. His mother opened the restaurant in 2005; Peter took over operations about seven years ago. He tells me the beef pho is a specialty of his mother's region in northern Vietnam. Peter learned to make it by watching her, although she never actually shared the recipe with him. But he's confident in his own take. "If I eat something, I know what's missing," he says.

During one of his frequent table visits, Peter tells me the harrowing story of how he escaped Vietnam in the 1980s by traveling to Malaysia and then to the Philippines before eventually making it to Portland, alone and without family. The trip was dangerous, and as he relives the tale he pulls back the sleeve of his sweater to show me the goose bumps on his arm. One by one, all his siblings escaped Vietnam through similar means and the family eventually reunited in Portland.

Every day Peter prepares enough of each soup for about 200 bowls. Sunday's beef pho and all its accoutrements can take upwards of 6 hours to prepare, but he is adamant about not taking shortcuts. This pho is remarkable in its clarity and intense, warm spice. On top of the deep beef flavor, which Peter achieves by slowly simmering beef shin bones and hunks of lean beef, hints of cinnamon, ginger, and star anise come through. The broth's delicate light-gray color belies its intensity, and each sip uncovers something new. It's deep but never heavy. "Light and fragrant. That's how it should be," Peter says.

During the COVID-19 crisis, Hà VL's lively, brightly colored dining room (above left) was closed for on-site meals, but the kitchen (below left) remained open for take-out service and delivery, keeping fans satisfied in the meantime.

Romesco is a garlicky Spanish sauce based on nuts and roasted red peppers.

A simple pantry sauce adds pizzazz to chicken cutlets.

by the editors of America's Test Kitchen

Quick Chicken Cutlets with Romesco Sauce

THE PANTRY IS a potential treasure trove of bold flavors, so ou goal with this weeknight supper was to make maximum use of what was in ours

Romesco, the classic Spanish sauce, brings together common ingredients with a wide range of flavors. Our version here combines the vibrancy of roasted red peppers, the sweetness of honey, the depth of sherry vinegar, the piquancy of cayenne, the pungency of garlic, the smokiness of smoked paprika and the comforting flavors of toasted hazelnuts and extra-virgin olive oil. (A bit of white bread adds body.) The best part: All it takes to make romesco is to drop everything in the food processor and give it a few pulses. The resulting sauce has a pleasing chunky texture; a complex mix of flavors; and a beautiful, saturated color. Talk about being more than the sum of its parts.

What to put it on? Chicken cutlets make a perfect canvas for this bold sauce. By slicing chicken breasts in hal horizontally and gently pounding ther to an even thickness, our homemade cutlets cook in less than 3 minutes and emerge from the skillet with beautiful brown edges and juicy interiors. They cook so quickly that you might want to call everyone to the table before you even put them in the skillet.

Should you find yourself with leftovers, a chicken cutlet and a swipe of sauce make for an excellent sandwich the next day.

SAUTÉED CHICKEN CUTLETS WITH ROMESCO SAUCE *Serves 4*
Estimated Time: 55 minutes
You will need one 12-ounce jar of roasted red peppers for this recipe.

CHICKEN
- 4 (6- to 8-ounce) boneless, skinless chicken breasts, trimmed
- 1 teaspoon table salt
- ¼ teaspoon pepper
- 4 teaspoons extra-virgin olive oil, divided

SAUCE
- 2 tablespoons extra-virgin olive oil, divided
- ½ slice hearty white sandwich bread, cut into ½-inch pieces
- ¼ cup hazelnuts, toasted and skinned
- 2 garlic cloves, sliced thin
- 1 cup jarred roasted red peppers, rinsed and patted dry
- 1½ tablespoons sherry vinegar
- 1 teaspoon honey
- ½ teaspoon smoked paprika
- ½ teaspoon table salt
- Pinch cayenne pepper

1. FOR THE CHICKEN: Place chicken breasts on large plate and freeze until firm, about 15 minutes.
2. FOR THE SAUCE: Meanwhile, add 1 tablespoon oil, bread, and hazelnuts to 12-inch nonstick skillet and cook over medium heat, stirring constantly, until bread and hazelnuts are lightly toasted, about 3 minutes. Add garlic and cook, stirring constantly, until fragrant, about 30 seconds.
3. Transfer bread mixture to food processor and pulse until coarsely chopped, about 5 pulses. Add red peppers, vinegar, honey, paprika, salt, cayenne, and remaining 1 tablespoon oil to processor. Pulse until finely chopped, 5 to 8 pulses. Transfer sauce to bowl and set aside for serving. (Sauce can be refrigerated for up to 2 days.)
4. Working with 1 chicken breast at a time, starting at thick end, cut breasts in half horizontally. Using meat pounder, gently pound each cutlet between 2 pieces of plastic wrap to even ¼-inch thickness. Pat cutlets dry with paper towels and sprinkle with salt and pepper.

5. Wipe now-empty skillet clean with paper towels. Heat 2 teaspoons oil in skillet over medium-high heat until just smoking. Place 4 cutlets in skillet and cook, without moving them, until browned on first side, about 2 minutes. Flip cutlets and continue to cook until opaque on second side, about 30 seconds longer. Transfer cutlets to serving platter and tent with aluminum foil. Repeat with remaining 4 cutlets and remaining 2 teaspoons oil. Serve with sauce.

Let's Cut Cutlets!
Cutlets from the grocery store are often ragged and of varying sizes; it's better to cut your own. Try to choose chicken breasts that are similarly sized. Briefly freeze the breasts to firm them up; then, starting at the thick end, carefully cut horizontally through each breast, using your guide (non-knife) hand to stabilize the breast as you cut. Then gently pound each half into an even thickness.

We use black beans here, but pinto and kidney beans work well, too.

Skillet Chipotle Beef Chili Bowls

A chili dinner in a skillet? Yes, please.

Recipe by Sara Mayer

CHILI IS ONE of our favorite dishes to make on the weekend. But does it have to be made only then? Could we find a way to make this hearty, spicy stew work on a weeknight? We were determined to do just that.

Our first move was to leave the Dutch oven on the shelf and instead reach for the trusty 12-inch nonstick skillet. Since we needed time to be on our side, we chose ground beef rather than chuck (or any other cut that would take longer to cook). But ground beef can be dry and pebbly in chili. To cut that possibility off at the pass, we treated the raw beef in a solution of salt and baking soda; this helped it remain moist, tender, and well seasoned.

We got the chili started by sautéing chopped onion and bell pepper. When the vegetables were softened and starting to brown, we added in the treated ground beef. Once the beef was no longer pink, we added our seasonings to the mix: minced garlic; earthy ground cumin; and smoky, spicy chipotle chile powder (see "A Powerhouse Ingredient"). We let these seasonings cook for about a minute in the hot pan to release their full flavors and aromas before adding a can of tomato sauce, a can of black beans, and a cup of thawed frozen corn kernels.

A lot of people like their chili over rice. We wanted to make the rice in the same skillet and found it best to do so while doing the prep work for the chili; after cooking the rice (and flavoring it with lime juice and zest), we portioned it into serving bowls that we kept warm in a low oven while we made the chili. A simple stir-together sauce of sour cream, fresh cilantro, and more lime zest and juice provided a refreshing burst of coolness to the fiery chili.

This was a perfect weeknight dinner, and it was easy to customize with our favorite toppings.

A Powerhouse Ingredient

Chili powder and chile powder are not the same thing. Chili powder—with an *i*—typically contains ground dried chile peppers plus seasonings such as cumin and oregano. Chile powder—with an *e*—is simply ground chile peppers. **Chipotle chile powder** is made from chipotle chiles, which are smoked and dried jalapeños. It has a bracing heat and rich, smoky flavor; a little goes a long way. Try some sprinkled on eggs; in beans; or as part of a barbecue rub for ribs, pork butt, or brisket.

SKILLET CHIPOTLE BEEF CHILI BOWLS WITH LIME-CILANTRO CREMA *Serves 4*
Estimated Time: 1¼ hours

You will need a 12-inch nonstick skillet with a tight-fitting lid for this recipe. Serve with pickled jalapeños, shredded cheese, and diced avocado, if desired.

- ½ cup sour cream
- ¼ cup minced fresh cilantro, divided
- 2 teaspoons grated lime zest, divided, plus 3 tablespoons juice (2 limes), divided
- 2 teaspoons table salt, divided
- 1 pound 90 percent lean ground beef
- 2 tablespoons plus 2 cups water, divided
- ¼ teaspoon baking soda
  Pinch pepper
- 2 tablespoons vegetable oil, divided
- 1 cup long-grain white rice
- 1 onion, chopped fine
- 1 red bell pepper, stemmed, seeded, and chopped
- 1 tablespoon ground cumin
- 2 garlic cloves, minced
- 2 teaspoons chipotle chile powder
- 1 (15-ounce) can tomato sauce
- 1 (15-ounce) can black beans, rinsed
- 1 cup frozen corn, thawed

1. Adjust oven rack to middle position, place 4 individual serving bowls on rack, and heat oven to 200 degrees. Whisk sour cream, 2 tablespoons cilantro, 1 teaspoon lime zest, 1 tablespoon lime juice, and ¼ teaspoon salt together in bowl; cover and refrigerate until ready to serve. Toss beef with 2 tablespoons water, baking soda, pepper, and ¼ teaspoon salt in bowl until thoroughly combined; let sit for 20 minutes.

2. Meanwhile, heat 1 tablespoon oil in 12-inch nonstick skillet over medium heat until shimmering. Add rice and cook, stirring often, until edges of grains begin to turn translucent, about 2 minutes. Add ½ teaspoon salt and remaining 2 cups water and bring to boil. Cover; reduce heat to low; and simmer until liquid is absorbed and rice is tender, about 20 minutes.

3. Off heat, add remaining 1 teaspoon lime zest and remaining 2 tablespoons lime juice and fluff gently with fork to incorporate. Portion rice into warmed serving bowls, cover with aluminum foil, and keep warm in oven.

4. Heat remaining 1 tablespoon oil in now-empty skillet over medium heat until shimmering. Add onion and bell pepper and cook until just beginning to brown, 5 to 7 minutes. Add beef, breaking up meat with wooden spoon, and cook until no longer pink, 6 to 8 minutes.

5. Stir in cumin, garlic, and chile powder and cook until fragrant, about 1 minute. Stir in tomato sauce, beans, corn, and remaining 1 teaspoon salt and cook until slightly thickened, about 3 minutes. Spoon chili over rice in bowls; sprinkle with remaining 2 tablespoons cilantro; and serve, passing sour cream–cilantro mixture separately.

"Even More Banana" Banana Bread

We put in more bananas than we thought our bread could hold. Then we added more. **by Matthew Fairman**

WHAT MAKES A really good banana bread? That's what my colleagues and I were asking ourselves as we dug in to the five banana breads I had baked to kick off testing for this recipe. After studying dozens of recipes, I had prepared five so that we could zero in on what we wanted.

The consensus we arrived at—after much tasting and discussing—was that we overwhelmingly prefer banana breads that are big on banana flavor and that aren't really "bready" at all. We were after a slice that was tender, moist, buttery, just the right amount of sweet, and (most important) heavy with the aroma and flavor of bananas. So I took a look at our favorite sample (not surprisingly the one with the most bananas in it) and asked myself a question: "Can it take even more bananas?"

Some 30 or so loaves later, the answer was a resounding yes; this version includes more than a pound of them. It also includes just a bit more butter, four fewer ingredients, and a simplified method (no more stand mixer). What's more, we think it tastes a lot better, too.

The Perfect Overripe Banana

Heavily speckled—or even black—bananas are best in this recipe. Why? As bananas age, their starch turns to sugar. If you have darkening bananas on the counter and wish to freeze them for making banana bread later, we recommend peeling them before freezing them.

JUST RIGHT FOR BANANA BREAD

DIY Overripe Bananas

No overripe bananas? Make your own by baking just-ripe, unpeeled yellow bananas in a 325-degree oven for 20 minutes, until they're entirely black. Be sure to let them cool completely before using them in this recipe.

BANANA BREAD

Makes 1 loaf; Estimated Time: 1½ hours, plus 1 hour cooling

Be sure to use very ripe, heavily speckled (or even black) bananas in this recipe. Use a potato masher to thoroughly mash the bananas. The test kitchen's preferred loaf pan measures 8½ by 4½ inches; if you use a 9 by 5-inch loaf pan, start checking for doneness 5 minutes earlier than advised in the recipe. We place the loaf pan on a rimmed baking sheet in case the batter overflows in the oven.

▢ BANANA BREAD

- 1½ cups (7½ ounces) all-purpose flour
- 1¼ teaspoons baking soda
- ¾ teaspoon table salt
- 2½ cups mashed very ripe bananas (about 5 bananas)
- 1 cup packed (7 ounces) dark brown sugar
- 10 tablespoons unsalted butter, melted and cooled slightly
- 2 large eggs
- 2 tablespoons granulated sugar

1. Adjust oven rack to middle position and heat oven to 350 degrees. Spray 8½ by 4½-inch loaf pan with vegetable oil spray.
2. Whisk flour, baking soda, and salt together in bowl. Whisk bananas, brown sugar, melted butter, and eggs in large bowl until thoroughly combined, making sure to break up any clumps of brown sugar with whisk. Add flour mixture to banana mixture and whisk gently until just combined (batter will be lumpy).
3. Place prepared pan on rimmed baking sheet. Transfer batter to prepared pan and sprinkle granulated sugar over top. Bake until toothpick inserted in center comes out clean, about 1 hour 10 minutes.
4. Let bread cool in pan on wire rack for 30 minutes. Tilt pan and gently remove bread. Let bread continue to cool on wire rack at least 30 minutes longer. Serve warm or at room temperature. (Cooled bread can be wrapped tightly in plastic wrap and stored at room temperature for up to 5 days.)

▢ DOUBLE-CHOCOLATE BANANA BREAD

- 1¼ cups (6¼ ounces) all-purpose flour
- ¼ cup (¾ ounce) Dutch-processed cocoa powder
- 1¼ teaspoons baking soda
- ¾ teaspoon table salt
- 2 cups mashed very ripe bananas (about 4 bananas)
- 1 cup packed (7 ounces) dark brown sugar
- 10 tablespoons unsalted butter, melted and cooled slightly
- 2 large eggs
- 4 ounces bittersweet chocolate, chopped
- 2 tablespoons granulated sugar

1. Adjust oven rack to middle position and heat oven to 350 degrees. Spray 8½ by 4½-inch loaf pan with vegetable oil spray.
2. Whisk flour, cocoa, baking soda, and salt together in bowl. Whisk bananas, brown sugar, melted butter, and eggs in large bowl until thoroughly combined, making sure to break up any clumps of brown sugar with whisk. Add flour mixture to banana mixture and whisk gently until just combined (batter will be lumpy). Fold in chocolate.
3. Place prepared pan on rimmed baking sheet. Transfer batter to prepared pan and sprinkle granulated sugar over top. Bake until toothpick inserted in center comes out clean, about 1 hour 10 minutes.
4. Let bread cool in pan on wire rack for 30 minutes. Tilt pan and gently remove bread. Let bread continue to cool on wire rack at least 30 minutes longer. Serve warm or at room temperature. (Cooled bread can be wrapped tightly in plastic wrap and stored at room temperature for up to 5 days.)

A SPRINKLE OF SUGAR ON TOP Provides crunch and a pop of sweetness

Using both cocoa powder and chopped bittersweet chocolate gives our chocolate variation a big punch of richness.

We like loaf pans with folded-metal (not pressed) constructions; they make baked goods with sharp corners.

If the bread doesn't easily tip out after 30 minutes of cooling, gently run a butter knife around the perimeter of the pan and try again.

■ PARKER HOUSE ROLLS

Makes 24 rolls
Estimated Time: 4 to 5 hours,
plus 15 minutes cooling

4	cups (20 ounces) all-purpose flour
2¼	teaspoons instant or rapid-rise yeast
1½	teaspoons table salt
1¼	cups (10 ounces) whole milk, room temperature
14	tablespoons unsalted butter, melted, divided
1	large egg, room temperature
2	tablespoons sugar

1. Whisk flour, yeast, and salt together in bowl of stand mixer. Whisk milk, 8 tablespoons melted butter, egg, and sugar in 4-cup liquid measuring cup until sugar has dissolved.

2. Fit mixer with dough hook. Slowly add milk mixture to flour mixture on low speed and mix until cohesive dough starts to form and no dry flour remains, about 2 minutes, scraping down bowl as needed. Increase speed to medium-low and knead until dough is smooth and elastic and clears sides of bowl but sticks to bottom, about 8 minutes.

3. Transfer dough to lightly floured counter and knead by hand to form smooth, round ball, about 30 seconds. Place dough seam side down in lightly greased large bowl or container; cover tightly with plastic wrap; and let rise until doubled in size, 1 to 1½ hours.

4. Line 2 rimmed baking sheets with parchment paper. Press down on dough to deflate. Transfer dough to clean counter and use bench scraper to divide in half. Stretch each half into even 12-inch log, cut each log into 12 equal pieces (about 1½ ounces each), and cover loosely with greased plastic. Working with 1 piece of dough at a time (keep remaining pieces covered), form into rough ball by stretching dough with your thumbs and pinching edges together on bottom so top is smooth. Place ball seam side down on clean counter and, using your cupped hand, drag in small circles until dough feels taut and round. Cover dough balls loosely with greased plastic and let rest for 15 minutes.

5. Working with few dough balls at a time, press balls into ¼-inch-thick rounds. Using thin handle of wooden spoon or dowel, firmly press down across width of rounds to create crease in center.

6. Brush tops of rounds with 3 tablespoons melted butter. Fold in half along crease and gently press edges to seal.

7. Arrange rolls on prepared sheets, spaced about 2 inches apart. Cover loosely with greased plastic and let rise until nearly doubled in size and dough springs back minimally when poked gently with your knuckle, 1 to 1½ hours. (Unrisen rolls can be refrigerated for at least 8 hours or up to 16 hours; let rolls sit at room temperature for 1 hour before baking.)

8. Adjust oven racks to upper-middle and lower-middle positions and heat oven to 350 degrees. Gently brush rolls with remaining 3 tablespoons melted butter, then mist with water. Bake until golden brown, 20 to 25 minutes, switching and rotating sheets halfway through baking. Transfer rolls to wire rack and let cool for 15 minutes. Serve warm or at room temperature.

Parker House Rolls

These tender, buttery rolls may have originated at Boston's Parker House Hotel, but now they belong to the entire country. **by the editors of America's Test Ki**

A Delicious Place to Stay

Harvey D. Parker arrived in Boston from the backwoods of Maine in 1825 as a poor but ambitious 20-year-old. He soon found work as a coachman, and by 1832 he had saved up enough money to purchase a tavern, which he called Parker's. By 1854, he was successful enough for a dramatic expansion: the Parker House Hotel on School Street. The hotel hosted guests including Charles Dickens, who stayed for five months, and John Wilkes Booth, who checked out just a week before his infamous visit to Ford's Theatre in Washington, D.C. Bakers in the Parker House kitchen were

widely renowned for their inventiveness; besides the signature Parker House roll, they also developed the Boston cream pie. Past employees of the hotel include Emeril Lagasse and Malcolm X.

...ess for Success

...a little effort into pushing the center
...ach dough round with a wooden spoon
...dle in step 5 of the recipe; the point is
...ctually thin the dough in that spot, not
...t to mark it. The thinning helps prevent
...rolls from losing their folded shape
...en they expand in the oven.

CENTER
Place the spoon
handle over
the middle of
each round.

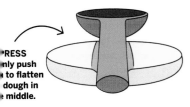

PRESS
...nly push
...t to flatten
...dough in
...middle.

Whisk dry ingredients

...bowl of stand mixer, whisk together
...ur, yeast, and salt. In 4-cup liquid mea-
...ring cup, whisk together milk, melted
...tter, egg, and sugar.
...y? Whisking ensures even distribution
...ingredients.

2. Knead dough in stand mixer

Fit mixer with dough hook. Slowly add milk mixture on low speed and mix for 2 minutes. Increase speed to medium-low and knead until dough is smooth and elastic, about 8 minutes.
Why? Kneading for 8 minutes produces just enough gluten for good structure but not so much that the rolls become tough.

3. Knead by hand

Transfer dough to counter and knead to form smooth ball, about 30 seconds. Then transfer to greased bowl and let rise until doubled in size, 1 to 1½ hours.
Why? Briefly kneading the dough by hand makes it more compact for its rise.

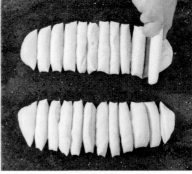

4. Divide into 24 pieces

Press dough to deflate, then transfer to clean counter and use bench scraper to divide it in half. Stretch each piece into 12-inch log, then cut each log into 12 pieces. Form each piece into taut ball and let rest for 15 minutes.
Why? This is the easiest way to divide the dough into 24 rolls.

Start shaping

...orking with few dough balls at a time,
...e your palm to flatten balls. Then use
...ndle of wooden spoon to firmly press
...ddle of each flattened round; press
...rd enough to thin dough in center.
...hy? The firm indent creates a
...ep-enough fold line to prevent the rolls
...m opening up in the oven.

6. Fold over

Brush tops of rounds with melted butter, then fold in half along depression and gently press edges to seal.
Why? This fold creates the signature Parker House shape. Sealing prevents the rolls from opening in the oven.

7. Let rolls rise

Space rolls 2 inches apart on baking sheets. Cover loosely with greased plastic wrap and let rise until doubled in size and dough springs back minimally when poked gently with knuckle, 1 to 1½ hours.
Why? This second rise creates the finished shape and contributes to the rolls' light crumb.

8. Prep and bake

Brush rolls with more melted butter, then mist with water and bake until golden brown, 20 to 25 minutes. Let rolls cool for 15 minutes before serving.
Why? The melted butter adds flavor and a nice sheen. The water enhances the crust.

Cutting the pears into small pieces releases more pectin, which helps this chutney hold together.

Pear-Cranberry **Chutney**

Traditional cranberry sauce is great. This year, we wanted a little something extra. **Recipe by Danielle DiSiato**

PEAR-CRANBERRY CHUTNEY

Serves 8 to 10 (Makes about 2 cups)
Estimated Time: 50 minutes,
plus 30 minutes cooling

For the best texture, buy pears that a ripe but firm; they should yield sligh when pressed. You will need two 1-c jars for this recipe.

2	tablespoons plus 1½ cups water, divided
1	shallot, minced
½	teaspoon table salt
2	garlic cloves, minced
½	teaspoon ground coriander
¼	teaspoon pepper
⅛	teaspoon ground allspice
1	pound ripe but firm Bartlett or Anj◌ pears, halved, cored, and cut into ¼-inch pieces
½	cup sugar, plus extra for seasoning
4	ounces (1 cup) fresh or thawed froz cranberries
2	tablespoons white wine vinegar

1. Combine 2 tablespoons water, shallot, and salt in large saucepan ov◌ medium heat; cover and cook until shallot begins to soften, about 3 min◌ utes. Uncover; stir in garlic, coriand◌ pepper, and allspice; and cook until fragrant, about 1 minute.
2. Stir in pears, sugar, and remainin◌ 1½ cups water. Cover and simmer, stirring occasionally, until pears are j◌ softened, 10 to 15 minutes.
3. Stir in cranberries and vinegar. Increase heat to medium-high and sim◌ mer, uncovered, until cranberries bur◌ and mixture is thickened, about 10 mi◌ utes. Season with salt, pepper, and ext◌ sugar to taste and let cool slightly.
4. Spoon chutney into two 1-cup jars Let cool completely. Serve. (Chutney can be refrigerated for up to 2 months

A GREAT HOLIDAY cranberry sauce offers so much: bright flavor, festive color, and a refreshing sense of balance to an otherwise heavy meal. While straightforward cranberry sauce will always be welcome, we thought that this year we'd add another option to the table—something with a bit more complexity and a little sweetness, too.

A great chutney combines sweet fruit, tangy vinegar, and warm spices with a few extra ingredients such as aromatics or sweeteners to even things out; it's bold but balanced.

This recipe starts by cooking minced shallot with a little water over medium heat to soften its texture and bring out its sweetness. Next, minced garlic and ground spices (corian-der, pepper, and allspice) enter the saucepan and cook just long enough to bloom and amplify their aromas before the subtly sweet pears are introduced. It's important to choose pears that are just ripe and not too soft so that the resulting chutney is chunky, not complete mush. Some sugar in the mix boosts the sweetness of the pears

without being cloying; more water helps everything meld and achieve the right consistency.

After the pears soften in the sauce-pan, cranberries join the party to cook through and burst, releasing their tart juices and a bit of pectin to thicken the mixture into something more jammy. What's more, the berries add a vibrant jewel-toned color.

Serve this beautiful chutney alongside your savory supper, as an accompaniment to a cheese platter, or spread on a turkey sandwich.

A Fine Pair

We call for Anjou (bottom left) and Bartlett (bottom right) pears here. Both have sweet, fragrant flesh and a smooth texture (other varieties can be gritty). Unripe pears have taut, shiny skin; as they ripen, their skin becomes more matte.

Like it hot? Then use hot Italian sausage instead of sweet.

Italian Sausage with White Beans and Kale

A few pantry staples helped us create a wholesome, rustic dinner in an hour. **Recipe by Sara Mayer**

IT'S HARD TO imagine a more comforting supper than a dish of soft, brothy beans; hearty kale; and punchy sausage. And that comfort level only increases when you have to clean just one pot afterward.

The trouble with greens such as kale is that you need a vessel with a large capacity so that they'll fit inside it when raw. A Dutch oven is the best choice here. To ensure that the kale emerges superflavorful, we sear the sausages in the pot first and then remove them and cook pungent onion and garlic in the savory fat left behind. After these steps we're left with delicious brown bits, aka fond, to scrape up into the cooking liquid and infuse the greens with meaty flavor.

About that cooking liquid: It's not just broth. Instead, we bolster chicken broth with canned tomatoes and their juice for flavor and pureed beans for a silky texture. We pile the kale into the pot, cover it, and simmer it for 15 minutes to cook down and mingle with the powerful flavors inside.

Remember those sausages? It's time for them to go back into the pot along with the rest of the beans to cook through and soak up maximum savory flavor. Another 10 minutes and dinner is ready for the table.

All that's left to do is put out some crusty bread to mop up all those delicious juices and open a bottle of wine.

Canned Cannellini?
While you could cook dried beans and add them to the pot here, using canned beans makes this dish much less work—without compromising the flavor or texture of the dish.

ONE-PAN ITALIAN SAUSAGE WITH WHITE BEANS AND KALE
Serves 4
Estimated Time: 1 hour
Serve with crusty bread.

- 2 (15-ounce) cans cannellini beans, rinsed, divided
- 1 (28-ounce) can diced tomatoes, drained, divided, with juice reserved
- 1 cup chicken broth
- 2 tablespoons extra-virgin olive oil
- 1 pound sweet or hot Italian sausage, pricked all over with fork
- 1 onion, chopped fine
- 3 garlic cloves, minced
- 1 pound kale, stemmed and chopped
- ¼ teaspoon table salt

1. Process ½ cup beans, ½ cup tomatoes, reserved tomato juice, and broth in food processor until smooth, about 30 seconds.
2. Heat oil in Dutch oven over medium heat until shimmering. Add sausages and brown on all sides, about 5 minutes; transfer to plate.
3. Add onion to fat left in pot and cook until softened, 5 to 7 minutes. Stir in garlic and cook until fragrant, about 30 seconds. Stir in kale, salt, pureed bean-tomato mixture, and remaining tomatoes, scraping up any browned bits. Cover and simmer, stirring occasionally, until kale is wilted and tender, about 15 minutes.
4. Stir in remaining beans, then nestle sausages into pot along with any accumulated juices. Cover and simmer until sausages register 160 degrees and sauce is slightly thickened, about 10 minutes. Season with salt and pepper to taste, and serve.

Word on Kale
...e call for a full pound of kale here (pictured at right), which is a lot. ...hether you use curly kale, red kale, or Lacinato (dinosaur) kale, ...u have to take the leaves off the tough stems before chopping ...em and adding them to the pot. We've found that the easiest way ... do this is with your hands. Grasp a leaf by the bottom (fat end) of ...e stem and run the fingers of your other hand up the side of the ...em, pinching as you go; it's OK to leave a little bit of the thinner, ...nder stem imbedded toward the top of the leaf.

KALE AND HEARTY
We slipped a quarter into the frame to show you just how much room a pound of uncooked kale takes up. Don't worry! Like most leafy greens, kale shrinks dramatically as it cooks.

Chicken Noodle Soup

A cup of raw egg noodles is just enough for two hearty bowls of soup.

Bone-In, Skin-On for Flavor

We like breast meat in this recipe, but we wanted more fat and flavor than a bone-less, skinless breast could provide. A single bone-in, skin-on split breast solved that problem, giving us clean white meat and a rich, flavorful broth.

CHICKEN NOODLE SOUP FOR TWO

Estimated Time: 1¼ hours

You can substitute fresh dill for the parsley, if desired.

- 1 (12-ounce) bone-in split chicken breast, trimmed
- ½ teaspoon pepper, divided
- ¼ teaspoon table salt
- 1 tablespoon extra-virgin olive oil
- ½ cup chopped onion
- ⅓ cup chopped carrot
- ⅓ cup chopped celery
- 1 garlic clove, minced
- ½ teaspoon dried thyme
- 4 cups chicken broth
- 2 ounces (1 cup) egg noodles
- 1 tablespoon chopped fresh parsley

1. Pat chicken dry with paper towels and sprinkle with ¼ teaspoon pepper and salt. Heat oil in large saucepan over medium-high heat until shimmering. Add chicken, skin side down, and cook until well browned on skin side, about 5 minutes. Transfer to plate, skin side up.

2. Add onion, carrot, celery, garlic, thyme, and remaining ¼ teaspoon pepper to fat left in saucepan. Cook until vegetables are softened, about 5 minutes. Stir in broth, scraping up any browned bits. Add chicken and bring to boil. Cover; reduce heat to low; and simmer until chicken registers 160 degrees, 14 to 17 minutes.

3. Remove saucepan from heat. Transfer chicken to plate and let cool slightly, about 10 minutes. Using 2 forks, shred chicken into bite-size pieces; discard skin and bones.

4. Return soup to boil over high heat and add noodles. Cook, uncovered, until noodles are tender, 7 to 9 minutes, stirring often. Add chicken and parsley and cook until chicken is warmed through, about 1 minute. Season with salt and pepper to taste. Serve.

Soup doesn't have to be made in huge quantities—sometimes you want just enough for dinner. **by Morgan Bolling**

WHENEVER I HAD a cold as a child, my mom made a massive batch of chicken noodle soup. It was as if the bigger the pot of soup, the better I'd feel. Clearly she is the kindest.

As an adult I still crave that same comforting elixir of a soup whenever I'm under the weather. But nowadays, with limited freezer space in my apartment, I want just enough for dinner.

My mother's recipe for chicken noodle soup starts like many recipes do: You make a homemade chicken stock by gently cooking a whole chicken and aromatics (carrot, onion, celery, garlic, herbs, etc.) in water for hours. To mimic this on a weeknight and on a smaller scale, I seared a single bone-in, skin-on split chicken breast before simmering it in store-bought chicken broth. Browning the chicken first added roasty flavor and helped render the flavorful fat out of the skin (and into my broth). And since chicken bones also contain a ton of flavor, they bolstered the store-bought broth with deep savory richness. Garlic and dried thyme, ingredients I always keep on hand, brought further depth and complexity to the broth.

After a couple tests, I decided to sauté a mix of onion, celery, and carrot in the residual fat left after searing the chicken before simmering the broth. Softening these aromatics in that fat added an extra level of depth to my quicker, smaller-batch soup.

Thick, chunky egg noodles felt like an obvious choice. They could not only soak up the rich, chicken-y soup base but also were easier to portion into a 1-cup measure than longer pastas such as spaghetti. With just enough comforting, deeply flavored soup and only one saucepan to clean, all I had left to do was add some fresh parsley, cuddle up on my couch with a blanket, and eat.

Classic Pot Roast

For the best flavor and texture, it pays to do a little work up front. **by the editors of America's Test Kitchen**

IF THERE WAS ever a dish that was a perfect fit for the slow cooker, it would be pot roast. And while you could certainly just pile your beef roast, vegetables, and broth in the cooker and let it "go," we found a better path to fuller flavor and better texture.

We started with a hefty chuck-eye roast, an affordable cut with lots of marbling and great beefy flavor. This cut has a seam of fat running through the middle, and our move here was to pull the raw roast in two along that seam, clean out the excess fat (if left in, this fat would make the resulting sauce greasy), and then tie the two halves up into separate tidy bundles with kitchen twine. Making two smaller roasts out of one big one not only helped control the fat level but also allowed the two pieces to cook faster and more evenly. We did find that it was best to briefly sear the roasts in a skillet on the stovetop to build deeper flavor before plunking them in the slow cooker.

With a skillet full of nice beef drippings, why not give the vegetables a head start on the stovetop, too? Through testing we found that the denser vegetables, carrots and potatoes, didn't really benefit from this maneuver, but the onion and celery definitely did. When the onion and celery were lightly browned, we stirred flour (for thickening), tomato paste, garlic, and thyme into the skillet, followed by equal amounts of red wine and beef broth. Scraping the skillet helped incorporate the flavorful fond (the browned bits left over from searing the meat and sautéing the vegetables) into the liquid.

At this point it was time to carefully pour the contents of the skillet into the slow cooker, stir in the potatoes and carrots, and nestle in the tied beef roasts. After 9 to 10 hours on low or 6 to 7 hours on high (it depends on how long you want your house to smell amazing), the beef became silky-soft, the vegetables tender, and the sauce superbeefy and flavorful. All that was left to do was to quickly skim the fat from the sauce, slice the meat, and serve up. A beautiful, comforting meal.

▪ SLOW-COOKER CLASSIC POT ROAST WITH CARROTS AND POTATOES

Serves 8 to 10
Estimated Time: 9 to 10 hours on low or 6 to 7 hours on high
Use small Yukon Gold potatoes measuring 1 to 2 inches in diameter; if using larger potatoes, cut them into 1-inch pieces. You can substitute ¼ teaspoon of dried thyme for the fresh, if desired.

- 1 **(4- to 5-pound) boneless beef chuck-eye roast, pulled into 2 pieces at natural seam and trimmed**
- 2 **teaspoons table salt, divided**
- 1¼ **teaspoons pepper, divided**
- 2 **tablespoons vegetable oil**
- 1 **onion, chopped**
- 2 **celery ribs, chopped**
- 2 **tablespoons all-purpose flour**
- 1 **tablespoon tomato paste**
- 3 **garlic cloves, minced**
- 1 **teaspoon minced fresh thyme**
- ½ **cup dry red wine**
- ½ **cup beef broth**
- 2 **pounds small Yukon Gold potatoes, unpeeled**
- 1 **pound carrots, peeled and halved crosswise, thick ends halved lengthwise**
- 2 **bay leaves**
- 2 **tablespoons minced fresh parsley**

1. Pat beef dry with paper towels and sprinkle with 1½ teaspoons salt and 1 teaspoon pepper. Tie 3 pieces of kitchen twine around each piece of beef to create 2 evenly shaped roasts. Heat oil in 12-inch skillet over medium-high heat until just smoking. Brown roasts all over, 7 to 10 minutes; transfer to plate.
2. Add onion, celery, remaining ½ teaspoon salt, and remaining ¼ teaspoon pepper to fat left in skillet and cook over medium heat until vegetables are softened and lightly browned, 8 to 10 minutes. Stir in flour, tomato paste, garlic, and thyme and cook until fragrant, about 1 minute. Slowly stir in wine and broth, scraping up any browned bits and smoothing out any lumps; transfer to slow cooker.
3. Stir potatoes, carrots, and bay leaves into slow cooker. Nestle roasts into slow cooker, adding any accumulated juices.

Cover and cook until beef is tender and fork slips easily in and out of meat, 9 to 10 hours on low or 6 to 7 hours on high.
4. Transfer roasts to carving board, tent with aluminum foil, and let rest for 20 minutes.
5. Discard bay leaves. Transfer vegetables to serving dish and tent with foil. Using large spoon, skim fat from surface of sauce. Stir parsley into sauce and season with salt and pepper to taste.
6. Remove twine from roasts, slice meat against grain ½ inch thick, and arrange on serving dish with vegetables. Spoon 1 cup sauce over meat and serve, passing remaining sauce separately.

What's the key to tender beef? Time.

Breaking It Down
We love the big, beefy flavor and affordable price of chuck-eye roast. This roast has a seam of fat running through its center; we call for pulling the roast apart, trimming out the fat, and tying up each of the two halves with kitchen twine before cooking. This helps prevent the braising liquid from becoming too greasy.

Jarred Medium Salsa

Supermarket shelves are crowded with salsas. We couldn't pick just one—but we'll help you find the right one for you.

by Carolyn Grillo

PLENTY OF ROASTED, SMOKY FLAVORS

GOOD HEAT, CRUNCHY VEGGIES

GARLIC AND CUMIN FLAVORS

SLIGHTLY SWEET

WE ALWAYS HAVE a jar (or two) of salsa in our pantries for when we need a quick snack or condiment. We especially like medium-heat salsas because they provide bold flavor without scorching our palates. There are tons of options at the store, and new brands have entered the market since we last tasted them. We wondered which medium-heat salsa should become our new go-to.

We identified 10 top-selling, nationally available salsa brands based on sales data from IRI, a Chicago-based market research firm. Many of these brands make multiple versions of medium-heat salsa, so we rounded up all the options from each company, tasted them against each other, and included our favorite from each brand in our final lineup of 10 salsas. A group of 21 staffers sampled the

The salsas ranged from thick and chunky to thin and pureed. When we strained a jar of each, some released ½ cup of liquid and others released more than 1 cup. All styles had fans.

½ cup of liquid

More than 1 cup of liquid

salsas plain and with our favorite tortilla chips and compared their flavors, textures, and heat levels.

Even though all the salsas we tasted were labeled as medium heat, some were considerably spicier than others. The flavors of the salsas also varied a lot. The most important variables were the type of pepper used in the salsa, the amount of sodium per serving, and the presence of additional spices or seasonings. Those made with jalapeños or a mix of jalapeños and milder pasilla peppers were the spiciest. Salsas containing bell peppers and those that didn't specify the types of pepper used tended to be more mild.

As for sodium, the levels ranged from

80 milligrams to upwards of 230 milligrams per serving. Tasters described salsas with less sodium as tasting a little "sweet," but the salsa with the most sodium didn't taste too salty, even when paired with tortilla chips.

A few salsas were garlicky, tasted strongly of cumin, or had bold smoky flavors from roasted ingredients. The rest tasted mostly like tangy, sweet tomatoes, with heat from the peppers.

The textures of the salsas in our lineup also varied, from thick and chunky to pureed. Some were almost saucy, like marinara. We strained one jar of each salsa (all the jars were around 16 ounces) and compared the amount of liquid they shed. The volume of liquid ranged from ½ cup to more than a full cup. Tasters had strong texture preferences, but each texture had its admirers.

Although the basic ingredients for tomato salsa are simple—tomatoes, onions, and peppers plus salt and maybe a little garlic and/or spices—the way manufacturers prepared and combined those ingredients resulted in salsas that tasted wildly different. Fortunately, we found something we liked in each of the salsas we tasted. Instead of picking a favorite, we've listed tasting notes for each one so that you can find the salsa that's right for you.

Web subscribers can see the full tasting results and complete chart at CooksCountry.com/nov20.

Even though all the salsas we tasted are labeled as medium heat, the spiciness of the salsas varied greatly. The salsas' textures varied, too. Below the salsas are listed from hottest to mildest. Spicier or milder; thicker or thinner; sweet, garlicky, or roasted—use the tasting notes below to find out which salsa is right for you.

HOTTEST

Mateo's Gourmet Medium Salsa
Price: $5.99 for 16 oz   **Pepper Type:** Jalapeño   **Amount of Liquid Shed:** ¾ cup
Buy This If You Like: A pureed salsa with intense heat and strong garlic and cumin flavors

Green Mountain Gringo Medium Salsa
Price: $4.99 for 16 oz   **Pepper Type:** Jalapeño, pasilla   **Amount of Liquid Shed:** ⅔ cup
Buy This If You Like: A thinner salsa that starts sweet and has a strong heat that builds

Pace Medium Chunky Salsa
Price: $2.99 for 16 oz   **Pepper Type:** Jalapeño   **Amount of Liquid Shed:** ½ cup
Buy This If You Like: Salsa with crunchy pieces of vegetables and a good amount of heat

Chi-Chi's Thick & Chunky Salsa Medium
Price: $2.99 for 16 oz   **Pepper Type:** Jalapeño   **Amount of Liquid Shed:** ½ cup
Buy This If You Like: Chunky salsa with a bit of sweetness and bright tomato flavor

Tostitos Chunky Salsa (Medium)
Price: $3.79 for 15.5 oz   **Pepper Type:** Jalapeño   **Amount of Liquid Shed:** ½ cup
Buy This If You Like: A thick salsa with medium-diced vegetables and moderate heat

La Victoria Thick 'n Chunky Salsa Medium
Price: $3.49 for 16 oz   **Pepper Types:** Jalapeño, green chiles   **Amount of Liquid Shed:** ½ cup
Buy This If You Like: A thicker, marinara-like salsa with a touch of smoke and mild heat

On the Border Original Salsa, Medium
Price: $2.99 for 16 oz   **Type of Pepper:** Jalapeño   **Amount of Liquid Shed:** ⅔ cup
Buy This If You Like: A thinner salsa and a sweet-and-smoky flavor combination

Frontera Double Roasted Gourmet Tomato Salsa
Price: $4.29 for 16 oz   **Pepper Type:** Fire-roasted jalapeño
Amount of Liquid Shed: Slightly less than 1 cup
Buy This If You Like: A thin salsa with roasted, smoky, charred flavors

Newman's Own Medium Salsa
Price: $2.99 for 16 oz   **Pepper Type:** Green chili, green bell, red jalapeño, red bell
Amount of Liquid Shed: ½ cup
Buy This If You Like: A thick salsa with tender pieces of tomato and mild heat

Herdez Salsa Casera Medium
Price: $3.49 for 16 oz   **Pepper Type:** Chile
Amount of Liquid Shed: Slightly more than 1 cup
Buy This If You Like: A thinner salsa that tastes mild and fresh like pico de gallo

MILDEST

Braise the Roof!
Why We Love This Pot

You can use a braiser for simmering, roasting, and searing, which makes it a much more versatile pot than you might expect. **by Riddley Gemperlein-Schirm**

addition to braising meats, we use ours for steaming kale.

A RECENT ATK Reviews team meeting, we played a fun game: Each us named our five must-have pieces cookware. My number one pick s my braiser, which pretty much es on my stovetop. With its sloped es, wide cooking surface, and heavy it's ready to tackle anything from li to sautéed greens to shakshuka to st chicken.

To find the best braiser, we selected ur enameled cast-iron models and e ceramic model, all priced from ut $59 to about $330 and all with acities close to 3.5 quarts. In each del, we braised chicken thighs, de meatballs in tomato sauce, ised green beans, roasted a whole cken, and made pork ragu. All the braisers made well-cooked d, but the cast-iron pans browned

food better than the ceramic braiser (ceramic is not as good a conductor of heat). And at about 7 pounds, the ceramic braiser felt flimsy compared with the cast-iron models, which weighed between 12 and 14 pounds.

The shape of each braiser was a key determinant of its performance. We liked pans with cooking surfaces that measured at least 10 inches across (the 4-pound whole chickens didn't fit as well in smaller pans). Liquids also evaporated more slowly in the models with smaller cooking surfaces.

When using a braiser that weighs more than 10 pounds when empty, it's important to have handles that are easy to grab with oven mitts. The handles of our two favorites were looped and easy to grasp. We also liked lids with wide, grippy knobs.

We washed all the braisers by hand after each cooking test, and they were all easy to clean. To see if they'd hold up over time, we did a couple things we don't recommend but that home cooks often do: We whacked the rim of each braiser with a metal spoon 50 times and slammed their lids down repeatedly. Only one, an enameled cast-iron model, chipped minimally.

Our winner, the Le Creuset Signature Enameled Cast-Iron 3.5-Quart Round Braiser, which costs about $300, produced great food, and its light interior made it easy for us to monitor progress. We really liked its wide, looped handles and its large lid knob. Its surface didn't chip or crack after being whacked.

Our Best Buy, the Tramontina Enameled Cast Iron Covered Braiser, which costs about $62, produced great food, but its handles were smaller and therefore slightly tougher to grip than our winner's.

While we'll still use our Dutch oven for braising large roasts, making soups and stews, deep frying, and baking bread, we really like braisers for their low sides, which made it easy to add and retrieve food. Another plus? Our favorite is almost 2 pounds lighter than our favorite Dutch oven, which makes it easier to maneuver in and out of the oven when full. So while a braiser won't replace our Dutch oven, we do think it makes a worthy addition to any cookware collection.

WHAT DO YOU GET WHEN YOU CROSS A DUTCH OVEN WITH A SKILLET?

The answer is our favorite braiser. It combines the best traits of our favorite Dutch oven and our favorite enameled cast-iron skillet in one pan. Like the Dutch oven, the braiser has two handles for easy transport, a lid to retain moisture, and a light-colored interior that makes it easy to monitor food as it browns. Like the enameled cast-iron skillet, our favorite braiser has a wide cooking surface, and its cast-iron core retains heat well, which translates into great searing capability. Not only is our favorite braiser good for braising, but it is a go-to pan for many other kitchen tasks. Here are a few.

1. ROASTING
It's ovensafe, its looped handles make it easy to lift, and it's wide enough to fit a 4-pound whole chicken.

2. SEARING
Its cast-iron core retains heat, and its enameled surface means that you don't have to worry about seasoning the pan.

3. SHALLOW FRYING
Its high sides and wide surface make it great for shallow-frying pork chops, chicken cutlets, egg rolls, and more.

4. STEAMING
The combination of the lid and the wide cooking surface makes it a good pan for braising vegetables such as kale.

5. SERVING
Our winner is as pretty as it is functional, so it can go straight from the stovetop or oven to the table.

Web subscribers can read the full testing at **CooksCountry.com/nov20.**

OUR TESTING RESULTS

KEY **Good** ★★★ **Fair** ★★ **Poor** ★

RECOMMENDED

Our Favorite ◄

Le Creuset Signature Enameled Cast-Iron 3.5-Quart Round Braiser
Model: LS2532-305HSS
Price: $299.95
Cooking: ★★★ **Ease of Use:** ★★★
Cleanup: ★★★ **Durability:** ★★★

Comments: Our top-ranked braiser had a light interior that made it easy to monitor browning; a generous cooking surface; and large, comfortable looped handles. It was easy to use and produced great food.

Staub Cast Iron 3.5-Quart Braiser
Model: ME7118
Price: $329.95
Cooking: ★★★
Ease of Use: ★★
Cleanup: ★★★ **Durability:** ★★★

Comments: This model cooked food evenly and browned it thoroughly. Plus, it had large handles. Two downsides: its dark interior and its rather small lid knob.

Best Buy ◄

Tramontina Enameled Cast Iron Covered Braiser
Model: 80131/050DS
Price: $61.97
Cooking: ★★★ **Ease of Use:** ★½
Cleanup: ★★★ **Durability:** ★★★

Comments: This pan performed on par with our favorite, but its handles were smaller. It had the largest cooking surface area, was easy to clean, and didn't chip or crack. It delivered great results at a bargain price.

RECOMMENDED WITH RESERVATIONS

Lodge 3.6-Quart Enamel Cast Iron Casserole Dish with Lid
Model: EC3CC13
Price: $59.90
Cooking: ★★½ **Ease of Use:** ★½
Cleanup: ★★★ **Durability:** ★★

Comments: This pan cooked decent food, but it had smaller handles that were tough to grasp. Its enameled coating chipped when we whacked it with a metal spoon.

NOT RECOMMENDED

Emile Henry Made in France Flame Braiser, 12"
Model: 34 4593
Price: $179.95
Cooking: ★½
Ease of Use: ★
Cleanup: ★★ **Durability:** ★★

Comments: This ceramic pan didn't retain heat well, so it browned food unevenly. It also had a smaller surface area. Its handles were short, stubby, and hard to grasp.

Maple-Pecan Skillet Granola

MAPLE-PECAN SKILLET GRANOLA

Serves 4 (Makes about 3 cups)
Estimated Time: 45 minutes

Do not substitute quick or instant oats in this recipe; old-fashioned oats provide the perfect amount of chew. It's important to stir the granola frequently in step 2 to ensure that the mixture cooks evenly.

- ¼ cup maple syrup
- 1 teaspoon vanilla extract
- ½ teaspoon ground cinnamon
- ¼ teaspoon table salt
- 2 tablespoons vegetable oil
- ½ cup pecans, chopped coarse
- 1½ cups (4½ ounces) old-fashioned rolled oats

1. Combine maple syrup, vanilla, cinnamon, and salt in bowl; set aside. Line baking sheet with parchment paper.
2. Heat oil in 12-inch nonstick skillet over medium heat until shimmering. Add pecans and cook, stirring frequently, until fragrant and just starting to darken in color, about 4 minutes. Add oats and cook, stirring frequently, until oats are golden and pecans are toasted, about 6 minutes.
3. Add maple syrup mixture to skillet and cook, stirring frequently, until absorbed and mixture turns shade darker, about 3 minutes. Transfer granola to prepared sheet, spread into even layer, and let cool for 20 minutes. Break granola into bite-size pieces and serve.

We're looking for recipes that you treasure—the ones that have been handed down in your family for a generation or more, that always come out for the holidays, and that have earned a place at your table and in your heart through many years of meals. Send us the recipes that spell home to you. Visit CooksCountry.com/recipe_submission (or write to Heirloom Recipes, Cook's Country, 21 Drydock Avenue, Suite 210E, Boston, MA 02210) and tell us a little about the recipe, and be sure to include your name and address.

COMING NEXT ISSUE

Our December/January 2021 issue features a splendid menu including **Cast Iron Pork Fajitas, Shrimp Piccata Pasta,** and **Portuguese-Style Bolos Lêvedos (right).** And for your holiday table, whether big or small, we offer **Easier Boneless Prime Rib** and **Snickerdoodles.** Plus, a roundup of our favorite cookie-baking ingredients and equipment will help you outfit yourself for the season. We hope you'll join us.

RECIPE INDEX

FIND THE ROOSTER!

A tiny version of this rooster has been hidden in a photo in the pages of this issue. Write to us with its location, and we'll enter you in a random drawing. Th[e] first correct entry drawn will win a copy [of] The Complete Cook's Country TV Sho[w] Cookbook, and each of the next five wil[l] receive a free one-year subscription to [our] website. To enter, visit CooksCountry.co[m/] rooster by October 31, 2020, or write to [Find the] Rooster ON20, Cook's Country, 21 Drydock Avenue, Suite 210E, Boston, MA 02210. Include your name and address [...] Mary Ellen Court of Miami, Florida, fou[nd] the rooster in the June/July 2020 issue [on] page 16.

WEB EXTRAS

Free for four months online at
CooksCountry.com

Make-Ahead Turkey Gravy

READ US ON IPAD

Download the Cook's Country app for i[Pad] and start a free trial subscription or pur chase a single issue of the magazine. G[o to] CooksCountry.com/iPad to download [the] app through the App Store.

Chocolate Cream Pie in a Jar

Time for something fun! **by Camila Chaparro**

● **NO LUMPS**
Be sure to whisk the corn-starch into the egg yolks thoroughly to avoid lumps.

● **TEMPER, TEMPER**
Take care when whisking the half-and-half mixture into the egg yolk mixture. Go slow or the yolks will scramble.

● **TWO CHOCOLATES**
We bolstered our semisweet chocolate with just a little unsweetened chocolate to add complexity and depth.

CHOCOLATE CREAM PIE IN A JAR
Serves 12
Estimated Time: 35 minutes, plus 1 hour cooling

You can either use store-bought whipped cream or whip 1 cup of chilled heavy cream, 1 tablespoon of sugar, 1 teaspoon of vanilla extract, and a pinch of table salt in a stand mixer on medium speed for 1 to 3 minutes, until soft peaks form. You will need twelve 4-ounce wide-mouth Mason jars for this recipe; for larger servings, use eight 6-ounce ramekins.

- 2½ cups half-and-half
- ⅓ cup (2⅓ ounces) sugar, divided
- Pinch table salt
- 6 large egg yolks
- 2 tablespoons cornstarch
- 6 tablespoons unsalted butter, cut into 6 pieces
- 6 ounces semisweet chocolate, chopped fine
- 1 ounce unsweetened chocolate, chopped fine
- 1 teaspoon vanilla extract
- 10 Oreo cookies, broken into coarse crumbs, divided
- 2 cups whipped cream

1. Bring half-and-half, 3 tablespoons sugar, and salt to simmer in medium saucepan over medium heat, stirring occasionally. Whisk egg yolks, cornstarch, and remaining sugar in medium bowl until smooth. Slowly whisk 1 cup warm half-and-half mixture into yolk mixture to temper, then slowly whisk tempered yolk mixture into remaining half-and-half mixture in saucepan.

2. Cook half-and-half mixture over medium heat, whisking constantly, until mixture is thickened and registers 180 degrees, about 30 seconds. Off heat, whisk in butter, semisweet chocolate, unsweetened chocolate, and vanilla until smooth. Strain pudding through fine-mesh strainer into clean bowl. Spray piece of parchment paper with vegetable oil spray and press directly against surface of pudding. Re-frigerate until chilled, at least 1 hour or up to 3 days.

3. Just before serving, add 1 tablespoon cookie crumbs to each of twelve 4-ounce wide-mouth Mason jars followed by approximately ½ cup pudding. Top with whipped cream and sprinkle with remaining cookie crumbs. Serve.

INSIDE THIS ISSUE

Cook's Country

STACK 'EM HIGH!

hese supremely
uffy malted milk
ancakes will take
our holiday
reakfast plans
ver the top.
AGE 33

NUTELLA
MAPLE
SYRUP

MALTED
MILK
PANCAKES

CEMBER/JANUARY 2021
95 U.S./$7.95 CANADA

DISPLAY UNTIL
JANUARY 4, 2021

7 71486 02742 3

01>

CHOUCROUTE GARNIE

Three cheers for meat

PAGE 4

CAST IRON PORK FAJITAS

One-pan fan favorite

PAGE 10

COOKIE BAKING 101

Key ingredients and
equipment **PAGE 30**

AMERICA'S
TEST KITCHEN

Letter from the EDITOR

AS THIS ISSUE goes to press, we still don't know what the holidays will hold for us. Will we be gathering in groups this year or celebrating in smaller bubbles? Will we have a big meal or a more modest one? Will we travel or stick close to home?

It's impossible to know for sure. But I have faith that no matter the circumstances, it will still feel special.

Even in difficult times, holidays help us stop, look around, celebrate each other, and embrace the kind of thoughtful gratitude that can get lost in the workaday world. This year, we'll all be holding each other a little extra close—literally if we can, figuratively if we must.

We've filled this issue of *Cook's Country* with a few new favorites that I hope add some festive feelings to your holidays, such as our foolproof Easier Prime Rib (page 19), our Torn and Fried Potatoes (page 20), and our refreshed recipe for Snickerdoodles (page 22). Plus, of course, there are plenty of quicker recipes for those in-between nights. I hope you'll find something inspiring in these pages.

On a personal note, this is my last issue as editor in chief of *Cook's Country*. I want to thank you for your readership over the years. *Cook's Country* has a dazzling future ahead, and I'm so excited to see it unfold.

TUCKER SHAW

Editor in Chief

Illustration: Hannah Jacobs

Cook's Country

Chief Executive Officer David Nussbaum
Chief Creative Officer Jack Bishop
Editor in Chief Tucker Shaw
Executive Managing Editor Todd Meier
Executive Food Editor Bryan Roof
Deputy Editor Scott Kathan
Deputy Food Editor Morgan Bolling
Senior Editor Cecelia Jenkins
Associate Editors Matthew Fairman, Jessica Rudolph
Test Cooks Mark Huxsoll, Amanda Luchtel
Photo Team Manager Alli Berkey
Lead Test Cook, Photo Team Eric Haessler
Test Cooks, Photo Team Hannah Fenton, Jacqueline Goche
Assistant Test Cooks, Photo Team Gina McCreadie, Christa
Lead Copy Editor Rachel Schowalter
Copy Editors Christine Campbell, April Poole
Managing Editor, Web Mari Levine
Digital Content Producer Danielle Lapierre
Contributing Editor Eva Katz
Senior Science Research Editor Paul Adams
Hosts & Executive Editors, Television Bridget Lancaster,
  Julia Collin Davison

Executive Editors, ATK Reviews Hannah Crowley, Lisa McM
Deputy Editor, ATK Reviews Kate Shannon
Associate Editors, ATK Reviews Miye Bromberg,
  Riddley Gemperlein-Schirm, Carolyn Grillo
Assistant Editor, ATK Reviews Chase Brightwell

Creative Director John Torres
Photography Director Julie Cote
Art Director Maggie Edgar
Associate Art Director Kristen Jones
Art Director, ATK Reviews Marissa Angelone
Senior Staff Photographers Steve Klise, Daniel J. van Acker
Photographer Kevin White
Photography Producer Meredith Mulcahy

Senior Director, Creative Operations Alice Carpenter
Deputy Editor, Culinary Content & Curriculum Christie Me
Senior Manager, Publishing Operations Taylor Argenzio
Imaging Manager Lauren Robbins
Production & Imaging Specialists Tricia Neumyer, Dennis
  Amanda Yong
Deputy Editor, Editorial Operations Megan Ginsberg
Assistant Editors, Editorial Operations Tess Berger, Sara Z
Test Kitchen Director Erin McMurrer
Assistant Test Kitchen Director Alexxa Benson
Test Kitchen Manager Meridith Lippard
Test Kitchen Shopping & Receiving Lead Heather Tolmie
Senior Kitchen Assistant Shopper Avery Lowe

Chief Financial Officer Jackie McCauley Ford
Senior Manager, Customer Support Tim Quinn
Customer Support Specialist Mitchell Axelson

Chief Digital Officer Fran Middleton
VP, Marketing Natalie Vinard
Director, Audience Acquisition & Partnerships Evan Steine
Director, Social Media Marketing & Emerging Platforms
  Kathryn Przybyla
Social Media Manager Charlotte Errity
Social Media Coordinators Sarah Sandler, Norma Tentori

Chief Revenue Officer Sara Domville

Director, Public Relations & Communications Brian Frankl

**Senior VP, Human Resources & Organizational
  Development** Colleen Zelina
Human Resources Manager Jason Lynott

Food Stylists Ashley Moore, Elle Simone Scott

Circulation Services PubWorX ProCirc

 Find us on **Facebook**
facebook.com/CooksCountry

 Find us on **Instagram**
instagram.com/CooksCountry

 Follow us on **Pinterest**
pinterest.com/TestKitchen

 Follow us on **Twitter**
twitter.com/TestKitchen

AMERICA'S TEST KITCHEN ®

America's Test Kitchen has been teaching home cooks how to be successful in the kitchen since 1993. Our mission is to empower and inspire confidence, community, and creativity in the kitchen. Millions watch our two shows on public television; read our two flagship magazines (Cook's Country and Cook's Illustrated); and rely on our books, websites, videos, podcasts, and educational products for children. America's Test Kitchen is located in a state-of-the-art Boston facility with 15,000 square feet of test kitchen and studio space. Learn more at americasTestKitchen.com.

18, 20, and 21

IN EVERY ISSUE

FEATURES

14

13

Cook's Country magazine (ISSN 1552-1990), number 96, is published bimonthly by America's Test Kitchen Limited Partnership, 21 Drydock Avenue, Suite 210E, Boston, MA 02210. Copyright 2020 America's Test Kitchen Limited Partnership. Periodicals postage paid at Boston, MA, and additional mailing offices, USPS #023453. Publications Mail Agreement No. 40020778. Return undeliverable Canadian addresses to P.O. Box 875, Station A, Windsor, ON N9A 6P2. POSTMASTER: Send address changes to Cook's Country, P.O. Box 6018, Harlan, IA 51593-1518. For subscription and gift subscription orders, subscription inquiries, or change of address notices, visit AmericasTestKitchen.com/support, call 800-526-8447 in the U.S. or 515-237-3663 from outside the U.S., or write to us at Cook's Country, P.O. Box 6018, Harlan, IA 51593-1518. PRINTED IN THE USA.

Compiled by Cecelia Jenkins and Mark Huxsoll

Holiday Libations
Get festive with a cocktail garnish!

How to Rim a Glass with Salt (or Sugar)

Moisten about ½ inch of the glass rim by running a citrus wedge around the outer edge (or by dipping the edge of the glass in a small saucer of water). Spread ½ cup of kosher salt or sugar (for up to four glasses) into an even layer on a small saucer, and then dip the moistened rim in the salt or sugar to coat.

How to Garnish with Citrus Zest

For a citrus zest twist, use a citrus zester/channel knife to remove a 3- to 4-inch strand of citrus peel, working around the circumference of the fruit in a spiral pattern to ensure a continuous piece. Curl the strand tightly to establish a uniform twist, and then place it directly in the cocktail or on the edge of the glass.

The Differences Between Types of Oats

Why do steel-cut oats take so much longer to cook than old-fashioned oats?

–Joanne Glidden, Augusta, Maine

The difference between steel-cut oats and old-fashioned ("rolled") oats lies in the manufacturing process. Steel-cut oats are full oat groats (whole oat kernels with the hull, or outer shell, removed) sliced into small pieces with steel blades. This leaves much of the kernel intact and helps give steel-cut oats their signature chewy texture. Rolled oats are oat kernels that have been steamed and flattened using large disks, which makes the oats thin, flaky, soft, and able to readily absorb liquid. Quick-cooking and instant oats are processed the same way that rolled oats are, but they are rolled thinner and are sometimes precooked and then dried so that they cook even more quickly.

Because steel-cut oats are physically more dense, they require more liquid during cooking and typically take about 25 minutes to cook (although soaking them in water overnight will shorten their cooking time); rolled oats take about 5 minutes to cook.

THE BOTTOM LINE: Since steel-cut oats are less processed than old-fashioned rolled oats and aren't flattened, they take longer to absorb liquid and therefore take longer to cook than old-fashioned rolled oats.

STEEL-CUT OATS
Chewy texture, nutty flavor; they take about 25 minutes to cook.

ROLLED OATS
The classic; they cook in about 5 minutes. Best choice for cookies.

INSTANT OATS
A bit mushy; we don't recommend them.

Beet It

I don't want to spend an hour roasting beets. Is there a quicker way to cook them?
–Tom Slate, Harrisburg, Pa.

We love sweet and tender roasted beets, but you're right—roasting them can take more than an hour, and then you have to factor in the time for cooling and peeling.

Is there a faster way to cook beets? Yes, in the microwave. Simply peel the beets, cut them into pieces (whole beets do not cook efficiently in the microwave), put them in a bowl, and add a bit of water to create steam and prevent the beet chunks from drying out. After microwaving for about 12 minutes, stir the beets and continue to microwave for about 12 minutes or until the beets are perfectly tender. Here's the recipe.

MICROWAVED BEETS
Serves 6
Total Time: 50 minutes

If you're using a Pyrex bowl and need to set the hot bowl down, avoid placing it on a cool or wet surface, as it may crack; place it on a dry cloth instead. Wear gloves when peeling and dicing the beets to prevent staining your hands.

> 2 pounds beets, trimmed, peeled, and cut into ¾-inch pieces
> ½ teaspoon table salt

In largest bowl your microwave will accommodate, stir together beets, ⅓ cup water, and salt. Cover bowl with plate and microwave until beets can be easily pierced with paring knife, 25 to 30 minutes, stirring halfway through microwaving. Drain beets. Serve. (Beets can be refrigerated for up to 3 days.)

...itten and compiled by Matthew Fairman

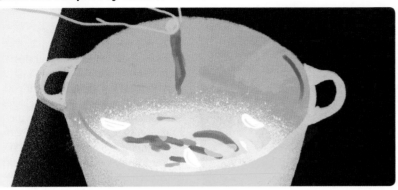

...elf-Mincing Anchovies

...ove using anchovies to add a savory punch to dishes such as stews and ...sta sauces, but I've never enjoyed the messy task of mincing them (or the ...gering odor they can leave on cutting boards). Recently, while I was making ...ecipe that called for minced anchovies, I fished out a couple fillets to chop ...em up and noticed that one of them broke in half as I tried to grab it with a ...rk. It occurred to me that most anchovy fillets are fragile enough to dissolve ...their own with just a little sautéing and stirring. So I stirred them into the ...t oil whole with the garlic. They essentially dissolved on their own, and ...ice then I've found that for most recipes that call for sautéing the ancho-...es, I don't need to mince them first. (Of course, it's always best practice to ...llow the recipe!)

...asy Shrimp ...eveining

...ark Johnson of Savannah, Ga., loves ...cluding peel-and-eat shrimp in his ...afood boils, and he's found a smart ...iy to devein the shrimp without hav-...g to shell them first or use seafood ...issors: He uses a thin wooden ...ewer to pull the vein out of the back ...the shell-on shrimp. He presses the ...p of the skewer through the shrimp ...a joint in the shell halfway down ...e shrimp's back, just deep enough ...travel under the vein. Then he lifts ...e skewer out of the shrimp's back, ...illing the vein out with it.

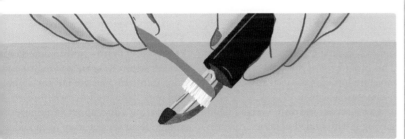

...ot Just for Teeth Anymore

...eth Gabriel of Waipahu, Hawaii, has a smart strategy for cleaning sharp kitch-...1 tools such as serrated vegetable peelers and food processor blades, which ...nd to snag or cut dish towels or sponges and have hard-to-clean nooks and ...annies. She uses a toothbrush: She just squeezes a drop of dish soap on the ...othbrush, gives the tools a scrub, and lets the toothbrush dry before storing it.

The Best Large Plastic Cutting Boards *by Miye Bromberg*

ATK REVIEWS

WE LOVE LARGE plastic cutting boards because they're inexpensive, relatively lightweight, and easy to clean and maneuver; unlike wood or bamboo cutting boards, they require no maintenance. We had never devoted an entire review solely to these practical boards, so we bought seven models, priced from about $19 to about $70, and used them as we chopped onions, minced parsley, pounded chicken breasts, and cleaved chicken parts for stock. We also washed each model by hand or in the dishwasher 50 times.

In the end, we found that the best large plastic cutting board for most home cooks is the Winco Statik Board Cutting Board 15" x 20" x ½". This utilitarian board is about ½ inch thick, so it didn't flex or bounce during use, and it didn't warp even after all those washes. Best of all, it sat ultrasecurely on the counter, thanks to its moderate weight and the four rubberized feet that helped stabilize it. If portability is your great-est priority, we also recommend the new OXO Good Grips Carving and Cutting Board. Weighing just over 3 pounds, it was the lightest board we tested, making it especially easy to move and clean.

What We Love About Our Winner

• Moderate weight that contributes to stability without sacrificing portability

• Rubber grips for optimal stability

• Moderate thickness for warp resistance and security while chopping

• Dishwasher-safe

KEY **Good** ★★★ **Fair** ★★ **Poor** ★

RECOMMENDED	CRITERIA

Our Favorite

Winco Statik Board Cutting Board
15" x 20" x ½"
Model: CBN-1520RD **Price:** $45.00
Thickness: 0.53 in **Weight:** 4 lb, 14 oz
Grips: Yes **Extra Features:** None

Ease of Use ★★½
Stability ★★★
Durability ★★½

Comments: Our favorite wowed us with its rock-solid stability and excellent durability. Thanks to its moderate weight and four small rubberized grips, it never budged. At about ½ inch thick, it didn't flex during use or warp, but it did scar a bit. Any stains and odors cleared up after a wash or two. Our one quibble: Some found it a tad heavy and thus slightly tricky to maneuver.

San Jamar Saf-T-Grip Cutting Board
Model: CBG152012WH **Price:** $23.99
Thickness: 0.48 in **Weight:** 4 lb, 8 oz
Grips: Yes **Extra Features:** Ruler

Ease of Use ★★½
Stability ★★★
Durability ★★½

Best Lightweight Board

OXO Good Grips Carving and Cutting Board
Model: 11272900 **Price:** $27.99
Thickness: 0.35 in **Weight:** 3 lb, 1 oz
Grips: Yes **Extra Features:** Trench

Ease of Use ★★½
Stability ★★½
Durability ★★½

RECOMMENDED WITH RESERVATIONS	

Winco Cutting Board 15" x 20" x 1", White
Model: CBXH-1520 **Price:** $34.26
Thickness: 1.00 in **Weight:** 9 lb, 1 oz

Ease of Use ★★
Stability ★★½
Durability ★★½

Stanton Trading Plastic Cutting Board
15 x 20 x ¾"
Model: 799-2075 **Price:** $25.46
Thickness: 0.75 in **Weight:** 6 lb, 14 oz

Ease of Use ★★
Stability ★★½
Durability ★★½

NOT RECOMMENDED	

San Jamar QuadGrip Cutting Board with
Smart-Check Visual Indicator
Model: CBQGSCSK1520
Price: $69.49 for plastic frame and 2 boards

Ease of Use ★
Stability ★★★
Durability ★

Dexas Polysafe NSF Certified Cutting Board
Model: 411-133 **Price:** $19.54

Ease of Use ★★
Stability ★
Durability ★

Web subscribers can see the complete results chart at **CooksCountry.com/jan21**.

The pork belly's soft fat adds luxe flavor and texture to the dish.

Choucroute Garnie

We're all in for pork. **by Bryan Roof**

A T ITS SIMPLEST, choucroute garnie is a rustic, rib-sticking, country-style dish that puts the focus on the meat. You might not guess it from the name: "Choucroute" means "sauerkraut" in French (the dish has roots in the Alsace region of France). And while there's plenty of sauerkraut in this dish, it's not exactly the first thing you see on your plate. Look at those sausage links! Look at that pork!

The trick with choucroute garnie is to create a dish that is rich and meaty but not overwhelming. You want clear and present pork flavor, tempered with just enough acidity (from wine and sauerkraut) to keep things in balance. And you want to tie all these flavors together with accents such as thyme, garlic, and caraway.

The specific meats and sausages used in choucroute garnie can change from kitchen to kitchen and are often very local (in Alsace, for example, you may find Strasbourg sausages or blood sausages), but I found that a combination of garlicky kielbasa, sweet and herbal bratwurst, smoky ham hock, and rich pork belly provided the range of flavors I sought. It sounds like a lot of meat, and it is. But that's what this dish is all about.

If you have lard on hand, this is a great place to use it (the recipe calls for only 2 tablespoons) to give the choucroute garnie a little extra something. But the dish is great with extra-virgin olive oil, too. Do seek out pork belly for this recipe; ask for it at the butcher counter if you don't see it

in the case. But if you just can't find it, you can substitute pork blade chops, pork butt, or slab bacon.

After experimenting with sauerkraut straight from the jar, drained sauerkraut, and rinsed sauerkraut, I chose rinsed sauerkraut, which I squeezed dry. This provided just the right texture and moisture level for the dish and kept its brininess in check.

To round out the dish, I recommend serving it with boiled potatoes; turn to page 32 for our recipe for **Boiled Potatoes with Butter and Parsley**.

This recipe serves eight, but keep in mind that it makes excellent leftovers, to be enjoyed cold or gently warmed up. I've even used the leftovers for sandwiches, much to the delight of my kids.

■ **CHOUCROUTE GARNIE**

Serves 8 Total Time: 3¼ hours

Note that we call for fully cooked bratwurst here. We developed this recipe with 12 ounces of bratwurst and 14 ounces of kielbasa, but if you can find only slightly larger packages of these sausages, it's OK to use the whole package. You can substitute tw 8- to 10-ounce bone-in blade-cut por chops; 1 pound of boneless pork butt cut in half; or 1 pound of slab bacon for the pork belly. Serve with Boiled Potatoes with Butter and Parsley (page 32), if desired.

- 2   tablespoons lard, bacon fat, or extra-virgin olive oil
- 1   onion, sliced thin
- 1   teaspoon kosher salt, divided
- 1   (12-ounce) smoked ham hock
- 1   cup dry white wine
- 5   garlic cloves, smashed and peeled
- 6   sprigs fresh thyme
- 1   pound skinless pork belly, cut into 2 equal pieces, fat cap trimmed to ¼ inch
- ½   teaspoon pepper
- 2   pounds sauerkraut, rinsed and squeezed dry
- 1   teaspoon caraway seeds
- 14 ounces kielbasa sausage, cut into 6 equal pieces (about 3-inch segments)
- 12 ounces cooked bratwurst, each sausage halved crosswise
   Whole-grain mustard

1. Adjust oven rack to middle position and heat oven to 325 degrees. Heat lar in Dutch oven over medium heat until shimmering. Add onion and ¼ teaspoc salt and cook until just softened, about 6 minutes. Remove pot from heat.
2. Add ham hock, wine, garlic, and thyme sprigs to pot. Sprinkle pork bell with pepper and remaining ¾ teaspoo salt, then add to pot. Cover contents o pot with sauerkraut, then sprinkle with caraway seeds. Cover pot, transfer to oven, and cook for 1½ hours.
3. Remove pot from oven and nestle kielbasa and bratwurst into sauerkrau Cover; return to oven; and continue t cook until sausages are hot throughou and pork belly is tender when pierced with paring knife, about 45 minutes longer. Remove pot from oven and le rest, covered, for 20 minutes.
4. Transfer sauerkraut to shallow platter; place sausages on top. Discarc thyme sprigs. Slice pork belly thin crosswise and add to platter. Remove meat from ham hock, slice thin, and add to platter; discard bone. Serve with mustard.

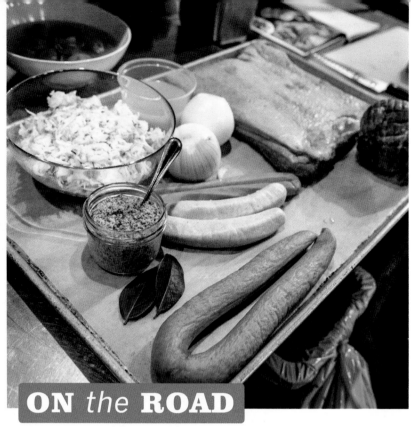

A Portland Meat Empire

Text by Bryan Roof; photos by Steve Klise

"CHOUCROUTE IS A local dish that everybody kind of puts their own spin on," says Eric Joppie, culinary director at Olympia Provisions in Portland, Oregon. "I've seen big pieces of salt pork, big pieces of smoked bacon, everything from different types of sausages to also having whole pieces of hocks and shanks. I've even seen some recipes that contain duck confit or goose fat."

In other words, according to Eric, choucroute garnie is a flexible, elastic, and ultimately personal dish.

At Olympia Provisions, it's even more personal than most, because here the cooks create nearly every ingredient—from the sauerkraut to the cured meats to the butter for the bread that's served alongside the dish—either in the restaurant itself or at a large facility dubbed the "Meat Plant." There, employees produce a wide variety of charcuterie for Olympia's several outposts as well as some retail outlets.

Elias Cairo opened Olympia Provisions in 2009 after developing a passion for handcrafted charcuterie during a European culinary apprenticeship. Over the years, he assembled a team to turn that passion into a local empire, including the NW Portland location we visited. It features an open

kitchen behind the bar and a refrigerated case displaying all manner of cured meats. Everything seems to be served on wooden boards. It's a rustic, welcoming environment.

Eric grew up in southern Texas, near San Antonio. "Slow-cooking meats is in my DNA," he says. But after moving to Oregon to cook in a small restaurant in the early 2000s, he was thrilled by the access to fresh, local ingredients, sourced directly from producers who would visit the restaurant.

After a decade in California's wine country, Eric moved back to Oregon and reconnected with Elias, a former neighbor. He started working at Olympia Provisions in 2016, and today he is the culinary director for all the company's operations, from restaurants to retail. It's a big job that takes him in many directions, but he loves getting behind the stove to cook. Choucroute garnie remains one of his favorite things to prepare.

"You can add in any kind of meat that you want. Apples would be good in this, I think. Other root vegetables would be good. Sauerkraut made with kohlrabi." Eric continues to brainstorm, the ideas flowing like water. "It's a nice dish."

Eric Joppie, top left, prepares choucroute at Olympia Provisions. During the COVID-19 crisis, Olympia temporarily closed some locations for in-person dining, focusing instead on takeout.

The large strips of orange peel add flavor and fragrance, but we don't recommend eating them.

Orange Chicken

An easy recipe for this crowd-pleaser? It's in the (brown paper) bag. **by Matthew Fairman**

■ ORANGE CHICKEN

Serves 4 Total Time: 1¼ hours

You can substitute ¾ cup of bottled orange juice for the freshly squeezed juice, if desired. If your oranges are small, you may need more than two to yield ¾ cup of juice. The chicken will be somewhat pale when fried in step 5; it will get more color when you toss it in the sauce. Serve with rice and steamed broccoli.

SAUCE

- 2 **oranges, divided**
- ¾ **cup chicken broth**
- ⅓ **cup distilled white vinegar**
- ⅓ **cup packed brown sugar**
- ¼ **cup soy sauce**
- 2 **tablespoons cornstarch**
- 3 **garlic cloves, minced**
- 1 **tablespoon grated fresh ginger**
- 1 **tablespoon sriracha**
- 1 **tablespoon toasted sesame oil**

CHICKEN

- 1½ **pounds boneless, skinless chicken thighs, trimmed and cut into 1-inch pieces**
- 2 **large egg whites**
- ½ **teaspoon table salt**
- 1½ **cups cornstarch**
- ½ **cup all-purpose flour**
- 1 **teaspoon baking powder**
- 1 **quart peanut or vegetable oil for frying**
- 2 **scallions, sliced thin on bias**

1. FOR THE SAUCE: Using vegetable peeler, remove eight 2-inch strips of zest from 1 orange. Using rasp-style grater, grate 1½ teaspoons zest from remaining orange. Halve both oranges and squeeze to get ¾ cup juice. Combine orange zest (strips and grated) and juice, broth, vinegar, sugar, soy sauce, cornstarch, garlic, ginger, sriracha, and oil in medium saucepan and whisk to dissolve cornstarch.

2. Bring sauce to simmer over medium-high heat, stirring frequently. Cook until dark brown and thickened, about 2 minutes. Cover and set aside.

3. Combine chicken, egg whites, and salt in bowl. Place cornstarch, flour, and baking powder in double-bagged large paper shopping bag. Roll top of bag to seal and shake gently to combine. Add chicken mixture to cornstarch mixture in bag, roll top of bag to seal, and shake vigorously to thoroughly coat chicken; set aside.

4. Line rimmed baking sheet with triple layer of paper towels. Add oil to large Dutch oven and heat over medium-high heat to 350 degrees.

5. Shake chicken in bag once more. Add half of chicken to hot oil and fry until cooked through (chicken will sti be somewhat pale), 4 to 6 minutes, stirring frequently. Adjust burner, if necessary, to maintain oil temperatur between 300 and 350 degrees. Using slotted spoon or spider skimmer, tran fer fried chicken to prepared sheet. Return oil to 350 degrees and repeat with remaining chicken.

6. Warm sauce over medium heat unt simmering, about 1 minute. Toss sauce and chicken in large bowl until chicke is evenly coated. Serve, sprinkling indi vidual portions with scallions.

Chicken Before and After

1. Breaded The bag makes easy work of dredging the chicken pieces.

2. Fried Presaucing, the fried chicken pieces are paler than you might expect.

FOR ME, THE appeal of orange chicken is undeniable. Crispy fried bits of juicy boneless chicken tossed in a vibrant, sweet-sour, slightly spicy orange sauce—what's not to like? According to Panda Express cofounder Andrew Cherng, orange chicken was invented by chef Andy Kao in Hawaii in 1987. The layers of flavor that permeated the satisfying dish have made it a favorite ever since.

On a recent evening in my tiny kitchen, I looked around halfway through cooking a batch of orange chicken and found that I'd used nearly every mixing bowl in my cupboard and covered the entirety of my limited counter space with prep equipment and cornstarch—and I hadn't even begun to fry.

The end product—savory pieces of chicken tossed in a beautifully complex citrus sauce—tasted really good, but I wondered if I could find a way to make it without my wife (and my cat) looking askance at the mess.

I examined my working recipe and started asking some hard questions and doing a bit more testing to find out the answers. I'd been marinating the chicken and then patting it dry before coating and frying it, but after making a batch without the marinating step, I didn't miss it in the final dish. I would rely on the sauce to deliver the flavor.

What I really wanted was a way to coat the chicken with a mixture that would fry up crispy and crunchy but that didn't involve me dirtying several bowls and covering my kitchen in cornstarch. I turned to a technique we've used in the past for coating small pieces of chicken: shaking them together with the dredge ingredients in a large paper shopping bag.

After experimenting with different amounts of oil, from a couple cups to a couple quarts, I found that just 1 quart of oil (which measured about ¾ inch deep in my Dutch oven) worked perfectly. What's more, the frying oil could be strained and reused several times.

This orange chicken is a winner. The orange juice and zest make the sticky, sweet-and-sour sauce sing; the hot, freshly fried chicken stays crunchy until the end of the meal; and a side of rice soaks up all that lovely sauce, so every bite is vibrant.

Our potent finishing dressing is studded with minced shallot and grated citrus zest.

Spiced Citrus Chicken Breasts

Fast, easy, and incredibly flavorful? This recipe has it covered. **by Morgan Bolling**

CHICKEN BREAST PROS: It's readily available, relatively inexpensive, tender, quick cooking, and takes well to lots of different seasonings. Chicken breast cons: It's not exactly packed with flavor, and it can be dry.

My goal was to create a fast, easy dish that elevated chicken breasts from "just OK" to "fantastic." If you've ever had a salad topped with sliced chicken breast, you know that the salad dressing does a great job of adding flavor and moisture to this mild cut. I decided to steer my recipe down a similar path by topping simply seared chicken breasts with a vibrant vinaigrette.

I started by seasoning four boneless, skinless chicken breasts with salt and pepper and searing them in a little oil in a skillet. I let the cooked chicken rest while I stirred together a simple vinaigrette of olive oil, wine vinegar, minced shallot, and salt and pepper. I then sliced the breasts and poured the dressing over them.

It tasted pretty good, but the thinner, tapered ends of the chicken breasts dried out a little, and the dressing needed a bit more oomph. For my next test, I pounded the fatter ends of the breasts so that the pieces were all of an even thickness. This would help them cook at the same rate and stay juicy throughout. Next, I dredged the chicken breasts in flour before searing them to protect their exteriors from becoming tough; the seared flour also created a textured surface for the vinaigrette to cling to.

For an intense hit of citrus flavor in the dressing, I swapped out the vinegar for lemon juice enhanced with both lemon and orange zest. A little cinnamon and cumin rubbed onto the chicken before flouring contributed deep flavor and fragrance to the dish. A sprinkling of cilantro added a fresh herbal counterpoint to finish it off.

Rasp-Style Graters

The rasp-style grater shown here looks like a woodworking file, and there's a good reason for that: The company that invented it, Grace Manufacturing, also makes woodworking tools. We use this tool, the Microplane Premium Classic Zester/Grater ($15), to grate all sorts of foods, from citrus zest, garlic, and ginger to chocolate, nutmeg, and cheese.

■ SPICED CITRUS CHICKEN

Serves 4 to 6 Total Time: 50 minutes

We recommend using a rasp-style grater to grate the citrus zest.

DRESSING

- ¼ cup extra-virgin olive oil
- 3 tablespoons minced shallot
- 1 teaspoon sugar
- 1 teaspoon grated orange zest
- ½ teaspoon grated lemon zest plus 2 tablespoons juice
- ¼ teaspoon table salt

CHICKEN

- 1½ teaspoons table salt
- 1½ teaspoons ground cumin
- ¾ teaspoon ground cinnamon
- ½ teaspoon pepper
- ⅓ cup all-purpose flour
- 4 (6- to 8-ounce) boneless, skinless chicken breasts, trimmed
- 2 tablespoons extra-virgin olive oil
- 2 tablespoons fresh cilantro leaves

1. FOR THE DRESSING: Combine all ingredients in bowl; set aside.

2. FOR THE CHICKEN: Combine salt, cumin, cinnamon, and pepper in small bowl. Spread flour in shallow dish. Place chicken between 2 sheets of plastic wrap. Using meat pounder, gently pound thick part of breasts to ¾-inch thickness.

3. Sprinkle spice mixture all over chicken. Working with 1 breast at a time, dredge in flour, shaking off excess, and transfer to large plate.

4. Heat oil in 12-inch nonstick skillet over medium heat until shimmering. Add chicken to skillet and cook until well browned and registering 160 degrees, about 8 minutes per side. Transfer to carving board and let rest for 5 minutes.

5. Slice chicken crosswise on bias and transfer to serving platter. Stir dressing to recombine and spoon over chicken. Sprinkle with cilantro and serve.

NUTELLA
RUGELACH

APRICOT JAM
RUGELACH

CINNAMON-WALNUT
RUGELACH

RASPBERRY JAM
RUGELACH

Rugelach

These little roll-up cookies hold treasures inside. **by Mark Huxsoll**

RUGELACH, SWEET ROLLED cookies popular in Jewish bakeries around the world, come in at least two distinct variations. The first is built on a yeasted dough and is most often found in Israel and among Mizrahi and Sephardic Jewish communities in many countries. The second is made from a dough that's highly enriched with cream cheese and is much more common in the United States (see "Backstory"). Both share the same name, rugelach, which is derived from the Yiddish and connotes the idea of a "twist."

I first fell in love with rugelach as a kid, when the bakery attendant at my local grocery store would slip me (and other well-behaved youngsters) a cookie. On lucky days, it would be a chocolate-filled rugelach, the kind made with cream cheese in the dough. I brought these memories with me into the test kitchen as I began work on my own recipe.

I started, of course, with the dough. After researching several recipes and carefully adjusting the amounts of flour, fat, and sugar, I had a dough that was lightly sweet with a pleasant tanginess from the cream cheese (and some sour cream, too). The dough came together quickly in the food processor. I set it in

the refrigerator to chill for an hour.

I rolled the chilled dough into a 12-inch circle, spread it with Nutella, and then used a pizza wheel to cut the circle into 16 equal wedges. I then rolled up each wedge from the edge to the center of the circle, creating the little "twists." Brushed with egg wash for shine and sprinkled with demerara sugar for sparkle, my rugelach baked up to a deep golden brown, and my Nutella filling didn't ooze. Picture perfect.

Rugelach Construction

We use a pizza wheel to cut equal-size wedges for rolling up.

■ NUTELLA RUGELACH

Serves 8 (Makes 32 cookies)
Total Time: 1¾ hours, plus 1 hour 20 minutes chilling and cooling

The demerara sugar adds a nice crunch to these rugelach, but they are still great without it. If you have packets of Sugar in the Raw at home, you can use those in place of the demerara. When brushing the rugelach with the egg wash, brush only a few cookies at a time and then sprinkle them with the demerara sugar immediately. If you brush the egg wash onto all the rugelach at once, it will begin to dry by the time you get to the last rugelach, and the sugar won't stick.

1½	cups (7½ ounces) all-purpose flour
¼	cup (1¾ ounces) granulated sugar
¼	teaspoon table salt
6	ounces cream cheese, cut into 3 pieces and chilled
10	tablespoons unsalted butter, cut into ½-inch pieces and chilled
¼	cup sour cream
⅔	cup Nutella, divided
1	large egg, beaten with 1 tablespoon water
1	tablespoon demerara sugar

1. Process flour, granulated sugar, and salt in food processor until combined, about 3 seconds. Add cream cheese and pulse until large, irregularly sized chunks of cream cheese form with some small pieces interspersed throughout, about 5 pulses. Scatter butter over top and pulse until butter is size of large peas, 5 to 7 pulses.

2. Add sour cream and process until dough forms little clumps that hold together when pinched with your fingers (dough will look crumbly), about 10 seconds.

3. Transfer dough to clean counter and knead briefly until dough just comes together, about 3 turns. Divide dough in half (each piece should weigh about 11 ounces) and form each piece into 4-inch disk. Wrap disks individually with plastic wrap and refrigerate for at least 1 hour or up to 2 days.

4. Adjust oven rack to middle position and heat oven to 375 degrees. Line baking sheet with parchment paper. Roll 1 dough disk into 12-inch circle on lightly floured counter. Using offset spatula, spread ⅓ cup Nutella evenly over entire surface of circle. Using pizza wheel or sharp knife, cut through center of circle to form 16 equal wedges. Starting at wide edge of each wedge, roll dough toward point and transfer to prepared sheet, seam side down.

5. Wipe counter clean, dust counter with additional flour, and repeat with remaining dough disk and remaining ⅓ cup Nutella. Arrange rugelach in 8 rows of four on sheet.

6. Working with few rugelach at a time, brush tops with egg wash, then sprinkle with demerara sugar. Bake until golden brown, 30 to 35 minutes. Let cookies cool completely on sheet, about 20 minutes. Serve.

CINNAMON-WALNUT RUGELACH

Omit Nutella. Pulse ½ cup walnuts, ½ cup packed brown sugar, 1½ teaspoons ground cinnamon, and ¼ teaspoon table salt in food processor until finely ground, about 20 pulses. Sprinkle half of filling over each dough circle.

JAM RUGELACH

Substitute raspberry or apricot jam for Nutella. (If jam contains large chunks of fruit, process jam in food processor to smooth, spreadable consistency before using.) Be sure to check for doneness at 30 minutes; jam tends to accelerate browning on bottom of rugelach.

BACKSTORY
The Rise of Cream Cheese Dough

The family tree of rolled pastries in the European tradition sprawls from French croissants to Viennese kipfel. Rugelach share roots with some of these treats, but according to food writer Tami Ganeles Weiser, the style of rugelach most common in the United States—made with a nonyeasted dough built on rich cream cheese—is a relatively new American twist. As she writes in *Tablet* magazine, ". . . the creation of rugelach, as we know them today—cookies made from yeast-free dough, rather than yeasted pastries—happened in the United States, less than a century ago, as a result of the commercialization of one of its key ingredients: cream cheese."

Cream cheese was first developed commercially in the United States in the late 19th century, when dairies proliferated across the Northeast (especially in New York, New Jersey, and Pennsylvania). Soft, creamy cheeses similar to French Neufchâtel were in vogue, particularly in Philadelphia.

Grocers in other parts of the country wanted to stock the good stuff, too, but a lack of reliable refrigerated transportation prohibited this. Things changed over the ensuing decades as factories expanded and refrigeration techniques improved. By the 1920s, big companies, including Kraft, whose "Philadelphia" brand became a market leader, had stepped into the market. Sales grew through the 1930s.

But the real coming-out party for cream cheese dough was the 1939 World's Fair in New York, which attracted some 44 million visitors. There, Kraft distributed thousands of booklets (pictured here) filled with recipes using marquee products such as Velveeta, Miracle Whip, and Philadelphia Cream Cheese. A recipe for apricot tarts featured a dough made with cream cheese. Home cooks loved the dough, which inspired countless new recipes, including a new twist on rugelach.

Through the middle of the 20th century, recipes for rugelach made with cream cheese dough appeared frequently in American cookbooks and magazines. And today, while you may still come across beautiful versions of rugelach made with yeasted dough in the United States, the cream cheese version, like the one in our pages here, is more common.

The Largest-Selling Packaged Cheese in the World!

PHILADELPHIA PASTEURIZED CREAM CHEESE
A Kraft-Phenix Cheese
Guaranteed Fresh!

A cheese with a flavor that's both delicate and rich! So soft you can spread it with a knife . . . or, with a fork and a little milk, whip it up like cream! It's "Philadelphia Brand" Cream Cheese!

Cream cheese, like milk, must be fresh if it is to have rich, delicate flavor. Exquisite freshness is the secret of "Philadelphia Brand's" marvelous flavor and texture. Kraft makes this famous brand of cream cheese in a spotless plant near your home! . . . rushes it new-made to grocers in fast service trucks! Kraft guarantees the freshness of "Philadelphia Brand".

Always look for the name "Philadelphia Brand" on the little silver foil package you buy.

Cast Iron Pork Fajitas

The goal: a satisfying supper in just one pan. **by Amanda Luchtel**

Cooking over medium heat allows us to achieve great browning without setting off the smoke alarm.

EVERY TIME I visit my local Tex-Mex restaurant, I contemplate ordering several different dishes, but inevitably I hear the familiar, mesmerizing sizzle of fajitas being delivered to a neighboring table. I smell the tantalizing aromas from the searing-hot grilled meat and charred vegetables, and I am overcome with what I like to call "Fajita FOMO" (fear of missing out). I order the fajitas.

Restaurants have an advantage with multipart dishes such as fajitas—a team of cooks. There may be a cook at the meat station, a cook overseeing vegetables, and still another responsible for tortillas. But I wanted a weeknight version at home, where it's just me doing the cooking, and I wanted to use only one pan: my trusty cast-iron skillet.

The most challenging part of fajitas is the meat. Chicken, steak, and shrimp are the usual suspects because they're tender and cook quickly. I wanted to branch out with another popular quick-cooking, tender cut: pork tenderloin. With a flavorful spice rub (mine would include pepper, cumin, chili powder, granulated garlic, dried oregano, allspice, and plenty of salt), it would be a hit.

A Serious Pan

This recipe calls for a 12-inch cast-iron skillet (you can also use a nonstick skillet); cast iron retains heat well and thus is a good option for browning foods. When properly maintained, a cast-iron pan develops a nonstick surface. We use these heavy pans—our winning 12-inch model weighs more than 7 pounds—for shallow frying; baking cornbread; searing steaks and chops; and, yes, making fajitas.

LODGE CLASSIC CAST IRON SKILLET, 12"
Our testing winner

Pepper Prepping

Here's an easy way to cut bell peppers into strips: Stand the pepper stem side up and cut down to remove a plank (try to avoid the ribs and seeds inside). Rotate the pepper and repeat cutting around it, and then cut the planks into strips.

To make enough for four to six people, I needed to use two tenderloins. I cut them in half crosswise to create pieces that would fit side by side in my cast-iron pan. But I still wasn't achieving the even browning I wanted with the cylindrical pieces. Pounding them into ¾-inch-thick steaks helped achieve more browning; plus, it increased their surface area, so the pork held more of the spice rub.

The next thing to figure out was how to make the rest of the dish in the same pan. First searing the pork and then cooking the vegetables while the pork rested was an easy call to make; because the skillet is already hot, the peppers and onion blister, soften, and brown very quickly. And in a happy twist, I found that the bits of delicious spice rub left behind after removing the meat adhered easily to the vegetables, distributing more flavor throughout the dish.

A smoky kitchen is a real pitfall when it comes to fajitas, especially when cooking at high heat. Restaurants have ventilation systems to handle this, but I needed to find a way to avoid setting off the smoke alarm. After a few tests, I realized that cast iron, with its strong heat retention, would allow me to cook everything just right even if I lowered my heat to medium—no need for an industrial Vent-A-Hood.

After slicing the succulent pork into fajita-size strips, I pushed the vegetables to one side of the skillet to make room for the pork and brought the cast-iron pan straight to the table to serve.

Go to CooksCountry.com/fajitas to find our recipe for Grilled Steak Fajitas and our On the Road story on Ninfa's in Houston, Texas.

■ CAST IRON PORK FAJITAS

Serves 4 to 6 Total Time: 55 minutes

Serve the fajitas with pico de gallo, avocado or guacamole, sour cream, your favorite hot sauce, and lime wedges. A nonstick skillet can also be used here; in step 3, add 2 tablespoons of oil to the skillet, swirl to coat, and heat until the oil is just smoking.

2½ teaspoons kosher salt, divided
1½ teaspoons pepper, divided
1 teaspoon ground cumin
1 teaspoon chili powder
1 teaspoon granulated garlic
1 teaspoon dried oregano
⅛ teaspoon ground allspice
2 (12- to 16-ounce) pork tenderloins, trimmed
3 tablespoons vegetable oil, divided
2 yellow, red, orange, or green bell peppers, stemmed, seeded, and cut into ¼-inch-wide strips
1 onion, halved and sliced ¼ inch thick
2 garlic cloves, minced
¼ cup chopped fresh cilantro
1 tablespoon lime juice
12 (6-inch) flour tortillas, warmed

1. Combine 2 teaspoons salt, 1 teaspoon pepper, cumin, chili powder, granulated garlic, oregano, and allspice in bowl.
2. Cut tenderloins in half crosswise. Working with 1 piece at a time, cover pork with plastic wrap and, using meat pounder, pound to even ¾-inch thickness. Pat pork dry with paper towels and sprinkle with spice mixture.
3. Heat 12-inch cast-iron skillet over medium heat for 3 minutes. Add 2 tablespoons oil to skillet and swirl to coat. Place pork in skillet and cook until meat is well browned on both sides and registers 135 to 140 degrees, 5 to 7 minutes per side. Transfer to carving board, tent with aluminum foil, and let rest while preparing pepper mixture.
4. Add remaining 1 tablespoon oil and bell peppers to now-empty skillet and cook for 3 minutes. Stir in onion, remaining ½ teaspoon salt, and remaining ½ teaspoon pepper and cook until vegetables are just softened, 3 to 5 minutes. Stir in garlic and cook until fragrant, about 30 seconds. Off heat, stir in cilantro and lime juice.
5. Slice pork thin crosswise. Stir any accumulated pork juices from carving board into vegetables. Push vegetables to 1 side of skillet and place pork on empty side. Serve pork and vegetables with tortillas.

Testing Colanders
by Kate Shannon

A GOOD COLANDER is a kitchen asset—and not just for pasta lovers. We use ours for draining many foods, from blanched vegetables to produce we've salted to shed liquid. We wondered if our previous favorite was still the best. We skipped silicone models (they're tippy) and those with a few big clusters of holes (food slips out and liquid drains slowly) and focused on stainless-steel colanders covered in tiny perforations. We bought six models, priced from about $15 to about $26, and used each to drain angel hair pasta; orzo; and diced, salted cucumbers.

We noticed big differences when using the colanders to drain pasta. Here's what mattered: bowl and base heights. If their bowls were too shallow, orzo sloshed up and out of them. Meanwhile, models with short bases were temporarily submerged in the draining cooking water and any gunk in the sink. Our previous favorite and a nearly identical model had 4¼-inch-tall bowls and 1⅛-inch-tall bases that kept foods both contained and clean. We're sticking with our longtime winner, the RSVP International Endurance Precision Pierced 5 Qt. Colander, because we have nearly two decades of experience using it. However, the other model, by Bellemain, would also be a welcome addition to any kitchen.

Anatomy of a Winner
The many positive attributes of the RSVP International model we tested made it our winner again.

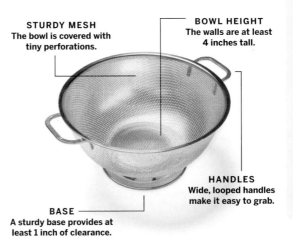

STURDY MESH
The bowl is covered with tiny perforations.

BOWL HEIGHT
The walls are at least 4 inches tall.

HANDLES
Wide, looped handles make it easy to grab.

BASE
A sturdy base provides at least 1 inch of clearance.

Skip These Styles

Clustered Perforations
Large holes grouped together with lots of solid patches of metal mean food escapes and liquid drains very slowly.

Over-the-Sink Strainers
Expandable handles can keep these models off the sink's floor, but only if they're a perfect fit. Otherwise, they fall into the sink.

Collapsible Models
Soft models that collapse for storage and expand for use are likely to collapse or tip over during use. They are also prone to fading.

KEY   Good ★★★   Fair ★★   Poor ★

HIGHLY RECOMMENDED

RSVP International Endurance Precision Pierced 5 Qt. Colander
Model: PUNCH-5   **Price:** $25.60
Capacity: 5 qt   **Height of Bowl:** 4¼ in
Style of Base: Metal ring   **Height of Base:** 1⅛ in

Performance ★★★
Feet and Handles ★★★
Cleanup and Durability ★★★

Comments: This simple colander is the best we've ever tested. Liquids drained quickly from the bowl's many tiny perforations. Its tall base lifted it high in the sink. We also like that it's dishwasher-safe and didn't dent when we dropped it.

Bellemain 5 Quart Stainless Steel Colander
Model: 82391   **Price:** $17.50
Capacity: 5 qt   **Height of Bowl:** 4¼ in
Style of Base: Metal ring   **Height of Base:** 1⅛ in

Performance ★★★
Feet and Handles ★★★
Cleanup and Durability ★★★

Comments: The only noticeable difference between this model and our favorite is that its handles are attached with rivets. Like our favorite, it drained quickly, it's dishwasher-safe, and its tall base lifted it high above draining water in the sink.

Web subscribers can see the complete results chart at CooksCountry.com/jan21.

One-Pot Shrimp Piccata Pasta

Improve your scampi game with this lively mash-up of two classic dishes.

by Matthew Fairman

IMAGINE A ONE-POT shrimp pasta dish: a cross between a garlicky scampi and a zippy, lemony piccata, with a little bit of creamy sauce tossed in for good measure.

That's what I was craving when I started work on this recipe. I wanted tender, succulent shrimp (they easily turn rubbery if they're overcooked) and lots of rich, silky sauce balanced with just enough vibrant lemon and briny capers. The sauce needed to be fully flavored with garlic and white wine, but it also needed to support (not upstage) the star of the show: the shrimp.

You see, I love shrimp. I grew up in coastal South Carolina eating shrimp for dinner that had been caught on day boats that very morning. Those shrimp boils were my favorite meals of the year, so every time I eat shrimp, I compare them to those superfresh morsels. Now, I know that most of the time you can't find shrimp that fresh at the market, but I also know that if you're careful to buy the right thing, you can find excellent flash-frozen shrimp in many grocery stores. That's why, now that I've moved away from South Carolina, I look for individually quick frozen (IQF) shell-on shrimp that are wild caught in U.S. waters. They should be untreated, meaning the only ingredient listed on the package should be shrimp (not salt or additives such as sodium tripolyphosphate). And I always, always use the shells to make a simple shrimp stock—why throw away all that flavor?

My recipe for shrimp piccata pasta begins with lightly browning the shrimp shells in oil with garlic and anchovies and then adding wine and water and simmering them for just 5 minutes to build a flavorful base for the pasta sauce. Using the shells like this is an easy way to cook the flavor of shrimp into the sauce without ever having to worry about overcooking the shrimp themselves. Shrimp are best when cooked gently for just a couple minutes.

Cooking the pasta in the garlicky shrimp stock (after you've removed the shells) does a lot for this recipe. For one thing, it means that you need only one pot and you never have to pull out the colander to drain the pasta, so you end up with fewer dishes to wash. More important, cooking the pasta (I like orecchiette here for the way it cups and captures the sauce) in just enough flavorful stock means that the starches from the pasta thicken the cooking liquid, yielding a luscious, creamy sauce. When the pasta is just al dente, you add the seasoned shrimp and gently poach them for 2 minutes in the garlicky sauce.

Adding fresh, citrusy parsley; a squeeze of lemon juice along with grated lemon zest; and a sprinkling of capers provides just enough of an acidic counterpoint to balance the richness of the creamy sauce, and grated Parmesan adds a salty, savory finishing touch that takes this shrimp pasta from delicious to irresistible.

I've gotten hungry just thinking about it, so I think I'm going to make it again for dinner tonight. I hope you will, too.

Turn Trash into Treasure

You could throw away the shells after prepping the shrimp, but you'd be doing yourself a disservice. This recipe calls for using these leftover materials to make an easy shrimp stock; it takes only about 15 minutes, and the flavor and body this stock adds to the final dish is substantial.

SHRIMP SHELLS
Brown the shells, add liquid, simmer, and strain. The resulting stock is deeply flavorful.

"Orecchiette" means "little ears" in Italian.

■ ONE-POT SHRIMP PICCATA PASTA

Serves 4 Total Time: 1 hour 5 minutes

You can substitute 12 ounces (4½ cups) of medium pasta shells for the orecchiette, if desired. We prefer untreated shrimp (those not treated with salt or additives such as sodium tripolyphosphate). Most frozen E-Z peel shrimp have been treated (the ingredient list should tell you). If you're using treated shrimp, do not salt the shrimp in step 1. You can use medium or large shrimp, but you may need to reduce the cooking time in step 5. The pasta will not absorb all the cooking liquid in step 4; stirring vigorously in step 5 helps thicken the sauce so that it coats the pasta.

- 1 pound extra-large shrimp (21 to 25 per pound), peeled, deveined, and tails removed, shells reserved
- 2½ teaspoons table salt, divided
- ¼ cup extra-virgin olive oil
- 7 garlic cloves, peeled (6 smashed, 1 minced)
- 2 anchovy fillets, rinsed (optional)
- ½ cup dry white wine
- 3½ cups water
- 12 ounces (3⅓ cups) orecchiette
- ⅓ cup chopped fresh parsley
- 2 tablespoons capers, rinsed
- ½ teaspoon grated lemon zest plus 1 tablespoon juice
- ½ teaspoon red pepper flakes
  Grated Parmesan cheese

1. Cut shrimp crosswise into thirds. Sprinkle shrimp with ½ teaspoon salt; set aside. Combine reserved shrimp shells; oil; smashed garlic; and anchovies, if using, in large Dutch oven and cook over medium heat until shells are spotty brown, 5 to 7 minutes.

2. Stir in wine and cook until liquid is nearly evaporated, about 2 minutes. Add water and remaining 2 teaspoons salt, increase heat to high, and bring to boil. Reduce heat to medium-low, cover, and simmer for 5 minutes.

3. Using spider skimmer or slotted spoon, remove shells from shrimp stock and transfer to bowl. (Some garlic cloves may be inadvertently removed at this point; this is OK.) Pour any stock that has accumulated in bottom of bowl back into pot. Discard shells.

4. Stir pasta into stock and bring to simmer. Cover; reduce heat to medium-low; and simmer, stirring occasionally, until pasta is al dente, 10 to 14 minutes (some liquid will remain in bottom of pot when pasta is al dente).

5. Stir in shrimp and cook, uncovered, until opaque, about 2 minutes, stirring often. Off heat, stir in parsley, capers, lemon zest and juice, pepper flakes, and minced garlic. Stir vigorously until sauce is thickened, about 1 minute. Serve with Parmesan.

Garlicky Broccoli Salad

What's the best way to add deep flavor to broccoli florets? Char them. **by Mark Huxsoll**

BROCCOLI DOESN'T NEED to be bland or boring. It shouldn't be overcooked to mush, underseasoned, or gray, either.

I wanted to create a broccoli salad that brought out the best in broccoli by highlighting its mildly bitter flavor. My goal was a salad that would be bold; flavorful; and substantial enough to work as a starter, side, or even a main dish.

To augment the broccoli's flavor, I turned to a method we've used before with great success—skillet roasting. While moist cooking methods such as boiling or steaming discourage browning and don't add much flavor, skillet roasting builds deep flavor by using dry, relatively high heat to create tasty char.

I found that by fully filling the pan (a nonstick skillet is best here) with florets, usually something we discourage, the broccoli on top steamed and began to soften while the broccoli on the bottom picked up considerable browning and deep flavor. The key was to stir the florets well, at 5-minute intervals throughout the cooking, so that all the broccoli was redistributed from the bottom to the top and had a perfect balance of crispy char and tender texture.

To turn the charred and tender broccoli into a salad, I needed to add a few more components. For savoriness, I added one medium red onion, halved and sliced thin, that I quickly softened in the skillet (and transferred to a bowl) before the broccoli went in. And for a bold, creamy dressing, I started with a silky combination of mayonnaise and olive oil and then layered in grated Parmesan, minced garlic, lemon juice, and red pepper flakes for heat.

The dressed broccoli and onion tasted great, but I was looking for one more element to add bulk and flavor. I tested cubed potatoes, cooked rice,

and different shapes of pasta, but in the end, beans were the ticket. I tried both white and red beans before landing on a test kitchen staple: canned chickpeas. The chickpeas, simply drained, rinsed, and left to absorb flavor in the dressing while the onion and broccoli cooked, brought an earthy savor and made the salad truly substantial. Delicious.

GARLICKY BROCCOLI AND CHICKPEA SALAD
Serves 4 to 6
Total Time: 50 minutes
The skillet will look very full when you add the broccoli in step 3, but the broccoli will shrink as it cooks. The broccoli pieces will begin to look very dark during cooking. This is OK.

- 1 ounce Parmesan cheese, grated (½ cup)
- ½ cup extra-virgin olive oil, divided
- 2 tablespoons lemon juice
- 3 garlic cloves, minced
- 1 tablespoon mayonnaise
- ½ teaspoon red pepper flakes
- 1 (15-ounce) can chickpeas, rinsed
- 1 red onion, halved and sliced ½ inch thick
- 1 teaspoon table salt, divided
- 1 teaspoon pepper, divided
- 1½ pounds broccoli florets, cut into 2-inch pieces

1. Whisk Parmesan, ¼ cup oil, lemon juice, garlic, mayonnaise, and pepper flakes together in large bowl. Add chickpeas and toss to combine; set aside.
2. Heat 1 tablespoon oil in 12-inch nonstick skillet over medium heat until shimmering. Add onion, ¼ teaspoon salt, and ½ teaspoon pepper and cook until onion is tender and beginning to brown, 6 to 8 minutes, stirring occasionally. Transfer onion to bowl with chickpea mixture.
3. Heat remaining 3 tablespoons oil in now-empty skillet over medium heat until shimmering. Add broccoli, remaining ¾ teaspoon salt, and remaining ½ teaspoon pepper. Cook until broccoli is dark brown and crispy in spots, about 20 minutes, stirring every 5 minutes.
4. Transfer broccoli to bowl with chickpea mixture and toss to combine. Serve warm.

Broccoli Stalks and Leaves
We call for just the florets here, but the stalks and leaves are fully delicious, too. Lightly peel and slice the stalks and add them raw to salads or sauté or steam them. The leaves have a strong flavor reminiscent of kale and are best lightly cooked.

Charred edges add dimension and complexity to broccoli.

One Pan, Two Cooking Methods
We usually advise against overcrowding a skillet, but with this technique—cooking over medium heat in a nonstick skillet, stirring occasionally—it works, producing tender florets with nice charring.

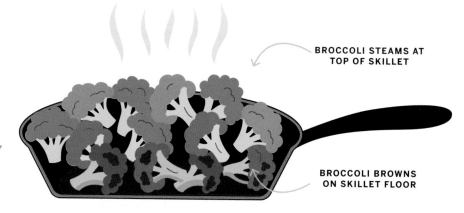

BROCCOLI STEAMS AT TOP OF SKILLET

BROCCOLI BROWNS ON SKILLET FLOOR

Bolos are bigger and richer than English muffins, and they're great for sandwiches and burgers, too.

Building the Bolos
Here's how we shape the muffins.

1. Portion After first rise, divide dough into 8 equal pieces.

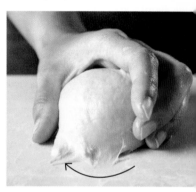

2. Round Cup each piece and roll in circles to create taut dough balls.

3. Flatten Use your hand to flatten each ball into disk.

4. Weight Top with baking sheet so disks don't puff too much before browning.

Bolos Lêvedos

Once you have these Portuguese breakfast treats around the house, you'll find dozens of ways to enjoy them.   **by Mark Huxsoll**

BOLOS LÊVEDOS, AT first glance, look a lot like English muffins. But these Portuguese treats ("bolos" means "cakes," and "lêvedos" means "yeast"), originally from the Azores, are denser, sweeter, and richer than English muffins, thanks to whole milk, eggs, and butter. To get their classic look, they are cooked on two sides on a dry griddle or skillet. They're often eaten for breakfast, but they can also be used as burger buns or sandwich bread.

Inspired by a visit to Central Bakery, a Portuguese bakery in Tiverton, Rhode Island (see "A Mighty Muffin"), that turns out hundreds of bolos lêvedos a day, I set out to create a small-scale recipe for the home kitchen.

After a few experiments with existing recipes, I zeroed in on some techniques we've used with other rich yeasted doughs that I knew would help here.

First, to ensure that the dough would be well hydrated enough to create a tender finished product, I followed a method called tang-zhong, which involves heating a small portion of flour and liquid to form a paste before mixing in the rest of the ingredients. This method helped the flour more readily absorb the liquid from the milk, eggs, and butter, creating a more workable dough and more tender and moist bolos (it also helped the cooked bolos stay fresh longer).

Second, I found that the additions of sugar and salt, essential to bolos, were impeding the absorption of the liquid. To solve the issue, I introduced an autolyse step, mixing everything together (except for the sugar and salt) and allowing it to rest for 15 minutes to fully hydrate and get a head start on gluten development. Only then did I incorporate the sugar and salt and finish kneading the dough.

With these two extra steps, plus a traditional two-part rise (first all together and then in individual portions; see "Building the Bolos" for information on portioning), I was able to brown my bolos in a nonstick skillet for that signature exterior color and then transfer them to a baking sheet and finish them off in the oven. You wouldn't believe how incredible my kitchen smelled as they baked; waiting for them to cool down was almost intolerable.

BOLOS LÊVEDOS (PORTUGUESE MUFFINS)

Makes 8 muffins
Total Time: 1½ hours, plus 2½ hours rising and cooling

If you don't own a microwave, the flour paste can also be made in a small saucepan over medium heat. Just be sure to whisk it constantly so that the ingredients don't scorch. Split the muffins with a knife. Serve them with butter or use them as sandwich bread or burger buns.

FLOUR PASTE
- ⅔ cup water
- ¼ cup (1¼ ounces) all-purpose flour

DOUGH
- 6 tablespoons whole milk
- 4 tablespoons unsalted butter, cut into 4 pieces and softened
- 2 large eggs
- 3 cups (15 ounces) all-purpose flour, plus extra for shaping
- 1 teaspoon instant or rapid-rise yeast
- ½ cup (3½ ounces) sugar
- 1 teaspoon table salt
- 1 teaspoon vegetable oil

1. FOR THE FLOUR PASTE: Whisk water and flour in medium bowl until no lumps remain. Microwave, whisking every 20 seconds, until mixture thickens to stiff, smooth, pudding-like consistency, 40 to 50 seconds. Transfer paste to bowl of stand mixer.

2. FOR THE DOUGH: Whisk milk into flour paste in bowl of stand mixer until combined. Whisk in butter until fully incorporated. Whisk in eggs until fully incorporated.

3. Add flour and yeast to paste mixture. Fit mixer with dough hook and mix on low speed until dough comes together and no dry flour remains, about 2 minutes. Turn off mixer, cover bowl with dish towel or plastic wrap, and let dough stand for 15 minutes.

4. Add sugar and salt to dough and mix on low speed until incorporated, about 1 minute. Increase speed to medium and mix until dough is elastic and pulls away from sides of bowl but still sticks to bottom (dough will be sticky), about 8 minutes. Transfer dough to greased large bowl; cover tightly with plastic wrap; and let rise until doubled in size, about 1½ hours.

5. Line rimmed baking sheet with parchment paper. Turn out dough onto clean counter and divide into 8 equal pieces, about 4 ounces each. Working with 1 piece of dough at a time, cup dough with your palm and roll against counter in circular motion into smooth, tight ball.

6. Sprinkle ¼ cup flour on counter. Working with 1 dough ball at a time, turn dough ball in flour and press with your hand to flatten into 3½- to 4-inch disk. Transfer dough disks to prepared sheet. Lay second sheet of parchment over dough disks, then place second rimmed baking sheet on top to keep disks flat during second rise. Let rise for 30 minutes. Adjust oven rack to middle position and heat oven to 350 degrees.

7. Heat oil in 12-inch nonstick skillet over medium-low heat until shimmering. Using paper towels, carefully wipe out oil from skillet.

8. Transfer 4 dough disks to skillet and cook until deeply browned on both sides, 2 to 4 minutes per side. Return toasted disks to sheet. Repeat with remaining 4 dough disks.

9. Bake until muffins register 190 degrees in center, 11 to 14 minutes. Transfer muffins to wire rack and let cool for 30 minutes. Serve. (Muffins can be stored in airtight container for up to 3 days or frozen for up to 1 month.)

BOLOS LÊVEDOS (PORTUGUESE MUFFINS) WITH LEMON AND CINNAMON

Add 1½ teaspoons grated lemon zest and ¼ teaspoon ground cinnamon with flour in step 3.

Easy Techniques

In this recipe we use a technique called **tangzhong**, which involves heating a mixture of water and flour (we use the microwave) until it forms a paste and then mixing it into the dough. This method helps the flour absorb the liquid it is cooked with, resulting in a moister final product. We also employ a technique called **autolyse**, giving the dough a short, 15-minute rest before we add the salt and sugar. This rest allows the flour to fully absorb the liquid and develop just the right amount of gluten for a satisfyingly chewy bolo.

A Mighty Muffin

Text by Bryan Roof; photos by Steve Klise

CENTRAL BAKERY IN Tiverton, Rhode Island, makes only one thing: bolos lêvedos. But brothers Paul and David Lopes believe this laser focus is the key to their 30-plus years of success.

"My mom and dad came to the United States and realized no one was making the muffins. In 1974, they started making them in their garage, then opened up their first bakery," Paul says. The muffins were based on the recipe Lopes's grandmother used back on São Miguel, an island in the Azores.

Business took off, thanks to word of mouth. "One of my dad's first big hits was on Cape Cod [in the late 1970s]," Paul says. Vacationing New Yorkers brought word of the muffins back to the city, starting a sales boom.

Paul credits the company's evolution to his customers. "In Portugal, the only thing they used the muffins for was breakfast. But the American public got really creative," Paul says. "Now, the number one use for this product is a hamburger bun." Central Bakery, an exclusively wholesale operation today, supplies Madison Square Garden and Yankee Stadium, among others.

Sticking to a single product confounds some customers. "I'll talk to a retailer and he'll say, 'What else do you have?' and I'll say, 'This is it,' and he'll say, 'You make just one product since 1974?' But it's keeping our doors open."

That extreme focus extends to the recipe and process, too. The brothers keep the specifics top secret. "We've tried to adapt, but it's not the same."

The Lopes brothers (left), second-generation operators of Central Bakery, based their recipe for bolos lêvedos (also called Portuguese muffins) on a family recipe brought from the Azores. Their mother, Leonor (above), and father, Tiberio, started the business in 1974.

Enjoy this flavorful dip at brunch or during cocktail hour. You can even serve it as a light supper.

Smoked Salmon Dip

To add excitement to our smoked salmon dip, we assembled a strong supporting cast. **by Amanda Luchtel**

I LOVE A FULLY loaded bagel on a weekend morning. I'm talking a schmear of cream cheese, smoked salmon, sliced onions, briny capers, fresh dill—the whole nine yards. It's a perfect combination of flavors, so I wanted to bring it to cocktail hour, too. I set my sights on a dip that would highlight the subtle sweet and smoky flavors of the salmon, with a boost from a few complementary ingredients.

I started with an 8-ounce block of chilled cream cheese, which I cut into eight pieces. Then, in the food processor, I layered 4 ounces of smoked salmon on top of the cream cheese, added lemon zest and juice, and seasoned it with a twist of freshly ground black pepper (because smoked salmon is already salted, there was no need to add more salt here). The lemon helped cut the richness of the fatty salmon and cream cheese without disguising their flavors.

But my dip wasn't dippable: Crackers kept breaking in half. What's more, the lemon and smoked salmon weren't evenly distributed. So I decided to start with softened cream cheese, which meant taking it out of the refrigerator 30 minutes before processing it (or microwaving it—out of the foil package—for 20 to 30 seconds). This gave me a much more cohesive and easily scoopable dip that was ready for an array of flavorful toppings that would really make it sing.

Briny, pungent capers and chopped fresh dill were definitely in, but the raw red onion was overwhelming the other flavors in the dip. After a few taste tests, I found the delicate flavor of a shallot—just enough oniony flavor, but not too much—to be less harsh and more appealing. A finishing drizzle of extra-virgin olive oil helped smooth out the texture and tied everything together.

■ BAGEL CHIPS

Serves 4 to 6
Total Time: 50 minutes
Any type of savory bagel can be used in this recipe. Look for unsliced bagels, which are often available in the bakery section of the grocery store. This recipe can easily be doubled; to do so, divide the slices between two baking sheets and bake one sheet at a time.

  2 **(4- to 5-inch) bagels**
 ¼ **cup extra-virgin olive oil, divided**
 ¼ **teaspoon kosher salt, divided**

1. Adjust oven rack to middle position and heat oven to 350 degrees. Place bagels on cutting board. Using serrated knife, slice bagels vertically, ¼ inch thick (slices will vary in length). Cut any slices that barely hang together in center (from bagel's hole) in half.
2. Spread slices in single layer on rimmed baking sheet. Brush tops with 2 tablespoons oil and sprinkle with ⅛ teaspoon salt. Flip slices and repeat brushing and sprinkling on second side with remaining 2 tablespoons oil and remaining ⅛ teaspoon salt.
3. Bake until crisp and light golden brown, 13 to 17 minutes. Let cool on sheet for 5 minutes. Serve. (Chips can be stored in airtight container for up to 3 days.)

■ SMOKED SALMON DIP

Serves 4 to 6 (Makes about 1½ cups) *Total Time: 25 minutes*
To quickly soften the cream cheese, microwave it in a large bowl for 20 to 30 seconds. This recipe can easily be doubled. Serve with cucumber slices, crackers, toasted baguette, and/or our Bagel Chips.

  8 **ounces cream cheese, cut into 8 pieces and softened**
  4 **ounces smoked salmon**
  1 **teaspoon grated lemon zest plus 1 tablespoon juice**
 ¼ **teaspoon pepper**
  1 **tablespoon minced shallot**
  1 **tablespoon capers, rinsed**
  1 **tablespoon coarsely chopped fresh dill**
  1 **tablespoon extra-virgin olive oil**

1. Process cream cheese, salmon, lemon zest and juice, and pepper in food processor until smooth, about 30 seconds, scraping down sides of bowl as needed. Transfer to serving dish and spread into even layer.
2. Sprinkle with shallot, capers, and dill. Drizzle with oil and serve.

TO MAKE AHEAD
Dip can be made through step 1, covered with plastic wrap, and refrigerated for up to 3 days. Let come to room temperature before proceeding with step 2.

Buying Smoked Salmon
Our taste test winner is **Spence & Co. Traditional Scottish Style Smoked Salmon**. If you can't find it, look for a product without added sweeteners or color.

Broccoli Rabe with Polenta and Fried Eggs

QUICK DINNERS

Chicken and Cauliflower in Garam Masala Tomato Sauce

QUICK DINNERS

Kimchi, Beef, and Tofu Soup

QUICK DINNERS

Wedge Salad with Steak Tips

QUICK DINNERS

Chicken and Cauliflower in Garam Masala Tomato Sauce

Serves 4 Total Time: 30 minutes
Serve over basmati rice, sprinkled with fresh cilantro leaves.

- 1 tablespoon garam masala
- ¾ teaspoon table salt
- ½ teaspoon pepper
- 4 (6- to 8-ounce) boneless, skinless chicken breasts, trimmed and cut into 1-inch pieces
- 2 tablespoons vegetable oil, divided
- ½ head cauliflower (1 pound), cored and cut into ½-inch florets
- 1 onion, chopped fine
- 2 tablespoons grated fresh ginger
- 3 garlic cloves, minced
- 1 (28-ounce) can crushed tomatoes
- ¼ cup heavy cream

1. Combine garam masala, salt, and pepper in small bowl. Toss chicken, 1 tablespoon oil, and 1 tablespoon spice mixture together in medium bowl.
2. Heat remaining 1 tablespoon oil in Dutch oven over medium-high heat until shimmering. Add cauliflower and onion and cook until onion is softened, about 5 minutes. Stir in ginger, garlic, and remaining spice mixture and cook until fragrant, about 30 seconds. Add tomatoes and chicken to pot and bring to boil. Reduce heat to medium-low and simmer, uncovered, until chicken is cooked through and cauliflower is tender, 10 to 12 minutes.
3. Off heat, stir in cream. Season with salt and pepper to taste. Serve.

Broccoli Rabe with Polenta and Fried Eggs

Serves 4 Total Time: 30 minutes
Pecorino Romano cheese can be substituted for the Parmesan.

- 3 cups water
- ¾ cup instant polenta
- 2½ ounces Parmesan cheese, grated (1¼ cups), divided
- ½ cup oil-packed sun-dried tomatoes, chopped coarse
- 1 teaspoon table salt, divided
- ½ teaspoon pepper, divided
- 5 tablespoons extra-virgin olive oil, divided
- 1 pound broccoli rabe, trimmed and cut into 1-inch pieces
- 1 garlic clove, minced
- ¼ teaspoon red pepper flakes
- 4 large eggs

1. Adjust oven rack 4 inches from broiler element and heat broiler. Bring water to boil in large saucepan over high heat. Whisk in polenta; reduce heat to medium-low; and cook until thickened, about 3 minutes. Off heat, stir in 1 cup Parmesan, tomatoes, ½ teaspoon salt, and ¼ teaspoon pepper. Cover to keep warm.
2. Brush rimmed baking sheet with 1 tablespoon oil. Toss broccoli rabe, garlic, pepper flakes, ¼ teaspoon salt, and 3 tablespoons oil together in bowl; transfer to prepared sheet. Broil broccoli rabe until most leaves are lightly charred and stems are crisp-tender, about 5 minutes, tossing halfway through broiling. Tent with foil.
3. Heat remaining 1 tablespoon oil in 12-inch nonstick skillet over medium-high heat until shimmering. Crack eggs into skillet and sprinkle with remaining ¼ teaspoon salt and remaining ¼ teaspoon pepper. Cover and cook for 1 minute. Remove from heat and let sit for 15 to 45 seconds for runny yolks, 45 to 60 seconds for soft but set yolks, or about 2 minutes for medium-set yolks. Serve polenta with broccoli rabe and eggs, sprinkling individual portions with remaining ¼ cup Parmesan.

Wedge Salad with Steak Tips

Serves 4 Total Time: 30 minutes
Sirloin steak tips, also known as flap meat, can be sold as whole steaks, cubes, and strips. To ensure uniform pieces, we prefer to purchase whole steaks and cut them ourselves.

- 1½ pounds sirloin steak tips, trimmed and cut into 2-inch pieces
- 1 teaspoon table salt, divided
- ¾ teaspoon pepper, divided
- 2 tablespoons vegetable oil
- ¾ cup plain yogurt
- 3 ounces Stilton cheese, crumbled (¾ cup), divided
- 1 garlic clove, minced
- 1 teaspoon red wine vinegar
- 1 head iceberg lettuce (9 ounces), cored and cut into 8 wedges
- 10 ounces cherry tomatoes, halved
- 4 slices cooked bacon, crumbled into ½-inch pieces
- 2 tablespoons minced fresh chives

1. Pat steak dry with paper towels and sprinkle with ¾ teaspoon salt and ½ teaspoon pepper. Heat oil in 12-inch skillet over medium-high heat until just smoking. Add steak and cook until meat is well browned on all sides and registers 125 degrees (for medium-rare), about 7 minutes. Transfer to plate, tent with foil, and let rest for 5 minutes.
2. Meanwhile, whisk yogurt, ½ cup Stilton, garlic, vinegar, remaining ¼ teaspoon salt, and remaining ¼ teaspoon pepper together in bowl.
3. Arrange lettuce wedges and steak tips on 4 plates and drizzle with dressing. Top with tomatoes, bacon, and remaining ¼ cup Stilton. Sprinkle with chives and season with salt and pepper to taste. Serve.

Kimchi, Beef, and Tofu Soup

Serves 4 Total Time: 30 minutes
If there's not enough brine in the kimchi jar to yield ¼ cup, add water to compensate. Make sure to use firm (not soft) tofu here.

- 1 pound 85 percent lean ground beef
- ½ teaspoon table salt
- ½ teaspoon pepper
- 1 tablespoon grated fresh ginger
- ½ cup mirin
- 3 cups water
- 3 cups kimchi, drained with ¼ cup brine reserved, chopped coarse
- 2 cups chicken broth
- 8 ounces firm tofu, cut into ½-inch cubes
- 2 tablespoons soy sauce
- 4 scallions, sliced thin
- 1 tablespoon toasted sesame oil

1. Combine beef, salt, and pepper in Dutch oven; cook over medium-high heat, breaking up meat with wooden spoon, until moisture evaporates and beef begins to sizzle, 8 to 10 minutes.
2. Add ginger and cook until fragrant, about 30 seconds. Stir in mirin, scraping up any browned bits. Stir in water, kimchi and reserved brine, broth, tofu, and soy sauce and bring to boil. Reduce heat to low; cover; and simmer to allow flavors to meld, about 15 minutes.
3. Off heat, stir in scallions and oil. Serve.

Crispy Chicken with Spicy Carrot Salad

QUICK DINNERS

Bucatini with Peas, Kale, and Pancetta

QUICK DINNERS

Garlicky Roasted Shrimp with Napa Cabbage and Orange Salad

QUICK DINNERS

Chorizo, Corn, and Tomato Tostadas with Lime Crema

QUICK DINNERS

Bucatini with Peas, Kale, and Pancetta

Serves 4 Total Time: 30 minutes
You can substitute spaghetti or linguine for the bucatini.

2	ounces pancetta, cut into ½-inch pieces
2	garlic cloves, minced
1	tablespoon grated lemon zest, divided
½	cup dry white wine
2½	cups water
2	cups chicken broth
1	pound bucatini
½	cup panko bread crumbs
1	tablespoon extra-virgin olive oil
⅛	teaspoon table salt
⅛	teaspoon pepper
1½	ounces Parmesan cheese, grated (¾ cup), divided
5	ounces (5 cups) baby kale
1	cup frozen peas

1. Cook pancetta in Dutch oven over medium heat until crispy, 6 to 8 minutes; using slotted spoon, transfer pancetta to paper towel–lined plate. Add garlic and 2 teaspoons lemon zest to fat left in pot and cook until fragrant, about 30 seconds. Stir in wine, scraping up any browned bits, and cook until nearly evaporated, about 3 minutes. Stir in water and broth.
2. Increase heat to high and bring to boil. Stir in pasta; reduce heat to medium; and simmer vigorously, stirring often, until pasta is nearly tender, 8 to 10 minutes. Meanwhile, toss panko, oil, salt, and pepper together in bowl. Microwave, stirring often, until crumbs are golden brown, 3 to 5 minutes. Stir in ¼ cup Parmesan and remaining 1 teaspoon lemon zest; set aside.
3. Stir kale and peas into pasta and continue to simmer until pasta is tender, about 4 minutes longer. Add remaining ½ cup Parmesan and stir vigorously until pasta is creamy and well coated, about 30 seconds. Season with salt and pepper to taste. Serve, sprinkling each portion with pancetta and panko mixture.

Crispy Chicken with Spicy Carrot Salad

Serves 4 Total Time: 30 minutes
Use the large holes of a box grater to shred the carrots.

4	(10- to 12-ounce) bone-in split chicken breasts, trimmed and pounded to ¾-inch thickness
1½	teaspoons table salt, divided
1	teaspoon pepper, divided
1	pound carrots, shredded
1	(15-ounce) can chickpeas, rinsed
3	ounces feta cheese, cut into ½-inch pieces (¾ cup)
2	oranges, peeled and segmented
2	tablespoons harissa
2	tablespoons chopped fresh mint
2	tablespoons extra-virgin olive oil
1	tablespoon lemon juice

1. Pat chicken dry with paper towels and sprinkle with ¾ teaspoon salt and ½ teaspoon pepper. Place chicken, skin side down, in 12-inch nonstick skillet. Cover skillet and place over medium heat. Cook chicken, without moving it, until skin is light golden brown, about 15 minutes.
2. Meanwhile, combine carrots, chickpeas, feta, oranges, harissa, mint, oil, lemon juice, remaining ¾ teaspoon salt, and remaining ½ teaspoon pepper in bowl. Season with salt and pepper to taste.
3. Increase heat to medium-high and continue to cook chicken, covered, until skin is deep golden brown and chicken registers 160 degrees, 10 to 15 minutes longer, rotating skillet halfway through cooking. Transfer chicken to platter and let rest for 5 minutes. Serve chicken with salad.

Chorizo, Corn, and Tomato Tostadas with Lime Crema

Serves 4 Total Time: 30 minutes
Top these tostadas with fresh cilantro leaves and crumbled queso fresco.

1	(14-ounce) bag green coleslaw mix
1	tablespoon minced jarred jalapeños, plus ¼ cup brine, divided
¾	teaspoon plus ⅛ teaspoon table salt, divided
½	cup sour cream
3	tablespoons lime juice (2 limes), divided
1	tablespoon vegetable oil
3	cups frozen corn, thawed
8	ounces Spanish-style chorizo sausage, halved lengthwise and sliced ¼ inch thick
6	ounces cherry tomatoes, quartered
1	(15-ounce) can black beans, rinsed
¼	cup chicken broth
12	(6-inch) corn tostadas

1. Adjust oven racks to upper-middle and lower-middle positions; heat oven to 450 degrees. Combine coleslaw, 3 tablespoons jalapeño brine, and ¼ teaspoon salt in bowl. Combine sour cream, 2 tablespoons lime juice, and ⅛ teaspoon salt in second bowl; set aside slaw and crema.
2. Heat oil in 12-inch nonstick skillet over medium-high heat until shimmering. Add corn, chorizo, and ¼ teaspoon salt and cook until warmed through, about 5 minutes. Off heat, stir in tomatoes and remaining 1 tablespoon lime juice.
3. Microwave beans, broth, jalapeños and remaining 1 tablespoon brine, and remaining ¼ teaspoon salt in bowl until hot, about 2 minutes. Mash beans with potato masher until spreadable, then spread evenly over tostadas. Divide tostadas between 2 rimmed baking sheets and bake until warmed through, about 5 minutes. Divide corn mixture among tostadas, then top with slaw and crema. Serve.

Garlicky Roasted Shrimp with Napa Cabbage and Orange Salad

Serves 4 Total Time: 30 minutes
One large or two small bunches of basil will yield the ½ cup needed here.

¼	cup table salt for brining
2	pounds shell-on jumbo shrimp (16 to 20 per pound)
6	tablespoons extra-virgin olive oil, divided
3	scallions, white and green parts separated and sliced thin
2	garlic cloves, minced
1	teaspoon fennel seeds
½	teaspoon red pepper flakes
½	small head napa cabbage, cored and sliced thin
3	oranges, peeled, quartered, and sliced crosswise ½ inch thick
½	cup shredded fresh basil
1	tablespoon cider vinegar
¼	teaspoon table salt

1. Dissolve ¼ cup salt in 1 quart cold water in large container. Using kitchen shears, cut through shells of shrimp; devein shrimp but do not remove shell. Using paring knife, cut ½-inch-deep slit in each shrimp along vein line, taking care not to cut shrimp in half completely. Submerge shrimp in brine, cover, and refrigerate for 15 minutes.
2. Adjust oven rack 4 inches from broiler element and heat broiler. Combine ¼ cup oil, scallion greens, garlic, fennel seeds, and pepper flakes in large bowl. Remove shrimp from brine and pat dry with paper towels. Toss shrimp with oil mixture. Spread shrimp on wire rack set in rimmed baking sheet.
3. Broil shrimp until opaque and just browned, 2 to 4 minutes per side, rotating sheet halfway through broiling; transfer shrimp to serving platter. Combine cabbage, oranges, basil, vinegar, salt, scallion whites, and remaining 2 tablespoons oil in bowl. Serve shrimp with cabbage salad.

Wine IN THE KITCHEN

This precious fermented juice adds brightness and complexity to countless dishes. **by Scott Kathan**

CHOOSING WINES FOR COOKING

First off, since flavor nuances are diminished with cooking, it makes sense to save superexpensive wines for sipping. That said, the rule of "cook only with wines you'd be happy drinking" has merit; as such, avoid the salty "cooking wine" sold next to the vinegar in the supermarket.

For red wines, we generally recommend medium-bodied wines for cooking and found that blends, such as **Côtes du Rhône** or "table" wines, produced more complex results. If you prefer single varietals, **Pinot Noir** and **Merlot** are good choices. Steer clear of heavily oaked reds (those that have been aged in oak barrels that confer a strong, aromatic flavor) such as **Cabernet Sauvignon**, as the oak flavor can intensify through cooking and dominate the dish.

When cooking with white wine, we prefer dry, clean-tasting wines such as **Sauvignon Blanc** or a dry **Riesling**; as with red wines, we advise steering clear of oaky whites (like many **Chardonnays**).

Finally, boxed wines—both reds and whites—can be a great option in the kitchen, as many are high quality, affordable, and, once opened, keep for much longer than bottled wines.

* Do you *need* an electric wine opener? Well, no . . . but our winner, the **Cuisinart Cordless Electric Wine Opener** ($44) works great and is fun to use.

WHAT ARE TANNINS?

Tannins are polyphenols, a group of chemical compounds that occur in naturally high concentrations in foods like pomegranates, cranberries, and—you guessed it—grape skins. Tannins taste bitter and have an astringent quality that makes your tongue feel dry. They are an invaluable component in bold red wines where the bitterness is just one piece of the flavor puzzle. The more time the grape juice spends in contact with the grape skins (before the skins are filtered out), the more tannic the wine will be.

THE COLOR OF WINE

White grapes produce white juice. Red grapes also produce white juice. Wait, what? Almost all grapes have light-colored flesh. Thus, red wine gets its color from the contact the pale juice has with the crushed red grape skins, which contain high levels of pigment; redness is only skin deep. So you can actually make white wines from red grapes—as long as you don't let the pressed juice stay in contact with the crushed skins. Rosé wines get their pink hue from the juice having only a short stay with the red skins; orange wines are made from crushed white grapes that ferment with their skins (and seeds), which impart a light orange hue.

WHAT WINE BRINGS TO FOOD

RED WINE
Red wine adds a brawny, tannic, complex, fruit-forward flavor and a twist of acidity to many recipes, most commonly sauces and braising liquids for flavorful red meats. With a few exceptions (such as short ribs braised in ruby port), we do not cook with sweet red wines.

SUBSTITUTION FOR RED WINE IN RECIPES
Black tea mixed with vinegar. Steep one tea bag (black tea, regular or decaf) in ½ cup of boiling water until the tea is completely cooled; then remove the bag and stir in 1 teaspoon of white vinegar. The tea adds a similarly savory, tannic depth as wine, while the vinegar brings acidity.

WHITE WINE
White wine brings brightness and acidity to recipes. It is typically used in recipes for poultry, seafood, or vegetables, all lighter foods more suited to white wine's lighter flavor.

SUBSTITUTION FOR WHITE WINE IN RECIPES
Dry vermouth (which keeps for months in the refrigerator), or chicken or vegetable broth mixed with vinegar; use ½ cup of broth mixed with a teaspoon of apple cider vinegar.

* Not all wine is vegetarian; some winemakers use animal-derived products to help clarify and process their wines.

SHERRY

We often call for dry (not sweet) sherry in recipes. This Spanish wine is fortified with brandy, giving it a rich flavor and big kick. Not sure which one to buy? Our taste test winner, from Lustau, was praised by our tasting panel for its "nice warmth" and "very nutty" flavor. Taylor Dry Sherry is a good less-expensive option.

SMOOTH AND NUTTY
Lustau Palo Cortado Península Sherry

Walk-Away Boneless Prime Rib

A holiday roast creates a splendid centerpiece. It shouldn't also create anxiety. **by Bryan Roof**

A BEAUTIFUL PRIME RIB roast is usually a special-occasion centerpiece, one that's surrounded by equally special side dishes. All that makes for a busy day in the kitchen, and when you add in the worry of an overcooked roast, it can be overwhelming.

I set out to establish a new method that would allow me to do the prep work, start the roast, and then leave it alone and, more important, not worry about it overcooking while I attended to the rest of the meal. I could focus on finishing up my stovetop side dishes, such as **Torn and Fried Potatoes** (page 20) and **Creamed Spinach** (page 21).

I selected a boneless roast for ease of carving. To ensure a well-seasoned exterior, I brushed it with Dijon mustard, which I chose for its sharp flavor and crust-enhancing qualities, and sprinkled the roast with salt and pepper.

From there I knew I had a few options. I could sear the roast on the stovetop first and then finish it in the oven, but maneuvering a roast of that size in a skillet is an unwieldy endeavor. I could bring the roast up to temperature slowly in a relatively low oven and then blast it at the end, but that would mean I'd have to constantly monitor its temperature as it came up.

A little research turned up an interesting hack: Start the roast in a hot oven for a predetermined amount of time based on its weight, and then shut off the oven and let the roast climb slowly to medium-rare over the course of the next 2 hours in the oven's residual heat. The promise was that with a little elementary math, this method would work for any size roast. And since it's seared in the oven rather than on the stovetop, the process is far less messy.

The recipe I found online called for cooking a bone-in prime rib for 5 minutes per pound at 500 degrees. In that scenario, the bone offers some protection against the meat overcooking, so for a boneless roast I would have to adjust the active oven time.

I tinkered with the equation and ended up with 3 minutes of "on" time per pound for a boneless roast. For a 3½-pound roast this walk-away method requires 11 minutes at 500 degrees before turning off the oven completely and leaving it alone for 2 hours.

After a 20-minute rest out of the oven, the roast yielded perfectly juicy, medium-rare slices. What's more, I had 2 hands-free, worry-free hours to prepare side dishes to go with it. Happy holidays, indeed.

COOKING TIME CHEAT SHEET FOR MEDIUM-RARE MEAT

Weigh your roast and round up to the nearest ½ pound. Triple that number and, if necessary, round up again to the nearest whole number. This is your oven-on roasting time. Place the roast into a 500-degree oven and set your timer to the time you calculated. When the time's up, turn off the oven and leave the roast alone for 2 hours. Perfect.

EXAMPLE FORMULA

Your roast is 3.3 pounds. Round that to 3.5 pounds. Triple the rounded weight to 10.5, and then round this up to 11. There's your oven-on roasting time: 11 minutes.

ROAST WEIGHT	OVEN-ON ROASTING TIME	WALK-AWAY TIME
2.6–3.0 pounds	9 minutes	2 hours
3.1–3.5 pounds	11 minutes	2 hours
3.6–4.0 pounds	12 minutes	2 hours
4.1–4.5 pounds	14 minutes	2 hours
4.6–5.0 pounds	15 minutes	2 hours

■ EASIER PRIME RIB

Serves 6 to 8
*Total Time: 3 hours 5 minutes,
plus 20 minutes resting*

It is critical that you not open the oven door at all while the roast is cooking. If you do, the heat will escape from the oven and the calculated cooking time will be ineffective. It's good to use an oven thermometer to ensure that your oven truly reaches 500 degrees before starting. This technique works for roasts outside of the weight range given here; see "Cooking Time Cheat Sheet for Medium-Rare Meat" to calculate the correct oven time for roasts of different weights. You'll find our recipe for homemade **Prepared Horseradish** on page 29.

1½   tablespoons kosher salt
1½   tablespoons pepper
  1   (3- to 3½-pound) boneless
      prime rib roast
  2   tablespoons Dijon mustard
      Prepared horseradish

1. Adjust oven rack to middle position and heat oven to 500 degrees. Line rimmed baking sheet with aluminum foil and set wire rack in sheet; spray rack with vegetable oil spray. Combine salt and pepper in bowl.
2. Using scale, weigh prime rib. Round weight up to nearest ½ pound. Multiply rounded weight by 3, then round that number up to nearest whole number. Record that number; this will be your oven-on roasting time.
3. Pat prime rib dry with paper towels. Brush all over with mustard. Sprinkle salt and pepper mixture evenly on all sides. Transfer to prepared wire rack, fat side up.
4. Transfer sheet with prime rib to oven and roast for time recorded in step 2. Without opening oven door, turn off oven and leave roast in oven, undisturbed, for 2 hours. Do not open oven during this time.
5. Remove sheet from oven and let prime rib rest on rack for 20 minutes. Transfer prime rib to carving board. Slice ¼ to ½ inch thick. Serve with horseradish.

These spuds are fluffy on the inside and crunchy on the outside.

Torn and Fried Potatoes

With a little planning and a little frying, you'll have the most satisfying spuds ever. **by Bryan Roof**

FEW INGREDIENTS ARE as adaptable and versatile as potatoes. You can boil, bake, mash, fry, or grill them—just about any method you can think of, you can use it on potatoes. But I'm extra-excited about a process I've been tinkering with a lot in my home kitchen: tearing and frying them.

By baking potatoes first and then letting them cool before tearing them into pieces and frying them, you get soft, fluffy interiors with crispy-crunchy exteriors, a compelling mix of textures.

Be prepared: This recipe takes a while. But most of that time is inactive—waiting for the potatoes to bake and then waiting for them to cool. Once that chunk of time is out of the way (the baking and cooling can be done a

couple days ahead), all that's left is to fry and serve them.

It's essential that your frying oil is at the right temperature: 375 degrees. It takes a few minutes to get the oil that hot, but don't shortchange this step, because when you add the cold potatoes the oil temperature will drop dramatically. You'll need to increase the heat after adding the potatoes to bring the oil back up to temperature quickly. This ensures crispy potatoes and keeps them from drying out or cooking unevenly.

Russets work best here, not only because their starchy centers create just the right texture but also because their skins provide beautiful earthy flavors. The result is a mashup of baked potatoes, potato skins, and french fries.

My top tip: Make sure that everyone is at the table and ready to eat when these potatoes come out of the oil. For the best experience, they must be eaten hot. To let them go cold would be a real disappointment. If you're serving these for a holiday dinner, have everything

else ready to go as soon as you start frying. Your fellow celebrants can sit down, cool their heels, and prepare their forks for the moment when you set these gorgeous potatoes down in front of them. Talk about a reason to celebrate.

■ TORN AND FRIED POTATOES

Serves 4
Total Time: 2¼ hours,
plus 3½ hours cooling

Since you eat the potato skins in this recipe, make sure to scrub them well before cooking. In addition to the salt, these potatoes can be seasoned with any variety of seasoning or herb blend; they're also great dipped in ketchup or aioli.

2½	pounds russet potatoes, unpeeled, scrubbed
1	quart vegetable oil for frying
1	teaspoon kosher salt

1. Adjust oven rack to middle position and heat oven to 400 degrees. Prick

each potato 6 times with fork. Place potatoes on rack and bake until tip of paring knife can be easily inserted into potatoes, about 1 hour 20 minutes. Let potatoes cool completely and then refrigerate until cold throughout, at least 3 hours. (Potatoes can be refrigerated for up to 2 days.)

2. Keeping skins on potatoes, use your hands to break potatoes into approximate 1½-inch pieces; transfer to bowl. Line rimmed baking sheet with triple layer of paper towels.

3. Add oil to Dutch oven and heat over medium-high heat to 375 degrees. Carefully add potatoes to hot oil and increase heat to high to compensate for oil cooling. Cook, stirring occasionally with metal spoon and taking care to scrape bottom of pot to prevent sticking, until potatoes are consistently browned and crispy, 13 to 15 minutes. Using spider skimmer or slotted spoon, transfer potatoes to prepared sheet. Sprinkle with salt. Serve.

Creamed **Spinach**

*Time to bring
this steakhouse
favorite home.*

by Mark Huxsoll

**We thicken the
sauce by stirring in
a beurre manié—a
paste of flour and
softened butter.**

CREAMED SPINACH IS a favorite side dish from fancy white-tablecloth steakhouses to more casual restaurants specializing in Sunday afternoon prime rib specials. I wanted to make this legendary side come alive in my kitchen. To do that would involve zeroing in on a couple things to get this dish just right: verdant spinach flavor and a rich, creamy sauce.

Some recipes for creamed spinach call for very complex sauces, but I didn't want the spinach flavor to be muddied by too many additions, so I chose carefully, including only a handful of complementary ingredients. I'd use pungent garlic; subtly sweet shallot; and Parmesan cheese, which would add its unmistakable umami depth. And I'd use cream, of course. The challenge would lie in how, and when, to include each ingredient.

Since spinach contains an extraordinary amount of water, I found that unless I wilted it down and cooked off the excess liquid before adding the cream, I would end up with soup. I started the spinach with butter along with the garlic and shallot. Then, when the water cooked out, I added the cream and cooked it down. Unfortunately, by the time the sauce reduced sufficiently, my spinach was terribly overcooked.

To remedy this, I introduced a simple thickening trick: a paste of butter and flour, called beurre manié, which helped create a luscious sauce. A bit of pepper, nutmeg, and the Parmesan were my finishing touches. Just right for the holiday table—or any table.

CREAMED SPINACH

Serves 4 to 6 Total Time: 30 minutes

Baby spinach comes in a wide range of package sizes; this recipe works with anywhere from 15 to 18 ounces of baby spinach. You can substitute half-and-half for the heavy cream, if desired, but the resulting dish will be less rich and slightly more soupy. Preheat your serving dish in a 200-degree oven for 10 minutes so that the spinach stays warm on the table.

- 2 **tablespoons unsalted butter, softened, plus 2 tablespoons unsalted butter**
- 1 **tablespoon all-purpose flour**
- 1 **shallot, minced**
- 1 **garlic clove, minced**
- 1 **pound (16 cups) baby spinach**
- ½ **teaspoon table salt**
- ½ **cup heavy cream**
- 2 **ounces Parmesan cheese, grated (1 cup)**
- ½ **teaspoon pepper**
  Pinch ground nutmeg

1. Using fork, mash 2 tablespoons softened butter and flour together in bowl to form smooth paste; set aside. Melt remaining 2 tablespoons butter in Dutch oven over medium heat. Add shallot and garlic and cook until shallot is translucent, 1 to 2 minutes. Add spinach and salt and turn with tongs to coat with butter, shallot, and garlic. Cook until just wilted, about 4 minutes.

2. Add cream and bring to simmer. Stir in flour mixture until incorporated. Cook until cream thickens and clings to spinach, about 3 minutes. Off heat, stir in Parmesan, pepper, and nutmeg. Season with salt and pepper to taste. Transfer to warm shallow dish and serve.

Browning the butter gives our snickerdoodles more depth.

Snickerdoodles

How to improve on a classic? For one thing, butter.

by Cecelia Jenkins

UNTIL RECENTLY, HERE'S what I knew about snickerdoodles: They have a great name, there's cinnamon sugar involved, and I love them. But they also have a subtly tangy flavor and a signature crinkly look, and therein lies their mystery. I wanted a clear path to all these hallmarks in a recipe streamlined enough for the busy holiday season.

Many recipes for snickerdoodles call for whipping shortening together with sugar in a stand mixer to incorporate air, which expands in the heat of the oven and then retreats into collapsed crinkles. I wanted to use butter, though, because butter tastes better. Plus, I wanted to mix by hand, not by machine. Melting the butter first made the dough easy to mix with just a spoon, no electricity needed. And to achieve the crinkled effect, I relied on baking soda: It reacted with the moisture and acidic ingredients in the dough and created enough carbon dioxide gas to make the cookies rise in the oven and then collapse to form a crinkled exterior.

Cream of tartar, an acidic powdered by-product of wine making, gives these cookies their tanginess, but using too much can leave behind a harsh, too-tart flavor. After a few tests, I learned that just 1 teaspoon gave the cookies the right tangy backbone. A bit of cream cheese in the dough bolstered the tangy flavor and added a bit of richness, too.

A few final details refined the flavor and texture. To make the cookies supremely buttery, I decided to keep the melted butter on the heat until the water in the butter evaporated and the milk solids took on a caramelized hue. The rich, nutty flavor that came from gently browning the butter complemented the cookies' sweetness and tang. And adding just a bit of oil to the cookie dough, in combination with the butterfat, yielded cookies with satisfyingly chewy centers but crispy, crunchy edges for irresistible textural contrast.

Here's what I know about snickerdoodles now: These knockout cookies are a breeze to make, and they belong on your holiday table.

■ SNICKERDOODLES

Makes 24 cookies   Total Time: 1¼ hours

When browning the butter in step 3, avoid using a nonstick skillet; the dark color of the skillet's nonstick coating makes it difficult to gauge when the butter has correctly browned. The cream cheese doesn't have to be at room temperature for this recipe; pouring the hot butter over it in step 4 will soften it enough to make it easy to mix. The final dough will be slightly softer than most cookie doughs. Trust the times in the recipe and don't overbake the cookies. They may seem underbaked when you pull them from the oven, but they will deflate and set as they cool.

2¼	cups (11¼ ounces) all-purpose flour
1	teaspoon cream of tartar
1	teaspoon baking soda
¾	teaspoon table salt
1½	cups (10½ ounces) sugar, plus ⅓ cup for rolling
3	ounces cream cheese, cut into 3 pieces
8	tablespoons unsalted butter
¼	cup vegetable oil
1	large egg
1	teaspoon vanilla extract
1	tablespoon ground cinnamon

1. Adjust oven rack to middle position and heat oven to 350 degrees. Line 2 rimless baking sheets with parchment paper.

2. Whisk flour, cream of tartar, baking soda, and salt together in bowl; set aside. Place 1½ cups sugar and cream cheese in large heatproof bowl.

3. Melt butter in 8-inch skillet over medium heat. Cook, swirling skillet constantly, until milk solids in butter are color of milk chocolate and have toasty aroma, 3 to 5 minutes.

4. Immediately remove skillet from heat and scrape browned butter into bowl with sugar and cream cheese. Stir and mash with rubber spatula until combined. Whisk in oil. Whisk in egg and vanilla until smooth. Stir in flour mixture with rubber spatula until soft, homogeneous dough forms.

5. Mix cinnamon and remaining ⅓ cup sugar together in shallow dish. Divide dough into 24 equal pieces, about 2 tablespoons each. Using your hands, roll dough into balls. Working in batches, roll balls in cinnamon sugar to coat, then evenly space balls on prepared sheets, 12 balls per sheet. Using bottom of drinking glass, flatten balls into 2-inch-wide disks, about ½ inch thick.

6. Bake cookies, 1 sheet at a time, until puffed and covered with small cracks (cookies will look raw between cracks and seem underdone; they will deflate and set as they cool), 11 to 13 minutes, rotating sheet halfway through baking.

7. Let cookies cool on sheet for 5 minutes, then transfer to wire rack and let cool completely. Serve. (Cookies can be stored in airtight container for up to 3 days.)

TO MAKE AHEAD

Follow recipe through step 5, then place dough disks on parchment paper–lined plate and freeze until very firm, at least 1 hour. Transfer disks to 1-gallon zipper-lock bag and freeze for up to 1 month. Increase baking time to about 15 minutes.

M&M Cookies

This fun and playful cookie deserves to be the best it can be. **by Matthew Fairman**

FOR A FEW years as a teenager I had a flawless routine for Friday lunch at school. I'd hit up the cafeteria for two slices of cheese pizza and then, instead of sitting down with the other kids to eat, my best friend and I would carry our lunches straight to the library. Because as soon as the bell rang for lunch, the cheerleaders would start setting up the bake sale there, and if you wanted to get one of Katie Johnson's M&M cookies, you needed to get there early. I can still remember feeling for the coins in my pocket as I walked to the library, searching for the ridged edges of the quarters, nervous to talk to the cheerleaders but glad to have an excuse all the same. I always made sure that I had exactly 75 cents so that I could keep the exchange brief, because for me, talking to Katie Johnson was like running into the ocean in January. Get in, gasp for air, get out. Totally worth it.

I'd all but forgotten about those Friday lunches until, just recently, I walked into a little bakery in Portland, Oregon, where they were selling M&M cookies. In my memory, there wasn't a cookie baked that could be better than Katie Johnson's. But these were.

They were big and colorful, soft and chewy, sweet and buttery, and just salty enough to bring me back to the counter to buy more. The crackly contrast of the M&M shells rocketed me back to high school. When the cashier gave me my change, I asked her why the cookies were so delicious. She smiled and said that she was the pastry chef. She said the real answer is probably that they have more salt, butter, and sugar, but that if I wanted to get technical, then I needed to increase the oven temperature and add more baking soda so that the cookies puff up quickly and then deflate for just the right texture. And then, with keen enthusiasm she exclaimed, "And you need to take them out of the oven way before you think they're done. *Way* before!" All these choices, she explained, made for soft, chewy cookies that would stay that way for days.

So that's the inspiration for this recipe. I followed her advice, but without her recipe, I needed to employ some test kitchen know-how and techniques. To start, I skipped the creaming of the butter and sugar, because that adds air that produces taller, more tender cookies. Instead, I whisked together brown sugar, granulated sugar, and melted butter; the extra moisture in the brown sugar made for moist, chewy cookies.

And as the pastry chef in Portland had instructed me to do, I added a bit more baking soda and salt, upped the oven temperature to 425 degrees, and pulled the cookies out of the oven after only 8 minutes. She gave good advice, and now I pass it on to you. Follow it, and I'd bet you'll get a lot more than 75 cents per cookie at your next bake sale.

Rolling the dough into balls before baking creates nice round cookies.

M&M COOKIE

■ M&M COOKIES
Makes 16 cookies
Total Time: 1 hour 40 minutes

Use standard, not mini, M&M'S in this recipe. The cookies will seem underdone when you pull them from the oven. This is OK; they will continue baking as they cool on the baking sheet for 5 minutes. This method ensures that the cookies remain chewy once they are cooled.

- 2¼ cups (11¼ ounces) all-purpose flour
- 1 teaspoon table salt
- ¾ teaspoon baking soda
- 12 tablespoons unsalted butter, melted
- 1 cup packed (7 ounces) light brown sugar
- ½ cup (3½ ounces) granulated sugar
- 1 large egg plus 1 large yolk
- 2 teaspoons vanilla extract
- 1¼ cups (9 ounces) M&M'S

1. Adjust oven rack to middle position and heat oven to 425 degrees. Line 2 baking sheets with parchment paper. Combine flour, salt, and baking soda in bowl.

2. Whisk melted butter, brown sugar, and granulated sugar in large bowl until thoroughly combined, about 30 seconds. Whisk in egg and yolk and vanilla until fully combined and mixture looks emulsified, about 30 seconds. Stir in half of flour mixture with rubber spatula or wooden spoon. Stir in candies and remaining flour mixture.

3. Divide dough into sixteen 2¼-ounce portions, about 2 heaping tablespoons each; divide any remaining dough evenly among dough portions. Roll dough portions between your hands to make smooth balls.

4. Evenly space dough balls on prepared sheets, 8 balls per sheet. Using your hand, flatten balls to ¾-inch thickness.

5. Bake cookies, 1 sheet at a time, until centers of cookies are puffed and still very blond, about 8 minutes; cookies will seem underdone. Let cookies cool on sheet for 5 minutes. Using spatula, transfer cookies to wire rack and let cool for 10 minutes before serving.

TO MAKE AHEAD
At end of step 4, transfer flattened dough balls to parchment paper–lined plate and freeze until very firm, at least 1 hour. Transfer balls to 1-gallon zipper-lock bag and freeze for up to 1 month. Bake from frozen, increasing baking time to 12 minutes.

Double-Crust Chicken Pot Pie

This hearty, delicious pie—a favorite from the Cook's Country archives—feels like a celebration on the table. **by Katie Leaird**

■ DOUBLE-CRUST CHICKEN POT PIE

Serves 6 to 8
Total Time: 2 hours, plus 2¼ hours chilling and cooling

The pie may seem loose when it comes out of the oven; it will set up as it cools. You can substitute 3 cups of turkey meat for the chicken, if desired.

CRUST

- ½ cup sour cream, chilled
- 1 large egg, lightly beaten
- 2½ cups (12½ ounces) all-purpose flour
- 1½ teaspoons table salt
- 12 tablespoons unsalted butter, cut into ½-inch pieces and chilled

FILLING

- 4 tablespoons unsalted butter
- 1 onion, chopped fine
- 2 carrots, peeled and cut into ¼-inch pieces (²/₃ cup)
- 2 celery ribs, cut into ¼-inch pieces (½ cup)
- ½ teaspoon table salt
- ½ teaspoon pepper
- 6 tablespoons all-purpose flour
- 2¼ cups chicken broth
- ½ cup half-and-half
- 1 small russet potato (6 ounces), peeled and cut into ¼-inch pieces (1 cup)
- 1 teaspoon minced fresh thyme
- 1 (2½-pound) rotisserie chicken, skin and bones discarded, meat shredded into bite-size pieces (3 cups)
- ¾ cup frozen peas
- 1 large egg, lightly beaten

1. FOR THE CRUST: Combine sour cream and egg in bowl. Process flour and salt in food processor until combined, about 3 seconds. Add butter and pulse until only pea-size pieces remain,

1. Make dough in processor
Pulse flour and salt with butter in food processor. Add sour cream and egg and pulse to combine.
Why? The sour cream adds richness and makes the dough easy to work with. The food processor ensures even distribution of the ingredients in the dough.

2. Knead, divide, and refrigerate
Turn out dough onto counter and knead until it comes together. Shape dough into 2 disks, wrap in plastic, and refrigerate for 1 hour.
Why? The crusts need to be chilled for easy rolling; the chilling time allows the gluten to relax and the butter to firm up.

3. Roll and place bottom crust
Let 1 crust sit on counter for 10 minutes, then roll into 12-inch circle on floured counter. Use rolling pin to transfer to pie plate.
Why? Moving the rolled dough with the rolling pin is a handy trick that lessens the chance of the dough stretching or tearing.

4. Fit into plate
Use your hands to gently lift and press edges of dough so it can sink into bottom corners of pie plate without stretching and thinning.
Why? The bottom dough needs to be strong and of uniform thickness to contain the wet filling.

5. Make filling on stovetop
Sauté vegetables, then add flour. Stir in broth and half-and-half. Add potatoes and cook until tender. Stir in chicken and peas.
Why? The flour thickens the filling. Using a rotisserie chicken saves time and produces great results here.

about 10 pulses. Add half of sour cream mixture and pulse until combined, about 5 pulses. Add remaining sour cream mixture and pulse until dough begins to form, about 10 pulses.

Transfer dough to lightly floured counter and knead briefly until dough comes together. Divide dough in half and form each half into 4-inch disk. Wrap disks tightly in plastic wrap and refrigerate for 1 hour. (Wrapped dough can be refrigerated for up to 2 days or frozen for up to 2 months. If frozen, let dough thaw completely on counter before rolling.)

Let chilled dough sit on counter to soften slightly, about 10 minutes, before rolling. Roll 1 disk of dough into 12-inch circle on lightly floured counter. Loosely roll dough around rolling pin and gently unroll it onto 9-inch pie plate, letting excess dough hang over edge. Ease dough into plate by gently lifting edge of dough with your hand while pressing into plate bottom with your other hand.

Roll other disk of dough into 12-inch circle on lightly floured counter, then transfer to parchment paper–lined baking sheet; cover with plastic. Refrigerate both doughs for 30 minutes.

FOR THE FILLING: Meanwhile, adjust oven rack to lowest position and heat oven to 450 degrees. Melt butter in large saucepan over medium heat. Add onion, carrots, celery, salt, and pepper and cook until vegetables begin to soften, about 6 minutes. Add flour and cook, stirring constantly, until golden, 1 to 2 minutes. Slowly stir in broth and half-and-half and bring to boil over medium-high heat.

6. Stir in potato and thyme. Reduce heat to medium and simmer until sauce is thickened and potato is tender, about 8 minutes. Off heat, stir in chicken and peas.

7. Transfer filling to dough-lined pie plate. Loosely roll remaining dough round around rolling pin and gently unroll it onto filling. Trim overhang to ½ inch beyond lip of plate. Pinch edges of top and bottom crusts firmly together. Tuck overhang under itself; folded edge should be flush with edge of plate. Crimp dough evenly around edge of plate using your fingers. Cut four 2-inch slits in top of dough.

8. Brush top of pie with egg. Place pie on rimmed baking sheet. Bake until top is light golden brown, 18 to 20 minutes. Reduce oven temperature to 375 degrees; rotate sheet; and continue to bake until crust is deep golden brown, 12 to 15 minutes longer. Let pie cool on wire rack for at least 45 minutes. Serve.

TO MAKE AHEAD

At end of step 6, transfer filling to bowl and refrigerate until fully chilled, about 1½ hours. Continue with step 7, then wrap pie tightly in plastic wrap and then aluminum foil. Freeze for up to 1 month. When ready to bake, unwrap frozen pie, cover with foil, and place on rimmed baking sheet (do not thaw). Place sheet on middle rack of cold oven and set oven to 375 degrees. Bake for 1¼ hours. Uncover pie and brush with egg. Rotate sheet and continue to bake until crust is golden brown and filling is beginning to bubble up through slits and registers at least 150 degrees, 55 minutes to 1¼ hours longer. Let cool for 45 minutes before serving.

ROLLING PIN

The test kitchen has two winning rolling pins: the straight **J.K. Adams Plain Maple Rolling Dowel** ($14) and the tapered **Fante's Tapered Baker's Pin** ($25), which is also made by J.K. Adams. The straight pin has more heft and is great for rolling out large, springy doughs; the tapered pin offers more precision and control.

PIE PLATE

We highly recommend the **Williams Sonoma Goldtouch Nonstick Pie Dish** ($19). It browned crusts beautifully, and its nonstick surface worked as advertised. A Pyrex pie plate (as shown in the steps below) also works well here.

PASTRY BRUSH

We like natural-bristle pastry brushes for pastry work because their bristles are more delicate when brushing egg wash or butter on fragile doughs; our favorite is the **Winco Flat Pastry and Basting Brush, 1½ Inch** ($7). We prefer silicone brushes for basting because they can withstand high heat and are easier to clean; our winner is the **OXO Good Grips Silicone Pastry Brush** ($8). For a sturdy pastry dough like the one in this recipe, either brush works just fine.

BEST NATURAL-BRISTLE BRUSH

BEST SILICONE-BRISTLE BRUSH

Rotisserie Chicken Stock

So you've picked the meat from a rotisserie chicken for this recipe. What do you do with what's left? Make stock! We found that the average rotisserie chicken carcass and skin (plus the jellied bits in the tray) weigh about 1 pound. To make a quick stock, simply throw all of that into a large saucepan with 5 cups of water, half an onion, and a bay leaf (plus whatever else you like: peppercorns, garlic, etc.). Simmer for 30 minutes, strain, and voilà: a small but tasty batch of stock.

In Praise of Frozen Peas

Some frozen vegetables (broccoli, carrots) are acceptable in a pinch, while others (green beans) are downright awful. But some, like peas, are great. In fact, almost every test kitchen recipe that calls for peas was developed using frozen peas. Why are they so good? Because they are picked when they're perfectly ripe and sweet and then quickly flash frozen to lock in flavor. Peas are soft and moist, so there's not much difference in texture between cooked fresh and frozen peas either.

6. Fill pie and place top crust
Transfer hot filling to bottom crust in pie plate, then use rolling pin to position second crust on top of filled pie.
Why? Our sturdy crust won't be compromised by the hot filling. The rolling pin method is the safest way to transfer the dough.

7. Trim overhang and seal
Use scissors to trim extra dough to ½ inch over edge of pie plate. Then pinch bottom and top crusts firmly together.
Why? Trimming ensures the correct thickness of the crust edge. Pinching the dough seals the crusts together.

8. Tuck overhang under
Fold overhang under itself so it sits on top edge of pie plate.
Why? This fold forms the thick ring of dough circumnavigating the top of the pie.

9. Crimp edge
Using 2 fingers of 1 hand and 1 finger of the other, press into dough edge from opposite sides to create crimped edge.
Why? Crimping seals the top and bottom pieces of dough together, minimizing leaks. Plus, it makes the pie look great.

10. Prep and bake
Cut 4 vent holes on top of pie, brush with egg, and bake.
Why? The vent holes allow steam to escape so that it doesn't cause the crust to puff and tear. The egg gives the crust an attractive glossy sheen.

The rich color of the roux carries over to the finished sauce.

■ SLOW-COOKER PORK GRILLADES

Serves 6 to 8
Total Time: 5 hours 55 minutes

We developed this recipe using Tony Chachere's Original Creole Seasoning. Pork butt roast is often labeled Boston butt in the supermarket.

- ½ cup vegetable oil
- ½ cup all-purpose flour
- 1 onion, chopped
- 1 green bell pepper, stemmed, seeded, and chopped
- 1 celery rib, chopped
- 2 slices bacon, chopped
- 2 garlic cloves, minced
- 2 tablespoons Louisiana seasoning
- 1 (3-pound) boneless pork butt roast, trimmed and cut into 1½-inch pieces
- 1¾ teaspoons table salt
- 1 teaspoon pepper
- 1 (14.5-ounce) can diced tomatoes, drained
- ½ cup water
- 1 tablespoon Worcestershire sauce
- 1 teaspoon Tabasco sauce, plus extra for serving
- 4 cups cooked white rice
- 3 scallions, sliced thin

1. Heat oil in large saucepan over medium-high heat until just smoking. Carefully stir in flour and cook, stirring constantly, until roux is color of milk chocolate, about 5 minutes. Add onion, bell pepper, celery, bacon, and garlic and cook, stirring frequently, until vegetables are softened, about 5 minutes.
2. Stir in Louisiana seasoning and cook until fragrant, about 1½ minutes. Transfer roux mixture to slow cooker.
3. Sprinkle pork with salt and pepper. Add pork, tomatoes, water, and Worcestershire to roux mixture in slow cooker and stir to combine. Cook until fork slips easily into and out of pork, 5 to 6 hours on high or 7 to 8 hours on low.
4. Skim excess fat from surface of grillades. Stir in Tabasco sauce and season with salt and pepper to taste. Serve over rice, sprinkled with scallions, passing extra Tabasco sauce separately.

Louisiana Seasoning

The best Louisiana seasonings are a bit salty and a bit prickly from cayenne. Our taste test winner is Tony Chachere's Original Creole Seasoning. Our web subscribers can find our recipe for Louisiana Seasoning at **CooksCountry. com/LAs.**

Pork Grillades

We love oven-braised grillades. Would we love a slow-cooked version, too?

by Mark Huxsoll

PORK GRILLADES, A Louisiana favorite of pork (usually chops) braised in a spicy gravy, is one of my favorite dishes from the state. To make it, you cook a roux of flour and oil until it's dark and fragrant to help form a rich, cohesive sauce base, and then you add the trinity (chopped bell pepper, onion, and celery), plenty of garlic, and Louisiana seasoning. You thin it out with broth and tomato to make a sauce that you use to slowly braise the chops. This dish sounded like a great candidate for the slow cooker.

The test kitchen has an oven-braised version of pork grillades that I used as my starting point. That recipe calls for braising thin-cut pork blade chops in the oven for an hour to tenderize them. But there's not much point in a slow-cooker recipe that cooks for only an hour—the machine is just getting warmed up at that point. So I turned to a flavorful cut of pork that we know lends itself well to longer cooking: pork shoulder, aka pork butt roast. Rather than cutting the shoulder into thin slices to mimic the chops, I decided to cube it for easier eating.

I started my grillades by making a roux in a saucepan on the stovetop; there's simply no way to shortcut this process and still have the grillades taste right. Once the roux was browned to the color of milk chocolate, I added the trinity, garlic, and some chopped bacon for another layer of flavor. When the vegetables had softened, I scraped this mixture right into the slow cooker and turned my attention to the pork.

Browning the cubed pork before it went into the cooker seemed like a good idea to build flavor, but in a side-by-side test of browned and unbrowned pork slow-cooked to tenderness, my tasters couldn't tell much difference. Score one for convenience, since I could just toss the cubed raw pork in with the other ingredients. One pitfall of some slow-cooker recipes is too much liquid, which results in washed-out flavor. Sautéing the trinity helped here, as it cooked some of the water out of the vegetables, but I also found it necessary to drain the can of diced tomatoes before adding it to the slow cooker.

That's all there is to it—except, of course, for making some steamed white rice, slicing up a few scallions, and twisting the cap off the Tabasco bottle.

Butternut Squash Soup

This rich, silky soup comes together in less than an hour. **by the editors of America's Test Kitchen**

WHEN PUREED WITH broth and maybe a bit of cream, roasted butternut squash makes a fantastic, hearty soup—one that's a little sweet, pleasantly rich and earthy, and deliciously savory. But let's face it: With the peeling, seeding, and chopping of the hard flesh, butternut squash isn't the easiest vegetable to prep, and then (if you follow the path of most recipes) you must roast the squash pieces until they're caramelized and sweet before pureeing them. Beyond that, sometimes you just want enough soup for two people—or even for one person, with a little left over for lunch. We sought an easier and quicker path to a smaller portion of butternut squash soup.

Browning pieces of butternut squash makes them taste sweeter and more complex, and it's a must-do step for this recipe; we made versions without browning the squash and they tasted wan and dull (even when we added extra sugar). Once we determined that we needed only 1¼ pounds of squash for our soup, we decided to brown the pieces in a saucepan on the stovetop instead of turning on the oven, which cut down the cooking time. To round out the soup's flavor, we found that using a chopped medium shallot (instead of part of an onion) provided just the right amount of savory-sweet base flavor. A minced garlic clove and teaspoon of squash's favorite herb, piney sage, provided nice accents.

Now that the vegetables and seasonings were all in the saucepan, we simply added a bit of chicken broth and simmered the soup until the squash was fully tender, which took about 15 minutes. Then we tipped the contents of the saucepan into the blender (an immersion blender works great here, too), buzzed them, and returned the now-smooth soup to the pan. Stirring in a little heavy cream added richness and gave the soup a silky texture.

The soup was great on its own, but we're always looking to take our recipes to the next level. So after testing a few different garnishes, we landed on crumbling some pungent blue cheese (a time-tested pairing with squash) over the top and sprinkling on some salty, crunchy roasted pepitas for contrasting texture.

▪ BUTTERNUT SQUASH SOUP WITH BLUE CHEESE AND PEPITAS FOR TWO
Total Time: 55 minutes

A medium shallot is a little larger than a golf ball and should yield about 3 tablespoons when it's chopped. To make this soup vegetarian, use vegetable broth instead of the chicken broth. We prefer crumbling a block of blue cheese ourselves, but store-bought blue cheese crumbles will work fine here. If you don't have a blender, an immersion blender will also work; just puree the soup right in the saucepan. Serve with crusty bread, if desired.

1	tablespoon extra-virgin olive oil
½	large butternut squash (1¼ pounds), peeled, seeded, and cut into 1-inch pieces (3 cups)
1	shallot, chopped
1	garlic clove, minced
1	teaspoon minced fresh sage
2	cups chicken broth, plus extra as needed
⅛	teaspoon table salt
⅛	teaspoon pepper
2	tablespoons heavy cream
¼	cup crumbled blue cheese
2	tablespoons roasted, salted pepitas

1. Heat oil in medium saucepan over medium heat until shimmering. Add squash and shallot and cook until vegetables are softened and lightly browned, about 10 minutes. Stir in garlic and sage and cook until fragrant, about 30 seconds.
2. Stir in broth, salt, and pepper and bring to simmer, scraping up any browned bits. Reduce heat to medium-low; cover; and cook until squash is tender, about 15 minutes.
3. Process soup in blender until smooth, about 2 minutes. Return soup to saucepan over medium-low heat and stir in cream. Adjust consistency with extra broth as needed. Off heat, season with salt and pepper to taste. Serve, sprinkled with blue cheese and pepitas. (Soup can be refrigerated for up to 3 days.)

A garnish of pepitas adds crunch and reinforces the squash flavor.

Prepping the Squash

1. Peel Use sharp vegetable peeler to remove skin from entire surface of squash.

2. Halve Cut peeled squash in two and save 1 half for another use. To use rounded end, simply halve it and seed it.

■ ONE-PAN BRAISED CHICKEN THIGHS WITH POTATOES, SHALLOTS, AND OLIVES

Serves 4
Total Time: 1 hour 50 minutes
Use small red potatoes measuring 1 to 2 inches in diameter.

- 8 (5- to 7-ounce) bone-in chicken thighs, trimmed
- 1 teaspoon table salt, divided
- ½ teaspoon pepper
- 1 teaspoon herbes de Provence
- 1 pound small red potatoes, unpeeled, halved
- 5 shallots, halved through root end
- 3 garlic cloves, sliced thin
- ¾ cup chicken broth
- ⅓ cup pitted kalamata olives, halved
- ¼ cup dry white wine
- ¼ cup oil-packed sun-dried tomatoes, chopped
- 3 sprigs fresh thyme
- ¼ cup chopped fresh parsley
   Lemon wedges

1. Adjust oven rack to middle position and heat oven to 350 degrees. Pat chicken dry with paper towels. Sprinkle all over with ½ teaspoon salt and pepper. Sprinkle undersides of thighs (sides without skin) with herbes de Provence.
2. Place chicken, skin side down, in cold 12-inch ovensafe nonstick skillet. Cook over medium-high heat until fat is rendered and skin is well browned, 8 to 11 minutes. Transfer chicken to plate, skin side up.
3. Pour off all but 2 tablespoons fat from skillet. Heat fat over medium heat until shimmering. Add potatoes, shallots, and remaining ½ teaspoon salt and cook until beginning to brown, about 5 minutes, stirring occasionally. Stir in garlic and cook until fragrant, about 30 seconds. Stir in broth, olives, wine, tomatoes, and thyme sprigs.
4. Return chicken to skillet, skin side up, along with any accumulated juices on plate and bring to boil. Transfer skillet to oven and cook, uncovered, until chicken registers at least 185 degrees, 30 to 35 minutes.
5. Transfer chicken to serving platter. Place skillet over high heat (skillet handle will be hot) and bring to boil. Cook until sauce is thick enough to coat back of spoon and potatoes are completely tender, about 7 minutes. Off heat, discard thyme sprigs and stir in parsley. Spoon sauce over chicken and serve with vegetables, passing lemon wedges separately.

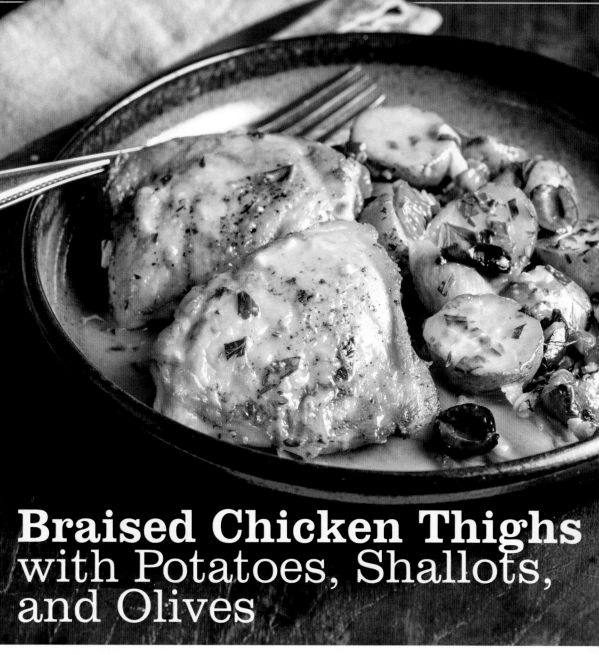

Braised Chicken Thighs
with Potatoes, Shallots, and Olives

This bold braise is sure to become a favorite in your regular repertoire.

by Jessica Rudolph

Herbes de Provence

Most supermarkets sell this herb blend, but if you prefer to make your own, here's our formula.

- 2 teaspoons dried marjoram
- 2 teaspoons dried thyme
- 1 teaspoon dried basil
- 1 teaspoon dried rosemary, crumbled
- 1 teaspoon dried sage
- ¼ teaspoon dried lavender (optional)
- ⅛ teaspoon ground fennel

Combine all ingredients in bowl.

CHICKEN AND POTATOES are a classic pair: humble and hearty, with lots of room for gussying up. Here I was after a simple one-pan chicken and potato dish with deep flavor.

I chose bone-in chicken thighs, a great cut for braising because they stay juicy and tender while rendering plenty of flavorful fat (which would deeply flavor the potatoes). I first browned the chicken, starting the thighs skin side down in a cold nonstick skillet to gently render the fat and get the skin golden and crispy. Then I removed the chicken and browned some potatoes (halved small, waxy potatoes held up best) in the rendered fat left in the skillet. I added halved shallots for their subtle sweetness, along with garlic and thyme for depth. Just a cup of liquid was all I needed to partially cover the potatoes—I opted for chicken broth, plus some white wine for acidity. I popped

the chicken back in the skillet skin side up so that the skin didn't sog, and then I stuck the whole thing in the oven until the thighs were cooked through.

Thirty minutes later, I had crisp, juicy chicken . . . and a skilletful of undercooked potatoes and shallots swimming in watery broth. I removed the chicken and brought everything else to a boil on the stovetop. In just a few minutes, the braising liquid reduced to velvety, rich pan sauce that cloaked the buttery-tender potatoes and meltingly soft shallots. The textures were spot-on but the dish needed some vibrancy.

So I brought some big-flavor add-ins to the braise: briny kalamata olives and savory sun-dried tomatoes, plus herbes de Provence to season the chicken itself. Chopped parsley and a spritz of fresh lemon finished off the dish; it was now deeply comforting but also lively and bright. Just what I wanted.

Prepared Horseradish

The prickly heat of prepared horseradish is incredibly compelling—especially when you try our easy homemade version. **by the editors of America's Test Kitchen**

Horseradish root, salt, and vinegar—prepared horseradish is really just a simple pickle.

RY IT ON ROAST BEEF
rn to page 18 for our
cipe for Easier Prime Rib.

PREPARED HORSERADISH

Serves 8 to 10 (Makes about 2 cups)
Total Time: 15 minutes

We call for canning and pickling salt here, which is often called preserving salt. Noniodized table salt can be used in an equal amount. To substitute Morton Kosher Salt for the canning and pickling salt, increase the amount to 1½ teaspoons; to use Diamond Crystal Kosher Salt, increase the amount to 2 teaspoons.

- 10 ounces fresh horseradish root, peeled and cut into 1-inch pieces (2 cups)
- 1 teaspoon canning and pickling salt
- 1 cup cider vinegar

1. Pulse horseradish and salt in food processor until coarsely chopped, about 15 pulses, scraping down sides of bowl as needed. With processor running, slowly add vinegar until incorporated and mixture has pulp-like consistency, about 1 minute, scraping down sides of bowl as necessary.
2. Spoon horseradish into two 1-cup jars; seal jars. (Horseradish can be refrigerated for up to 3 weeks; flavor will deepen over time.)

A Root of No Evil

People have been cooking with horseradish for a long time; it was popular with the ancient Greeks. It is the root of a plant in the Brassicaceae family, and it loses its mustardy pungency when exposed to heat and air, so grate it just before using it.

USES FOR PREPARED HORSERADISH

- Stir into mayonnaise or mustard and spread onto sandwiches
- Serve with roast beef
- Stir into ketchup to make cocktail sauce
- Vinaigrettes
- Potato salad
- Deviled eggs
- Mashed potatoes
- Creamy dips

F YOU'RE A fan of tastebud-prickling, sinus-tingling horseradish, ou're in for a treat. We're here with e news that making your own version f prepared horseradish is supersimple d yields a product that's fresher and righter than anything you can buy a store. And it's perfect next to a oliday roast.

The hardest part of this recipe is nding fresh horseradish root; thank-lly, it's becoming more common in .S. markets. These roots are fibrous d need to be broken down. While ou could use a knife to mince the tough root, a food processor makes the job much easier (you do need to cut the horseradish into 1-inch pieces before tossing it in the processor).

We found that a heavy pour of vinegar—our tasters preferred the cider variety for its hint of sweetness—was needed to balance the horseradish's sharp bite. A little salt (see "Canning and Pickling Salt") enhanced the flavor. And that's it—just three ingredients. This prepared horseradish keeps for three weeks in the refrigerator, where you'll be glad to have it at the ready for Bloody Marys and countless other uses.

Canning and Pickling Salt

Canning and pickling salt, often called preserving salt, is specifically designed for pickle making and doesn't have any iodine or anticaking agents that can produce hazy brines. It also has a very fine grain, which dissolves quickly in water. If you can't find it, use noniodized table salt or kosher salt; see the recipe headnote for measurements.

Cookie Baking 101

Using the right equipment and the very best ingredients can prevent common baking mishaps. We've gathered years of test kitchen knowledge to help ensure your cookie-baking success. **Compiled by Carolyn Grillo**

EIGHT KEY INGREDIENTS AND HOW TO STORE THEM

① UNSALTED BUTTER

When baking cookies, we reach for unsalted butter. The sodium level of salted butter can vary, and we prefer to control the seasoning of our cookies. Plus, salted butter almost always contains more water than unsalted butter, which can interfere with gluten development.

Store: Butter can pick up off-flavors when it's refrigerated for longer than a month, and it can turn rancid as its fat oxidizes. For longer storage (up to four months), move it to the freezer.

② COCOA POWDER

When we want big chocolate flavor, we turn to cocoa powder, which has a higher proportion of flavorful cocoa solids, ounce for ounce, than any other form of chocolate. There are two styles: Dutch-processed and natural. The Dutching process—treating the cocoa with an alkalizing agent—neutralizes some of the cocoa's acidity. We prefer high-fat Dutched cocoa in our cookie recipes because the fat adds richness and flavor. It can also help ensure that cookies bake up moist and tender.

Store: Cocoa powder should be stored in an airtight container in a cool, dry place.

③ VANILLA

There are two varieties of vanilla: pure extract and imitation. In our tests, we've found that there's not much flavor difference between the real thing and a well-made imitation vanilla, especially when they're used in cookies and other baked goods. The additional flavor and aroma compounds in pure vanilla extract begin to bake off and dissipate at higher temperatures, so the subtleties are lost. One clear difference is the price; pure vanilla extract costs about 25 times more than imitation vanilla.

Store: Vanilla should keep indefinitely when stored in its original container.

④ EGGS

Egg yolks and whites have different properties and functions; together they can bind, thicken, emulsify, and leaven. They also provide fat and moisture.

Store: Eggs can be stored in the refrigerator for up to three months. Store eggs in the back of the refrigerator (the coldest area), not in the door (the warmest area), and keep them in their carton; this prevents the eggs from drying out and protects them from odors.

⑤ CHEMICAL LEAVENERS

A majority of cookie recipes call for some kind of chemical leavener, such as baking powder or baking soda, to help the cookies rise during baking. Without the transformative powers of leavening, many baked goods would emerge from the oven dense, flat, or hard.

Store: Baking powder will begin to lose its effectiveness six months after its container is opened, so we suggest labeling your container with the date you opened it. Store baking soda intended for baking in an airtight container at room temperature.

⑥ GRANULATED SUGAR

In addition to providing a cookie's requisite sweetness, sugar also contributes to its moisture level, chewiness, structure, and browning. Granulated sugar is generally incorporated into cookies, while confectioners' sugar and turbinado sugar are used primarily to decorate and add crunch to the exteriors of cookies, respectively.

Store: Sugar should be stored in an airtight container.

⑦ BROWN SUGAR

Brown sugar is granulated sugar that has been combined with molasses. Light brown sugar is made with less molasses than dark brown sugar. If the choice of light or dark brown sugar is important in one of our recipes, we call for that specific sugar. either type can be used, we simply call for brown sugar.

Store: Brown sugar should be stored in an airtight container to prevent it from drying out. We use the *Sugar Bears Inc. Brown Sugar Bear* ($3.25) to keep our brown sugar soft.

TIP: If your brown sugar has dried out and hardened, place it a bowl with a slice of sandwich bread, cover it, and microwave for 10 to 20 seconds to revive it.

⑧ FLOUR

Flour gives cookies structure and affects their crumb and chewiness. We call for all-purpose flour in most of our cookie recipes, but we sometimes use cake flour, which has a low amount of protein, when making fine-crumbed, delicate cookies.

Store: Store flour in an airtight container away from light and heat. Whole-wheat flour contains more fat than refined flours and quickly turns rancid at room temperature, so it should be stored in the freezer. Make sure to let flour kept in the freezer come to room temperature before using it.

MEASURING AND PREPPING TIPS

Using an accurate kitchen scale to measure dry ingredients, such as flour and sugar, is the best way to ensure that your baked goods turn out as intended. Alternatively, we recommend the dip-and-sweep method. First, dip the dry measuring cup (or measuring spoon) into a dry ingredient until it's overflowing, and then sweep across the bowl of the cup (or spoon) with a straight edge such as the back of a knife to return the excess back to its container.

STORING BAKED COOKIES

Drop Cookies: Store for about three days in an airtight container at room temperature.

Slice-and-Bake Cookies: Store for about one week in an airtight container at room temperature.
TIP: Store chewy cookies with a piece of bread to keep them from drying out.

Brownies and Blondies: Store for about five days in an airtight container at room temperature. Items with perishable ingredients, such as cream cheese, may require refrigeration.
TIP: Leave brownies and blondies uncut to help retain their freshness.

Storage Equipment We Recommend

We like to store dry ingredients, such as flour and sugar, in the *Cambro 6-Quart Square Storage Container ($23.74)*. It's sturdy, spacious, and easy to clean.

Our favorite cookie jar is the *OXO Good Grips Pop Storage Container, Big Square 4 Quart ($16.99)*. This container has an airtight seal that is activated by a pop-up button on the lid. We also like that the clear plastic jar shows off what's inside.

MAKING THE MOST OF YOUR OVEN

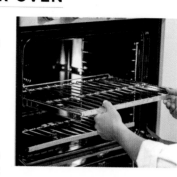

Adjust oven racks as directed: When we're baking just one sheet of cookies at a time, we nearly always bake them on the middle rack. When we're baking two sheets at a time, we tend to move the racks to the upper-middle and lower-middle positions. The closer to the bottom of the oven, the browner the bottoms of the cookies will be relative to the tops.

Rotate baking sheets: Even the best ovens have cold and hot spots, so rotating the baking sheet (the cookies that were in the front will now be in the back of the oven) is essential. And if you're baking two sheets at once, switch their positions halfway through baking in addition to rotating their orientation. This will further ensure even baking.

Choose your baking sheet wisely: Heat rises from the element at the bottom of the oven and circulates in currents to warm the entire chamber. A rimmed baking sheet's raised edges divert hot air currents from the cookies to the top of the oven. A rimless cookie sheet allows hot air to immediately sweep over the cookies. That means cookies baked on a cookie sheet brown more quickly and can finish sooner than those baked on a rimmed baking sheet. We like baking cookies with both types of sheets; just be aware of the type of baking sheet you're using and the timing. We like to check on cookies a few minutes before the timer goes off.

To learn how to make our irresistible brownie cookies, visit CooksCountry.com/browniecookie

EIGHT MUST-HAVE PIECES OF EQUIPMENT

Measuring Spoons
The narrow measuring spoons of our favorite set fit in the openings of most spice jars, and their design also allows for accurate measurements when employing the dip-and-sweep method, which is our preferred method of volume measuring.
Winner: *Cuisipro Stainless Steel 5-Piece Measuring Spoons ($12.33)*

Digital Kitchen Scale
Our winning kitchen scale is not only accurate but also sturdily constructed and responsive. It features a removable platform for easy cleaning. Plus, it's simple to switch between imperial and metric systems of measurement.
Winner: *OXO Good Grips 11 lb Food Scale with Pull Out Display ($49.99)*

Wire Racks
Wire racks allow air to circulate all around the cookies as they cool. Our winner fits snugly inside our favorite rimmed baking sheet, so it can be used for tasks beyond cooling (we use ours to bake slices of Almond Biscotti and when drizzling melted chocolate over cookies such as Florentines).
Winner: *Checkered Chef Cooling Rack ($12.95)*

Parchment Paper
We line baking sheets with parchment paper to ensure that cookies release effortlessly. We like precut sheets, which are sized to fit standard rimmed baking sheets.
Winner: *King Arthur Flour Parchment Paper 100 Half-Sheets ($19.95 per package)*
TIP: We've found that a single piece of parchment can be used to make up to five batches of cookies without any issues. Reach for a fresh sheet if your parchment becomes messy or dry and brittle.

Inexpensive Stand Mixer
This stand mixer has a powerful motor and a highly efficient mixing arm that can mix stiff or chunky cookie dough with ease.
Winner: *KitchenAid KSM75WH Classic Plus Series 4.5-Quart Tilt-Head Stand Mixer ($254.99)*

Rimmed Baking Sheets and Cookie Sheets
We bake cookies on rimmed baking sheets as well as cookie sheets. The main difference between the two is that cookie sheets are flat and rimless. Both sheets are made from thick aluminum, so they're sturdy and warp-resistant. They also both produce evenly baked cookies. See "Making the Most of Your Oven" for more information.
Winners: *Nordic Ware Baker's Half Sheet ($14.97)* and *Vollrath Wear-Ever Cookie Sheet (Natural Finish) ($15.99)*

Silicone Spatula
This all-silicone spatula is firm enough to scrape down the sides of bowls and fold ingredients into cookie dough yet flexible and agile enough to spread batter.
Winner: *Di Oro Living Seamless Silicone Spatula—Large ($10.97)*

Boiled Potatoes with Butter and Parsley

BOILED POTATOES WITH BUTTER AND PARSLEY
Serves 4 to 6 Total Time: 35 minutes
Use potatoes that measure 1 to 2 inches in diameter.

- 1½ **pounds small Yukon Gold potatoes, peeled**
- ½ **teaspoon table salt, plus salt for cooking potatoes**
- 4 **tablespoons unsalted butter**
- 2 **tablespoons chopped fresh parsley**

1. Place potatoes and 2 tablespoons salt in large saucepan and cover with water by 1 inch. Bring to boil over medium-high heat. Reduce heat to medium and simmer until potatoes can be easily pierced with tip of paring knife, about 15 minutes.

2. Drain potatoes in colander. Add butter to now-empty saucepan and melt over low heat. Remove saucepan from heat; add potatoes, parsley, and salt to butter; and stir gently with rubber spatula to combine. Transfer to platter and serve.

U.S. POSTAL SERVICE STATEMENT OF OWNERSHIP, MANAGEMENT AND CIRCULATION

1. Publication Title: Cook's Country; 2. Publication No. 1552-1990; 3. Filing date: 10/01/20; 4. Issue frequency: Dec/Jan; Feb/Mar; Apr/May; Jun/Jul; Aug/Sept; Oct/Nov; 5. No. of issues published annually: 6; 6. Annual Subscription Price is $35.70; 7. Complete mailing address of known office of publication: 21 Drydock Avenue, Suite 210E, Boston, MA 02210; 8. Complete mailing address of headquarters or general business office of publisher: 21 Drydock Avenue, Suite 210E, Boston, MA 02210; 9. Full names and complete mailing addresses of publisher, editor, and managing editor. Publisher, David Nussbaum, 21 Drydock Avenue, Suite 210E, Boston, MA 02210, Editor, Tucker Shaw, 21 Drydock Avenue, Suite 210E, Boston, MA 02210, Managing Editor, Todd Meier, 21 Drydock Avenue, Suite 210E, Boston, MA 02210; 10. Owner: America's Test Kitchen LP; 21 Drydock Avenue, Suite 210E, Boston, MA 02210; 11. Known bondholders, mortgages, and other securities: NONE; 12. Tax status: Has Not Changed During Preceding 12 Months; 13. Publication title: Cook's Country; 14. Issue date for circulation data below: August/September 2020; 15A. Total number of copies: Average number of copies each issue during the preceding 12 months: 327,787 (Aug/Sep 2020: 309,456); B. Paid circulation: 1. Mailed outside-county paid subscriptions. Average number of copies each issue during the preceding 12 months: 267,900 (Aug/Sep 2020: 267,851); 2. Mailed in-county paid subscriptions. Average number of copies each issue during the preceding 12 months: 0 (Aug/Sep 2020: 0); 3. Sales through dealers and carriers, street vendors and counter sales. Average number of copies each issue during the preceding 12 months: 9,812 (Aug/Sep 2020: 7,000); 4. Paid distribution through other classes mailed through the USPS. Average number of copies each issue during the preceding 12 months: 0 (Aug/Sep 2020: 0); C. Total paid distribution. Average number of copies each issue during preceding 12 months: 277,712 (Aug/Sep 2020: 274,851); D. Free or nominal rate distribution (by mail and outside mail); 1. Free or nominal Outside-County. Average number of copies each issue during the preceding 12 months: 1,523 (Aug/Sep 2020: 1,575); 2. Free or nominal rate in-county copies. Average number of copies each issue during the preceding 12 months: 0 (Aug/Sep 2020: 0); 3. Free or nominal rate copies mailed at other Classes through the USPS. Average number of copies each issue during preceding 12 months: 0 (Aug/Sep 2020: 0); 4. Free or nominal rate distribution outside the mail. Average number of copies each issue during preceding 12 months: 725 (Aug/Sep 2020: 725); E. Total free or nominal rate distribution. Average number of copies each issue during the preceding 12 months: 2,248 (Aug/Sep 2020: 2,300); F. Total free distribution. Average number of copies each issue during preceding 12 months: 279,960 (Aug/Sep 2020: 277,151); G. Copies not Distributed. Average number of copies each issue during preceding 12 months: 47,927 (Aug/Sep 2020: 32,305); H. Total. Average number of copies each issue during preceding 12 months: 327,887 (Aug/Sep 2020: 309,459); I. Percent paid. Average percent of copies paid for the preceding 12 months: 99.20% (Aug/Sep 2020: 99.17%)

FIND THE ROOSTER!

A tiny version of this rooster has been hidden in a photo in the pages of this issue. Write to us with its location, and we'll enter you in a random drawing. Th first correct entry drawn will win a copy The Complete Cook's Country TV Sho Cookbook, and each of the next five wi receive a free one-year subscription to website. To enter, visit CooksCountry.c rooster by December 31, 2020, or write Rooster DJ21, Cook's Country, 21 Dryd Avenue, Suite 210E, Boston, MA 0221C Include your name and address. Maria Yocum of Richlandtown, Pa., found the rooster in the August/September 2020 issue on page 7.

WEB EXTRAS

Free for four months online at
CooksCountry.com/jan21

Chocolate Brownie Cookies

READ US ON IPAD

Download the Cook's Country app for iPad and start a free trial subscription o purchase a single issue of the magazin to CooksCountry.com/iPad to downloa our app through the App Store.

Malted Milk Pancakes with Nutella Maple Syrup

These tall, tangy cakes raise the bar for your holiday breakfast. **by Matthew Fairman**

MALTED MILK PANCAKES WITH NUTELLA MAPLE SYRUP

Serves 4
(Makes twelve 4-inch pancakes)
Total Time: 1 hour

Do not stir the batter after letting it rest in step 3. Stirring bursts the bubbles created when the baking soda reacts with the buttermilk; these bubbles give the pancakes lift as they cook. The pancakes can be cooked on an electric griddle; set the griddle temperature to 350 degrees and cook the pancakes as directed. This recipe can easily be halved to serve two or doubled to serve a crowd.

PANCAKES

1½	cups (7½ ounces) all-purpose flour
¼	cup (1¾ ounces) sugar
¼	cup (1⅛ ounces) malted milk powder
1	tablespoon baking powder
½	teaspoon baking soda
1¼	teaspoons table salt
1¼	cups plus 2 tablespoons buttermilk
2	large eggs
4	tablespoons unsalted butter, melted and cooled slightly
1	teaspoon vegetable oil, plus extra as needed

NUTELLA MAPLE SYRUP

½	cup maple syrup
¼	cup Nutella
½	teaspoon table salt

1. FOR THE PANCAKES: Adjust oven rack to middle position and heat oven to 200 degrees. Set wire rack in rimmed baking sheet and place sheet in oven.

2. Whisk flour, sugar, milk powder, baking powder, baking soda, and salt together in medium bowl. Whisk buttermilk, eggs, and melted butter together in separate bowl (butter may form clumps; this is OK).

3. Make well in center of flour mixture and pour in buttermilk mixture; gently whisk until just combined (batter should remain lumpy, with few streaks of flour). Do not overmix. Let batter sit for 10 minutes. (Do not stir batter after resting.)

4. FOR THE NUTELLA MAPLE SYRUP: Meanwhile, whisk maple syrup, Nutella, and salt in bowl until combined.

5. Heat oil in 12-inch nonstick skillet over medium heat for 3 minutes. Using paper towels, carefully wipe out oil, leaving thin film on bottom and sides of skillet.

6. Using ¼-cup dry measuring cup, portion batter into skillet in 3 places. Cook until edges of pancakes are set, bubbles on surface are just beginning to break, and underside is golden brown, about 3 minutes.

7. Using thin, wide spatula, flip pancakes and continue to cook until second side is golden brown, 1 to 2 minutes longer. Transfer pancakes to prepared wire rack in oven (or serve as they're ready). Repeat with remaining batter, using extra oil and adjusting heat as necessary if pancakes begin to darken too quickly. Serve with Nutella maple syrup.

INSIDE THIS ISSUE